D0066440

DISCOVERING
The Humanities

THIRD EDITION

Henry M. Sayre
OREGON STATE UNIVERSITY

PEARSON

Boston Columbus Indianapolis New York San Francisco
Amsterdam Cape Town Dubai London Madrid Milan Munich Paris Montréal Toronto
Delhi Mexico City São Paulo Sydney Hong Kong Seoul Singapore Taipei Tokyo

In memory of Norwell "Bud" Therien, who first envisioned this project, and for whose friendship I will always be grateful. I miss him.

Editor-in-Chief: Sarah Touborg
Sponsoring Editor: Helen Ronan
Editorial Assistant: Victoria Engros
Executive Marketing Manager: Wendy Albert
Project Management Team Lead: Melissa Feimer
Production Project Manager: Joe Scordato
Program Manager: Barbara Marttine Cappuccio
Senior Operations Supervisor: Mary Fischer
Senior Operations Specialist: Diane Peirano
Cover Designer: Kathryn Foot
Senior Digital Media Director: David Alick
Digital Media Project Manager: Rich Barnes
Digital Imaging Specialist: Corin Skidds
Art Management and Manuscript Development: Laurence King Publishing, Ltd.

Full-Service Project Management: Lumina Datamatics, Inc.
Composition: Lumina Datamatics, Inc.
Printer/Binder: Courier/Kendallville
Cover Printer: Courier/Kendallville
Commissioning Editor: Kara Hattersley-Smith
Senior Editor: Melissa Danny
Picture Researchers: Julia Ruxton, Sarah Hopper
Text Permissions Editor: Nicholas Jewitt
Front cover image: Diego Velázquez, *Las Meninas (The Maids of Honor)*. Detail. 1656. Oil on canvas, 10'¾" × 9'¾". Museo del Prado, Madrid, Spain/Bridgeman Images.
Back cover image: *Las Meninas* shown in full. © Photo Scala, Florence.

Copyright © 2016, 2013, 2010 by Pearson Education, Inc. or its affiliates. All Rights Reserved. Printed in the United States of America. This publication is protected by copyright, and permission should be obtained from the publisher prior to any prohibited reproduction, storage in a retrieval system, or transmission in any form or by any means, electronic, mechanical, photocopying, recording, or otherwise. For information regarding permissions, request forms and the appropriate contacts within the Pearson Education Global Rights & Permissions department, please visit www.pearsoned.com/permissions/.

Acknowledgements of third party content appear on pages C-1–C-3, which constitute an extension of this copyright page.

PEARSON, ALWAYS LEARNING, and MYARTSLAB are exclusive trademarks in the U.S. and/or other countries owned by Pearson Education, Inc. or its affiliates.

Unless otherwise indicated herein, any third-party trademarks that may appear in this work are the property of their respective owners and any references to third-party trademarks, logos or other trade dress are for demonstrative or descriptive purposes only. Such references are not intended to imply any sponsorship, endorsement, authorization, or promotion of Pearson's products by the owners of such marks, or any relationship between the owner and Pearson Education, Inc. or its affiliates, authors, licensees or distributors.

Library of Congress Cataloging-in-Publication Data
Sayre, Henry M.
    Discovering the humanities / Henry M. Sayre, Oregon State University. — Third edition.
        pages cm
Includes bibliographical references and index.
ISBN 978-0-13-387770-0
1. Civilization—History. 2. Humanities—History. 3. Social change—History. I. Title.
CB69.S288 2014
306—dc23

                                        2014008986

10 9 8 7 6 5 4 3 2 1
V011

Student Edition:
ISBN-10: 0-13-387770-1
ISBN-13: 978-0-13-387770-0

Instructor's Resource Copy:
ISBN-10: 0-13-387832-5
ISBN-13: 978-0-13-387832-5

à la carte
ISBN-10: 0-13-387833-3
ISBN-13: 978-0-13-387833-2

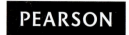

ALWAYS LEARNING

CONTENTS

SEE CONTEXT AND MAKE CONNECTIONS...

DEAR READER,

It has been fifteen years since I first sat down to write this book, and now, with the publication of this third edition, I'd like to take the opportunity to reflect a moment on this book and the value of the humanities in general.

The great question facing the humanities fifteen years ago was simple and direct: Do we or do we not include the cultures of the world, beyond the West, in the text? Many of us teaching the course felt unequipped to take on the arts and cultures of Asia, Africa, and Central and South America. Others felt that there was already too much to cover in simply addressing the Western world. But as work on the book proceeded, it became evident to me that taking a global perspective was not only important but essential to the humanistic enterprise in general.

And what, you might well ask, is the humanistic enterprise in the first place? At the most superficial level, a humanities course is designed to help you identify the significant works of art, architecture, music, theater, philosophy, and literature of distinct cultures and times, and to recognize how these different expressions of the human spirit respond to and reflect their historical contexts. More broadly, you should arrive at some understanding of the creative process and how what we—and others—have made and continue to value reflects what we all think it means to be human. But in studying other cultures—entering into what the British-born, Ghanaian-American philosopher and novelist Kwame Anthony Appiah has described as a "conversation between people from different ways of life"—we learn even more. We turn to other cultures because to empathize with others, to willingly engage in discourse with ideas strange to ourselves, is perhaps the fundamental goal of the humanities. The humanities are, above all, disciplines of openness, inclusion, and respectful interaction. What we see reflected in other cultures is usually something of ourselves, the objects of beauty that delight us, the weapons and the wars that threaten us, the melodies and harmonies that soothe us, the sometimes troubling but often penetrating thoughts that we encounter in the ether of our increasingly digital globe. Through the humanities we learn to seek common ground.

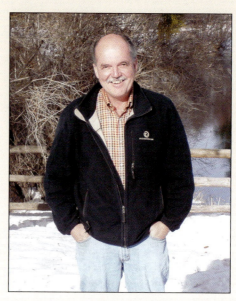

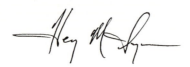

ABOUT THE AUTHOR

Henry M. Sayre is Distinguished Professor of Art History at Oregon State University–Cascades Campus in Bend, Oregon. He earned his Ph.D. in American Literature from the University of Washington. He is producer and creator of the 10-part television series *A World of Art: Works in Progress*, which aired on PBS in the fall of 1997; and author of seven books, including *A World of Art*; *The Visual Text of William Carlos Williams*; *The Object of Performance: The American Avant-Garde since 1970*; and an art history book for children, *Cave Paintings to Picasso*.

WHAT'S NEW

Discovering the Humanities helps students see context and make connections across the humanities by tying together the entire cultural experience through a narrative storytelling approach. Written around Henry Sayre's belief that students learn best by remembering stories rather than memorizing facts, it captures the voices that have shaped and influenced human thinking and creativity throughout our history.

For this new edition, we've created an extraordinary new learning architecture: REVEL. Every feature that students formerly accessed through MyArtsLab is now embedded in this new cross-platform environment—music, architectural panoramas, Closer Looks, studio technique videos, self-tests, and so on. You can zoom in on a piece of art, switch on the chapter audio, and listen to the text being read to you while you look at the image. You can begin your day at home, working with a chapter on your laptop, get on the bus, and continue working on your iphone, arrive at school, and open the chapter on your ipad. REVEL is as fully mobile as you are, and you can use it on any device, anywhere, and anytime.

We firmly believe that this new learning architecture will help students engage even more meaningfully in the critical thinking process, helping them to understand how cultures influence one another, how ideas are exchanged and evolve over time, and how this collective process has led us to where we stand today. With several new features, this third edition helps students to understand context and make connections across time, place, and culture.

To prepare the third edition, we partnered with our current users to hear what was successful and what needed to be improved. The feedback we received through focus groups, online surveys, and reviews helped shape and inform this new edition. For instance, many users felt that more literature needed to be included in the book, and we have tried to accommodate that desire by adding discussion of Chaucer, Shakespeare, Alexander Pope, and many modern authors. Where some felt that our coverage fell short—on Hellenic Greece, Mannerism and Postmodernism, for instance—we have extended our discussions. Here are some examples of these changes:

1. Chapter 1 introduces the new research at Çatalhöyük.
2. Chapter 2 expands the coverage of Hellenic sculpture, including a third image of the Pergamon frieze and the second sculpture from the "Vanquished Gauls" grouping.
3. Chapter 6 has significant new coverage of the Limbourg brothers, focusing on *January* and *February* from *Les Très Riches Heures*, and an extended discussion of Chaucer's *Canterbury Tales* has been added, including a Reading

from the Prologue, the first instance of an effort to include much more literature in this edition.
4. Chapter 7 expands on the coverage of women in Italian humanist society by incorporating Paola Tinagli's arguments in her book *Women in Italian Renaissance Art: Gender, Representation, Identity*.
5. Chapter 8 now includes a much fuller discussion of Shakespeare, including the "O, what a rogue and peasant slave am I" speech from *Hamlet* Act II, Scene 2, and the "To be, or not to be" soliloquy from Act III, Scene 1.
6. Chapter 9 includes additional material on African ritual practice, including two new images.
7. Chapter 10 further clarifies Mannerism with a new introduction and the addition of Arcimboldo's *Summer*, Michelangelo's Pietà, and Parmigianino's *The Madonna with the Long Neck*.
8. Chapter 11 now includes an extended discussion of Alexander Pope's *An Essay on Man*, and a new section on the English Garden including Pope's Villa at Twickenham.
9. Chapter 14 now includes a long section on early twentieth-century literature, including works by Apollinaire, Pound, and Williams. Three long excerpts from *The Waste Land* have been added to the section on The Great War and Its Aftermath. Finally a new section on The Stream-of-Consciousness Novel has been added, including a long excerpt from the Molly Bloom soliloquy at the end of *Ulysses* and the madeleine moment from Proust's *Swann's Way*.
10. In Chapter 15, the concluding section on The Postmodern Era has been expanded from 3 to 12 pages including a discussion of Borges (and his story "Borges and I" in full), paintings by Gerhard Richter, Pat Steir, and David P. Bradley, and video works by Bill Viola, Pipilotti Rist, Isaac Julien, Phil Collins, and Janine Antoni.

These changes reflect what we have learned about how humanities courses are constantly evolving. We have learned that more courses are being taught online and that instructors are exploring new ways to help their students engage with course material. An edition ago, we developed MyArtsLab with these needs in mind. Now, REVEL moves us in an even more interactive and compelling direction. With powerful learning tools integrated into the book, the textbook experience is now a seamless environment in which all of these tools are available at your fingertips.

All of these changes can be seen through the new, expanded, or improved features shown here.

NEW!
CONTINUING PRESENCE OF THE PAST

This new feature helps students to understand how the arts of the past remain relevant today. Designed to underscore the book's emphasis on continuity and change, the Continuing Presence of the Past in each chapter, identified with a special icon, connects an artwork from that period to a contemporary artwork in a dynamic digital feature found in REVEL as well as in MyArtsLab.

For example, in Chapter 3, Continuing Presence of the Past focuses on Cai Guo-Qiang's *Project to Extend the Great Wall of China by 10,000 Meters: Project for Extraterrestrials, No. 10* in which the artist detonated a series of explosions from the western end of the Great Wall that slithered in a red line on the horizon to form an ephemeral extension of the Great Wall itself. Gunpowder, originally a force for destruction, had now become an act of creation.

LEARNING OBJECTIVES AND THINKING BACK QUESTIONS

Learning Objectives and Thinking Back questions in each chapter focus on learning objectives and reflect the larger learning objectives of not only *Discovering the Humanities* but also national course outcomes. In addition, the Thinking Back features pose critical-thinking questions as well as reviewing the material covered in the chapter.

CLOSER LOOK

These highly visual features offer an in-depth look at a particular work from one of the disciplines of the humanities. The annotated discussions give students a personal tour of the work—with informative captions and labels—to help students understand its meaning. Critical-thinking questions, *Something to Think About*, prompt students to make connections and further apply this detailed knowledge of the work.

CONTINUITY & CHANGE ESSAYS

These full-page essays at the end of each chapter illustrate the influence of one cultural period upon another and show cultural changes over time.

PRIMARY SOURCE EXCERPTS

Each chapter of *Discovering the Humanities* includes primary source readings in the form of brief excerpts from important works included within the body of the text.

CONTINUITY & CHANGE ICONS

These in-text references provide a window into the past. The eye-catching icons enable students to refer to material in other chapters that is relevant to the topic at hand.

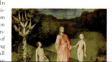

THINKING BACK

1.1 Discuss the rise of culture and how developments in art and architecture reflect the growing sophistication of prehistoric cultures.

The widespread use of stone tools and weapons by *Homo sapiens*, the hominid species that evolved around 120,000–100,000 years ago, gives rise to the name of the earliest era of human development, the Paleolithic era. Carvers fashioned stone figures, both in the round and in relief. In cave paintings, such as those discovered at Chauvet Cave, the artists' great skill in rendering animals helps us to understand that the ability to represent the world with naturalistic fidelity is an inherent human skill, unrelated to cultural sophistication. If culture can be defined as a way of living—religious, social, and/or political—formed by a group of people and passed on from one generation to the next, what can the earliest art tell us about the first human cultures? What do the dwellings at Çatalhöyük suggest about the growing sophistication of Neolithic peoples? What questions remain a mystery?

1.2 Describe the role of myth in prehistoric culture.

Much of our understanding of the role of myth in prehistoric cultures derives from the traditions that survive

1.3 Distinguish among the ancient civilizations of Mesopotamia, and focus on how they differ from that of the Hebrews.

The royal tombs at the Sumerian city of Ur reveal a highly developed Bronze Age culture, based on the social order of the city-state, which was ruled by a priest-king acting as the intermediary between the gods and the people. The rulers also established laws and encouraged record keeping, which in turn required the development of a system of writing known as cuneiform script. In Sumer and subsequent Mesopotamian cultures, monumental structures such as ziggurats were dedicated to the gods, and in each city-state one of the gods rose to prominence as the city's protector. How would you characterize the general relationship between Mesopotamian rulers and the gods? The Hebrews practiced a monotheistic religion. They considered themselves the "chosen people" of God, whom they called Yahweh. The written word is central to their culture, and it is embodied in a body of law, the Torah. What does the Torah have in common with the Law Code of Hammurabi? How does it differ? How do the stories in Genesis, the first book of the Hebrew Bible, compare to the *Epic of Gilgamesh?*

1.4 Account for the stability of Egyptian culture.

CLOSER LOOK

Hieronymus Bosch's *Garden of Earthly Delights* is full of strange hybrid organisms, part animal or bird, part human, part plant, sometimes part mechanical contraption. In the left panel of the triptych, we see the Garden of Eden, populated with such strange creatures as albino giraffes and elephants, unicorns, and flying fish. In the right panel, we see Bosch's deeply disturbing vision of hell, in which fire spits from the skyline and tortured souls are impaled on musical instruments or eaten alive by monsters. The central panel presents an image of life on earth, with hundreds of naked young men and women frolicking in a garden full of giant berries and other fruits. Lovers are

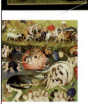

... of God's command to Adam and Eve

CONTINUITY & CHANGE

Egyptian and Greek Sculpture

Freestanding Greek sculpture of the Archaic period—that is, sculpture dating from about 600–480 BCE—is notable for its stylistic connections to 2,000 years of Egyptian tradition. The Late Period statue of Mentuemhet (Fig. 1.27), from Thebes, dating from around 660 BCE, differs hardly at all from Old Kingdom sculpture at Giza (see Fig. 1.24), and even though the *Anavysos Kouros* (Fig. 1.28), from a cemetery near Athens, represents a significant advance in relative naturalism over the Greek sculpture of just a few years before, it still resembles its Egyptian ancestors. Remarkably, since it follows upon the *Anavysos Kouros* by only 75 years, the *Doryphoros (Spear Bearer)* (Fig. 1.29) is significantly more naturalistic. Although this is a Roman copy of a lost fifth-century BCE bronze Greek statue, we can assume it reflects the original's naturalism, since the original's sculptor, Polyclitus, was renowned for his ability to render the human body realistically. But this advance, characteristic of Golden Age Athens, represents more than just a cultural taste for naturalism. It also represents a heightened cultural sensitivity to the worth of the individual, a belief that as much as we value what we have in common with one another—the bond that creates the city-state—our individual contributions are at least of equal value. By the fifth century BCE, the Greeks clearly understood that individual genius and achievement could be a matter of civic pride. ■

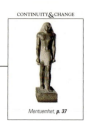
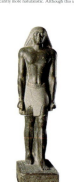
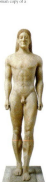
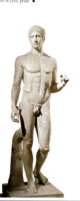

CONTINUITY & CHANGE

Mentuemhet, p. 37

PEARSON CHOICES AND RESOURCES

GIVE YOUR STUDENTS CHOICES

Pearson humanities titles are available in the following formats to give your students more choices—and more ways to save.

Explore REVEL—dynamic content matched to the way today's students read, think, and learn.

Ideal for Sayre's approach to the humanities, REVEL includes

- spoken audio,
- pan/zoom and scale markers for nearly every image,
- 360-degree architectural panoramas and simulations of major monuments,
- media interactives and videos, including "students on site" videos shot and narrated by proficient student learners, and
- quizzing that allows students to check their understanding at regular intervals.

Fully mobile, REVEL enables students to interact with course material on the devices they use, anywhere and anytime.

REVEL's assignability and tracking tools help educators

- ensure that students are completing their reading and understanding core concepts
- establish a clear, detailed schedule that helps students stay on task
- monitor both class assignment completion and individual student achievement

Build your own Pearson Custom course material.
For enrollments of at least 25, the Pearson Custom Library allows you to create your own textbook by

- combining chapters from best-selling Pearson textbooks in the sequence you want
- adding your own content, such as a guide to a local art museum, a map of monuments in your area, your syllabus, or a study guide you've created.

A Pearson Custom Library book is priced according to the number of chapters and may even save your students money. *To begin building your custom text, visit* www.pearsoncustomlibrary.com *or contact your Pearson representative.*

Explore additional cost-saving options.

The Books à la Carte edition offers a convenient, three-hole-punched, loose-leaf version of the traditional text at a discounted price—allowing students to take only what they need to class. Books à la Carte editions are available both with and without access to MyArtsLab. *Students save 35% over the list price of the traditional book.* ISBN: 0-13-387833-3

The CourseSmart eTextbook offers the same content as the printed text in a convenient online format—with highlighting, online search, and printing capabilities. With a CourseSmart eText, students can search the text, make notes online, print out reading assignments that incorporate lecture notes, and bookmark important passages for later review. *Students save 60% over the list price of the traditional book.* www.coursesmart.com

ADDITIONAL RESOURCES

Support Students with MyArtsLab—a robust companion study environment

For those customers who prefer companion study resources, MyArtsLab offers:

- Writing Space, providing a single place to create and evaluate graded writing assignments, featuring tools for developing and assessing concept mastery and critical thinking
- media assignments such as Closer Look tours, panoramas, videos, and simulations
- study resources such as flashcards
- links to book specific test banks for quizzes

INSTRUCTOR RESOURCES

PowerPoints
Instructors who adopt the text may gain access to a robust collection of PowerPoints illustrated with images from the text, additional media, and class discussion prompts.

Instructor's Manual and Test Item File
This is an invaluable professional resource and reference for new and experienced faculty. Each chapter contains the following sections: Chapter Overview, Chapter Objectives, Key Terms, Lecture and Discussion Topics, Resources, and Writing Assignments and Projects. The test bank includes multiple-choice, short-answer, and essay questions. Available for download from www.pearsonhighereducation.com

MyTest
This flexible online test-generating software includes all questions found in the Test Item File. Instructors can quickly and easily create customized tests with MyTest at www.pearsonmytest.com

DEVELOPING *DISCOVERING THE HUMANITIES*

DISCOVERING THE HUMANITIES

is the result of an extensive development process involving the contributions of over 100 instructors and their students. We are grateful to all who participated in shaping the content, clarity, and design of this text. Manuscript reviewers and focus group participants for the third edition include:

Laura Stevens, *Northwest Florida College*
Cheryl Boots, *Boston University*
Margaret Browning, *Hampton University*
Margaret Chaplin, *Richland College*
Marilyn Edwards, *Athens Technical College*
Billie Gateley, *Jackson State Community College*
Lisette Gibson, *Capital University*
Karen Guerin, *Bossier Parish Community College*
Nat Hardy, *Savannah State University*
Mike Vanden Heuvel, *University of Wisconsin-Madison*
Ira Holmes, *College of Central Florida*
Richard Kortum, *East Tennessee State University*
Carolyn Lawrence, *Chattahoochee Technical College*
Pamela Payne, *Palm Beach Atlantic University*
Chad Redwing, *Modesto Junior College*
Bonnie Smith, *Gwinnett Technical College*
Gary Zaro, *Paradise Valley Community College*

We are also grateful to all who reviewed the earlier editions of this title:

FIRST EDITION:
Mindi Bailey, *Collin County Community College*
Peggy Brown, *Collin County Community College*
Terre Burton, *Dixie College*
Elizabeth Cahaney, *Elizabethtown Community and Technical College*
Rick Davis, *Brigham Young University–Idaho*
Christa DiMaio Richie, *Salem Community College*
Tiffany Engel, *Tulsa Community College*
Gabrielle Fennmore, *St. Thomas University*
Michael Fremont Redfield, *Saddleback College*
Nat Hardy, *Savannah State University*
Thelma Ithier-Sterling, *Hostos Community College*
Stuart Kendall, *Eastern Kentucky University*
Maria Miranda, *Hostos Community College*
Nathan Poage, *Houston Community College*
Aditi Samarth, *Richland College*
Cheryl Smart, *Pima Community College*
Lynn Spencer, *Brevard Community College*
Alice Taylor, *West Los Angeles College*

Paul Van Heuklom, *Lincoln Land Community College*
Leila Wells, *Griffin Technical College*
Deborah J. Wickering, *Aquinas College*

SECOND EDITION:
Paul Beaudoin, *Fitchburg State University*
Terre Burton, *Dixie College*
Katherine Harrell, *South Florida Community College*
Scott Keeton, *Chattahoochee Technical College*
Sandi Landis, *St. Johns River Community College*
Aditi Samarth, *Richland College*
Frederick Smith, *Florida Gateway College*

In addition, while this revision was in development, I had the chance to learn from a special group of faculty who attended the Pearson Forum for Humanities:

Natalie Biscalia, *Hillsborough Community College*
Joanne Bock, *Palm Beach State College*
Elaine Dale, *Santa Fe College*
Cristy Furr, *St. Johns River State College*
Alyson Gill, *Arkansas State University*
Steven Godby, *Broward College: South Campus*
Eugene Greco, *Miami Dade College: Kendall Campus*
Bobby Hom, *Santa Fe College*
Dale Hoover, *Edison State College*
Michael Hurlburt, *Broward College: South Campus*
Theresa James, *South Florida State College*
Sandi Landis, St. *Johns River State College*
David Luther, *Edison State College*
Brandon Montgomery, *State College of Florida*
Pavel Murdzhev, *Santa Fe Collge*
Christie Rinck, *University of South Florida*
Susan Ross, *St. Johns River State College*
Joseph Savage, *St. Johns River State College*
Henry Sayre, *Oregon State University–Cascades Campus*
Maira Spelleri, *State College of Florida*
Greg Thompson, *Hillsborough Community College-Brandon*
Krista Ubbels, *St. Johns River State College*
Jason Whitmarsh, *St. Johns River State College*

ACKNOWLEDGMENTS

Discovering the Humanities is a brief version of the larger text, *The Humanities: Culture, Continuity and Change*, Third Edition, and is inevitably indebted to all who contributed to that revision. No project of this scope could ever come into being without the hard work and perseverance of many more people than its author. In fact, this author has been humbled by a team at Pearson that never wavered in their confidence in my ability to finish this enormous undertaking (or if they did, they had the good sense not to let me know); never hesitated to cajole, prod, and massage me to complete the project in something close to on time; and always gave me the freedom to explore new approaches to the materials at hand. At the down-and-dirty level, I am especially grateful to fact-checker Julia Moore; to Mary Ellen Wilson for the pronunciation guides; for the more specialized pronunciations offered by David Atwill (Chinese and Japanese), Jonathan Reynolds (African), Nayla Muntasser (Greek and Latin), and Mark Watson (Native American); to Margaret Gorenstein for tracking down the readings; to Laurel Corona for her extraordinary help with Africa; to Arnold Bradford for help with critical thinking questions; and to Francelle Carapetyan for her remarkable photo research. The maps and some of the line art are the work of cartographer and artist Peter Bull, with Precision Graphic drafting a large portion of the line art for the book. I find both in every way extraordinary.

In fact, I couldn't be more pleased with the look of the book, which is the work of Pat Smythe, senior art director. Cory Skidds, senior imaging specialist, worked on image compositing and color accuracy of the artwork. The production of the book was coordinated by Melissa Feimer, managing editor, Barbara Cappuccio, program manager and Joe Scordato, project manager, who oversaw with good humor and patience the day-to-day, hour-to-hour crises that arose. And I want to thank Lindsay Bethoney and the staff at

Lumina Datamatics for working so hard to make the book turn out the way I envisioned it.

The marketing and editorial teams at Pearson are beyond compare. On the marketing side, Jonathan Cottrell, vice president of marketing, and Wendy Albert, executive marketing manager, helped us all to understand just what students want and need. On the editorial side, my thanks to Sarah Touborg, editor-in-chief; Roth Wilkofsky, publisher; Helen Ronan, senior editor; my friend, the late Bud Therien, special projects manager; and Christopher Fegan, editorial assistant. The combined human hours that this group has put into this project are staggering. This book was Bud's idea in the first place, and I know that he would be pleased to see how the project is continuing to flourish; Sarah has supported me every step of the way in making it as good, or even better, than I envisioned. I need to thank, especially, the extraordinary team that has developed the extraordinary new learning architecture that is REVEL. REVEL takes the entire, innovative set of learning tools that was introduced in MyArtsLab and makes it immediately and seamlessly available to the student. Over the course of the last decade, as technology has increasingly encroached on the book as we know it—with the explosion, that is, of the internet, digital media, and new forms of publishing, like the iPad and Kindle—I worried that books like *Discovering the Humanities* might one day lose their relevance. I envisioned it being supplanted by some as yet unforeseen technological wizardry that would transport my readers, like some machine in a science fiction novel, into a three- or four-dimensional learning space "beyond the book." Well, little did I know that Pearson Education was developing just such a space, one firmly embedded in the book, not beyond it.

Deserving of special mention is the editorial team at Laurence King Publishers in London, particularly Kara Hattersley-Smith, commissioning editor; Melissa Danny, senior editor; Simon Walsh, production; and Julia Ruxton, picture editor. A special thanks to the faculty at Collin County Community College and St. John's River College. Their feedback over the course of the book's development was tremendously valuable and helped shape many of the changes you now see.

Finally, I want to thank, with all my love, my beautiful wife, Sandy Brooke, who has supported this project in every way. She has continued to teach, paint, and write, while urging me on, listening to my struggles, humoring me when I didn't deserve it, and being a far better wife than I was a husband. In some ways, enduring what she did in the first edition must have been tougher in the second, since she knew what was coming from the outset. She was, is, and will continue to be, I trust, the source of my strength.

In memory of Norwell "Bud" Therien, who first envisioned this project, and for whose friendship I will always be grateful. I continue to miss his wisdom and good humor.

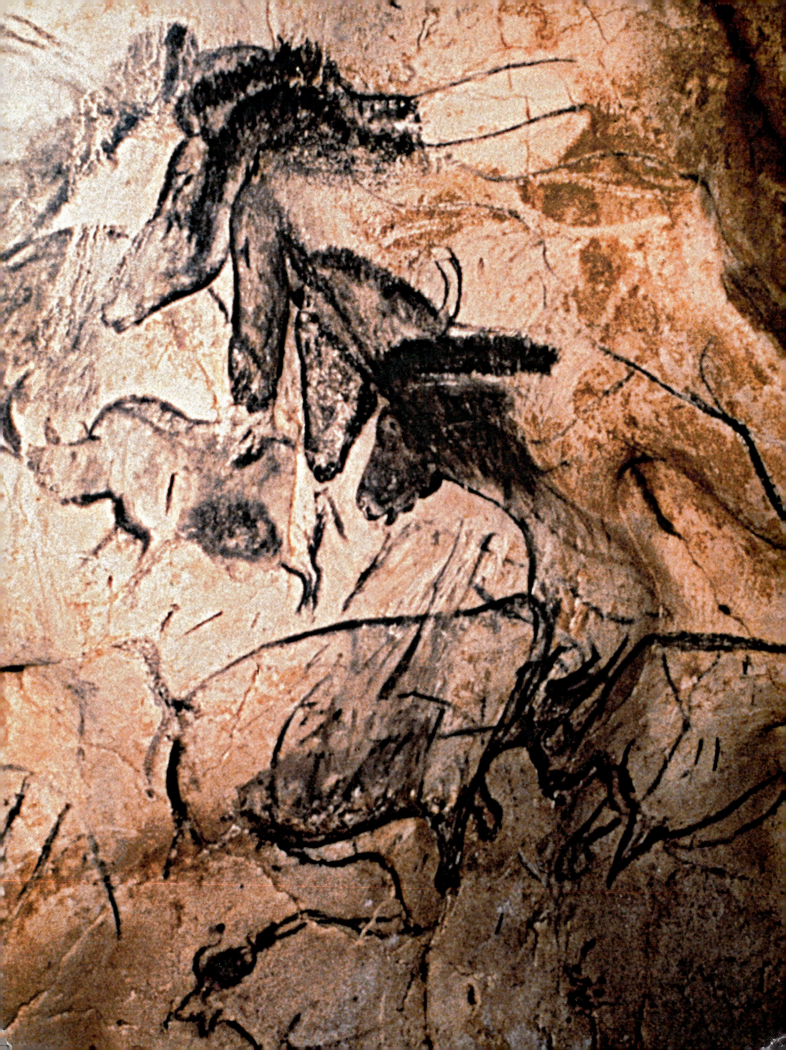

The Prehistoric Past and the Earliest Civilizations

The River Cultures of the Ancient World

1

LEARNING OBJECTIVES

1.1 Discuss the rise of culture and how developments in art and architecture reflect the growing sophistication of prehistoric cultures.

1.2 Describe the role of myth in prehistoric culture.

1.3 Distinguish among the ancient civilizations of Mesopotamia, and focus on how they differ from that of the Hebrews.

1.4 Account for the stability of Egyptian culture.

On a cold December afternoon in 1994, Jean-Marie Chauvet and two friends were exploring the caves in the steep cliffs along the Ardèche River gorge in southern France. After descending into a series of narrow passages, they entered a large chamber. There, beams from their headlamps lit up a group of drawings that would astonish the three explorers—and the world (Fig. **1.1**).

Since the late nineteenth century, we have known that **prehistoric** peoples—peoples who lived before the time of writing and so of recorded history—drew on the walls of caves. Twenty-seven such caves had already been discovered in the cliffs along the 17 miles of the Ardèche gorge (Map **1.1**). But the cave found by Chauvet and his friends transformed our thinking about prehistoric peoples. Where previously discovered cave paintings had appeared to modern eyes as childlike, this cave contained drawings comparable to those a contemporary artist might have done. We can only speculate that other comparable artworks were produced in prehistoric times but have not survived, perhaps because they were made of wood or other perishable materials. It is even possible that art may have been made earlier than 30,000 years ago, perhaps as people began to inhabit the Near East, between 90,000 and 100,000 years ago.

At first, during the Paleolithic era, or "Old Stone Age" (from the Greek *palaios,* "old," and *lithos,* "stone") the cultures of the world sustained themselves on game and wild plants. The cultures themselves were small, scattered, and nomadic, although evidence suggests some interaction among the

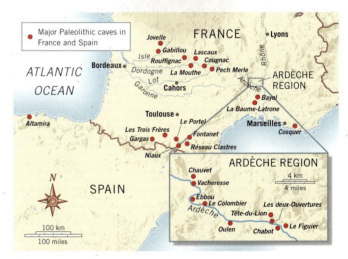

Map 1.1 Major Paleolithic Caves in France and Spain.

◄ **Fig. 1.1 Cave painting with horses, Chauvet Cave, Vallon-Pont-d'Arc, Ardèche gorge, France. ca. 30,000 BCE.** Ministère de la Culture et de la Communication. Direction Régionale des Affaires Culturelles de Rhône-Alpes. Service Régional de l'Archéologie. Paint on limestone, approx. height 6'. In the center of this wall are four horses, each behind the other in a startlingly realistic space. Below them, two rhinoceroses fight.

1

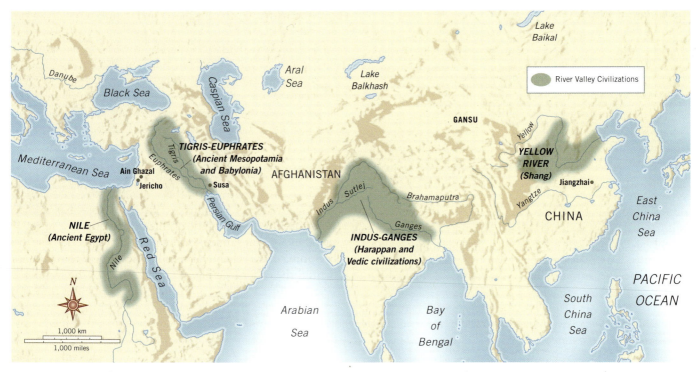

Map 1.2 The Great River Valley Civilizations, ca. 2000 BCE. Agriculture thrived in the great river valleys throughout the Neolithic era, but by the end of the period, urban life had developed there as well, and civilization as we know it had emerged.

various groups. As the ice covering the Northern Hemisphere began to recede, around 10,000 BCE, agriculture began to replace hunting and gathering, and with it, a nomadic lifestyle gave way to a more sedentary way of life. The consequences of this shift were enormous, and ushered in the Neolithic era, or "New Stone Age."

In the great river valleys of the Middle East and Asia (Map **1.2**), distinct centers of people involved in a common pursuit began to form more and more sophisticated civilizations. (The rise of these civilizations in India and China is discussed in Chapter 3.) A **civilization** is a social, economic, and political entity distinguished by the ability to express itself through images and written language. Civilizations develop when the environment of a region can support a large and productive population. An increasing population requires increased production of food and other goods, not only to support itself, but also to trade for other commodities. Organizing this level of trade and production also requires an administrative elite to form and to establish priorities. The existence of such an elite is another characteristic of civilization. Finally, as the history of cultures around the world makes abundantly clear, one of the major ways that societies have acquired the goods they want and simultaneously organized themselves is by means of war.

We begin this book, then, with the first inklings of civilized cultures in prehistoric times, evidence of which survives in cave paintings and in small sculptures dating back more than 25,000 years. Before the invention of writing, sometime after 10,000 BCE, these cultures created myths and legends that explained their origins and relation to the world. Then,

beginning about 4000 BCE, across the ancient world, the science of metallurgy developed. As people learned to separate metals from their ores and then work or treat them to create objects, the stone and bone tools and weapons of the prehistoric world were replaced by metal ones, inaugurating the era archeologists have named the Bronze Age.

THE BEGINNINGS OF CULTURE

How do cultures arise, and how do art and architecture reflect their growing sophistication?

A **culture** encompasses the values and behaviors shared by a group of people, developed over time, and passed down from one generation to the next. Culture manifests itself in the laws, customs, ritual behavior, and artistic production common to the group. The cave paintings at Chauvet suggest that, as early as 30,000 years ago, the Ardèche gorge was a *center of culture*, a focal point of group living in which the values of a community find expression. There were others like it: In northern Spain, the first decorated cave was discovered in 1879 at Altamira. In the Dordogne region of southern France, to the west of the Ardèche, schoolchildren discovered the famous Lascaux Cave in 1940 when their dog disappeared down a hole. And in 1991, along the French Mediterranean coast, a diver discovered the entrance to the beautifully decorated Cosquer Cave below the waterline near Marseille.

Agency and Ritual: Cave Art

Ever since cave paintings were first discovered, scholars have been marveling at the skill of the people who produced them, but we have been equally fascinated by their very existence. Why were these paintings made? Most scholars believe that they possessed some sort of **agency**—that is, they were created to exert some power or authority over the world of those who came into contact with them. Until recently, it was generally accepted that such works were associated with the hunt. Perhaps the hunter, seeking game in times of scarcity, hoped to conjure it up by depicting it on cave walls. Or perhaps such drawings were magic charms meant to ensure a successful hunt. But at Chauvet, fully 60 percent of the animals painted on its walls were never, or rarely, hunted—such animals as lions, rhinoceroses, bears, panthers, and woolly mammoths. One drawing depicts two rhinoceroses fighting horn to horn beneath four horses that appear to be looking on (see Fig. 1.1).

What role, then, did these drawings play in the daily lives of the people who created them? The caves may have served as some sort of **ritual** space. A ritual is a rite or ceremony habitually practiced by a group, often in religious or quasi-religious contexts. The caves, for instance, might be understood as gateways to the underworld and death, as symbols of the womb and birth, or as pathways to the world of dreams experienced in the dark of night, and rites connected with such passage might have been conducted in them. The general arrangement of the animals in the paintings by species or gender, often in distinct chambers of the caves, suggests to some that the paintings may have served as lunar calendars for predicting the seasonal migration of the animals. Whatever the case, surviving human footprints indicate that these caves were ritual gathering places and in some way served the common good.

At Chauvet, the use of color suggests that the paintings served some sacred or symbolic function. For instance, almost all the paintings near the entrance to the cave are painted with natural red pigments derived from ores rich in iron oxide. Deeper inside the cave, in areas more difficult to reach, the vast majority of the animals are painted in black pigments derived from ores rich in manganese dioxide. This shift in color appears to be intentional, but we can only guess its meaning.

The skillfully drawn images at Chauvet raise even more important questions. The artists seem to have understood and practiced a kind of **perspectival drawing**—that is, they were able to convey a sense of three-dimensional space on a two-dimensional surface. In the painting reproduced at the beginning of this chapter, several horses appear to stand one behind the other (see Fig. 1.1). The head of the top horse overlaps a black line, as if peering over a branch or the back of another animal. In no other cave yet discovered do drawings show the use of shading, or **modeling**, so that the horses' heads seem to have volume and dimension. And yet these cave paintings, rendered more than 30,000 years ago, predate other cave paintings by at least 10,000 years, and some by as much as 20,000 years.

One of the few cave paintings that depict a human figure is found at Lascaux, in the Dordogne region of southwestern France. What appears to be a male wearing a bird's-head mask lies in front of a disemboweled bison (Fig. 1.2). Below him is a bird-headed spear thrower, a device that enabled hunters to throw a spear farther and with greater force. (Several examples of spear throwers have survived.) In the Lascaux painting, the hunter's spear has pierced the bison's

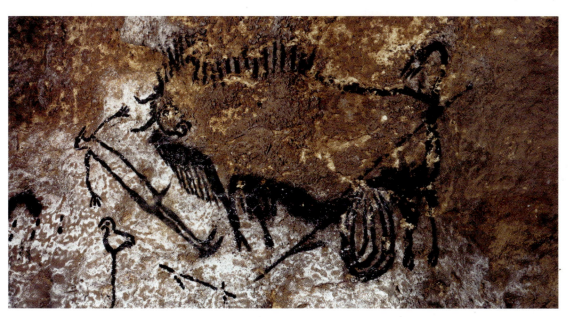

Fig. 1.2 Cave painting with bird-headed man, bison, and rhinoceros, Lascaux Cave, Dordogne, France. ca. 15,000–13,000 BCE. Paint on limestone, length approx. 9′. In 1963, Lascaux was closed to the public so that conservators could fight a fungus attacking the paintings. Most likely, the fungus was caused by carbon dioxide exhaled by visitors. An exact replica called Lascaux II was built and can be visited.

hindquarters, and a rhinoceros charges off to the left. We have no way of knowing whether this was an actual event or an imagined scene. One of the painting's most interesting and inexplicable features is the discrepancy between the relatively naturalistic representation of the animals and the highly stylized, almost abstract realization of the human figure. Was the sticklike man added later by a different, less talented artist? Or does this image suggest that man and beast are different orders of being?

Before the discovery of Chauvet, historians divided the history of cave painting into a series of successive styles, each progressively more realistic. But Chauvet's paintings, by far the oldest known, are also the most advanced in their realism, suggesting the artist's conscious quest for visual **naturalism**, that is, for representations that imitate the actual appearance of the animals. Not only were both red and black animals outlined, but their shapes were also modeled by spreading paint, either with the hand or with a tool, in gradual gradations of color. Such modeling is extremely rare or unknown elsewhere. In addition, the artists further defined many of the animals' contours by scraping the wall behind so that the beasts seem to stand out against a deeper white ground. Three handprints in the cave were evidently made by spitting paint at a hand placed on the cave wall, resulting in a stenciled image.

Art, the Chauvet drawings suggest, does not necessarily evolve in a linear progression from awkward beginnings to more sophisticated representations. On the contrary, already in the earliest artworks, people obtained a very high degree of sophistication. Apparently, even from the earliest times, human beings could choose to represent the world naturalistically or not, and the choice not to represent the world in naturalistic terms should be attributed not necessarily to lack of skill or sophistication but to other, more culturally driven factors.

Paleolithic Culture and Its Artifacts

Footprints discovered in South Africa in 2000 and fossilized remains uncovered in the forest of Ethiopia in 2001 suggest that, about 5.7 million years ago, the earliest upright humans, or hominins (as distinct from the larger classification of **hominids**, which includes great apes and chimpanzees as well as humans), roamed the continent of Africa. Ethiopian excavations further indicate that sometime around 2.5 or 2.6 million years ago, hominid populations began to make rudimentary stone tools, although long before, between 14 million and 19 million years ago, the *Kenyapithecus* ("Kenyan ape"), a hominin, made stone tools in east central Africa. Nevertheless, the earliest evidence of a culture coming into being are the stone artifacts of *Homo sapiens* (Latin for "one who knows"). *Homo sapiens* evolved about 100,000–120,000 years ago and can be distinguished from earlier hominids by the lighter build of their skeletal structure and larger brain. A 2009 study of genetic diversity among Africans found the San people of Zimbabwe to be the most diverse, suggesting

that they are the most likely origin of modern humans from which others gradually spread out of Africa, across Asia, into Europe, and finally to Australia and the Americas.

Homo sapiens were **hunter-gatherers**, whose survival depended on the animals they could kill and the foods they could gather, primarily nuts, berries, roots, and other edible plants. The tools they developed were far more sophisticated than those of their ancestors. They included cleavers, chisels, grinders, hand axes, and arrow- and spearheads made of flint, a material that also provided the spark to create an equally important tool—fire. In 2004, Israeli archeologists working at a site on the banks of the Jordan River reported the earliest evidence yet found of controlled fire created by hominids—cracked and blackened flint chips, presumably used to light a fire, and bits of charcoal dating from 790,000 years ago. Also at the campsite were the bones of elephants, rhinoceroses, hippopotamuses, and small species, demonstrating that these early hominids cut their meat with flint tools and ate steaks and marrow. *Homo sapiens* cooked with fire, wore animal skins as clothing, and used tools as a matter of course. They buried their dead in ritual ceremonies, often laying them to rest accompanied by stone tools and weapons.

The Paleolithic era is the period of *Homo sapiens*'s ascendancy. These people carved stone tools and weapons that helped them survive in an inhospitable climate. They carved small sculptural objects as well, which, along with the cave paintings we have already seen, appear to be the first instances of what we have come to call "art." Among the most remarkable of these sculptural artifacts are a large number of female figures, found at various archeological sites across Europe. The most famous of these is the limestone statuette *Woman*, found at Willendorf, in modern Austria (Fig. **1.3**), dating from between about 25,000 to 20,000 BCE and sometimes called the *Venus of Willendorf*. Markings on the *Woman* and other similar figures indicate that they were originally colored, but what these small sculptures meant and what they were used for remains unclear. Most are 4 to 5 inches high and fit neatly into a person's hand. This suggests that they may have had a ritual purpose. Their exaggerated breasts and bellies and their clearly delineated genitals support a connection to fertility and childbearing. We know, too, that the *Woman* from Willendorf was originally painted in red ochre, suggestive of menses. And, her navel is not carved; rather, it is a natural indentation in the stone. Whoever carved her seems to have recognized, in the raw stone, a connection to the origins of life. But such figures may have served other purposes as well. Perhaps they were dolls, guardian figures, or images of beauty in a cold, hostile world where having body fat might have made the difference between survival and death.

Female figurines vastly outnumber representations of males in the Paleolithic era, which suggests that women played a central role in Paleolithic culture. Most likely, they had considerable religious and spiritual influence, and their preponderance in the imagery of the era suggests that Paleolithic culture may have been *matrilineal* (in which descent is

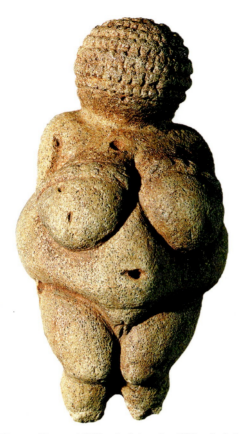

Fig. 1.3 *Woman (Venus of Willendorf)*, **found at Willendorf, Austria. ca. 25,000–20,000 BCE.** Limestone, height 4". Naturhistorisches Museum, Vienna. For many years, modern scholars called this small statue the *Venus of Willendorf*. They assumed that its carvers attributed to it an ideal of female beauty comparable to the Roman ideal of beauty implied by the name Venus.

determined through the female line) and *matrilocal* (in which residence is in the female's tribe or household). Such traditions exist in many primal societies today.

The Rise of Agriculture

For 2,000 years, from 10,000 to 8000 BCE, the ice covering the Northern Hemisphere receded farther and farther northward. As temperatures warmed, life gradually changed. During this period of transition, areas once covered by vast regions of ice and snow developed into grassy plains and abundant forests. Hunters developed the bow and arrow, which were easier to use than the spear at longer range on the open plains. They fashioned dugout boats out of logs to facilitate fishing, which became a major food source. They domesticated dogs to help with the hunt as early as 11,000 BCE, and soon other animals as well—goats and cattle particularly. Perhaps most important, people began to cultivate the more edible grasses. Along the eastern shore of the Mediterranean, they harvested wheat; in Asia, they cultivated millet and rice; and in the Americas, they grew squash, beans, and corn. Gradually,

farming replaced hunting as the primary means of sustaining life. A culture of the fields developed—an agriculture, from the Latin *ager*, "farm," "field," or "productive land."

The rise of agricultural society defines the Neolithic era. Beginning in about 8000 BCE, Neolithic culture concentrated in the great river valleys of the Middle East and Asia, and gradually, as the climate warmed, Neolithic culture spread across Europe. By about 5000 BCE, the valleys of Spain and southern France supported agriculture, but not until about 4000 BCE is there evidence of farming in the northern reaches of the European continent and England.

Meanwhile, the great rivers of the Middle East and Asia provided a consistent and predictable source of water, and people soon developed irrigation techniques that fostered organized agriculture and animal husbandry. As production outgrew necessity, members of the community were freed to occupy themselves in other endeavors—complex food preparation (bread, cheese, and so on), construction, religion, even military affairs. Soon, permanent villages began to appear, and villages began to look more and more like cities.

Neolithic Çatalhöyük

Sometime around 7400 BCE, at Çatalhöyük (also known as Chatal Huyuk) in central Turkey, a permanent village began to take shape that would flourish for nearly 1,200 years. At one point or another, as many as 3,000 people lived in close proximity to one another in rectangular houses made of mud bricks held together with plaster. These houses stood side by side, one wall abutting the next, with entrances through the roof and down a ladder. There were no windows, and the only natural light in the interior came from the entryway. The roof appears to have served as the primary social space, especially in the summer months. Domed ovens were placed both on the roof and in the interior.

The people of Çatalhöyük were apparently traders, principally of obsidian, a black, volcanic, and glasslike stone that can be carved into sharp blades and arrowheads, which they mined at Hasan Dag, a volcano visible from the village. The rows of windowless houses that composed the village, the walls of which rose to as high as 16 feet, must have served a defensive purpose, but they also contained what archeologists have come to view as an extraordinary sense of communal history. Their interior walls and floors were plastered and re-plastered, then painted and repainted with a white lime-based paint, again and again over hundreds of years. Beneath the floors of some—but not all—of the houses were burials, averaging about six per house, but sometimes rising to between 30 and 62 bodies. For reasons that are not entirely clear, from time to time, these bodies were exhumed, and the skulls of long-deceased ancestors were removed. The skulls were then reburied in new graves or in the foundations of new houses as they were built and rebuilt. Whatever the rationale for such ceremonies, they could not have helped but create a sense of historical continuity in the community.

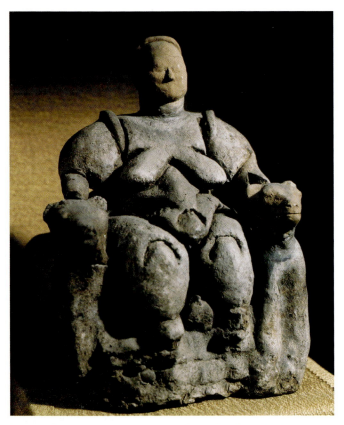

Fig. 1.4 Woman seated between two felines, Çatalhöyük, Turkey. ca. 6850–6300 BCE. Terra cotta, height 4⅝". Museum of Anatolian Civilizations, Ankara. The woman's head in this sculpture is a modern addition.

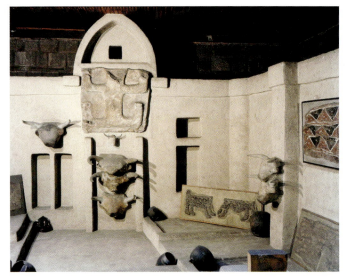

Fig. 1.5 Reconstruction of a "shrine," Çatalhöyük, Turkey. ca. 6850–6300 BCE. Museum of Anatolian Civilizations, Ankara. The relief sculpture below the arch in the center of the room appears to be a decapitated animal or even, possibly, human form.

Çatalhöyük was first extensively excavated from 1958 by Sir James Mellaart, who concluded that the village's culture was matrilineal, based in no small part on his discovery of a number of female figurines including a clay sculpture of a seated woman (Fig. **1.4**), who represented, he believed, a Fertility or Mother Goddess. Found in a grain bin—evidence of the community's growing agricultural sophistication—she sits enthroned between two felines, perhaps in the process of giving birth. But Ian Hodder of Cambridge University, who took up the excavation of the site in 1993, after a nearly 30-year hiatus, has recently concluded that she is something other than a Fertility Goddess. "There are full breasts on which the hands rest," he wrote in 2005,

and the stomach is extended in the central part. There is a hole in the top for the head which is missing. As one turns the figurine around one notices that the arms are very thin, and then on the back of the figurine one sees a depiction of either a skeleton or the bones of a very thin and depleted human. The ribs and vertebrae are clear, as are the scapulae and the main pelvic bones. The figurine can be interpreted in a number of ways—as a woman turning into an ancestor, as a woman associated with death, or as death and life conjoined. . . . Perhaps the importance of female imagery

was related to some special role of the female in relation to death as much as to the roles of mother and nurturer.

Supporting Hodder's theories is a burial of a deceased woman who holds in her arms the plastered and painted skull of a male. Similarly, Mellaart believed that many of the rooms that contained large numbers of bodies were shrines or temples (Fig. **1.5**). The walls of these rooms were decorated with the skulls of cows and the heads and horns of bulls. Found under the floors of some houses were boar tusks, vulture skulls, and fox and weasel teeth. But Hodder has found evidence that these houses—he calls them "history houses"—were not shrines at all, but more or less continuously occupied, suggesting that art and decoration were integral to the daily lives of the community's residents.

Neolithic Pottery Across Cultures

The transition from cultures based on hunting and fishing to cultures based on agriculture led to the increased use of pottery vessels. Ceramic vessels are fragile, so hunter-gatherers would not have found them practical for carrying food, but people living in the more permanent Neolithic settlements could have used them to carry and store water, and to prepare and store certain types of food.

Some of the most remarkable Neolithic painted pottery comes from Susa, on the Iranian plateau. The patterns on one particular beaker (Fig. **1.6**) from around 5000 to 4000 BCE are highly stylized animals. The largest of these is an ibex, a popular decorative feature of prehistoric ceramics from Iran. Associated with the hunt, the ibex may have been a symbol of plenty. The front and hind legs of the ibex are rendered by two triangles, the tail hangs behind it like a feather, the head

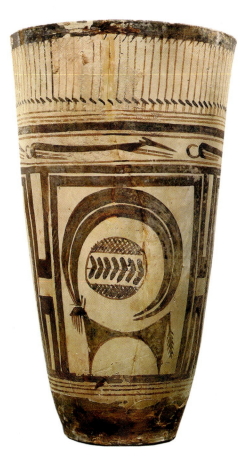

Fig. 1.6 Beaker with ibex, dogs, and long-necked birds, from Susa, southwestern Iran. ca. 5000–4000 BCE. Baked clay with painted decoration, height 11¼″. Musée du Louvre, Paris. The ibex was the most widely hunted game in the ancient Middle East, a fact that probably accounts for its centrality in this design.

is only marginally connected to the body, and the horns rise in a large, exaggerated arc to encircle a decorative circular form. Hounds race around the band above the ibex, and wading birds form a decorative band across the beaker's top.

In Europe, the production of pottery apparently developed some time later, around 3000 BCE. By this time, the potter's wheel was in use in the Middle East as well as China. A machine created expressly to produce goods, the potter's wheel represents the first mechanical and technological breakthrough in history. As skilled individuals specialized in making and decorating pottery, and traded their wares for other goods and services, the first elemental forms of manufacturing began to emerge.

Neolithic Ceramic Figures

It is a simple step from forming clay pots and firing them to modeling clay sculptural figures and submitting them to the same firing process. Examples of clay modeling can be found in some of the earliest Paleolithic cave sites, where, at Altamira, for instance, in Spain, an artist added clay to an existing rock outcropping in order to underscore the rock's natural resemblance to an animal form. At Le Tuc d'Audoubert,

south of Lascaux, in France, an artist shaped two clay bison, each 2 feet long, as if they were leaning against a rock ridge.

But these Paleolithic sculptures were never fired. One of the most interesting examples of Neolithic fired clay figurines was the work of the so-called Nok peoples who lived in modern Nigeria. We do not know what they called themselves—they are identified instead by the name of the place where their artifacts were discovered. In fact, we know almost nothing about the Nok. We do not know how their culture was organized, what their lives were like, or what they believed. But while most Neolithic peoples in Africa worked in materials that were not permanent, the Nok fired clay figures of animals and humans that were approximately life-size.

These figures were first unearthed early in the twentieth century by miners over an area of about 40 square miles. Carbon-14 and other forms of dating revealed that some of these objects had been made as early as 800 BCE and others as late as 600 CE. Little more than the hollow heads has survived intact, revealing an artistry based on abstract geometric shapes (Fig. **1.7**). In some cases, the heads are represented as ovals; in others they are cones, cylinders, or spheres. Facial features are combinations of ovals, triangles, graceful arches, and straight lines. These heads were probably shaped with wet clay and then, after firing, finished by carving details into the hardened clay. Some scholars

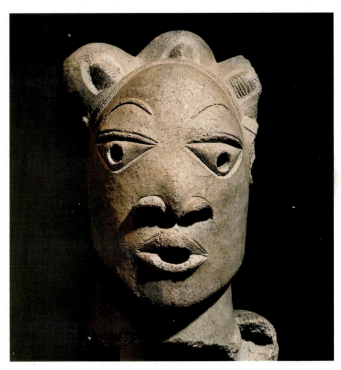

Fig. 1.7 Head, Nok. ca. 500 BCE–200 CE. Terra cotta, height 14³⁄₁₆″. This slightly larger-than-life-size head was probably part of a complete body, and shows the Nok people's interest in abstract geometric representations of facial features and head shape. Holes in the eyes and nose were probably used to control temperature during firing.

 View the Closer Look for the Nok head on **MyArtsLab**

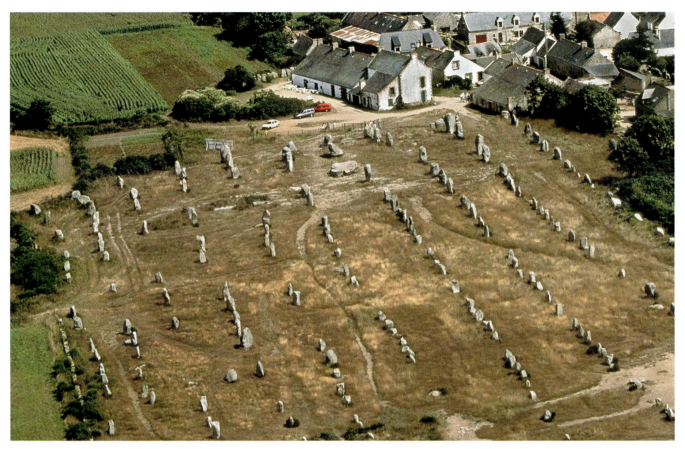

Fig. 1.8 Neolithic menhir alignments at Ménec, Carnac, Brittany, France. ca. 4250–3750 BCE. According to an ancient legend, the Carnac menhirs came into being when a retreating army was driven to the sea. Finding no ships to aid their escape, they turned to face their enemy and were transformed into stone.

have argued that the technical and artistic sophistication of works by the Nok and other roughly contemporaneous groups suggests that it is likely there are older artistic traditions in West Africa that have not yet been discovered. Certainly, farther to the east, in the sub-Saharan regions of the Sudan, Egyptian culture had exerted considerable influence for centuries, and it may well be that Egyptian technological sophistication had worked its way westward.

The Neolithic Megaliths of Northern Europe

A distinctive kind of monumental stone architecture appears late in the Neolithic period, particularly in what is now Britain and France. Known as **megaliths**, or "big stones," these works were constructed without the use of mortar and represent the most basic form of architectural construction. Sometimes, they consisted merely of posts— upright stones stuck into the ground—called **menhirs**, from the Celtic words *men*, "stone," and *hir*, "long." These single stones occur in isolation or in groups. The largest of the groups is at Carnac, in Brittany (Fig. **1.8**), where some 3,000 menhirs arranged east to west in 13 straight rows, called alignments, cover a 2-mile stretch of plain. The stones stand about 3 feet tall at the east end, and gradually get larger and larger until, at the west end, they attain a

height of 13 feet. This east–west alignment suggests a connection to the rising and setting of the sun and to fertility rites. Scholars disagree about the stones' significance: some speculate that they may have marked out a ritual procession route, while others think they symbolized the human body and the process of growth and maturation. But there can be no doubt that megaliths were designed to be permanent structures, where domestic architecture was not. Quite possibly the megaliths stood in tribute to the strength of the leaders responsible for assembling and maintaining the considerable labor force required to construct them.

Perhaps the best-known type of megalithic structure is the **cromlech**, from the Celtic *crom*, "circle," and *lech*, "place." Without doubt, the most famous megalithic structure in the world is the cromlech known as Stonehenge (Fig. **1.9**), on Salisbury Plain, about 100 miles west of London. A henge is a special type of cromlech, a circle surrounded by a ditch with built-up embankments, presumably for fortification.

The site at Stonehenge reflects four major building periods, extending from about 2750 to 1500 BCE. By about 2100 BCE, most of the elements visible today were in place. In the middle was a U-shaped arrangement of ten posts grouped in pairs, each pair topped by a capstone— what we today call **post-and-lintel** construction. The one at the bottom of the U stands taller than the rest, rising

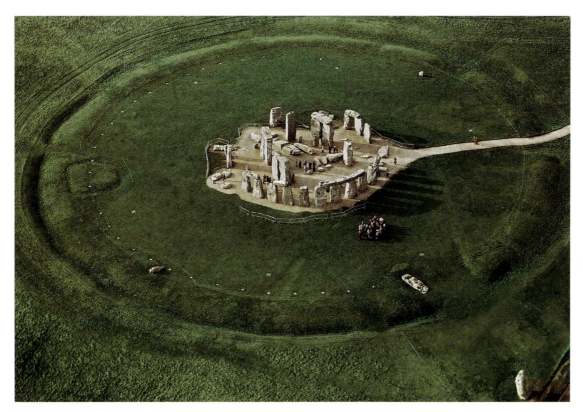

Fig. 1.9 Stonehenge, Salisbury Plain, Wiltshire, England. ca. 2750–1500 BCE. Like most Neolithic sites, Stonehenge invites speculation about its significance. Of this, however, we are certain: At the summer solstice, the longest day of the year, the sun rises directly over the Heel Stone, visible at the bottom right of this photograph. This suggests that the site was intimately connected to the movement of the sun.

 View the Closer Look for Stonehenge on **MyArtsLab**

to a height of 24 feet, with a 15-foot lintel 3 feet thick. A continuous circle of sandstone posts, each weighing up to 50 tons and all standing 20 feet high, surrounded the five trilithons. Across their top was a continuous lintel 106 feet in diameter. This is the Sarsen Circle. Just inside the Sarsen Circle was once another circle, made of bluestone—a bluish dolerite—found only in the mountains of southern Wales, some 120 miles away.

Why Stonehenge was constructed remains something of a mystery, although a recent discovery at nearby Durrington Walls has shed new light on the problem. Durrington Walls lies about 2 miles northeast of Stonehenge itself (see Map **1.3**). It consists of a circular ditch surrounding a ring of postholes out of which very large timber posts would have risen. The circle was the center of a village of as many as 300 houses. The site is comparable in scale to Stonehenge itself. These discoveries—together with the ability to carbon-date human remains found at Stonehenge with increased accuracy—suggest that Stonehenge was itself a burial ground. Archeologist Mike Parker Pearson of the University of Sheffield speculates that villagers would have transported their dead down an avenue leading to the River Avon, then journeyed downstream in a ritual symbolizing the passage to the afterlife, finally arriving at an avenue leading up to Stonehenge from the river. "Stonehenge wasn't set in isolation," Parker

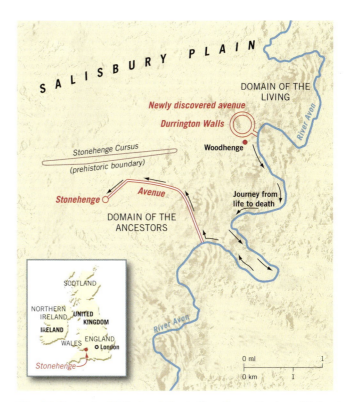

Map 1.3 Durrington Walls in relation to Stonehenge. Courtesy of National Geographic.

Pearson says, "but was actually one-half of this monumental complex. We are looking at a pairing—one in timber to represent the transience of life, the other in stone marking the eternity of the ancestral dead."

MYTH IN PREHISTORIC CULTURAL LIFE

What role does myth play in prehistoric cultures?

Much of our understanding of prehistoric cultures comes from stories that have survived in cultures around the world that developed without writing—that is, **oral cultures**—such as the San cultures of Zimbabwe and the Oceanic peoples of Tahiti in the South Pacific. These peoples passed down their myths and histories over the centuries, from generation to generation, by word of mouth. Although, chronologically speaking, many of these cultures are contemporaneous with the medieval, Renaissance, and even modern cultures of the West, they are actually closer to the Neolithic cultures in terms of social practice and organization. Especially in terms of myths and the rituals associated with them, they can help us to understand the outlook of actual Neolithic peoples.

A **myth** is a story that a culture assumes is true. It also embodies the culture's views and beliefs about its world, often serving to explain otherwise mysterious natural phenomena. Myths stand apart from scientific explanations of the nature of reality, but as a mode of understanding and explanation, myth has been one of the most important forces driving the development of culture. Although myths are speculative, they are not pure fantasy. They are grounded in observed experience. They serve to rationalize the unknown and to explain to people the nature of the universe and their place within it.

Both nineteenth-century and more recent anthropological work among the San people suggests that their belief systems can be traced back for thousands of years. As a result, the meaning of their rock art that survives in open-air caves below the overhanging stone cliffs atop the hills of what is now Matobo National Park in Zimbabwe (Fig. **1.10**), some of which dates back as far as 5,000 to 10,000 years ago, is not entirely lost. A giraffe stands above a group of smaller giraffes crossing a series of large, white, lozenge-shaped forms with brown rectangular centers, many of them overlapping one another. To the right, six humanlike figures are joined hand in hand, probably in a trance dance. For the San people, prolonged dancing activates *num*, a concept of personal energy or potency that the entire community can acquire. Led by a **shaman**, a person thought to have special ability to communicate with the spirit world, the dance encourages the *num* to heat up until it boils over and rises up through the spine to explode, causing the dancers to enter a trance. Sweating and trembling, the dancers variously convulse or become rigid. They might run, jump, or fall. The San believe that in many instances, the dancer's spirit leaves the body, traveling far away, where it might enter into battle with supernatural forces. At any event, the trance imbues the dancer with almost supernatural agency. The dancers' *num* is capable of curing illnesses, managing game, or controlling the weather.

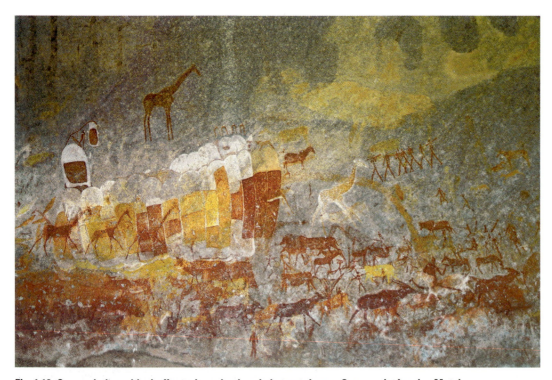

Fig. 1.10 Cave painting with giraffes, zebra, eland, and abstract shapes, San people, Inanke, Matobo National Park, Zimbabwe. Before 1000 CE. Photo: Christopher and Sally Gable © Dorling Kindersley. The animals across the bottom are elands, the largest species of antelope, resembling cattle.

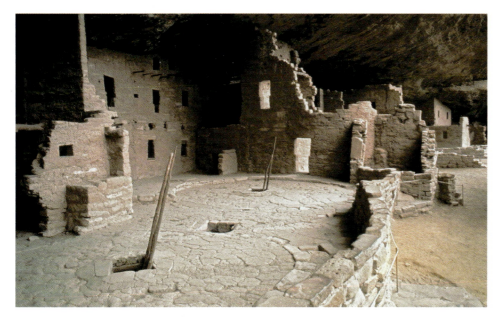

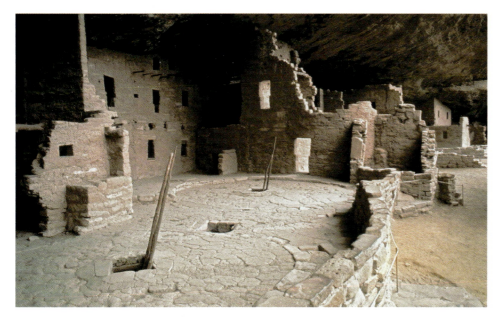

Fig. 1.12 Roof construction of a kiva. After a National Park Service pamphlet.

Fig. 1.11 Spruce Tree House, Mesa Verde. Anasazi culture, ca. 1200–1300 CE.
The courtyard was formed by the restoration of the roofs over two underground kivas.

Myth in the Native American Cultures of the Southwest

The Pueblo peoples of the American Southwest trace their ancestry back to the Anasazi, who lived in the region from about 900 to 1300 CE, a time roughly contemporaneous with the late Middle Ages in Europe. They have maintained the active practice of their ancient Anasazi religious rites and ceremonies, which they have chosen not to share with outsiders.

The Anasazi left us no written record of their culture, only ruins and artifacts. As William M. Ferguson and Arthur H. Rohn, two prominent scholars of the Anasazi, have described them, "They were a Neolithic people without a beast of burden, the wheel, metal, or a written language, yet they constructed magnificent masonry housing and ceremonial structures, irrigation works, and water impoundments." At Mesa Verde, in what is today southwestern Colorado, their cliff dwellings (Fig. 1.11) resemble many of the Neolithic cities of the Middle East, such as 'Ain Ghazal ("spring of the gazelles"), just outside what is now Amman, Jordan. Although 'Ain Ghazal flourished from about 7200 to 5000 BCE, thousands of years before the Mesa Verde community, both complexes were constructed with stone walls sealed with a layer of mud plaster. Their roofs were made of wooden beams cross-layered with twigs and branches and sealed with mud. Like other Neolithic cultures, the Anasazi were accomplished in pottery making, decorating their creations with elaborately abstract, largely geometric shapes and patterns.

The Anasazi abandoned their communities in the late thirteenth century, perhaps because of a great drought that lasted from about 1276 to 1299. Today, their descendants include the Hopi and the Zuni. (*Anasazi* is in fact a Navajo word meaning "enemy ancestors"—we do not know what the Anasazi called themselves.) What is remarkable about the Pueblo peoples, who despite the fact that they speak several different languages share a remarkably common culture, is that many aspects of their culture have survived and are practiced today much as they were in ancient times. For all Pueblo peoples, the village is not just the center of culture but the very center of the world. And the cultural center of the village life is the **kiva** (Fig. 1.12), two of which have been restored at Spruce Tree House to form the plaza visible in Fig. 1.11. They are constructed of horizontally laid logs built up to form a dome with an access hole. The roof thus created is used as a common area. Down below, in the enclosed kiva floor, was a *sipapu*, a small, round hole symbolic of the Anasazi creation myth, which told of the emergence of the Anasazi's ancestors from the depths of the earth. In the parched Southwestern desert country, it is equally true that water, like life itself, also seeps out of small fissures in the earth. Thus, it is as if the Anasazi community, and everything necessary to its survival, emerged from Mother Earth.

Most Pueblo peoples do not allow their ceremonial dances to be photographed. These dance performances tell stories that relate to the experiences of the Pueblo peoples, from planting, hunting, and fishing in daily life, to the larger experiences of birth, puberty, maturity, and death. Still other stories explain the origin of the world, the emergence of a particular Pueblo people into the world, and their history. Most Pueblo people believe that they originated in the womb of Mother Earth and, like seeds sprouting from the soil in the springtime, were called out into the daylight by their Sun Father. This belief about origins is embodied in a type of narrative known as an **emergence tale**, a form of creation myth (**Reading 1.1**).

Zuni Emergence Tale, *Talk Concerning the First Beginning*

Yes, indeed. In this world there was no one at all. Always the sun came up; always he went in. No one in the morning gave him sacred meal; no one gave him prayer sticks; it was very lonely. He said to his two children: "You will go into the fourth womb. Your fathers, your mothers, kä·eto·we, tcu-eto·we, mu-eto·we, le-eto·we, all the society priests, society pekwins, society bow priests, you will bring out yonder into the light of your sun father."

So begins this emergence tale, which embodies the fundamental principles of Zuni religious society. The Zuni, or "Sun People," are organized into groups, each responsible for a particular aspect of the community's well-being, and each group is represented by a particular *-eto·we*, or fetish, connecting it to its spiritual foundation in the Earth's womb. The pekwins mentioned here are sun priests, who control the ritual calendar. Bow priests oversee warfare and social behavior. In return for corn and breath given them by the Sun Father, the Zuni offer him cornmeal and downy feathers attached to painted prayer sticks symbolizing both clouds—the source of rain—and breath itself. Later in the tale the two children of the Sun Father bring everyone out into the daylight for the first time:

Into the daylight of their sun father they came forth standing. Just as early dawn they came forth. After they came forth there they set down their sacred possessions in a row. The two said, "Now after a little while when your sun father comes forth standing to his sacred place you will see him face to face. Do not close your eyes." Thus he said to them. After a little while the sun came out. When he came out they looked at him. From their eyes the tears rolled down. After they had looked at him, in a little while their eyes became strong. "Alas!" Thus they said. They were covered all over with slime. With slimy tails and slimy horns, with webbed fingers, they saw one another. "Oh dear! is this what we look like?" Thus they said.

Then they could not tell which was which of their sacred possessions.

From this point on in the tale, the people and priests, led by the two children, seek to find the sacred "middle place," where things are balanced and orderly. Halona-Itiwana it is called, the sacred name of the Zuni Pueblo, "the Middle Ant Hill of the World." In the process they are transformed from indeterminate salamander-like creatures into their ultimate human form, and their world is transformed from chaos to order.

At the heart of the Zuni emergence tale is a moment when, to the dismay of their parents, many children are transformed into water creatures—turtles, frogs, and the like—and the Hero Twins instruct the parents to throw these children back into the river. Here they become *kachinas* or *katcinas*, deified spirits, who explain:

May you go happily. You will tell our parents, "Do not worry." We have not perished. In order to remain thus forever we stay here. To Itiwana but one day's travel remains. Therefore we stay nearby. . . . Whenever the waters are exhausted and the seeds are exhausted you will send us prayer sticks. Yonder at the place of our first beginning with them we shall bend over to speak to them. Thus there will not fail to be waters. Therefore we shall stay quietly nearby.

The Pueblo believe that kachina spirits, not unlike the *num* of the San people of Africa, manifest themselves in performance and dance. Masked male dancers impersonate the kachinas, taking on their likeness as well as their supernatural character. Through these dance visits the kachinas, although always "nearby," can exercise their powers for the good of the people. The nearly 250 kachina personalities embody clouds, rain, crops, animals, and even ideas such as growth and fertility. Although kachina figurines are made for sale as art objects, particularly by the Hopi, the actual masks worn in ceremonies are not considered art objects by the Pueblo people. Rather, they are thought of as active agents in the transfer of power and knowledge between the gods and the men who wear them in dance. In fact, kachina dolls made for sale are considered empty of any ritual power or significance.

Pueblo emergence tales, and the ritual practices that accompany them, reflect the general beliefs of most Neolithic peoples. These include the following:

- belief that the forces of nature are inhabited by living spirits, which we call **animism**;
- belief that nature's behavior can be compared to human behavior (we call the practice of investing plants, animals, and natural phenomena with human form or attributes **anthropomorphism**), thus explaining what otherwise would remain inexplicable;
- belief that humans can communicate with the spirits of nature, and that, in return for a sacrificial offering or a prayer, the gods might intercede on their behalf.

Japan and the Role of Myth in the Shinto Religion

A culture's religion—that is, its understanding of the divine—is thus closely tied to and penetrated by mythical elements. Its beliefs, as embodied in its religion, stories, and myths, have always been closely tied to seasonal celebrations and agricultural production—planting and harvest in particular, as well as rain—the success of which was understood to be inextricably linked to the well-being of the community. In a fundamental sense, myths reflect the community's ideals, its history (hence the preponderance of creation myths in both ancient societies and contemporary religions), and its aspirations. Myths also tend to mirror the culture's moral and political systems, its social organization, and its most fundamental beliefs.

A profound example is the indigenous Japanese religion of Shinto. Before 200 CE, Japan was fragmented; its various regions were separated by sea and mountain, and ruled by numerous competing and often warring states. The *Records of Three Kingdoms*, a classic Chinese text dating from about 297 CE, states that in the first half of the third century CE many or most of these states were unified under the rule of Queen Himiko. According to the *Records*, "The country formerly had a man as ruler. For some 70 or 80 years after that there were disturbances and warfare. Thereupon the people agreed upon a woman for their ruler. Her name was Himiko." After her rule, Japan was more or less united under the Yamato emperors, who modeled their rule on the Chinese, and whose imperial court ruled from modern-day Nara Prefecture, then known as Yamato province. Its peoples shared a mythology that was finally collected near the end of the Yamato period, in about 700 CE, called the *Kojiki* or *Chronicles of Japan*.

According to the *Kojiki*, the islands that constitute Japan were formed by two *kami*, or gods—Izanagi and his consort, Izanami. Among their offspring was the sun goddess, Amaterasu Omikami, from whom the Japanese Imperial line later claimed to have descended. In other words, Japanese emperors could claim not merely to have been put in position by the gods; they could claim to be direct descendants of the gods, and hence divine.

Amaterasu is the principal goddess of the early indigenous religious practices that came to be known as Shinto. She is housed in a shrine complex at Ise, a sacred site from prehistoric times. In many respects, Shinto shares much with Pueblo religions. In Shinto, trees, rocks, water, and mountains—especially Mount Fuji, the volcano just outside Tokyo, which is said to look over the country, as its protector—are all manifestations of the *kami*, which, like kachinas, are the spirits that are embodied in the natural world. Even the natural materials with which artists work, such as clay, wood, and stone, are imbued with the *kami* and are to be treated with the respect and reverence due to a god. The *kami* are revered in *matsuri*, festivals that usually occur annually, in which, it is believed, past and present merge into one, everyday reality fades away, and people come face to face with their gods. The *matsuri* serve to purify the territory and community associated with the *kami*, restoring them from the degradation inevitably worked upon them by the passing of time. During the festival, people partake of the original energies of the cosmos, which they will need to restore order to their world. Offerings such as fish, rice, and vegetables, as well as music and dancing, are presented to the *kami*, and the offerings of food are later eaten.

The main sanctuary, or *shoden*, at Ise consists of undecorated wooden beams and a thatched roof (Fig. **1.13**). Ise is exceptional in its use of these plain and simple materials, which embody not only the basic tenet of Shinto—reverence for the natural world—but also the continuity and renewal of a tradition where wood, rather than stone, has always been the principal building material. The most prominent festival at Ise is the *shikinen-sengu* ceremony, which involves the installation of the deity in a

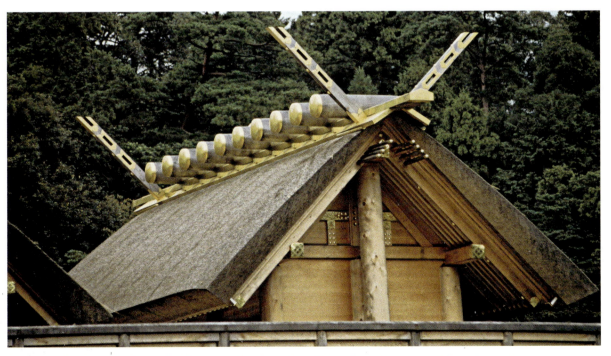

Fig. 1.13 Naiku (Inner) Shrine housing Amaterasu, Ise, Japan. Late fifth–early sixth century CE. Although the site has been sacred to Shinto since prehistoric times, beginning in the reign of the emperor Temmu (r. 673–86 CE), the Shinto shrine at Ise has been rebuilt by the Japanese ruling family, with some inevitable lapses, every 20 years. The most recent reconstruction occurred in 2013; it will be rebuilt again in 2033.

 View the Closer Look for the Ise shrine on **MyArtsLab**

new shrine in a celebration of ritual renewal held every 20 years. The shrine buildings are rebuilt on empty ground adjacent to the older shrine, the deity is transferred to the new shrine, and the older shrine is razed, creating empty ground where the next shrine will be erected. The empty site is strewn with large white stones and is left totally empty except for a small wooden hut containing a sacred wooden pole, a practice that scholars believe dates back to very ancient times. This cycle of destruction and renewal connects the past to the present, the human community to its gods and their original energies.

The three sacred treasures of Shinto—a sword, a mirror, and a jewel necklace—were said to be given by Amaterasu to the first emperor, and they are traditionally handed down from emperor to emperor in the enthronement ceremony. The mirror is housed at Ise, the sword at the Atsuta Shrine in Nagoya, and the jewel necklace at the Imperial Palace in Tokyo. These imperial regalia are not considered mere symbols of the divine but "deity-bodies" in which the powers of the gods reside, specifically wisdom in the mirror, valor in the sword, and benevolence in the jewel necklace. To this day, millions of Japanese continue to practice Shinto, and they undertake pilgrimages to Ise each year.

MESOPOTAMIA: POWER AND SOCIAL ORDER IN THE EARLY MIDDLE EAST

What characteristics distinguish the ancient civilizations of Mesopotamia, and how do they differ from that of the Hebrews?

In September 1922, British archeologist C. Leonard Woolley boarded a steamer, beginning a journey that would take him to Iraq. There, Woolley and his team would discover one of the richest treasure troves in the history of archeology in the ruins of the ancient city of Ur. Woolley concentrated his energies on the burial grounds surrounding the city's central **ziggurat**, a pyramidal temple structure consisting of successive platforms with outside staircases and a shrine at the top (Figs. **1.14**, **1.15**). Digging there in the winter of 1927, he unearthed a series of tombs with several rooms, many bodies, and spectacular objects—vessels, crowns, necklaces, statues, and weapons—as well as jewelry and lyres made of electrum and the deep blue stone lapis lazuli. With the same sense of excitement that was felt by Jean-Marie Chauvet and

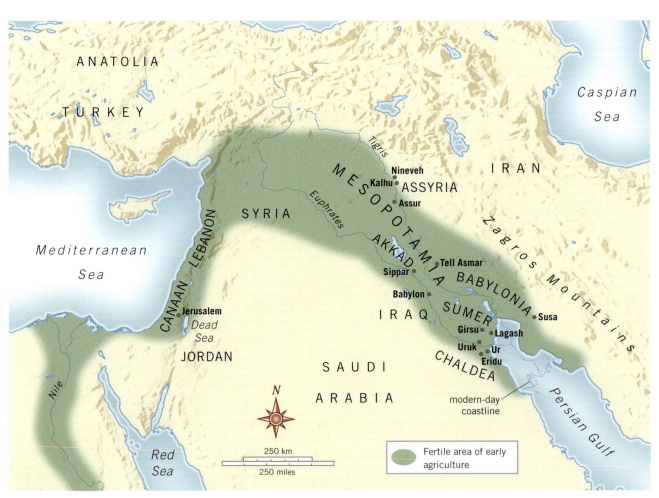

Map 1.4 Major Mesopotamian capitals, ca. 2600–500 BCE.

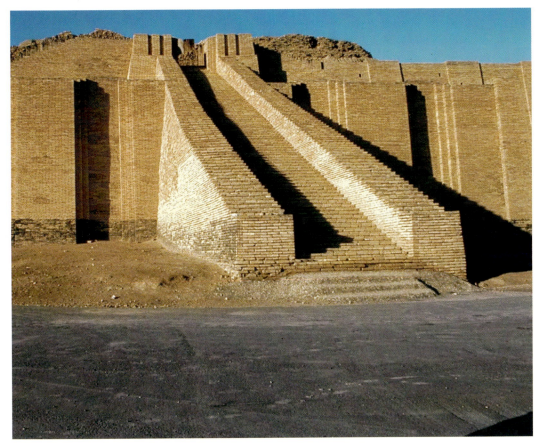

Fig. 1.14 The ziggurat at Ur (present-day Muqaiyir, Iraq). ca. 2100 BCE. The best-preserved and most fully restored of the ancient Sumerian temples, this ziggurat was the center of the city of Ur, on the banks of the Euphrates River.

his companions when they first saw the paintings on the wall of Chauvet Cave, Woolley was careful to keep what he called the "royal tombs" secret. On January 4, 1928, he telegrammed his colleagues in Latin. Translated to English, his message read:

> I found the intact tomb, stone built, and vaulted over with bricks of queen Shubad [later known as Puabi] adorned with a dress in which gems, flower crowns and animal figures are woven. Tomb magnificent with jewels and golden cups.
> —Woolley

When Woolley's discovery was made public, it was worldwide news for years.

Archeologists and historians were especially excited by Woolley's discoveries because they opened a window onto the larger region we call Mesopotamia, the land between the Tigris and Euphrates rivers. Ur was one of 30 or 40 cities that arose in Sumeria, the southern portion of Mesopotamia (Map **1.4**). In fact, its people abandoned Ur more than 2,000 years ago, when the course of the Euphrates moved away from the city.

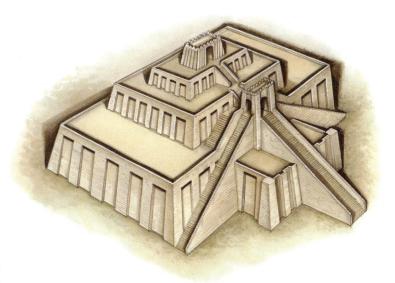

Fig. 1.15 Reconstruction drawing of the ziggurat at Ur (present-day Muqaiyir, Iraq). ca. 2100 BCE. British archeologist Sir Leonard Woolley undertook reconstruction of the ziggurat in the 1930s. In his reconstruction, a temple on top, which was the home of the patron deity of the city, crowned the three-tiered platform, the base of which measures 140 by 200 feet. The entire structure rose to a height of 85 feet. Woolley's reconstruction was halted before the second and third platforms were completed.

Sumerian Ur

Ur is not the oldest city to occupy the southern plains of Mesopotamia, the region known as Sumer. That distinction belongs to Uruk, just to the north. But the temple structure at Ur is of particular note because it is the most fully preserved and restored. It was most likely designed to evoke the mountains surrounding the river valley, which were the source of the water that flowed through the two rivers and, so, the source of life. Topped by a sanctuary, the ziggurat might also have symbolized a bridge between heaven and earth. Woolley, who supervised the reconstruction of the first platform and stairway of the ziggurat at Ur, speculated that the platforms of the temple were originally not paved but covered with soil and planted with trees, an idea that modern archeologists no longer accept.

Visitors—almost certainly limited to members of the priesthood—would climb the stairs to the temple on top. They might bring an offering of food or an animal to be sacrificed to the resident god—at Ur, it was Nanna or Sin, god of the moon. Visitors often placed in the temple a statue that represented themselves in an attitude of perpetual prayer. We know this from the inscriptions on many of the statues. One, dedicated to the goddess Tarsirsir, protector of Girsu, a city-state across the Tigris and not far upstream from Ur, reads:

> To Bau, gracious lady, daughter of An, queen of the holy city, her mistress, for the life of Nammahani . . . has dedicated as an offering this statue of the protective goddess of Tarsirsir which she has introduced to the courtyard of

Bau. May the statue, to which let my mistress turn her ear, speak my prayers.

A group of such statues, found in 1934 in the shrine room of a temple at Tell Asmar, near present-day Baghdad, includes seven men and two women (Fig. **1.16**). The men wear belted, fringed skirts. They have huge eyes, inlaid with lapis lazuli (a blue semiprecious stone) or shell set in bitumen. The single arching eyebrow and crimped beard (only the figure at the right is beardless) are typical of Sumerian sculpture. The two women wear robes. All figures clasp their hands in front of them, suggestive of prayer when empty and of making an offering, when holding a cup. Scholars once believed that the tallest man represents Abu, god of vegetation, because of his especially large eyes. Today this theory is discounted, but all the figures are probably worshipers.

Religion in Ancient Mesopotamia Although power struggles among the various city-states dominate Mesopotamian history, with one civilization succeeding another, and with each city-state or empire claiming its own particular divinity as chief among the Mesopotamian gods, the nature of Mesopotamian religion remained relatively constant across the centuries. With the exception of the Hebrews, the religion of the Mesopotamian peoples was polytheistic, consisting of multiple gods and goddesses connected to the forces of nature—sun and sky, water and storm, earth and its fertility. We know many of them by two names, one in Sumerian and the other in the Semitic language of the later, more powerful Akkadians.

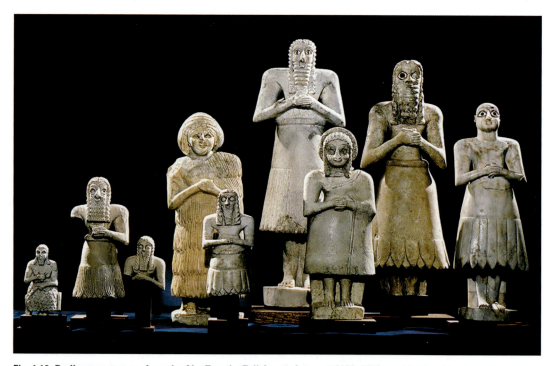

Fig. 1.16 Dedicatory statues, from the Abu Temple, Tell Asmar, Iraq. ca. 2900–2700 BCE. Marble, alabaster, and gypsum, height of tallest figure approx. 30". Excavated by the Iraq Expedition of the Oriental Institute of the University of Chicago, February 13, 1934. Courtesy of the Oriental Institute of the University of Chicago. The wide-eyed appearance of these figures is probably meant to suggest that they are gazing in perpetual awe at the deity.

To the Mesopotamians, human society was merely part of the larger society of the universe governed by these gods, and a reflection of it. Anu, father of the gods, represents the authority, which the ruler emulates as lawmaker and giver. Enlil, god of the air—the calming breeze as well as the violent storm—is equally powerful, but he represents force, which the ruler emulates in his role as military leader. The active principles of fertility, birth, and agricultural plenty are those of the goddess Belitili, while water, the life force itself, the creative element, is embodied in the god Ea, or Enki, who is also god of the arts. Both Belitili and Ea are subject to the authority of Anu. Ishtar, goddess of both love and war, is subject to Enlil, ruled by his breezes (in the case of love) and by his storm (in the case of war). A host of lesser gods represented natural phenomena, or, in some cases, abstract ideas, such as truth and justice.

The Mesopotamian ruler, often represented as a "priest-king," and often believed to possess divine attributes, acts as the intermediary between the gods and humankind. His ultimate responsibility is the behavior of the gods—whether Ea blesses the crop with rains, Ishtar his armies with victory, and so on.

Royal Tombs of Ur Religion was central to the people of Ur, and the cemetery there, discovered by Sir Leonard Woolley in 1928, tells us a great deal about the nature of their beliefs. Woolley unearthed some 1,840 graves, most dating from between 2600 and 2000 BCE. The greatest number of graves were individual burials of rich and poor alike. However, some included a built burial chamber rather than just a coffin and contained more than one body, in some cases as many as 80. These multiple burials, and the evidence of elaborate burial rituals, suggest that members of a king or queen's court accompanied the ruler to the grave. The two richest burial sites, built one behind the other, are now identified as royal tombs, one belonging to Queen Puabi, the other to an unknown king (but it is not that of her husband, King Meskalamdug, who is buried in a different grave).

One of Woolley's most important discoveries in the Royal Cemetery was the so-called *Standard of Ur* (Fig. **1.17**). The main panels of this rectangular box of unknown function are called "War" and "Peace," because they illustrate, on one side, a military victory and, on the other, the subsequent

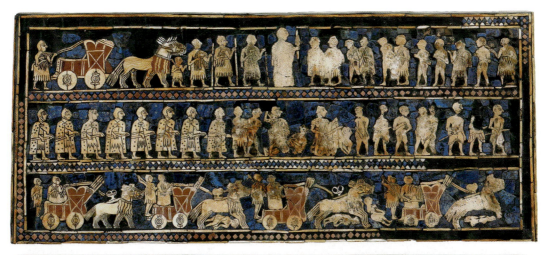

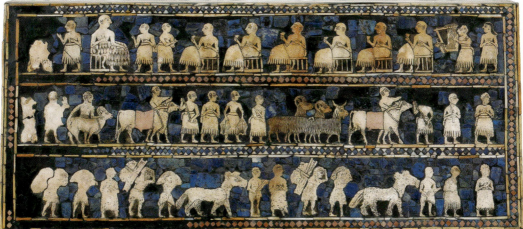

Fig. 1.17 *Standard of Ur*, front ("War") and back ("Peace") sides, from tomb 779, cemetery at Ur (present-day Muqaiyir, Iraq). ca. 2600 BCE. Shell, lapis lazuli, and red limestone, originally on a wooden framework, height 8′, length 19″. © The Trustees of the British Museum. For all its complexity of design, this object is not much bigger than a sheet of legal paper. Its function remains a mystery, although it may have served as a pillow or headrest. Woolley's designation of it as a standard was purely conjectural.

 View the Closer Look for the *Standard of Ur* on **MyArtsLab**

banquet celebrating the event, or perhaps a cult ritual. Each panel is composed of three **registers**, or self-contained horizontal bands, within which the figures stand on a **ground line**, or baseline.

At the right side of the top register of the "Peace" panel (the lower half of Fig. 1.17), a musician plays a lyre, and behind him another, apparently female, sings. The king, at the left end, is recognizable because he is taller than the others and wears a tufted skirt, his head breaking the register line on top. In this convention, known as **social perspective**, or **hieratic scale**, the most important figures are represented as larger than the others. In other registers on the "Peace" side of the *Standard*, servants bring cattle, goats, sheep, and fish to the celebration. These represent the bounty of the land and perhaps even delicacies from lands to the north. (Notice that the costumes and hairstyles of the figures carrying sacks in the lowest register are different from those in the other two.) This display of consumption and the distribution of food may have been intended to dramatize the power of the king by showing his ability to control trade routes.

On the "War" side of the *Standard*, the king stands in the middle of the top register. War chariots trample the enemy on the bottom register. (Note that the chariots have solid wheels; spoked wheels were not invented until approximately 1800 BCE.) In the middle register, soldiers wearing leather cloaks and bronze helmets lead naked, bound prisoners to the king in the top register, who will presumably decide their fate. Many of the bodies found in the royal tombs were wearing similar military garments. The importance of the *Standard of Ur* is not simply as documentary evidence of Sumerian life but as one of the earliest examples we have of historical narrative.

Akkad

At the height of the Sumerians' power in southern Mesopotamia, a people known as the Akkadians arrived from the north and settled in the area around present-day Baghdad. Their capital city, Akkad, has never been discovered, and in all likelihood lies under Baghdad itself. Under Sargon I (r. ca. 2332–2279 BCE), the Akkadians conquered virtually all other cities in Mesopotamia, including those in Sumer, to become the region's most powerful city-state. Sargon named himself "King of the Four Quarters of the World" and equated himself with the gods, a status bestowed upon Akkadian rulers from his time forward. Legends about Sargon's might and power survived in the region for thousands of years. Indeed, the legend of his birth gave rise to what amounts to a **narrative genre** (a class or category of story with a universal theme) that survives to the present day: the boy from humble origins who rises to a position of might and power, the so-called rags-to-riches story.

As depicted on surviving clay tablets, Sargon was an illegitimate child whose mother deposited him in the Euphrates River in a basket. There, a man named Akki (after whom Akkad itself is named) found him while drawing water from the river and raised him as his own son. Such stories of

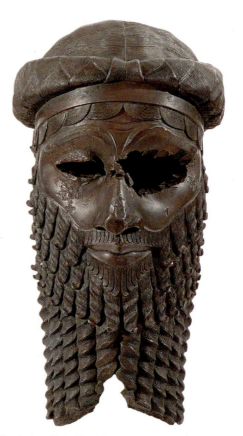

Fig. 1.18 *Head of an Akkadian Man*, from Nineveh (present-day Kuyunjik, Iraq). ca. 2300–2200 BCE. Copper alloy, height 14⅛". Iraq Museum, Baghdad. Note that the figure is life-size.

abandonment, orphanhood, and being a foundling raised by foster parents have become a standard feature in the narratives of mythic heroes.

Although the Akkadian language was very different from Sumerian, through most of the third millennium BCE—that is, until Sargon's dynastic ambitions altered the balance of power in the region—the two cultures coexisted peacefully. The Akkadians adopted Sumerian culture and customs and their style of **cuneiform writing**, a script made of wedge-shaped characters, although not their language. In fact, many bilingual dictionaries and Sumerian texts with Akkadian translations survive. The Akkadian language was Semitic in origin, having more in common with other languages of the region, particularly Hebrew, Phoenician, and Arabic. It quickly became the common language of Mesopotamia, and peoples of the region spoke Akkadian, or dialects of it, throughout the second millennium and well into the first.

Although Akkad was arguably the most influential of the Mesopotamian cultures, few Akkadian artifacts survive, perhaps because Akkad and other nearby Akkadian cities have disappeared under Baghdad and the alluvial soils of the Euphrates plain. Two impressive sculptural works do remain, however. The first is the bronze head of an Akkadian man (Fig. **1.18**), found at Nineveh. It was once believed to be Sargon the Great himself, but many modern scholars now think it was part of a statue of Sargon's grandson

Naram-Sin (ca. 2254–2218 BCE). It may be neither, but it is certainly the bust of a king. Highly realistic, it depicts a man who appears both powerful and majestic. In its damaged condition, the head is all that survives of a life-size statue that was destroyed in antiquity. Its original gemstone eyes were removed, perhaps by plundering soldiers, or possibly by a political enemy who recognized the sculpture as an emblem of absolute majesty. In the fine detail surrounding the face—in the beard and elaborate coiffure, with its braid circling the head—it testifies to the Akkadian mastery of the lost-wax casting technique, which originated in Mesopotamia as early as the third millennium BCE. It is the earliest monumental work made by that technique that we have.

Babylon

The Akkadians dominated Mesopotamia for just 150 years, their rule collapsing not long after 2200 BCE. For the next 400 years, various city-states thrived locally. No one in Mesopotamia matched the Akkadians' power until the first decades of the eighteenth century BCE, when Hammurabi of Babylon (r. 1792–1750 BCE) gained control of most of the region.

Hammurabi imposed order on Babylon, where laxity and disorder, if not chaos, reigned. A giant **stele**—an upright stone slab carved with a commemorative design or inscription—survives, upon which is inscribed the so-called Law Code of Hammurabi (Fig. **1.19**). By no means the first of its kind, although by far the most complete, the stele is a record of decisions and decrees made by Hammurabi over the course of some 40 years of his reign. Its purpose was to celebrate his sense of justice and the wisdom of his rule. Atop the stele, in sculptural relief, Hammurabi receives the blessing of Shamash, the sun god; notice the rays of light coming from his shoulders. The god is much larger than Hammurabi; in fact, he is to Hammurabi as Hammurabi, the patriarch, is to his people. If Hammurabi is divine, he is still subservient to the greater gods. At the same time, the phallic design of the stele, like such other Mesopotamian steles as the *Stele of Naram-Sin*, asserts the masculine prowess of the king.

Below the relief, 282 separate "articles" cover both sides of the basalt monument. One of the great debates of legal history is the question of whether these articles actually constitute a code of law. If by *code* we mean a comprehensive, systematic, and methodical compilation of all aspects of Mesopotamian law, then it is not. It is instead selective, even eccentric, in the issues it addresses. Many of its articles seem to be "reforms" of already existing law, and as such they define new principles of justice.

Chief among these is the principle of *talion*—an eye for an eye, a tooth for a tooth—which Hammurabi introduced to Mesopotamian law. (Sections of earlier codes from Ur compensate victims of crimes with money.) This principle punished the violence or injustice perpetrated by one free person upon another, but violence by an upper-class person on a lower-class person was penalized much less severely. Slaves

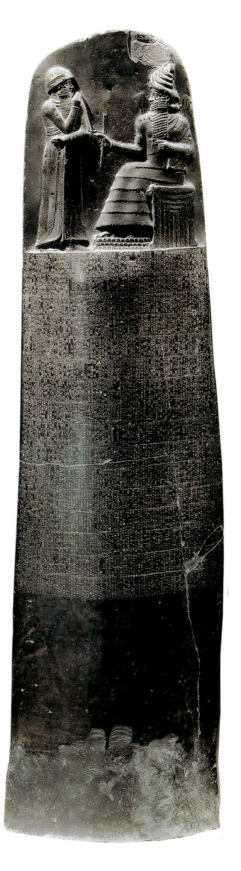

Fig. 1.19 *Stele of Hammurabi*, from Susa (present-day Shush, Iran). ca. **1760** BCE. Diorite, height of stele approx. 7'; height of relief 28". Musée du Louvre, Paris. This stele was stolen by invading Elamites and removed to Susa, where it was excavated by the French in 1898.

(who might be either war captives or debtors) enjoyed no legal protection at all—only the protection of their owner.

The code tells us much about the daily lives of Mesopotamian peoples, including conflicts great and small. In rules governing family relations and class divisions in Mesopotamian society, inequalities are sharply drawn. Women are inferior to men, and wives, like slaves, are the personal property of their husbands (although protected from the abuse of neglectful or unjust husbands). Incest is strictly forbidden. Fathers cannot arbitrarily disinherit their sons—a son must have committed some "heavy crime" to justify such treatment. The code's strongest concern is the maintenance and protection of the family, although trade practices and property rights are also of major importance.

The following excerpts from the code, beginning with Hammurabi's assertion of his descent from the gods and his status as their favorite (**Reading 1.2**), give a sense of the code's scope. But the code is, finally and perhaps above all, the gift of a king to his people, as Hammurabi's epilogue, at the end of the excerpt, makes clear:

READING 1.2

from the *Law Code of Hammurabi* (ca. 1760 BCE)

When the august god Anu, king of the Anunnaku deities, and the god Enlil, lord of heaven and earth, who determines the destinies of the land, allotted supreme power over all peoples to the god Marduk, the firstborn son of the god Ea, exalted him among the Igigu deities, named the city of Babylon with its august name and made it supreme exalted within the regions of the world, and established for him within it eternal kingship whose foundations are as fixed as heaven and earth, at that time, the gods Anu and Bel, for the enhancement of the well-being of the people, named me by my name, Hammurabi, the pious prince, who venerates the gods, to make justice prevail in the land, to abolish the wicked and the evil, to prevent the strong from oppressing the weak, to rise like the Sun-god Shamash over all humankind, to illuminate the land. . . .

1. If a man accuses another man and charges him with homicide but cannot bring proof against him, his accuser shall be killed. . . .

8. If a man steals an ox, a sheep, a donkey, a pig, or a boat—if it belongs either to the god or to the palace, he shall give thirtyfold; if it belongs to a commoner, he shall replace it tenfold; if the thief does not have anything to give, he shall be killed. . . .

32. If there is either a soldier or a fisherman who is taken captive while on a royal campaign, a merchant redeems him, and helps him get back to his city—if there are sufficient in his own estate for the redeeming, he himself shall redeem himself: if there are not sufficient means in his estate to redeem him he shall be redeemed by his city's temple; if there are not sufficient means in his city's temple to redeem him, the palace shall redeem him; but his field, orchard, or house shall not be given for his redemption. . . .

143. If [a woman] is not circumspect, but is wayward, squanders her household possessions, and disparages her husband, they shall cast that woman into the water. . . .

195. If a child should strike his father, they shall cut off his hand.

196. If an *awilu* [in general, a person subject to law] should blind the eye of another *awilu*, they shall blind his eye.

197. If he should break the bone of another *awilu*, they shall break his bone. . . .

229. If a builder constructs a house for a man but does not make his work sound, and the house he constructs collapses and causes the death of the householder, that builder shall be killed. . . .

282. If a slave should declare to his master, "You are not my master," he (the master) shall bring charge and proof against him that he is indeed his slave, and his master shall cut off his ear. . . .

These are the decisions which Hammurabi, the able king, has established, and thereby has directed the land along the course of truth and the correct way of life.

I am Hammurabi, noble king . . .

May any king who will appear in the land in the future, at any time, observe the pronouncements of justice that I have inscribed upon my stele. May he not alter the judgments that I rendered and verdicts that I gave, nor remove my engraved image. If that man has discernment, and is capable of providing just ways for his land, may he heed the pronouncements I have inscribed upon my stele, may the stele reveal for him the traditions, the proper conduct, the judgments of the land that I rendered, the verdicts of the land that I gave and may he, too, provide just ways for all humankind in his care. . . .

I am Hammurabi, king of justice. . . .

Even if Hammurabi meant only to assert the idea of justice as the basis for his own divine rule, the stele established what amounts to a uniform code throughout Mesopotamia. It was repeatedly copied for more than 1,000 years, long after it was removed to Susa in 1157 BCE, and it established the rule of law in Mesopotamia for a millennium. From this point on, the authority and power of the ruler could no longer be capricious, subject to the whim, fancy, and subjective interpretation of his singular personality. The law was now, at least ostensibly, more objective and impartial. The ruler was required to follow certain prescribed procedures. But the law, so prescribed in writing, was now also hard to change, much less flexible, and much more impersonal. Exceptions to the rule were few and difficult to justify. Eventually, written law would remove justice from the discretion of the ruler and replace it with a legal establishment of learned judges charged with enacting the king's statutes.

Mesopotamian Literature and the *Epic of Gilgamesh*

Sumerian literature survives on nearly 100,000 clay tablets and fragments. Many deal with religious themes in the form of poems, blessings, and incantations to the gods. One of the great surviving manuscripts of Mesopotamian culture, and the oldest story ever recorded, is the *Epic of Gilgamesh*. An **epic** is a long narrative poem in elevated language. It follows characters of a high position through a series of adventures, often including a visit to the world of the dead. For many literary scholars, the epic is the most exalted poetic form. The central figure is a legendary or historical figure of heroic proportion, in this case the Sumerian king Gilgamesh. Homer's *Iliad* and *Odyssey* (see Chapter 2) had been considered the earliest epics until late in the nineteenth century, when *Gilgamesh* was discovered in the library of King Ashurbanipal at Nineveh, believed to be the first library of texts systematically collected and organized in history.

The scope of an epic is large. The supernatural world of gods and goddesses usually plays a role in the story, as do battles in which the hero demonstrates his strength and courage. The poem's language is suitably dignified, often consisting of many long, formal speeches. Lists of various heroes or catalogs of their achievements are frequent.

Epics are often compilations of preexisting myths and tales handed down from generation to generation, often orally, and finally unified into a whole by the epic poet. Indeed, the outline of the story is usually known to its audience. The poet's contribution is the artistry brought to the subject, demonstrated through the use of epithets, metaphors, and similes. **Epithets** are words or phrases that characterize a person (for example, "Enkidu, the protector of herdsmen," or "Enkidu, the son of the mountain"). **Metaphors** are words or phrases used in place of another to suggest a similarity between the two, as when Gilgamesh is described as a "raging flood-wave who destroys even walls of stone." **Similes** compare two unlike things by the use of the word "like" or "as" (for example, "the land shattered like a pot").

Perhaps most important, the epic illuminates the development of a nation or race. It is a national poem, describing a people's common heritage and celebrating its cultural identity. It is hardly surprising, then, that the Assyrian king Ashurbanipal (r. 668–627 BCE), preserved the *Epic of Gilgamesh* in his great library, a collection of 20,000 to 30,000 cuneiform tablets containing approximately 1,200 distinct texts. The *Epic of Gilgamesh* preserves the historical lineage of all Mesopotamian kings—Sumerian, Akkadian, Assyrian, and Babylonian. The tale embodies their own heroic grandeur, and thus the grandeur of their peoples.

Gilgamesh consists of some 2,900 lines written in Akkadian cuneiform script on 11 clay tablets, none of them completely whole. It was composed sometime before Ashurbanipal's reign, possibly as early as 1200 BCE, by Sinleqqiunninni, a scholar-priest of Uruk. This would make Sinleqqiunninni the oldest known author. We know that Gilgamesh was the fourth king of Uruk, ruling sometime between 2700 and 2500 BCE. (The dates of his rule were recorded on a clay tablet, the *Sumerian King List*.) Recovered fragments of his story date back nearly to his actual reign, and the story we have, known as the Standard Version, is a compilation of these earlier versions.

At the center of the poem, in Tablet VI, Ishtar, goddess of both love and war, offers to marry Gilgamesh. Gilgamesh refuses, which unleashes Ishtar's wrath. She sends the Bull of Heaven to destroy Gilgamesh and Enkidu, but they slay it instead (**Reading 1.3a**).

READING 1.3a

from the *Epic of Gilgamesh*, Tablet VI (late 2nd millennium BCE)

A Woman Scorned

. . . When Gilgamesh placed his crown on his head Princess,
   Ishtar raised her eyes to the beauty of Gilgamesh.
"Come along, Gilgamesh, be you my husband,
   to me grant your lusciousness.[1]
Be you my husband, and I will be your wife.
I will have harnessed for you a chariot of lapis
   lazuli and gold,
with wheels of gold . . .
Bowed down beneath you will be kings, lords,
   and princes.
The Lullubu people[2] will bring you the produce of the
   mountains and countryside as tribute.
Your she-goats will bear triplets, your ewes twins,
your donkey under burden will overtake the mule,
your steed at the chariot will be bristling to gallop,
your ox at the yoke will have no match."
Gilgamesh addressed Princess Ishtar saying:
"Do you need oil or garments for your body?
Do you lack anything for food or drink?
I would gladly feed you food fit for a god,
I would gladly give you wine fit for a king . . .
a half-door that keeps out neither breeze nor blast,
a palace that crushes down valiant warriors,
an elephant who devours its own covering,
pitch that blackens the hands of its bearer,
a waterskin that soaks its bearer through,
limestone that buckles out the stone wall,
a battering ram that attracts the enemy land,
a shoe that bites its owner's feet!
Where are your bridegrooms that you keep forever? . . .
You loved the supremely mighty lion,
yet you dug for him seven and again seven pits.
You loved the stallion, famed in battle,
yet you ordained for him the whip, the goad,
   and the lash,
ordained for him to gallop for seven and seven hours,
ordained for him drinking from muddied waters,[3]
you ordained for his mother Silili to wail continually.
You loved the Shepherd, the Master Herder,
who continually presented you with bread
   baked in embers,
and who daily slaughtered for you a kid.
Yet you struck him, and turned him into a wolf,

[1]Literally "fruit."
[2]The Lullubu were a wild mountain people living in the area of modern-day western Iran. The meaning is that even the wildest, least controllable of peoples will recognize Gilgamesh's rule and bring tribute.
[3]Horses put their front feet in the water when drinking, churning up mud.

so his own shepherds now chase him
and his own dogs snap at his shins.
You loved Ishullanu, your father's date gardener,
who continually brought you baskets of dates,
and brightened your table daily.
You raised your eyes to him, and you went to him:
   'Oh my Ishullanu, let us taste of your strength,
   stretch out your hand to me, and touch our
   "vulva."'[4]
Ishullanu said to you:
   'Me? What is it you want from me? . . .'
As you listened to these his words
   you struck him, turning him into a dwarf(?),[5] . . .
   And now me! It is me you love, and you will ordain
for me as for them!"

Her Fury

When Ishtar heard this
in a fury she went up to the heavens,
going to Anu, her father, and crying,
going to Antum, her mother, and weeping:
   "Father, Gilgamesh has insulted me over and over,
   Gilgamesh has recounted despicable deeds about me,
   despicable deeds and curses!"
Anu addressed Princess Ishtar, saying:
   "What is the matter? Was it not you who provoked
     King Gilgamesh?
   So Gilgamesh recounted despicable deeds about you,
   despicable deeds and curses!"
Ishtar spoke to her father, Anu, saying:
   "Father, give me the Bull of Heaven,
   so he can kill Gilgamesh in his dwelling.
   If you do not give me the Bull of Heaven,
   I will knock down the Gates of the Netherworld,
   I will smash the door posts, and leave the doors
     flat down,
   and will let the dead go up to eat the living!
   And the dead will outnumber the living!"
Anu addressed Princess Ishtar, saying:
   "If you demand the Bull of Heaven from me,
   there will be seven years of empty husks for the land
     of Uruk.
   Have you collected grain for the people?
   Have you made grasses grow for the animals?"
Ishtar addressed Anu, her father, saying:
   "I have heaped grain in the granaries for the people,
   I made grasses grow for the animals,
   in order that they might eat in the seven years of empty
     husks.
   I have collected grain for the people,
   I have made grasses grow for the animals. . . ."
When Anu heard her words,
he placed the nose-rope of the Bull of Heaven in her hand.
Ishtar led the Bull of Heaven down to the earth.
When it reached Uruk . . .
It climbed down to the Euphrates . . .

[4] This line probably contains a word play on *hurdatu* as "vulva" and "date palm," the latter being said (in another unrelated text) to be "like the vulva."
[5] Or "frog"?

At the snort of the Bull of Heaven a huge pit opened up,
and 100 Young Men of Uruk fell in.
At his second snort a huge pit opened up,
and 200 Young Men of Uruk fell in.
At his third snort a huge pit opened up,
and Enkidu fell in up to his waist.
Then Enkidu jumped out and seized the Bull of Heaven by
   its horns.
The Bull spewed his spittle in front of him,
with his thick tail he flung *his dung behind him*(?).
Enkidu addressed Gilgamesh, saying:
   "My friend, we can be bold(?) . . .
   Between the nape, the horns, and . . . thrust your
     sword."
Enkidu stalked and *hunted down* the Bull of Heaven.
He grasped it by the thick of its tail
and held onto it with both his hands(?),
while Gilgamesh, like an *expert butcher*,
boldly and *surely approached the Bull of Heaven.*
Between the nape, the horns, and . . . he thrust his sword. . . .
Ishtar went up onto the top of the Wall of Uruk-Haven,
cast herself into the pose of mourning, and hurled her
   woeful curse:
   "Woe unto Gilgamesh who slandered me and killed the
     Bull of Heaven!"
When Enkidu heard this pronouncement of Ishtar,
he wrenched off the Bull's hindquarter and flung it in her face:
   "If I could only get at you I would do the same to you!
   I would drape his innards over your arms!" . . .
Gilgamesh said to the palace retainers:
   "Who is the bravest of the men?
   Who is the boldest of the males?
   —Gilgamesh is the bravest of the men,
   the boldest of the males!
   She at whom we flung the hindquarter of the Bull of
     Heaven in anger,
   Ishtar has no one that pleases her . . . "

But Gilgamesh and Enkidu cannot avoid the wrath of the gods altogether. One of them, the gods decide, must die, and so Enkidu suffers a long, painful death, attended by his friend Gilgamesh, who is terrified (**Reading 1.3b**):

READING 1.3b

from the *Epic of Gilgamesh*, Tablet X (late 2nd millennium BCE)

My friend. . . . Enkidu, whom I love deeply, who went
   through every hardship with me,
the fate of mankind has overtaken him.
Six days and seven nights I mourned over him
and would not allow him to be buried
until a maggot fell out of his nose.
I was terrified by his appearance,
I began to fear death, and so roam the wilderness.
The issue of Enkidu, my friend, oppresses me,
so I have been roaming long trails through the wilderness.

How can I stay silent, how can I be still?
My friend whom I love has turned to clay.
Am I not like him? Will I lie down, never to get up again?

Dismayed at the prospect of his own mortality, Gilgamesh embarks on a journey to find the secret of eternal life from the only mortal known to have attained it, Utnapishtim, who tells him the story of the Great Flood. Several elements of Utnapishtim's story deserve explanation. First of all, this is the earliest known version of the flood story that occurs also in the Hebrew Bible, with Utnapishtim in the role of the biblical Noah. The motif of a single man and wife surviving a worldwide flood brought about by the gods occurs in several Middle Eastern cultures, suggesting a single origin or shared tradition. In the Sumerian version, Ea (Enki) warns Utnapishtim of the flood by speaking to the wall, thereby technically keeping the agreement among the gods not to warn mortals of their upcoming disaster. The passage in which Ea tells Utnapishtim how to explain his actions to his people without revealing the secret of the gods is one of extraordinary complexity and wit (**Reading 1.3c**). The word for "bread" is *kukku*, a pun on the word for "darkness," *kukkû*. Similarly, the word for "wheat," *kibtu*, also means "misfortune." Thus, when Ea says, "He will let loaves of bread shower down,/ and in the evening a rain of wheat," he is also telling the truth: "He will let loaves of darkness shower down, and in the evening a rain of misfortune."

READING 1.3c

from the *Epic of Gilgamesh*, Tablet XI (late 2nd millennium BCE)

Utnapishtim spoke to Gilgamesh, saying:
"I will reveal to you, Gilgamesh, a thing that is hidden,
a secret of the gods I will tell you!
Shuruppak, a city that you surely know,
situated on the banks of the Euphrates,
that city was very old, and there were gods inside it.
The hearts of the Great Gods moved them to inflict the
   Flood. . . .
Ea, the Clever Prince, was under oath with them
so he repeated their talk to the reed house:
'Reed house, reed house! Wall, wall!
Hear, O reed house! Understand, O wall!
O man of Shuruppak, son of Ubartutu:
Tear down the house and build a boat!
Abandon wealth and seek living beings!
Spurn possessions and keep alive human beings!
Make all living beings go up into the boat.
The boat which you are to build,
its dimensions must measure equal to each other:
its length must correspond to its width,
Roof it over like the Apsu.'
I understood and spoke to my lord, Ea:
'My lord, thus is your command.
I will heed and will do it.

But what shall I answer the city, the populace, and the
   Elders?'

Ea spoke, commanding me, his servant:
'. . . this is what you must say to them:
"It appears that Enlil is rejecting me
so I cannot reside in your city,
nor set foot on Enlil's earth.
I will go . . . to live with my lord, Ea,
and upon you he will rain down abundance,
a profusion of fowls, myriad fishes.
He will bring you a harvest of wealth,
in the morning he will let loaves of bread shower down,
and in the evening a rain of wheat."' . . .

I butchered oxen for the meat(?),
and day upon day I slaughtered sheep.
I gave the workmen(?) ale, beer, oil, and wine, as if it were
   river water,
so they could make a party like the New Year's Festival. . . .
The boat was finished. . . .
Whatever I had I loaded on it:
whatever silver I had I loaded on it,
whatever gold I had I loaded on it.
All the living beings that I had I loaded on it,
I had all my kith and kin go up into the boat,
all the beasts and animals of the field and the craftsmen I
   had go up. . . .

I watched the appearance of the weather—
the weather was frightful to behold!
I went into the boat and sealed the entry. . . .
Just as dawn began to glow
there arose on the horizon a black cloud.
Adad rumbled inside it. . . .
Stunned shock over Adad's deeds overtook the heavens,
and turned to blackness all that had been light.
The . . . land shattered like a . . . pot.

All day long the South Wind blew . . . ,
blowing fast, submerging the mountain in water,
overwhelming the people like an attack.
No one could see his fellow,
they could not recognize each other in the torrent.
The gods were frightened by the Flood,
and retreated, ascending to the heaven of Anu.
The gods were cowering like dogs, crouching by the outer
   wall.
Ishtar shrieked like a woman in childbirth. . . .
Six days and seven nights
came the wind and flood, the storm flattening the land.
When the seventh day arrived, the storm was pounding,
the flood was a war—struggling with itself like a woman
   writhing (in labor).
The sea calmed, fell still, the whirlwind (and) flood stopped
   up.
I looked around all day long—quiet had set in
and all the human beings had turned to clay!

 Read the document from the *Epic of Gilgamesh* on **MyArtsLab**

> The terrain was flat as a roof.
> I opened a vent and fresh air (daylight?) fell upon the side
>   of my nose.
>
> I fell to my knees and sat weeping,
> tears streaming down the side of my nose.
> I looked around for coastlines in the expanse of the sea,
> and at twelve leagues there emerged a region (of land).
> On Mt. Nimush the boat lodged firm,
> Mt. Nimush held the boat, allowing no sway."

When the gods discover Utnapishtim alive, smelling his incense offering, they are outraged. They did not want a single living being to escape. But since he has, they grant him immortality and allow him to live forever in the Faraway. As a reward for Gilgamesh's own efforts, Utnapishtim tells Gilgamesh of a secret plant that will give him perpetual youth. "I will eat it," he tells the boatman who is returning him home, "and I will return to what I was in my youth." But when they stop for the night, Gilgamesh decides to bathe in a cool pool, where the scent of the plant attracts a snake who steals it away, an echo of the biblical story of Adam and Eve, whose own immortality is stolen away by the wiles of a serpent—and their own carelessness. Broken-hearted, Gilgamesh returns home empty-handed.

The *Epic of Gilgamesh* is the first known literary work to confront the idea of death, which is, in many ways, the very embodiment of the unknown. Although the hero goes to the very ends of the earth in his quest, he ultimately leaves with nothing to show for his efforts except an understanding of his own, very human, limitations. He is the first hero in Western literature to yearn for what he can never attain, to seek to understand what must always remain a mystery. And, of course, until the death of his friend Enkidu, Gilgamesh had seemed, in his self-confident confrontation with Ishtar and in the defeat of the Bull of Heaven, as near to a god as a mortal might be. In short, he embodied the Mesopotamian hero-king. Even as the poem asserts the hero-king's divinity—the poem first introduces him as two parts god, one part human—it emphasizes his humanity and the mortality that accompanies it. By making literal the first words of the *Sumerian King List*—"After the kingship had descended from heaven"—the *Epic of Gilgamesh* acknowledges what many Mesopotamian kings were unwilling to admit, at least publicly: their own, very human, limitations, and their own powerlessness in the face of the ultimate unknown—death.

The Hebrews

The Hebrews (from *Habiru*, "outcast" or "nomad") were a people forced out of their homeland in the Mesopotamian basin in about 2000 BCE. According to their tradition, it was in the delta of the Tigris and Euphrates rivers that God created Adam and Eve in the Garden of Eden. It was there that Noah survived the same great flood that Utnapishtim survived in the *Epic of Gilgamesh*. And it was out of there that Abraham of Ur led his people into Canaan, in order to escape the warlike Akkadians and the increasingly powerful

Babylonians. There is no actual historical evidence to support these stories. We know them only from the Hebrew Bible—a word that derives from the Greek *biblia*, "books"—a compilation of hymns, prophecies, and laws transcribed by its authors between 800 and 400 BCE, some 1,000 years after the events the Hebrew Bible describes. Although the archeological record in the Near East confirms some of what these scribes and priests wrote, especially about more contemporaneous events, the stories themselves were edited and collated into the stories we know today. They recount the Assyrian conquest of Israel, the Jews' later exile to Babylon after the destruction of Jerusalem by the Babylonian king Nebuchadnezzar in 587 BCE, and their eventual return to Jerusalem after the Persians conquered the Babylonians in 538 BCE. The stories represent the Hebrews' attempt to maintain their sense of their own history and destiny. But it would be a mistake to succumb to the temptation to read the Hebrew Bible as an accurate account of the historical record. Like all ancient histories, passed down orally through generation upon generation, it contains its fair share of mythologizing.

The Hebrews differed from other Near Eastern cultures in that their religion was *monotheistic*—they worshiped a single god, whereas others in the region tended to have gods for their clans and cities, among other things. According to Hebrew tradition, God made an agreement with the Hebrews, first with Noah after the flood, later renewed with Abraham and each of the subsequent **patriarchs** (scriptural fathers of the Hebrew people): "I am God Almighty; be fruitful and multiply; a nation and a company of nations shall come from you. The land which I gave to Abraham and Isaac I will give to you, and I will give the land to your descendants after you" (Genesis 35:11–12). In return for this promise, the Hebrews, the "chosen people," agreed to obey God's will. "Chosen people" means that the Jews were chosen to set an example of a higher moral standard ("a light unto the nations")—not chosen in the sense of favored, which is a common misunderstanding of the term.

Genesis, the first book of the Hebrew Bible, tells the story of the creation of the world out of a "formless void." It describes God's creation of the world and all its creatures, and his continuing interest in the workings of the world, an interest that would lead, in the story of Noah, to God's near-destruction of all things. It also posits humankind as easily tempted by evil. It documents the moment of the introduction of sin (and shame) into the cosmos, associating these with the single characteristic separating humans from animals—knowledge. And it shows, in the example of Noah, the reward for having "walked with God," the basis of the covenant.

Moses and the Ten Commandments   The biblical story of Moses and the Ten Commandments embodies the centrality of the written word to Jewish culture. The Hebrew Bible claims that in about 1600 BCE drought forced the Hebrew people to leave Canaan for Egypt, where they prospered until the Egyptians enslaved them in about 1300 BCE. Defying the rule of the pharaohs, the Jewish patriarch Moses led his people out of Egypt. According to tradition, Moses led the Jews across the Red Sea (which miraculously parted to facilitate the escape) and into the desert of the Sinai peninsula. (The story became the basis for the book of Exodus.) Most likely, they crossed a large tidal flat, called the Sea of Reeds; subsequently that body of water was misidentified as the Red Sea. Unable to return to Canaan, which was now occupied by local tribes of considerable military strength, the Jews settled in an arid region of the Sinai desert near the Dead Sea for a period of 40 years, which archeologists date to sometime between 1300 and 1150 BCE.

In the Sinai desert, the Hebrews forged the principal tenets of a new religion that would eventually be based on the worship of a single god. There, too, the Hebrew god supposedly revealed a new name for himself—YHWH, a name so sacred that it could neither be spoken nor written. The name is not known and YHWH is a cipher for it. There are, however, many other names for God in the Hebrew Bible, among them Elohim, which is plural in Hebrew, meaning "gods, deities"; Adonai ("Lord"); and El Shaddai, literally "God of the fields" but usually translated "God Almighty." Some scholars believe that this demonstrates the multiple authorship of the Bible. Others argue that the Hebrews originally worshiped many gods, as did other Near Eastern peoples. Still other scholars suggest that God has been given different names to reflect different aspects of his divinity, or the different roles he might assume—the guardian of the flocks in the fields, or the powerful master of all. Translated into Latin as "Jehovah" in the Middle Ages, the name is now rendered in English as "Yahweh." This God also gave Moses the Ten Commandments, carved onto stone tablets, as recorded in Deuteronomy 5:6–21. Subsequently, the Hebrews carried the commandments in a sacred chest, called the Ark of the Covenant (Fig. 1.20), which was lit by seven-branched candelabras known as *menorahs*. The centrality to Hebrew culture of these written words is even more apparent in the words of God that follow the commandments (**Reading 1.4**):

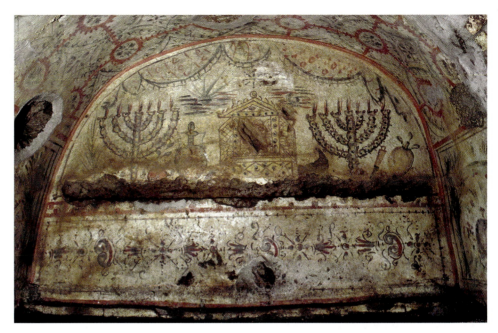

Fig. 1.20 Menorahs and Ark of the Covenant, wall painting in a Jewish catacomb, Villa Torlonia, Rome. 3rd century CE. 3'11" × 5'9". Two menorahs (seven-branched candelabras) flank the Ark. The menorah is considered a symbol of the nation of Israel and its mission to be "a light unto the nations" (Isaiah 42:6). Instructions for making it are outlined in Exodus 25:31–40. Relatively little ancient Jewish art remains. Most of it was destroyed as the Jewish people were conquered, persecuted, and exiled.

READING 1.4

from the Hebrew Bible (Deuteronomy 6:6–9)

6 Keep these words that I am commanding you today in your heart.

7 Recite them to your children and talk about them when you are at home and when you are away, when you lie down and when you rise.

8 Bind them as a sign on your hand, fix them as an emblem on your forehead,

9 and write them on the doorposts of your house and on your gates.

Whenever the Hebrews talked, wherever they looked, wherever they went, they focused on the commandments of their God. Their monotheistic religion was thus also an ethical and moral system derived from an omnipotent God. The Ten Commandments were the centerpiece of the Torah, or Law (literally "instructions"), consisting of Genesis, Exodus, Leviticus, Numbers, and Deuteronomy. (Christians would later incorporate these books into their Bible as the first five books of the Old Testament.) The Hebrews considered these five books divinely inspired and attributed their original authorship to Moses himself, although, as we have noted, the texts as we know them were written much later.

The body of laws outlined in the Torah is quite different from the code of Hammurabi. The code was essentially a list of punishments for offenses; it is not an *ethical* code (see Fig. 1.19 and Reading 1.2). Hebraic and Mesopotamian laws are distinctly different. Perhaps because the Hebrews were once themselves aliens and slaves, their law treats the lowest members of society as human beings. As Yahweh declares in Exodus 23:6: "You will not cheat the poor among you of their rights at law." At least under the law, class distinctions, with the exception of slaves, did not exist in Hebrew society, and punishment was levied equally. Above all else, rich and poor alike were united for the common good in a common enterprise, to follow the instructions for living as God provided.

After 40 years in the Sinai had passed, it is believed that the patriarch Joshua led the Jews back to Canaan, the Promised Land, as Yahweh had pledged in the covenant. Over the next 200 years, they gradually gained control of the region through a protracted series of wars described in

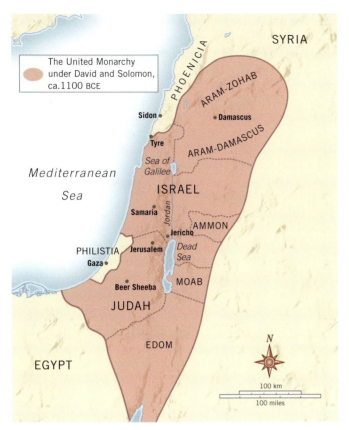

Map 1.5 The United Monarchy of Israel under David and Solomon, ca. 1100 BCE.

the books of Joshua, Judges, Samuel, and Kings in the Bible, which together make up a theological history of the early Jewish peoples. The Jews named themselves the Israelites, after Israel, the name that was given by God to Jacob. The nation consisted of 12 tribes, each descended from one of Jacob's 12 sons. By about 1000 BCE, Saul had established himself as king of Israel, followed by David, who as a boy rescued the Israelites from the Philistines by killing the giant Goliath with a stone thrown from a sling, as described in First Samuel, and later united Israel and Judah into a single state (Map **1.5**).

Solomon, the Prophets, and the Diaspora Solomon undertook to complete the building campaign begun by his father, and by the end of his reign, Jerusalem was, by all reports, one of the most beautiful cities in the Near East. A magnificent palace and, most especially, a splendid temple dominated the city. First Kings claims that Yahweh himself saw the temple and approved of it.

The scriptural covenant between God and the Hebrews was the model for the relationship between the Hebrew king and his people. Each provided protection in return for obedience and fidelity. The same relationship existed between the family patriarch and his household. His wife and children were his possessions, whom he protected in return for their unerring faith in him.

After Solomon's death, the United Monarchy of Israel split into two separate states. To the north was Israel, with its capital in Samaria, and to the south, Judah, with its capital in Jerusalem. In this era of the two kingdoms, Hebrew culture was dominated by **prophets**, men who were prophetic not in the sense of foretelling the future, but rather in the sense of serving as mouthpieces and interpreters of Yahweh's purposes, which they claimed to understand through visions. The prophets instructed the people in the ways of living according to the laws of the Torah, and they more or less freely confronted anyone guilty of wrongful actions, even the Hebrew kings. They attacked, particularly, the wealthy Hebrews whose commercial ventures had brought them unprecedented material comfort and who were inclined to stray from monotheism and worship Canaanite fertility gods and goddesses. The moral laxity of these wealthy Hebrews troubled the prophets, who urged the Hebrew nation to reform spiritually.

In 722 BCE, Assyrians attacked the northern kingdom of Israel and scattered its people, who were thereafter known as the Lost Tribes of Israel. The southern kingdom of Judah survived another 135 years, until Nebuchadnezzar and the Babylonians overwhelmed it in 587 BCE, destroying the Temple of Solomon in Jerusalem and deporting the Hebrews to Babylon. Not only had the Hebrews lost their homeland and their temple, but the Ark of the Covenant itself disappeared. For nearly 70 years, the Hebrews endured what is known as the Babylonian Captivity, as recorded in Psalm 137: "By the rivers of Babylon, there we sat down, yea we wept, when we remembered Zion."

Finally, invading Persians, whom they believed had been sent by Yahweh, freed them from the Babylonians in 520 BCE. They returned to Judah, known now, for the first time, as the Jews (after the name of their homeland). They rebuilt a Second Temple of Jerusalem, with an empty chamber at its center, meant for the Ark of the Covenant should it ever return. And they welcomed back other Jews from around the Mediterranean, including many whose families had left the northern kingdom almost 200 years earlier. Many others, however, were by now permanently settled elsewhere, and they became known as the Jews of the Diaspora or the "dispersion."

Hebrew culture would have a profound impact on Western civilization. The Jews provided the essential ethical and moral foundation for religion in the West, including Christianity and Islam, both of which incorporate Jewish teachings into their own thought and practice. In the Torah, we find the basis of the law as we understand and practice it today. So moving and universal are the stories recorded in the Torah that over the centuries they have inspired—and continue to inspire—countless works of art, music, and literature. Most important, the Hebrews introduced to the world the concept of ethical monotheism: the idea that there is only one God, and that God demands that humans behave in a certain way, and rewards and punishes accordingly. Few, if any, concepts have had a more far-reaching effect on history and culture.

The Persian Empire

In 520 BCE, the Persians, formerly a minor nomadic tribe that occupied the plateau of Iran, defeated the Babylonians and freed the Jews. Their imperial adventuring had begun in 559 BCE with the ascension of Cyrus II (called the Great, r. 559–530 BCE), the first ruler of the Achaemenid dynasty, named after Achaemenes, a warrior-king whom Persian legend says ruled on the Iranian plateau around 700 BCE. By the time of Cyrus' death, the Persians had taken control of the Greek cities in Ionia on the west coast of Anatolia. Under King Darius (r. 522–486 BCE), they soon ruled a vast empire that stretched from Egypt in the south, around Asia Minor, to the Ukraine in the north. The capital of the empire was Parsa, which the Greeks called Persepolis, or city of the Persians, located in the Zagros highlands of present-day Iran. Built by artisans and workers from all over the Persian Empire, including Greeks from Ionia, it reflected Darius' multicultural ambitions. If he was, as he said, "King of Kings, King of countries, King of the earth," his palace should reflect the diversity of his peoples.

Rulers are depicted at Persepolis in relief sculptures with Assyrian beards and headdresses (Fig. 1.21). In typical Mesopotamian fashion, they are larger than other people in the works. These decorations further reflect the Persians' sense that all the peoples of the region owed them allegiance. Mesopotamian, Assyrian, Egyptian, and Greek styles all intermingle in the palace's architecture and decoration. The relief in Fig. 1.21, from the stairway to the audience hall where Darius and his son Xerxes received visitors, is covered with images of their subjects bringing gifts to the palace—23 subject nations in all, including Ionian, Babylonian, Syrian, and Susian, each culture recognizable by its beards and costumes. Darius can be seen receiving tribute as Xerxes stands behind him, as if waiting to take his place as the Persian ruler. These are the same two Persian leaders who, in the first decades of the fifth century BCE, would invade Greece, the son destroying, as we will see in the next chapter, the city of Athens, but in his destruction of the Greek capital, ushering in the great building campaign that was the hallmark of the Greek Golden Age.

THE STABILITY OF ANCIENT EGYPT: FLOOD AND SUN

What accounts for the stability of Egyptian culture?

Civilization in Mesopotamia developed across the last three millennia BCE almost simultaneously with civilization in Egypt. The two civilizations have much in common. Both formed around river systems—the Tigris and Euphrates in Mesopotamia; the Nile in Egypt. Both were agrarian societies that depended on irrigation, and their economies were

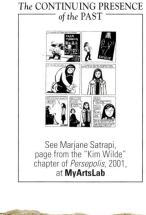

The CONTINUING PRESENCE
of the PAST

See Marjane Satrapi,
page from the "Kim Wilde"
chapter of *Persepolis*, 2001,
at **MyArtsLab**

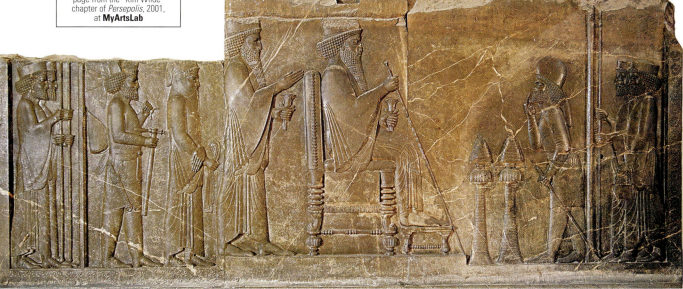

Fig. 1.21 *Darius and Xerxes Receiving Tribute*, detail of a relief from a stairway leading to the Hall of One Hundred Columns, ceremonial complex, Persepolis, Iran. 491–486 BCE. Limestone, height 8'4". Iranbastan Museum, Teheran. This panel was originally painted in blue, scarlet, green, purple, and turquoise. Objects such as Darius' necklace and crown were covered in gold.

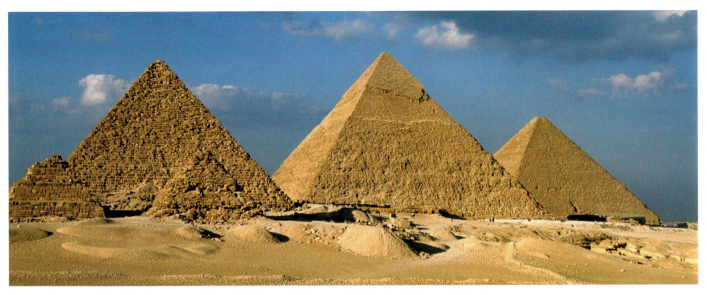

Fig. 1.22 The pyramids of Menkaure (ca. 2470 BCE), Khafre (ca. 2500 BCE), and Khufu (ca. 2530 BCE) at Giza. Giza was an elaborate complex of ritual temples, shrines, and ceremonial causeways, all leading to one or another of the three giant pyramids.

Watch the architectural simulation of the pyramids on **MyArtsLab**

hostage to the sometimes fickle, sometimes violent flow of their respective river systems. As in Mesopotamia, Egyptians learned to control the river's flow by constructing dams and irrigation canals, and it was probably the need to cooperate with one another in such endeavors that helped Mesopotamia to thrive and Egypt to create the civilization that would eventually arise in the Nile Valley.

The Mesopotamians and the Egyptians built massive architectural structures dedicated to their gods—the ziggurats in Mesopotamia (see Fig. 1.15) and the pyramids in Egypt (Fig. **1.22**). Although the former appears to be dedicated, at least in part, to water and the latter to the sun, both unite earth and sky in a single architectural form. Indeed, the earliest Egyptian pyramids were stepped structures on the model of the Mesopotamian ziggurat. Both cultures developed forms of writing, although the cuneiform script of Mesopotamian culture and the hieroglyphic script of Egyptian society were very different. There is ample evidence that the two civilizations traded with each other, and to a certain degree influenced each other.

What most distinguishes Egyptian from Mesopotamian culture, however, is the relative stability of the former. Mesopotamia was rarely, if ever, united as a single entity. Whenever it was united, it was through force, the power of an army, not the free will of a people striving for the common good. In contrast, political transition in Egypt was dynastic—that is, rule was inherited by members of the same family, sometimes for generations. As in Mesopotamia, however, the ruler's authority was cemented by his association with divine authority. He was, indeed, the manifestation of the gods on Earth. In fact, there is clear reason to believe that the sculptural image of a ruler was believed to be, in some sense, the ruler himself.

The Nile and Its Culture

Like the Tigris and Euphrates in Mesopotamia, the Nile could be said to have made Egypt possible. The river begins in the heart of Africa, one tributary in the mountains of Ethiopia and another at Lake Victoria in Uganda, from which it flows north for over 4,000 miles. Egyptian civilization developed along the last 750 miles of the river's banks, extending from the granite cliffs at Aswan north to the Mediterranean Sea (Map **1.6**).

Nearly every year, torrential rains caused the river to rise dramatically. Most years, from July to November, the Egyptians could count on the Nile flooding their land. When the river receded, deep deposits of fertile silt covered the valley floor. Fields would then be tilled, and crops planted and tended. If no flood occurred for a period of years, famine could result. The cycle of flood and sun made Egypt one of the most productive cultures in the ancient world, and one of the most stable. For 3,000 years, from 3100 BCE until the defeat of Mark Antony and Cleopatra by the Roman general Octavian in 31 BCE, Egypt's institutions and culture remained remarkably unchanged.

As a result of the Nile's annual floods, Egypt called itself Kemet, meaning "Black Land." In Upper Egypt, from Aswan to the Delta, the black, fertile deposits of the river covered an extremely narrow strip of land. Surrounding the river's alluvial plain were the "Red Lands," the desert environment that could not support life, but where rich deposits of minerals and stone could be mined and quarried. Lower Egypt, consisting of the Delta itself, began some 13 miles north of Giza, the site of the Great Pyramids, across the river from what is now Cairo.

In this land of plenty, great farms flourished, and wildlife abounded in the marshes. In fact, the Egyptians linked the

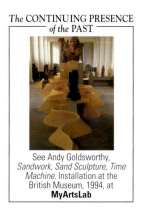

The CONTINUING PRESENCE
of the PAST

See Andy Goldsworthy,
*Sandwork, Sand Sculpture, Time
Machine*. Installation at the
British Museum, 1994, at
MyArtsLab

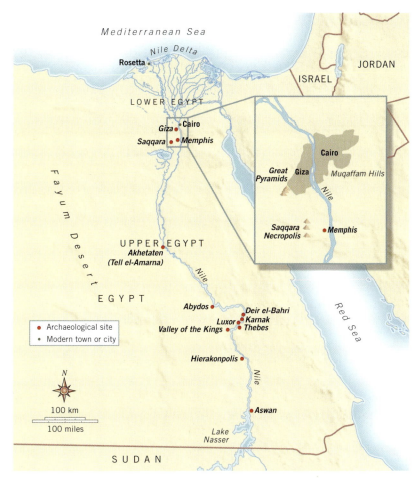

Map 1.6 Nile River Basin with archeological sites in relation to present-day Cairo. The broad expanse of the Lower Nile Delta was crisscrossed by canals, allowing easy transport of produce and supplies.

marsh to the creation of the world, and represented it that way in the famous hunting scene that decorates the tomb of Nebamun at Thebes (Fig. **1.23**). Nebamun is about to hurl a snake-shaped throwing stick into a flock of birds as his wife and daughter look on. The painting is a sort of visual pun, referring directly to procreation. The verb "to launch a throwing stick" also means "to ejaculate," and the word for "throwing stick" itself, to "create." The hieroglyphs written between Nebamun and his wife translate as "enjoying oneself, viewing the beautiful, . . . at the place of constant renewal of life."

Scholars divide Egyptian history into three main periods of achievement. Almost all the conventions of Egyptian art were established during the first period, the Old Kingdom. During the Middle Kingdom, the "classical" literary language that would survive through the remainder of Egyptian history was first produced. The New Kingdom was a period of prosperity that saw a renewed interest in art and architecture. During each of these periods, successive dynasties—or royal houses—brought peace and stability to the country. Between them were "Intermediate Periods" of relative instability.

Egypt's continuous cultural tradition—lasting more than 3,000 years—is history's clearest example of how peace and prosperity go hand in hand with cultural stability. As opposed to the warring cultures of Mesopotamia, where city-state vied with city-state and empire with successive empire, Egyptian culture was predicated on unity. It was a theocracy, a state ruled by a god or by the god's representative—in this case a king (and very occasionally a queen), who ruled as the living representative of the sun god, Re. Egypt's government was indistinguishable from its religion, and its religion manifested itself in nature, in the flow of the Nile, the heat of the sun, and in the journey of the sun through the day and night and through the seasons. In the last judgment of the soul

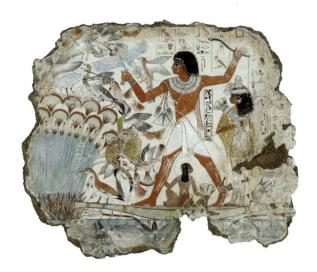

Fig. 1.23 *Nebamun Hunting Birds*, from the tomb of Nebamun, Thebes. Dynasty 18, ca. 1400 BCE. Fresco on dry plaster, height approx. 2'8". © The Trustees of the British Museum. The fish and the birds, and the cat, are completely realistic, but this is not a realistic scene. It is a conventional representation of the deceased, in this case Nebamun, spearing fish or hunting fowl, almost obligatory for the decoration of a tomb.

after death, Egyptians believed that the heart was weighed to determine whether it was "found true by trial of the Great Balance." Balance in all things—in nature, in social life, in art, and in rule—this was the constant aim of the individual, the state, and, Egyptians believed, the gods.

Whereas in Mesopotamia the flood was largely a destructive force, in Egypt it had a more complex meaning. It could, indeed, be destructive, sometimes rising so high that great devastation resulted. But without it, the Egyptians knew, their culture could not endure. So, in Egyptian art and culture, a more complex way of thinking about nature, and about life itself, developed. Every aspect of Egyptian life is countered by an opposite and equal force, which contradicts and negates it, and every act of negation gives rise to its opposite again. As a result, events are cyclical, as abundance is born of devastation and devastation closely follows abundance. Likewise, just as the floods brought the Nile Valley back to life each year, the Egyptians believed that rebirth necessarily followed death. So their religion, which played a large part in their lives, reflected the cycle of the river itself.

Egyptian Religion: Cyclical Harmony The religion of ancient Egypt, like that of Mesopotamia, was *polytheistic*, consisting of many gods and goddesses who were associated with natural forces and realms. When represented, gods and goddesses have human bodies and human or animal heads, and wear crowns or other headgear that identifies them by their attributes. The religion reflected an ordered universe in which the stars and planets, the various gods, and basic human activities were thought to be part of a grand and harmonious design. A person who did not disrupt this harmony did not fear death because his or her spirit would live on forever.

At the heart of this religion were creation stories that explained how the gods and the world came into being. Chief among the Egyptian gods was Re, god of the sun. According to these stories, at the beginning of time, the Nile created a great mound of silt, out of which Re was born. It was understood that Re had a close personal relationship with the king, who was considered the son of Re. But the king could also identify closely with other gods. The king was simultaneously believed to be the personification of the sky god, Horus, and was identified with deities associated with places like Thebes or Memphis when his power resided in those cities. Although not a full-fledged god, the king was *netjer nefer*, literally, a "junior god." That made him the representative of the people to the gods, whom he contacted through statues of divine beings placed in all temples. Through these statues, Egyptians believed, the gods manifested themselves on earth. Not only did the orderly functioning of social and political events depend upon the king's successful communication with the gods, but so did events of nature—the ebb and flow of the river chief among them.

Like the king, all the other Egyptian gods descend from Re, as if part of a family. As we have said, many can be traced back to local deities of predynastic times who later assumed greater significance at a given place—at Thebes, for instance, the trinity of Osiris, Horus, and Isis gained a special

significance. Osiris, ruler of the underworld and god of the dead, was at first a local deity in the eastern Delta. According to myth, he was murdered by his wicked brother Seth, god of storms and violence, who chopped his brother into pieces and threw them into the Nile. But Osiris's wife and sister, Isis, the goddess of fertility, collected all these parts, put the god back together, and restored him to life. Osiris was therefore identified with the Nile itself, with its annual flood and renewal. The child of Osiris and Isis was Horus, who defeated Seth and became the mythical first king of Egypt. The actual, living king was considered the earthly manifestation of Horus (as well as the son of Re). When the living king died, he became Osiris, and his son took the throne as Horus. Thus, even the kingship was cyclical.

At Memphis, the triad of Ptah, Sekhmet, and Nefertum held sway. A stone inscription at Memphis describes Ptah as the supreme artisan and creator of all things (**Reading 1.5**):

READING 1.5

"This It Is Said of Ptah," from Memphis, ca. 2300 BCE

This it is said of Ptah: "He who made all and created the gods." And he is Ta-tenen, who gave birth to the gods, and from whom every thing came forth, foods, provisions, divine offerings, all good things. This it is recognized and understood that he is the mightiest of the gods. Thus Ptah was satisfied after he had made all things and all divine words.

He gave birth to the gods, He made the towns,
He established the nomes [provinces],
He placed the gods in their shrines,
He settled their offerings,
He established their shrines,
He made their bodies according to their wishes,
Thus the gods entered into their bodies,
Of every wood, every stone, every clay,
Every thing that grows upon him
In which they came to be.

Sekhmet is Ptah's female companion. Depicted as a lioness, she served as protector of the king in peace and war. She is also the mother of Nefertum, a beautiful young man whose name means "perfection," small statues of whom were often carried by Egyptians for good luck.

The cyclical movement through opposing forces, embodied in stories such as that of Osiris and Isis, is one of the earliest instances of a system of religious and philosophic thought that survives even in contemporary thought. Life and death, flood and sun, even desert and oasis, were part of a larger harmony of nature, one that was predictable both in the diurnal cycle of day and night and in its seasonal patterns of repetition. A good deity, such as Osiris, was necessarily balanced by a bad deity, such as Seth. The fertile Nile Valley was balanced by the harsh desert surrounding it. The narrow reaches of the upper Nile were balanced by the broad marshes of the Delta. All things were predicated upon the return of their opposite, which negates them, but which in the process completes the whole and regenerates the cycle of being and becoming once again.

Pictorial Formulas in Egyptian Art

This sense of duality, of opposites, informs even the earliest Egyptian artifacts, such as the *Palette of Narmer*, found at Hierakonpolis in Upper Egypt (see *Closer Look*, pages 32–33). A palette is technically an everyday object used for grinding pigments and making body or eye paint. The scenes on the *Palette of Narmer* are in low relief. Like the *Standard of Ur* (see Fig. 1.17), they are arranged in registers that provide a ground line upon which the figures stand (the two lion-tamers are an exception). The figures typically face to the right, although often, as is the case here, the design is balanced left and right. The artist represents the various parts of the human figure in what the Egyptians thought was their most characteristic view. So, the face, arms, legs, and feet are in profile, with the left foot advanced in front of the right. The eye and shoulders are in front view. The mouth, navel and hips, and knees are in three-quarter view. As a result, the viewer sees each person in a **composite** view, the integration of multiple perspectives into a single unified image.

In Egyptian art, not only the figures but also the scenes themselves unite two contradictory points of view into a single image. In the *Palette of Narmer*, the king approaches his dead enemies from the side, but they lie beheaded on the ground before him as seen from above. Egyptian art often represents architecture in the same terms. At the top center of the *Palette of Narmer*, the external facade of the palace is depicted simultaneously from above, in a kind of ground plan, with its niched facade at the bottom. The design contains Narmer's Horus-name, consisting of a catfish and a chisel. The hieroglyphic signs for Narmer could not be interpreted until the nineteenth century, but we are still not sure whether it is to be read "Narmer," which are the later phonetic values of the signs. In fact, later meanings of these signs suggest that it might be read "sick catfish," which seems rather unlikely.

The Old Kingdom

Although the *Palette of Narmer* probably commemorates an event in life, as a votive object it is, like most surviving Egyptian art and architecture, chiefly concerned with burial and the afterlife. The Egyptians buried their dead on the west side of the Nile, where the sun sets, a symbolic reference to death and rebirth, since the sun always rises again. The pyramid was the first monumental royal tomb. A massive physical manifestation of the reality of the king's death, it was also the symbolic embodiment of his eternal life. It would endure for generations, as, Egyptians believed, would the king's **ka**. This idea is comparable to an enduring "soul" or "life force," a concept found in many other

Some of the Principal Egyptian Gods

A Horus, son of Osiris, a sky god closely linked with the king; pictured as a hawk, or hawk-headed man.
B Seth, enemy of Horus and Osiris, god of storms; pictured as an unidentifiable creature (some believe a wild donkey), or a man with this animal's head.
C Thoth, a moon deity and god of writing, counting, and wisdom; pictured as an ibis, or ibis-headed man, often with a crescent moon on his head.
D Khnum, originally the god of the source of the Nile, pictured as a bull who shaped men out of clay on his potter's wheel; later, god of pottery.
E Hathor, goddess of love, birth, and death; pictured as a woman with cow's horns and a sun disk on her head.
F Sobek, the crocodile god, associated both with the fertility of the Nile, and, because of the ferocity of the crocodile, with the army's power and strength.
G Re, the sun god in his many forms; pictured as a hawk-headed man with a sun disk on his head.

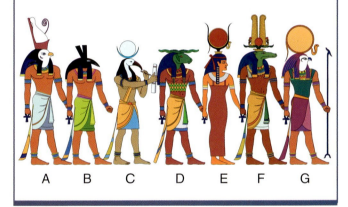

A   B   C   D   E   F   G

religions. The *ka*, which all persons possessed, was created at the same time as the physical body, itself essential for the person's existence since it provided the *ka* with an individual identity in which its personality, or **ba**, might also manifest itself. This meant that it was necessary to preserve the body after death so that the *ba* and *ka* might still recognize it for eternity. All the necessities of the afterlife, from food to furniture to entertainment, were placed in the burial chamber of the pyramid with the king's body.

Monumental royal sculpture was designed to embody the enduring nature of the royal *ka*. The word for sculpture in Egyptian is the same as that for giving birth. Indeed, funerary sculpture served the same purpose as the pyramids themselves—to preserve and guarantee the king's existence after death, thereby providing a kind of rebirth. The stone materials used for funerary images had to be the hardest, most durable kind, as enduring as the *ka* itself. Sandstone or limestone would not do. The materials of choice were diorite, schist, and granite, stones that can also take on a high polish and,

The Egyptians created a style of writing very different from that of their northern neighbors in Mesopotamia. It consists of **hieroglyphs**, "writing of the gods," from the Greek *hieros*, meaning "holy," and *gluphein*, "to engrave." Although the number of signs increased over the centuries from about 700 to nearly 5,000, the system of symbolic communication underwent almost no major changes from its advent in the fourth millennium BCE until 395 CE, when Egypt was conquered by the Roman Empire. It consists of three kinds of sign: **pictograms**, or stylized drawings that represent objects or beings, which can be combined to express ideas; **phonograms**, which are pictograms used to represent sounds; and **determinatives**, signs used to indicate which category of objects or beings is in question. The *Palette of Narmer* is an early example of the then-developing hieroglyphic style. It consists largely of pictograms, though in the top center of each side, Narmer's name is represented as a phonogram.

The circle formed by the two elongated lions' necks intertwined on the *recto*, or front, of the palette is a bowl for mixing pigments. The palette celebrates the defeat by Narmer (r. ca. 3000 BCE) of his enemies and his unification of both Upper and Lower Egypt, which before this time had been at odds. So on the recto side, Narmer wears the red cobra crown of Lower Egypt, associated with the cobra goddess Wadjir of Buto in the Delta, and on the *verso*, or back, he wears the white crown of Upper Egypt, associated with Wadjit's sister, the vulture goddess Nekhbet of Nekheb in southern Egypt—representing his ability (and duty) to harmonize antagonistic elements.

Flanking the top of each side of the palette is a goddess wearing cow's horns; such headdresses represent the divine attributes of the figure. Later, **Hathor**, the sky mother, a goddess embodying all female qualities, would possess these attributes, but this early image probably represents the cow goddess, **Bat**.

The **mace** was the chief weapon used by the king to strike down enemies, and the scene here is emblematic of his power.

As on the other side of the palette, the king is here accompanied by his sandal-bearer, who stands on his own ground line. He carries the king's sandals to indicate that the king, who is barefoot, stands on **sacred ground**, and that his acts are themselves sacred.

Narmer, wearing the white crown of Upper Egypt, strikes down his enemy, probably the embodiment of **Lower Egypt** itself, especially since he is, in size, comparable to Narmer himself, suggesting that he is likewise a leader.

Two more figures represent the defeated enemy. Behind the one on the left is a small aerial view of a **fortified city**; behind the one on the right, a **gazelle trap**. Perhaps together they represent Narmer's victory over both city and countryside.

The hawk is a symbolic representation of the god **Horus**. The king was regarded as the earthly embodiment of Horus. Here, Horus has a human hand with which he holds a rope tied to a symbolic representation of a conquered land and people.

A human head grows from the same ground as six **papyrus** blossoms, possibly the symbol of Lower Egypt.

This hieroglyph identifies the man that Narmer is about to kill, a name that is otherwise unknown.

Palette of Narmer, verso side, from Hierakonpolis. Dynasty 1, ca. 3000 BCE. Schist, height 25¼". Egyptian Museum, Cairo.

 View the Closer Look for the *Palette of Narmer* on **MyArtsLab**

Narmer's Palette was not meant for actual use. Rather, it is a **votive**, or ritual object, a gift to a god or goddess that was placed in a temple to ensure that the king, or perhaps some temple official, would have access to a palette throughout eternity. It may or may not register actual historical events, although, in fact, Egypt marks its beginnings with the unification of its Upper and Lower territories. Subsequent kings, at any rate, presented themselves in almost identical terms, as triumphing over their enemies, mace in hand, even though they had had no role in a similar military campaign. It is even possible that by the time of Narmer such conventions were already in place, although our system of numbering Egyptian dynasties begins with him. Whatever the symbolism of the scene depicted, the **pictorial formulas**, or conventions of representation, that Egyptian culture used for the rest of its history are fully developed in this piece.

Something to Think About . . .

Do you see any connection between the Egyptian king Narmer and the depiction of kings in Mesopotamia?

These are two instances of the hieroglyphic sign for **Narmer**, consisting of a catfish above a chisel. Each individual hieroglyph is a pictogram but is utilized here for its phonetic sound. **Nar** is the word for "catfish," and **mer** is the word for "chisel" (or, perhaps, "sickly")—hence "Narmer." In the lower instance, the hieroglyph identifies the king. In the instance at the top, the king's name is inside a depiction of his palace seen simultaneously from above, as a ground plan, and from the front, as a facade. This device, called a **serekh**, is traditionally used to hold the king's name.

We are able to identify **Narmer** not only from his hieroglyphic name, next to him, but by his relative size. As befits the king, he is larger than anyone else.

Similarly positioned on the other side of the palette and identified by the accompanying hieroglyph, this is the king's **sandal-bearer**.

The **bull** here strikes down his victim and is another representation of the king's might and power. Note that in the depictions of Narmer striking down his victim and in procession, a bull's tail hangs from his waistband.

The defeated **dead** lie in two rows, their decapitated heads between their feet. Narmer in sacred procession reviews them, while above them, a tiny Horus (the hawk) looks on.

This is the **mixing bowl** of the palette. The lions may represent competing forces brought under control by the king. Each is held in check by one of the king's **lion-tamers**, figures that in some sense represent state authority.

This is a representation of a **fortified city** as seen both from above, as a floor plan, and from the front, as a facade. It is meant to represent the actual site of Narmer's victory.

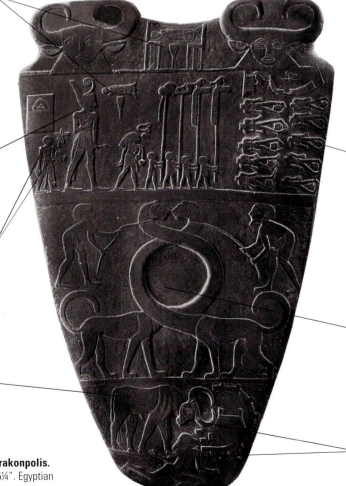

Palette of Narmer, recto side, from Hierakonpolis. **Dynasty 1, ca. 3000 BCE.** Schist, height 25¼". Egyptian Museum, Cairo.

because they are not prone to fracture, can be finely detailed when carved. Most Egyptian statues were monolithic (carved out of a single piece of stone), even those depicting more than a single figure. such as the statue of Menkaure with a woman—perhaps his queen, his mother, or even a goddess—that was found at his valley temple at Giza (Fig. **1.24**). Here, the deep space created by carving away the side of the stone to expose fully the king's right side seems to free him from the stone. He stands with one foot ahead of the other in the second traditional pose, the conventional depiction of a standing figure. He is not walking. Both feet are planted firmly on the ground (and so his left leg is, of necessity, slightly longer than his right). His back is firmly implanted in the stone panel behind him, but he seems to have emerged farther from it than the female figure who accompanies him, as if to underscore his power and might. Although the woman is almost the same size as the king, her stride is markedly shorter than his. She embraces him, her arm reaching round his back, in a gesture that suggests the simple marital affection of husband and wife. The ultimate effect of this sculpture—its solidity and unity, its sense of resolution—testifies finally to its purpose, which is to endure for eternity.

The New Kingdom and Its Moment of Change

Throughout the Middle Kingdom and well into the New Kingdom, Egyptian artistic and religious traditions remained intact. But toward the end of the Eighteenth Dynasty, Egypt experienced one of the few real crises of its entire history when, in 1353 BCE, Amenhotep IV (r. 1353–1337 BCE) assumed the throne of his father, Amenhotep III (r. 1391–1353 BCE).

Although previous Egyptian kings may have associated themselves with a single god whom they represented in human form, Egyptian religion supported a large number of gods. Even the Nile was worshiped as a god. Amenhotep IV abolished the pantheon of Egyptian gods and established a monotheistic religion in which the sun disk Aten was worshiped exclusively. Other gods were still acknowledged, but they were considered too inferior to Aten to be worth worshiping. Whether Amenhotep's religion was *henotheistic*—the belief and worship of a single god while accepting that other deities might also exist and be worshiped—or truly monotheistic is a matter of some debate. But his religion may well have influenced the Hebrews, whose stay in Egypt was contemporaneous with Amenhotep's rule.

Amenhotep IV believed that the sun was the creator of all life, and he was so dedicated to Aten that he changed his own name to Akhenaten ("The Shining Spirit of Aten") and moved the capital of Egypt from Thebes to a site many miles north that he named Akhetaten (modern Tell el-Amarna). This move transformed Egypt's political and cultural as well as religious life. At this new capital he presided over the worship of Aten as a divine priest and his queen as a divine priestess. Temples to Aten were open courtyards, where the altar received the sun's direct rays.

Why would Amenhotep IV/Akhenaten have substituted a brand of monotheism for Egypt's traditional polytheistic religion? Many Egyptologists argue that the switch had to do with enhancing the power of the pharaoh. With the pharaoh representing the one god who mattered, all religious justification for the power held by a priesthood dedicated to the traditional gods was gone. As we have seen, the pharaoh was traditionally associated with the sun god Re. Now, in the form of the sun disk Aten, Re was the supreme deity, embodying the characteristics of all the other gods, therefore rendering them superfluous. By analogy, Amenhotep IV/Akhenaten was now supreme priest, rendering all other

Fig. 1.24 Menkaure with a Queen, probably Khamerernebty, from the valley temple of Menkaure, Giza. Dynasty 4, ca. 2460 BCE. Schist, height 54¼". Museum of Fine Arts, Boston. Harvard University–Boston Museum of Fine Arts Expedition, 11.1738. Photograph © 2014 Museum of Fine Arts, Boston. Note that the woman's close-fitting attire is nearly transparent, indicating a very fine weave of linen.

priests superfluous as well. Simultaneously, the temples dedicated to the other gods lost prestige and influence. These changes also converted the priests into dissidents.

A New Art: The Amarna Style Such significant changes had a powerful effect on the visual arts as well. Previously, Egyptian art had been remarkably stable because its principles were considered a gift of the gods—thus perfect and eternal. But now, the perfection of the gods was in question, and the principles of art were open to re-examination as well. A new art replaced the traditional canon of proportion—the familiar poses of king and queen—with realism, and a sense of immediacy, even intimacy. So Akhenaten allowed himself to be portrayed with startling realism, in what has become known, from the present-day name for the new capital, as the Amarna style.

For example, in a small relief from his new capital, Akhenaten has a skinny, weak upper body, and his belly protrudes over his skirt; his skull is elongated behind an extremely long, narrow facial structure; and he sits in a slumped, almost casual position (Fig. 1.25). (One theory holds that Akhenaten had Marfan's Syndrome, a genetic disorder that leads to skeletal abnormalities.) This depiction contrasts sharply with the idealized depictions of the pharaohs in earlier periods. Akhenaten holds one of his children in his arms and seems to have just kissed her. His two other children sit with the queen across from him, one turning to speak with her mother, the other touching the queen's cheek. The queen herself, Nefertiti, sits only slightly below her husband and appears to share his position and authority. In fact, one of the most striking features of the Amarna style is Nefertiti's prominence in the decoration of the king's temples. In one, for example, she is shown slaughtering prisoners, an image traditionally reserved for the king himself. It is likely that her prominence was part of Akhenaten's desire to encourage the veneration of his own family (who, after all, represented Aten on earth).

The Return to Thebes and to Tradition Akhenaten's revolution was short-lived. Upon his death, Tutankhaten (r. 1336–1327 BCE), probably Akhenaten's son, assumed the throne and changed his name to Tutankhamun (indicating a return to the more traditional gods, in this case Amun). The new king abandoned Tell el-Amarna, moved the royal family to Memphis in the north, and reaffirmed Thebes as the nation's religious center. He died shortly afterward, and was buried on the west bank of the Nile at Thebes.

Tutankhamun's is the only royal tomb in Egypt to have escaped the total pillaging of looters. When Howard Carter and Lord Carnarvon discovered it under the tomb of the Twentieth Dynasty king Ramses VI in the Valley of the Kings near Deir el-Bahri, they found a coffin consisting of three separate coffins placed one inside the other (Fig. 1.26). These were in turn encased in a quartzite sarcophagus, a rectangular stone coffin that was encased in four gilded, boxlike wooden

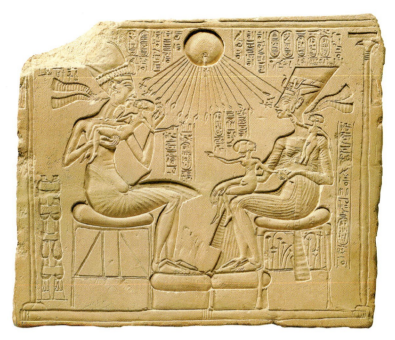

Fig. 1.25 *Akhenaten and His Family*, from Akhetaten (modern Tell el-Amarna). Dynasty 18, ca. 1345 BCE. Painted limestone relief, 12¾" × 14⅞". Staatliche Museen, Berlin, Preussischer Kulturbesitz, Ägyptisches Museum. Between Akhenaten and his queen Nefertiti, the sun disk Aten shines down beneficently. Its rays end in small hands, which hold the ankh symbol for life before both the king and queen.

View the Closer Look for *Akhenaten and his Family* on **MyArtsLab**

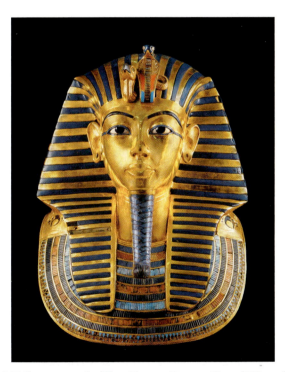

Fig. 1.26 Funerary mask of Tutankhamun. Dynasty 18, ca. 1327 BCE. Gold inlaid with glass and semiprecious stones, height 21¼". Egyptian Museum, Cairo. This death mask was placed over the upper body of the mummified king, which rested inside three other coffins, the innermost of which was made of solid gold.

shrines, also placed one inside the other. In their rigid formality, the coffins within, each depicting the king, hark back to the traditional Egyptian art of the Middle Kingdom.

The elaborate burial process was not meant solely to guarantee survival of the king's *ka* and *ba*. It also prepared him for a "last judgment," a belief system that would find expression in the Hebrew faith as well. In this two-part ritual, deities first questioned the deceased about their behavior in life. Then their hearts, the seat of the *ka*, were weighed against an ostrich feather, symbol of Maat, the goddess of truth, justice, and order. Egyptians believed the heart contained all the emotions, intellect, and character of the individual, and so represented both the good and bad aspects of a person's life. If the heart did not balance with the feather, then the dead person was condemned to nonexistence, to be eaten by a creature called Ammit, the vile "Eater of the Dead," part crocodile, part lion, and part hippopotamus. Osiris, wrapped in his mummy robes, oversaw this moment of judgment. Tut himself, depicted on his sarcophagus with his crossed arms holding crook and flail, was clearly identified with Osiris.

THINKING BACK

1.1 Discuss the rise of culture and how developments in art and architecture reflect the growing sophistication of prehistoric cultures.

The widespread use of stone tools and weapons by *Homo sapiens*, the hominid species that evolved around 120,000–100,000 years ago, gives rise to the name of the earliest era of human development, the Paleolithic era. Carvers fashioned stone figures, both in the round and in relief. In cave paintings, such as those discovered at Chauvet Cave, the artists' great skill in rendering animals helps us to understand that the ability to represent the world with naturalistic fidelity is an inherent human skill, unrelated to cultural sophistication. If *culture* can be defined as a way of living—religious, social, and/or political—formed by a group of people and passed on from one generation to the next, what can the earliest art tell us about the first human cultures? What do the dwellings at Çatalhöyük suggest about the growing sophistication of Neolithic peoples? What questions remain a mystery?

1.2 Describe the role of myth in prehistoric culture.

Much of our understanding of the role of myth in prehistoric cultures derives from the traditions that survive in such contemporary Native American tribes as the Hopi and Zuni, who are the direct descendants of the Anasazi. Their legends encapsulate the fundamental religious principles of the culture. Such stories, and the ritual practices that accompany them, reflect the general beliefs of most Neolithic peoples. Can you describe some of these beliefs? What role do sacred sites play, such as those at Ise in Japan?

1.3 Distinguish among the ancient civilizations of Mesopotamia, and focus on how they differ from that of the Hebrews.

The royal tombs at the Sumerian city of Ur reveal a highly developed Bronze Age culture, based on the social order of the city-state, which was ruled by a priest-king acting as the intermediary between the gods and the people. The rulers also established laws and encouraged record keeping, which in turn required the development of a system of writing known as cuneiform script. In Sumer and subsequent Mesopotamian cultures, monumental structures such as ziggurats were dedicated to the gods, and in each city-state one of the gods rose to prominence as the city's protector. How would you characterize the general relationship between Mesopotamian rulers and the gods? The Hebrews practiced a monotheistic religion. They considered themselves the "chosen people" of God, whom they called Yahweh. The written word is central to their culture, and it is embodied in a body of law, the Torah. What does the Torah have in common with the Law Code of Hammurabi? How does it differ? How do the stories in Genesis, the first book of the Hebrew Bible, compare to the *Epic of Gilgamesh*?

1.4 Account for the stability of Egyptian culture.

The annual cycle of flood and sun, the inundation of the Nile River valley that annually deposited deep layers of silt, followed by months of sun in which crops could grow in the fertile soil, helped to define Egyptian culture. This predictable cycle helped to create a cultural belief in the stability and balance of all things that lasted for more than 3,000 years. Can you describe this belief in terms of cyclical harmony? How does the Egyptian religion reflect this belief system? Most surviving Egyptian art and architecture was devoted to burial and the afterlife, the cycle of life, death, and rebirth. In what way do the statues of Egyptian kings and queens reflect this?

✓ Study and review on MyArtsLab

Egyptian and Greek Sculpture

Freestanding Greek sculpture of the Archaic period—that is, sculpture dating from about 600–480 BCE—is notable for its stylistic connections to 2,000 years of Egyptian tradition. The Late Period statue of Mentuemhet (Fig. **1.27**), from Thebes, dating from around 660 BCE, differs hardly at all from Old Kingdom sculpture at Giza (see Fig. 1.24), and even though the *Anavysos Kouros* (Fig. **1.28**), from a cemetery near Athens, represents a significant advance in relative naturalism over the Greek sculpture of just a few years before, it still resembles its Egyptian ancestors. Remarkably, since it follows upon the *Anavysos Kouros* by only 75 years, the *Doryphoros (Spear Bearer)* (Fig. **1.29**) is significantly more naturalistic. Although this is a Roman copy of a lost fifth-century BCE bronze Greek statue, we can assume it reflects the original's naturalism, since the original's sculptor, Polyclitus, was renowned for his ability to render the human body realistically. But this advance, characteristic of Golden Age Athens, represents more than just a cultural taste for naturalism. It also represents a heightened cultural sensitivity to the worth of the individual, a belief that as much as we value what we have in common with one another—the bond that creates the city-state—our *individual* contributions are at least of equal value. By the fifth century BCE, the Greeks clearly understood that individual genius and achievement could be a matter of civic pride. ■

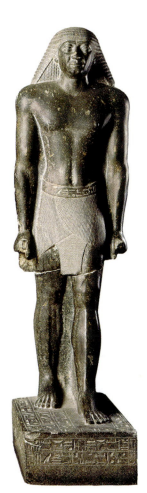

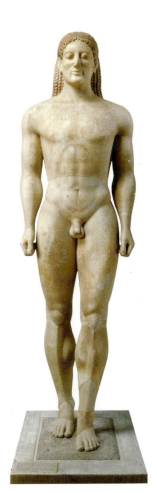

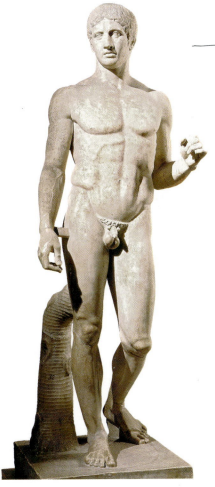

Fig. 1.27 *Mentuemhet*, from Karnak, Thebes, Egypt. ca. 660 BCE. Granite, height 54". Egyptian Museum, Cairo.

Fig. 1.28 *Anavysos Kouros*, from Anavysos cemetery, near Athens. ca. 525 BCE. Marble with remnants of paint, height 6'4". National Archeological Museum, Athens.

Fig. 1.29 *Doryphoros (Spear Bearer)*, Roman copy after the original bronze by Polyclitus of ca. 450–440 BCE. Marble, height 6'6". Museo Archeologico Nazionale, Naples.

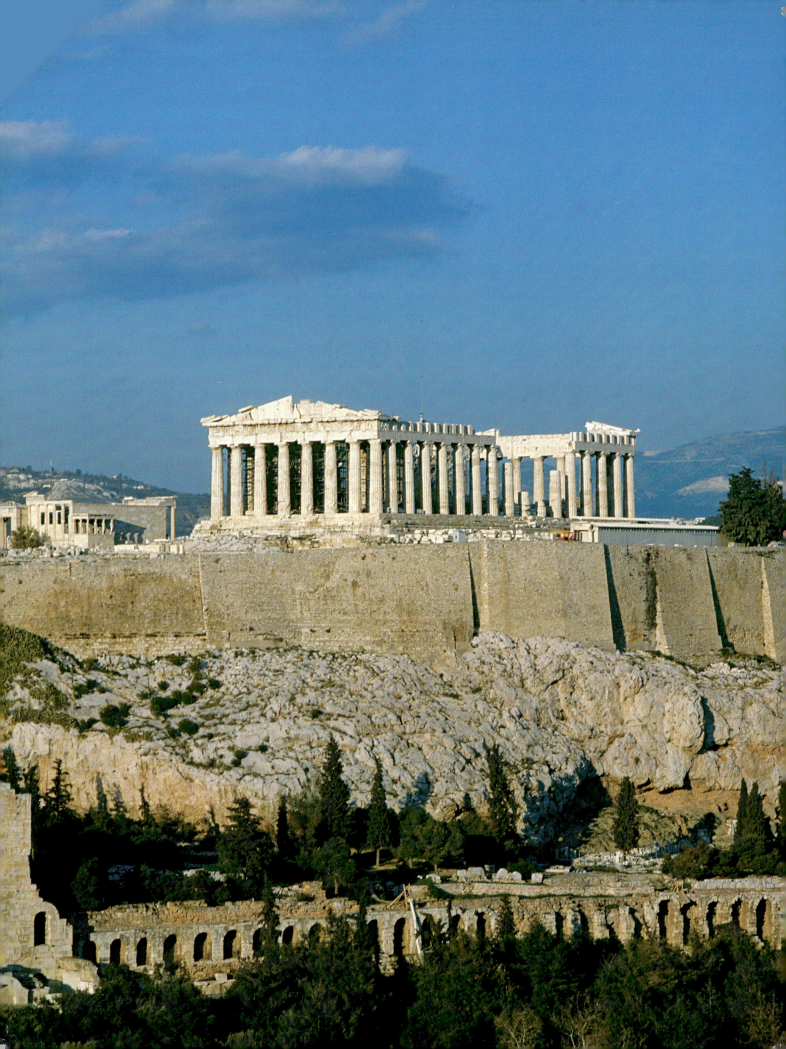

The Greek World
The Classical Tradition

2

LEARNING OBJECTIVES

2.1 Outline how the Cycladic, Minoan, and Mycenaean cultures contributed to the later Greeks' sense of themselves.

2.2 Define the polis and explain how it came to reflect the values of Greek culture.

2.3 Describe how Pericles defined and shaped Golden Age Athens.

2.4 Characterize the values of the Hellenistic world in terms of politics, philosophy, and art.

In the fourth and fifth centuries BCE, Athens was the center of the Greek world. Still predominantly rural and agricultural, it was one **polis** among some 8,000 *poleis*—or city-states—that stretched across the Greek Peloponnese, the islands of the Aegean Sea, and even farther around the Mediterranean to the Italian peninsula and the mainland of Asia Minor (Map **2.1**). In fact, the Greek poleis are distinguished by their isolation from one another and their fierce sense of independence. The Greek mainland is a very rugged country of mountains separating small areas of arable land. The sea naturally separates each of the Greek islands from the mainland and one another. In this fractured geography, each polis came to think of itself less as a place and more as a cultural center in its own right. Each citizen owed allegiance and loyalty to the polis. They depended upon and served in its military. And they asserted their identity, first of all, by participating in the affairs of their own particular city-state. And yet, curiously, they maintained an identity as Greeks.

Like most poleis, the polis of Athens consisted of an urban center, small by modern standards, surrounding a natural citadel that could serve as a fortification, but which usually functioned as the city-state's religious center (Fig. **2.1**). The Greeks called this citadel an **acropolis**—literally, the "top of the city." On lower ground, at the foot of the acropolis, was the **agora**, a large open space that served as public meeting place, marketplace, and civic center. The principal architectural feature of the agora was the **stoa** (Fig. **2.2**), a

long, open arcade supported by **colonnades**, rows of columns. While Athenians could buy grapes, figs, flowers, and lambs in the agora, it was far more than just a shopping center. It was the place where citizens congregated, debated the topics of

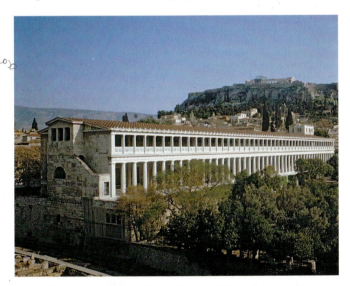

Fig. 2.2 The Stoa of Attalus, Athens, Greece. 150 BCE. This stoa, reconstructed at the eastern edge of the modern agora, retains traditional form. The broad causeway on the right was the Panathenaic Way, the route of the ritual processions to the Acropolis in the distance. The original agora buildings lie farther to the right and overlook the Panathenaic Way.

◀ **Fig. 2.1 The Acropolis, Athens, Greece. Rebuilt in the second half of the 5th century BCE.** After the Persians destroyed Athens in 479 BCE, the entire city, including the Acropolis, had to be rebuilt. This afforded the Athenians a unique opportunity to create one of the greatest monumental spaces in the history of Western architecture.

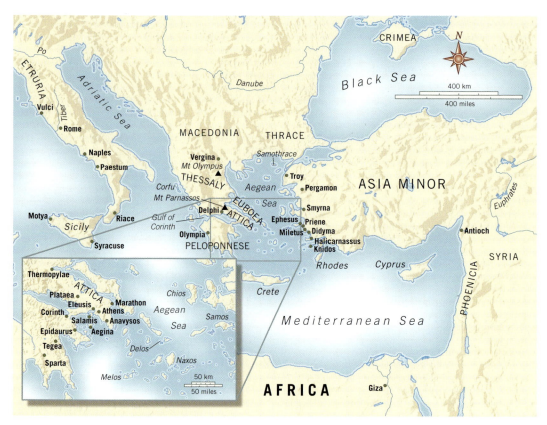

Map 2.1 The City-states of Ancient Greece.

the day, argued points of law, settled disputes, and presented philosophical discourse. In short, it was the place where they practiced their politics.

The Greek philosopher Aristotle (384–322 BCE) described the Athenian polis in his *Politics*: "The partnership finally composed of several villages is the *polis*; it has at last attained the limit of virtually complete self-sufficiency, and thus while it comes into existence for the sake of mere life, it exists for the sake of the good life." For Aristotle, the essential purpose of the polis was to guarantee, barring catastrophe, that each of its citizens might flourish. Writing in the fourth century BCE, Aristotle is thinking back to the Athens of the fifth century BCE, the so-called Golden Age. During these years the pursuit of what Aristotle called *eudaimonia*, "the good or flourishing life," resulted in a culture of astonishing sophistication and diversity. For *eudaimonia* is not simply a happy or pleasurable existence; rather, the polis provides the conditions in which each individual may pursue an "activity of soul in accordance with complete excellence." For Aristotle, this striving for "complete excellence" defines Athens in the Golden Age. The polis produced a body of philosophical thought so penetrating and insightful that the questions it posed—on the relationship between individual freedom and civic responsibility, the nature of the beautiful, the ideal harmony between the natural world and the intellectual or spiritual realm, to name a few—and the conclusions it reached dominated Western inquiry for centuries to come.

This chapter traces the rise of Greek culture from its earliest roots in the pre-literary cultures of the Aegean Sea, from whom the Greeks believed their own great culture sprang, through its Golden Age in the fifth century BCE, when Athens became a place of absolute cultural ascendancy, to Greece's cultural domination of the Eastern Mediterranean world and beyond, until, in the first century BCE, Rome came to challenge Greek ascendancy across the Mediterranean basin.

BRONZE AGE CULTURE IN THE AEGEAN

What differentiates the cultures of the Aegean from one another, and how did they contribute to the later Greeks' sense of themselves?

The Aegean Sea, in the eastern Mediterranean, is filled with islands. Here, beginning in about 3000 BCE, seafaring cultures took hold. So many were the islands, and so close to one another, that navigators were always within sight of land. In the natural harbors where seafarers came ashore, port communities developed and trade began to flourish.

The later Greeks thought of the Bronze Age Aegean peoples as their ancestors—particularly those who inhabited the Cyclades islands, the island of Crete, and

Mycenae, on the Peloponnese—and considered their activities and culture as part of their own prehistory. They even had a word for the way they knew them—*archaiologia*, "knowing the past." They did not practice archeology as we do today, excavating ancient sites and scientifically analyzing the artifacts discovered there. Rather, they learned of their past through legends passed down, at first orally and then in writing, from generation to generation. Interestingly, the modern practice of archeology has confirmed much of what was legendary to the Greeks.

The Cyclades

The Cyclades are a group of more than 100 islands in the Aegean Sea between mainland Greece and the island of Crete. They form a roughly circular shape, giving them their name, from the Greek word *kyklos*, "circle" (also the origin of our word "cycle"). No written records of the early Cycladic people remain, although archeologists have found a good deal of art in and around hillside burial chambers. The most famous of these artifacts are marble figurines in a highly simplified and abstract style that appeals to the modern eye (Fig. 2.3). The Cycladic figures originally looked quite different because they were painted. Most of the figurines depict females, but male figures, including seated harpists and acrobats, also exist. The figurines range in height from a few inches to life-size, but anatomical detail in all of them is reduced to essentials. With their toes pointed down, their heads tilted back, and their arms crossed across their chests, the fully extended figures are corpselike. Their function remains unknown, but some scholars suggest they were used for home worship and then buried with their owner.

By about 2200 BCE, trade with Crete to the south brought the Cyclades into the larger island's political orbit and radically altered late Cycladic life. Evidence of this influence survives in the form of wall paintings such as the *Miniature Ship Fresco*, a frieze at the top of at least three walls, which suggests a prosperous seafaring community engaged in a celebration of the sea (Fig. 2.4). People lounge on terraces and rooftops as boats glide by, accompanied by leaping dolphins. The painting was discovered in 1967 on the island of Thera (today known as Santorini), at Akrotiri,

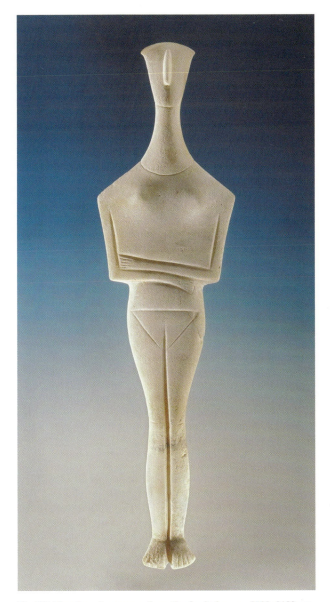

Fig. 2.3 Figurine of a woman from the Cyclades. ca. 2400–2100 BCE. Marble, height 17". Antikensammlung, Staatliche Museen, Berlin. Larger examples of such figurines may have been objects of worship.

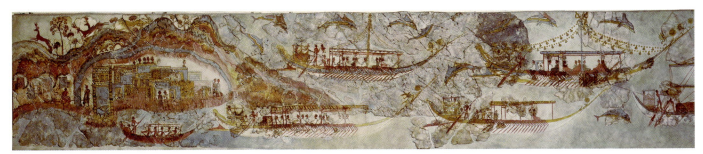

Fig. 2.4 *Miniature Ship Fresco* (detail from the left section), from Room 5, West House, Akrotiri, Thera (Santorini). Before 1623 BCE. Height 14⁵⁄₁₆". National Archeological Museum, Athens. The total length of this fresco is over 24 feet. Harbors such as this one provided shelter to traders who sailed between the islands of the Aegean Sea as early as 3000 BCE.

 View the Closer Look on the *Miniature Ship Fresco* (*"Flotilla Fresco"*) on **MyArtsLab**

a community that had been buried beneath one of the largest volcanic eruptions in the last 10,000 years. About 7 cubic miles of magma spewed forth, and the ash cloud that resulted during the first phase of the eruption was about 23 miles high. The enormity of the eruption caused the volcano at the center of Thera to collapse, producing a caldera, a large basin or depression that filled with seawater. The present island of Thera is actually the eastern rim of the original volcano (small volcanoes are still active in the center of Thera's crescent sea).

The eruption was so great that it left evidence worldwide—in the stunted growth of tree rings as far away as Ireland and California, and in ash taken from ice core samples in Greenland. With this evidence, scientists have dated the eruption to 1623 BCE. In burying the city of Akrotiri, it also preserved it. Not only were the community's homes elaborately decorated—with mural paintings such as the *Miniature Ship Fresco*, which was made with water-based pigments on wet plaster, and which extended across the top of at least three walls in a second-story room, suggesting a prosperous, seafaring community—but its citizens also enjoyed a level of personal hygiene unknown elsewhere in Western culture until Roman times. Clay pipes led from interior toilets and baths to sewers built under winding, paved streets. Straw reinforced the walls of the houses, protecting them against earthquakes and insulating them from the heat of the Mediterranean sun.

Minoan Culture in Crete

Just to the south of the Cyclades lies Crete, the largest of the Aegean islands. Bronze Age civilization developed there as early as 3000 BCE. Trade routes from Crete established communication with such diverse areas as Turkey, Cyprus, Egypt, Afghanistan, and Scandinavia, from which the island imported copper, ivory, amethyst, lapis lazuli, carnelian, gold, and amber. From Britain, Crete imported the tin necessary to produce bronze. A distinctive culture called Minoan flourished on Crete from about 1900 to 1375 BCE. The name comes from the legendary king Minos, who was said to have ruled the island's ancient capital of Knossos.

Many of the motifs in the frescoes at Akrotiri, in the Cyclades, also appear in the art decorating Minoan palaces on Crete, including the palace at Knossos. This suggests the mutual influence of Cycladic and Minoan cultures by the start of the second millennium BCE. Unique to Crete, however, is emphasis on the bull, the central element of one of the best-preserved frescoes at Knossos, the *Toreador Fresco* (Fig. 2.5). Three almost nude figures appear to toy with a charging bull. (As in Egyptian art, women are traditionally depicted with light skin, men with a darker complexion.) The woman on the left holds the bull by the horns, the man vaults over its back, and the woman on the right seems to have either just finished a vault or to have positioned herself to catch the man. It is unclear whether this is a ritual

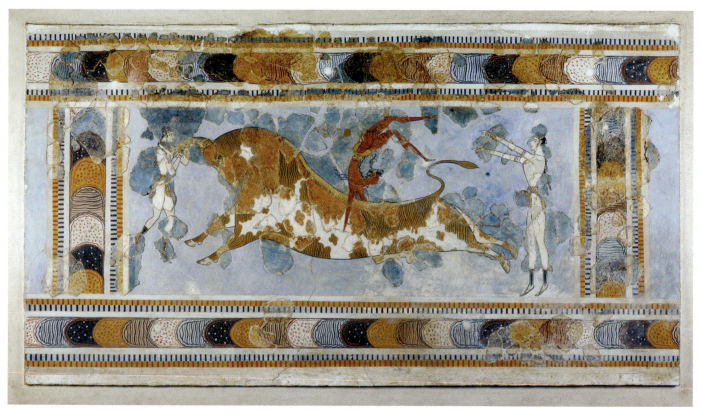

Fig. 2.5 *Bull Leaping* (*Toreador Fresco*), **from the palace complex at Knossos, Crete. ca. 1450–1375 BCE.** Fresco, height approx. 24½". Archeological Museum, Iráklion, Crete. The darker patches of the fresco are original fragments. The lighter areas are modern restorations.

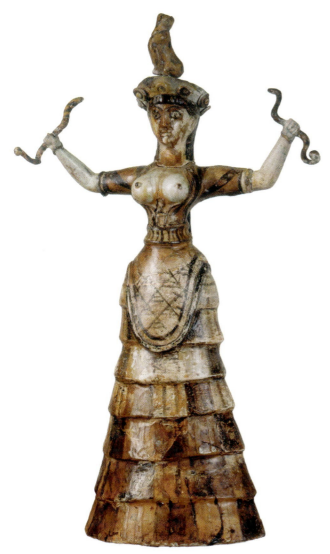

Fig. 2.6 *Snake Goddess or Priestess*, **from the palace at Knossos, Crete. ca. 1500 BCE.** Faience, height 11⅝". Archeological Museum, Iráklion, Crete. Faience is a kind of earthenware ceramic decorated with glazes. Modern faience is easily distinguishable from ancient because it is markedly lighter in tone.

 View the Closer Look on the *Snake Goddess* on **MyArtsLab**

activity, perhaps part of a rite of passage. What we do know is that the Minoans regularly sacrificed bulls, as well as other animals, and that the bull was at least symbolically associated with male virility and strength.

Female Deities The people of Thera and Crete seem to have shared the same religion as well as similar artistic motifs. Ample archeological evidence tells us that the Minoans in Crete worshiped female deities. We do not know much more than that, but some students of ancient religions have proposed that the Minoan worship of one or more female deities is evidence that in very early cultures the principal deity was a goddess rather than a god.

It has long been believed that one of the Minoan female deities was a snake goddess, but recently, scholars have questioned the authenticity of most of the existing snake goddess figurines. Sir Arthur Evans (1851–1941), who first excavated at the Palace of Minos on Crete, identified images of the Cretan goddess as "Mountain Goddess," "Snake Goddess," "Dove Goddess," "Goddess of the Caves," "Goddess of the Double Axes," "Goddess of the Sports," and "Mother Goddess." Evans saw all these as different aspects of a single deity, or Great Goddess. A century after he introduced the Snake Goddess (Fig. **2.6**) to the world, scholars are still debating its authenticity. In his book *Mysteries of the Snake Goddess* (2002), Kenneth Lapatin makes a convincing case that craftspeople employed by Evans manufactured artifacts for the antiquities market. He believes that the body of the statue is an authentic antiquity, but the form in which we see it is largely the imaginative fabrication of Evans's restorers. Many parts were missing when the figure was unearthed, and so an artist working for Evans fashioned new parts and attached them to the figure. The snake in the goddess's right hand lacked a head, leaving its identity as a snake open to question. Most of the goddess's left arm, including the snake in her hand, were absent and later fabricated. When the figure was discovered, it lacked a head, and this one is completely fabricated. The cat on the goddess's head is original, although it was not found with the statue. Lapatin believes that Evans, eager to advance his own theory that Minoan religion was dedicated to the worship of a Great Goddess, never questioned the manner in which the figures were restored. As interesting as the figure is, its identity as a snake goddess is at best questionable. We cannot even say with certainty that the principal deity of the Minoan culture was female, let alone that she was a snake goddess. There are no images of snake goddesses in surviving Minoan wall frescoes, engraved gems, or seals, and almost all the statues depicting her are fakes or imaginative reconstructions.

It is likely, though, that Minoan female goddesses were closely associated with a cult of vegetation and fertility, and the snake is an almost universal symbol of rebirth and fertility. We do know that the Minoans worshiped on mountaintops, closely associated with life-giving rains, and deep in caves, another nearly universal symbol of the womb in particular and origin in general. And in early cultures, the undulations of the earth itself—its hills and ravines, caves and riverbeds—were (and often still are) associated with the curves of the female body and genitalia. But until early Minoan writing is deciphered, the exact nature of Minoan religion will remain a mystery.

The Palace of Minos The *Snake Goddess* was discovered along with other ritual objects in a storage pit in the Palace of Minos at Knossos. The palace as Evans found it is enormous, covering more than 6 acres. There were originally two palaces at the site—an "old palace," dating from 1900 BCE, and a "new palace," built over the old one after an enormous earthquake in 1750 BCE. This "new palace" was the focus of Evans's attention.

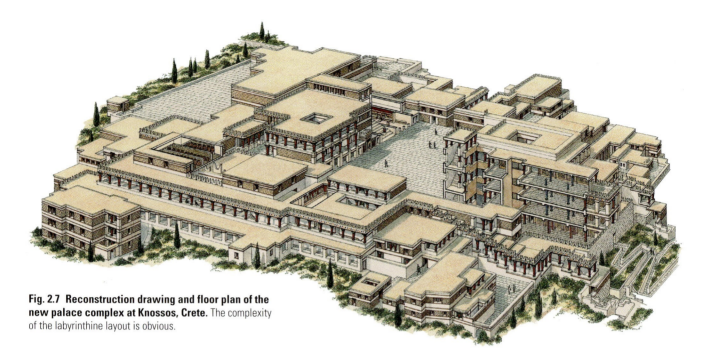

Fig. 2.7 Reconstruction drawing and floor plan of the new palace complex at Knossos, Crete. The complexity of the labyrinthine layout is obvious.

The palace at Knossos was only loosely organized around a central, open courtyard, as a reconstruction drawing makes clear (Fig. **2.7**). Leading from the courtyard were corridors, staircases, and passageways that connected living quarters, ritual spaces, baths, and administrative offices, in no discernable order or design. Workshops surrounded the complex, and vast storerooms could easily provide for the needs of both the palace population and the population of the surrounding countryside. In just one storeroom, excavators discovered enough ceramic jars to hold 20,000 gallons of olive oil.

Hundreds of wooden columns decorated the palace. Only fragments have survived, but we know from paintings and ceramic house models how they must have looked. Evans created concrete replicas, which are displayed today at the West Portico and the Grand Staircase (Fig. **2.8**). The originals were made of huge timbers cut on Crete and then turned upside down so that the top of each is broader than the base. The columns were painted bright red with black **capitals**, the sculpted blocks that top them. The capitals are shaped like pillows or cushions. (In fact, they are very close to the shape of an evergreen's root ball, as if the original design were suggested by trees felled in a storm.) Over time, as the columns rotted or were destroyed by earthquakes or possibly burned by invaders, they must have become increasingly difficult to replace, for Minoan builders gradually deforested the island. This may be one reason why the palace complex was abandoned sometime around 1450 BCE.

Representations of double axes decorated the palace at every turn, and indeed the Palace of Minos was known in Greek times as the House of the Double Axes. In fact, the Greek word for the palace was *labyrinth*, from *labrys*, "double ax." Over time, the Greeks came to associate the House of the Double Axes with its inordinately complex layout, and *labyrinth* came to mean "maze."

The Legend of Minos and the Minotaur The Greeks solidified the meaning of the labyrinth in a powerful legend. King Minos boasted that the gods would grant him anything he wished, so he prayed that a bull might emerge from the sea that he might sacrifice to the god of the sea, Poseidon. A white bull did emerge from the sea, one so beautiful that Minos decided to keep it for himself and sacrifice a different one from his herd instead. This angered Poseidon, who took revenge by causing Minos' queen, Pasiphae, to fall in love

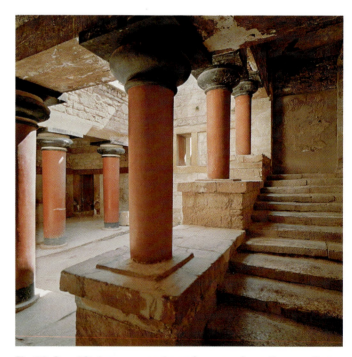

Fig. 2.8 Grand Staircase, east wing, palace complex at Knossos, Crete. ca. 1500 BCE, as reconstructed by Sir Arthur Evans. The staircase served as a light well and linked all five stories of the palace.

with the bull. To consummate her passion, she convinced Minos' chief craftsperson, Daedalus, to construct a hollow wooden cow into which she might place herself and attract the bull. The result of this union was a horrid creature, half man, half bull: the Minotaur.

To appease the monster's appetite for human flesh, Minos ordered the city of Athens, which he also ruled, to send him 14 young men and women each year as sacrificial victims. Theseus, son of King Aegeus of Athens, vowed to kill the Minotaur. As he set sail for Crete with 13 others, he promised his father that he would return under white sails (instead of the black sails of the sacrificial ship) to announce his victory. At Crete, he seduced Ariadne, daughter of Minos. Wishing to help Theseus, she gave him a sword with which to kill the Minotaur and a spindle of thread to lead himself out of the maze in which the Minotaur lived. Victorious, Theseus sailed home with Ariadne but abandoned her on the island of Naxos, where she was discovered by the god of wine, Dionysus, who married her and made her his queen. Theseus, sailing into the harbor at Athens, neglected to raise the white sails, perhaps intentionally. When his father, King Aegeus, saw the ship still sailing under black sails, he threw himself into the sea, which from then on took his name, the Aegean. Theseus, of course, then became king.

The story is a creation or origin myth, like the Zuni emergence tale (see Reading 1.1 in Chapter 1) or the Hebrew story of Adam and Eve in Genesis. But it differs from them in one important point: Rather than narrating the origin of humankind in general, it tells the story of the birth of one culture out of another. It is the Athenian Greeks' way of knowing their past, their *archaiologia*. The tale of the labyrinth explained to the later Greeks where and how their culture came to be. It correctly suggests a close link to Crete, but it also emphasizes Greek independence from that powerful island. It tells us, furthermore, much about the emerging Greek character, for Theseus would, by the fifth century BCE, achieve the status of a national hero. The great tragedies of Greek theater represent Theseus as wily, ambitious, and strong. He stops at nothing to achieve what he thinks he must. If he is not altogether admirable, he mirrors behavior the Greeks attributed to their gods. Nevertheless, he is anything but idealized or godlike. He is, almost to a fault, completely human.

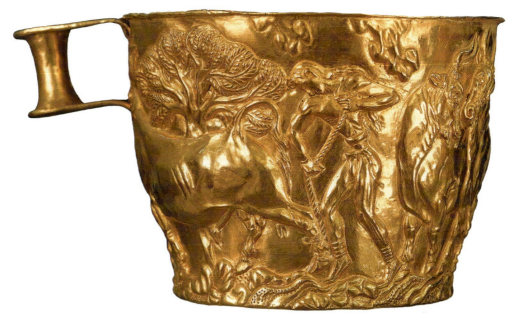

Fig. 2.9 *Vaphio Cup*, **from a tomb at Vaphio, south of Sparta, Greece. ca. 1650–1450 BCE.** Gold, height 3½″. National Archeological Museum, Iráklion, Crete. Mycenaean invaders used Crete as a base for operations for several centuries, and probably acquired the cup there.

It was precisely this search for the origins of Greek culture that led Sir Arthur Evans to the discovery of the Palace of Minos in Crete. He confirmed "the truth" in the legend of the Minotaur. If there was no actual monster, there was indeed a labyrinth. And that labyrinth was the palace itself.

Mycenaean Culture on the Mainland

When the Minoans abandoned the palace at Knossos in about 1450 BCE, warriors from the mainland culture of Mycenae, on the Greek mainland, quickly occupied Crete (see Map 2.1). One reason for the abandonment of Knossos was suggested earlier—the deforestation of the island. Another might be that Minoan culture was severely weakened in the aftermath of the volcanic eruption on Thera, and therefore susceptible to invasion or internal revolution. A third might be that the Mycenaean army simply overwhelmed the island. The Mycenaeans were certainly acquainted with the Minoan culture some 92 miles to their south, across the Aegean.

Minoan metalwork was prized on the mainland. Its fine quality is very evident in the *Vaphio Cup*, one of two golden cups found in the nineteenth century in a tomb at Vaphio, just south of Sparta, on the Peloponnese (Fig. **2.9**). This cup was executed in **repoussé**, a technique in which the artist hammers out the design from the inside. It depicts a man in an olive grove capturing a bull by tethering its hind legs. The bull motif is classically Minoan. The Mycenaeans, however, could not have been more different from the Minoans. Whereas Minoan towns were unfortified, and battle scenes were virtually nonexistent in their art, the Mycenaeans lived in communities surrounding fortified hilltops, and battle and hunting scenes dominate their art. Minoan culture appears to

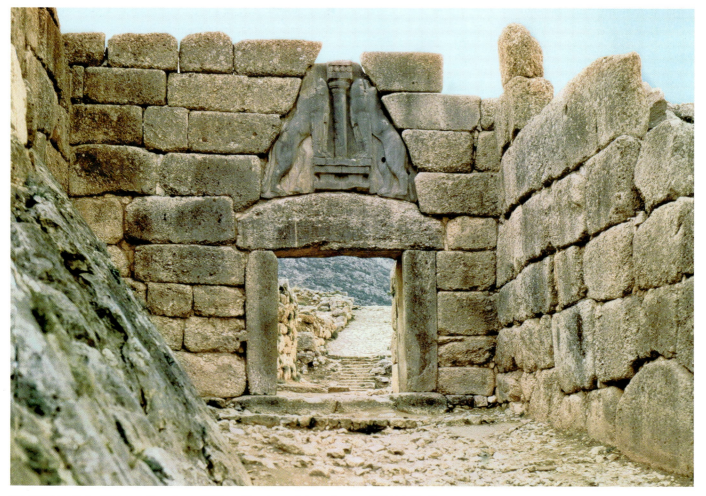

Fig. 2.10 Lion Gate, Mycenae, Greece. ca. 1300 BCE. Limestone relief, panel approx. 9'6" high. The lionesses are carved on a triangle of stone that relieves the weight of the massive doorway from the lintel. The original heads, which have never been found, were attached to the bodies with dowels.

have been peaceful, while the warlike Mycenaeans lived and died by the sword.

The ancient city of Mycenae, which gave its name to the larger Mycenaean culture, was discovered by German archeologist Heinrich Schliemann (1822–1890) in the late nineteenth century, before Sir Arthur Evans discovered Knossos. Its citadel looks down across a broad plain to the sea. Its walls—20 feet thick and 50 feet high—were built from huge blocks of rough-hewn stone, in a technique called **cyclopean masonry** because it was believed by later Greeks that only a race of monsters known as the Cyclopes could have managed them. Visitors to the city entered through a massive Lion Gate at the top of a steep path that led from the valley below (Fig. **2.10**). The lionesses that stood above the gate's lintel were themselves 9 feet high. It is likely that their missing heads originally turned in the direction of approaching visitors, as if to ward off evil or, perhaps, humble them in their tracks. They were probably made of a different stone from the bodies and may have been plundered at a later time. From the gate, a long, stone street wound up the hill to the citadel itself. Here, overseeing all, was the king's palace.

Mycenae was only one of several fortified cities on mainland Greece that were flourishing by 1500 BCE and that have come to be called Mycenaean. Mycenaean culture was the forerunner of ancient Greek culture and was essentially **feudal** in nature—that is, a system of political organization held together by ties of allegiance between a lord and those who relied on him for protection. Kings controlled not only their own cities but also the surrounding countryside. Merchants, farmers, and artisans owed their own prosperity to the king and paid high taxes for the privilege of living under his protection. More powerful kings, such as those at Mycenae itself, also expected the loyalty (and financial support) of other cities and nobles over whom they exercised authority. A large bureaucracy of tax collectors, civil servants, and military personnel ensured the state's continued prosperity. Like the Minoans, they engaged in trade, especially for the copper and tin required to make bronze.

The feudal system allowed Mycenae's kings to amass enormous wealth, as Schliemann's excavations confirmed. He discovered gold and silver death masks of fallen heroes (Fig. **2.11**), as well as swords and daggers inlaid with imagery of

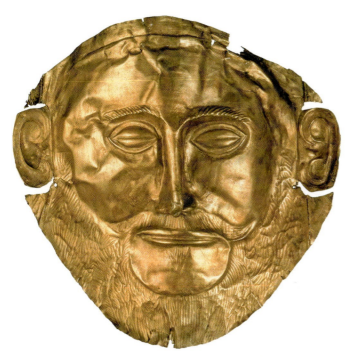

Fig. 2.11 Funerary mask (*Mask of Agamemnon*), from Grave Circle A, Mycenae, Greece. ca. 1600–1550 BCE. Gold, height approx. 12″. National Archeological Museum, Athens. When Schliemann discovered this mask, he believed it was the death mask of King Agamemnon, but it predates the Trojan War by some 300 years. Recent scholarship suggests that Schliemann may have added the handlebar mustache and large ears, perhaps to make the mask appear more "heroic."

events such as a royal lion hunt. He also found delicately carved ivory, from the tusks of hippopotamuses and elephants, suggesting if not the breadth of Mycenae's power, then the extent of its trade, which clearly included Africa. It seems likely, in fact, that the Mycenaean taste for war, and certainly its occupation of Crete, was motivated by the desire to control trade routes throughout the region.

The Homeric Epics

In about 800 BCE, the Greeks began to write down the stories from and about their past—their *archaiologia*—that had been passed down, generation to generation, by word of mouth. The most important of these stories were composed by an author whom history calls Homer. Homer was most likely a bard, a singer of songs about the deeds of heroes and the ways of the gods. His stories were part of a long-standing oral tradition that dated back to the time of the Trojan War, which we believe occurred sometime around 1200 BCE. Out of the oral materials he inherited, Homer composed two great epic poems, the *Iliad* and the *Odyssey*. The first narrates an episode in the ten-year Trojan War, which, according to Homer, began when the Greeks launched a large fleet of ships under King Agamemnon of Mycenae to bring back Helen, the wife of his brother King Menelaus of Sparta, who had eloped with Paris, son of King Priam of Troy. The *Odyssey* narrates the adventures of one of the principal Greek leaders, Odysseus (also known as Ulysses), on his return home from the fighting.

Most scholars believed that these Homeric epics were pure fiction until the discovery by Heinrich Schliemann in the 1870s of the actual site of Troy, a multilayered site near modern-day Hissarlik, in northwestern Turkey. The Troy of Homer's epic was discovered in the sixth layer. (Schliemann also believed that the shaft graves at Mycenae, where he found so much treasure, were those of Agamemnon and his royal family, but modern dating techniques have ruled that out.) Suddenly, the *Iliad* assumed, if not the authority, then the aura of historical fact.

By the sixth century BCE, the *Iliad* was recited every four years in Athens (without omission, according to law), and many copies of it circulated in Greece in the fifth and fourth centuries BCE. Finally, in Alexandria, Egypt, in the late fourth century BCE, scribes wrote the poem on papyrus scrolls, perhaps dividing it into the 24 manageable units we refer to today as the poem's books.

The poem was so influential that it established certain epic conventions, standard ways of composing an epic that were followed for centuries to come. Examples include starting the poem *in medias res*, Latin for "in the middle of things," that is, in the middle of the story; invoking the muse at the poem's outset; and stating the poem's subject at the outset.

The *Iliad* tells but a small fraction of the story of the Trojan War, which was launched by Agamemnon of Mycenae and his allies to attack Troy around 1200 BCE. The tale begins after the war is under way and narrates what is commonly called "the rage of Achilles," a phrase drawn from the first line of the poem. Already encamped on the Trojan plain, Agamemnon has been forced to give up a girl that he has taken in one of his raids, but he takes the beautiful Briseis from Achilles as compensation. Achilles, by far the greatest of the Greek warriors, is outraged. He suppresses his urge to kill Agamemnon, but withdraws from the war. He knows that the Greeks cannot succeed without him, and in his rage he believes they deserve their fate. Indeed, Hector, the great Trojan prince, soon drives the Greeks back to their ships, and Agamemnon sends ambassadors to Achilles to offer him gifts and beg him to return to the battle. Achilles refuses: "His gifts, I loathe his gifts. . . . I wouldn't give you a splinter for that man! Not if he gave me 10 times as much, 20 times over." When the battle resumes, things become desperate for the Greeks. Achilles partially relents, permitting Patroclus, his close friend and perhaps his lover, to wear his armor in order to put fear into the Trojans. Led by Patroclus, the Achaeans, as Homer calls the Greeks, drive the Trojans back.

The most notable feature of the poem is the unflinching verbal picture Homer paints of the realities of war, not only its cowardice, panic, and brutality, but also its compelling attraction. In this arena, the Greek soldier is able to demonstrate one of the most important values in Greek culture, his *areté*, often translated as "virtue," but actually meaning something closer to "being the best you can be" or "reaching your highest human potential." Homer uses the term to describe

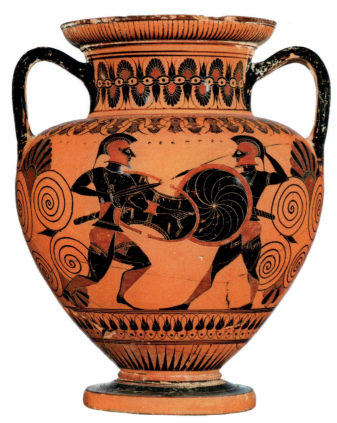

Fig. 2.12 Botkin Class Amphora. ca. 540–530 BCE. Black figure decoration on ceramic, height 11⁹⁄₁₆", diameter 9½". Museum of Fine Arts, Boston, Henry Lillie Pierce Fund, 98.923. Photograph © 2014 Museum of Fine Arts, Boston. On the other side of this vase are two heavily armed warriors, one pursuing the other.

both Greek and Trojan heroes, and it refers not only to their bravery but also to their effectiveness in battle.

The sixth-century BCE painting on the side of the *Botkin Class Amphora*—an **amphora** is a Greek jar, with an egg-shaped body and two curved handles, used for storing oil or wine—embodies the concept of *areté* (Fig. **2.12**). Here, two warriors, one armed with a sword, the other with a spear, confront each other with unwavering determination and purpose. At one point in the *Iliad*, Homer describes two such warriors, holding their own against each other, as "rejoicing in the joy of battle." They rejoice because they find themselves in a place where they can demonstrate their *areté*. The following passage, from Book 24, the final section of the *Iliad*, shows the other side of war and the other side of the poem, the compassion and humanity that distinguish Homer's narration (**Reading 2.1**). Hector, son of the king of Troy, has struck down Patroclus with the aid of the god Apollo. On hearing the news, Achilles is devastated and finally enters the fray. Until now, fuming over Agamemnon's insult, he has sat out the battle, refusing, in effect, to demonstrate his own *areté*. But now, he redirects his rage from Agamemnon to the Trojan warrior Hector, whom he meets and kills. He then ties Hector's body to his chariot and drags it to his tent. The

act is pure sacrilege, a violation of the dignity due the great Trojan warrior and an insult to his memory. Late that night, Priam, the king of Troy, steals across enemy lines to Achilles' tent and begs for the body of his son:

READING 2.1

from Homer, *Iliad*, Book 24 (ca. 750 BCE)

"Remember your own father, great godlike Achilles—
as old as I am, past the threshold of deadly old age!
No doubt the countrymen round about him plague him now,
with no one there to defend him, beat away disaster.
No one—but at least he hears you're still alive
and his old heart rejoices, hopes rising, day by day,
to see his beloved son come sailing home from Troy.
But I—dear god, my life so cursed by fate . . .
I fathered hero sons in the wide realm of Troy
and now not a single one is left, I tell you.
Fifty sons I had when the sons of Achaea came,
nineteen born to me from a single mother's womb
and the rest by other women in the palace. Many,
most of them violent Ares cut the knees from under.
But one, one was left me, to guard my wall, my people—
the one you killed the other day, defending his fatherland,
my Hector! It's all for him I've come to the ships now,
to win him back from you—I bring a priceless ransom.
Revere the gods, Achilles! Pity me in my own right,
remember your own father! I deserve more pity . . .
I have endured what no one on earth has ever done before—
I put to my lips the hands of the man who killed my son."

Those words stirred within Achilles a deep desire
to grieve for his own father. Taking the old man's hand
he gently moved him back. And overpowered by memory
both men gave way to grief. Priam wept freely
for man-killing Hector, throbbing, crouching
before Achilles's feet as Achilles wept himself,
now for his father, now for Patroclus once again,
and their sobbing rose and fell throughout the house. . . .
Then Achilles called the serving-women out:
"Bathe and anoint the body—
bear it aside first. Priam must not see his son."
He feared that, overwhelmed by the sight of Hector,
wild with grief, Priam might let his anger flare
and Achilles might fly into fresh rage himself,
cut the old man down and break the laws of Zeus.
So when the maids had bathed and anointed the body
sleek with olive oil and wrapped it round and round
in a braided battle-shirt and handsome battle-cape,
then Achilles lifted Hector up in his own arms
and laid him down on a bier, and comrades helped him
raise the bier and body onto a sturdy wagon. . . .
Then with a groan he called his dear friend by name:
"Feel no anger at me, Patroclus, if you learn—
ever there in the House of Death—I let his father
have Prince Hector back. He gave me worthy ransom
and you shall have your share from me, as always,
your fitting, lordly share."

Homer clearly recognizes the ability of these warriors to exceed their mere humanity, to raise themselves not only to a level of great military achievement, but also to a state of compassion, nobility, and honor. It is this exploration of the "doubleness" of the human spirit, its cruelty and its humanity, its blindness and its insight, that perhaps best defines the power and vision of the Homeric epic.

Homer's second epic, the *Odyssey*, narrates the adventures of Odysseus on his ten-year journey home from the war in Troy—his encounters with monsters, giants, and a seductive enchantress, a sojourn on a floating island and another in the underworld. But above all the poem's subject is Odysseus' passionate desire once more to see his wife, Penelope, and Penelope's fidelity to him. Where anger and lust drive the *Iliad*—from Achilles' angry sulk to Helen's fickleness—love and familial affection drive the *Odyssey*. Penelope is gifted with *areté* in her own right, since for the 20 years of her husband's absence she uses all the cunning in her power to ward off the suitors who flock to marry her, convinced that Odysseus is never coming home.

In later Greek culture, the *Iliad* and the *Odyssey* were the basis of Greek education. Every schoolchild learned the two poems by heart. They were the principal vehicles through which the Greeks came to know the past, and through the past, they came to know themselves. The poems embodied what might be called the Greeks' own cultural as opposed to purely personal *areté*, their desire to achieve a place of preeminence among all states. But in defining this larger cultural ambition, the *Iliad* and *Odyssey* laid out the individual values and responsibilities that all Greeks understood to be their personal obligations and duties if the state were ever to realize its goals.

THE RISE OF THE GREEK POLIS

How are the values of the Greek polis reflected in its art and architecture?

The Greek city-state, or polis, arose during the ninth century BCE, around the time of Homer. Colonists set sail from cities on the Greek mainland to establish new settlements. Eventually, there were as many as 1,500 Greek city-states scattered around the Mediterranean and the Black Sea from Spain to the Crimea, including large colonies in Italy (Fig. **2.13**). Since the fall of Mycenae in about 1100 BCE, some 100 years after the Trojan War, Greece had endured a long period of cultural decline that many refer to as the Dark Ages. Greek legend has it that a tribe from the North, the Dorians, overran the Greek mainland and the Peloponnese. Historical evidence suggests that the Dorians possessed iron weapons and easily defeated the bronze-armored Greeks. Scattered and in disarray, the Greek people almost forgot the rudiments of culture, and reading and writing fell into disuse. For the most part, the Greeks lived in small rural communities that often warred with one another. But despite these conditions, which hardly favored the development of art and architecture, the Greeks managed to sustain a sense of identity and even, as the survival of the Trojan War legends suggests, some idea of their cultural heritage.

Gradually, across Greece, communities began to organize themselves and exercise authority over their own limited geographical regions, which were defined by natural boundaries—mountains, rivers, and plains. The population of even the largest communities was largely dedicated to agriculture, and agricultural values—a life of hard, honest

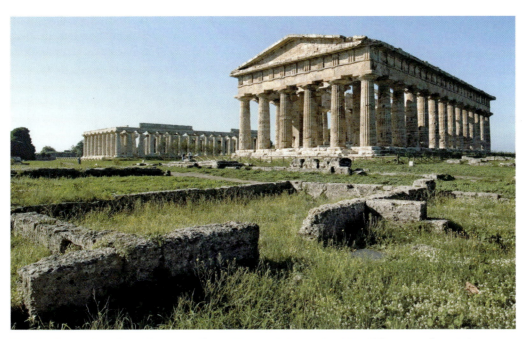

Fig. 2.13 The Temple of Hera I (background), ca. 560 BCE, and the Temple of Hera II (foreground), ca. 460 BCE, Paestum, Italy. Two of the best-preserved Greek temples can be found in Italy, at Paestum, south of Naples, in a place the Greeks called Poseidonia, after the god of the sea, Poseidon.

work and self-reliance—predominated. The great pastoral poem of the poet Hesiod (flourished ca. 800 BCE), *Works and Days*, testifies to this. *Works and Days* was written at about the same time as the Homeric epics in Boeotia, the region of Greece dominated by the city-state of Thebes. Hesiod gives us a clear insight not only into many of the details of Greek agricultural production, but into social conditions as well. He mentions that all landowners possessed slaves (taken in warfare), who comprised over half the population. He also speaks of the Greek gods Zeus, king of the gods and master of the sky, and Demeter, goddess of agriculture and grain, and the necessity of working hard in order to please them. In fact, it was Hesiod, in his *Theogony* (*The Birth of the Gods*), who first detailed the Greek **pantheon** (literally, "all the gods").

The Greek Gods

The religion of the Greeks informed almost every aspect of daily life. The gods watched over the individual at birth, nurtured the family, and protected the city-state. They controlled the weather, the seasons, health, marriage, longevity, and the future, which they could foresee. Each polis traced its origins to a particular founding god—Athena for Athens, Zeus for Sparta. Sacred sanctuaries were dedicated to others.

The Greeks believed that the 12 major gods lived on Mount Olympus, in northeastern Greece. While the number of gods on Olympus was fixed at 12, over time different gods were included and others excluded, so that some 15 gods were considered "major" at one time or another. There they ruled over the Greeks in a completely human fashion. They quarreled and meddled, loved and lost, exercised justice or not—and they were depicted by the Greeks in human form. There was nothing special about them except their power, which was enormous, sometimes frighteningly so. But the Greeks believed that as long as they did not overstep their bounds and try to compete with the gods—the sin of **hubris**, or pride—the gods would protect them.

Among the major gods (with their later Roman names in parentheses) are:

Zeus (Jupiter): King of the gods, usually bearded, and associated with the eagle and thunderbolt.

Hera (Juno): Wife and sister of Zeus, and the goddess of marriage and maternity.

Athena (Minerva): Goddess of war, but also, through her association with Athens, of civilization; the daughter of Zeus, born from his head; often helmeted, shield and spear in hand; the owl (wisdom) and the olive tree (peace) are sacred to her.

Ares (Mars): God of war, and son of Zeus and Hera, usually armored.

Aphrodite (Venus): Goddess of love and beauty; Hesiod says she was born when the severed genitals of Uranus, the Greek personification of the sky, were cast into the sea and his sperm mingled with sea foam to create her. Eros is her son.

Apollo (Phoebus): God of the sun, light, truth, prophecy, music, and medicine; he carries a bow and arrow, sometimes a lyre; he is often depicted riding a chariot across the sky.

Artemis (Diana): Goddess of the hunt and the moon; Apollo's sister, she carries bow and arrow, and is accompanied by hunting dogs.

Demeter (Ceres): Goddess of agriculture and grain.

Dionysus (Bacchus): God of wine and inspiration, closely aligned to myths of fertility and sexuality.

Hermes (Mercury): Messenger of the gods, but also god of fertility, theft, dreams, commerce, and the marketplace; usually wearing winged sandals and a winged hat, he carries a wand with two snakes entwined around it.

Hades (Pluto): God of the underworld, accompanied by his monstrous dog Cerberus.

Hephaestus (Vulcan): God of the forge and fire; son of Zeus and Hera and husband of Aphrodite; wears a blacksmith's apron and carries a hammer.

Hestia (Vesta): Goddess of the hearth and sister of Zeus.

Poseidon (Neptune): Brother of Zeus and god of the sea; carries a trident (a three-pronged spear); the horse is sacred to him.

Persephone (Proserpina): Goddess of fertility, Demeter's daughter, carted off each winter to the underworld by her husband Hades, but released each spring to restore the world to plenty.

Of particular interest here—as in Homer's *Iliad*—is that the gods are as susceptible to Eros, or Desire, as is humankind. In fact, the Greek gods are sometimes more human than humans—susceptible to every human foible. Like many a family on Earth, the father, Zeus, is an all-powerful philanderer, whose wife, Hera, is watchful, jealous, and capable of inflicting great pain on rivals for her husband's affections. Their children are scheming and self-serving in their competition for their parents' attention. The gods think like humans, act like humans, and speak like humans. They sometimes seem to differ from humans only in the fact that they are immortal. Unlike the Hebrew God, who is admittedly sometimes portrayed as arbitrary—consider the Book of Job—the Greek gods present humans with no clear principles of behavior, and the priests and priestesses who oversaw the rituals dedicated to them produced no scriptures or doctrines. The gods were capricious, capable of changing their minds, susceptible to argument and persuasion, alternately obstinate and malleable. If these qualities created a kind of cosmic uncertainty, they also embodied the intellectual freedom and the spirit of philosophical inquiry that would come to define the Greek state.

The Greek Architectural Tradition

The Greek poleis were distinguished by their physical isolation from one another and their fierce independence. In competition for the few really fertile lands on the mainland, they often warred with one another. And inevitably certain city-states became more powerful than others. Before the ninth century BCE, many Athenians had migrated to Ionia in southwestern Anatolia (modern Turkey), and relations with the Near East helped Athens to flourish. Corinth, situated on the isthmus

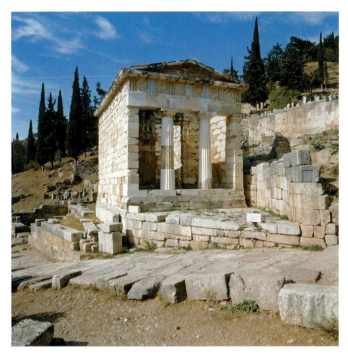

Fig. 2.14 The Athenian Treasury, Delphi, and plan. ca. 510 BCE. The sculptural program around the Treasury, just below the roof line, depicts the adventures of two great Greek mythological heroes, Theseus and Heracles.

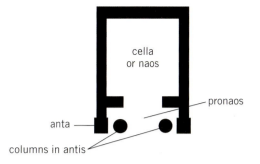

between the Greek mainland and the Peloponnese, controlled north–south trade routes from early times, but after it built a towpath to drag ships over the isthmus on rollers, it soon controlled the sea routes east and west as well. The Spartans, on the Peloponnese, traced their ancestry back to the legendary Dorians, whose legacy was military might. But despite their many differences, a common architectural tradition began to arise among the poleis, one that not only demonstrated their common cultural heritage, but has also had a lasting influence on Western architecture as a whole.

As early as the eighth century BCE, various poleis began to establish sanctuaries where they could come together to share music, religion, poetry, and athletics. The sanctuary was a large-scale reflection of another Greek invention, the **symposium**, literally a "coming together" of men (originally of the same military unit) to share poetry, food, and wine. At the sanctuaries, people from different city-states came together to honor their gods and, by extension, to celebrate, in the presence of their rivals, their own accomplishments.

Delphi The sanctuaries were sacred religious sites. They inspired the city-states, which were always trying to outdo one another, to create the first monumental architecture since Mycenaean times. At Delphi, high in the mountains above the Gulf of Corinth, and home to the Sanctuary of Apollo, the city-states, in their usual competitive spirit, built monuments and statues dedicated to the god, and elaborate treasuries to store offerings. Many built hostels so that pilgrims from home could gather. Delphi was an especially important site. Here, the Greeks believed, the Earth was attached to the sky by its navel. Here, too, through a deep crack in the

ground, Apollo spoke, through the medium of a woman called the Pythia. Priests interpreted the cryptic omens and messages she delivered. The Greek author Plutarch, writing in the first century CE, said that the Pythia entered a small chamber beneath the temple, smelled sweet-smelling fumes, and went into a trance. This story was dismissed as fiction until recently, when geologists discovered that two faults intersect directly below the Delphic temple, allowing hallucinogenic gases to rise through the fissures, specifically ethylene, which has a sweet smell and produces a narcotic effect described as a floating or disembodied euphoria.

The facade of the Athenian Treasury at Delphi consisted of two columns standing in *antis* (that is, between two-squared stone pilasters, called **antae**). Behind them is the **pronaos**, or enclosed vestibule, at the front of the building, with its doorway leading into the **cella** (or naos), the principal interior space of the building (see the floor plan, Fig. 2.14).

We can see the antecedents of this building type in a small ceramic model of an early Greek temple dating from the eighth century BCE and found at the Sanctuary of Hera near Argos (Fig. 2.15). Its projecting porch supported by two columns anticipates the antis columns and pronaos of the Athenian Treasury. The triangular area over the porch created by the pitch of the roof, called the **pediment**, is not as steeply pitched in the Treasury.

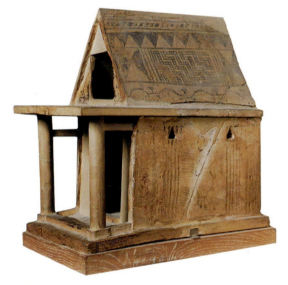

Fig. 2.15 Model of a temple, found in the Sanctuary of Hera, Argos. Mid-8th century BCE. Terra cotta, length 4½". National Archeological Museum, Athens. We do not know if later temples were painted like the model here.

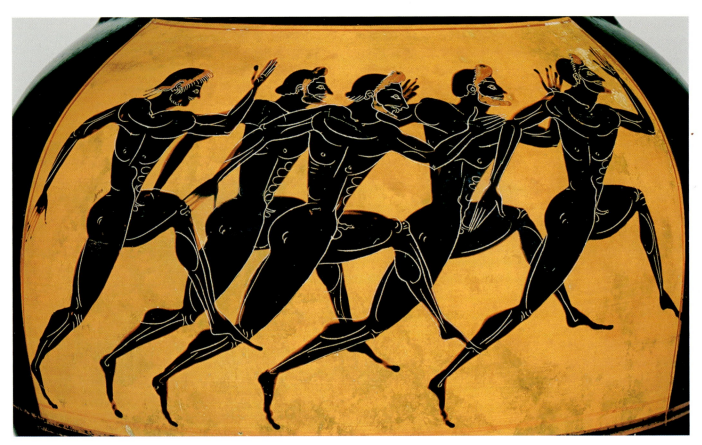

Fig. 2.16 The Euphiletos Painter, Black-figure amphora showing a foot-race at the Panathenaic Games in Athens (detail). ca. 530 BCE. Terra cotta, height 24½". The Metropolitan Museum of Arts, New York. Rogers Fund, 1914 (14.130.12). Greek athletes competed nude. In fact, our word *gymnasium* derives from the Greek word for "naked," *gymnos.*

The Temples of Hera at Paestum From this basic form, surviving in the small treasuries at Delphi, the larger temples of the Greeks would develop. Two distinctive **orders**—systems of proportion that include the building's plan, its **elevation** (the arrangement and appearance of the temple's foundation, columns, and lintels), and decorative scheme—developed before 500 BCE, the **Doric order** and the **Ionic order** (see *Closer Look*, pages 54–55). Later, a third, **Corinthian order** would emerge. Among earliest surviving examples of a Greek temple of the Doric order are the Temples of Hera I and II in the Sanctuary of Hera at Paestum, a Greek colony established in the seventh century BCE in Italy, about 50 miles south of present-day Naples (see Fig. 2.13). As the plan of the Temple of Hera I makes clear, the earlier of the two temples was a large, rectangular structure, with a pronaos containing three (as opposed to two) columns and an elongated cella, behind which is an **adyton**, the innermost sanctuary housing the place where, in a temple with an oracle, the oracle's message was delivered. Surrounding this inner structure was the **peristyle**, a row of columns that stands on the **stylobate**, the raised platform of the temple. The columns swell about one-third of the way up and contract again at the top, a characteristic known as **entasis**, and are topped by the two-part capital of the Doric order with its rounded **enchinus** and tabletlike **abacus**.

Olympia and the Olympic Games The Greeks date the beginning of their history to the first formal Panhellenic ("all-Greece") athletic competition, held in 776 BCE. These first Olympic Games were held at Olympia. There, a sanctuary dedicated to Hera and Zeus also housed an elaborate athletics facility. The first contest of the first games was a 200-yard dash the length of the Olympia stadium, a race called the *stadion* (Fig. 2.16). Over time, other events of solo performance were added, including chariot racing, boxing, and the pentathlon (from Greek *penta*, "five," and *athlon*, "contest"), consisting of discus, javelin, long jump, sprinting, and wrestling. There were no second or third prizes. Winning was all. The contests were conducted every four years during the summer months and were open only to men (married women were forbidden to attend, and unmarried women probably did not attend). The Olympic Games were held for more than 1,000 years, until the Christian Byzantine emperor Theodosius banned them in 394 CE. They were revived in 1896 to promote international understanding and friendship.

The Olympic Games were only one of numerous athletic festivals held in various locations. These games comprised a defining characteristic of the developing Greek national identity. As a people, the Greeks believed in *agonizesthai*, a verb meaning "to contend for the prize." They were driven by competition. Potters bragged that their work was better than any other's. Playwrights competed for best play, poets for best recitation, athletes for best performance. As the city-states themselves competed for supremacy, they began to understand the spirit of competition as a trait shared by all.

Greek Sculpture and the Taste for Naturalism

Greek athletes performed nude, so it is not surprising that athletic contests gave rise to what may be called a "cult of the body." The physically fit male not only won accolades in athletic contests, but also represented the conditioning and strength of the military forces of a particular polis. The male body was also celebrated in a widespread genre of sculpture known as the *kouros*, meaning "young man" (Figs. **2.17** and **2.18**). This celebration of the body was uniquely Greek. No other Mediterranean culture so emphasized the depiction of the male nude. Several thousand *kouroi* (plural of *kouros*) appear to have been carved in the sixth century BCE alone. They could be found in sanctuaries and cemeteries, most often serving as votive offerings to the gods or as commemorative grave markers. Their resolute features suggest their determination in their role as ever-watchful guardians.

Although we would never mistake an early Greek figure (such as Fig. 2.17) for the work of an Egyptian sculptor—its nudity and much more fully realized anatomical features are clear differences—still, its Egyptian influences are obvious, as can be seen in the comparison between a late Egyptian sculpture and the two *kouroi* dating from 600 BCE and 525 BCE respectively (see Fig. 1.27).

CONTINUITY & CHANGE

Mentuemhet, p. 37

In fact, as early as 650 BCE, the Greeks were in Egypt, and by the early sixth century BCE, 12 cooperating city-states had established a trading outpost in the Nile Delta. The Greek sculpture serves much the same funerary function as its Egyptian ancestors. In fact, an inscription on the base of Fig. 2.17 reads: "Stop and grieve at the dead Kroisos, slain by wild Ares in the front rank of battle. This is a monument to a fallen hero, killed in the prime of youth."

During the course of the sixth century, *kouroi* became distinguished by *naturalism*. That is, they increasingly reflect the artist's desire to represent the human body as it appears in nature. This in turn probably reflects the growing role of the individual in Greek political life. We do not know why sculptors wanted to realize the human form more naturalistically,

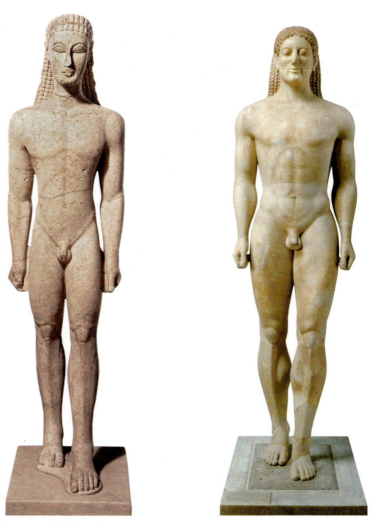

Fig. 2.17 (left) *New York Kouros*. **ca. 600** BCE. Marble, height 6'4". The Metropolitan Museum of Art, New York. Fletcher Fund, 1932 (32.11.1).

Fig. 2.18 (right) *Anavysos Kouros*, **from Anavysos cemetery, near Athens. ca. 525** BCE. Marble with remnants of paint, height 6'4". National Archeological Museum, Athens. The sculpture on the left is one of the earliest known life-size standing sculptures of a male in Greek art. The one on the right represents 75 years of Greek experimentation with the form. Note its closed-lip "Archaic smile," a symbol of liveliness and vitality.

but we can surmise that the reason must be related to *agonizesthai*, the spirit of competition so dominant in Greek society. Sculptors must have competed against one another in their attempts to realize the human form. Furthermore, since it was believed that the god Apollo manifested himself as a well-endowed athlete, the more lifelike and natural the sculpture, the more nearly it could be understood to resemble the god himself.

At the center of Athenian life was the worship, on the Acropolis, of the goddess Athena, the city's protector. Just as the *kouros* statue seems related to Apollo, statues of *korai*, or "maidens" (singular *kore*), appear to have been votive offerings to Athena and were apparently conceived as gifts to the goddess. Male citizens dedicated *korai* to her as a gesture of both piety and evident pleasure in the beauty of the sculpture itself. From the mid-sixth century BCE on, the sculptural production of *korai* flourished in Athens.

Classical Greek architecture is composed of three vertical elements—the **platform**, the **column**, and the **entablature**—which comprise its elevation. The relationship of these three units is referred to as the elevation's order. There are three orders—Doric, Ionic, and Corinthian—each distinguished by its specific design.

The Classical Greek orders became the basic design elements for architecture from ancient Greek times to the present day. A major source of their power is the sense of order, predictability, and proportion that they embody. Notice how the upper elements of each order—the elements comprising the entablature—change as the column supporting them becomes narrower and taller. In the Doric order, the **architrave** (the bottom layer of the entablature) and the frieze (the flat band just above the architrave decorated with sculpture, painting, or moldings) are comparatively massive. The Doric is the heaviest of the columns. The Ionic is lighter and noticeably smaller. The Corinthian is smaller yet, seemingly supported by mere leaves.

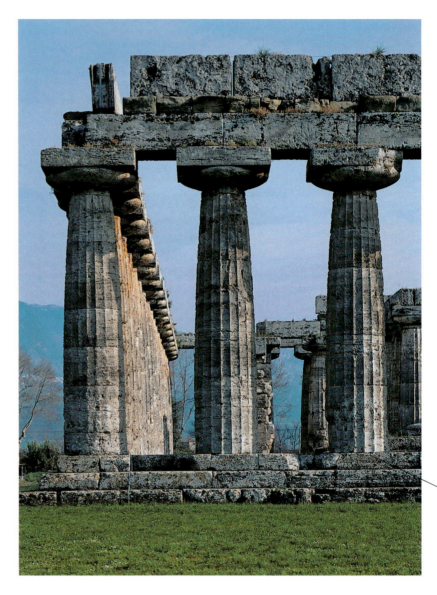

Doric columns at the Temple of Hera I, and plan. Paestum, Italy. ca. 540 BCE.
The floor plan of all three orders is essentially the same, although in the Doric order the last two columns were set slightly closer together—corner contraction, as it is known—resulting in the corner gaining a subtle visual strength and allowing regular spacing of sculptural elements in the entablature above.

Something to Think About . . .

The base, shaft, and capital of a Greek column have often been compared to the feet, body, and head of the human figure. How would you compare the Doric, Ionic, and Corinthian orders to Figs. 2.17, 2.18, and 2.27?

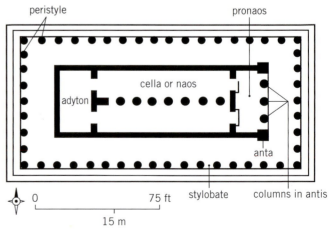

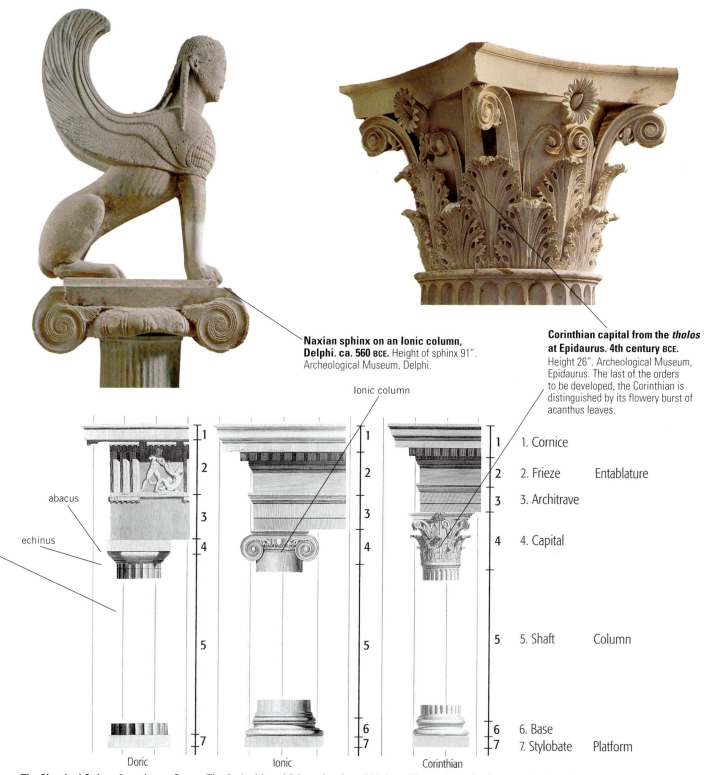

Naxian sphinx on an Ionic column, Delphi. ca. 560 BCE. Height of sphinx 91". Archeological Museum, Delphi.

Corinthian capital from the *tholos* at Epidaurus. 4th century BCE. Height 26". Archeological Museum, Epidaurus. The last of the orders to be developed, the Corinthian is distinguished by its flowery burst of acanthus leaves.

Ionic column

abacus

echinus

Doric

Ionic

Corinthian

1. Cornice

2. Frieze   Entablature

3. Architrave

4. Capital

5. Shaft   Column

6. Base

7. Stylobate   Platform

The Classical Orders, from James Stuart, *The Antiquities of Athens*, London, 1794. An architectural order lends a sense of unity and structural integrity to a building as a whole. By the century BCE, the Greeks had developed the Doric and the Ionic orders. The former is sturdy and simple. The latter is lighter in proportion and more elegant in detail, its capital characterized by a scroll-like motif called a **volute**. The Corinthian order, which originated in the last half of the century BCE, is the most elaborate of all. It would become a favorite of the Romans.

👁 **Watch** an architectural simulation of the Greek orders on **MyArtsLab**

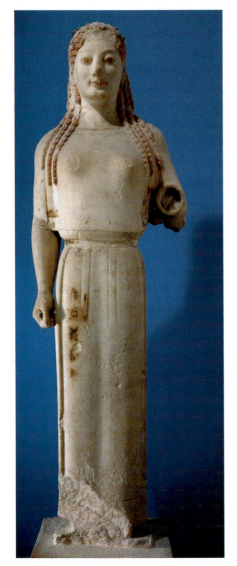

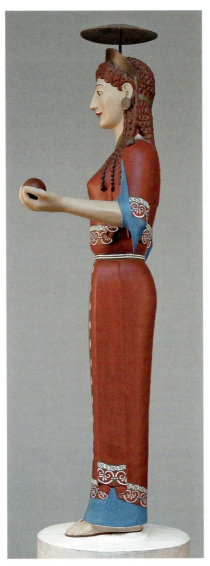

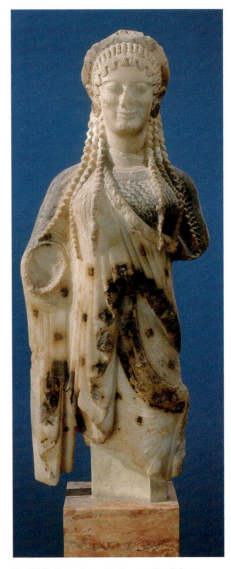

Fig. 2.19 *Peplos Kore* **and cast reconstruction of the original, from the Acropolis, Athens. Dedicated 530 BCE.** Polychromed marble, height 47½". Acropolis Museum, Athens (original), and Museum of Classical Archaeology, University of Cambridge, UK (cast). The extended arm, probably bearing a gift, was originally a separate piece, inserted in the round socket at her elbow. Note the small size of this sculpture, more than 2 feet shorter than the male *kouros* sculptures (Fig. 2.17 and Fig. 2.18).

Fig. 2.20 *Kore*, **from the Acropolis, Athens. ca. 520 BCE.** Polychromed marble, height 21". Acropolis Museum, Athens. Although missing half its height, the sculpture gives us a clear example of the elaborate dress of the last years of the sixth century BCE.

As with the *kouros* statues, the *korai* also became more naturalistic during the century. This trend is especially obvious in their dress. In the sculpture known as the *Peplos Kore* (Fig. **2.19**), anatomical realism is suppressed by the straight lines of the sturdy garment known as a *peplos*. Usually made of wool, the *peplos* is essentially a rectangle of cloth folded down at the neck, pinned at the shoulders, and belted. Another *kore*, also remarkable for the amount of original paint on it, is the *Kore* dating from ca. 520 BCE found on the Athenian Acropolis (Fig. **2.20**). This one wears a *chiton*, a garment that by the last decades of the century had become much more popular than the pelos. Made of linen, the chiton clings more closely to the body and is gathered to create pleats and folds that allow the artist to show off his virtuosity.

Athenian Pottery

The same trend toward increasing naturalism is also evident in the decorative painting on Greek pottery. By the middle of the sixth century BCE, Athens had become a major center of pottery making. Athenian potters were helped along by the extremely high quality of the clay available in Athens, which turned a deep orange color when fired.

As with Athenian sculpture, the decorations on Athenian vases grew increasingly naturalistic and detailed until, generally, only one scene filled each side of the vase. The Greeks soon developed two types of vase, characterized by the relationship of figure to ground: black- and red-figure vases. The figures on **black-figure** vases are painted with slip, a mixture of clay and water, so that after firing they

Many Greek pots depict gods and heroes, including representations of the *Iliad* and *Odyssey*. An example of this tendency is a **krater**, or vessel in which wine and water were mixed, that shows the *Death of Sarpedon*. It was made by the potter Euxitheos and painted by Euphronius by 515 BCE (Fig. **2.22**). Euphronius was praised especially for his ability to render human anatomy accurately. Here Sarpedon has just been killed by Patroclus (see Reading 2.1). Blood pours from his leg, shoulder, and carefully drawn abdomen. The winged figures of Hypnos (Sleep) and Thanatos (Death) are about to carry off his body as Hermes, messenger of the gods, who guides the dead to the underworld, looks on. But the naturalism of the scene is not the source of its appeal. Rather, its perfectly balanced composition transforms the tragedy into a rare depiction of death as an instance of dignity and order. The spears of the two warriors left and right mirror the edge of the vase, the design formed by Sarpedon's stomach muscles is echoed in the decorative bands at top and bottom, and the handles of the vase mirror the arching backs of Hypnos and Thanatos.

The *Death of Sarpedon* is an example of a **red-figure** vase. The process is the reverse of the black-figure process, and more complicated. Here, the slip is used to paint the background, outlining the figures. Using the same slip, Euphronius also drew details on the figure (such as Sarpedon's abdomen) with a brush. The vase was then fired in three stages, each with a different amount of oxygen allowed into

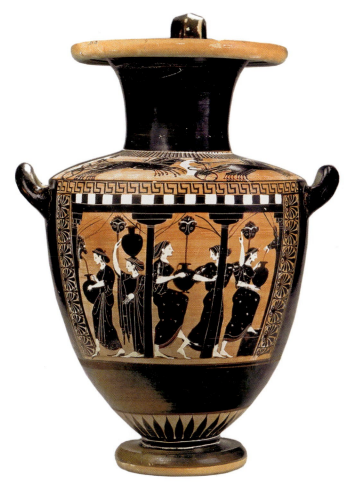

Fig. 2.21 Priam Painter, *Women at the Fountain.* ca. 520–510 BCE.
Black-figure decoration on a hydria (water jug). Height 20⅞, diameter 14⁹⁄₁₆″. Museum of Fine Arts, Boston. Reproduced with permission. Photograph © 2014 Museum of Fine Arts, Boston. All rights reserved. The convention of depicting women's skin as white is also found in Egyptian and Minoan art.

remain black against an unslipped red background. *Women at the Fountain* (Fig. **2.21**) is an example. Here, the artist, whom scholars have dubbed the Priam Painter, has added touches of white by mixing white pigment into the slip. By the second half of the sixth century, new motifs, showing scenes of everyday life, became increasingly popular. This *hydria*, or water jug, shows women carrying similar jugs as they chat at a fountain house of the kind built by the tyrant Pisistratus in the sixth century BCE at the ends of the aqueducts that brought water into the city. Such fountain houses were extremely popular spots, offering women, who were for the most part confined to their homes, a rare opportunity to gather socially. Water flows from animal-head spigots at both sides and across the back of the scene. The composition's strong vertical and horizontal framework, with its Doric columns, is softened by the rounded contours of the women's bodies and the vases they carry. This vase underscores the growing Greek taste for realistic scenes and naturalistic representation.

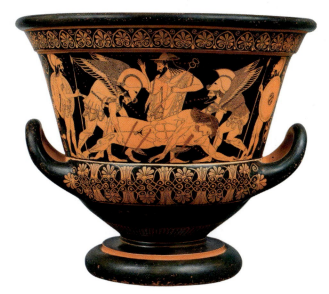

Fig. 2.22 Euphronius (painter) and Euxitheos (potter), *Death of Sarpedon.* ca. 515 BCE. Red-figure decoration on a calyx krater. Ceramic, height of krater 18″. Museo Nazionale di Villa Giulia, Rome. This type of krater is called a *calyx krater* because its handles curve up like the calyx flower. The krater was housed in the collection of the Metropolitan Museum of Art in New York until it became clear that it was illegally excavated in Italy in the early 1970s. The Museum returned the piece to Italy in 2008.

🔍 **View** the Closer Look on the *Euphronius Krater* on **MyArtsLab**

the kiln. In the first stage, oxygen was allowed into the kiln, "fixing" the whole vase in one overall shade of red. Then, oxygen in the kiln was reduced to the absolute minimum, turning the vessel black. At this point, as the temperature rose, the slip became vitrified, or glassy. Finally, oxygen entered the kiln again, turning the unslipped areas—in this case, the red figures—back into a shade of red. The areas painted with the now vitrified slip were not exposed to oxygen, so they remained black.

The Poetry of Sappho

The poet Sappho (ca. 610–ca. 580 BCE) was hailed throughout antiquity as "the tenth Muse," and her poetry celebrated as a shining example of female creativity. We know little of Sappho's somewhat extraordinary life. She was born on the island of Lesbos, and probably married. She mentions both a brother and a daughter, Cleis, in her poetry. As an adult poet, she surrounded herself with a group of young women who together engaged in the celebration of Aphrodite (love), the Graces (beauty), and the Muses (poetry). Her own poetry gives rise to the suggestion that her relation to these women was erotic. It seems clear that her circle shared their lives with one another only for a brief period before marriage.

Sappho produced nine books of **lyric poems** on themes of love and personal relationships, often with other women. Only fragments of Sappho's poetry have survived. It is impossible to convey the subtlety and beauty of her poems in translation, but their astonishing economy of feeling does come across. In the following poem (**Reading 2.2a**), one of the longest surviving fragments, she expresses her love for a married woman:

READING 2.2a
Sappho, lyric poetry

He is more than a hero
He is a god in my eyes
the man who is allowed
to sit beside you—he
who listens intimately
to the sweet murmur of
your voice, the enticing
laughter that makes my own
heart beat fast. If I meet
you suddenly, I can't
speak—my tongue is broken;
a thin flame runs under
my skin; seeing nothing
hearing only my ears
drumming, I drip with sweat;
trembling shakes my body
and I turn paler than
dry grass. At such times
death isn't far from me.

Such poems such were sung to the accompaniment of a lyre, as depicted in a red-figure vase by Polygnotos (Fig. 2.23). We have little knowledge of what Greek music actually sounded like. The only complete work of music to have survived is a *skolion*, or drinking song, by Seikolos, found chiseled on the first-century BCE gravestone of his wife, Euterpe. The Greek system for writing musical notation, apparently borrowed from the Phoenicians, marked the position of the fingers on the strings of the instrument.

Sappho's talent is the ability to condense the intensity of her feelings into a single breath, a breath that, as the following poem suggests, lives on (**Reading 2.2b**). Even in so short a poem, Sappho realizes concretely the Greek belief that we can achieve immortality through our words and deeds:

READING 2.2b
Sappho, lyric poetry

Although they are
only breath, words
which I command
are immortal.

Sappho's work was collected into nine volumes (arranged according to meter) by the Library of Alexandria, but these are now lost, like most of the rest of the library's 700,000 volumes. After Homer, she was probably the most admired poet in antiquity, but where Homer's poetry was concerned with creating a national, Hellenic identity, Sappho's lyrics were more personal, establishing her own, individual sense of self.

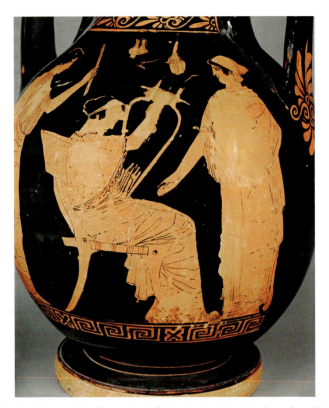

Fig. 2.23 Polygnotos (vase painter), Two women, one playing a lyre. 5th century BCE. Red-figure decoration on a *pelike* (two-handled vase similar to an amphora). Musée du Louvre, Paris. Most of Sappho's poems were written to be sung by a performer accompanying herself on the lyre.

The Rise of Democracy and the Threat of Persia

The growing naturalism of sixth-century BCE sculpture, to say nothing of the highly personal poetry of Sappho, coincides with the rise of democratic institutions in Athens, and reflects this important development. Both bear witness to a growing Greek spirit of innovation and accomplishment, and both testify to a growing belief in the dignity and worth of the individual.

In 508 BCE, the Athenian aristocrat Cleisthenes instituted the first Athenian political democracy—from the Greek *demokratia*, the rule (*kratia*) of the people (*demos*)—an innovation in self-government that might not have been possible had the Athenians not just endured more than 50 years of tyranny, beginning in 560 BCE when Pisistratus assumed rule in Athens. Then, the urban and rural regions of the Athenian polis were wracked by division. Wealthy landowners from the plains, poorer hill people living on the mountainsides, Athenian merchants, and aristocracy, all vied for power. Pisistratus had controlled this division with a heavy hand, ruling as a tyrant—that is, as a dictator—without consulting the people. Although he succeeded in providing jobs for the entire population by commissioning large-scale public works, he exiled aristocrats who did not support him, and he often kept sons of noble families as his personal hostages to guarantee their families' loyalty. His son Hippias, who followed him to power in 527 BCE, was harsher still, exiling more nobles and executing many others. In 510 BCE the exiled nobles revolted with aid from Sparta, Hippias escaped to Persia, and Cleisthenes took over.

"Nothing is worse for a city than a tyrant," the Greek playwright Euripides would later write in his play *The Suppliant Women*. "One man rules, and frames the law himself. Equality doesn't exist. But when laws are written down, both rich and poor have the same right to justice. This is freedom's rallying cry: 'What man has good advice to give the city? Make it public, and earn a reputation. . . . For the city's sake, what could be better than that? When the people are the pilots of the city, they control their own destiny.'" In other words, politics—a dedication to the well-being of the polis through discussion, consensus, and united action—depends upon democracy. In a tyranny, there can be no politics because there can be no debate. Whatever their diverging views, the citizens of the polis were free to debate the issues, to speak their minds. They spoke as individuals, and they cherished the freedom to think as they pleased. But they spoke out of a concern for the common good, for the good of the polis, which, after all, gave them the freedom to speak in the first place. When Aristotle says, in his *Politics*, that "man is a political animal," he means that man is a creature of the polis, bound to it, dedicated to it, determined by it, and, somewhat paradoxically, liberated by it as well.

These principles were well understood by Cleisthenes, who reorganized the Athenian political system into **demes**, small local areas comparable to precincts or wards in a modern city. Because all citizens—remember, only males were citizens—registered in their given *deme*, landowners and merchants had equal political rights. Cleisthenes then grouped the *demes* into ten political "tribes," whose membership cut across all family, class, and regional lines, thus effectively diminishing the power and influence of the noble families. Each tribe appointed 50 of its members to a Council of Five Hundred, which served for 36 days. There were thus ten separate councils per year, and no citizen could serve on the council more than twice in his lifetime. With so many citizens serving on the council for such short times, it is likely that nearly every Athenian citizen participated in the government at some point during his lifetime.

The new Greek democracy was immediately threatened by the rise of the Persian Empire in the east (see Chapter 1). In 499 BCE, probably aware of the newfound political freedoms in Athens and certainly chafing at the tyrannical rule of the Persians, the Ionian cities rebelled, burning down the city of Sardis, the Persian headquarters in Asia Minor. In 495 BCE, the Persian ruler Darius struck back. He burned down the most important Ionian city, Miletus, slaughtering the men and taking its women and children into slavery. Then, probably influenced by Hippias, who lived in exile in his court, Darius set his sights on Athens, which had sent a force to Ionia to aid the rebellion.

In 490 BCE, a huge Persian army, estimated at 90,000, landed at Marathon, on the northern plains of Attica. They were met by a mere 10,000 Greeks, led by a professional soldier named Miltiades, who had once served under Darius in Persia, and who understood the weakness of Darius' military strategy. Miltiades struck Darius' forces at dawn, killing 6,000 Persians and suffering minimal losses himself. The Persians were routed. The anxious citizens of Athens heard news of the victory from Phidippides, who ran the 26 miles between Marathon and Athens, thus completing the original marathon, a run that the Greeks would soon incorporate into their Olympic Games. (Contrary to popular belief, Phidippides did not die in the effort.)

Darius may have been defeated, but the Persians were not done. Even as the Greeks basked in victory, Darius and his son Xerxes were once again solidifying their power at Persepolis, and after Darius died fighting in Egypt in 486 BCE, Xerxes (r. 486–465 BCE) assumed the throne. By 481 BCE, it was apparent that Xerxes was preparing to attack Greece once again. Themistocles (ca. 524–ca. 460 BCE), an Athenian statesman and general, had been anticipating the invasion for a decade. He convinced the Athenians to unite with the other Greek poleis under the direction of the Spartans, the strongest military power. When a large supply of silver was discovered in 483 BCE, Themistocles, convinced that the Persians could not be defeated on land, persuaded Athens to use its newfound wealth to build a fleet.

Finally, in 480 BCE, Xerxes led a huge army into Greece. In his nine-volume *Histories* (430 BCE), written 50 years after the events, Herodotus, the first Greek historian, says that Xerxes' army numbered five million men and that whole rivers were dried up when the army stopped to drink. These are doubtless exaggerations, but Xerxes' army was probably the largest ever assembled until that time. Modern estimates suggest that it was composed of at least 150,000 men. Herodotus also tells us that the Delphic oracle had prophesied that Athens would be destroyed and advised the Athenians to put their trust in "wooden walls." Themistocles knew that the Persians had to be delayed so that the Athenians would have time to abandon the city and take to the sea. At a narrow pass between the sea and the mountains called Thermopylae, a band of 300 Spartans, led by their king, Leonidas, gave their lives so that the Athenians could escape.

The Persians sacked Athens, and, as Themistocles hoped, quickly pursued the Athenians out to sea. At Salamis, off the Athenian coast, the Greeks won a stunning victory, led by Themistocles. The Persian fleet, numbering about 800 galleys, faced the Greek fleet of about 370 smaller and more maneuverable *triremes*, galleys with three tiers of oars on each side. Themistocles lured the Persian fleet into the narrow waters of the strait at Salamis. The Greek triremes then attacked the crowded Persian fleet and used the great curved prows of their galleys to ram and sink about 300 Persian vessels. The Greeks lost only about 40 of their own fleet, and Xerxes was forced to retreat, never to threaten the Greek mainland again.

THE GOLDEN AGE

What did Pericles believe to be the source of Athenian greatness, and how is that greatness reflected in the art of the Golden Age?

After the Persian invasion, the Athenians returned to a devastated city. They initially vowed to keep the Acropolis in a state of ruin as a reminder of the horrible price of war; however, the statesman Pericles (ca. 495–429 BCE) convinced them to rebuild it, ushering in a "Golden Age." No person dominated Athenian political life in the fifth century BCE more than Pericles. An aristocrat by birth, he was nonetheless democracy's strongest advocate. Late in his career, in 431 BCE, he delivered a speech honoring soldiers who had fallen in early battles of the Peloponnesian War, a struggle for power between Sparta and Athens that would eventually result in Athens's defeat in 404 BCE, long after Pericles' own death. Pericles begins his speech by saying that, in order to honor the dead properly, he would like "to point out by what principles of action we rose to power, and under what institutions and through what manner of life our empire became great." First and foremost in his mind is Athenian democracy. But Pericles is not concerned with politics alone. He praises the Athenians' "many relaxations from toil." He acknowledges that life in Athens is as good as it is because "the fruits of the whole earth flow in upon us." And, he insists, Athenians are "lovers of the beautiful" who seek to "cultivate the mind." "To sum up," he concludes (**Reading 2.3**):

READING 2.3

Thucydides, *History of the Peloponnesian Wars*, Pericles' Funeral Speech (ca. 410 BCE)

I say that Athens is the school of Hellas, and that the individual Athenian in his own person seems to have the power of adapting himself to the most varied forms of action with the utmost versatility and grace. This is no passing and idle word, but truth and fact; and the assertion is verified by the position to which these qualities have raised the state. . . . I have dwelt upon the greatness of Athens because I want to show you that we are contending for a higher prize than those who enjoy none of these privileges, and to establish by manifest proof the merit of these men whom I am now commemorating. Their loftiest praise has been already spoken. For in magnifying the city, I magnify them, and men like them whose virtues made her glorious.

When Pericles says that Athens is "the school of Hellas," he means that it teaches all of Greece by its example. He insists that the greatness of the state is a function of the greatness of its individuals. The quality of Athenian life depends on this link between individual freedom and civic responsibility—which most of us in the Western world recognize as the foundation of our own political idealism (if, too often, not our political reality).

As for rebuilding the Acropolis, Pericles argued that, richly decorated with elaborate architecture and sculpture, the Acropolis could become a fitting memorial not simply to the Persian war but especially to Athena's role in protecting the Athenian people. Furthermore, at Persepolis, the defeated Xerxes and then his son and successor Artaxerxes I (r. 465–424 BCE), were busy expanding their palace, and Athens was not about to be outdone. Pericles placed the sculptor Phidias in charge of the sculptural program for the new buildings on the Acropolis, and Phidias may have been responsible for the architectural project as well.

The Architectural Program at the Acropolis

The cost of rebuilding the Acropolis was enormous, but despite the reservations expressed by many over such extravagant expenditure, financed mostly by tributes that Athens assessed upon its allies, the project had the virtue of employing thousands of Athenians—citizens, metics (free men who were not citizens because they came from somewhere in the Greek world other than Athens), and slaves alike—thus guaranteeing its popularity. Writing a *Life of Pericles* five centuries later, the Greek-born biographer Plutarch (ca. 46–after 119 CE) gives us some idea of the project and its effects (**Reading 2.4**):

READING 2.4

Plutarch, *Life of Pericles* (75 CE)

The raw materials were stone, bronze, ivory, gold, ebony, and cypress wood. To fashion them were a host of craftsmen: carpenters, molders, coppersmiths, stonemasons, goldsmiths, ivory-specialists, painters, textile-designers, and sculptors in relief. Then there were the men detailed for transport and haulage: merchants, sailors, and helmsmen at sea; on land, cartwrights, drovers, and keepers of traction animals. There were also the rope-makers, the flax-workers, cobblers, roadmakers, and miners. Each craft, like a commander with his own army, had its own attachments of hired laborers and individual specialists organized like a machine for the service required. So it was that the various commissions spread a ripple of prosperity throughout the citizen body.

The Parthenon The centerpiece of the project was the Parthenon (Fig. 2.24), which was completed in 432 BCE after 15 years of construction. As Pericles had argued, it was built to give thanks to Athena for the salvation of Athens and Greece in the Persian Wars, but it was also a tangible sign of the power and might of the Athenian state, designed to impress all who visited the city. It was built on the foundations and platform of an earlier structure, but the architects Ictinus and Callicrates clearly intended it to represent the Doric order in its most perfect form. It has 8 columns at the ends and 17 on the sides. The entasis of each column (a feature also used in the Temple of Hera I at Paestum more than 100 years earlier) counters the eye's tendency to see the uninterrupted parallel columns as narrowing as they rise and to give a sense of "breath" or liveliness to the stone. The columns also slant slightly inward, so that they appear to the eye to rise straight up. And since horizontal lines appear to sink in the middle, the platform beneath them rises nearly 5 inches from each corner to the middle. There are no true verticals or horizontals in the building, a fact that lends its apparently rigid geometry a sense of liveliness and animation.

In the clarity of its parts, the harmony among them, and its overall sense of proportion and balance, the Parthenon represents the epitome of Classical architecture. The building's Classical sense of beauty manifests itself in the architects' use of a system of proportionality in order to coordinate

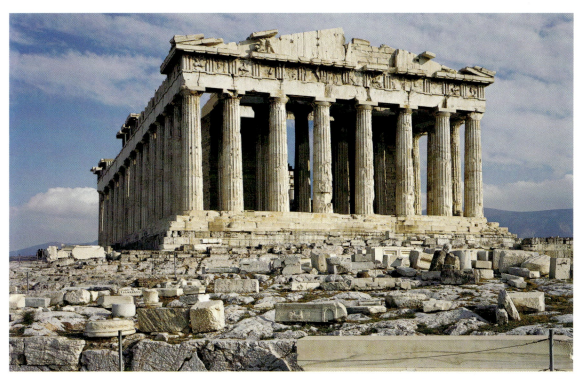

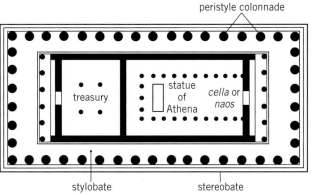

peristyle colonnade

treasury

statue of Athena

cella or naos

stylobate   stereobate

Explore an architectural panorama of the Parthenon on **MyArtsLab**

Fig. 2.24 Ictinus, with contributions by Callicrates, the Parthenon and its plan, Acropolis, Athens. 447–438 BCE. Sculptural program completed 432 BCE. The temple measures about 228′ × 101′ on the top step. The temple remained almost wholly intact (although it served variously as a church and then a mosque) until 1687, when the attacking Venetians exploded an Ottoman powder magazine housed in it. The giant, 40-foot-high sculpture of Athena Parthenos was located in the Parthenon's *cella* or *naos,* the central interior room of a temple in which the cult statue was traditionally housed.

the construction process in a way that resulted in a harmonious design. The ratio controlling the Parthenon's design can be expressed in the algebraic formula $x = 2y + 1$. The temple's columns, for instance, reflect this formula: There are 8 columns on the short ends and 17 on the sides, because $17 = (2 \times 8) + 1$. The ratio of the stylobate's length to width is 9:4, because $9 = (2 \times 4) + 1$. This mathematical regularity is central to the overall harmony of the building.

Other Architectural Projects on the Acropolis One of the architects employed in the project, Mnesicles, was charged with designing the **propylon**, or large entry way, where the Panathenaic Way approached the Acropolis from below. Instead of a single gate, he created five, an architectural tour de force named the Propylaia (the plural of *propylon*), flanked with porches and colonnades of Doric columns. The north wing included a picture gallery featuring paintings of Greek history and myth, none of which survive. Contrasting with the towering mass of the Propylaia was the far more delicate Temple of Athena Nike (Fig. **2.25**), situated on the promontory just to the west and overlooking the entrance way. Graced by slender Ionic columns, the diminutive structure (it measures a mere 27 by 19 feet) was designed by Callicrates and built in 425 BCE, not long after the death of Pericles. It was probably meant to celebrate what the Athenians hoped would be their victory in the Peloponnesian Wars, as *nike* is Greek for "victory." Before the end of the wars, between 410 and 407 BCE, it was surrounded by a **parapet**, or low wall, faced with panels depicting Athena together with her winged companions, the Victories.

To the left of the Parthenon, visitors would have seen the Erechtheion (Fig. **2.26**). Its asymmetrical and multileveled structure is unique, resulting from the rocky site on which it is situated. Flatter areas were available on the Acropolis, so its demanding position is clearly intentional. The building surrounds a sacred spring dedicated to Erechtheus, the first

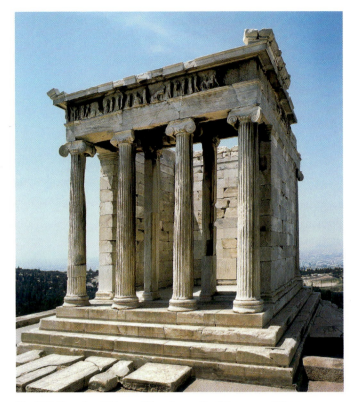

Fig. 2.25 Temple of Athena Nike, Acropolis, Athens. ca. 425 BCE. Overlooking the approach to the Propylaia, the temple's lighter Ionic columns contrast dramatically with the heavier, more robust Doric columns of the gateway.

legendary king of Athens, after whom the building is named. Work on the building began after the completion of the Parthenon, in the 430s BCE, and took 25 years. Among its unique characteristics is the famous Porch of the Maidens, facing the Parthenon. It is supported by six **caryatids**, female figures serving as columns. These figures illustrate both the idea of the temple column as a kind of human figure and the idea that the stability of the polis depends on the conduct of its womenfolk. All assume a classic *contrapposto* pose, the three on the left with their weight over the right leg, the three on the right with their weight over the left. Although each figure is unique—the folds on their chitons fall differently, and their breasts are different sizes and shapes—together they create a sense of balance and harmony.

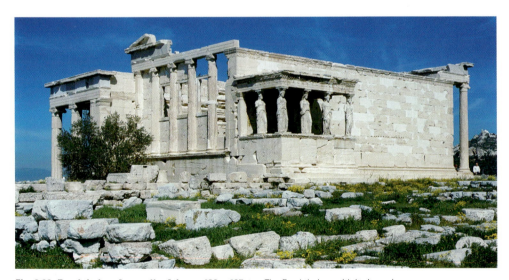

Fig. 2.26 Erechtheion, Acropolis, Athens. 430s–405 BCE. The Erechtheion, with its irregular and asymmetrical design, slender Ionic columns, and delicate Porch of the Maidens, contrasts dramatically and purposefully with the more orthodox and highly regular Parthenon across the Acropolis to the south.

The Sculptural Program at the Parthenon

If Phidias' hand was not directly involved in carving the sculpture decorating the Parthenon, most of the decoration is probably his design. He was, of course, heir to the ever-increasing interest in naturalistic representation that had developed at the end of the sixth century BCE in Athenian *kouros* sculpture (see Figs. 2.17 and 2.18). A sculpture attributed to Kritios (Fig. **2.27**), found in 1865 in a pile of debris on the Acropolis pushed aside by Athenians cleaning up after the Persian invasion (its head was found 25 years later in a separate location), demonstrates the increasing naturalism of Greek sculpture during the first 20 years of the fifth century BCE. The boy's head is turned slightly to the side. His weight rests on the left leg, and the right leg extends forward, bent slightly at the knee. The figure seems to twist around its **axis**, or imaginary central line, the natural result of balancing the body over one supporting leg. The term for this stance, coined during the Italian Renaissance, is **contrapposto** ("counterpoise"), or weight-shift. The inspiration for this development seems to have been a growing desire by Greek sculptors to dramatize the stories narrated in the decorative programs of temples and sanctuaries. Liveliness of posture and gesture and a sense of capturing the body in action became their primary sculptural aims and the very definition of classical beauty.

An even more developed version of the *contrapposto* pose can be seen in the *Doryphoros*, or *Spear Bearer* (Fig. **2.28**), whose weight falls on the forward right leg. An idealized portrait of an athlete or warrior, originally done in bronze, the *Doryphoros* is a Roman copy of the work of Polyclitus, one of the great artists of the Golden Age. The sculpture was famous throughout the ancient world as a demonstration of Polyclitus' treatise on proportion known as *The Canon* (from the Greek *kanon*, meaning "measure" or "rule"). In Polyclitus' system, the ideal human form was determined by the height of the head from the crown to the chin. The head was one-eighth the total height, the width of the shoulders was one-quarter the total height, and so on, each measurement reflecting these ideal proportions. For Polyclitus, these relations resulted in the work's *symmetria*, the origin of our word "symmetry," but meaning, in Polyclitus' usage, "commensurability," or "having a common measure." Thus, the figure, beautifully realized in great detail, right down to the veins on

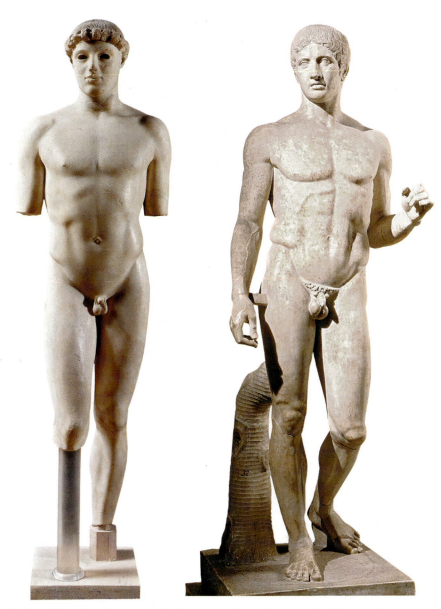

Fig. 2.27 *Kritios Boy*, **from Acropolis, Athens. ca. 480 BCE.** Marble, height 46". Acropolis Museum, Athens. The growing naturalism of Greek sculpture is clear when one compares the *Kritios Boy* to the *kouros* figures discussed earlier in the chapter. Although more naturalistic, this figure still served a votive function.

Fig. 2.28 *Doryphoros (Spear Bearer)*, **Roman copy after the original bronze by Polyclitus of ca. 450–440 BCE.** Marble, height 6'6". Museo Archeologico Nazionale, Naples. There is some debate about just what "measure" Polyclitus employed to achieve his ideal figure. Some argue that his system of proportions is based on the length of the figure's index finger or the width of the figure's hand across the knuckles. The idea that it is based on the distance between the chin and the hairline derives from a much later discussion of proportion by the Roman writer Vitruvius, who lived in the first century CE. It is possible that Vitruvius had firsthand knowledge of Polyclitus' *Canon*, which was lost long ago.

the back of the hand, reflects a higher mathematical order and embodies the ideal harmony between the natural world and the intellectual or spiritual realm.

The sculptures decorating the Parthenon proper were in three main areas—in the pediments at each end of the building, on the **metopes**, or the square panels between the beam

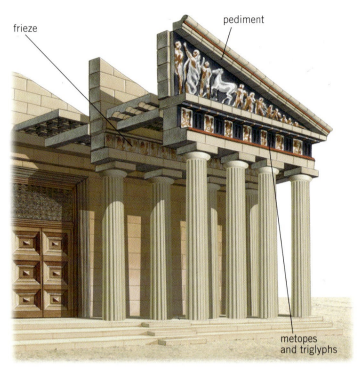

frieze

pediment

metopes
and triglyphs

Fig. 2.29 Cutaway drawing of the Parthenon porch showing friezes, metopes, and pediment. Evident here is the architect Ictinus' juxtaposition of the Doric order, used for the columns with their capitals and the entablature on the outside, with the lighter Ionic order of its continuous frieze, used for the entablature inside the colonnade.

ends under the roof, and on the frieze that runs across the top of the outer wall of the cella (Fig. **2.29**). Brightly painted, these sculptures must have appeared strikingly lifelike. The 3-foot-high frieze that originally ran at a height of nearly 27 feet around the central block of the building depicts a ceremonial procession (Fig. **2.30**). Traditionally, the frieze has been interpreted as a depiction of the Panathenaic procession, a civic festival occurring every four years in honor of

Athena. Some 525 feet long, the frieze consists of horsemen, musicians, water carriers, maidens, and sacrificial beasts. All the human figures have the ideal proportions of the *Doryphoros* (see Fig. 2.28).

The sculptural program in the west pediment depicts Athena battling with Poseidon to determine who was to be patron of Athens. Scholars debate the identity of the figures in the east pediment, but it seems certain that overall it portrays the birth of Athena with gods and goddesses in attendance (Fig. **2.31**). The 92 metopes, each separated from the next by **triglyphs**, square blocks divided by grooves into three sections, narrate battles between the Greeks and four enemies—the Trojans on one side, and on the other three, giants, Amazons (perhaps symbolizing the recently defeated Persians), and centaurs, mythological beasts with the legs and bodies of horses and the trunks and heads of humans. Executed in high relief (Fig. **2.32**), these metopes represent the clash between the forces of civilization—the Greeks—and their barbarian, even bestial opponents. The male nude reflects not only physical but also mental superiority, a theme particularly appropriate for a temple to Athena, goddess of both war and wisdom.

Philosophy and the Polis

The extraordinary architectural achievement of the Acropolis is matched by the philosophical achievement of the great Athenian philosopher Socrates, born in 469 BCE, a decade after the Greek defeat of the Persians. His death in 399 BCE arguably marks the end of Athens's Golden Age. Socrates' death was not a natural one. His execution was ordered by a polis in turmoil after its defeat by the Spartans in 404 BCE. The city had submitted to the rule of the oligarchic government installed by the victorious Spartans, the so-called Thirty Tyrants, whose power was ensured by a gang of "whip-bearers." They deprived the courts of their power and initiated a set of trials against rich men and democrats

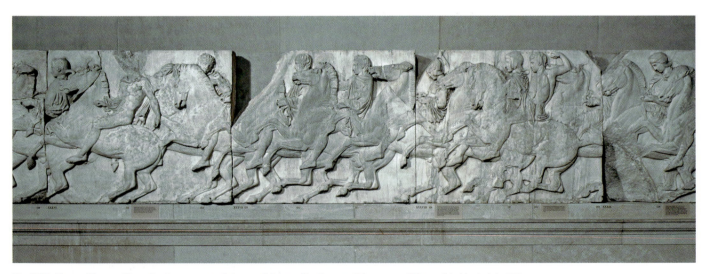

Fig. 2.30 *Young Men on Horseback*, segment of the north frieze, Parthenon, Athens. ca. 440 BCE. Marble, height 41".
© The Trustees of the British Museum. This is just a small section of the entire procession, which extends completely around the Parthenon.

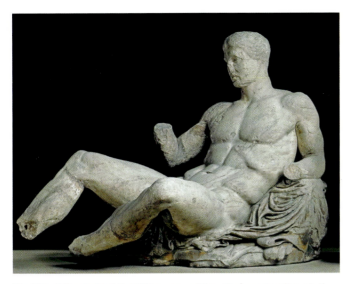

Fig. 2.31 A Recumbent God (Dionysus or Heracles), east pediment of the Parthenon. ca. 435 BCE. Length approx. 51". © The Trustees of the British Museum. In 1801, Thomas Bruce, Earl of Elgin and British ambassador to Constantinople, brought the marbles from the east pediment, as well as some from the west pediment and the south metopes, and a large part of the frieze, back to England—the source of their name, the *Elgin Marbles*. The identities of the figures are much disputed, but the greatness of their execution is not. Now exhibited in the round, in their original position on the pediment, they were carved in high relief. As the sun passed over the three-dimensional relief on the east and west pediments, the sculptures would have appeared almost animated by the changing light and the movement of their cast shadows.

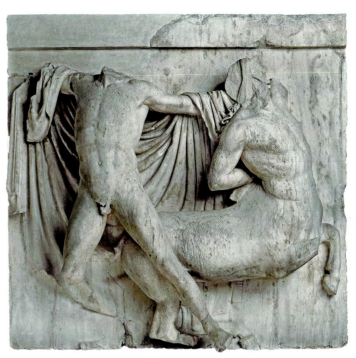

Fig. 2.32 Lapith Overcoming a Centaur, south metope 27, from the Parthenon. 447–438 BCE. Marble relief, height 4'5". © The Trustees of the British Museum. The Lapiths are a people in Greek myth who defeated drunken centaurs at the wedding of their king, Pirithous. The Greeks identified centaurs with the Persians, whom they considered the embodiment of chaos, possessing centaur-like forces of irrationality.

who opposed their tyranny. Over 1,500 Athenians were subsequently executed. Socrates was brought to trial, accused of subversive behavior, corrupting young men, and introducing new gods, though these charges may have been politically motivated. He antagonized his jury of citizens by insisting that his life had been as good as anyone's and that far from committing any wrongs, he had greatly benefited Athens. He was convicted by a narrow majority and condemned to die by drinking poisonous hemlock. His refusal to flee and his willingness to submit to the will of the polis and drink the potion testify to his belief in the very polis that condemned him. His eloquent defense of his decision to submit is recorded in the *Crito*, a dialogue between Socrates and his friend Crito, actually written by Plato, Socrates' student and fellow philosopher. Although the Athenians would continue to enjoy relative freedom for many years to come, the death of Socrates marks the end of their great experiment with democracy. Although Socrates was no defender of democracy—he did not believe that most people were really capable of exercising good government—he became the model of good citizenship and right thinking for centuries to come.

The Philosophical Tradition in Athens To understand Socrates' position, it is important to recognize that the crisis confronting Athens in 404 BCE was not merely political, but deeply philosophical. Furthermore, a deep division existed between the philosophers and the polis. Plato, Socrates' student, through whose writings we know Socrates' teachings,

believed that good government was unattainable "unless either philosophers become kings in our cities or those whom we now call kings and rulers take to the pursuit of philosophy." He well understood that neither was likely to happen, and that good government was, therefore, something of a dream. To complicate matters further, there were two distinct traditions of Greek *philosophia*—literally, "love of wisdom"—pre-Socratic and Sophist.

The oldest philosophical tradition, that of the **pre-Socratics**, the Greek philosophers who preceded Socrates, was chiefly concerned with describing the natural universe—the tradition inaugurated by Thales of Miletus. "What," the pre-Socratics asked, "lies behind the world of appearance? What is everything made of? How does it work? Is there an essential truth or core at the heart of the physical universe?" In some sense, then, they were scientists who investigated the nature of things, and they arrived at some extraordinary insights. Pythagoras (ca. 570–490 BCE) was one such pre-Socratic thinker. He conceived of the notion that the heavenly bodies appear to move in accordance with the mathematical ratios and that these ratios also govern musical intervals producing what was later called "the harmony of the spheres." Leucippus (fifth century BCE) was another. He conceived of an atomic theory in which everything is made up of small, indivisible particles and the empty space, or void, between them (the Greek word for "indivisible" is *atom*). Democritus of Thrace (ca. 460–ca. 370 BCE) furthered the theory by applying it to the mind. He taught that everything from feelings and ideas to the physical sensations of taste, sight, and smell could be explained by the movements of atoms in the brain. Heraclitus of Ephesus (ca. 540–ca. 480 BCE) argued for the impermanence of all things. Change, or flux, he said, is the basis of reality, although an underlying Form or Guiding Force (*logos*) guides the process, a concept that later informs the Gospel of John in the Christian Bible, where *logos* is often mistranslated as "word."

Socrates was heir to the second tradition of Greek philosophy, that of the **Sophists**, literally "wise men." The Sophists no longer asked, "What do we know?" but, instead, "How do we know what we think we know?" and, crucially, "How can we trust what we think we know?" In other words, the Sophists concentrated not on the natural world but on the human mind, fully acknowledging the mind's many weaknesses. The Sophists were committed to what we have come to call **humanism**—that is, a focus on the actions of human beings, political action being one of the most important.

Protagoras (ca. 485–410 BCE), a leading Sophist, was responsible for one of the most famous of all Greek dictums: "Man is the measure of all things." By this he meant that each individual human, not the gods, not some divine or all-encompassing force, defines reality. All sensory appearances and all beliefs are true for the person whose appearance, or belief, they are. The Sophists believed that there were two sides to every argument. Protagoras' attitude about the gods is typical: "I do not know that they exist or that they do not exist."

The Sophists were teachers who traveled about, imparting their wisdom for pay. Pericles championed them, encouraging the best to come to Athens, where they enjoyed considerable prestige despite their status as metics. Their ultimate aim was to teach political virtue—*areté*—emphasizing skills useful in political life, especially rhetorical persuasion, the art of speaking eloquently and persuasively. Their emphasis on rhetoric—their apparent willingness to assume either side of any argument merely for the sake of debate—as well as their critical examination of myths, traditions, and conventions, gave them a reputation for cynicism. Thus, their brand of argumentation came to be known as *sophistry*—subtle, tricky, superficially plausible, but ultimately false and deceitful reasoning.

Socrates and the Sophists Socrates despised everything the Sophists stood for, except their penchant for rhetorical debate, which was his chief occupation. He roamed the streets of Athens, engaging his fellow citizens in dialogue, wittily and often bitingly attacking them for the illogic of their positions. He employed the **dialectic method**—a process of inquiry and instruction characterized by continuous question-and-answer dialogue intent on disclosing the unexamined premises held implicitly by all reasonable beings. Unlike the Sophists, he refused to demand payment for his teaching, but like them, he urged his fellow men not to mistake their personal opinions for truth. Our beliefs, he knew, are built mostly on a foundation of prejudice and historical conditioning. He differed from the Sophists most crucially in his emphasis on virtuous behavior. For the Sophists, the true, the good, and the just were relative things. Depending on the situation or one's point of view,

anything might be true, good, or just—the point, as will become evident in the next section, of many a Greek tragedy.

For Socrates, understanding the true meaning of the good, the true, and the just was prerequisite for acting virtuously, and the meaning of these things was not relative. Rather, true meaning resided in the **psyche**, the seat of both intelligence and character. Through **inductive reasoning**—moving from specific instances to general principles, and from particular to universal truths—it was possible, he believed, to understand the ideals to which human endeavor should aspire. Neither Socrates nor the Sophists could have existed without the democracy of the polis and the freedom of speech that accompanied it. Even during the reign of Pericles, Athenian conservatives had charged the Sophists with the crime of impiety. In questioning everything, from the authority of the gods to the rule of law, they challenged the stability of the very democracy that protected them. It is thus easy to understand how, when democracy ended, Athens condemned Socrates. He was democracy's greatest defender, and if he believed that the polis had forsaken its greatest invention, he himself could never betray it. Thus, he chose to die.

Plato's *Republic* and Idealism So far as we know, Socrates himself never wrote a single word, and his thinking is known only through the writings of Plato (ca. 428–347 BCE). Thus, it may be true that the Socrates we know is the one Plato wanted us to have, and that when we read Socrates' words, we are encountering Plato's thought more than Socrates'.

As Plato presents Socrates to us, the two philosophers, master and pupil, have much in common. They share the premise that the psyche is immortal and immutable. They also share the notion that we are all capable of remembering the psyche's pure state. But Plato advances Socrates' thought in several important ways. Plato's philosophy is a brand of **idealism**—it seeks the eternal perfection of pure ideas, untainted by material reality. He believes that there is an invisible world of eternal Forms, or Ideas, beyond everyday experience, and that the psyche, trapped in the material world and the physical body, can catch only glimpses of this higher order. Through a series of mental exercises, beginning with the study of mathematics and moving on to the contemplation of the Forms of Justice, Beauty, and Love, the student can arrive at a level of understanding that amounts to superior knowledge.

Socrates' death deeply troubled Plato—not because he disagreed with Socrates' decision, but because of the injustice of his condemnation. The result of Plato's thinking is *The Republic*. In this treatise, Plato outlines his model of the ideal state. Only an elite cadre of the most highly educated men were to rule—those who had glimpsed Plato's ultimate Form, or Idea—the Good. In *The Republic*, in a section known as the "Allegory of the Cave," Socrates addresses Plato's older brother, Glaucon, in an attempt to describe the difficulties the psyche encounters in its attempt to understand the higher Forms. The Form of Goodness, Socrates says, is "the universal author of all things beautiful and right, parent of light and of the lord of light in this visible world, and the immediate source of reason and truth in the intellectual; and . . . this is the power upon which he who would act rationally, either in public or private life, must have his eye fixed." The Form of Goodness, then, is something akin to the common understanding of God (although not God, from whom imperfect objects such as human beings descended, but more like an aspect of the Ideal, of which, one supposes, God must have some superior knowledge). The difficulty is that, once having attained an understanding of the Good, the wise individual will appear foolish to the people, who understand not at all. And yet, Plato argues, it is precisely these individuals, blessed with wisdom, who must rule the commonwealth.

In many ways, Plato's ideal state is reactionary—it certainly opposes the individualistic and self-aggrandizing world of the Sophists. Plato is indifferent to the fact that his wise souls will find themselves ruling what amounts to a totalitarian regime. He believes their own sense of Goodness will prevail over their potentially despotic position. Moreover, rule by an intellectual philosopher king is superior to rule by any person whose chief desire is to satisfy his own material appetites.

To live in Plato's *Republic* would have been dreary indeed. Sex was to be permitted only for purposes of procreation. Everyone would undergo physical and mental training. Although he believed in the intellectual pursuit of the Form or Idea of Beauty, Plato did not champion the arts. He condemned certain kinds of lively music because they affected not the reasonable mind of their audience but the emotional and sensory tendencies of the body. (But even for Plato, a man who did not know how to dance was uneducated—Plato simply preferred more restrained forms of music.) He also condemned sculptors and painters, whose works, he believed, were mere representations of representations—for if an actual bed is once removed from the Idea of Bed, a painting of a bed is twice removed, the

faintest shadow. Furthermore, the images created by painters and sculptors appealed only to the senses. Thus he banished them from his ideal republic. Because they gave voice to tension within the state, poets were banned as well.

The Theater of the People

The Dionysian aspects of the symposium—the drinking, the philosophical dialogue, and sexual license—tell us something about the origins of Greek drama. The drama was originally a participatory ritual, tied to the cult of Dionysus (god of wine and inspiration). A chorus of people participating in the ritual would address and respond to another chorus or to a leader, such as a priest, perhaps representing (thus "acting the part" of) Dionysus. These dialogues usually occurred in the context of riotous dance and song—befitting revels dedicated to the god of wine. Sexual license was the rule of the day. On a mid-sixth-century amphora used as a wine container (Fig. 2.33) we see five satyrs, minor deities with characteristics of goats or horses, making wine, including one playing pipes. Depicted in the band across the top is Dionysus himself, sitting in the midst of a rollicking band of satyrs and maenads—the frenzied women with whom he cavorted.

This kind of behavior gave rise to one of the three major forms of Greek drama, the **satyr play**. Always the last event of the daylong performances, the satyr play was **farce**, that is, broadly satirical comedy, in which actors disguised themselves as satyrs, replete with extravagant genitalia, and generally honored the "lord of misrule," Dionysus, by misbehaving themselves. One whole satyr play survives, the *Cyclops* of Euripides, and half of another, Sophocles' *Trackers*. The spirit of these plays can perhaps be summed up best by Odysseus' first words in the *Cyclops* as he comes ashore on the island of Polyphemus (the same story as that related by Homer in the *Odyssey*): "What? Do I see right? We must have come to the city of Bacchus. These are satyrs I see around the cave." The play, in other words, spoofs or lampoons traditional Greek legend by setting it in a world turned topsy-turvy, a world in which Polyphemus is stronger than Zeus because his farts are louder than Zeus' thunder.

Comedy Closely related to the satyr plays was **comedy**, an amusing or lighthearted play designed to make its audience laugh. The word itself is derived from the *komos*, a phallic dance, and nothing is sacred to comedy. It freely slandered, buffooned, and ridiculed politicians, generals, other public figures, and especially the gods. Foreigners, as always in Greek culture, are subject to particular abuse, as are women; in fact, by our standards, the plays are racist and sexist. Most of what we know about Greek comedies comes from two sources: vase painting and the plays of the playwright Aristophanes.

Comedic action was a favorite subject of vase painters working at Paestum in Italy in the fourth century BCE. They depict actors wearing masks and grotesque costumes distinguished by padded bellies, buttocks, and enlarged genitalia.

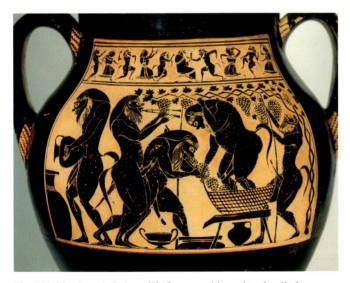

Fig. 2.33 The Amasis Painter (?), *Satyrs making wine,* **detail of Athenian black-figure amphora. ca. 540–530 BCE.** Martin von Wagner Museum, University of Würzburg. The entire ritual of wine production is depicted here, from harvesting the grapes, to stomping them to render their juice, to pouring the juice into large vats for fermentation. All lead to the state of ecstasy (ekstasis) painted across the top band.

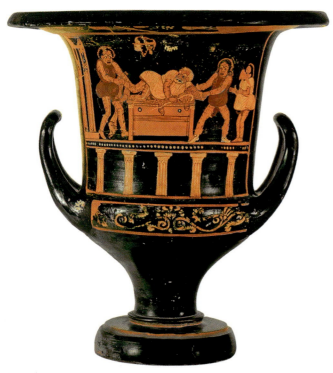

Fig. 2.34 Assteas, red-figure krater depicting a comedy, from Paestum, Italy. ca. 350 BCE. Staatliche Museen, Berlin. On a stage supported by columns, with a scenic backdrop to the left, robbers try to separate a man from his strongbox.

These vases show a theater of burlesque and slapstick that relied heavily on visual gags (Fig. **2.34**).

The works of Aristophanes (ca. 445–388 BCE) are the only comedies to have survived, and only 11 of his 44 plays have come down to us. *Lysistrata* is the most famous. Sexually explicit to a degree that can still shock a modern audience, it takes place during the Peloponnesian Wars and tells the story of an Athenian matron who convinces the women of Athens and Sparta to withhold sex from their husbands until they sign a peace treaty. First performed in 411 BCE, seven years before Sparta's victory over Athens, it has its serious side, begging both Athenians and Spartans to remember their common traditions and put down their arms. Against this dark background, the play's action must have seemed absurd and hilarious to its Athenian audience, ignorant of what the future would hold for them.

Tragedy It was at **tragedy** that the Greek playwrights truly excelled. As with comedy, the basis for tragedy is conflict, but the tensions at work in tragedy—murder and revenge, crime and retribution, pride and humility, courage and cowardice—have far more serious consequences. Tragedies often explore the physical and moral depths to which human life can descend. The form also has its origins in the Dionysian rites—the name itself derives from *tragoidos*, the "goat song" of the half-goat, half-man satyrs—and tragedy's seriousness of purpose is not at odds with its origins. Dionysus was also the god of immortality, and an important aspect of his cult's influence is that he promised his followers life after death, just as the grapevine

regenerates itself year after year. If tragedy can be said to have a subject, it is death—and the lessons the living can learn from the dead.

The original chorus structure of the Dionysian rites survives as an important element in tragedy. Thespis, a playwright from whom we derive the word *thespian*, "actor," first assumed the conscious role of an actor in the mid-sixth century BCE and apparently redefined the role of the **chorus**. At first, the actor asked questions of the chorus, perhaps of the "tell me what happened next" variety, but when two, three, and sometimes four actors were introduced to the stage, the chorus began to comment on their interaction. In this way, the chorus assumed its classic function as an intermediary between actors and audience. Although the chorus's role diminished noticeably in the fourth century BCE, it remained the symbolic voice of the people, asserting the importance of the action to the community as a whole.

Greek tragedy often focused on the friction between the individual and his or her community, and, at a higher level, between the community and the will of the gods. This conflict manifests itself in the weakness or "tragic flaw" of the play's **protagonist**, or leading character, which brings the character into conflict with the community, the gods, or some **antagonist** who represents an opposing will. The action occurs in a single day, the result of a single incident that precipitates the unfolding crisis. Thus the audience feels that it is experiencing the action in real time, that it is directly involved in and affected by the play's action.

During the reign of the tyrant Pisistratus, the performance of all plays was regularized. An annual competitive festival for the performance of tragedies called the City Dionysia was celebrated for a week every March as the vines came back to life, and a separate festival for comedies occurred in January. At the City Dionysia, plays were performed in sets of four—**tetralogies**—all by the same author, three of which were tragedies, performed during the day, and the fourth a satyr play, performed in the evening. The audiences were as large as 14,000, and audience response determined which plays were awarded prizes. Slaves, metics, and women judged the performances alongside citizens.

Aeschylus Although many Greek playwrights composed tragedies, only those of Aeschylus, Sophocles, and Euripides have come down to us. Aeschylus (ca. 525–ca. 456 BCE), the oldest of the three, is reputed to have served in the Athenian armies during the Persian Wars and fought in the battles at Marathon and Salamis. He won the City Dionysia 13 times. It was Aeschylus who introduced a third actor to the tragic stage, and his chorus plays a substantial role in drawing attention to the underlying moral principles that define or determine the action. He also was a master of the visual presentation of his drama, taking full advantage of stage design and costume. Three of his plays, known as the *Oresteia*, form the only complete set of tragedies from a **tetralogy** that we have.

The plays narrate the story of the Mycenaean king Agamemnon, murdered by his adulterous wife Clytemnestra and mourned and revenged by their children, Orestes and Electra. In the first play, *Agamemnon*, Clytemnestra murders her husband, partly in revenge for his having sacrificed their daughter Iphigenia to ensure good weather for the invasion of Troy, and partly to marry her lover, Aegisthus. In the second play, *The Libation Bearers*, Orestes murders Aegisthus and Clytemnestra, his mother, to avenge his father's death. Orestes is subsequently pursued by the Furies, a band of *chthonian* gods (literally "gods of the earth," a branch of the Greek pantheon that is distinguished from the Olympian, or "heavenly" gods), whose function is to seek retribution for wrongs and blood-guilt among family members. The Furies form the Chorus of the last play in the cycle, the *Eumenides*, in which the seemingly endless cycle of murder comes to an end. In this play, Athens institutes a court to hear Orestes' case. The court absolves him of the crime of matricide, with Athena herself casting the deciding vote.

None of the violence in the plays occurs on stage—either the chorus or a messenger describes it. And in fact, the ethical dimension of Aeschylus' trilogy is underscored by the triumph of civilization and law, mirrored by the transformation of the Furies—the blind forces of revenge—into the Eumenides, or "Kindly Ones," whose dark powers have been neutralized.

Sophocles Playwright, treasurer for the Athenian polis, a general under Pericles, and advisor to Athens on financial matters during the Peloponnesian Wars, Sophocles (ca. 496–406 BCE) was an almost legendary figure in fifth-century BCE Athens. He wrote over 125 plays, of which only 7 survive, and he won the City Dionysia 18 times. In *Oedipus the King*, Sophocles dramatizes how the king of Thebes, a polis in east central Greece, mistakenly kills his father and marries his mother, then finally blinds himself to atone for his crimes of patricide and incest. In *Antigone*, Sophocles dramatizes the struggle of Oedipus' daughter, Antigone, with her uncle, Creon, the tyrannical king who inherited Oedipus' throne. Antigone struggles for what amounts to her democratic rights as an individual to fulfill her familial duties, even when this opposes what Creon argues is the interest of the polis. Her predicament is doubly complicated by her status as a woman.

As the play opens, Antigone's brothers, Polynices and Eteocles, have killed each other in a dispute over their father's throne. Creon, Oedipus' brother-in-law, who has inherited the throne, has forbidden the burial of Polynices, believing Eteocles to have been the rightful heir. Antigone, in the opening scene, defends her right to bury her brother, and this willful act, which she then performs in defiance of Creon's authority, leads to the tragedy that follows. She considers the burial her duty, since no unburied body can enjoy an afterlife. The play begins as Antigone explains her action to her sister, Ismene, who thoroughly disapproves of what she has done (**Reading 2.5a**):

READING 2.5a

Sophocles, *Antigone*

ISMENE Oh my sister, think—
think how our own father died, hated,
his reputation in ruins, driven on

---

by the crimes he brought to light himself
to gouge out his eyes with his own hands—
then mother . . . his mother and wife, both in one,
mutilating her life in the twisted noose—
and last, our two brothers dead in a single day,
both shedding their own blood, poor suffering boys,
battling out their common destiny hand-to-hand.
Now look at the two of us, left so alone. . . .
think what a death we'll die, the worst of all
if we violate the laws and override
the fixed decree of the throne, its power—
we must be sensible. Remember we are women,
we're not born to contend with men. Then too,
we're underlings, ruled by much stronger hands,
so we must submit in this, and things still worse.
I, for one, I'll beg the dead to forgive me—
I'm forced, I have no choice—I must obey
the ones who stand in power. Why rush to extremes?
It's madness, madness.

The conflict between Antigone and Creon is exacerbated by their gender difference. The Greek male would expect a female to submit to his will. But it is, in the end, Antigone's "rush to extremes" that forces the play's action—that, and Creon's refusal to give in. Creon's "fatal flaw"—his pride (hubris)—leads to the destruction of all whom he loves, and Antigone herself is blindly dedicated to her duty to honor her family. Her actions in the play have been the subject of endless debate. Some readers feel that she is far too hard on Ismene, and certainly a Greek audience would have found her defiance of male authority shocking. Nevertheless, her strength of conviction seems to many—especially modern audiences—wholly admirable.

But beyond the complexities of Antigone's personality, one of Sophocles' greatest achievements, the play really pits two forms of idealism against each other: Antigone's uncompromising belief in herself plays off Creon's equally uncompromising infatuation with his own power and his dedication to his political duty, which he puts above devotion even to family.

The philosophical basis of the play is clearly evident in the essentially Sophist debate between Creon and his son Haemon, as Haemon attempts to point out the wrong in his father's action (**Reading 2.5b**):

READING 2.5b

Sophocles, *Antigone*

HAEMON Father, the gods implant reason in men, the highest of all things that we call our own. Not mine the skill—far from me be the quest!—to say wherein thou speakest not aright; and yet another man, too, might have some useful thought. . . . No, though a man be wise, 'tis no shame for him to learn many things, and to bend in season. Seest thou, beside the wintry torrent's course, how the trees that yield to it save every twig, while the stiffnecked perish root and branch? And even thus he

---

who keeps the sheet of his sail taut, and never slackens it, upsets his boat, and finishes his voyage with keel uppermost.

Nay, forego thy wrath; permit thyself to change. For if I, a younger man, may offer my thought, it were far best, I ween, that men should be all-wise by nature; but, otherwise—and oft the scale inclines not so—'tis good also to learn from those who speak aright. . . .

CREON Men of my age are we indeed to be schooled, then, by men of his?

HAEMON In nothing that is not right; but if I am young, thou shouldest look to my merits, not to my years.

CREON Is it a merit to honour the unruly?

HAEMON I could wish no one to show respect for evil-doers.

CREON Then is not she tainted with that malady?

HAEMON Our Theban folk, with one voice, denies it. . . .

CREON Am I to rule this land by other judgment than mine own?

HAEMON That is no city which belongs to one man.

CREON Is not the city held to be the ruler's?

HAEMON Thou wouldst make a good monarch of a desert.

CREON This boy, it seems, is the woman's champion.

HAEMON If thou art a woman; indeed, my care is for thee.

CREON Shameless, at open feud with thy father!

HAEMON Nay, I see thee offending against justice.

CREON Do I offend, when I respect mine own prerogatives?

HAEMON Thou dost not respect them, when thou tramplest on the gods' honours. . . .

CREON Thou shalt rue thy witless teaching of wisdom.

HAEMON Wert thou not my father, I would have called thee unwise.

CREON Thou woman's slave, use not wheedling speech with me.

HAEMON Thou wouldest speak, and then hear no reply?

CREON Sayest thou so? Now, by the heaven above us—be sure of it—thou shalt smart for taunting me in this opprobrious strain. Bring forth that hated thing, that she may die forthwith in his presence—before his eyes—at her bridegroom's side!

Finally, the play demonstrates the extreme difficulty of reconciling the private and public spheres—one of Greek philosophy's most troubling and troubled themes—even as it cries out for the rational action and sound judgment that might have spared its characters their tragedy.

Euripides The youngest of the three playwrights, Euripides (ca. 480–406 BCE), writing during the Peloponnesian Wars, brought a level of measured skepticism to the stage. Eighteen of his 90 works survive, but Euripides won the City Dionysia only four times. His plays probably angered more conservative Athenians, which may be why he moved from Athens to Macedonia in 408 BCE. In *The Trojan Women*, for instance, performed in 415 BCE, he describes, disapprovingly, the Greek enslavement of the women of Troy, drawing an unmistakable analogy to the contemporary Athenian victory at Melos, where women were subjected to Athenian abuse.

Euripides' darkest play, and his masterpiece, is *The Bacchae*, which describes the introduction to Thebes of the worship of Dionysus by the god himself, disguised as a mortal. Pentheus, the young king of the city, opposes the Dionysian rites both because all the city's women have given themselves up to Dionysian ecstasy and because the new religion disturbs the larger social order. Performed at a festival honoring Dionysus, the play warns of the dangers of Dionysian excess as the frenzied celebrants, including Pentheus' own mother, mistake their king for a wild animal and murder him. Euripides' play underscores the fact that the rational mind is unable to comprehend, let alone control, all human impulses.

Greek theater itself, particularly the tragedies of Aeschylus, Sophocles, and Euripides, would become the object of study in the fourth century BCE, when the philosopher Aristotle, Plato's student, attempted to account for tragedy's power in his *Poetics*. And despite the fact that the tragedies were largely forgotten in the Western world until the sixteenth century, they have had a lasting impact on Western literature, deeply influencing writers from William Shakespeare to the modern American novelist William Faulkner.

The Performance Space During the tyranny of Pisistratus, plays were performed in an open area of the Agora called the *orchestra*, or "dancing space." Spectators sat on wooden planks laid on portable scaffolding. Sometime in the fifth century BCE, the scaffolding collapsed, and many people were injured. The Athenians built a new theater (*theatron*, meaning "viewing space"), dedicated to Dionysus, into the hillside on the side of the Acropolis away from the Agora and below the Parthenon. Architecturally, it was very similar to the best preserved of all Greek theaters, the one at Epidaurus (Figs. **2.35** and **2.36**), built in the early third century BCE. The *orchestra* has been transformed into a circular performance space, approached on each side by an entry way called a **parados**, through which the chorus would enter the *orchestra* area. Behind this was an elevated platform, the **proscenium**, the stage on which the actors performed and where painted backdrops could be hung. Behind the proscenium was the *skene*, literally a "tent," and originally a changing room for the actors. Over time, it was transformed into a building, often two stories tall. Actors on the roof could portray the gods, looking down on the action below. By the time of Euripides, it housed a rolling or rotating platform that could suddenly reveal an interior space.

Artists were regularly employed to paint stage sets, and evidence suggests that they had at least a basic knowledge of perspective (although the geometry necessary for a fully realized perspectival space would not be developed until around 300 BCE, in Euclid's *Optics*). Their aim was, as in sculpture, to approximate reality as closely as possible. We know from literary sources that the painter Zeuxis "invented" ways to shade or model the figure in the fifth

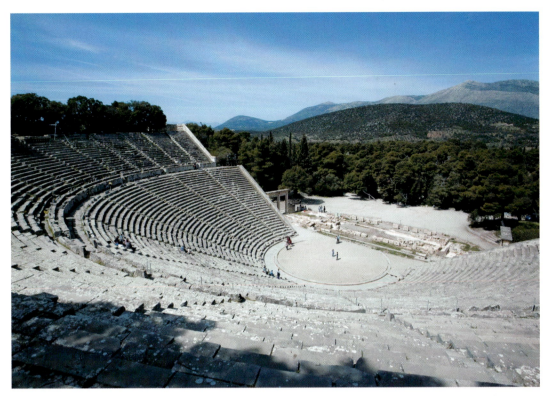

Fig. 2.35 Theater, Epidaurus. Early 3rd century BCE. This theater is renowned for its democratic design—not only is every viewer equally well situated, but also the acoustics of the space are unparalleled. A person sitting in the very top row can hear a pin drop on the *orchestra* floor.

century BCE. Legend also had it that he once painted grapes so realistically that birds tried to eat them. The theatrical sets would have at least aimed at this degree of naturalism.

THE HELLENISTIC WORLD

How are the values of the Hellenistic world reflected in its politics, philosophy, and art?

Both the emotional drama of Greek theater and the sensory appeal of its music reveal a growing tendency in the culture to value emotional expression at least as much as, and sometimes more than, the balanced harmonies of Classical art. During the Hellenistic age in the fourth and third centuries BCE, the truths that the culture increasingly sought to understand were less idealistic and universal, and more and more empirical and personal. This shift is especially evident in the new empirical philosophy of Aristotle (384–322 BCE), whose investigation into the workings of the real world supplanted, or at least challenged, Plato's idealism. In many ways, however, the ascendancy of this new aesthetic standard can be attributed to the daring, the audacity, and the sheer awe-inspiring power of a single figure, Alexander of Macedonia, known as Alexander the Great (356–323 BCE). Alexander aroused the emotions and captured the imagination of not just a theatrical audience, but an entire people—perhaps even the entire Western world—and created a legacy that established Hellenic Greece as the model against which all cultures in the West had to measure themselves.

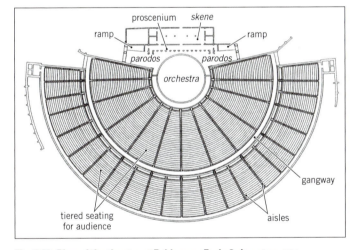

Fig. 2.36 Plan of the theater at Epidaurus. Early 3rd century BCE.

The Empire of Alexander the Great

Alexander was the son of Philip II (382–336 BCE) of Macedonia, a relatively undeveloped state to the north whose inhabitants spoke a Greek dialect unintelligible to Athenians. Recognizing that after the Peloponnesian Wars, the Greek poleis were in disarray, in 338 BCE Philip defeated the combined forces of Athens and Thebes and unified all of Greece, with the exception of Sparta. He then turned his attention to Persia, and when he was assassinated in 336 BCE, Alexander quickly took control.

Within two years of conquering Thebes, Alexander had crossed the Hellespont into Asia and defeated Darius III of Persia at the battle of Issus (just north of modern Iskenderon, Turkey). The victory continued Philip's plan to repay the Persians for their role in the Peloponnesian Wars and to conquer Asia as well. By 332 BCE, Alexander had conquered Egypt, founding the great city of Alexandria (named, of course, after himself) in the Nile Delta (Map **2.2**). Then he marched back into Mesopotamia, where he again defeated Darius III and then marched into both Babylon and Susa without resistance. After making the proper sacrifices to the Akkadian god Marduk—and thus gaining the admiration of the locals—he advanced on Persepolis, the Persian capital, which he burned after seizing its royal treasures. Then he entered present-day Pakistan.

Alexander's object was India, which he believed was relatively small. He thought if he crossed it, he would find what he called Ocean, and an easy sea route home. Finally, in 326 BCE, his army reached the Indian Punjab. Under Alexander's leadership, it had marched over 11,000 miles without a defeat. It had destroyed ancient empires, founded many cities (in the 320s BCE, Alexandrias proliferated across the world), and created the largest empire the world had ever known.

When Alexander and his army reached the banks of the Indus River in 326 BCE, he encountered a culture that had long fascinated him. His teacher Aristotle had described it, wholly on hearsay, as had Herodotus before him, as the farthest land mass to the east, beyond which lay the Endless Ocean that encircled the world. Alexander stopped first at Taxila (20 miles north of present-day Islamabad, Pakistan; see Map 2.2), where King Omphis greeted him with a gift of 200 silver talents, 3,000 oxen, 10,000 sheep, and 30 elephants, and bolstered Alexander's army by giving him 700 Indian cavalry and 5,000 infantry.

While Alexander was in Taxila, he became acquainted with the Hindu philosopher Calanus. Alexander recognized in Calanus and his fellow Hindu philosophers a level of wisdom and learning that he valued highly, one clearly reminiscent of Greek philosophy, and his encounters with them represent the first steps in a long history of the cross-fertilization of Eastern and Western cultures.

But in India the army encountered elephants, whose formidable size proved problematic. East of Taxila, Alexander's troops managed to defeat King Porus, whose army was equipped with 200 elephants. Rumor had it that farther to the east, the kingdom of the Ganges, their next logical opponent, had a force of 5,000 elephants. Alexander pleaded with his troops: "Dionysus, divine from birth, faced terrible tasks—and we have outstripped him! . . . Onward, then: let us add to our empire the rest of Asia!" The army refused to budge. His conquests thus concluded, Alexander himself sailed down the Indus River, founding the city that would later become Karachi. As he returned home, he contracted fever in Babylon and died in 323 BCE. Alexander's life was brief, but his influence on the arts was long-lasting.

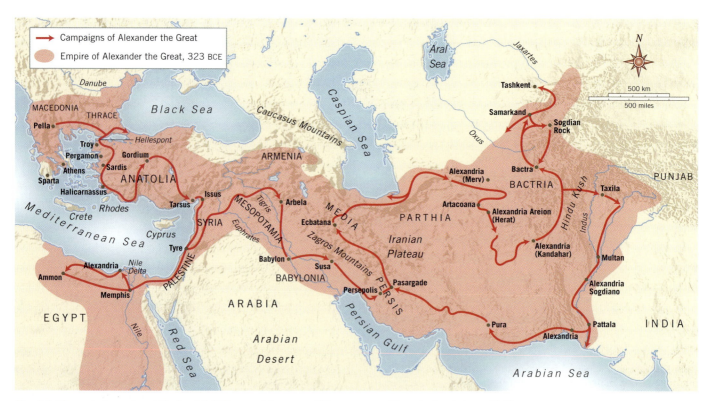

Map 2.2 Alexander's empire at his death in 323 BCE and the route of his conquests. Alexander founded over 70 cities throughout his empire, naming many after himself.

Toward Hellenistic Art: Sculpture in the Late Classical Period

During Alexander's time, sculpture flourished. Ever since the fall of Athens to Sparta in 404 BCE, Greek artists had continued to develop the **Classical** style of Phidias and Polyclitus, but they modified it in subtle yet innovative ways. Especially notable was a growing taste for images of men and women in quiet, sometimes dreamy and contemplative moods, which increasingly replaced the sense of nobility and detachment characteristic of fifth-century Classicism and found its way even into depictions of the gods. The most admired sculptors of the day were Lysippus, Praxiteles, and Skopas. Very little of the last's work has survived, although he was noted for high-relief sculpture featuring highly energized and emotional scenes. The work of the first two is far better known.

The Heroic Sculpture of Lysippus Alexander hired the sculptor Lysippus (flourished fourth century BCE) to do all his portraits. Despite his cruel treatment of the Thebans early in his career, Alexander was widely admired by the Greeks. Even during his lifetime, but especially after his death, sculptures celebrating the youthful hero abounded, almost all of them modeled on Lysippus' originals. Alexander is easily recognizable—his disheveled hair long and flowing, his gaze intense and melting, his mouth slightly open, his head alertly turned on a slightly tilted neck (Fig. **2.37**).

Lysippus dramatized his hero. That is, he did not merely represent Alexander as naturalistically as possible, he also animated him, showing him in the midst of action. In all likelihood, he idealized him as well. The creation of Alexander's likeness was a conscious act of propaganda. Early in his conquests the young hero referred to himself as "Alexander the Great," and Lysippus' job was to embody that greatness. Lysippus challenged the Classical *kanon* of proportion created by Polyclitus: smaller heads and more slender bodies lent his heroic sculptures a sense of greater height. In fact, he transformed the Classical tradition in sculpture and began to explore new possibilities that, eventually, would define Hellenistic art, with its sense of animation, drama, and psychological complexity. In a Roman copy of a lost original by Lysippus known as the *Apoxyomenos* (Fig. **2.38**), or *The Scraper,* an athlete removes oil and dirt from his body

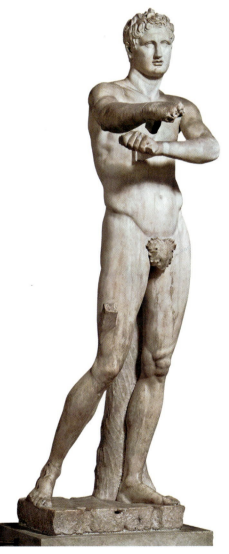

Fig. 2.38 Lysippus, ***Apoxyomenos (The Scraper),*** **Roman copy of an original Greek bronze of ca. 350–325 BCE.** Museo Pio Clementino, Vatican Museums, Vatican State. Marble, height 6'8". According to the Roman Pliny the Elder, writing in his *Natural History* in the first century CE, Lysippus "made the heads of his figures smaller than the old sculptors used to do." In fact, the ratio of the head size to the body in Lysippus' sculpture is 1:9, compared to Polyclitus' Classical proportions of 1:8.

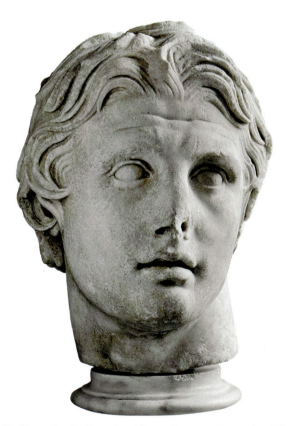

Fig. 2.37 ***Alexander the Great,*** **head from a Pergamene copy (ca. 200 BCE) of a statue, possibly after a 4th-century BCE original by Lysippus.** Marble, height 16⅛". Archaeological Museum, Istanbul. Alexander is traditionally portrayed as if looking beyond his present circumstances to greater things.

with an instrument called a strigil. Compared to the *Doryphoros* (*Spear Bearer*) of Polyclitus (see Fig. 2.28), *The Scraper* is much slenderer, his legs much longer, his torso shorter. *The Scraper* seems much taller, although in fact the sculptures are very nearly the same height. The arms of *The Scraper* break free of his frontal form and invite the viewer to look at the sculpture from the sides as well as the front. He seems detached from his circumstances, as if recalling his athletic performance. All in all, he seems both physically and mentally uncontained by the space in which he stands.

The Sensuous Sculpture of Praxiteles Competing with Lysippus for the title of greatest sculptor of the fourth century BCE was the Athenian Praxiteles (flourished 370–330 BCE). Praxiteles was one of the 300 wealthiest men in Athens, thanks to his skill, but he also had a reputation as a womanizer. The people of the port city of Knidos, a Spartan colony in Asia Minor, asked him to provide them with an image of their patron goddess, Aphrodite, in her role as the protectress of sailors and merchants. Praxiteles responded with a sculpture of Aphrodite as the goddess of love, here reproduced in a later Roman copy (Fig. **2.39**). She stands at her bath, holding her cloak in her left hand. The sculpture is a frank celebration of the body—reflecting in the female form the humanistic appreciation for the dignity of the human body in its own right. (Images of it on local coins suggest that her original pose was far less modest than that of the Roman copy, her right hand not shielding her genitals.) The statue made Knidos famous, and many people traveled there to see it. She was enshrined in a circular temple, easily viewed from every angle, the Roman scholar Pliny the Elder (23–79 CE) tells us, and she quickly became an object of religious attention—and openly sexual adoration. The reason for this is difficult to assess in the rather mechanical Roman copies of the lost original.

Praxiteles' *Aphrodite of Knidos* may be the first fully nude depiction of a woman in Greek sculpture, which may be why it caused such a sensation. Its fame elevated female nudity from a sign of low moral character to the embodiment of beauty, even truth itself. Paradoxically, it is also one of the earliest examples of artwork designed to appeal to what some art historians describe as the male gaze that regards woman as its sexual object. Praxiteles' canon for depicting the female nude—wide hips, small breasts, oval face, and centrally parted hair—remained the standard throughout antiquity.

Aristotle: Observing the Natural World

We can only guess what motivated Lysippus and Praxiteles so to dramatize and humanize their sculptures, but it is likely that the aesthetic philosophy of Aristotle played a role. Aristotle was a student of Plato's. Recall that, for Plato, all reality is a mere reflection of a higher, spiritual truth, a higher dimension of Ideal Forms that we glimpse only through philosophical contemplation.

Aristotle disagreed. Reality was not a reflection of an ideal form, but existed in the material world itself, and by observing the material world, one could come to know universal truths. So Aristotle observed and described all aspects of the

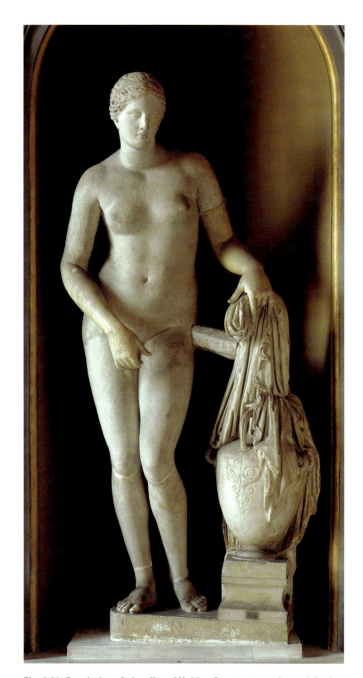

Fig. 2.39 Praxiteles, *Aphrodite of Knidos,* Roman copy of an original of ca. 350 BCE. Marble, height 6'8". Vatican Museums, Vatican State. The head of this figure is from one Roman copy, the body from another. The right forearm and hand, the left arm, and the lower legs of the *Aphrodite* are all seventeenth- and eighteenth-century restorations. There is reason to believe that her hand was not so modestly positioned in the original.

world in order to arrive at the essence of things. His methods of observation came to be known as *empirical investigation*. And although he did not create a formal **scientific method**, he and other early empiricists did create procedures for testing their theories about the nature of the world that, over time, would lead to the great scientific discoveries of Bacon, Galileo, and Newton. Aristotle studied biology, zoology, physics, astronomy, politics, logic, ethics, and the various genres of literary expression. Based on his observations of lunar eclipses, he concluded as early as 350 BCE that the Earth was spherical, an observation that may have motivated Alexander to cross India in order to sail back to Greece. He described over 500 animals in his *Historia Animalium*, including many that he dissected himself. In fact, Aristotle's observations of marine biology were unequaled until the seventeenth century and were still much admired by Charles Darwin in the nineteenth.

Aristotle also understood the importance of formulating a reasonable hypothesis to explain phenomena. His *Physics* is an attempt to define the first principles governing the behavior of matter—the nature of weight, motion, physical existence, and variety in nature. At the heart of Aristotle's philosophy is a question about the relation of *identity* and *change* (not far removed, incidentally, from one of the governing principles of this text—the idea of continuity and change in the humanities). To discuss the world coherently, we must be able to say what it is about a thing that makes it the thing it is, that separates it from all the other things in the world. In other words, what is the attribute that we would call its material identity or *essence*? What it means to be human, for instance, does not depend on whether one's hair turns gray. Such "accidental" changes matter not at all. At the same time, our experience of the natural world suggests that any coherent account requires us to acknowledge process and change—the change of seasons, the changes in our understanding associated with gaining knowledge in the process of aging, and so on. For Aristotle, any account of a thing must accommodate both aspects: We must be able to say what changes a thing undergoes while still retaining its essential nature. Aristotle thus approached all manner of things—from politics to the human condition—with an eye toward determining what constituted their essence.

Aristotle's *Poetics* What constitutes the essential nature of literary art, and the theater in particular, especially fascinated Aristotle. Like all Greeks, he was well acquainted with the theater of Aeschylus, Euripides, and Sophocles, and in his *Poetics* he defined their literary art as "the imitation of an action that is complete and whole." Including a whole action, or a series of events that ends with a crisis, gives the play a sense of unity. Furthermore, he argued (against Plato, who regarded imitation as inevitably degrading and diminishing) that such imitation elevates the mind ever closer to the universal.

One of the most important ideas that Aristotle expressed in the *Poetics* is **catharsis**, the cleansing, purification, or purgation of the soul. As applied to drama, it is not the tragic hero who undergoes catharsis, but the audience. The audience's experience of catharsis is an experience of change, just as change always accompanies understanding. In the theater, what moves the audience to change is its experience of the universality of the human condition—what it is that makes us human, our weaknesses as well as our strengths. At the sight of the action on stage, they are struck with "fear and pity." Plato believed that both these emotions were pernicious. But Aristotle argued that the audience's emotional response to the plight of the characters on stage clarified for them the fragility and mutability of human life. What happens in tragedy is universal—the audience understands that the action could happen to anyone at any time.

The Golden Mean In Aristotle's philosophy, such Classical aesthetic elements as unity of action and time, orderly arrangement of the parts, and proper proportion all have ethical ramifications. He argued for them by means of a philosophical method based on the **syllogism**, two premises from which a conclusion can be drawn. The most famous of all syllogisms is this:

> All men are mortal;
> Socrates is a man;
> Therefore, Socrates is mortal.

In the *Nicomachean Ethics*, written for and edited by his son Nicomachus, Aristotle attempts to define, once and for all, what Greek society had striven for since the beginning of the polis—the good life. The operative syllogism goes something like this:

> The way to happiness is through the pursuit of moral virtue;
> The pursuit of the good life is the way to happiness;
> Therefore, the good life consists in the pursuit of moral virtue.

The good life, Aristotle argued, is attainable only through balanced action. Tradition has come to call this the **Golden Mean**—not Aristotle's phrase but that of the Roman poet Horace—the middle ground between any two extremes of behavior. Thus, in a formulation that was particularly applicable to Aristotle's student Alexander the Great, the Golden Mean between cowardice and recklessness is courage. Like the arts, which imitate an action, human beings are defined by their actions: "As with a flute-player, a statuary [sculptor], or any artisan, or in fact anybody who has a definite function, so it would seem to be with humans. . . . The function of humans is an *activity* of soul in accordance with reason." This activity of soul seeks out the moral mean, just as "good artists . . . have an eye to the mean in their works."

Despite the measure and moderation of Aristotle's thinking, Greek culture did not necessarily reflect the balanced approach of its leading philosopher. In his emphasis on catharsis—the value of experiencing "fear and pity," the emotions that move us to change—Aristotle introduced the values that would define the age of Hellenism, the period lasting from 323 to 31 BCE, that is, from the death of Alexander to the Battle of Actium, the event that marks in the minds of many the beginning of the Roman Empire.

Alexandria

Perhaps the most spectacular of all Alexander's capitols was Alexandria in Egypt. Alexander conceived of all the cities he founded as centers of culture. They would be hubs of trade and learning, and Greek culture would radiate from them to the surrounding countryside. But Alexandria exceeded even Alexander's expectations.

The city's ruling family, the Ptolemies (heirs of Alexander's close friend and general, Ptolemy I), built the world's first museum—from the Greek *mouseion*, literally, "temple to the muses"—conceived as a meeting place for scholars and students. Nearby was the largest library in the world. It contained over 700,000 volumes. Plutarch later claimed that it was destroyed in 47 BCE, after Julius Caesar ordered his troops to set fire to the Ptolemaic fleet and winds spread the flames to warehouses and dockyards. We now know that the library survived—the Roman geographer Strabo worked there in the 20s BCE. But here were collected the great works of Greek civilization, the writings of Plato and Aristotle, the plays of the great tragedians Aeschylus, Sophocles, and Euripides, as well as the comedies of Aristophanes. Stimulated by the intellectual activity in the city, the great mathematician Euclid formulated the theorems of plane and solid geometry here.

The city was designed by Alexander's personal architect, Dinocrates of Rhodes (flourished fourth century BCE), laid out in a grid, enclosed by a wall, and accessible by four gates at the ends of its major avenues. It was blessed by three extraordinary harbors. One was connected to the Nile, allowing the transfer of the river's enormous agricultural wealth. It was a cosmopolitan city, exceeding even Golden Age Athens in the diversity of its inhabitants. As its population approached one million at the end of the first century BCE, commerce was its primary activity. Banks conducted transactions. Peoples of different ethnic backgrounds—Jews, Africans, Greeks, Egyptians, various races and tribes from Asia Minor—all came together with the single purpose of making money.

Gradually, Hellenistic and Egyptian cultures merged, a fact underscored by the Egyptian king Ptolemy I (r. 323–285 BCE) when he diverted the funeral train of Alexander the Great from its Macedonian destination to Egypt. Burying him either in Memphis or Alexandria (his tomb has never been found), Ptolemy guaranteed that the city would forever be associated with the cult of Alexander himself. Tomb decorations at Luxor depict Alexander in the traditional role and style of an Egyptian pharaoh.

Pergamon: Hellenistic Capital

Upon his death, Alexander left no designated successor, and his three chief generals divided his empire into three successor states: the kingdom of Macedonia (including all of Greece), the kingdom of the Ptolemies (Egypt), and the kingdom of the Seleucids (Syria and what is now Iraq). But a fourth, smaller kingdom in western Anatolia, Pergamon (present-day Bergama, Turkey), soon rose to prominence and became a center of Hellenistic culture. Ruled by the Attalids—descendants of a Macedonian general named Attalus—Pergamon was founded as a sort of treasury for the huge fortunes Alexander had accumulated in his conquests. It was technically under the control of the Seleucid kingdom. However, under the leadership of Eumenes I (r. 263–241 BCE), Pergamon achieved virtual independence.

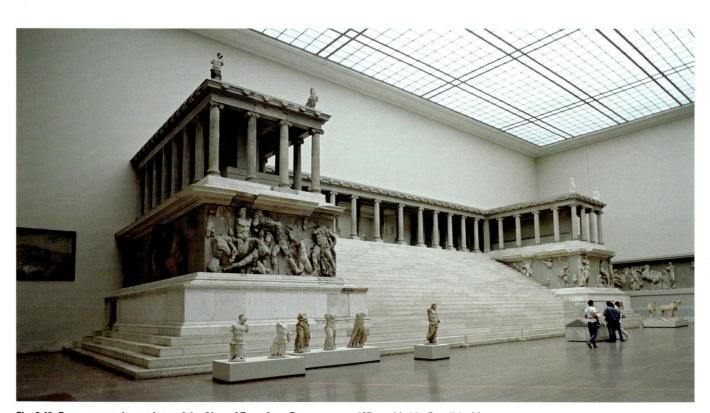

Fig. 2.40 Reconstructed west front of the Altar of Zeus, from Pergamon. ca. 165 BCE. Marble, Staatliche Museen, Berlin, Antikensammlung, Pergamonmuseum. The Pergamon altar was exported to Germany with the permission of the Ottoman authorities in 1899, but in recent years, Turkish authorities have expressed interest in its return with ever-increasing insistence.

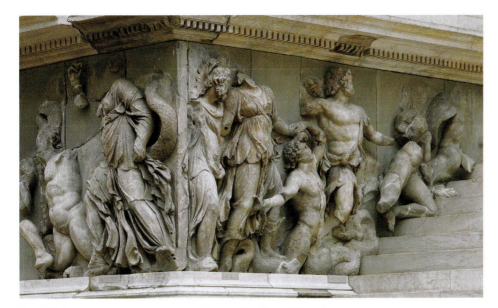

Fig. 2.41 Reconstructed west staircase frieze of the Altar of Zeus, from Pergamon. ca. 165 BCE. Marble. Staatliche Museen, Berlin, Antikensammlung, Pergamonmuseum. Particularly notable here is the extended arm of the kneeling warrior in the center, which reaches several feet into the viewer's space.

The CONTINUING PRESENCE
of the PAST

See Thomas Struth, *Pergamon Museum I, Berlin*, 2001, at **MyArtsLab**

C-print mounted on Plexiglas, 77¾" × 97¾". Marian Goodman Gallery. Inv. #8008

The Library at Pergamon The Attalids created a huge library filled with over 200,000 Classical Athenian texts. These were copied onto parchment, a word that derives from the Greek *pergamene*, meaning "from Pergamon," and refers to sheets of tanned leather. Pergamon's vast treasury allowed the Attalids the luxury of investing enormous sums of money in decorating their acropolis with art and architecture. Especially under the rule of Eumenes II (r. 197–160 BCE), the building program flourished. It was Eumenes II who built the library, as well as the theater and a gymnasium. And he was probably responsible for the Altar of Zeus (Fig. **2.40**), which is today housed in Berlin. The staircase entrance to the altar is 68 feet wide and nearly 30 feet deep. It rises to an Ionic colonnade. As opposed to the Parthenon, where the frieze is elevated above the colonnade, the first thing the viewer confronts at the Altar of Zeus is the frieze itself, a placement that draws attention to its composition of nearly 200 separate twisted, turning, and animated figures. Notice how, as the frieze narrows and rises up the stairs (Fig. **2.41**), the figures seem to break free of the architectural space that confines them and crawl out onto the steps of the altar.

A New Sculptural Style The altar is decorated with the most ambitious sculptural program since the

Parthenon, and is 7½ feet high. Its subject is a mythical battle of the gods and the giants for control of the world. The giants are depicted with snakelike bodies that coil beneath the feet of the triumphant gods (Fig. **2.42**). These figures represent one of the greatest examples of the Hellenized style of sculpture that depends for its effects on its **expressionism**, that is, the attempt to elicit an emotional response in the viewer. The theatrical effects of Lysippus are magnified into

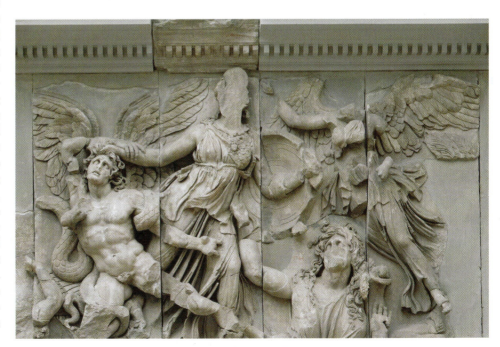

Fig. 2.42 Detail of the east frieze of the Altar of Zeus, from Pergamon. ca. 165 BCE. In this image, Athena grabs the hair of a winged, serpent-tailed monster, who is identified on the base of the monument as Alkyoneos, son of the earth goddess Ge. Ge herself rises up from the ground on the right to avenge her son. Behind Ge, a winged Nike flies to Athena's rescue.

a heightened sense of drama. Where Classical artists sought balance, order, and proportion, this frieze, with its figures twisting, thrusting, and striding in motion, stresses diagonal forces that seem to pull each other apart. Swirling bodies and draperies weave in and out of the sculpture's space, and the relief is so three-dimensional that contrasts of light and shade add to the dramatic effects. Above all, the frieze is an attempt to evoke the emotions of fear and pity that Aristotle argued led to catharsis in his *Poetics*, not the intellectual order of Classical tradition.

The relief was designed to celebrate Pergamon's role as the new center of Hellenism, its stature as the "new Athens." To that end, most authorities agree that the relief depicts the Attalid victory over the Gauls, a group of non-Greek-speaking and therefore "barbarian" central European Celts who had begun to migrate south through Macedonia as early as 300 BCE, and who had eventually settled in Galatia, just east of Pergamon. Sometime around 240–230 BCE, Attalos I (r. 241–197 BCE) defeated the Gauls in battle. Just as the Athenians had alluded to the battle between the forces of civilization and inhuman, barbarian aggressors in the metopes of the Parthenon (see Fig. 2.32), so too the Pergamenes suggested the nonhumanity of the Gauls by depicting the giants as snakelike and legless, unable even to begin to rise to the level of the Attalid victors.

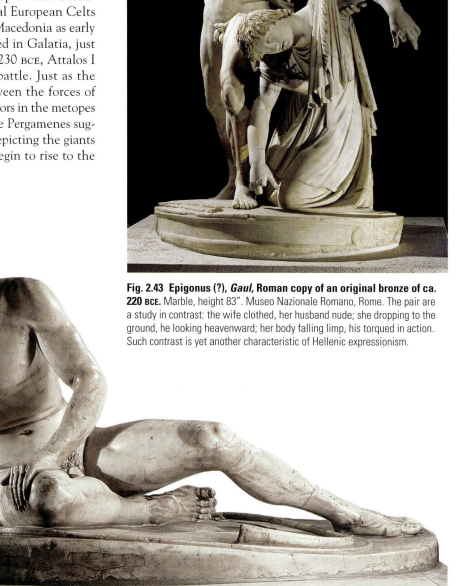

Fig. 2.43 Epigonus (?), ***Gaul,*** **Roman copy of an original bronze of ca. 220 BCE.** Marble, height 83". Museo Nazionale Romano, Rome. The pair are a study in contrast: the wife clothed, her husband nude; she dropping to the ground, he looking heavenward; her body falling limp, his torqued in action. Such contrast is yet another characteristic of Hellenic expressionism.

Fig. 2.44 Epigonus (?), ***Dying Gaul,*** **Roman copy of an original bronze of ca. 220 BCE.** Marble, height 37". Museo Capitolino, Rome. The Gaul seems both resigned to his fate—pressing against the ground to support himself as if pushing futilely against death—and also determined to show his valor and strength to the end—holding himself up as long as he can. Such emotional ambiguity is an integral aspect of Hellenistic art.

When Attalus I defeated the Gauls, he commissioned a group of three life-size figures to decorate the sanctuary of Athena Nikephoros (the "Victory-bringer") on the acropolis of Pergamon. Possibly the work of the sculptor Epigonus, the original bronze versions of these sculptures, which represent the vanquished Gauls, no longer exist, and how they related to one another is not clear. Nevertheless, the drama of their presentation and their appeal to the emotions of the viewer is unmistakable. In what was probably the centerpiece of the installation (Fig. 2.43), a Gallic chieftain, having just killed his wife in order to prevent her capture, possible abuse at the hands of the Pergamenes, and almost certain sale into slavery, now turns his sword on himself. He twists in an expressive theatricality, his arms and body rising to the task in marked contrast to the limp collapse of his wife beside him. A second sculpture, which probably flanked the suicide in the center of the installation, depicts a wounded Gallic trumpeter (Fig. 2.44). The Gaul's identity is established by the horn that lies at his feet, by his tousled hair and mustache (uncharacteristic of Greeks), and by his golden Celtic torc, or choker, the only item of clothing the Gauls wore in combat. He is dying from a chest wound that bleeds profusely below his right breast. The brutal realism together with the nobility and heroism of the defeated Gaul places this work among the earliest examples of Hellenistic expressionism.

One other Hellenistic sculpture deserves particular attention: the *Nike of Samothrace* (Fig. 2.45). Convincing arguments date it anywhere from 300 BCE to as late as 31 BCE, the preponderance of evidence suggesting the third or early second centuries BCE. Most agree that it was probably commissioned to celebrate a naval victory. It originally stood (with head and arms that have not survived, except for a single hand) upon the sculpted prow of a ship that was dramatically set in a pool of water at the top of a cliff on the island of Samothrace in the north Aegean. The dynamic forward movement of the striding figure is balanced dramatically by the open gesture of her extended wings and the powerful directional lines of her windblown gown across her body. When light rakes across the deeply sculpted forms of this figure, it emphasizes the contrasting textures of feathers, fabric, and flesh. With the *Altar of Zeus*, this sculpture reflects a new direction in art. Not only is this new art more interested in non-Greek subjects (Gauls and Trojans, for instance), but also the calm and restraint of Classical art have disappeared, replaced by the freedom to explore the emotional extremes of the human experience.

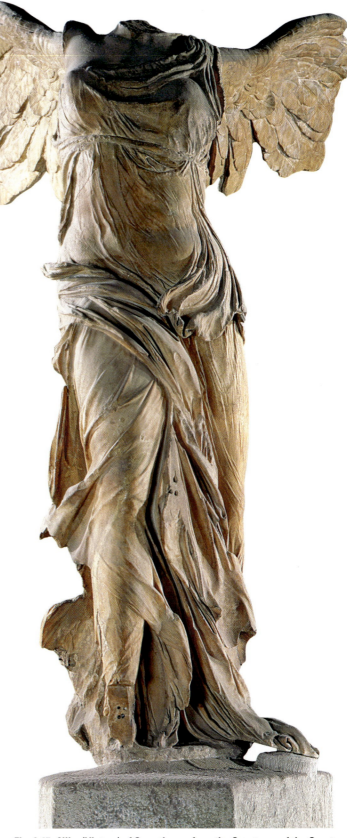

Fig. 2.45 *Nike (Victory) of Samothrace*, **from the Sanctuary of the Great Gods, Samothrace. ca. 300–190 BCE**. Marble, height 8′1″. Musée du Louvre, Paris. Discovered by French explorers in 1863, the Nike appears so immediate and alive that the viewer can almost feel the gust of wind that blows across her body.

THINKING BACK

2.1 Outline how the Cycladic, Minoan, and Mycenaean cultures contributed to the later Greeks' sense of themselves.

The later Greeks traced their ancestry to the cultures that arose in the islands of the Aegean Sea. The art of the Cyclades consisted of highly simplified Neolithic figurines and later, probably under the influence of Minoan culture to the south, elaborate wall frescoes depicting everyday events. Unique to Minoan culture is an emphasis on the bull, associated with the legend of King Minos and the Minotaur, and the double ax, symbol of the palace of Minos at Knossos, whose complex layout gives rise to the word "labyrinth." Mycenaean warriors from the Greek mainland invaded Crete in about 1450 BCE. There is abundant archeological evidence that they had valued Minoan artistry long before and had traded with the Minoans. But from all appearances their two cultures could not have been more different. In what ways did Minoan and Mycenaean cultures differ?

Around 800 BCE, Homer's great epics, the *Iliad* and the *Odyssey*, were transcribed. The stories had been passed down orally for generations. The *Iliad* tells of the anger of the Greek hero Achilles and its consequences during a war between Mycenae and Troy, which occurred sometime around 1200 BCE. The *Odyssey* follows the Greek commander Odysseus on his adventure-laden journey home to his faithful wife, Penelope. These stories, and such legends as the myth of the Minotaur, comprised for the Greeks their *archaiologia*, their way of knowing their past. How do the *Iliad* and the *Odyssey* both embody the Greek value of *areté*?

2.2 Define the polis and explain how it came to reflect the values of Greek culture.

The rural areas of Greece, separated from one another by mountainous geography, gradually began to form into a community—the polis, or city-state—that exercised authority over its region. Inevitably, certain of these poleis became more powerful than others. At Delphi, Olympia, and even in colonies such as Paestum on the Italian peninsula, the city-states came together to honor their gods at sanctuaries. What role did these sanctuaries play in the development of Greek culture?

2.3 Describe how Pericles defined and shaped Golden Age Athens.

In the fifth century, the statesman Pericles dominated Athenian political life. In his funeral speech honoring the war dead, delivered early in the Peloponnesian Wars, he claimed "excellence" for Athenians in all aspects of endeavor, leading Greece by its example. How would you

characterize the contributions of Pericles to the Greeks' sense of themselves?

The Athenians realized the excellence of their sculpture, which became increasingly naturalistic even as it embodied an increasingly perfect sense of proportion. They realized it even more dramatically on the Acropolis, where Pericles instituted a massive architectural program that included what is perhaps the highest expression of the Doric order, the Parthenon. How would you define the Idea of Beauty (a Platonic notion) as reflected in Greek sculpture? In Greek architecture as exemplified by the Parthenon? Why have we come to call this work "Classical"?

Pericles also championed the practice of philosophy in Athens. His Athens inherited two distinct philosophical traditions, that of the pre-Socratics, who were chiefly concerned with describing the natural universe, and that of the Sophists, who were primarily concerned with understanding the nature of human "knowing" itself. Pericles was particularly interested in the Sophists. Why? The Sophist philosophy was, however, rejected by Socrates. In what ways does the philosophy of Socrates differ from that of the Sophists? Socrates never wrote a word himself, but his student Plato recorded his thoughts. How does Plato extend Socratic thought in the *Republic*?

Greek theatrical practice arose out of rites connected with Dionysus, god of wine. In what ways do both Greek comedy and Greek tragedy reflect this common origin? What is the role of the chorus in tragedy? What tension does tragedy most often exploit?

2.4 Characterize the values of the Hellenistic world in terms of politics, philosophy, and art.

The influence of Alexander the Great extended across North Africa and Egypt, into the Middle East, and as far as the Indian subcontinent, creating the largest empire the world had ever known. During his reign, sculpture flourished as a medium, the two masters of the period being Lysippus and his chief competitor, Praxiteles. How does the work of the two sculptors compare? What new direction in sculpture did they introduce and how did later Hellenistic sculptors exploit that direction?

Alexander's tutor, the philosopher Aristotle, emphasized the importance of empirical observation in understanding the world, distinguishing between a thing's identity—its essence—and the changes that inevitably occur to it over time. How would you compare Aristotle's philosophy to Plato's? How does Aristotle's *Poetics* inform later Hellenistic sculpture?

✔ **Study** and **review** on **MyArtsLab**

Rome and Its Hellenistic Heritage

Rome traced its origins back to the Trojan warrior Aeneas, who at the end of the Trojan War sailed off to found a new homeland for his people. The Roman poet Virgil (70–19 BCE) would celebrate Aeneas' journey in his epic poem the *Aeneid*, written in the last decade of his life. There, he describes how the gods who supported the Greeks punished the Trojan priest Laocoön for warning his countrymen not to accept the "gift" of a wooden horse from the Greeks:

> I shudder even now,
> Recalling it—there came a pair of serpents
> With monstrous coils, abreast the sea, and aiming
> Together for the shore. . . .
> Straight toward Laocoön, and first each serpent
> Seized in its coils his two young sons, and fastened
> The fangs in those poor bodies. And the priest
> Struggled to help them, weapons in his hand.
> They seized him, bound him with the mighty coils,
> Twice round his waist, twice round his neck, they squeezed
> With scaly pressure, and still towered above him
> Straining his hands to tear the knots apart,
> His chaplets[1] stained with blood and the black poison,
> He uttered horrible cries, not even human,
> More like the bellowing of a bull when, wounded,
> It flees the altar, shaking from the shoulder
> The ill-aimed axe.

[1]Chaplets: Garlands for the head.

It is likely that as he wrote the *Aeneid*, Virgil had seen the sculpture of *Laocoön and His Sons* (Fig. **2.46**), carved in about 150 BCE. (Some argue that the sculpture, discovered in 1506 in the ruins of a palace belonging to the emperor Titus [r. 79–81 CE] in Rome, is a copy of the now-lost original.) Whatever the case, the drama and expressionism of the sculpture are purely Hellenic. So too are its complex interweaving of elements and diagonal movements reminiscent of Athena's struggle with the giants on the frieze of the Altar of Zeus at Pergamon (see Fig. 2.42).

In fact, even though Rome conquered Greece in 146 BCE (at about the time that the *Laocoön* was carved), Greece could be said to have "ruled" Rome, at least culturally. Rome was a fully Hellenized culture—it fashioned itself in the image of Greece almost from its beginnings. Indeed, many of the works of Greek art reproduced in this book are not Greek at all but later Roman copies of Greek originals. The emperor Augustus (r. 27 BCE–14 CE) sought to transform Rome into the image of Pericles' Athens. A sculpture by Lysippus was a favorite of the emperor Tiberius (r. 14–57 CE), who had it removed from public display and placed in his bedroom. So outraged were the public, who considered the sculpture theirs and not the emperor's, that he was forced to return it to its public place. Later Roman emperors, notably Caligula and Nero, raided Delphi and Olympia for works of art.

It was not, in the end, its art on which Rome most prided itself. "Others," Virgil would write in his poem, "no doubt, will better mold the bronze." He concludes:

> . . . remember, Roman,
> To rule the people under law, to establish
> The way of peace, to battle down the haughty,
> To spare the meek. Our fine arts, these, forever. ∎

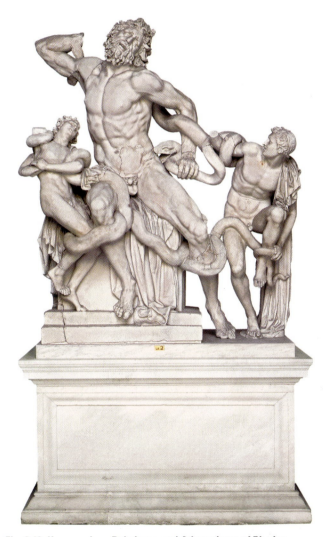

Fig. 2.46 Hagesandros, Polydoros, and Athanadoros of Rhodes, *Laocoön and His Sons*. Hellenistic, 2nd–1st century BCE, or marble copy of an original, Rome, 1st century CE. Marble, height 6'10". Museo Pio Clementino, Vatican Museums, Vatican State. Pliny the Elder attributes the sculpture to the three artists from Rhodes. If this is a copy of a lost original (and scholars debate the issue), it was probably inspired by Virgil's poem.

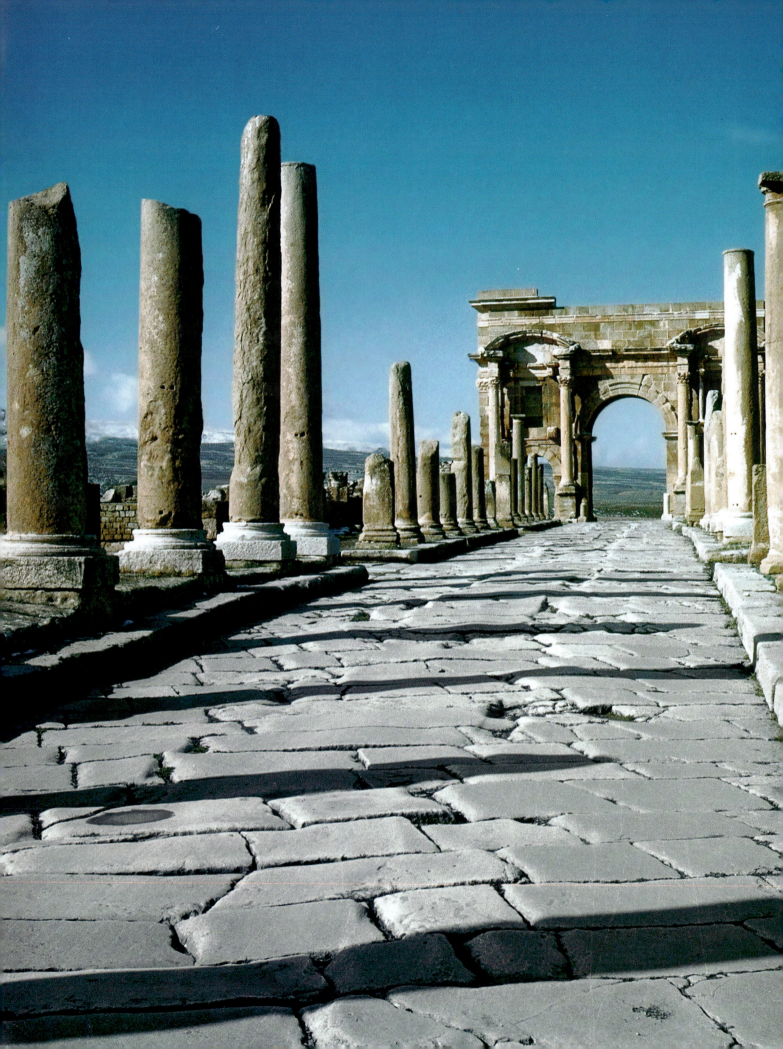

Empire 3

Urban Life and Imperial Majesty in Rome, China, and India

LEARNING OBJECTIVES

3.1 Characterize imperial Rome, its dual sense of origin, and its debt to the Roman Republic.

3.2 Describe the impact of the competing schools of thought that flourished in early Chinese culture—Daoism, Confucianism, and Legalism.

3.3 Discuss the ways in which both Hinduism and Buddhism shaped Indian culture.

Thamugadi, modern Timgad, Algeria, is one of the few totally excavated towns in the Roman Empire, and its ruins tell us as much or more about Roman civilization as any other Roman city, including Rome itself. It was founded in about 100 CE as a colony for retired soldiers of the Roman legions who had served the Empire as it constantly expanded its borders in Africa. Whereas Rome had grown haphazardly over hundreds of years and under many rulers, Thamugadi was an entirely new city and a model, if not of Rome itself, then of the Roman sense of order. It was based on the rigid grid of a Roman military camp and was divided into four quarters defined by east–west and north–south arteries, broad avenues lined with columns (Fig. **3.1**), with a forum, or public square, at their crossing. The town had 111 *insulae* (apartment blocks), and all the amenities of Roman life were available: 14 public baths, a library, a theater, and several markets, including one that sold only clothes (Fig. **3.2**).

Thamugadi is the product of the conscious Roman decision to "Romanize" the world, a symbol of empire itself. By the middle of the third century BCE, Rome had begun to seek control of the entire Mediterranean basin and its attendant wealth. The Roman military campaigns led to the building of these cities, with their amphitheaters, temples, arches, roads, fortresses, aqueducts, bridges, and monuments of every description. From Scotland in the north to the oases of the Sahara desert in the south, from the Iberian peninsula in the west to Asia Minor as far as the Tigris River in the east, local

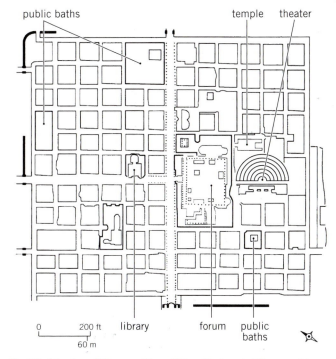

Fig. 3.2 City plan of Thamugadi. ca. 200 CE. The layout of Thamugadi is a symbol of Roman reason and planning—efficient and highly organized.

◀ **Fig. 3.1 Colonnaded street in Thamugadi, North Africa. View toward the Arch of Trajan. Late 2nd century CE.** Thamugadi was established in about 100 CE as a colony for retired soldiers of the Roman Third Legion. It represents the deep imprint Rome left upon its entire empire.

83

aristocrats took up Roman customs (Map 3.1). Roman law governed each region. Rome remained the center of culture all others at the periphery imitated.

If most empires, including Rome's but also Alexander the Great's before it (see Chapter 2) and those of the great maritime empires of the sixteenth and seventeenth centuries, including Portugal and Spain (see Chapter 9), begin with military campaigns designed to win territory and the wealth associated with that territory, the resulting empires are not usually held together by force. Rather, the conquered people—who may indeed suffer considerably as they are overcome, victimized by enslavement and even extermination (as would happen in both Africa and the Americas in the sixteenth century)—are often won over by the enhanced economic opportunities afforded them by the larger markets

opened up by participation in the empire's network of trade. But perhaps most importantly of all, empires like Rome's bring together diverse cultures, religions, philosophical ideas, and artistic tastes in an environment of mutual influence. As much as Rome imposed its will and ways of life on the entire Mediterranean, the cultures of the Mediterranean—especially those of Greece and the Near East—affected Rome as well. Empire is the first step in the globalization of world culture.

Rome admired Greece for its cultural achievements, from its philosophy to its sculpture, and, as we have seen, its own art developed from Greek-Hellenic models. But Rome admired its own achievements as well, and its art differed from that of its Hellenic predecessors in certain key respects. Instead of depicting mythological events and heroes,

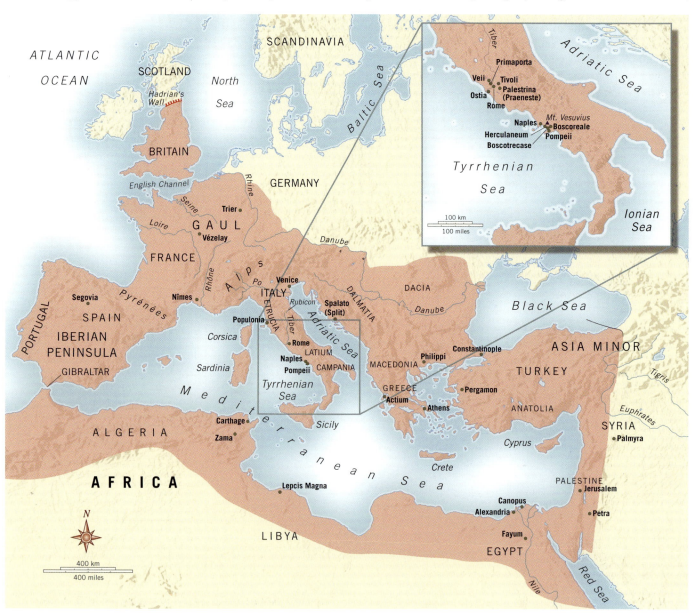

Map 3.1 The Roman Empire at its greatest extent, ca. 180 CE. By 180 CE the Roman Empire extended from the Atlantic Ocean in the west to Asia Minor, Syria, and Palestine in the east, and from Scotland in the north to the Sahara desert in North Africa.

Roman artists depicted current events and real people, from generals and their military exploits to leaders and recently deceased citizens. They celebrated the achievements of a state that was their chief patron, so that all the world might stand in awe of the state's accomplishments. And this sense of accomplishment is what cities like Thamugadi and the monuments of Rome itself also represent.

This chapter traces the rise of Roman civilization from its Greek and Etruscan origins in the sixth century BCE to about 313 CE, when the empire was Christianized. At roughly the same time, in China and in the river valleys of the Asian subcontinent of India, other empires took shape as well. In both China and India, national literatures arose, as did religious and philosophical practices that continue to this day and are influential worldwide; but in the ancient world, East and West had not yet met. The peoples of the Mediterranean world and those living in the Yellow and Indus river valleys were isolated from one another. As trade routes stretched across the Asian continent, these cultures would eventually cross paths. Gradually, Indian thought, especially Buddhism, would find its way into China, and Chinese goods would find their way to the West. Even more gradually, intellectual developments in ancient China and India, from Daoism to the teachings of Confucius and Buddha, would come to influence cultural practice in the Western world. But throughout most of the period studied in this chapter, until roughly 200 CE, the cultures of China and India developed independently of those in the West.

The Etruscan homeland, Etruria, occupied the part of the Italian peninsula that is roughly the same as present-day Tuscany. It was bordered by the Arno River to the north (which runs through Florence) and the Tiber River to the south (which runs through Rome). Rome itself developed geographically between two cultures—the Greek colonies to the south of the Tiber and the Etruscan settlements to the north. Its situation, in fact, is geographically improbable. Rome was built on a hilly site (on seven hills, to be precise) on the east bank of the Tiber. Its low-lying areas were swampy and subject to flooding, while the higher elevations of the hillsides did not easily lend themselves to building. The River Tiber itself provides a sensible explanation for the city's original siting, since it gave the city a trade route to the north and access to the sea at its port of Ostia to the south. And so does one of the river's primary crossings from the earlier times, Tiber Island, next to the Temple of Portunus. Thus, Rome was physically and literally the crossing place of Etruscan and Greek cultures.

The city also had competing foundation myths. The first is embodied in Virgil's *Aeneid*, in the story of its founding by the Trojan warrior Aeneas, who at the end of the Trojan War sailed off to found a new homeland for his people (see *Continuity & Change*, Chapter 2). The other was Etruscan. Legend had it that twin infants named Romulus and Remus were left to die on the banks of the Tiber but were rescued by a she-wolf who suckled them (Fig. 3.3). Raised by a shepherd, the twins decided to build a city on the Palatine Hill above the spot where they had been saved (accounting, in the manner

ROME

What characterizes imperial Rome, and how did it continue to reflect its dual sense of origin and its Republican heritage?

The origins of Roman culture are twofold. On the one hand, there were the Greeks, who as early as the eighth century BCE colonized the southern coastal regions of the Italian peninsula and Sicily and whose Hellenic culture the Romans adopted for their own. On the other hand, there were the Etruscans. Scholars continue to debate whether the Etruscans were indigenous to Italy or whether they migrated from the Near East. In the ninth and eighth centuries BCE, the Etruscans became known to the outside world for their mineral resources, and by the seventh and sixth centuries they were major exporters of fine painted pottery, a black ceramic ware known as *bucchero*, bronzework, jewelry, oil, and wine. By the fifth century BCE, they were known throughout the Mediterranean for their skill as sculptors in both bronze and terra cotta.

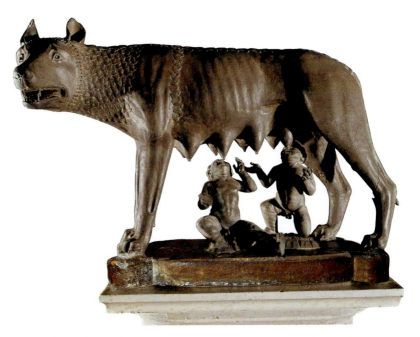

Fig. 3.3 *She-Wolf.* ca. 500–480 BCE. Bronze, with glass-paste eyes, height 33". Museo Capitolino, Rome. Scholars have recently suggested that the sculpture dates from medieval times. The two suckling figures representing Romulus and Remus are Renaissance additions. Nevertheless, the bronze, which became a symbol of Rome, combines a ferocious realism with the stylized portrayal of, for instance, the wolf's geometrically regular mane.

of foundation myths, for the unlikely location of the city).
Soon, the two boys feuded over who would rule the new city.
In his *History of Rome*, the Roman historian Livy (59 BCE–17 CE)
briefly describes the ensuing conflict:

> Then followed an angry altercation; heated passions led
> to bloodshed; in the tumult Remus was killed. The more
> common report is that Remus contemptuously jumped
> over the newly raised walls and was forthwith killed by
> the enraged Romulus, who exclaimed, "Shall it be hence-
> forth with every one who leaps over my walls." Romulus
> thus became sole ruler, and the city was called after him,
> its founder.

The date, legend has it, was 753 BCE.

Republican Rome

By the time of Virgil, the Greek and Etruscan myths had
merged. Thus, according to legend, Aeneas' son founded the
city of Alba Longa, just to the south of Rome, which was
ruled by a succession of kings until Romulus brought it under
Roman control.

Romulus, it was generally accepted, inaugurated the traditional Roman distinction between **patricians**, the land-
owning aristocrats who served as priests, magistrates, lawyers,
and judges, and **plebeians**, the poorer class who were craftspeople, merchants, and laborers. When, in 510 BCE, the
Romans expelled the last of the Etruscan kings and decided
to rule themselves without a monarch, the patrician/plebe-
ian distinction became very similar to the situation in fifth-
century BCE Athens. There, a small aristocracy who owned
the good land and large estates shared citizenship with a
much larger working class.

In Rome, as in the Greek model, every free male was a citizen, but in the Etruscan manner, not every citizen enjoyed
equal privileges. The Senate, the political assembly in charge
of creating law, was exclusively patrician. In reaction, the
plebeians formed their own legislative assembly, the Con-
silium Plebis (Council of Plebeians), to protect themselves
from the patricians, but the patricians were immune to any
laws the plebeians passed, known as *plebiscites*. Finally, in 287
BCE, the plebiscites became binding law for all citizens, and
something resembling equality of citizenship was assured.

The expulsion of the Etruscan kings and the dedication of
the Temple of Jupiter on the Capitoline Hill in 509 BCE mark
the beginning of actual historical records documenting the
development of Rome. They also mark the beginning of the
Roman Republic, a state whose political organization rested
on the principle that the citizens were the ultimate source
of legitimacy and sovereignty. Many people believe that the
Etruscan bronze head of a man (Fig. **3.4**) is a portrait of Lucius Junius Brutus, the founder and first consul of the Roman
Republic. However, it dates from approximately 100–200
years after Brutus' life, and it more likely represents a noble
"type," an imaginary portrait of a Roman founding father, or
pater, the root of the word *patrician*. This role is conveyed
through the figure's strong character and strength of purpose.

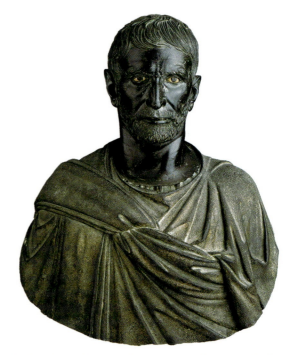

Fig. 3.4 Head of a Man (possibly a portrait of Lucius Junius Brutus).
ca. 300 BCE. Bronze, height 27½". Museo Capitolino, Palazzo dei Conservatori,
Rome. The eyes, which look slightly past the viewer, and the intensely furrowed
brow, give the figure an almost visionary force and suggest the influence of
Lysippus (compare Fig. 2.37 in Chapter 2).

In republican Rome, every plebeian chose a patrician as
his patron—and, indeed, most patricians were themselves
clients of some other patrician of higher status—whose
duty it was to represent the plebeian in any matter of law
and provide an assortment of assistance in matters, primarily economic. This paternalistic relationship—which we
call *patronage*—reflected the family's central role in Roman
culture. The *pater* protected not only his wife and family but
also his clients, who submitted to his patronage. In return
for the *pater*'s protection, family and client equally owed the
pater their total obedience—which the Romans referred to
as *pietas*, "dutifulness." So embedded was this attitude that
when toward the end of the first century BCE the Republic
declared itself an empire, the emperor was called *pater patriae*,
"father of the fatherland."

Roman Rule By the middle of the third century BCE, the
Republic had embarked on a series of military exploits known
as the Punic Wars that recall Alexander's imperial adventuring of the century before. Whenever Rome conquered a region, it established permanent colonies of veteran soldiers
who received allotments of land, virtually guaranteeing them
a certain level of wealth and status. These soldiers were citizens. If the conquered people proved loyal to Rome, they could
gain full Roman citizenship. Furthermore, when not involved
in combat, the local Roman soldiery transformed themselves
into engineers—building roads, bridges, and civic projects of
all types, significantly improving the region, as at Thamugadi
in Algeria (see Figs. 3.1 and 3.2). In this way, the Republic

diminished the adversarial status of its colonies and gained their loyalty.

The prosperity brought about by Roman expansion soon created a new kind of citizen in Rome. They called themselves *equites* ("equestrians") to connect them to the cavalry, the elite part of the military, since only the wealthy could afford the necessary horses. The *equites* were wealthy businessmen, but not often landowners and therefore not patricians. The patricians considered the commercial exploits of the *equites* crass and their wealth ill-gotten. Soon the two groups were in open conflict, the *equites* joining ranks with the plebeians.

The Senate was the patrician stronghold, and it feared any loss of power and authority. When the general Pompey the Great (106–48 BCE) returned from a victorious campaign against rebels in Asia Minor in 62 BCE, the Senate refused to ratify the treaties he had made in the region or to grant the land allotments he had given his soldiers. Outraged, Pompey joined forces with two other successful military leaders. One had put down the slave revolt of Spartacus in 71 BCE. The other was Gaius Julius Caesar (100–44 BCE), a military leader from a prestigious patrician family that claimed descent from Aeneas and Venus. The union of the three leaders became known as the First Triumvirate.

A Divided Empire Wielding the threat of civil war, the First Triumvirate soon dominated the Republic's political life, but theirs was a fragile relationship. Caesar accepted a five-year appointment as governor of Gaul, present-day France. By 49 BCE, he had brought all of Gaul under his control. He summed up this conquest in his *Commentaries* in the famous phrase "Veni, vidi, vici"—"I came, I saw, I conquered"—a statement that captures, perhaps better than any other, the militaristic nature of the Roman state as a whole. He was preparing to return home when Pompey joined forces with the Senate. They reminded Caesar of a long-standing tradition that required a returning commander to leave his army behind, in this case on the Gallic side of the Rubicon River, but Caesar refused. Pompey fled to Greece, where Caesar defeated him a year later. Again Pompey fled, this time to Egypt, where he was murdered. The third member of the Triumvirate had been captured and executed several years earlier.

Now unimpeded, Caesar assumed dictatorial control over Rome. He treated the Senate with disdain, and most of its membership counted themselves as his enemies. On March 15, 44 BCE, the Ides of March, he was stabbed 23 times by a group of 60 senators at the foot of a sculpture honoring Pompey on the floor of the Senate. This scene was memorialized in English by Shakespeare's great play *Julius Caesar* and Caesar's famous line, as he sees his ally Marcus Junius Brutus (85–42 BCE) among the assassins, "Et tu, Brute?"— "You also, Brutus?" Brutus and the others believed they had freed Rome of a tyrant, but the people were outraged, the Senate disgraced, and Caesar considered a martyr.

Cicero and the Politics of Rhetoric In times of such political upheaval, it is not surprising that one of the most powerful figures of the day would be someone who specialized in the art of political persuasion. In pre-Augustan Rome, that person was the **rhetorician** (writer and public speaker, or orator) Marcus Tullius Cicero (106–43 BCE). First and foremost, Cicero recognized the power of the Latin language to communicate with the people. Although originally used almost exclusively as the language of commerce, Latin, by the first century CE, was understood to be potentially a more powerful tool of persuasion than Greek, still the literary language of the upper classes. The clarity and eloquence of Cicero's style can be quickly discerned, even in translation, as an excerpt (**Reading 3.1**) from his essay *On Duty* demonstrates.

READING 3.1
_____

from Cicero, *On Duty* (44 BCE)

That moral goodness which we look for in a lofty, high-minded spirit is secured, of course, by moral, not physical strength. And yet the body must be trained and so disciplined that it can obey the dictates of judgment and reason in attending to business and in enduring toil. But that moral goodness which is our theme depends wholly upon the thought and attention given to it by the mind. And, in this way, the men who in a civil capacity direct the affairs of the nation render no less important service than they who conduct its wars: by their statesmanship oftentimes wars are either averted or terminated; sometimes also they are declared. . . . And so diplomacy in the friendly settlement of controversies is more desirable than courage in settling them on the battlefield; but we must be careful not to take that course merely for the sake of avoiding war rather than for the sake of public expediency. War, however, should be undertaken in such a way as to make it evident that it has no other object than to secure peace.

The dangers attending great affairs of state fall sometimes on those who undertake them, sometimes upon the state. In carrying out such enterprises, some run the risk of losing their lives, others their reputation and the good-will of their fellow-citizens. It is our duty, then, to be more ready to endanger our own than the public welfare and to hazard honor and glory more readily than other advantages. . . .

Philosophically, Cicero's argument extends back to Plato and Aristotle, but rhetorically—that is, in the structure of its argument—it is purely Roman. It is purposefully deliberative in tone—that is, its chief concern is to give sage advice rather than to engage in a Socratic dialogue to elicit that advice.

Portrait Busts, *Pietas*, and Politics This historical context helps us to understand a major Roman art form of the second and first centuries BCE, the portrait bust. These are generally portraits of patricians (and upper-middle-class citizens wishing to emulate them) rather than *equites*. Roman portrait busts share with their Greek ancestors an affinity for

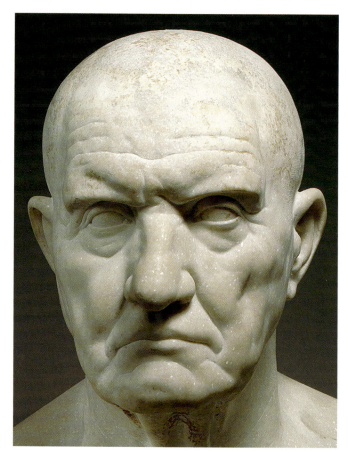

Fig. 3.5 *A Roman Man.* ca. 80 BCE. Marble, life-size. The Metropolitan Museum of Art, Rogers Fund, 1912 (12.233). His face creased by the wrinkles of age, this man is the very image of the *pater*, the man of *gravitas* (literally "weight," but also "presence" or "influence"), *dignitas* ("dignity," "worth," and "character"), and *fides* ("honesty" and "conscientiousness").

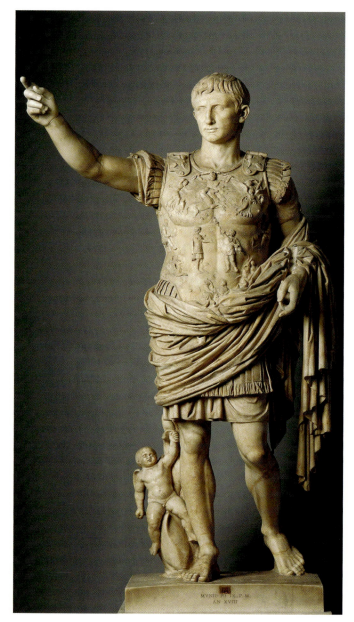

Fig. 3.6 *Augustus of Primaporta.* ca. 20 BCE. Marble, height 6'8". Vatican Museums, Vatican State. On the breastplate, a bearded Parthian from Asia Minor hands over Roman standards that had been lost in a battle of 53 BCE. In 20 BCE, when the original version of this statue was carved—most scholars believe this is actually a later copy—Augustus had won them back.

View the Closer Look for *Augustus of Primaporta* on **MyArtsLab**

naturalistic representation, but they are even more realistic, revealing their subjects' every wrinkle and wart (Fig. **3.5**). This form of realism is known as **verism** (from the Latin *veritas*, "truth"). Indeed, the high level of naturalism may have resulted from their original form, wax ancestral masks, usually made at the peak of the subject's power, called *imagines*, which were then transferred to stone.

Compared to the Greek Hellenistic portrait bust—recall Lysippus' portrait of Alexander (see Fig. 2.37 in Chapter 2), copies of which proliferated throughout the Mediterranean in the third century BCE—the Roman portrait differs particularly in the age of the sitter. Both the Greek and Roman busts are essentially propagandistic in intent, designed to extol the virtues of the sitter, but where Alexander is portrayed as a young man at the height of his powers, the usual Roman portrait bust depicts its subject at or near the end of life. The Greek portrait bust, in other words, signifies youthful possibility and ambition, while the Roman version claims for its subject the wisdom and experience of age. These images celebrate *pietas*, the deep-seated Roman virtue of dutiful respect toward the gods, fatherland, and parents. To respect one's parents was tantamount, for the Romans, to respecting

one's moral obligations to the gods. The respect one owed one's parents was, in effect, a religious obligation.

If the connection to Alexander—especially the emphasis on the power of the gaze—is worth considering, the Roman portrait busts depict a class under attack, a class whose virtues and leadership were being threatened by upstart generals and *equites*. They are, in other words, the very picture of conservative politics. Their furrowed brows represent their wisdom, their wrinkles their experience, and their extraordinarily naturalistic representation their character. They represent the Senate itself, which should be honored, not disdained.

Imperial Rome

On January 13, 27 BCE, Octavian came before the Senate and gave up all his powers and provinces. It was a rehearsed event. The Senate begged him to reconsider and take Syria, Gaul, and the Iberian Peninsula for his own (these provinces just happened to contain 20 of the 26 Roman legions, guaranteeing him military support). They also asked him to retain his title of consul of Rome, with the supreme authority of *imperium*, the power to give orders and exact obedience, over all of Italy and subsequently all Roman-controlled territory. He agreed "reluctantly" to these terms, and the Senate, in gratitude, granted him the semidivine title Augustus, "the revered one." Augustus (r. 27 BCE–14 CE) thereafter portrayed himself as a near-deity. The *Augustus of Primaporta* (Fig. **3.6**) is the slightly-larger-than-life-size sculpture named for its location at the home of Augustus' wife, Livia, at Primaporta, on the outskirts of Rome. Augustus is represented as the embodiment of the famous admonition given to Aeneas by his dead father (*Aeneid*, Book 6): "To rule the people under law, to establish/ The way of peace." Augustus, like Aeneas, is duty bound to exhibit *pietas*, the obligation to his ancestor "to rule earth's peoples."

The sculpture, though recognizably Augustus, is nevertheless idealized. It adopts the pose and ideal proportions of Polyclitus' *Doryphoros* (see Fig. 2.28 in Chapter 2). The gaze, reminiscent of the look of Alexander the Great, purposefully recalls the visionary hero of Greece who died 300 years earlier. The right arm is extended in the gesture of *ad locutio*—he is giving a (military) address. The military garb announces his role as commander-in-chief. Riding a dolphin at his feet is a small Cupid, son of the goddess Venus, laying claim to the Julian family's divine descent from Venus and Aeneas. Although Augustus was more than 70 years old when he died, he was always depicted as young and vigorous, choosing to portray himself, apparently, as the ideal leader rather than the wise, older *pater*.

Augustus was careful to maintain at least the trappings of the Republic. The Senate stayed in place, but Augustus soon eliminated the distinction between patricians and *equites*, and fostered the careers of all capable individuals, whatever their origin. Some he made provincial governors, others administrators in the city, and he encouraged still others to enter political life. Soon the Senate was populated with many men who had never dreamed of political power. All of them—governors, administrators, and politicians—owed everything to Augustus. Their loyalty further solidified his power.

Family Life Augustus also quickly addressed what he considered to be another crisis in Roman society—the demise of family life. Adultery and divorce were commonplace. There were more slaves and freed slaves in the city than citizens, let alone aristocrats. And family size, given the cost of living in the city, was diminishing. He reacted by criminalizing adultery and passed several other laws to promote family life. Men between the ages of 20 and 60 and women between the ages of 20 and 50 were required to marry. A divorced woman was required to remarry within six months, a widow within a year. Childless adults were punished with high taxes or deprived of inheritance. The larger an aristocrat's family, the greater his political advantage. It is no coincidence that when Augustus commissioned a large monument to commemorate his triumphal return after establishing Roman rule in Gaul and restoring peace to Rome, the *Ara Pacis Augustae* (Altar of Augustan Peace), he had its exterior walls on the south decorated with a retinue of his own large family, a model for all Roman citizens, in a procession of lictors (the class of citizens charged with guarding and attending to the needs of magistrates), priests, magistrates, senators, and other representatives of the Roman people (Fig. **3.7**).

Art historians believe that the *Ara Pacis Augustae* represents a real event, perhaps a public rejoicing for Augustus' reign (it was begun in 13 BCE when he was 50), or the dedication of the altar itself, which occurred on Livia's fiftieth birthday in 9 BCE. The realism of the scene is typically Roman. A sense of spatial depth is created by depicting figures farther

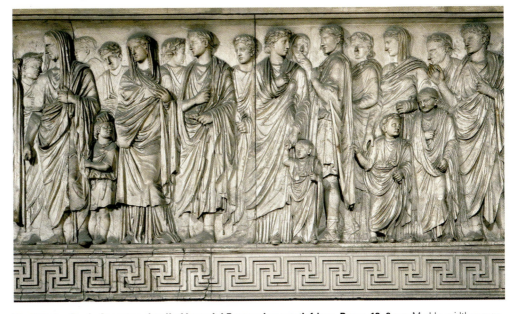

Fig. 3.7 *Ara Pacis Augustae*, **detail of Imperial Procession, south frieze, Rome. 13–9 BCE.** Marble, width approx. 35'. At the left is Marcus Agrippa, Augustus' son-in-law, married to his daughter Julia. The identities of the other figures are not secure, but scholars speculate that clinging to Agrippa's robe is either a foreign child belonging to Agrippa's household or Augustus' grandson Gaius Caesar, who with his brother Lucius often traveled with their grandfather and whom Augustus taught to imitate his own handwriting. The child looks backward and up at Augustus' wife, Livia, one of the most powerful people in Rome. Behind Livia is her son by an earlier marriage, Tiberius, who would succeed Augustus as emperor.

away from us in low relief and those closest to us in high relief, so high in fact that the feet of the nearest figures project over the architectural frame into our space. This technique would have encouraged viewers—the Roman public—to feel that they were part of the same space as the figures in the sculpture itself. The Augustan peace is the peace enjoyed by the average Roman citizen, the Augustan family a metaphor for the larger family of Roman citizens.

But perhaps above all, the *Ara Pacis Augustae* offers the peaceful continuity of family life from generation to generation as a metaphor and model for the peaceful continuity of the empire from one ruler to the next. Three generations of Augustus' family are depicted in the relief. It also demonstrates the growing prominence of women in Roman society. Augustus' wife, Livia, is depicted holding Augustus' family together, standing between her stepson-in-law, Marcus Agrippa, and her own sons, Tiberius and Drusus.

Livia became a figure of idealized womanhood in Rome. She was the "female leader" of Augustus' programs of reform, a sponsor of architectural projects, and a trusted advisor to both her husband and son. While Livia enjoyed greater power and influence than most Roman women, all possessed the rights of citizenship, although they could not vote or hold public office. Still, married women retained their legal identity. They controlled their own property and managed their own legal affairs. Elite women modeled themselves on Livia, wielding power through their husbands and sons.

Literary Rome: Virgil, Horace, and Ovid

When Augustus took control of Rome, he arranged for all artistic patronage to pass through his office. During the civil wars, the two major poets of the day, Virgil and Horace, had lost all their property, but Augustus' patronage allowed them to keep on with their writings. Because the themes they pursued were subject to Augustus' approval, they tended to glorify both the emperor and his causes. He was far less supportive of the poet Ovid, whom he banished permanently from Rome.

Virgil and the *Aeneid* After Augustus' triumph over Antony and Cleopatra at the battle of Actium in 31 BCE, Virgil retired to Naples, where he began work on an epic poem designed to rival Homer's *Iliad* and to provide the Roman state—and Augustus in particular—with a suitably grand founding myth. Previously he had been engaged with two series of pastoral idylls, the *Eclogues* (or *Bucolics*) and the *Georgics*. The latter poems (**Reading 3.2**) are modeled on Hesiod's *Works and Days* (see Chapter 2). They extol the importance of hard work, the

---

READING 3.2

from Virgil, *Georgics*

In early spring-tide, when the icy drip
Melts from the mountains hoar, and Zephyr's breath
Unbinds the crumbling clod, even then 'tis time;
Press deep your plow behind the groaning ox,

And teach the furrow-burnished share to shine.
That land the craving farmer's prayer fulfils,
Which twice the sunshine, twice the frost has felt;
Ay, that's the land whose boundless harvest-crops
Burst, see! the barns.

---

necessity of forging order in the face of a hostile natural world, and, perhaps above all, the virtues of agrarian life.

The political point of the *Georgics* was to celebrate Augustus' gift of farmlands to veterans of the civil wars, but in its exaltation of the myths and traditions of Italy, it served as a precursor to the *Aeneid*. It was written in **dactylic hexameter**, the verse form that Homer had used in the *Iliad* and *Odyssey*. (The metrical form of the translation above, however, is iambic pentameter—five rhythmic units, each short long, as in *dee-dum*—a meter much more natural to English than the Latin dactylic hexameter.) In dactylic hexameter each line consists of six rhythmic units, or **feet**, and each foot is either a **dactyl** (long, short, short, as in *dum-diddy*) or a **spondee** (long, long, as in *dum-dum*). Virgil reportedly wrote the *Georgics* at a pace of less than one line a day, perfecting his understanding of the metrical scheme in preparation for the longer poem.

The *Aeneid* opens in Carthage, where, after the Trojan War, Aeneas and his men have been driven by a storm, and where they are hosted by the Phoenician queen Dido. During a rainstorm Aeneas and Dido take refuge in a cave, where the queen, having fallen in love with the Trojan hero, gives herself willingly to him. She now assumes that she is married, but Aeneas, reminded by his father's ghost of his duty to accomplish what the gods have predetermined—a classic instance of *pietas*—knows he must resume his destined journey. An angry and accusing Dido begs him to stay. When Aeneas rejects her pleas, Dido vows to haunt him after her death and to bring enmity between Carthage and his descendants forever (a direct reference on Virgil's part to the Punic Wars). As his boat sails away, she commits suicide by climbing a funeral pyre and falling upon a sword. The goddesses of the underworld are surprised to see her. Her death, in their eyes, is neither deserved nor destined, but simply tragic. Virgil's point is almost coldly hardhearted: All personal feelings and desires must be sacrificed to one's responsibilities to the state. Civic duty takes precedence over private life.

The poem is, on one level, an account of Rome's founding by Aeneas, but it is also a profoundly moving essay on human destiny and the great cost involved in achieving and sustaining the values and principles upon which culture—Roman culture in particular, but all cultures by extension—must be based. Augustus, as Virgil well knew, claimed direct descent from Aeneas, and it is particularly important that the poem presents war, at which Augustus excelled, as a moral tragedy, however necessary.

In Book 7, Venus gives Aeneas a shield made by the god Vulcan. The shield displays the important events in the future history of Rome, including Augustus at the Battle of Actium. Aeneas is, Virgil writes, "without understanding . . . proud and happy . . . [at] the fame and glory of his children's children." But in the senseless slaughter that ends the poem, as Aeneas and the Trojans battle Turnus and the Italians, Virgil demonstrates that the only thing worse than not avenging the death of one's friends and family is, perhaps, avenging them. In this sense the poem is a profound plea for peace, a peace that Augustus would dedicate himself to pursuing.

The Horatian Odes Quintus Horatius Flaccus, known as Horace (65–8 BCE), was a close friend of Virgil. Impressed by Augustus' reforms, and probably moved by his patronage, Horace was won over to the emperor's cause, which he celebrated directly in two of his many odes, lyric poems of elaborate and irregular meter. Horace's odes imitated Greek precedents. The following lines open the fifth ode of Book 3 of the collected poems, known simply as the *Odes*:

> Jove [the Roman Zeus, also called Jupiter] rules
>   in heaven, his thunder shows;
> Henceforth Augustus earth shall own
> Her present god, now Briton foes
> And Persians bow before his throne.

The subject matter of the *Odes* ranges from these patriotic pronouncements to private incidents in the poet's own life, the joys of the countryside (Fig. **3.8**), the pleasures of wine, and so on. Horace's villa offered him an escape from the trials of daily life in Rome itself. But no Roman poet more gracefully harmonized the Greek reverence for beauty with the Roman concern with duty and obligation.

Ovid's *Art of Love* and *Metamorphoses* Augustus' support for poets did not extend to Publius Ovidius Naso, known as Ovid (43 BCE–17 CE). Ovid's talent was for love songs designed to satisfy the notoriously loose sexual mores of the Roman aristocrats, who lived in somewhat open disregard of Augustus and Livia's family-centered lifestyle. His *Ars Amatoria* (*Art of Love*) angered Augustus, as did some undisclosed indiscretion by Ovid. As punishment—probably more for the indiscretion than for the poem—Augustus permanently exiled him to the town of Tomis on the Black Sea, the remotest part of the Empire, famous for its wretched weather. The *Metamorphoses*, composed in the years just before his exile, is a collection of stories describing or revolving around one sort of supernatural change of shape or another, from the divine to the human, the animate to the inanimate, the human to the vegetal.

In the *Ars Amatoria*, the poet describes his desire for the fictional Corinna. Ovid outlines the kinds of place in Rome where one can meet women, from porticoes to gaming houses, from horse races to parties, and especially anywhere wine, that great banisher of inhibition, can be had. Women,

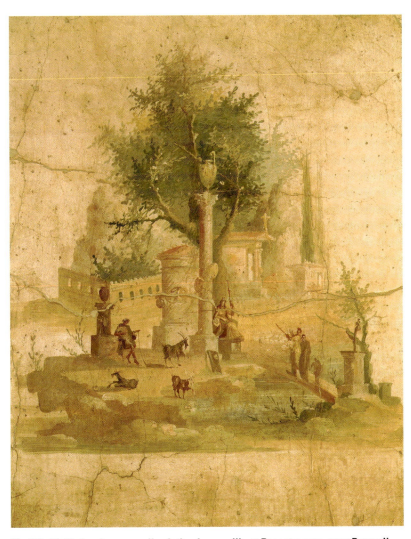

Fig. 3.8 *Idyllic Landscape*, wall painting from a villa at Boscotrecase, near Pompeii. **1st century BCE.** Museo Archeologico Nazionale, Naples. This landscape depicts the love of country life and the idealizing of nature that is characteristic of the Horatian *Odes*. It contrasts dramatically with urban life in Rome.

he says, love clandestine affairs as much as men; they simply do not chase after men, "as a mousetrap does not chase after mice." Become friends with the husband of a woman you desire, he advises. Lie to her—tell her that you only want to be her friend. Nevertheless, he says, "If you want a woman to love you, be a lovable man."

Ovid probably aspired to Virgil's fame, although he could admit, "My life is respectable, but my Muse is full of jesting." His earliest major work, the *Amores* (*Loves*), begins with many self-deprecating references to Virgil's epic, which begins with the famous phrase, "Arms and the man I sing":

> Arms, warfare, violence—I was winding up to produce
> A regular epic, with verse-form to match—
> Hexameters, naturally. But Cupid (they say) with a
>   snicker
> Lopped off one foot from each alternate line.
> "Nasty young brat," I told him, "who made *you* Inspector
>   of Metres?"

Nevertheless, Ovid uses dactylic hexameter for the *Metamorphoses* and stakes out an epic scope for the poem in its opening lines:

My intention is to tell of bodies changed
To different forms; the gods, who made the changes,
Will help me—or I hope so—with a poem
That runs from the world's beginning to our own days!

If the *Metamorphoses* is superficially more a collection of stories than an epic, few poems in any language have contributed so importantly to later literature. It is so complete in its survey of the best-known Classical myths, plus stories from Egypt, Persia, and Italy, that it remains a standard reference work. At the same time, it tells its stories in an utterly moving and memorable way. The story of Actaeon, for instance, is a cautionary tale about the power of the gods. Actaeon happens to see the virgin goddess Diana bathing one day when he is out hunting with his dogs. She turns him into a stag to prevent him from ever telling what he has seen. As his own dogs turn on him and savagely tear him apart, his friends call out for him, lamenting his absence from the kill. But he is all too present:

Well might he wish not to be there, but he was there,
    and well might he wish to see
And not to feel the cruel deeds of his dogs.

In the story of Narcissus, Echo falls in love with the beautiful youth Narcissus, but when Narcissus spurns her, she fades away. He in turn is doomed to fall in love with his own image reflected in a pool, according to Ovid, the spring at Clitumnus. So consumed, he finally dies beside the pool, his body transformed into the narcissus flower. In such stories, the duality of identity and change, Aristotle's definition of the essence of a thing, becomes deeply problematic. Ovid seems to deny that any human characteristic is essential, asserting that all is susceptible to change. To subsequent generations of readers, from Shakespeare to Freud, Ovid's versions of myths would raise the fundamental questions that lie at the heart of human identity and psychology.

Augustus and the City of Marble

Of all the problems facing Augustus when he assumed power, the most overwhelming was the infrastructure of Rome. The city was, quite simply, a mess. Seneca reacted by preaching Stoicism. He argued that Rome was what it was, and one should move on as best one can. Augustus reacted by calling for a series of public works, which would serve the people of Rome and, he well understood, himself. The grand civic improvements Augustus planned would be a kind of imperial propaganda, underscoring not only his power but also his care for the people in his role as *pater patriae*. Public works could—and indeed did—elicit the public's loyalty.

Rome had developed haphazardly, without any central plan, spilling down the seven hills it originally occupied into

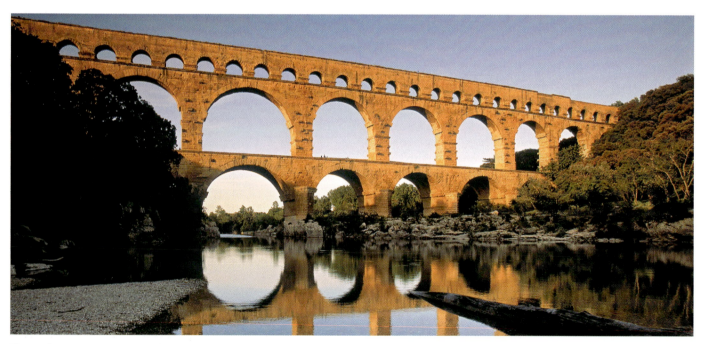

Fig. 3.9 Pont du Gard, near Nîmes, France. Late 1st century BCE–early 1st century CE. Height 180'. The Roman city of Nîmes received 8,000–12,000 gallons of water a day via this aqueduct.

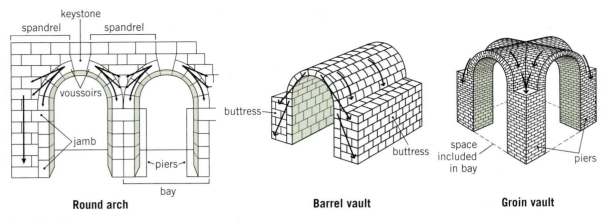

spandrel keystone spandrel

voussoirs

jamb

piers

bay

Round arch

buttress

buttress

Barrel vault

space included in bay

piers

Groin vault

Fig. 3.10 Arches.

👁 **Watch** an architectural simulation of the round arch on **MyArtsLab**

the valleys along the Tiber. By contrast, all the Empire's provincial capitals were conceived on a strict grid plan, with colonnaded main roads leading to an administrative center, and were adorned with public works such as baths, theaters, and triumphal arches. In comparison, Rome was pitiable. Housing conditions were dreadful, water was scarce, and food was in short supply. Because the city was confined by geography to a small area, space was at a premium.

Augustus could not do much about the housing situation, although he did build aqueducts to bring more water into the city. But most of all he implemented an ambitious building program designed to provide elegant public spaces where city dwellers could escape from their cramped apartments. He once claimed that he had restored 82 temples in one year. But if he could boast, "I found a city of brick, and left it a city of marble," that was largely because he had put a lot of marble veneer over brick walls. By the second century CE, the city would be one of the most beautiful in the world, but the beauty was only skin-deep. The housing situation that Augustus inherited had barely improved.

Public Works: The Aqueduct and the Arch Augustus inaugurated what amounted to an ongoing competition among the emperors to outdo their predecessors in the construction of public works and monuments. His ambitions are reflected in the work of the architect Vitruvius (flourished late first century BCE to early first century CE). A military engineer for Julius Caesar, under Augustus' patronage, Vitruvius wrote the ten-volume *On Architecture*. The only work of its kind to have survived from antiquity, it would become extremely influential more than 1,000 years later, when Renaissance artists became interested in classical design. In its large scale, the work matches its patron's architectural ambitions, dealing with town planning, building materials and construction methods, the construction of temples, the Classical orders, and the rules of proportion.

Vitruvius also wrote extensively about one of Rome's most pressing problems—how to satisfy the city's need for water. In fact, one of the most significant contributions of the Julio-Claudian dynasty, which extends from Augustus through Nero (r. 54–68 CE), was an enormous aqueduct, the Aqua Claudia. Such aqueducts depended on Roman ingenuity in perfecting the arch and vault so that river gorges could be successfully spanned to carry the pipes bringing water to a city miles away. The Aqua Claudia delivered water from 40 miles away into the very heart of the city, not so much for private use as for the fountains, pools, and public baths.

Aqueduct construction depended largely on the arch. While the arch was known to cultures such as the Mesopotamians, the Egyptians, and the Greeks, it was the Romans who perfected it, evidently learning its principles from the Etruscans but developing those principles further. The Pont du Gard, a beautiful Roman aqueduct near the city of Nîmes in southern France (Fig. 3.9), is a good example.

The Romans understood that much wider spans than the Etruscans had bridged could be achieved with the **round arch** (left, Fig. 3.10) than with post-and-lintel construction. The weight of the masonry above the arch is displaced to the supporting upright elements (**piers** or **jambs**). The arch is constructed with a supporting scaffolding that is formed with wedge-shaped blocks, called **voussoirs**, and capped with a large, wedge-shaped stone, called the **keystone**, the last element put in place. The space inside the arch is called a **bay**, and the wall areas between the arches of an **arcade** (a succession of arches, such as seen on the Pont du Gard) are called **spandrels**.

When a round arch is extended, it forms a **barrel vault** (middle, Fig. 3.10). To ensure that the downward pressure from the arches does not collapse the walls, a **buttress** support is often added. When two barrel vaults meet each other at a right angle, they form a **groin vault** (right, Fig. 3.10).

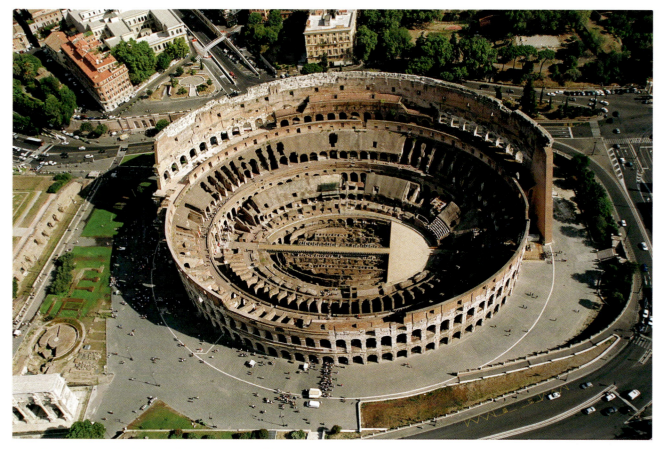

Fig. 3.11 Aerial view of Colosseum, Rome. Constructed 72–80 CE. The opening performance at the Colosseum in 80 CE lasted 100 days. During that time, 9,000 wild animals—lions, bears, snakes, boars, even elephants, imported from all over the Empire—were killed, and so were 2,000 gladiators.

✳ **Explore** an architectural panorama of the Colosseum on **MyArtsLab**

The Colosseum The interior corridors of the Colosseum in Rome make use of both barrel and groin vaulting. This huge arena (Fig. **3.11**) was built by Vespasian (r. 69–79 CE), the former commander in Palestine, who succeeded Nero when the latter's lavish lifestyle led to his ouster and subsequent suicide. Vespasian built the Colosseum across from Nero's ostentatious palace, known as the Golden House. He named it after the Colossus, a 120-foot-high statue of Nero as sun god that stood in front of it. The Colosseum formed a giant oval, 615 feet long, 510 feet wide, and 159 feet high, and audiences, estimated at 50,000, entered and exited through its 76 vaulted arcades in a matter of a few minutes.

These vaults were made possible by the use of concrete, which, like the arch itself, was known to the Mesopotamians, the Egyptians, and the Greeks, but perfected by the Romans, who evidently learned its principles from the Etruscans. Mixed with volcanic aggregate from nearby Naples and Pompeii, it set more quickly and was stronger than any building material yet known. The Colosseum's wooden floor, the *arena* (Latin for "sand," which covered the floor), lay over a maze of rooms and tunnels that housed the gladiators, athletes, and wild animals that entertained the masses. The top story of the building housed an awning system that could be

extended on an array of pulleys and ropes to shield part of the audience from the hot Roman sun. Each level employed a different architectural order: the Tuscan order on the ground floor, the Ionic on the second, and the Corinthian, the Romans' favorite, on the third. All the columns are engaged and purely decorative, serving no structural purpose. The facade thus moves from the heaviest and sturdiest elements at the base to the lightest, most decorative at the top, a logic that is both structurally and visually satisfying.

The Imperial Roman Forum The Colosseum stands at the eastern end of the *Forum Romanum,* or Roman Forum (Fig. **3.12**). This vast building project was among the most ambitious undertaken in Rome by the Five Good Emperors, under whose rule Rome thrived: Nerva (r. 96–98 CE), Trajan (r. 98–117 CE), Hadrian (r. 117–38 CE), Antoninus Pius (r. 138–61 CE), and Marcus Aurelius (r. 161–180 CE). The *Forum Romanum* was the chief public square of Rome, the center of Roman religious, ceremonial, political, and commercial life. Originally, a Roman forum was comparable to a Greek *agora,* a meeting place in the heart of the city. Gradually, the forum took on a symbolic function as well, becoming a symbol of imperial power that testified to the

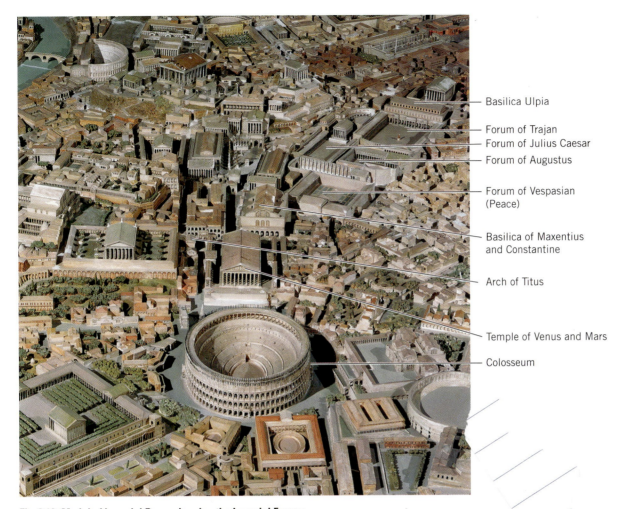

Basilica Ulpia

Forum of Trajan
Forum of Julius Caesar
Forum of Augustus

Forum of Vespasian
(Peace)

Basilica of Maxentius
and Constantine

Arch of Titus

Temple of Venus and Mars

Colosseum

Fig. 3.12 Model of Imperial Rome showing the Imperial Forums.

prosperity—and peace— bestowed by the emperor upon Rome's citizenry. Julius Caesar was the first to build a forum of his own, in 46 BCE, just to the north of the *Forum Romanum.* Augustus subsequently paved it over, restored its Temple of Venus, and proceeded to build his own forum with its Temple of Mars the Avenger. Thus began what amounted to a competition among successive emperors to outdo their predecessors by creating their own more spectacular forums. These imperial forums lined up north of and parallel to the great Roman Forum, which over the years was itself subjected to new construction. The result was an extremely densely built city center.

The last and largest of these forums was Trajan's. It sheltered the Column of Trajan (see Fig. 3.16), Trajan's Market, and the Basilica Ulpia (Fig. **3.13**) A **basilica** is a large rectangular building with a rounded extension, called an **apse**, at one or both ends, and easy access in and out. It was a general-purpose building that could be adapted to many uses. Designed by Trajan's favorite architect, the Greek Apollodorus of Damascus, the Basilica Ulpia was 200 feet wide and 400 feet long.

The stability and prosperity of the city was due, at least in part, to the fact that none of these emperors except Marcus

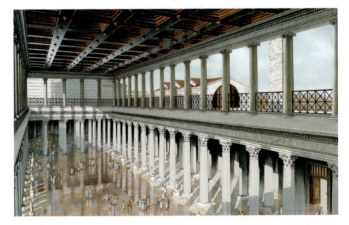

Fig. 3.13 Reconstruction drawing of the central hall, Basilica Ulpia, Forum of Trajan, Rome. 113 CE. Relatively plain and massive on the outside, the basilica is distinguished by its vast interior space, which would later serve as the model for some Christian churches.

 View the Closer Look on the Roman Forum on **MyArtsLab**

Aurelius had a son to whom he could pass on the Empire. Thus, each was handpicked by his predecessor from among the ablest men in the Senate. When, in 180 CE, Marcus

Aurelius' decadent and probably insane son Commodus (r. 180–92 CE) took control, the empire quickly learned that the transfer of power from father to son was not necessarily a good thing.

Triumphal Arches and Columns During Vespasian's reign, his son Titus defeated the Jews in Palestine, who were rebelling against Roman interference with their religious practices. Titus' army sacked the Second Temple of Jerusalem in 70 CE. To honor this victory and the death of Titus 11 years later, a memorial arch was constructed in Rome. Originally, the Arch of Titus was topped by a statue of a four-horse chariot and driver. Such arches, known as *triumphal arches* because triumphant armies marched through them, were composed of a simple barrel vault enclosed within a rectangle, and enlivened with sculpture and decorative engaged columns (Fig. **3.14**). They would deeply influence later architecture, especially the facades of Renaissance cathedrals. Hundreds of arches of similar form were built throughout the Roman Empire. Most were not technically triumphal, but, like all Roman monumental architecture, they were intended to symbolize Rome's political power and military might.

The Arch of Titus was constructed of concrete and faced with marble, its inside walls decorated with narrative reliefs. One of them shows Titus' soldiers marching with the treasures of the Second Temple in Jerusalem (Fig. **3.15**). In the foreground, the soldiers carry what some speculate might

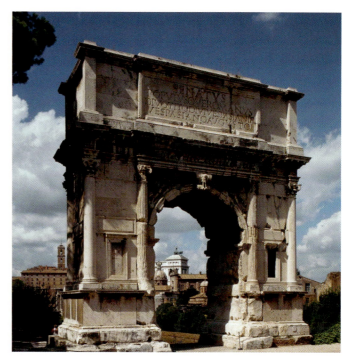

Fig. 3.14 Arch of Titus, Rome. ca. 81 CE. The inscription at the top of the arch, which reads "The Senate and the Roman people to the Deified Titus Vespasian Augustus, son of the Deified Vespasian," was chiseled deeply into the stone, so that it might catch the light, allowing it to be read from a great distance.

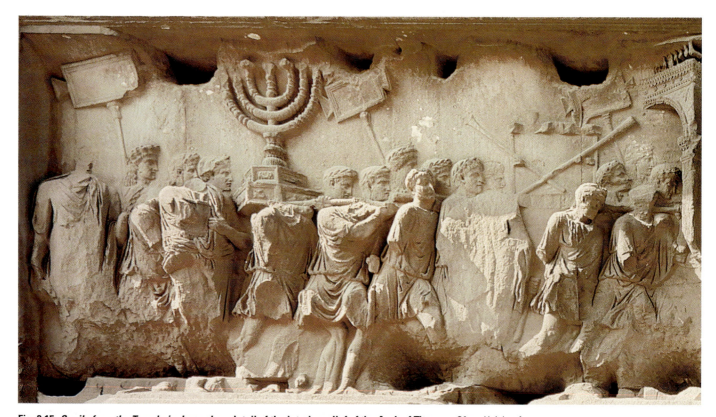

Fig. 3.15 *Spoils from the Temple in Jerusalem*, detail of the interior relief of the Arch of Titus. ca. 81 CE. Height of relief approx. 7'10". The figures in the relief are nearly life-size. The relief has been badly damaged, largely because in the Middle Ages, a Roman family used the arch as a fortress, constructing a second story in the vault. Holes for the floor beams appear at the top of the relief.

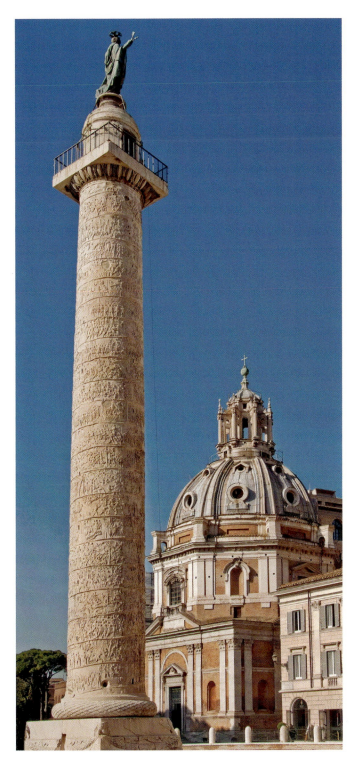

Fig. 3.16 Column of Trajan, Forum of Trajan, Rome. 106–113 CE. Marble, overall height with base 125′. Winding through the interior of the shaft is a staircase leading to a viewing platform at the top.

🔍 **View** the Closer Look for the Column of Trajan on **MyArtsLab**

be the golden Ark of the Covenant, and behind that a *menorah*, the sacred Jewish candelabrum, also made of gold. They bend under the weight of the gold and stride forward convincingly. The carving is extremely deep, with nearer figures and elements rendered with undercutting and in higher relief

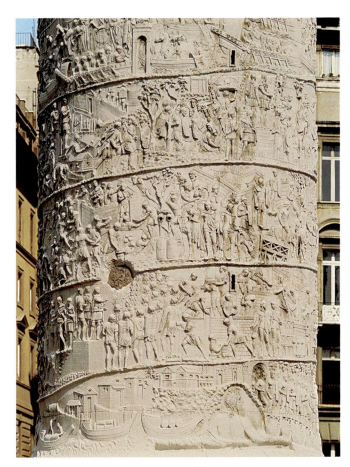

Fig. 3.17 Lower portion of the Column of Trajan, Forum of Trajan, Rome, 106–113 CE. To the left of the second band, Trajan addresses his troops. To the right of that scene, his troops build a fortification.

than more distant ones. This creates a sense of real space and, when light and shadow play over the sculptural relief, even a sense of movement.

Another type of monument favored by the Romans and with similar symbolic meaning—suggestive not only of power but also of virility—is the ceremonial column. Like the triumphal arch, it was a masonry and concrete platform for narrative reliefs. Two of the emperors who ruled during the era of the Five Good Emperors (96 CE–193 CE)—Trajan and Marcus Aurelius—built columns to celebrate their military victories. Trajan's Column, perhaps the most complete artistic statement of Rome's militaristic character, consists of a spiral of 150 separate scenes from his military campaign in Dacia, across the Danube River in what is now Hungary and Romania. If laid out end to end, the complete narrative would be 625 feet long (Figs. **3.16** and **3.17**). At the bottom of the column, the band is 36 inches wide; at the top it is 50 inches, so that the higher elements might be more readily visible. In order to eliminate shadow and increase the legibility of the whole, the carving is very low relief. At the bottom of the column, the story begins with Roman troops crossing the Danube on a pontoon bridge. A river god looks on with some interest. Battle scenes constitute less than a quarter of the entire narrative. Instead, we witness the Romans building fortifications, harvesting crops,

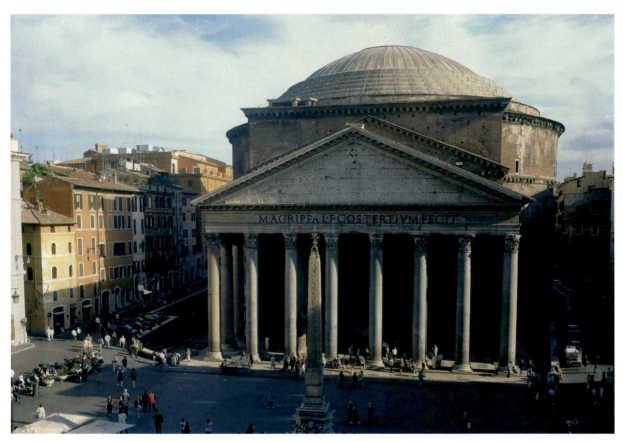

Fig. 3.18 The Pantheon, Rome. 118–125 CE. The Pantheon is an impressive feat of architectural engineering, and it would inspire architects for centuries to come. However, Hadrian humbly (and politically) refused to accept credit for it. He passed off the building as a "restoration" of a temple constructed on the same site by Augustus' closest friend, colleague, and son-in-law, Marcus Agrippa, in 27–25 BCE. Across the architrave (the bottom element in an entablature above the columns) of the facade is an inscription that serves both propagandistic and decorative purposes: "Marcus Agrippa, son of Lucius, three times consul, made this."

 View the Closer Look on the Pantheon on **MyArtsLab**

participating in religious rituals. All in all, the column's 2,500 figures are carrying out what Romans believed to be their destiny—they are bringing the fruits of civilization to the world.

The Pantheon Hadrian's Pantheon ranks with the Forum of Trajan as one of the most ambitious building projects undertaken by the Good Emperors. The Pantheon (from the Greek *pan*, "all," and *theoi*, "gods") is a temple to "all the gods," and sculptures representing all the Roman gods were set in recesses around its interior. The facade is a Roman temple, originally set on a high podium, with its eight massive Corinthian columns and deep portico, behind which are massive bronze doors (Fig. **3.18**). Photography presents little evidence of its monumental presence, elevated above its long forecourt (Fig. **3.19**). Today, both the forecourt and the elevation have disappeared beneath the streets of modern Rome. Figure 3.18 shows the Pantheon as it looks today.

The facade gives no hint of what lies beyond the doors. The interior of the Pantheon consists of a cylindrical space topped by a dome, the largest built in Europe before the twentieth century (Fig. **3.20**). The whole is a perfect hemisphere—the diameter of the rotunda is 144 feet, as is the height from floor to ceiling. The weight of the dome rests on eight massive

supports, each more than 20 feet thick. The dome itself is 20 feet thick at the bottom but narrows to only 6 feet thick at the *oculus*, the circular opening at the top. The *oculus* is 30 feet in diameter. Recessed panels, called **coffers**, further lighten the weight of the roof. The *oculus*, or "eye," admits light, which forms a round spotlight that moves around the building during

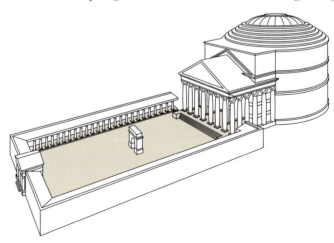

Fig. 3.19 The Pantheon, Rome. Schematic drawing showing the original forecourt.

Wall in the north of England to the Rock of Gibraltar in the south, across North Africa and Asia Minor, and encompassing all of Europe except what is now northern Germany and Scandinavia (see Map 3.1). Like Roman architecture, the Empire was built up of parts that were meant to harmonize in a unified whole, governed by rules of proportion and order. And if the monuments the Empire built to celebrate itself were grand, the Empire was grander still.

Pompeii

In 79 CE, during the rule of the Emperor Titus, the volcano Vesuvius erupted southeast of Naples, burying the seaside town of Pompeii in 13 feet of volcanic ash and rock. Its neighboring city Herculaneum was covered in 75 feet of a ground-hugging avalanche of hot ash that later solidified. Living in retirement nearby was Pliny the Elder, a commander in the Roman navy and the author of *The Natural History*, an encyclopedia of all contemporary knowledge. At the time of the eruption, his nephew Pliny the Younger (ca. 61–ca. 113 CE) was staying with him. This is his eyewitness account (**Reading 3.3**):

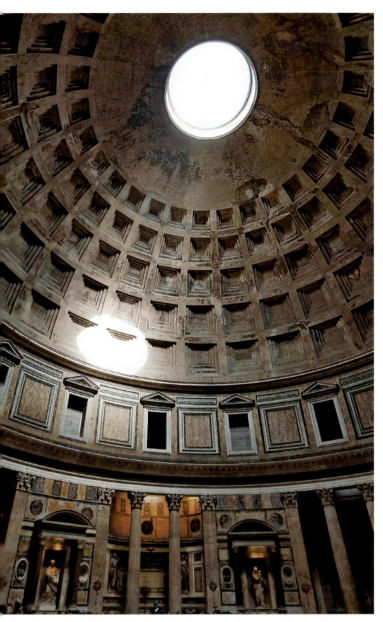

Fig. 3.20 Interior of the Pantheon, Rome. The sun's rays entering through the *oculus* form a spotlight on the Pantheon's interior, moving and changing intensity with the time of day.

the course of a day (it admits rain, as well, which is drained out through small openings in the floor). For the Romans, this light may well have symbolized Jupiter's ever-watchful eye cast over the affairs of state, illuminating the way.

In the vast openness of its interior, the Pantheon mirrors the cosmos, the vault of the heavens. Mesopotamian and Egyptian architecture had created monuments with exterior mass. Greek architecture was a kind of sculptural event, built up of parts that harmonized. But the Romans concentrated on sheer size, including the vastness of interior space. Like the Basilica Ulpia (see Fig. 3.13) in the Forum of Trajan, the Pantheon is concerned primarily with realizing a single, whole, uninterrupted interior space.

In this sense, the Pantheon mirrors the Empire. It too was a single, uninterrupted space, stretching from Hadrian's

READING 3.3

from *Letters of Pliny the Younger*

On 24 August, in the early afternoon, my mother drew his [Pliny the Elder's] attention to a cloud of unusual size and appearance. He had been out in the sun, had taken a cold bath, and lunched while lying down, and was then working at his books. He called for his shoes and climbed up to a place which would give him the best view of the phenomenon. It was not clear at that distance from which mountain the cloud was rising (it was afterwards known to be Vesuvius); its general appearance can best be expressed as being like an umbrella pine, for it rose to a great height on a sort of trunk and then split off into branches, I imagine because it was thrust upwards by the first blast and then left unsupported as the pressure subsided, or else it was borne down by its own weight so that it spread out and gradually dispersed. . . .

They debated whether to stay indoors or take their chance in the open, for the buildings were now shaking with violent shocks, and seemed to be swaying to and fro as if they were torn from their foundations. Outside, on the other hand, there was the danger of falling pumice-stones, even though these were light and porous; however, after comparing the risks they chose the latter. In my uncle's case one reason outweighed the other, but for the others it was a choice of fears. As a protection against falling objects they put pillows on their heads tied down with cloths. . . .

We also saw the sea sucked away and apparently forced back by the earthquake: at any rate it receded from the shore so that quantities of sea creatures were left stranded on dry sand. On the landward side a fearful black cloud was rent by forked and quivering bursts of flame, and parted to reveal great tongues of fire, like flashes of lightning magnified in size. . . .

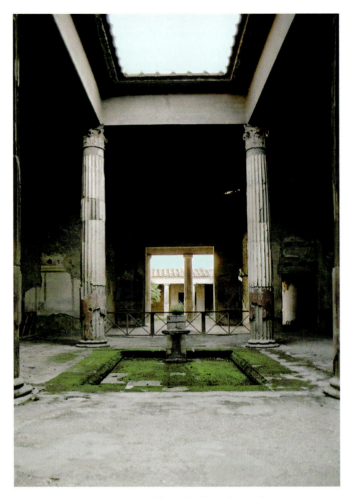

Fig. 3.21 Atrium, House of the Silver Wedding, Pompeii. 1st century BCE. Erich Lessing/akg-images. This view looks through the atrium to the main reception area and the peristyle court. The house gets its name from the silver wedding anniversary of Italy's King Humbert and his queen, Margaret of Savoy, in 1893, the year it was excavated. They actively supported archeological fieldwork at Pompeii, which began in the mid century.

> You could hear the shrieks of women, the wailing of infants, and the shouting of men; some were calling their parents, others their children or their wives, trying to recognize them by their voices. People bewailed their own fate or that of their relatives, and there were some who prayed for death in their terror of dying. Many besought the aid of the gods, but still more imagined there were no gods left, and that the universe was plunged into eternal darkness for evermore. . . .

Pliny the Elder, interested in what was happening, made his way toward Vesuvius, where he died, suffocated by the poisonous fumes. Pliny the Younger, together with his mother, survived. Of the 20,000 inhabitants of Pompeii, 2,000 died, mostly slaves and the poor left behind by the rich who escaped the city after early warning shocks.

Much of what we know today about everyday Roman life is the direct result of the Vesuvius eruption. Those who survived left their homes in a hurry, and were unable to recover

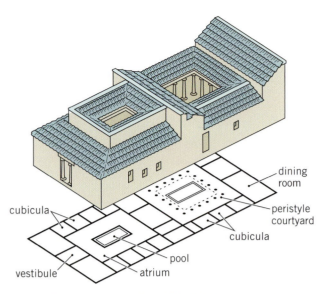

Fig. 3.22 Plan of the House of the Silver Wedding, Pompeii. 1st century BCE.

anything they left behind. Buried under the ashes were not only homes and buildings but also food and paintings, furniture and garden statuary, even pornography and graffiti. The latter include the expected—"Successus was here," "Marcus loves Spendusa"—but also the unexpected and perceptive—"I am amazed, O wall, that you have not collapsed and fallen, since you must bear the tedious stupidities of so many scrawlers." When Pompeii was excavated, beginning in the eighteenth century, many of the homes and artifacts were found to be relatively well preserved. The hardened lava and ash had protected them from the ravages of time. But eighteenth-century excavators also discovered something unexpected. By filling the hollows where the bodies of those caught in the eruption had decomposed, they captured images of horrific death.

Domestic Architecture: The *Domus* Although by no means the most prosperous town in Roman Italy, Pompeii was something of a resort, and, together with villas from other nearby towns, the surviving architecture gives us a good sense of the Roman *domus*—the townhouse of the wealthier class of citizen. The *domus* was oriented to the street along a central axis that extended from the front entrance to the rear of the house. The House of the Silver Wedding at Pompeii is typical in its design (Figs. **3.21** and **3.22**). An **atrium**, a large space with a shallow pool for catching rainwater below its open roof, extends directly behind the vestibule. The atrium was the symbolic heart of the house: the location for the *imagines*, the wax masks from which portrait busts were later made (see Fig. 3.5), and the main reception area. *Imagines* were also housed in the reception rooms just off the main one, which in turn opens onto a central **peristyle courtyard**, surrounded by a colonnaded walkway. The dining room faces into the courtyard, as do a number of *cubicula*, small general-purpose rooms often used for sleeping quarters. At the back of the house, facing into the courtyard, is a hall furnished with seats for discussion. Servants probably lived upstairs at the rear of the house.

The *domus* was a measure of a Roman's social standing, as the vast majority lived in apartment blocks or *insulae*. The house itself was designed to underscore the owner's reputation. Each morning, the front door was opened and left open. Gradually, the atrium would fill with clients—remember, the head of a Roman household was patron to many—who came to show their respect in a ritual known as the *salutatio*. Passersby could look in to see the crowded atrium, and the patron himself was generally seated in the open area between the atrium and the peristyle courtyard, silhouetted by the light from the peristyle court behind. Surrounded by the busts of his ancestors, the symbol of his social position and prestige, he watched over all who entrusted themselves to his patronage.

At the center of the Roman *domus* was the garden of the peristyle courtyard, with a fountain or pond in the middle. Thanks to the long-term research of the archeologist Wilhelmina Jashemski, we know a great deal about these courtyard gardens. At the House of G. Polybius in Pompeii, excavators carefully removed ash down to the level of the soil on the summer day of the eruption in 79 CE, when the garden would have been in full bloom. They were able to collect pollen, seeds, and other evidence, including root systems (obtained by pouring plaster into the surviving cavities), and thus determine what plants and trees were cultivated in it. Polybius' garden was lined, at one end, with lemon trees in pots, which were apparently trained and pruned to cover the wall in an *espalier*—a geometric trellis. Cherry, pear, and fig trees filled the rest of the space. Gardens at other homes suggest that most were planted with nut- and fruit-bearing trees, including olive, which would provide the family with a summer harvest. Vegetable gardens are sometimes found at the rear of the *domus*, a source of more fresh produce.

The garden also provided visual pleasure for the family. In the relatively temperate Roman climate, the garden was in bloom for almost three-quarters of the year. It was the focus of many rooms in the *domus*, which opened onto the garden. And it was evidently a symbol for the fertility, fecundity, and plenty of the household itself, for many a Roman garden was decorated with statuary referencing the cult of Dionysus.

Wall Painting Mosaics decorated many floors of the *domus*, and paintings adorned the walls of the atrium, the hall, the dining room, and other reception rooms throughout the villa. Artists worked with pigments in a solution of lime and soap, sometimes mixed with a little wax, polished with a special metal or glass, and then buffed with a cloth. Even the *cubicula* bedrooms were richly painted.

Writing in the second century CE, the satirist and rhetorician Lucian (ca. 120–after 180 CE) describes what he takes to be the perfect house—"lavish, but only in such degree as would suffice a modest and beautiful woman to set off her beauty." He continues, describing the wall paintings:

> The . . . decoration—the frescoes on the walls, the beauty of their colors, and the beauty, exactitude and truth of each detail—might well be compared with the face of spring and with a flowery field, except that those things fade and wither and change and cast their beauty, while this is spring eternal, field unfading, bloom undying.

Just outside Rome, at the villa of Livia at Primaporta, a wall painting depicting a garden full of fresh fruit, songbirds, and flowers reflects this sensibility (Fig. **3.23**). It is rendered as if it were an extension of the room itself, as if Livia and

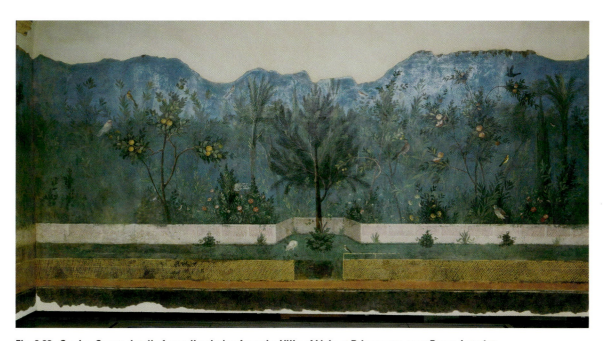

Fig. 3.23 *Garden Scene*, detail of a wall painting from the Villa of Livia at Primaporta, near Rome. Late 1st century BCE. Museo Nazionale Romano, Rome. The artist created a sense of depth by setting a wall behind a fence with its open gate.

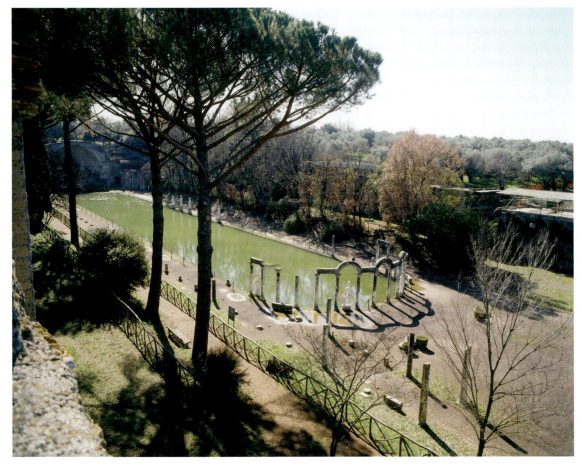

Fig. 3.24 The Canal (reflecting pool) at Hadrian's Villa, Tivoli. ca. 125–135 CE. At the far end of the pool is an outdoor dining room, with concrete benches. These would have been covered with cushions for comfort.

Augustus and their visitors could, at any time, step through the wall into their "undying" garden. Thus, although naturalistically rendered, it is an idealistic representation.

Hadrian's Villa at Tivoli If the domus was the urban townhouse of Rome's wealthier class of citizen, the villa, or country residence, was often far more luxurious, and among the most luxurious ever constructed was the emperor Hadrian's at Tivoli, some 18 miles east of Rome at the edge of the Sabine Hills. Situated in over 300 acres on a slope overlooking the surrounding countryside, it was a masterful blending of inventive buildings, waterworks, and gardens. At the turning of almost every corner, a surprising new vista reveals itself. The buildings themselves were copies of Hadrian's favorite places throughout the entire Empire, including the Stoa from the Athenian agora (see Fig. 2.2 in Chapter 2), the Ptolemaic capital of Egypt, Alexandria, and the Academia in Athens, where Plato conversed with his students in the shade of an olive grove. One of the complex's most attractive features is a long reflecting pool, called the Canal (Fig. 3.24). It was surrounded by a colonnade with alternating arched and linteled entablatures. Between the columns, Hadrian set copies of the most famous sculptures of ancient Greece, including a marble copy of the *Discobolus*, or *Discus Thrower*, originally cast in bronze by the Greek sculptor Myron in the middle of the fifth century BCE. Hadrian was so enamored of Greek sculpture that he had the caryatids from the Erechtheion on the Athenian Acropolis (see Fig. 2.26 in Chapter 2) copied for the villa. In its architectural and sculptural scope, the villa embodies the imperial reach of Rome itself.

CHINA

How did Daoism, Confucianism, and Legalism impact early Chinese culture?

The North China plain lies in the large, fertile valley of the Yellow River (Map 3.2). Around 7000 BCE, when the valley's climate was much milder and the land more forested than it is today, the peoples inhabiting this region began to cultivate the soil, growing primarily millet. Archeologists recognize at least three separate cultural groups in this region during this period, distinguished by their different pottery styles and works in jade. As Neolithic tribal people, they used stone tools, and although they domesticated

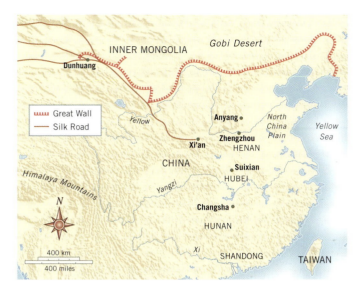

Map 3.2 Map of China, ca. 1600 CE.

animals very early on, they maintained the shamanistic practices of their hunter-gatherer heritage. Later inhabitants of this region would call this area the "Central Plain" because they believed it was the center of their country. During the ensuing millennia, Chinese culture in the Central Plain coalesced in ways that parallel developments in the Middle East and Greece during the same period, as China transformed itself from an agricultural society into a more urban-centered state.

By the third century BCE, at about the same time that Rome began establishing its imperial authority over the Mediterranean world, the government of China was sufficiently unified that it could build a Great Wall (Fig. **3.25**) across the hills north of the Central Plain to protect the realm from the intruding Central Asians who lived beyond its northern borders. Some sections of the wall were already in place, built in previous centuries to protect local areas. These were rebuilt and connected to define a frontier stretching some 1,500 miles from northeast to northwest China. New roads and canal systems were built linking the entire nation, a large salaried bureaucracy was established, and a new imperial government headed by an emperor collected taxes, codified the law, and exerted control over a domain of formerly rival territories. Unification—first achieved here by the Qin dynasty—has remained a preeminent problem throughout China's long history.

Early Chinese Culture

Very few of the built edifices of ancient Chinese civilization have been found. We know that by the middle of the second millennium BCE, Chinese leaders ruled from large capitals, rivaling those in the West in their size and splendor. Beneath present-day Zhengzhou, for instance, lies an early metropolitan center with massive earthen walls. Stone was scarce in this area, but abundant forests made wood plentiful, so it was used to build cities. As impressive as they were, cities built of wood were vulnerable to fire and military

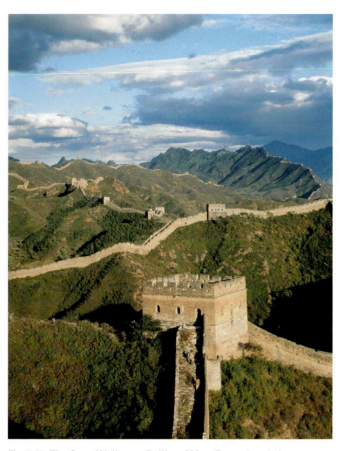

Fig. 3.25 The Great Wall, near Beijing, China. Begun late 3rd century BCE. Length approx. 4,100 miles, average height 25′. In the third century BCE, Qin Shihuangdi, the first emperor of China, ordered his army to reconstruct, link, and augment walls on the northern frontier of China in order to form a continuous barrier protecting his young country from northern peoples.

attack, and no sign of them remains. Nevertheless, we know a fair amount about early Chinese culture from the remains of its written language and the tombs of its rulers. Even the most ancient Chinese writing—found on oracle bones and ceremonial bronze vessels—is closely related to modern Chinese. And archeologists discovered that royal Chinese tombs, like Egyptian burial sites, contain furnishings, implements, luxury goods, and clothing that—together with the written record—give us a remarkably vivid picture of ancient China.

The CONTINUING PRESENCE
of the PAST

See Cai Guo-Qiang, *Project to Extend the Great Wall of China by 10,000 Meters: Project for Extraterrestrials No. 10,* 1993, at **MyArtsLab**

The Shang Dynasty (ca. 1700–1045 BCE) Chinese records say that King Tang established the Shang dynasty. The Shang state was a linked collection of villages, stretching across the plains of the lower Yellow River Valley. But it was not a contiguous state with distinct borders; other villages separated some of the Shang villages from one another, and were frequently at war with the Shang. The royal family surrounded itself with shamans, who soon developed into a kind of nobility, and, in time, walled urban centers formed around the nobles' palaces or temples. The proliferation of bronze vessels, finely carved jades, and luxury goods produced for the Shang elite suggests that well-organized centers of craft production were located nearby. The Shang nobility organized itself into armies—surviving inscriptions describe forces as large as 13,000 men—that controlled the countryside and protected the king.

The first classic of Chinese literature, *The Book of Changes*, or *Yi Jing*, compiled later from ideas that developed in the Shang era, is a guide to interpreting the workings of the universe. A person seeking to understand some aspect of his or her life or situation poses a question and tosses a set of straws or coins. The arrangement they make when they fall leads to one of 64 readings (or hexagrams) in the *Yi Jing*. (Fu Xi, the culture-hero who invented writing, is also said to have invented the eight trigrams that combine in pairs to form the 64 hexagrams.) Each hexagram describes the circumstances of the specific moment, which is, as the title suggests, always a moment of transition, a movement from one set of circumstances to the next. The *Yi Jing* prescribes certain behaviors appropriate to the moment. Thus, it is a book of wisdom.

This wisdom is based on a simple principle—that order derives from balance, a concept the Chinese share with the ancient Egyptians. The Chinese believe that over time, through a series of changes, all things work toward a condition of balance. Thus, when things are out of balance, diviners might reliably predict the future by understanding that the universe tends to right itself. For example, the eleventh hexagram, entitled *T'ai*, or "Peace," indicated the unification of heaven and earth. The image reads:

> Heaven and earth unite: the image
>   of PEACE.
> Thus the ruler
> Divides and completes the course of
>   heaven and earth,
> And so aids the people.

In fact, according to the Shang rulers, "the foundation of the universe" is based on the marriage of *Qian* (at once heaven and the creative male principle) and *Kun* (the earth, or the receptive female principle), symbolized by the Chinese symbol of yin yang (Fig. **3.26**). *Yin* is soft, dark, moist, and cool; *yang* is hard, bright, dry, and warm. The two combine to create the endless cycles of change, from night to day, across the four seasons of the year. They balance the five elements (wood, fire, earth, metal, and water) and the five powers of creation (cold, heat, dryness, moisture, and wind). The yin yang sign, then, is a symbol of harmonious integration, the perpetual interplay and mutual relation among all things. And note that each

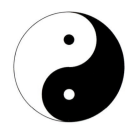

Fig. 3.26 *Yin yang* symbol.

side contains a small circle of the same value as its opposite—neither side can exist without the other.

The interlocking of opposites illustrated by the *yin yang* motif is also present in the greatest artistic achievement of the Shang, their bronze casting. In order to cast bronze, a negative shape must be perfected first, into which the molten metal is then poured to make a positive shape. Through the manufacture of ritual vessels, such as the *guang* or wine vessel illustrated here (Fig. **3.27**), the Shang developed an extremely sophisticated bronze-casting technology, as advanced as any ever used. Made for offerings of food, water, and wine during ceremonies of ancestor worship, these bronze vessels were kept in the ancestral hall and brought out for banquets. Like formal dinnerware, each type of vessel had a specific shape and purpose.

The conduct of the ancestral rites was the most solemn duty of a family head, with explicit religious and political significance. While the vessel shapes originally derived from the shapes of Neolithic pottery, in bronze they gradually became decorated with fantastic, supernatural creatures, especially

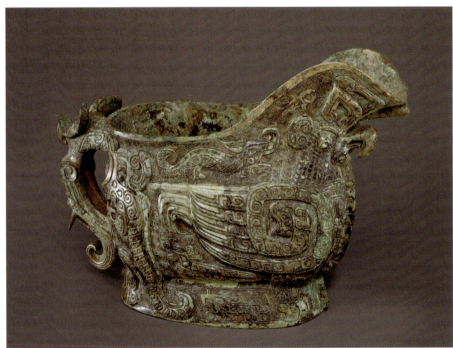

Fig. 3.27 Spouted Ritual Wine Vessel (*guang*). Shang dynasty, early Anyang period, 13th century BCE. Bronze, height 8½". The Metropolitan Museum of Art, New York. Rogers Fund, 1943. (43.25.4). Coiled serpents emerging from the wings and roaring tiger-dragons decorate the sides. Serving as a handle is a horned bird that is transformed into a dragon-serpent.

dragons. For the Shang, the bronzes came to symbolize political power and authority. Leaders made gifts of bronze as tokens of political patronage, and strict rules governed the number of bronzes a family might possess according to rank.

The Zhou Dynasty (1027–256 BCE) The Shang believed that their leaders were the sole conduit to the heavenly ancestors. However, in 1027 BCE, a rebel tribe known as the Zhou overthrew the Shang dynasty, claiming that the Shang had lost the Mandate of Heaven—that is, the right to rule as granted by the gods—by not ruling virtuously. The Zhou asserted that the legitimacy of a ruler derived from divine approval, and that the Shang had lost this favor because of their decadent extravagances. Even so, the Zhou took measures to intermarry with the elite whom they had overthrown, and took pains to conserve and restore what they admired of Shang culture. In fact, both the *Book of Changes* and the *yin yang* symbol were originated by the Shang but codified and written down by the Zhou.

The Zhou ushered in an era of cultural refinement and philosophical accomplishment. One example is the oldest collection of Chinese poetry, the *Book of Songs* (*Shi jing*), still taught in Chinese schools today. According to tradition, government officials were sent into the countryside to record the lyrics of songs that expressed the feelings of the people. The collection that survives, first compiled by the Zhou, consists of 305 poems from between the eleventh and seventh centuries BCE. The poems address almost every aspect of life. There are love poems, songs celebrating the king's rule, sacrificial hymns, and folk songs. Descriptions of nature abound—over 100 kinds of plant are mentioned, as well as 90 kinds of animal and insect. Marriage practices, family life, clothing, and food are all subjects of poems. One of the oldest celebrates the harvest as an expression of the family's harmony with nature, the symbol that the family's ancestors are part of the same natural cycle of life and death, planting and harvest, as the universe as a whole (**Reading 3.4**):

READING 3.4

from the *Book of Songs*

Abundant is the year, with much millet, much rice;
But we have tall granaries,
To hold myriads, many myriads and millions of grain.
We make wine, make sweet liquor,
We offer it to ancestor, to ancestress,
We use it to fulfil all the rites,
To bring down blessings upon each and all.

The songs in the *Shi jing* are contemporary with the poems that make up the *Dao de Jing* (*The Way of Life*), the primary philosophical treatise, written in verse, of Daoism, the Chinese mystical school of thought. The *Dao* ("the way") is deeply embedded in nature, and to attain it, the individual must practice the art of "not-doing." (It is said that those who speak about the Dao do not know of it, and those who know about the Dao do not speak of it.) The book, probably composed in the third century BCE, is traditionally ascribed to Lao Tzu ("the Old One"), who lived during the sixth century BCE. In essence, it argues for a unifying principle in all nature, the interchangeability of energy and matter, a principle the Chinese call *qi*. The *qi* can be understood only by those who live in total simplicity, and to this end the Daoist engages in strict dietary practices, breathing exercises, and meditation. In considering such images as the one expressed in the following poem, the first in the volume, the Daoist finds his or her way to enlightenment (**Reading 3.5**):

READING 3.5

from the *Tao Te Ching (or Dao de Jing)*

There are ways but the Way is uncharted;
There are names but not nature in words:
Nameless indeed is the source of creation
But things have a mother and she has a name.

The secret waits for the insight
Of eyes unclouded by longing;
Those who are bound by desire
See only the outward container.

These two come paired but distinct
By their names.
Of all things profound,
Say that their pairing is deepest,
The gate to the root of the world.

The final stanza seems to be a direct reference to the principle of *yin yang*, itself a symbol of the *qi*. But the chief argument here, and the outlook of Daoism as a whole, is that enlightenment lies neither in the visible world nor in language, although to find the "way" one must, paradoxically, pass through or use both. Daoism thus represents a spiritual desire to transcend the material world.

If Daoism sought to leave the world behind, another great canon of teachings developed during the Zhou dynasty sought to define the proper way to behave *in* the world. The Zhou controlled most of China until internal feuding and a *coup d'état* forced them to move their capital east in 771 BCE. From that point on, the power of the Zhou rulers gradually declined. For 515 years, until the final collapse of the Zhou in 256 BCE, China was subjected to ever greater political turmoil as warring political factions, with at best only nominal allegiance to the emperor, struggled for power. Reacting to this state of affairs was the man many consider China's greatest philosopher and teacher, Kong Fuzi, or, as he is known in the West, Confucius.

Confucius was born to aristocratic parents in the province of Shandong in 551 BCE, the year before Pisistratus came to power in Athens. By his early twenties, Confucius had begun to teach a way of life, now referred to as Confucianism, based on self-discipline and proper relations among people. If each individual led a virtuous life, then the family would live in harmony. If the family lived in harmony, then the village would follow its moral leadership. If the village exercised proper behavior toward its neighbor villages, then the country would live in peace and thrive.

Traditional Chinese values—values that Confucius believed had once guided the Zhou, such as self-control, propriety, reverence for one's elders, and virtuous behavior—lie at the core of this system. Tradition has it that Confucius compiled and edited the *Book of Changes*, the *Book of Songs* (which he edited down to 305 verses), and four other "classic" Chinese texts: the *Book of Documents*, containing speeches and pronouncements of historical rulers; the *Book of Rites*, which is essentially a code of conduct; the *Spring and Autumn Annals*, a history of China up to the fifth century BCE; and a lost treatise on music.

Confucius particularly valued the *Book of Songs*. "My little ones," he told his followers, "why don't you study the *Songs*? Poetry will exalt you, make you observant, enable you to mix with others, provide an outlet for your vexations; you learn from it immediately to serve your parents and ultimately to serve your prince. It also provides wide acquaintance with the names of birds, beasts, and plants."

After his death, in 479 BCE, Confucius' followers transcribed their conversations with him in a book known in English as the *Analects*. Where the *Dao de Jing* is a spiritual work, the *Analects* is a practical one. At the heart of Confucius' teaching is the principle of *li*—propriety in the conduct of the rites of ancestor worship. The courtesy and dignity required when performing the rites lead to the second principle, *ren*, or benevolent compassion and fellow feeling, the ideal relationship that should exist among all people. Based on respect for oneself, *ren* extends this respect to all others, manifesting itself as charity, courtesy, and, above all, justice. *De*, or virtue, is the power of moral example that an individual, especially a ruler, can exert through a life dedicated to the exercise of *li* and *ren*. Finally, *wen*, or culture, will result. Poetry, music, painting, and the other arts will all reveal an inherent order and harmony reflecting the inherent order and harmony of the state. Like an excellent leader, brilliance in the arts illuminates virtue. The Chinese moral order, like that of the Greeks (see Chapter 2), depended not upon divine decree or authority, but instead upon the people's own right actions. Its emphasis on respect for age, authority, and morality made Confucianism extremely popular among Chinese leaders and the artists they patronized. It embraced the emperor, the state, and the family in a single ethical system with a hierarchy that was believed to mirror the structure of the cosmos. By the early second century BCE, the Han dynasty (206 BCE–220 CE discussed later in this chapter), adopted Confucianism as the Chinese state religion, and a thorough knowledge of the Confucian classics was subsequently required of any politically ambitious person.

Imperial China

Whereas Rome's empire derived from outward expansion, China's empire arose from consolidation at the center. From about the time of Confucius onward, seven states vied for control. They mobilized armies to battle one another; iron weapons replaced bronze; they organized bureaucracies and established legal systems; merchants gained political power; and a "hundred schools of thought" flowered.

The Qin Dynasty (221–206 BCE): Organization and Control
This period of warring states culminated when the western state Qin (the origin of our name for China) conquered the other states and unified them under the Qin Empire in 221 BCE. Under the leadership of Qin Shihuangdi (r. 221–210 BCE), who declared himself "First Emperor," the Qin worked very quickly to achieve a stable society. To discourage nomadic invaders from the north, they built the Great Wall of China (see Fig. 3.25). The wall was constructed by soldiers, augmented by criminals, civil servants who found themselves in disfavor, and conscripts from across the countryside. Every family was required to provide one able-bodied adult male to work on the wall each year. It was made of rammed earth, reinforced by continuous horizontal courses of brushwood, and faced with stone. Watchtowers were built at high points, and military barracks were constructed in the valleys below. At the same time, the Chinese constructed nearly 4,350 miles of road, linking even the farthest reaches of the country to the Central Plain. By the end of the second century CE, China had some 22,000 miles of road serving a country of nearly 1.5 million square miles.

Such massive undertakings could only have been accomplished by an administrative bureaucracy of extraordinary organizational skill. Indeed, in the 15 years that the Qin ruled China, the written language was standardized, a uniform coinage was introduced, all wagon axles were required to be the same width so that they would uniformly fit in the existing ruts on the Chinese roads (thus accommodating trade and travel), a system of weights and measures was introduced, and the country was divided into the administrative and bureaucratic provinces much as they exist to the present day.

Perhaps nothing tells us more about Qin organization and control than the tomb of its first emperor, Qin Shihuangdi (see *Closer Look*, pages 108–109). When he died, battalions of life-size earthenware guards in military formation were buried in pits beside his tomb. (More than 8,000 have been excavated so far.) Like the Great Wall, this monumental undertaking required an enormous workforce, and we know that the Qin enlisted huge numbers of workers in this and its other projects.

To maintain control, in fact, the Qin suppressed free speech, persecuted scholars, burned classical texts, and otherwise exerted absolute power. They based their thinking on the writings of Han Feizi, who had died in 233 BCE, 12 years before the Qin took power. Orthodox Confucianism had been codified by Meng-zi, known as Mencius (ca. 370–300 BCE), an itinerant philosopher and sage who argued for the innate goodness of the individual. He believed that bad character was a result of society's inability to provide a positive, cultivating atmosphere in which individuals might realize their capacity for goodness. Han Feizi, on the other hand, argued that human beings were inherently evil and innately selfish (exactly the opposite of Mencius' point of view). **Legalism**, as Han Feizi's philosophy came to be called, required that the state exercise its power over the individual, because no agency other than the state could instill enough fear in the individual to elicit proper conduct. The Qin Legalist bureaucracy, coupled with an oppressive tax structure imposed to pay for their massive civil projects, soon led to rebellion, and after only 15 years in power, the Qin collapsed.

The Han Dynasty (206 BCE–220 CE): The Flowering of Culture

In place of the Qin, the Han dynasty came to power, inaugurating more than 400 years of intellectual and cultural growth. The Han emperors installed Confucianism as the official state philosophy and established an academy to train civil servants. Where the Qin had disenfranchised scholars, the Han honored them, even going so far as to give them an essential role in governing the country.

Under Emperor Wu, Chinese literary arts flourished. In 120 BCE, he established the *Yue fu*, the so-called Music Bureau, which would come to employ some 829 people charged with collecting the songs of the common people. The folk style of the *yuefu* songs was widely imitated by court poets during the Han and throughout the history of Chinese poetry. The lines are of uneven length, although often of five characters, and emphasize the joys and vicissitudes of daily life. A case in point is a poem by Liu Xijun, a Chinese princess who, around 110 BCE, was married for political reasons to the chief of the Wusun, a band of nomads who lived on the steppes of northwest China. Her husband, as it turned out when she arrived, was old and decrepit, spoke almost no Chinese, and by and large had nothing to do with her, seeing her every six months or so. This is her "Lament" (**Reading 3.6**):

READING 3.6

Liu Xijun, "Lament"

My family married me off
to the King of the Wusun.
and I live in an alien land
a million miles from nowhere.
My house is a tent,
My walls are of felt.
Raw flesh is all I eat,
with horse milk to drink.
I always think of home
and my heart stings,
O to be a yellow snow-goose
floating home again!

The poem's last two lines—what might be called the flight of Liu Xijun's imagination—are typical of Chinese poetry, where time and again the tragic circumstances of life are overcome through an image of almost transcendent natural beauty.

As Liu Xijun's poem suggests, women poets and scholars were common—and respected—during the Han dynasty. But as the circumstances surrounding Liu Xijun's poem also suggest, women did not enjoy great power in society. The traditional Chinese family was organized around basic Confucian principles: Elder family members were wiser, and therefore superior to the younger, and males were superior to females. Thus, while a grandmother might hold sway over her grandson, a wife owed unquestioning obedience to her husband. The unenviable plight of women is the subject of a poem by Fu Xuan, a male poet of the late Han dynasty who apparently was one of the most prolific poets of his day, although only 63 of his poems survive (**Reading 3.7**):

READING 3.7

Fu Xuan, "To Be a Woman"

It is bitter to be a woman,
the cheapest thing on earth.
A boy stands commanding in the doorway
like a god descended from the sky.
His heart hazards the four seas,
thousands of miles of wind and dust,
but no one laughs when a girl is born.
The family doesn't cherish her.
When she's a woman she hides in back rooms,
scared to look a man in the face.
They cry when she leaves to marry—
a brief rain, then mere clouds.
Head bowed, she tries to compose her face,
her white teeth stabbing red lips.
She bows and kneels endlessly,
even before concubines and servants.
If their love is strong as two stars
she is like a sunflower in the sun,
but when their hearts are water and fire
a hundred evils descend on her.
The years change her jade face
and her lord will find new lovers.
They who were close like body and shadow
will be remote as Chinese and Mongols.
Sometimes even Chinese and Mongols meet
but they'll be far as polar stars.

The poem is notable for the acuity and intensity of its imagery—her "white teeth stabbing red lips," the description of a close relationship as "like body and shadow," and, in the last lines, the estrangement of their relationship to a point as far apart as "polar stars," farther apart even than the Chinese and Mongols. (And who, one must ask, is more like the barbarian hordes, the male or the female?)

What we know about the domestic setting of Han dynasty society we can gather mostly from surviving poetic images describing everyday life in the home, but our understanding of domestic architecture derives from ceramic models. A model of a house found in a tomb, presumably provided for the use of the departed in the afterlife, is four stories high and

CLOSER LOOK

One day in 1974, peasants digging a well on the flat plain 1,300 yards east of the huge Qin dynasty burial mound of the Emperor Qin Shihuangdi in the northern Chinese province of Shaanxi unearthed parts of a life-size clay soldier—a head, hands, and body. Archeologists soon discovered an enormous subterranean pit beneath the fields containing an estimated 6,000 infantrymen, most standing four abreast in 11 parallel trenches paved with bricks. In 1976 and 1977, two smaller but equally spectacular sites were discovered north of the first one, containing another 1,400 individual warriors and horses, complete with metal weaponry.

Qin Shihuangdi's actual tomb has never been excavated. It rises 140 feet above the plain. Historical records indicate that below the mound is a subterranean palace estimated to be about 400 feet by 525 feet. According to the *Shi Ji* (*Historical Records*) of Sima Qian, a scholar from the Han dynasty, the emperor was buried there in a bronze casket surrounded by a river of mercury. Scientific tests conducted by Chinese archeologists confirm the presence of large quantities of

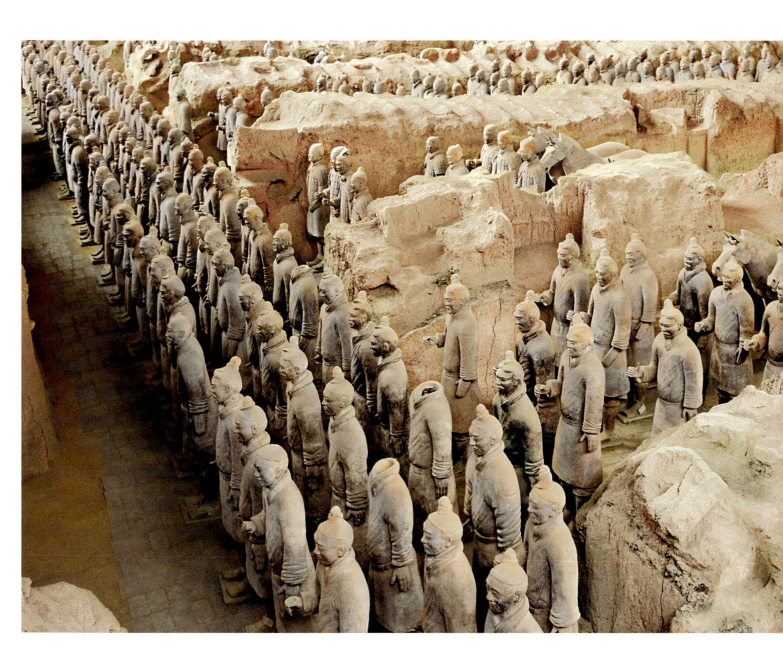

mercury in the soil of the burial mound. Magnetic scans of the tomb have also revealed large numbers of coins, suggesting the emperor was buried with his treasury.

Something to Think About . . .

Why do you suppose the ceramic army was deployed outside the tomb of Qin Shihuangdi and not in it?

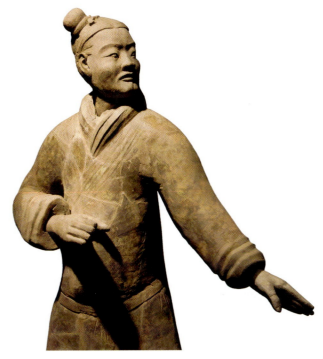

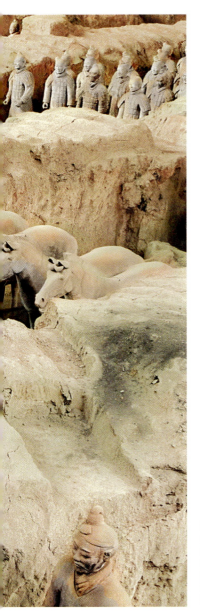

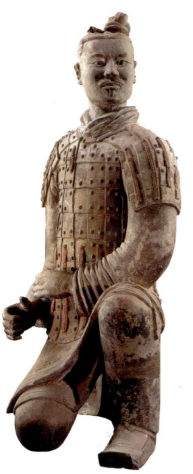

Two terra-cotta soldiers from the burial mound of Qin Shihuangdi, Shaanxi province, China. Both ca. 210 BCE. On the right, a kneeling archer, height 48"; above, an infantryman poised for hand-to-hand combat, height 70". The bodies of most of the soldiers in the tomb appear to have been mass-produced in molds. After each stylized body was baked, head and hands were added. No two heads are alike. Many seem to possess unique, individual facial features, and they exhibit a variety of hairstyles. They were subsequently painted in vivid colors, and most carried actual weapons. Knives, spears, swords, and arrowheads have been found at the site.

Soldiers and horses, from the pits near the tomb of Qin Shihuangdi, Shaanxi province, China. Qin dynasty, ca. 210 BCE. Terra cotta, life-size. The practice of fashioning clay replicas of humans for burial at mausoleum sites replaced an earlier practice of actual human sacrifice. Over 700,000 people were employed in preparing the tomb.

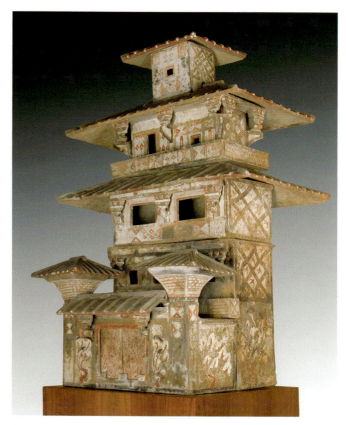

Fig. 3.28 Model of a house, Eastern Han dynasty (25–220 CE), 1st century CE. Painted earthenware with unfired pigments, 52" × 33½" × 27". The Nelson-Atkins Museum of Art, Kansas City, Missouri. This is one of the largest and most complete models of a Han house known.

topped by a watchtower (Fig. **3.28**). The family lived in the middle two stories, while livestock, probably pigs and oxen, were kept in the gated lower level with its courtyard extending in front of the house.

Architecturally, the basic form of the house is commonly found across the world—rectangular halls with columns supporting the roof or the floor above. The walls serve no weight-bearing function. Rather, they serve as screens separating the inside from the outside, or one interior room from another. Distinctive to Chinese architecture are the broad eaves of the roof, which would become a standard feature of East Asian construction. Adding playful charm is the elaborate decoration of the facade, including painted trees flanking the courtyard.

Aside from their military value, horses advanced the growth of trade along the Silk Road. Nearly 5,000 miles long, this trade route led from the Yellow River Valley to the Mediterranean, and along it, the Chinese traded their most exclusive commodity, silk. The quality of Han silk is evident in a silk banner from the tomb of the wife of the Marquis of Dai, discovered on the outskirts of present-day Changsha in Hunan (Fig. **3.29**). Painted with scenes representing the underworld, the earthly realm, and the heavens, it represents the Han conception of the cosmos. Long, sinuous lines representing dragons' tails, coiling serpents, long-tailed birds, and flowing draperies unify the three

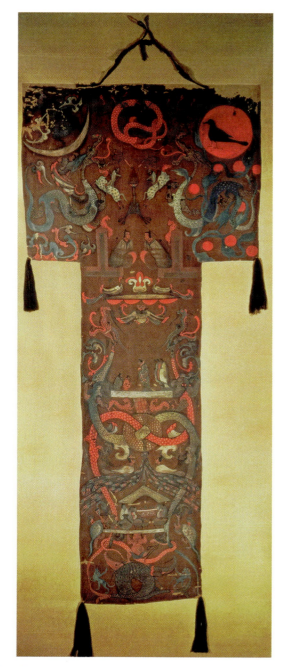

Fig. 3.29 Painted banner from the tomb of the wife of the Marquis of Dai, Mawangdui, Changsha, Hunan province. Han dynasty, ca. 160 BCE. Colors on silk, height 6'8½". Hunan Provincial Museum, Changsa. The banner was found in the innermost of the nested coffins opened in 1972.

realms. In the right corner of the heavenly realm, above the crossbar of the T, is an image of the sun containing a crow, and in the other corner is a crescent moon supporting a toad. Between them is a deity entwined within his own long, red serpent tail. The deceased noblewoman herself stands on the white platform in the middle region of the banner. Three attendants stand behind her and two figures kneel before her, bearing gifts. On a white platform in the lower realm, bronze vessels contain food and wine for the deceased.

The Han were especially inventive. In the West, the limitations of papyrus as a writing medium had led to the invention of parchment at Pergamon, but the Chinese invention of cellulose-based paper in 105 CE by Cai Lun, a eunuch and attendant to the Imperial Court who held a post responsible for manufacturing instruments and weapons, enabled China to develop widespread literacy much more quickly than the West. Although modern technology has simplified the process, his method remains basically unchanged—the suspension in water of softened plant fibers that are formed in molds into thin sheets, couched, drained, and then dried. Motivated by trade, the Han also began to make maps, becoming the world's first cartographers. They invented important agricultural technology such as the wheelbarrow and horse collar. They learned to measure the magnitude of earthquakes with a crude but functional seismograph. But persistent warring with the nomadic peoples to the north required money to support military and bureaucratic initiatives. Unable to keep up with increased taxes, many peasants were forced off the land and popular rebellion ensued. By the third century CE, the Han dynasty had collapsed. China reentered a period of political chaos lasting from 220 until 589 CE, when imperial rule finally regained its strength.

ANCIENT INDIA

How did the Hindu and Buddhist faiths help to shape the cultures of ancient India?

Indian civilization was born along the Indus River in the northwest corner of the Indian subcontinent in present-day Pakistan somewhere around 2700 BCE in an area known as Sind—from which the words *India* and *Hindu* originate (Map **3.3**).

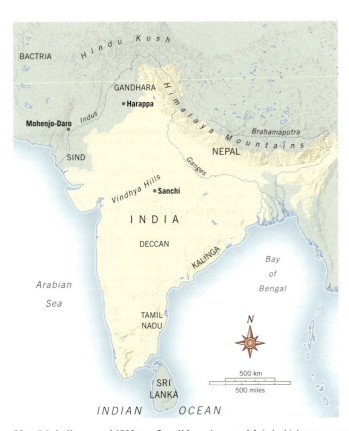

Map 3.3 **India around 1500 BCE.** Cut off from the rest of Asia by high mountains to the north, India was nevertheless a center of trade by virtue of its prominent maritime presence.

The earliest Indian peoples lived in at least two great cities in the Indus Valley—Mohenjo-Daro, on the banks of the Indus, and Harappa, on the River Ravi, downstream from present-day Lahore. These great cities thrived until around 1900 BCE and were roughly contemporaneous with Sumerian Ur, the Old Kingdom of Egypt, and Minoan civilization in the Aegean.

The cities were discovered by chance in the early 1920s and excavations have continued since. The best preserved of the sites is Mohenjo-Daro. Built atop a citadel is a complex of buildings, presumably a governmental or religious center, surrounded by a wall 50 feet high. Set among the buildings on the citadel is a giant pool (Fig. **3.30**). Perhaps a public bath or a ritual space, it has finely fitted bricks, laid on edge and bound together with gypsum plaster, which made it watertight. The bricks on the side walls of the tank were covered with a thick layer of bitumen (natural tar) to keep water from seeping through the walls and up into the superstructure. The pool was open to the air and surrounded by a brick colonnade.

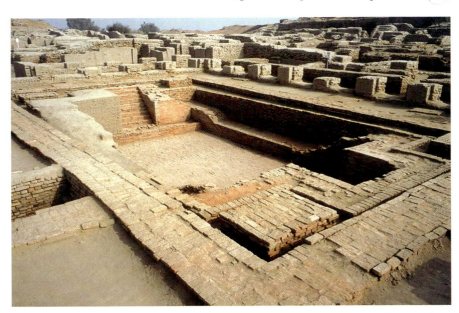

Fig. 3.30 Large water tank, possibly a public or ritual bathing area, from Mohenjo-Daro, Indus Valley civilization. ca. 2600–1900 BCE. It measures approximately 39½' north–south and 23' wide, with a maximum depth of almost 8'.

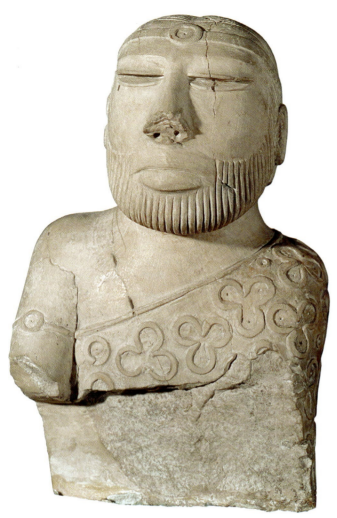

Fig. 3.31 Torso of a "priest-king" from Mohenjo-Daro, Indus Valley civilization. ca. 2000–1900 BCE. Steatite, height 6⅞". National Museum of Pakistan, Karachi. The look created by the figure's half-closed eyes suggests that this might be a death mask of some sort. The *trefoil*, or three-lobed decorations on the garment that crosses his chest were originally filled with red paint.

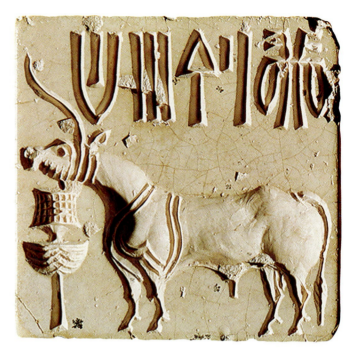

Fig. 3.32 Seal depicting a horned animal, Indus Valley civilization. ca. 2500–1900 BCE. Steatite, approx. 1¼" × 1¼". National Museum of Pakistan, Karachi. The function of seals like this remains unknown.

Outside the wall and below the citadel, a city of approximately 6 to 7 square miles, with broad avenues and narrow side streets, was laid out in a rough grid. It appears to have been home to a population of between 20,000 and 50,000. Most of the houses were two stories tall and built around a central courtyard. A network of covered drainage systems ran through the streets, channeling waste and rainwater into the river. The houses were built with standard sizes of baked brick, each measuring 2¾ × 5½ × 11 inches, a ratio of 1:2:4. A brick of identical ratio but larger—4 × 8 × 16 inches—was used in the building of platforms and city walls. Unlike the sun-dried bricks used in other cultures at the time, Mohenjo-Daro's bricks were fired, making them much more durable. All this suggests a civilization of considerable technological know-how and sophistication.

The arts of the Indus civilizations include human and animal figurines made of stone, terra cotta, bronze, and other materials—including the so-called priest-king found at Mohenjo-Daro (Fig. **3.31**)—terra-cotta pottery, and various styles of decorative ornament for human wear, including beads and stoneware bangles. Over 2,000 small seals have been unearthed. Carved from steatite stone, coated with alkali, and then fired to produce a luminous white surface, many depict animals with an extraordinary naturalism, especially considering that they are rendered in such miniature detail (Fig. **3.32**). Depictions of warfare or conquered enemies are strikingly absent in representational art. As the top of this seal shows, the peoples of the valley had a written language, although it remains undeciphered.

Sometime around 1500 BCE, the Aryas, nomads from the north, invaded the Indus River Valley and conquered its inhabitants, making them slaves. Thus began the longest-lasting set of rigid, class-based societal divisions in world history, the Indian caste system. By the beginning of the first millennium BCE, these castes consisted of five principal groups, based on occupation: At the bottom of the ladder was a group considered "out of caste," people whose occupations or habits were, by definition, impure or polluted. Next in line were the Shudras, unskilled workers. Then came the Vaishyas, artisans and merchants. They were followed by the Kshatriyas, rulers and warriors. At the highest level were the Brahmins, priests and scholars.

Hinduism and the Vedic Tradition

The social castes were sanctioned by the religion the Aryas brought with them, a religion based on a set of sacred hymns to the Aryan gods. These hymns, called *Vedas*, were written in the Aryan language, Sanskrit, and they gave their name to an entire period of Indian civilization, the Vedic period (ca. 1500–322 BCE). From the *Vedas* in turn came the *Upanishads*, a book of mystical and philosophical texts that date from sometime after 800 BCE. Taken together, the *Vedas* and the *Upanishads* form the basis of the Hindu religion, with Brahman, the universal soul, at its center. The religion has no single body of doctrine, nor any standard set of practices. It is defined above all by the diversity of its beliefs and deities. Indeed, several images of mother goddesses, stones in the phallic form, as well as a seal with an image that resembles the Hindu god Shiva, have been excavated at various Indus sites, leading scholars to believe that certain aspects and concepts of Hinduism survived from the Indus civilizations and were incorporated into the Vedic religion.

The *Upanishads* argue that all existence is a fabric of false appearances. What appears to the senses is entirely illusory. Only Brahman is real. Thus, in a famous story illustrating the point, a tiger, orphaned as a cub, is raised by goats. It learns, as a matter of course, to eat grass and make goat sounds. But one day it meets another tiger, who takes it to a pool to look at itself. There, in its reflection in the water, it discovers its true nature. The individual soul needs to discover the same truth, a truth that will free it from the endless cycle of birth, death, and rebirth and unite it with the Brahman in **nirvana**, a place or state free from worry, pain, and the external world.

Brahman, Vishnu, and Shiva As Hinduism developed, the functions of Brahman, the divine source of all being, were split among three gods: Brahma, the creator; Vishnu, the preserver; and Shiva, the destroyer. Vishnu was one of the most popular of the Hindu deities. In his role as preserver, he is the god of benevolence, forgiveness, and love, and like the other two main Hindu gods, he was believed capable of assuming human form, which he did more often than the other gods because of his great love for humankind. Among Vishnu's most famous incarnations is his appearance as Rama in the oldest of the Hindu epics, the *Ramayana* (*Way of Rama*), written by Valmiki in about 550 BCE. Like Homer in ancient Greece, Valmiki gathered together many existing legends and myths into a single story, in this case narrating the lives of Prince Rama and his queen, Sita. The two serve as models of Hindu life. Rama is the ideal son, brother, husband, warrior, and king, and Sita loves, honors, and serves her husband with absolute and unquestioning fidelity. These characters face moral dilemmas to which they must react according to **dharma**, good and righteous conduct reflecting the cosmic moral order that underlies all existence. For Hindus, correct actions can lead to cosmic harmony; and bad actions,

violating dharma, can trigger cosmic tragedies such as floods and earthquakes.

An equally important incarnation of Vishnu is as the charioteer Krishna in the later Indian epic the *Mahabharata*, composed between 400 BCE and 400 CE. In the sixth book of the *Mahabharata*, titled the *Bhagavad Gita*, Krishna comes to the aid of Arjuna, a warrior who is tormented by the conflict between his duty to fight and kill his kinsmen in battle and the Hindu prohibition against killing. Krishna explains to Arjuna that as a member of the Kshatriya caste—that is, as a warrior—he is freed from the Hindu sanction against killing. In fact, by fighting well and doing his duty, he can free himself from the endless cycle of birth, death, and reincarnation, and move toward spiritual union with the Brahman.

But Vishnu's popularity is probably most attributable to his celebration of erotic love, which to Hindus symbolizes the mingling of the self and the absolute spirit of Brahman. In the *Vishnu Puranas* (the "old stories" of Vishnu), collected about 500 CE, Vishnu, in his incarnation as Krishna, is depicted as seducing one after another of his devotees. In one story of the *Vishnu Puranas*, he seduces an entire band of milkmaids: "They considered every instant without him a myriad of years; and prohibited (in vain) by husbands, fathers, brothers, they went forth at night to sport with Krishna, the object of their affection." Allowing themselves to be seduced does not suggest that the milkmaids were immoral, but shows an almost inevitable manifestation of their souls' quest for union with divinity.

If Brahma is the creator of the world, Shiva takes what Brahma has made and embodies the world's cyclic rhythms. Since in Hinduism, the destruction of the old world is followed by the creation of a new world, Shiva's role as destroyer is both positive and necessary. In this sense, he possesses reproductive powers, and in this manifestation of his being, he is frequently represented as a *linga* (phallus), often carved in stone on temple grounds or at shrines.

The Goddess Devi Goddess worship is fundamental to Hindu religion. Villages usually recognize goddesses as their protectors, and the goddess Devi is worshiped in many forms throughout India. She is the female aspect without whom the male aspect, which represents consciousness or discrimination, remains impotent and void. For instance, in the *Devi Mahatmayam*, another of the Puranas, composed like the *Vishnu Puranas* around 500 CE, Vishnu was asleep on the great cosmic ocean, and because of his slumber, Brahma was unable to create. Devi intervenes, kills the demons responsible for Vishnu's slumber, and helps to wake up Vishnu. Thus continues the cycle of life.

Devi is synonymous with Shakti, the primordial cosmic energy, and represents the dynamic forces that move through the entire universe. Shaktism, a particular brand of Hindu faith that regards Devi as the Supreme Brahman itself, believes that all other forms of divinity, female or male, are themselves simply forms of Devi's diverse

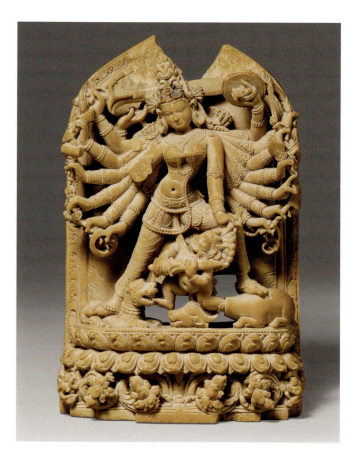

Fig. 3.33 *The Goddess Durga Killing the Buffalo Demon, Mahisha (Mahishasuramardini),* **Bangladesh or India. Pala period, 12th century** CE. Argillite, height 5⁵⁄₁₆". The Metropolitan Museum of Art, New York. Durga represents the warrior aspect of Devi.

the wilderness. For six years he meditated, finally attaining complete enlightenment while sitting under a banyan tree at Bodh Gaya. Shortly thereafter he gave his first teaching, at the Deer Park at Sarnath, expounding the Four Noble Truths:

1. Life is suffering.
2. This suffering has a cause, which is ignorance.
3. Ignorance can be overcome and eliminated.
4. The way to overcome this ignorance is by following the Eightfold Path of right view, right resolve, right speech, right action, right livelihood, right effort, right mindfulness, and right concentration.

Living with these truths in mind, one might overcome what Buddha believed to be the source of all human suffering—the desire for material things, which is the primary form of ignorance. In doing so, one would find release from the illusions of the world, from the cycle of birth, death, and rebirth, and ultimately reach nirvana. These principles are summed up in the *Dhammapada*, the most popular canonical text of Buddhism, which consists of 423 aphorisms, or sayings, attributed to Buddha and arranged by subject into 26 chapters. Its name is a compound consisting of *dhamma*, the vernacular form of the formal Sanskrit word *dharma*, mortal truth, and *pada*, meaning "foot" or "step"—hence it is "the path of truth." The aphorisms are widely admired for their wisdom and their sometimes stunning beauty of expression.

The Buddha (which means "Enlightened One") taught for 40 years until his death at age 80. His followers preached that anyone could achieve Buddhahood, the ability to see the ultimate nature of the world. Persons of very near total enlightenment, but who have vowed to help others achieve Buddhahood before crossing over to nirvana, came to be known as **bodhisattvas**, meaning "those whose essence is wisdom." In art, bodhisattvas wear the princely garb of India, while Buddhas wear a monk's robe.

The Maurya Empire Buddhism would become the official state religion of the Maurya Empire, which ruled India from 321 to 185 BCE. The Empire was founded by Chandragupta Maurya (r. ca. 321–297 BCE) in eastern India. Its capital was Pataliputra (present-day Patna) on the Ganges River, but Chandragupta rapidly expanded the Empire westward, taking advantage of the vacuum of power in the Indus Valley that followed Alexander the Great's invasion of 326 BCE. In 305 BCE, the Hellenistic Greek ruler Seleucus I, ruler of one of the three states that succeeded Alexander's empire, the kingdom of the Seleucids, tried to reconquer India once again. He and Chandragupta eventually signed a peace treaty, and diplomatic relations between Seleucid Greece and the Maurya Empire were established. Several Greeks ambassadors were soon residing in the Mauryan court, the beginning of substantial relations between East and West. Chandragupta was succeeded by his son Bindusara (r. ca. 297–273 BCE), who also had a Greek ambassador at his court, and who extended the Empire southward, conquering almost all the Indian peninsula and establishing the Maurya

manifestations. But she has a number of particular manifestations. In an extraordinary miniature carving from the twelfth century, Devi is seen in her manifestation as Durga (Fig. **3.33**), portrayed as the sixteen-armed slayer of a buffalo inhabited by the fierce demon Mahisha. Considered invincible, Mahisha threatens to destroy the world, but Durga comes to the rescue. In this image, she has just severed the buffalo's head and Mahisha, in the form of a tiny, chubby man, his hair composed of snake heads, emerges from the buffalo's decapitated body and looks up admiringly at her even as his toes are being bitten by her lion. Durga smiles serenely as she hoists Mahisha by his hair and treads gracefully on the buffalo's body.

Buddhism: "The Path of Truth"

Because free thought and practice mark the Hindu religion, it is hardly surprising that other religious movements drew on it and developed from it. Buddhism is one of those. Its founder, Shakyamuni Buddha, lived from about 563 to 483 BCE. He was born Prince Siddhartha Gautama, child of a ruler of the Shakya clan—Shakyamuni means "sage of the Shakyas"—and was raised to be a ruler himself. Troubled by what he perceived to be the suffering of all human beings, he abandoned the luxurious lifestyle of his father's palace to live in

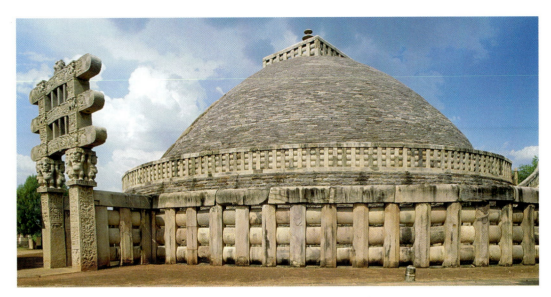

Fig. 3.34 The Great Stupa, Sanchi, Madhya Pradesh, India, view of the West Gateway.
Founded 3rd century BCE, enlarged ca. 150–50 BCE. Shrine height 50', diameter 105'. In India,
the stupa is the principal monument to Buddha. The stupa symbolizes, at once, the World Mountain,
the Dome of Heaven, and the Womb of the Universe.

✳ **Explore** an architectural panorama of the Great Stupa at Sanchi on **MyArtsLab**

Empire as the largest Empire of its time. He was in turn succeeded by his son Ashoka (r. ca. 273–232 BCE).

It was Ashoka who established Buddhism as the official state religion. On a battlefield in 261 BCE, he was appalled by the carnage he had inflicted in his role as a warrior king. As he watched a monk walking slowly among the dead, Ashoka was moved to decry violence and force of arms and to spread the teachings of Buddha. From that point, Ashoka, who had been described as "the cruel," began to be known as "the pious." At a time when Rome was engaged in the Punic Wars, Ashoka pursued an official policy of nonviolence. The unnecessary slaughter or mutilation of animals was forbidden. Sport hunting was banned, and although the limited hunting of game for the purpose of consumption was tolerated, Ashoka promoted vegetarianism. He built hospitals for people and animals alike, preached the humane treatment of all living things, and regarded all his subjects as equals, regardless of politics, religion, or caste. He also embarked on a massive Buddhist architectural campaign, erecting as many as 8,400 shrines and monuments to Buddha throughout the empire. Soon, Buddhism spread beyond India, and Buddhist monks from China traveled to India to observe Buddhist practices.

The Great Stupa Among the most famous of the Buddhist monuments that Ashoka erected is the Great Stupa at Sanchi (Fig. 3.34), which was enlarged in the second century BCE. A **stupa** is a kind of burial mound. The earliest eight of them were built around 483 BCE as reliquaries for Buddha's remains, which were themselves divided into eight parts. In the third century, Ashoka opened the original eight stupas and further divided Buddha's relics, scattering them among a great many other stupas, probably including that at Sanchi.

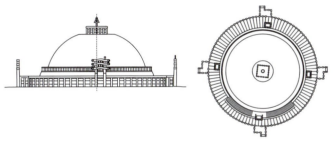

Fig. 3.35 Elevation and plan of the Great Stupa, Sanchi. One of the most curious aspects of the Great Stupa is that its four gates are not aligned on an axis with the four openings in the railing. Some scholars believe that this arrangement is derived from gates on farms, which were designed to keep cattle out of the fields.

The stupa as a form is deeply symbolic, consisting first and foremost of a hemispheric dome, built of rubble and dirt and faced with stone, evoking the Dome of Heaven (Fig. **3.35**). Perched on top of the dome is a small square platform, in the center of which is a mast supporting three circular discs or "umbrellas," called *chatras*. These signify both the banyan tree beneath which Buddha achieved enlightenment and the three levels of Buddhist consciousness—desire, form, formlessness—through which the soul ascends to enlightenment. The dome is set on a raised base, around the top of which is a walkway. As pilgrims to the stupa circle the walkway, they symbolically follow Buddha's path, awakening to enlightenment. The whole is a **mandala** (literally "circle"), the Buddhist diagram of the cosmos.

Ashoka's missionary ambition matched his father's and grandfather's military zeal, and he sent Buddhist emissaries as far west as Syria, Egypt, and Greece. No Western historical record of these missions survives, and their impact on Western thought remains a matter of speculation.

3.1 Characterize imperial Rome, its dual sense of origin, and its debt to the Roman Republic.

Roman culture developed out of both Greek and indigenous Etruscan roots. The Etruscans also provided the Romans with one of their founding myths, the legend of Romulus and Remus; Virgil's *Aeneid* was the other. According to legend, it was Romulus who inaugurated the traditional Roman distinction between patricians and plebeians with its system of patronage and *pietas*. Describe this system.

During the era of the Roman republic in the first century, the powerfully eloquent and persuasive writing of the rhetorician Cicero helped to make Latin the chief language of the empire. His essay *On Duty* helped to define *pietas* as a Roman value. How is this value evidenced in the portrait busts of the era?

In 27 BCE, the Senate granted Octavian the imperial name Augustus and the authority of *imperium* over all the empire. In what way did Augustus idealize himself in the monumental statues dedicated to him? How did he present his wife, Livia, and his family to the public, and what values did he wish his family to embody?

Under Augustus, Roman literature also thrived. But Augustus' greatest achievement, and that of the emperors to follow him, was the transformation of Rome into, in Augustus' words, "a city of marble." Why did the Roman emperors build so many public works? What did they symbolize or represent? In the private sphere, how does the architecture of the *domus* reflect Roman values?

3.2 Describe the impact of the competing schools of thought that flourished in early Chinese culture—Daoism, Confucianism, and Legalism.

During the Shang (ca. 1700–1045 BCE) and Zhou (1045-256 BCE) dynasties, the two great strains of Chinese philosophy—Daoism, a mystical quietism based on harmony with nature, and Confucianism, a pragmatic political

philosophy based on personal cultivation—came into full flower. The philosophical symbol of *yin yang* was devised during this early period, too. Can you detect the workings of the yin-yang philosophy in the poetry of the *Book of Songs* and in the later philosophy of Confucius? How did Confucianism contribute to the workings of the Chinese state? Why is Daoism less suited as a political philosophy?

Under the leadership of the first emperor, Qin Shihuangdi, the Qin dynasty (221–206 BCE) unified China and undertook massive building projects, including the 4,000-mile-long Great Wall, enormous networks of roads, and the emperor's own tomb, guarded by nearly 8,000 life-size ceramic soldiers, projects that required the almost complete reorganization of Chinese society. This reorganization was made possible by placing totalitarian authority in the hands of a ruthless dictator. How did Han Feizi's Legalism support the emperor's approach? How do the massive building projects of the Qin dynasty compare those of the Roman Empire in the West?

During the Han dynasty (206 BCE–220 CE), the scholars and writers disenfranchised by the Qin were restored to respectability. How does Han culture reflect Confucian values?

3.3 Discuss the ways in which both Hinduism and Buddhism shaped Indian culture.

Before 2000 BCE, in the Indus Valley, sophisticated cultures arose at cities such as Mohenjo-Daro. But after the invasion of the Aryans in about 1500 BCE, the Hindu religion took hold in India. The *Vedas* and *Upanishads* were its two basic texts. Its three major gods were Brahma, the creator; Vishnu, the preserver; and Shiva, the destroyer, who is also a great dancer, embodying the sacred rhythms of creation and destruction, birth, death, and rebirth. What does this religion share with Buddhism, the official Indian state religion adopted by the Maurya emperor Ashoka? In what ways did Ashoka seek to spread Buddhism as the dominant Indian faith?

✓ **Study** and **review** on **MyArtsLab**

CONTINUITY & CHANGE

Christian Rome

Throughout its history, the Roman Empire had been a polytheistic state in which literally dozens of religions were tolerated. But as Christianity became a more and more dominant force in the Empire, it threatened the political and cultural identity of the Roman citizen. No longer was a Roman first and foremost Roman. Increasingly, that citizen was first and foremost Christian.

In reaction to this threat to imperial authority, during the chaotic years after the fall of the Severan emperors in 235 CE, Christians were blamed, as their religion spread across the Empire (see Map 3.1), for most of Rome's troubles. By the end of the third century, there were about five million Christians in the Roman Empire, nearly a tenth of the population. Rome had a particularly large Christian congregation with

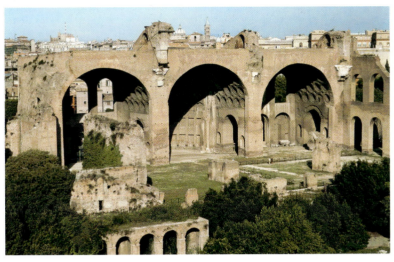

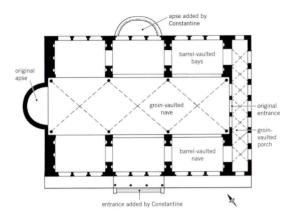

Figs. 3.36 and 3.37 The Basilica of Maxentius and Constantine, also known as the Basilica Nova, and plan.
Rome. 306–313 CE. Constantine added an imposing entrance on the southwest side of Maxentius' basilica and another apse across from it, perhaps to accommodate crowds.

considerable influence, since its leadership was believed to be descended from Jesus' original disciples, Peter and Paul. In 303, the emperor Diocletian (r. 284–305 CE) unleashed a furious persecution of Christians that lasted for eight years.

Diocletian saw the Roman Church as a direct threat to his own authority, recognizing that it had achieved an almost monarchical control over the other dioceses, or Church territories, in the Empire. He forbade Christian worship, ordered churches destroyed, burned books, and had all bishops arrested. Under penalty of death, Christians were compelled to make sacrifices to the emperor, whom non-Christian Romans considered divine. Thousands refused, and the martyrdom they thus achieved fueled rather than diminished the Church's strength.

In 305, Diocletian retired owing to bad health, ushering in a period of instability. Finally, Constantine I, known as "Constantine the Great" (r. 306–37), won a decisive battle at the Milvian Bridge, at the entrance to Rome, on October 28, 312, establishing himself as emperor. Two years earlier, as Constantine was advancing on Rome from Gaul, the story had circulated that he had seen a vision of the sun god Apollo accompanied by Victory (Nike) and the Roman numeral XXX symbolizing the 30 years he would reign. By the end of his life, he claimed to have seen, instead, above the sun, a single cross, by then an increasingly common symbol of Christ, together with the legend, "In this sign you shall conquer." At any rate, it seems certain that at the Battle of the Milvian Bridge, Constantine ordered that his troops decorate their shields with crosses, and perhaps the Greek

letters *chi* and *rho* as well. These letters stood for *Christos*, although *chi* and *rho* had long meant *chrestos*, "auspicious," and Constantine probably meant only this and not Jesus Christ. While Constantine himself reasserted his devotion to the Roman state religion, within a year, in 313, he issued the Edict of Milan, which granted religious freedom to all, ending religious persecution in the Empire.

Constantine's architectural program in Rome would leave a lasting mark on subsequent Christian architecture, particularly his work on a basilica at the southern end of the line of Imperial Forums (see Fig. 3.12). Originally built by Maxentius, it was the last of the great imperial buildings erected in Rome (Figs. **3.36** and **3.37**). Like all Roman basilicas, the Basilica of Maxentius and Constantine (also known as the Basilica Nova) was a large rectangular building with a rounded extension, called an *apse*, at one or both ends and easy access in and out. It was, similarly, an administrative center—courthouse, council chamber, and meeting hall—and its high vaulted ceilings were purposefully constructed on the model of large Roman baths. Its **nave**, the large central area, rose to an elevation of 114 feet. One entered through a triple portico at the southeast end and looked down the nave some 300 feet to the original apse at the other end of the building, which acted as a focal point. The basilica plan, with the apse as its focal point, would exert considerable influence on later Christian churches. These later churches would transform the massive interiors from administrative spaces to religious sanctuaries, whose vast interior spaces elicited religious awe. ■

Explore an architectural panorama of the Basilica of Maxentius and Constantine (Basilica Nova) on **MyArtsLab**

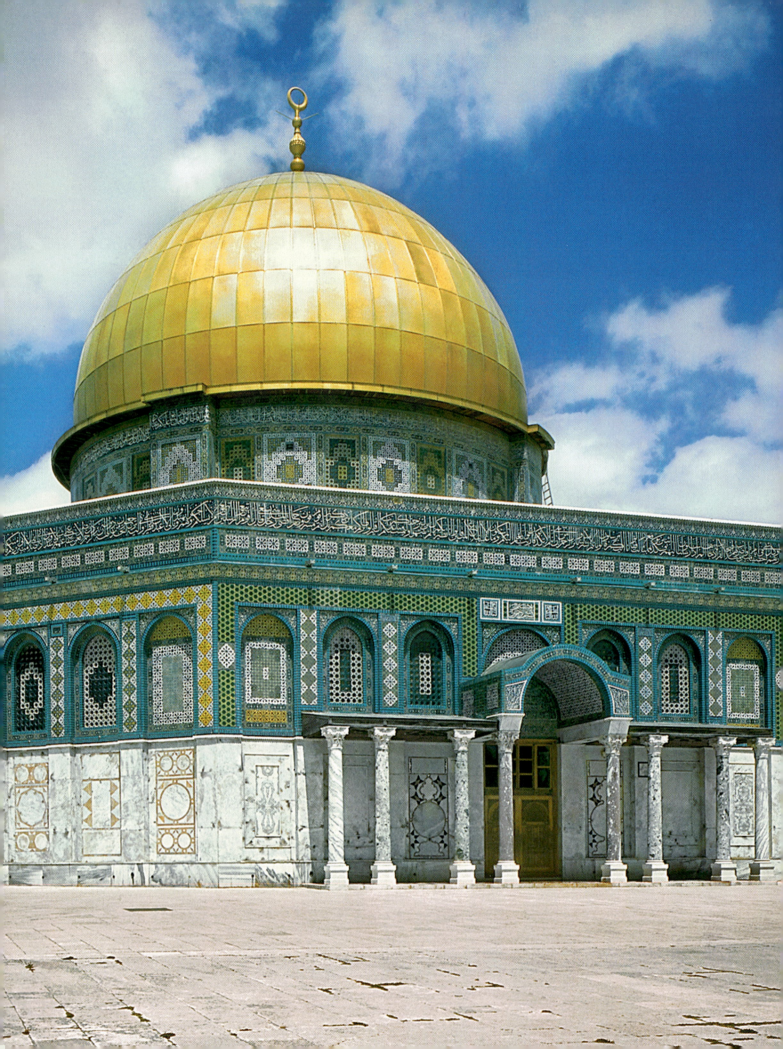

The Flowering of Religion

Faith and the Power of Belief in the Early First Millennium

LEARNING OBJECTIVES

4.1 Examine the impact of Roman rule on Judaic culture.

4.2 Discuss the development of Christianity from its Jewish roots to its rapid spread through the Roman world.

4.3 Describe the new Byzantine style of art and discuss how it reflects the values of the Byzantine emperors, especially Justinian.

4.4 Outline the principal tenets of the Muslim faith, and account for its rapid spread.

4.5 Characterize the spread of Buddhism from India north into China.

The Dome of the Rock (Fig. **4.1**) stands atop the Temple Mount in Jerusalem, on the site where, in Jewish tradition, Abraham prepared to sacrifice his son Isaac. The Jewish Temple of Solomon originally stood here, and the site is further associated—by Jews, Christians, and Muslims alike—with God's creation of Adam. The Second Temple of Jerusalem also stood on this spot until it was destroyed by Roman soldiers when they sacked the city in 70 CE, to put down a Jewish revolt, an event commemorated on the Arch of Titus in Rome (see Fig. 3.15 in Chapter 3). Only the Wailing Wall remains, part of the original retaining wall for the platform supporting the Temple Mount and for Jews the most sacred site in Jerusalem. To this day, the plaza in front of the wall functions as an open-air synagogue where daily prayers are recited and other Jewish rituals are performed. On Tisha B'Av, the ninth day of the month of Av, which occurs in either July or August, a fast is held commemorating the destruction of the successive temples on this site, and people sit on the ground before the wall reciting the Book of Lamentations.

One of the earliest examples of Muslim architecture, built in the 680s, the Dome encloses an **ambulatory**, a circular, colonnaded walkway that in turn encloses a projecting rock lying directly beneath the golden dome. By the sixteenth century, Islamic faithful claimed that the Prophet Muhammad ascended to heaven from this spot, on a winged horse named Buraq, but there is no evidence that this story was in circulation when the Dome was originally built. Others thought that it represents the ascendancy of Islam over Christianity in the Holy Land. Still others believed the rock is the center of the world, or that it could refer to the Temple of Solomon, the importance of which is fully acknowledged by Muslims, who consider Solomon a founding father of their own faith. All this suggests that the Dome was meant to proselytize, or convert both Jews and Christians to the Muslim faith.

The sanctity of this spot, then, at the heart of Jerusalem, is recognized equally by the three great faiths of the Western world—Judaism, Christianity, and Islam—and the intersection of these religions, together with the spread of Buddhism in Asia, is the subject of this chapter. As Christianity came to differentiate itself from its Judaic heritage, it came into increasing conflict with imperial Rome. Both Rome and the Church demanded absolute allegiance and loyalty of the citizen/believer. Until the Emperor Constantine granted religious freedom to all Romans in 313 CE,

◄ Fig. 4.1 The Dome of the Rock, Jerusalem. Late 680s–691. The golden dome of the building rises above a projecting rock that is surrounded by an ambulatory. The building's function remains unclear. It is not a mosque, although it is certainly some kind of religious memorial. Inscriptions from the Qur'an decorate its interior. These are the oldest excerpts from the text to have survived.

 View the Closer Look for the Dome of the Rock on **MyArtsLab**

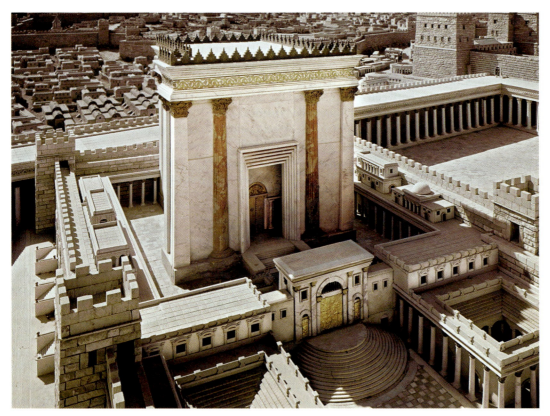

Fig. 4.2 Model of the Second Temple of Jerusalem. ca. 20 BCE. Only the Western Wall of Herod's temple survives today, and for Jews it remains the most sacred site in Jerusalem. It serves as a reminder of both the First Temple, totally destroyed by the Babylonians in 586 BCE, and, of course, the destruction of the Second Temple by the Romans. As a result of the sense of loss associated with the site and the lamentations it provokes, for centuries it has been known as the Wailing Wall.

building program. During his reign (37–4 BCE), he rebuilt the city of Jerusalem, constructing a large palace and enlarging the Second Temple (Fig. **4.2**). We can see the Hellenistic influence in its tall, engaged Corinthian columns and its decorative frieze, and its Roman roots in its triple-arched gateway. Herod also engaged in other massive building programs, including a port at Caesarea and the fortress at Masada. Although Herod's three sons ruled briefly after their father's death, Rome became less and less tolerant of the Jewish faith—the laws of Rome often coming into conflict with the Biblical law—and direct Roman rule was soon imposed.

Finally, in 66 CE, the Jews revolted. In 68 CE, the Romans destroyed Qumran. In 70 CE, they sacked the temple in Jerusalem, as depicted on the Arch of Titus in Rome (see Fig. 3.15 in Chapter 3). At Masada, a band of zealots held out until 74 CE. The Roman general Flavius Silva surrounded the mountain with a wall and eight encampments, then built a huge earthen ramp up the mountainside. Rather than submit to the Romans, the Jews inside the fortress committed mass suicide, each man responsible for killing his own family and then himself. The Romans changed the name of the province from Judea, "land of the Jews," to Palestine, "land of the Philistines"—the ancient enemy of the Jews, but a culture that had disappeared long before Herod's time (the giant Goliath, slain by David, as told in the Book of Samuel, had

been a Philistine). It was as if the history of the Jewish presence in the region were to be permanently erased. Finally, in 135 CE, after yet another Jewish revolt, the Emperor Hadrian rebuilt Jerusalem as a Roman city, which Jews were forbidden to enter. Hundreds of thousands of Jews were killed or sold into slavery, their land and property were confiscated, and the survivors fled throughout the Mediterranean and the Middle East. The diaspora that had begun with the Assyrian invasion of Israel in 722 BCE was now complete. Not until 1948, when the state of Israel was established by the United Nations, would Jews control their homeland again.

THE RISE OF CHRISTIANITY

How did Christianity develop from its Jewish roots to spread rapidly through the Roman world?

The development of Christianity, the religion that would have such a profound effect upon the history of the Western world, can be understood only in the context of Jewish history. It developed as one among many other minor sects of Judaism, at first so inconsequential that Josephus mentions it only briefly. Later theological writings, as opposed to actual historical accounts written at the time, tell us that in Judea's sectarian climate, Jesus of Nazareth was born to Mary and Joseph of Judea in about 4 BCE. At about the age of 30, Jesus began to lead the life of an itinerant rabbi. He preached repentance, compassion for the poor and meek, love of God and neighbor, and the imminence of the apocalypse, which he called the coming of the kingdom of God.

Although his teachings were steeped in the wisdom of the Jewish tradition, they antagonized both Jewish and Roman leaders. Jesus, in the spirit of reform, had challenged the commercialization of the Jewish Temple in Jerusalem, especially the practice of money-changing within its sacred precincts, alienating the Sadducee sect that managed it. After his followers identified him as the Messiah, or Savior—he did not make the claim for himself—both conservative Jewish leaders and Roman rulers were threatened. The proclamation by his followers that he was the son of God amounted to a crime against the Roman state, since the emperor was considered to be the only divine human on earth. In fact, since Jews were monotheistic and refused to worship other gods, including the emperor, their beliefs were a political threat to the Romans. The Christian sect's belief in the divinity of Jesus posed a special problem.

An enemy of the state, denounced by the other Jews that he had antagonized, betrayed by his disciple Judas (a betrayal now called into question with the publication of the Gospel of Judas), Jesus was crucified in about 30 CE, a degrading fate reserved for criminals and non-Roman citizens. Christian tradition has it—we possess no actual historical account—that the Crucifixion occurred outside the city walls on a hillside known as Golgotha, now the site of the Church of the Holy Sepulchre (Fig. 4.3), and that Jesus was buried in a rock tomb just behind the site. Three days later, his followers reported that he rose from the dead and reappeared among them. The promise of resurrection, already a fundamental tenet of the Pharisee and Essene sects, became the foundation of Christian faith.

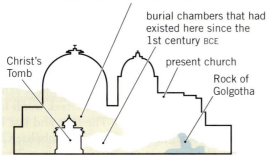

Fig. 4.3 Cutaway drawing of the Church of the Holy Sepulchre, Jerusalem, showing the site of Christ's Tomb. This site was originally a small rocky hill, Golgotha, upon which Jesus was crucified, and unused stone quarry in which tombs had been cut. The first basilica on the site was built by the emperor Constantine between 326 and 335 CE.

The Evangelists

Upon his death, Jesus' reputation grew as word of his life and resurrection was spread, first by his **evangelists** (the word "evangelist" comes from the Greek *evangelos*, meaning "bearer of good"—and note the root *angel* in the word as well) and then by his **apostles**, literally "those who have been sent" by God as his witnesses. Preeminent among the latter was Paul, who had persecuted Jews in Judea before converting to the new faith in Damascus (in present-day Syria) in 35 CE. Paul's epistles, or letters, are the earliest writings of the new Christian faith. In letters written to churches he founded or visited in Asia Minor, Greece, Macedonia, and Rome, which comprise 14 books of the Christian Scriptures, he argues the nature of religious truth and interprets the life of Christ—his preferred name for Jesus, one that he coined. "Christ" means, literally, "the Anointed One." It refers to the Jewish tradition of anointing priests, kings, and prophets with oil, and the fact that by Jesus' time Jews had come to expect a savior who embodied all the qualities of priest, king, and prophet. In true sectarian tradition, for Paul, the only correct expression of Judaism included faith in Christ. Paul conflated Jewish tradition, then, with his belief that Jesus' Crucifixion was the act of his salvation of humankind. He argued that Christ was blameless and suffered on the cross to pay for the sins of humanity. Resurrection, he believed, was at the heart of the Christian faith, but redemption was by no means automatic—sinners had to show their faith in Christ and his salvation. Faith, he argues in his Epistle to the Church in Rome, ensures salvation (**Reading 4.1**):

READING 4.1

from the Bible, Romans 5:1–11

[1]Therefore, since we are justified by faith, we have peace with God through our Lord Jesus Christ, [2]through whom we have obtained access to this grace in which we stand; and we boast in our hope of sharing the glory of God. [3]And not only that, but we also boast in our sufferings, knowing that suffering produces endurance, [4]and endurance produces character, and character produces hope, [5]and hope does not disappoint us, because God's love has been poured into our hearts through the Holy Spirit that has been given to us.

[6]For while we were still weak, at the right time Christ died for the ungodly . . . [8]But God proves his love for us in that while we still were sinners Christ died for us. [9]Much more surely then, now that we have been justified by his blood, will we be saved through him from the wrath of God. [10]For if while we were enemies, we were reconciled to God through the death of his Son, much more surely, having been reconciled, will we be saved by his life. [11]But more than that, we even boast in God through our Lord Jesus Christ, through whom we have now received reconciliation.

Fifteen centuries after Paul wrote these words, the Church would find itself divided between those who believed that salvation was determined by faith alone, as Paul argues, and those who believed in the necessity of good works to gain entry to

are illuminated by the soul of God. He adds to the Platonic emphasis on pure ideas a Christian belief in the sacred word of God, in which God's "light" is understood to shine. In the *Confessions*, too, Augustine codified the idea of typological readings of the Bible, proposing, for example, Eve, the biological mother of humanity, as a type for Mary, the spiritual mother. Similarly, he saw the deliverance of the Israelites from Egypt as a prefiguration of the redemption of Jesus.

Augustine was a prolific writer and thinker and a renowned teacher. One of his most important works is *The City of God*, written between 413 and 425. It is a reinterpretation of history from a theological point of view. In many ways, the book was a response to the sack of Rome by the Visigoths in 410. What had happened to the once powerful empire that had controlled the world, in a common phrase, "to its very edge?" How had such a disaster come to pass? Augustine attempts to answer these questions.

Many Romans blamed the Christians for the city's downfall, but Augustine argued, to the contrary, that pagan religion and philosophy, and particularly the hubris, or arrogance, of the emperors in assuming to be divine had doomed Rome from the beginning. Even more to the point, Augustine argued that the fall of Rome was inevitable, since the city was a product of humankind, and thus corrupt and mortal. Even a Christian Rome was inevitably doomed. History was a forward movement—at least in a spiritual sense—to the Day of Judgment, a movement from the earthly city, with its secular ways, to the heavenly city, untouched by worldly concerns (**Reading 4.3**):

READING 4.3

from Augustine, *The City of God*

The two cities were created by two kinds of love: the earthly city by a love of self even to the point of contempt for God, the heavenly city by a love of God carried even to the point of contempt for self. Consequently, the earthly city glories in itself while the heavenly city glories in the Lord. . . . In the one, the lust for dominion has dominion over its princes as well as over the nations it subdues; in the other, both those put in charge and those placed under them serve one another in love, the former by their counsel, the latter by their obedience. . . .

Augustine's world view is essentially dualistic, composed of two parts. In his writings, the movement of history (and that of life itself) follows a linear progression from darkness to light, from body to soul, from evil to goodness, from doubt to faith, and from blindness to understanding. His own life story, as described in *Confessions*, revealed him as the sinner saved. He saw himself, in fact, as a type for all Christians, whose ultimate place, he believed, would one day be the City of God.

THE BYZANTINE EMPIRE AND ITS CHURCH

What differentiates Byzantine art from earlier, Classical models and how does it reflect the values of the Empire and its church?

Constantine had built his new capital at Constantinople in 325 CE in no small part because Rome was too vulnerable to attack from Germanic tribes. Located on a highly defensible peninsula, Constantinople was far less susceptible to threat, and indeed, while Rome finally collapsed after successive Germanic invasions in 476, Constantinople would serve as the center of Christian culture throughout the early Middle Ages, surviving until 1453, when Ottoman Turks finally succeeded in overrunning it.

In Constantine's Constantinople, Christian basilicas stood next to Roman baths, across from a Roman palace and Senate, the former connected to a Roman hippodrome, all but the basilicas elaborately decorated with pagan art and sculpture gathered from across the Empire. Christians soon developed an important new understanding of these pagan works: They could ignore their pagan elements and think of them simply as *art*. This was the argument of Basil the Great (ca. 329–79), the major theologian of the day. In his twenties he had studied the classics of Greek literature in Athens and had fallen in love with them. He believed it was possible to understand them as literature, not theology, as great works of art, not as arguments for the existence of pagan gods.

Nonetheless, Roman pagan ways soon gave way to Christian doctrine. Constantine himself outlawed pagan sacrifices, and although the emperor Julian the Apostate (r. 361–63) briefly attempted to reinstate paganism, by the time of Theodosius I's rule (379–95), all pagan temples were closed throughout the Empire, and Christianity was the official religion. However, Roman law, not Biblical law, remained the norm in Byzantine culture, schools taught Classical Greek texts, especially Homer's *Iliad*, and important writers still modeled their work on Classical precedents. Nevertheless, by the middle of the sixth century, the emperor Justinian had closed the Academy of Athens, the last pagan school of philosophy in the Empire, and over 100 churches and monasteries stood in Constantinople alone.

Justinian's Empire

After Rome collapsed in 476, Odoacer, a Germanic leader, named himself king of Italy (r. 476–93), which he governed from the northern Italian city of Ravenna. Finally, the Ostrogothic ("Eastern Gothic") king Theodoric the Great overthrew Odoacer in 493 and ruled Italy until 526. The Byzantine emperors tolerated Theodoric's rule in Italy largely because he was Christian and had been raised in the imperial palace in Constantinople. But after a new young emperor, Justinian (r. 527–65), assumed the Byzantine throne, things quickly changed. Justinian launched a massive campaign to rebuild Constantinople, including the construction of a giant new Hagia Sophia (Fig. **4.13**) at the site of the old one when the latter

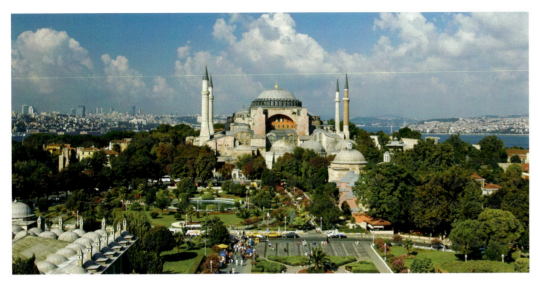

Fig. 4.13 Hagia Sophia, Istanbul (formerly Constantinople). 532–37. Originally dedicated to Christ as the personification of Holy (*hagia*) Wisdom (*sophia*), the church was transformed into a mosque by Muslim conquerors in 1453. Today, it serves as a museum, although it remains one of the oldest religious sanctuaries in the world.

View the Closer Look for the Hagia Sophia on **MyArtsLab**

was burned to the ground in 532 by rioting civic "clubs"—that probably were more like modern "gangs." The riots briefly caused Justinian to consider abandoning Constantinople, but his queen, Theodora, persuaded him to stay: "If you wish to save yourself, O Emperor," she is reported to have counseled, "that is easy. For we have much money, there is the sea, here

are the boats. But think whether after you have been saved you may not come to feel that you would have preferred to die." Justinian may well have begun construction of the new Hagia Sophia to divert attention from the domestic turmoil stirred up by the warring gangs. And he may have conceived his imperial adventuring to serve the same end (Map **4.3**). In 535, he retook

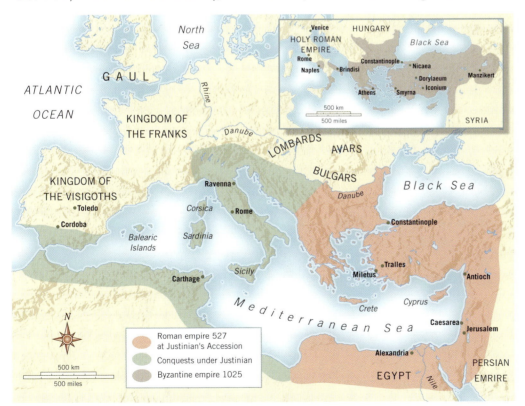

Map 4.3 The Byzantine Empire at the Death of Justinian in 565 and in 1025. The insert shows the Empire nearly 500 years after Justinian's reign, in 1025. Although it had shrunk, the Byzantine Empire remained a powerful force in the Eastern Mediterranean throughout the Middle Ages.

North Africa from the Visigoths, and a year later, he launched a campaign, headed by his general Belisarius, to retake Italy from the successors of Theodoric. But through his massive building program, especially, Justinian aimed to assert not only his political leadership but his spiritual authority also. His rule was divine, as his divine works underscored.

Hagia Sophia At the emperor's request, Procopius of Caesarea (ca. 490–ca. 560), Justinian's official court historian, wrote a treatise, *On Justinian's Buildings*, celebrating the emperor's building campaign. Book 1 is dedicated to the new Hagia Sophia, which Justinian erected on the site of the one that had burned down. As a result of Procopius' writings, we know a great deal about the building itself, including the identity of its architects, two mathematicians named Isidorus of Miletus and Anthemius of Tralles. Isidorus had edited the works of Archimedes, the third-century BCE geometrician who established the theory of the lever in mechanics, and both Isidorus and Anthemius had made studies of parabolas and curved surfaces. Their deep understanding of mathematics and physics is evident in their plan for Hagia Sophia.

Their completely original design consisted of a giant dome on a square base, the thrust of the dome carried on four giant arches that make up each side of the square (Figs. **4.14** and **4.15**). Between these arches are triangular curving vault sections, called **pendentives**, that spring from the corners of the base. The dome that rises from these pendentives has around its base 40 windows, creating a circle of light that makes the dome appear to float above the naos, underscoring its symbolic function as the dome of heaven. The sheer height of the dome adds to this effect—it is 184 feet high (41 feet higher than the Pantheon), and 112 feet in diameter. To the east and west, beneath the arches, are conch domes, or half domes, semicircular structures that spread out from a central dome, extending the space. These in turn are punctuated by yet smaller conch domes. Thus, a succession of curving spaces draws the visitor's eyes both upward to the symbolically heavenly space of the dome and forward to the sanctuary apse, seat of the altar and the liturgy. The intricate and lacy carving on the lower levels lends the stonework an almost ethereal lightness. The domes above are believed to have been covered with mosaics, probably consisting in the sixth century of plain gold grounds ornamented with crosses. Light from the windows around the base of the dome and conch domes would have ricocheted around the gold-covered interior, creating magical, even celestial light.

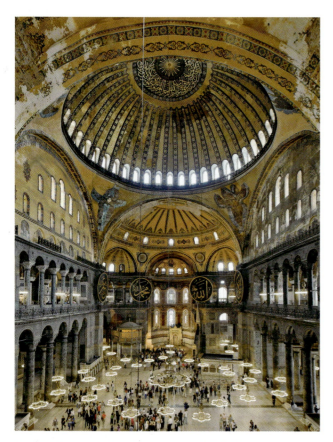

Fig. 4.14 Interior of Hagia Sophia, Istanbul. 532–37. So vast is the central dome of the church that it was likened, in its own time, to the Dome of Heaven. It was said that to look up at the dome from below was akin to experiencing the divine order of the cosmos.

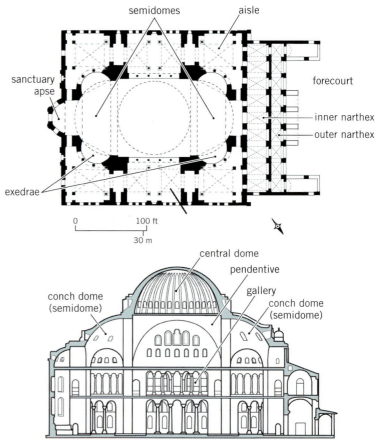

Fig. 4.15 Anthemius of Tralles and Isidorus of Miletus, Plan and section of Hagia Sophia, Istanbul. 532–37.

 Watch an architectural simulation about pendentives on **MyArtsLab**

Saint Catherine's Monastery Justinian was not content merely to rebuild Constantinople. Bridges, roads, aqueducts, monuments, churches, and monasteries sprang up around the Empire. Not the least important of these sixth-century works was the fortress and monastery known as Saint Catherine's, at the foot of Mount Sinai, in the desert near the tip of the Sinai peninsula, in modern Egypt. It was at Mount Sinai that, according to the Old Testament, God gave Moses the Ten Commandments. The monastery was sited on the spot of the burning bush, where tradition held that God had first addressed Moses and instructed him to go to Egypt and lead the Jews to the Promised Land. Thus, the monastery had great symbolic significance.

Especially important to Justinian's architectural program were the embellishments—**icons**, or images—that his artists added to church interiors. Among the earliest examples of icons are a set of paintings on wooden panels from Saint Catherine's, among them a *Theotokos and Child* (Fig. **4 .16**). *Theotokos* means "God-bearing," an epithet defining Mary as the Mother of God, an official Orthodox Church view after 431. If Mary is the mother of Jesus, the Church argued, and if Jesus is God, then Mary is the Mother of God. Such images, and the doctrine associated with them, were expected to stir the viewer to prayer. Mary's eyes are averted from the viewer's, but the Christ Child, like the two military saints, Theodore (left) and George, who flank the central pair, looks straight out. The two angels behind raise their eyes to the sky, from which God's hand descends in blessing. The words of the sixth-century Byzantine poet Agathias (ca. 536–82) are useful here: "The mortal man who beholds the image directs his mind to a higher contemplation. . . . The eyes encourage deep thoughts, and art is able by means of colors to ferry over the prayer of the mind." Thus, the icon was in some sense a vessel of prayer directed to the saint, and, given Mary's military escort, must have offered the viewer her protection.

But such imagery soon became the focus of controversy. The sudden rise of Islam as a powerful military force had a chilling effect on Byzantine art. The Byzantine emperor Leo III (r. 717–41), who came to power during the second Muslim siege of Constantinople, began to formulate a position opposing the use of holy images. He understood that the Muslims, who were still regarded as Christian heretics, had barred images from their mosques and, so the logic went, their military successes against the Byzantine Empire were a sign both of God's approval of their religious practice and of disapproval of Byzantium's. Like the Muslims, Leo argued that God had prohibited religious images in the Ten Commandments—"Thou shalt not make any graven image, or any likeness of any thing that is in heaven above, or that is in the earth beneath, or that is in the water under the earth: Thou shalt not bow down thyself to them nor serve them" (Exodus 20:4–5). Therefore, anyone worshiping such images was an idolater and was offending God. The solution was to ban images.

Thus was inaugurated a program of **iconoclasm**, from the Greek *eikon* ("icon" or "image") and *klao* (to "break" or

"destroy"), the practice of destroying religious images. While iconoclasts like Leo III set out to destroy religious images, iconophiles ("lovers of images") defended their use, usually in terms very similar to those expressed by the poet Agathias quoted above. But whatever position one assumed, the artistic style of the icons was employed in almost every form of artistic endeavor.

Byzantine icons employed a standardized shorthand to depict the events. It is as if their artistic vocabulary consisted of a limited repertoire of feet, hands, robes, and faces, all of which could be used over and over again in any context, the most important figure being the largest. We call this style, which is at once formally abstract and priestly, **hieratic**.

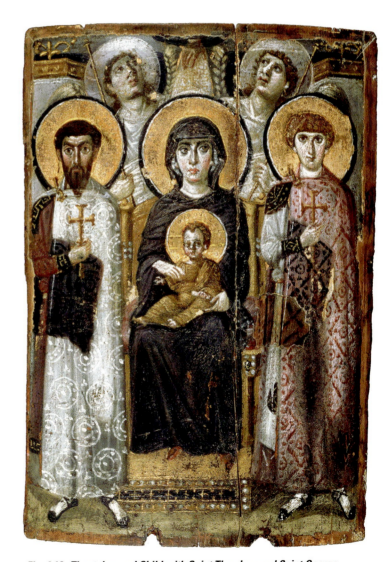

Fig. 4.16 *Theotokos and Child with Saint Theodore and Saint George.* **6th century.** Encaustic on board, 27" × 19¾". Saint Catherine's Monastery, Mount Sinai. Byzantine culture rarely, if ever, referred to Mary as "the Virgin." Instead she was the *Theotokos*, the "Mother of God."

Beowulf, the Oldest English Epic Poem

This rigidly hierarchical nature of feudal society is probably nowhere better demonstrated than in the oldest English epic poem, *Beowulf.* In the poem, a young hero, Beowulf, comes from afar to rid a community of monsters, headed by the horrific Grendel, who have been ravaging it. He returns home to his native Sweden and rules well for 50 years, until he meets a dragon who is menacing his people. Beowulf demonstrates his fierce courage and true loyalty to his vassals by taking the dragon on, but it kills him. The lesson drawn from his fate is a simple one: "So every man must yield/ the leasehold of his days."

Beowulf concludes with the hero's warriors burning his body along with his treasures on a funeral pyre, thus rounding out a story that opens with a burial as well. A treasure very much like that found in the Sutton Hoo ship burial is described just 26 lines into the poem, when the death of Danish king Shild Sheafson is described (**Reading 5.1**):

READING 5.1

Beowulf, trans. Burton Raffel

When his time was come the old king died,
Still strong but called to the Lord's hand.
His comrades carried him down to the shore,
Bore him as their leader had asked, their lord
And companion, while words could move on his tongue.
Shild's reign had been long; he'd ruled them well.
There in the harbor was a ring-prowed fighting
Ship, its timbers icy, waiting,
And there they brought the beloved body
Of their ring-giving lord, and laid him near
The mast. Next to that noble corpse
They heaped up treasures, jeweled helmets,
Hooked swords and coats of mail, armor
Carried from the ends of the earth; no ship
Had ever sailed so brightly fitted,
No king sent forth more deeply mourned.
Forced to set him adrift, floating
As far as the tide might run, they refused
To give him less from their hoards of gold
Than those who'd shipped him away, an orphan
And a beggar, to cross the waves alone.
High up over his head they flew
His shining banner, then sadly let
The water pull at the ship, watched it
Slowly sliding to where neither rulers
Nor heroes nor anyone can say whose hands
Opened to take that motionless cargo.

The findings at Sutton Hoo, as well as the ship discovered at Oseberg (see Fig. 5.1), suggest that *Beowulf* accurately reflects many aspects of life in the northern climates of Europe in the Middle Ages. The poem was composed in Anglo-Saxon, or Old English, sometime between 700 and 1000 CE, handed down first as an oral narrative and later transcribed. Its 3,000 lines represent a language that predates the merging of French and English tongues after 1066, when William

the Conqueror, a Norman duke, invaded England. The poem survived in a unique tenth-century manuscript, copied from an earlier manuscript and itself badly damaged by fire in the eighteenth century. It owes its current reputation largely to J.R.R. Tolkien, author of *The Lord of the Rings,* who in the 1930s argued for the poem's literary value. The source of Tolkien's attraction to the poem will be obvious to anyone who knows his own great trilogy.

Beowulf is an English poem, but the events it describes take place in Scandinavia. One of its most notable literary features, common to Old English literature, is its reliance on compound phrases, or **kennings**, substituted for the usual name of a person or thing. Consider, for instance, the following line:

> *Hwæt we Gar-Dena in gear-dagum*
> So. The Spear-Danes in days gone by

Instead of saying "the past," the poem says *gear-dagum,* which literally means "year-days." Instead of "the Danes," it says *Spear-Danes,* implying their warrior attributes. The poet calls the sea the *fifelstréam,* literally the "sea-monster stream," or "whale-path," and the king, the "ring-giver." A particularly poetic example is *beado-leoma,* "battle-light," referring to a flashing sword. In a sense, then, these compound phrases are metaphoric riddles that context helps to explain. *Beowulf* contains many such compounds that occur only once in all Anglo-Saxon literature—*hapax legomena,* as they are called, literally "said or counted once"—and context is our only clue to their meaning.

Some have interpreted phrases such as Shild Sheafson's crossing "over into the Lord's keeping" as evidence that the poem is a Christian allegory. But although Beowulf does indeed give "thanks to Almighty God," and admit that his victory over the monster Grendel would not have been possible "if God had not protected me," there is nothing in the poem to suggest that this is the Christian God. There are no overtly Christian references in the work. The poem teaches its audience that power, strength, fame, and life itself are fleeting—a theme consonant with Christian values, but by no means necessarily Christian. And although Beowulf, in his arguably foolhardy courage at the end of the poem, displays a Christlike willingness to sacrifice himself for the greater good, the honor and courage he exhibits are fully in keeping with the values of feudal warrior culture.

The Merging of Pagan and Christian Styles

Whatever *Beowulf*'s relation to Christian tradition, it is easy to see how the poem might have been read, even in its own time, in Christian terms. But after the Romans withdrew from Britain in 406, Christianity had survived only in the westernmost reaches of the British Isles—in Cornwall, in Wales, and in Ireland, where Saint Patrick had converted the population between his arrival in 432 and his death in 461. Around 563, an Irish monk, Columba, founded a monastery on the Scottish island of Iona. He traveled widely through Scotland and converted many northern Picts, a Scottish tribe, to Christianity. In about 635, almost simultaneously with the pagan burial at Sutton Hoo, in which only a few if any Christian artifacts were discovered, a monk from Iona built another monastery at Lindisfarne, an island off the coast of Northumbria in northeast England. The "re-Christianization" of Britain was underway.

Meanwhile, in 597, Pope Gregory I (papacy 590–604) sent a mission to England of 40 monks, headed by the Benedictine prior Augustine (d. 604)—not the same Augustine who had written *The Confessions* and *The City of God*—to convert the pagan Anglo-Saxons. Gregory urged Augustine not to eliminate pagan traditions overnight, but to incorporate them into Christian practice. In a letter sent to Augustine in 601, he wrote: "For it is certainly impossible to eradicate all errors from obstinate minds at one stroke, and whoever wishes to climb a mountaintop climbs gradually step by step, and not in one leap." This is one reason that the basic elements of the animal style, evident in the purse cover from Sutton Hoo (see Fig. 5.2), appear in a manuscript page from the *Lindisfarne Gospels*, designed by Bishop Eadfrith of Lindisfarne in 698 (Fig. **5.3**). Notice particularly how the geometric grids in the border decoration of the purse cover are elaborated in the central circle of the Lindisfarne **carpet page** (a descriptive term, not used in the Middle Ages, that refers to the resemblance between such pages and Turkish or Islamic carpets). The animal interlace of the purse cover reappears in the corner designs that frame the central circle of the carpet page, where two birds face outward and two inward. And the beasts that turn to face each other in the middle of the purse cover are echoed in the border figures of the carpet page, top and bottom, left and right. The pre-Christian decorative vocabulary of the Sutton Hoo treasure, created to honor a pagan king, has been transformed to honor the Christian conception of God.

This syncretic style—a style in which different practices and principles are combined—which flourished in England and Ireland during the early Middle Ages, is called *Hiberno-Saxon*

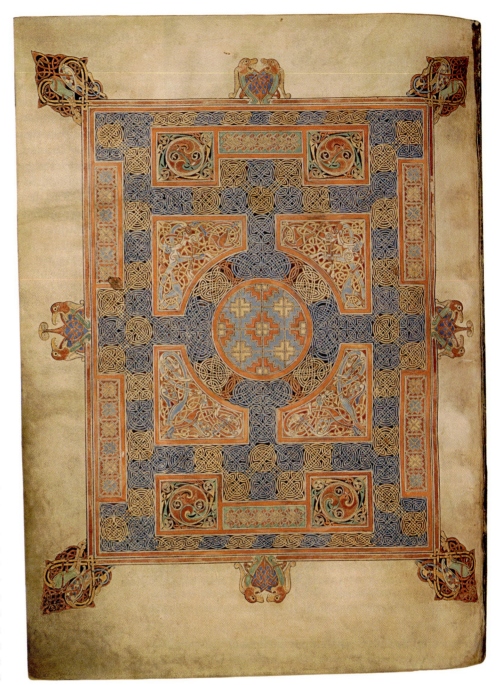

Fig. 5.3 Bishop Eadfrith, Carpet Page, from the *Lindisfarne Gospels*, Northumbria, England. ca. 698. Tempera on vellum, 13½″ × 9¾″. British Library, London. An inscription on the manuscript identifies Eadfrith as its scribe and decorator, Ethelwald as its binder, Billfrith as the monk who adorned it with gems, and Aldred as its translator into Anglo-Saxon: "Thou living God be mindful of Eadfrith, Ethelwald, Billfrith, and Aldred a sinner; these four have, with God's help, been engaged upon this book."

(*Hibernia* is the Latin name for Ireland). Hiberno-Saxon manuscript illustration is notable particularly for its unification of Anglo-Saxon visual culture with the textual tradition of Christianity. In the monastic scriptoria (singular **scriptorium**)—the halls in which monks worked to copy and decorate biblical texts—artists soon began to decorate the letterforms themselves, creating elaborate capitals at the beginning of important sections of a document. One of the

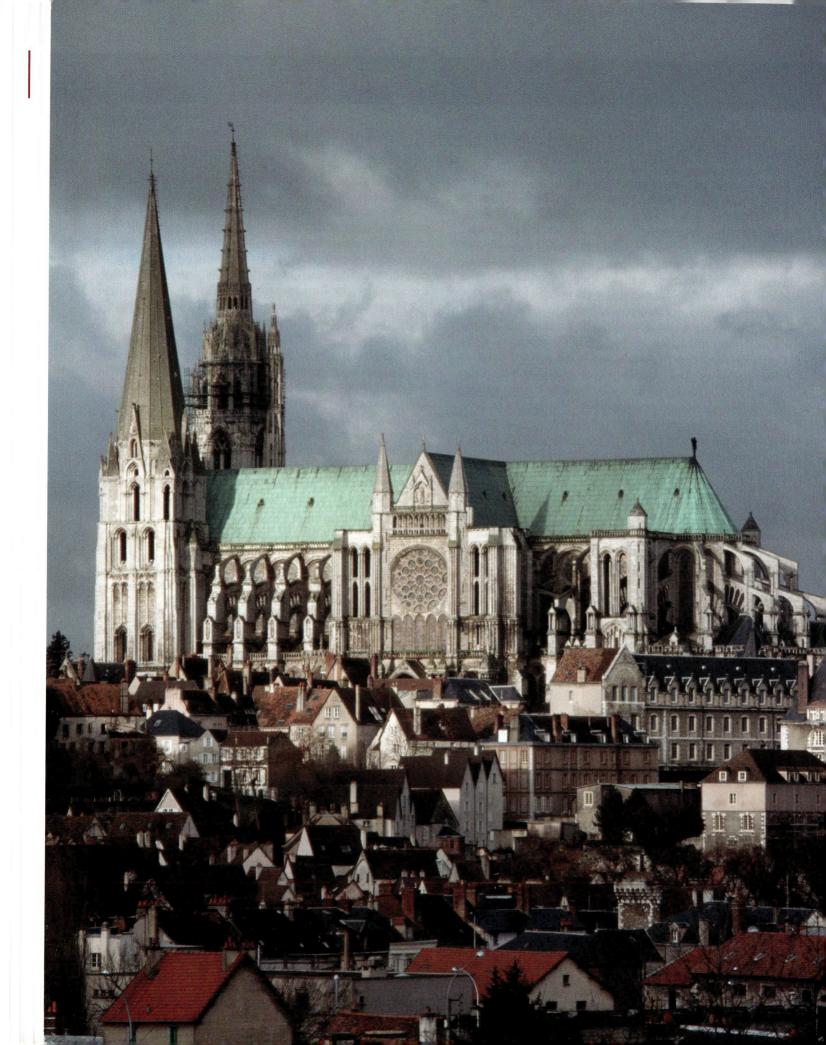

The Gothic and the Rebirth of Naturalism 6

Civic and Religious Life in an Age of Inquiry

LEARNING OBJECTIVES

6.1 Outline the ideas, technological innovations, and stylistic developments that distinguish the Gothic style in France.

6.2 Explain why the University of Paris was preeminent among medieval institutions of higher learning.

6.3 Define the Radiant style.

6.4 Compare and contrast art and civic life in Siena and Florence.

6.5 Examine the spread of a vernacular literary style in European culture.

On June 11, 1144, King Louis VII, his queen, Eleanor of Aquitaine, and a host of dignitaries traveled a few miles north of Paris to the royal Abbey of Saint-Denis, where they dedicated a new choir for the royal church. It would be the crowning achievement of the king's personal domain, the Île-de-France. Designed by Abbot Suger of Saint-Denis, the choir would quickly inspire a new style of architecture and decoration that came to be known as **Gothic**. *Gothic* was originally a derogatory term, adopted in sixteenth-century Italy to describe the art of Northern Europe, where, it was believed, Classical traditions had been destroyed by Germanic invaders—that is, by the Goths. In its own time, this style was known as *opus modernum* (modern work) or *opus francigenum* (French work). These terms highlight the style's decidedly new and contemporary flavor as well as its place of origin.

By the end of the twelfth century and the beginning of the thirteenth, town after town across northern France would imitate Suger's design at Saint-Denis. At Chartres, just to the west of the Île-de-France on the Eure River (Fig. **6.1**), to the

north at Rouen, Amiens, and Beauvais, to the east at Laon and Reims, to the south at Bourges, and in Paris itself, Gothic cathedrals sprang up with amazing rapidity. Much of the rest of Europe would soon follow suit.

With the rise of this new Gothic style came a new standard of beauty in Western architecture and decoration. A new masonry architecture developed, eventually resulting in intricate stonework that was almost skeletal in its lightness and soaring ever higher to create lofty interior spaces. Gothic architecture matched the decorative richness of stained glass with sculptural programs that were increasingly inspired by Classical models of naturalistic representation. A new, richer liturgy developed as well, and with it, polyphonic music that by the thirteenth century was accompanied by a new instrument—the organ. The Île-de-France was the center of all these developments. It was there, as well, at the University of Paris, founded in 1200, that a young Dominican monk named Thomas Aquinas initiated the most important theological debates of the age, inaugurating a style of intellectual inquiry that we associate with higher learning to this day.

◀ **Fig. 6.1 The Cathedral of Notre-Dame, Chartres, France. ca. 1134–1220.** Chartres Cathedral rises majestically, crowning the town surrounding it. Such cathedrals were the cultural centers of their communities, the source of the community's pride and prestige.

Even as an elaborate and flamboyant new style of Gothic architecture developed in the North, closely associated with the court of King Louis IX (r. 1226–70) in Paris, the Gothic arrived in Italy, where it was adapted to local traditions in Florence and Siena particularly. The two cities competed for preeminence during the thirteenth and fourteenth centuries. Out of this competition, the modern Western city as we know it—a more or less self-governing center of political, economic, and social activity, with public spaces, government buildings, and urban neighborhoods—was born. Republican Rome (see Chapter 3) and Golden Age Athens (see Chapter 2) were both models, but what distinguished Florence and Siena from these earlier republics was the role that the citizenry played in expressing their civic pride. The churches, monuments, and buildings of these late medieval cities were the work not of enlightened rulers but of the people themselves. Perhaps because the people were the great artistic patrons of the era, a new type of literature developed, written in Italian, not Latin, and often focusing on the more ordinary aspects of everyday life as lived by common people. The citizenry was genuinely thankful to God for its well-being and gave thanks by building, maintaining, and embellishing cathedrals. They built churches for the new monastic orders that served the cities' common folk. As in France, the cult of the Virgin inspired artists in both cities, and both cities placed themselves under her protection.

Until 1348, despite the ups and downs each city experienced, the Virgin seemed to bless both with good fortune. But that year, as many as half the population of both cities died of the plague. To many, the Black Death represented the vengeance of an angry God punishing the people for their sins. But, in its wake, artists, writers, merchants, and scholars discovered greater personal freedom and opportunity. Perhaps inspired by the harsh realities they confronted during the plague, artists created works of ever-greater realism and candor.

SAINT-DENIS AND THE GOTHIC CATHEDRAL

What ideas, technological innovations, and stylistic developments mark the rise of the Gothic style in France?

Even as a pupil at the monastery school, Abbot Suger had dreamed of transforming the Abbey of Saint-Denis into the most beautiful church in France. The dream was partly inspired by his desire to lay claim to the larger territories surrounding the Île-de-France. Suger's design placed the royal domain at the center of French culture, defined by an architecture surpassing all others in beauty and grandeur.

After careful planning, Suger began work on the Abbey in 1137, painting the walls, already almost 300 years old, with gold and precious colors. Then he added a new facade with twin towers and a triple portal. Around the back of the ambulatory he added a circular string of chapels, all lit with large stained-glass windows (Fig. **6.2**), "by virtue of

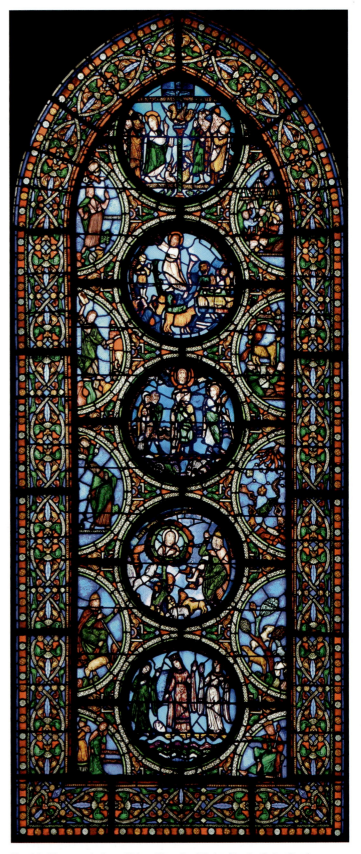

Fig. 6.2 Moses window, Abbey Church of Saint-Denis, Saint-Denis, France. 1140–44. This is the best preserved of the original stained-glass windows at Saint-Denis. Scholars have speculated that Moses was a prominent theme at the royal Abbey of Saint-Denis because his leadership of the Israelites was the model for the French king's leadership of his people.

which," Suger wrote, "the whole would shine with the miraculous and uninterrupted light."

This light proclaimed the new Gothic style. In preparing his plans, Suger had read what he believed to be the writings of the original Saint Denis. (We now know that he was reading the mystical tracts of a first-century Athenian follower of Saint Paul.) According to these writings, light is the physical and material manifestation of the Divine Spirit. Suger would later survey the accomplishments of his administration and explain his religious rationale for the beautification of Saint-Denis:

> Marvel not at the gold and the expense but at the craftsmanship of the work.
> Bright is the noble work; but being nobly bright, the work
> Should brighten the minds, so that they may travel, through the true lights,
> To the True Light where Christ is the true door.

The church's beauty, therefore, was designed to elevate the soul to the realm of God.

When Louis VII and Eleanor left France for the Second Crusade in 1147 (see Chapter 5), just three years after Suger's dedication of his choir, they also left the abbot without the funds necessary to finish his church. It was finally completed a century after he died in 1151. Much of its original sculptural and stained-glass decoration was destroyed in the late eighteenth century during the French Revolution. Although it was partially restored in the nineteenth and twentieth centuries, only five of its original stained-glass windows remain, and we must turn to other churches modeled on its design to comprehend its full effect. Chief among these is the Cathedral of Notre-Dame at Chartres, which, like the other Gothic cathedrals in both the Île-de-France and its surrounding territories, drew its inspiration from Paris.

The cathedral's spires can be seen for miles in every direction, lording over town and countryside as if it were the very center of its world (Fig. 6.3). Chartres was, in fact, located in the heart of France's grain belt, and its economy thrived as France exported grain throughout the Mediterranean basin. But more important, Chartres was the spiritual center of the cult of the Virgin, which throughout the twelfth and thirteenth centuries assumed an increasingly important role in the religious life of Western Europe. The popularity of this cult contributed, perhaps more than any other factor, to the ever-increasing size of the era's churches. Christians worshiped the Virgin as the Bride of Christ, Personification of the Church, Queen of Heaven, and prime Intercessor with God for the salvation of humankind. This last role was especially important, for in it the Virgin could intervene to save sinners from eternal damnation. The cult of the Virgin manifested itself especially in the French cathedrals, which are often dedicated to *Notre Dame*, "Our Lady."

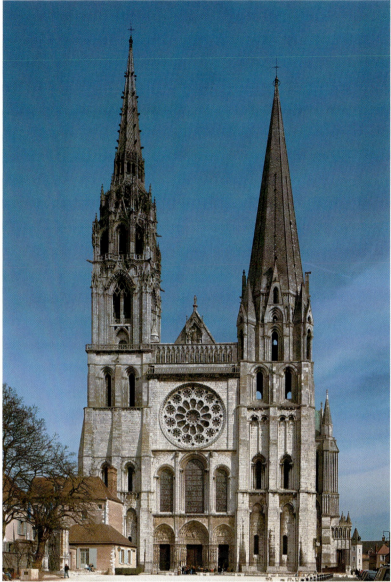

Fig. 6.3 West facade, Chartres Cathedral, France. ca. 1134–1220; south spire ca. 1160; north spire 1507–13. The different designs of the two towers reflect the Gothic dismissal of Romanesque absolute balance and symmetry as well as the growing refinements of the Gothic style. The later, north tower (left) was much more elaborately decorated and, in the more open framework of its stonework, more technically advanced.

Soon after the first building phase was completed at Chartres, between about 1140 and 1150, pilgrims thronged to the cathedral to pay homage to what the Church claimed was the Virgin's tunic, worn at Jesus' birth. This relic was housed in the cathedral and was believed to possess extraordinary healing powers. But in 1194, the original structure was destroyed by fire, except for the west facade, a few stained-glass windows, and the tunic of the Virgin. The survival of the window and the tunic was taken as a sign of divine providence, and a massive reconstruction project was begun in gratitude. Royalty and local nobility contributed

✳ **Explore** the architectural panorama for Chartres Cathedral on **MyArtsLab**

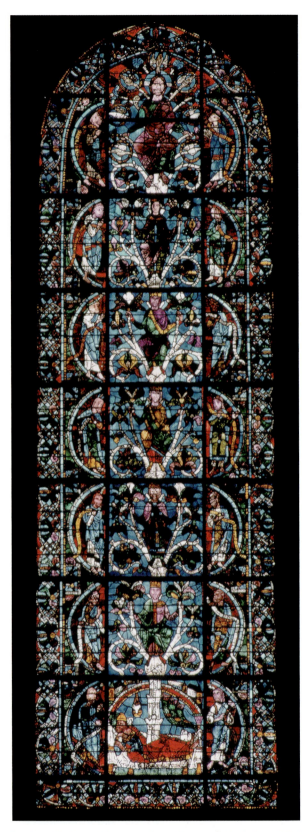

Fig. 6.4 *The Tree of Jesse* **window, Chartres Cathedral. ca. 1150–70.**
Jesse was the father of King David, who, according to the Gospels, was an ancestor of Mary. At the base of the window lies the body of Jesse, a tree growing out of him. The tree branches into the four kings of Judea, one on each row. Mary is just below Christ. Seven doves, representing the seven gifts of the Holy Spirit, encircle Christ. In half-moons flanking each section of the tree stand the 14 prophets.

their financial support, and the local guilds gave both money and work.

Behind the more-or-less Romanesque west facade, with its round-arch windows, rose what many consider to be the most magnificent of all Gothic cathedrals, its stained glass unrivaled in Europe.

Stained Glass

The stained-glass program at Chartres is immensely complex. The innovative engineering that marks Gothic architecture (discussed in the next section) freed the walls of the need to bear the weight of the structure. It also freed the walls to contain glass.

The purpose of the stained-glass programs in all Gothic cathedrals was to tell the stories of the Bible in a compelling way to an audience that was largely illiterate. The art allowed them to read the scriptural stories for themselves. At Chartres, 175 glass panels, containing more than 4,000 figures, are carefully designed, in Abbot Suger's words, "to show simple folk . . . what they ought to believe." Two windows are notable for their role in the cult of the Virgin. One of these depicts the so-called Tree of Jesse (Fig. **6.4**). Jesse trees are a common motif in twelfth- and thirteenth-century manuscripts, murals, sculpture, and stained glass, and their associated traditions are still celebrated by Christians during the season of Advent. They were thought to represent the genealogy of Christ, since they depict the Virgin Mary as descended from Jesse, the father of King David, thus fulfilling a prophecy in the book of Isaiah (11:1): "And there shall come forth a rod out of the stem of Jesse and a branch shall grow out of his roots." Most Jesse trees have at their base a recumbent Jesse with a tree growing from his side or navel. On higher branches of the tree are various kings and prophets of Judea. At the top are Christ and Mary. Sometimes the Virgin holds the infant Jesus, but here, as in a similar window at Saint-Denis, she appears in the register below Jesus. Since Jesse trees portray Mary as descending from royal lineage, they played an important role in the cult of the Virgin.

A second window in the north transept of the cathedral also evokes the Virgin (Fig. **6.5**). A **rose window**—a round window with mullions (framing elements) and traceries extending outward from its center in the manner of the petals of a rose—it is symbolic of the Virgin Mary in her role as the Mystic Rose—the root plant, it was believed, of the Jesse Tree. It measures 42 feet in diameter.

The stained glass at Chartres covers more than 32,000 square feet of surface area, and the overall effect of so many windows can hardly be imagined. The windows were donated by the royal family, by noblemen, and by merchant guilds. On an average day, the light outside the cathedral is approximately 1,000 times greater than the light inside. Thus the windows, backlit and shining in the relative darkness of the nave, seem to radiate with an ethereal and immaterial glow, suggesting a spiritual beauty beyond the here and now.

Gothic Architecture

As the Gothic style developed, important architectural innovations contributed to the goal of elevating the souls of worshipers to the spiritual realm. Key among these innovations was rib vaulting (Fig. **6.6**). The principles of rib vaulting were known to Romanesque architects, but Gothic architects used these techniques with increasing sophistication. Rib vaults are a form of groin vault (see Fig. 3.10 in Chapter 3). They are based on the pointed arch, which can reach to a greater height than a rounded arch. At the groins, structural moldings called ribs channel the vault's thrust outward and downward. These ribs were constructed first and supported the scaffolding upon which masonry webbing was built. These ribs were essentially a "skeleton" filled with a lightweight masonry "skin." Rib vaulting allowed the massive stonework of the Romanesque style to be replaced, inside and out, by an almost lacy play of thin columns and patterns of ribs and windows, all pointing upward in a gravity-defying crescendo that carries the viewer's gaze toward the heavens. Extremely high naves—Chartres' nave is 120 feet high, Reims' is 125, and the highest of all, Beauvais', is 157, the equivalent of a 15-story building—add to this emphasis on verticality, contributing a sense of elevation that is both physical and spiritual.

The preponderance of pointed rather than rounded arches contributes to this feeling as well. The pointed arch, in fact, possesses structural properties that contribute significantly to the Gothic style—the flatter or rounder an arch is, the greater outward thrust or pressure it puts on the supporting walls. By reducing outward thrust, the pointed arch allows larger windows and lighter **buttresses**, pillars traditionally built against exterior walls to brace them and strengthen the vault. **Flying buttresses** (Figs. **6.7**, **6.8**,

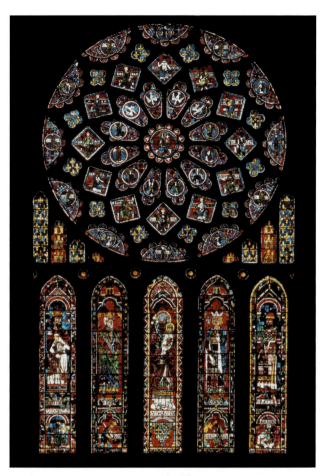

Fig. 6.5 Rose window and lancets, north transept, Chartres. ca. 1210–30. The rich blue colors of this rose window were especially treasured because legend had it that Abbot Suger had produced the blues by grinding up sapphires. The richness of the blues, however, derives from a cobalt oxide.

View the Closer Look for the Rose Window and Lancets from the North Transept of Chartres Cathedral on **MyArtsLab**

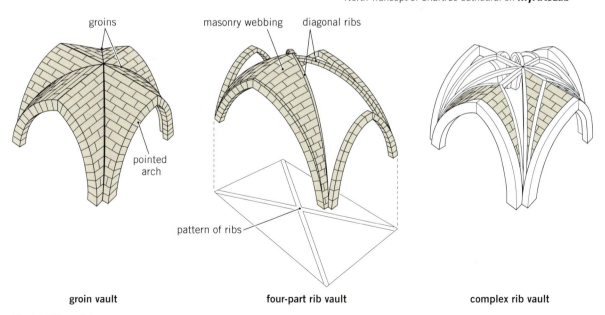

groins · masonry webbing · diagonal ribs

pointed arch

pattern of ribs

groin vault · four-part rib vault · complex rib vault

Fig. 6.6 Rib vaulting.

Watch an architectural simulation of the ribbed vault on **MyArtsLab**

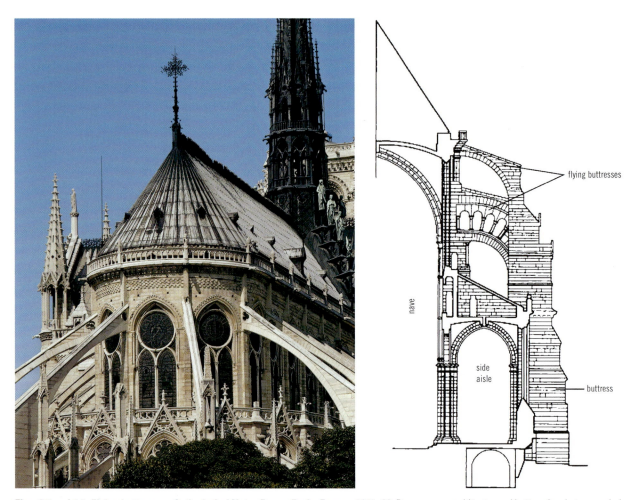

Figs. 6.7 and 6.8 Flying buttresses, Cathedral of Notre-Dame, Paris, France. 1211–90. Romanesque architects used buttressing, but concealed it under the aisle roofs. Moving the buttresses to the outside of the structure created a sense of light bridgework that contributed to the aesthetic appeal of the building as much as to its structural integrity.

and visible as well on the exterior of Chartres Cathedral, Fig. 6.1) allow even lighter buttressing and more windows. They extend away from the wall, employing an arch to focus the strength of the buttress's support at the top of the wall, the section most prone to collapse from the outward pressure of the vaulted ceiling. A flying buttress is basically a huge stone prop that pushes in against the walls with the same force with which the vaults push out. The thrust of the vaulted ceilings still comes down the piers and walls, but also moves down the arms of the flying buttresses, down the buttresses themselves, and into the ground. The flying buttresses help to spread the weight of the vaults over more supporting stone, allowing the walls to be thinner while still supporting as much weight as earlier, thicker walls. As the magnificent flying buttresses at Notre-Dame Cathedral in Paris demonstrate, they also create a stunning visual spectacle, arching winglike from the building's side as if defying gravity.

During the thirteenth century, architects began to adorn the exteriors of their cathedrals with increasingly elaborate decoration. Stone **crockets**, leaflike forms that curve

outward, their edges curling up, were added to the pinnacles, spires, and gables of the cathedrals. These were topped by **finials**, knoblike architectural forms also found on furniture. The textural richness of these forms is evident in the comparison of Chartres Cathedral (see Fig. 6.3), where they are relatively absent, and Amiens Cathedral, where they are abundant (Fig. **6.9**). The facade of Amiens is also elaborately decorated with sculpture. Most of the sculptures were made in a 20-year period by a large workshop in Amiens itself, lending the entire facade a sense of unity and coherence.

Gothic Sculpture

If we look at developments in architectural sculpture from the time of the decoration of the west portal of Chartres Cathedral (1145–70) to the time of the sculptural plan of the south transept portal (1215–20), and, finally, to the sculptures decorating the west front of Reims Cathedral (1225–55), we can see that, in a little over 100 years, Gothic sculptors had begun to reintroduce Classical principles of sculptural composition into Western art.

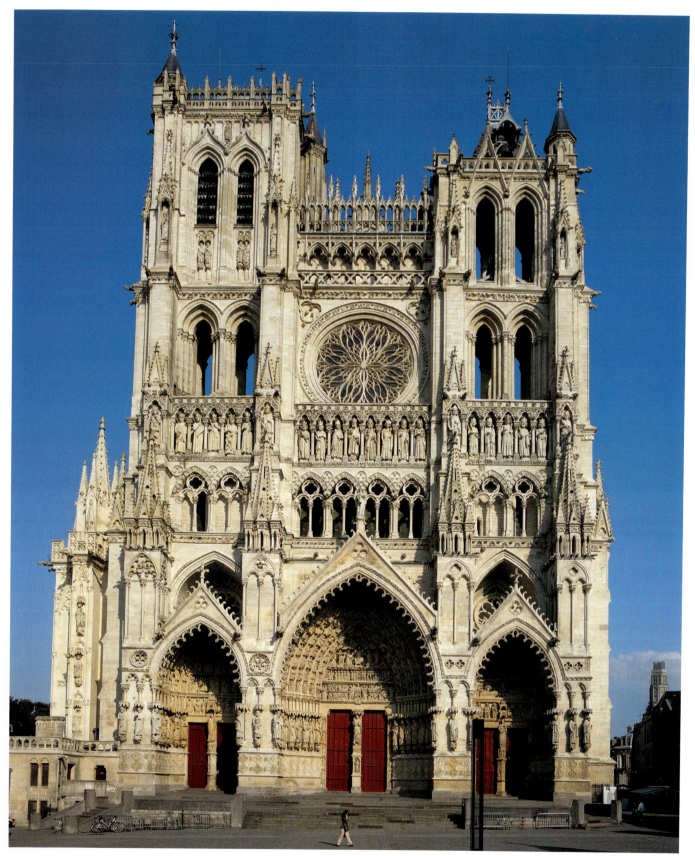

Fig. 6.9 West facade, Amiens Cathedral, Amiens, France. 1220–36/40, and continued through the 15th century. The sculptors who decorated the facade quickly became famous and traveled across Europe, carrying their style to Spain and Italy.

✳ **Explore** the architectural panorama for Amiens Cathedral on **MyArtsLab**

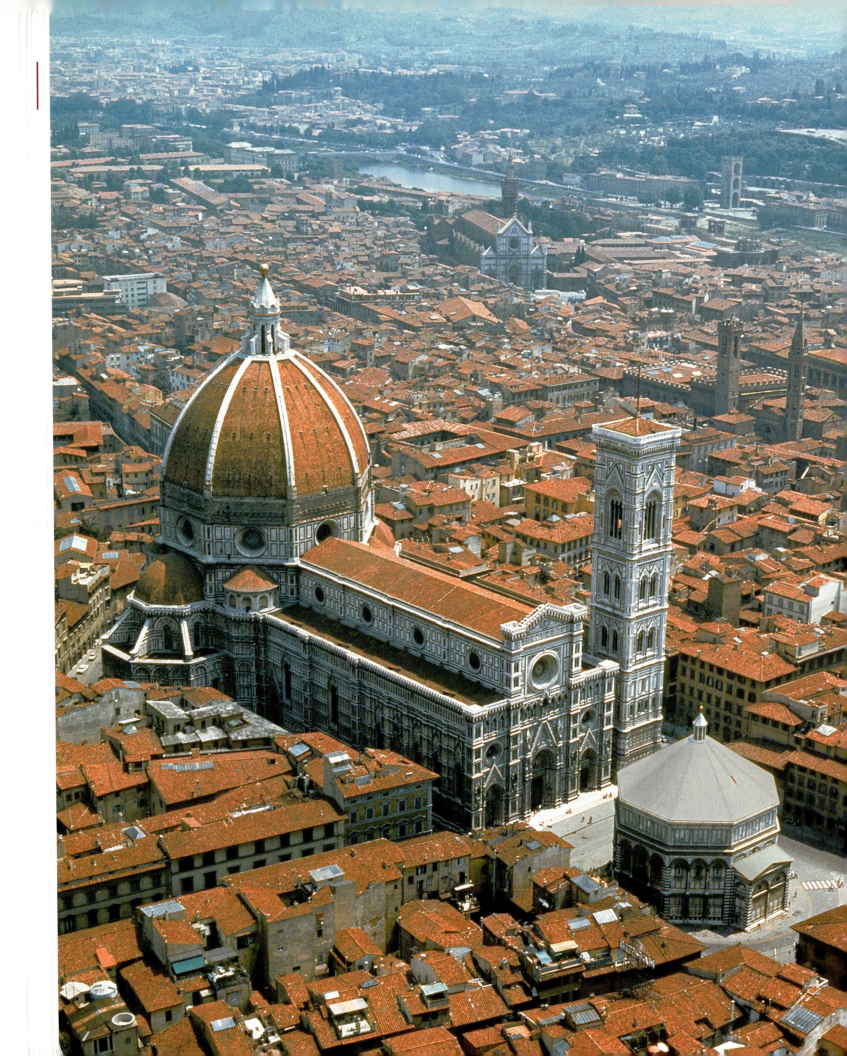

The Renaissance

Florence, Rome, and Venice

7

The word *Renaissance*, from the Italian *rinascita*, "rebirth," became widely used in the nineteenth century as historians began to assert that the beliefs and values of the medieval world were transformed in Italy, and in Florence particularly. Where the Middle Ages had been an age of faith, in which the salvation of the soul was an individual's chief preoccupation, the Renaissance was an age of intellectual exploration, inspired by a resurgence of interest in the art and literature of Classical antiquity, in which the **humanist** strove to understand in ever more precise and scientific terms the nature of humanity and its relationship to the natural world.

This chapter traces the rise of the humanist Renaissance city-state as a center of culture in Italy in the fifteenth century, concentrating on Florence, Rome, and Venice (Map 7.1). In Florence the Medici family, whose wealth derived from their considerable banking interests, did much to position the city as a model that others felt compelled to imitate.

In Rome, the wealth at the disposal of the papacy, and the willingness of the Church to bestow that wealth in the form of commissions to artists and architects in an effort to restore that city to the greatness it enjoyed more than a thousand years earlier at the height of the Roman Empire, essentially guaranteed its rebirth as a new and vital center of culture. And the citizenry of Venice—where goods from northern Europe flowed into the Mediterranean, and goods from the Mediterranean and points east flowed into Europe—thought of themselves as the most cosmopolitan and the most democratic people in the world. In this environment of enlightened leadership, the arts flourished.

THE STATE AS A WORK OF ART: FLORENCE AND THE MEDICI

How did the Medici family help shape humanist Florence?

The preeminent Italian city-state in the fifteenth century was Florence. Centered around its great cathedral (Fig. 7.1), it was so thoughtfully and carefully constructed by the ruling Medici family that later scholars would come to view it as a work of art in its own right. The Medici were the

◀ **Fig. 7.1 Florence, Italy.** The Duomo, Florence's magnificent cathedral, rises over the city. Its octagonal baptistery sits in the square before it. Just above and to the right of its bell tower, or campanile, designed by Giotto and built between 1334 and 1359, is the tower of the Palazzo Vecchio, the city hall.

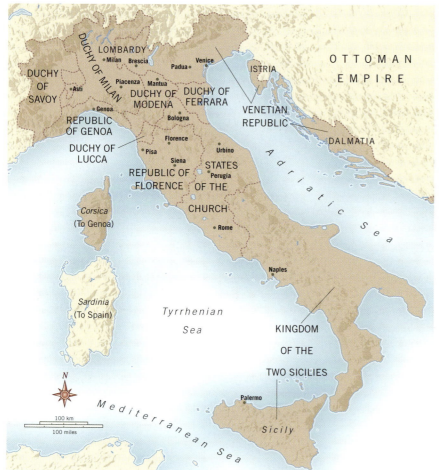

Map 7.1 Major Italian city-states during the Renaissance.

most powerful family in Florentine affairs from 1418, when they became bankers to the papacy, until 1494, when irate citizens removed them from power. A family of bankers with offices in Pisa, Rome, Bologna, Naples, Venice, Avignon, Lyon, Geneva, Basel, Cologne, Antwerp, Bruges, and London during the fifteenth century, the Medici never ruled Florence outright, but instead managed its affairs from behind the scenes.

No event better exemplifies the nature of the Italian Renaissance and anticipates the character of Florence under the Medici than a competition held in 1401 to choose a designer for a pair of bronze doors for the north entrance to the city's **baptistery** (see Fig. 7.1). The baptistery is a building standing in front of the cathedral and used for the Christian rite of baptism.

In many ways, it is remarkable that the competition to find the best design for the Baptistery doors could even take place. As much as four-fifths of the city-state's population had died in the Black Death of 1348, and the plague had returned, though less severely, in 1363, 1374, 1383, 1388, and 1400. Finally, in the summer of 1400, it came again, this time killing 12,000 Florentines, about one-fifth of the

remaining population. Perhaps the guild hoped that a facelift for the Baptistery might appease an evidently wrathful God. Furthermore, civic pride and patriotism were also at stake. Milan, the powerful city-state to the north, had laid siege to Florence, blocking trade to and from the seaport at Pisa and creating the prospect of famine. The fate of the Florentine Republic seemed to be in the balance.

So the competition was not merely about artistic talent. The general feeling was that if God looked with favor on the enterprise, the winner's work might well be the city's salvation. In fact, during the summer of 1402, as the competition was concluding, the duke of Milan died in his encampment outside the walls of Florence. The siege was over, and Florence was spared. If the Wool Guild could not take credit for these events, no one could deny the coincidence.

Thirty-four judges—artists, sculptors, and prominent citizens, including a Medici—chose the winner from among the seven entrants. Each artist was asked to create a bronze relief panel depicting the Hebrew Bible's story of the Sacrifice of Isaac (Genesis 22) in a 21-by-17½-inch *quatrefoil* (a four-leaf clover shape set on a diamond). All but two designs were eliminated, both by little-known 24-year-old goldsmiths: Filippo Brunelleschi (1377–1446) and Lorenzo Ghiberti (1378–1455).

The Sacrifice of Isaac is the story of how God tested the faith of the patriarch Abraham by commanding him to sacrifice Isaac, his only son. Abraham took Isaac into

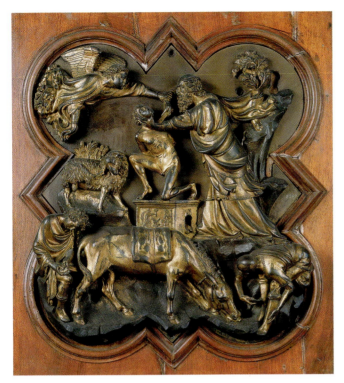

Fig. 7.2 Filippo Brunelleschi, *Sacrifice of Isaac,* **competition relief commissioned for the doors of the Baptistery. 1401–02.** Parcel-gilt bronze, 21″ × 17½″. Museo Nazionale del Bargello, Florence. Brunelleschi's background seems to be little more than a flat surface against which his forms are set.

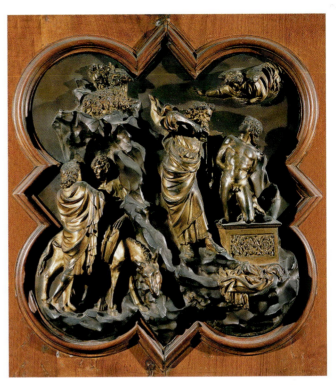

Fig. 7.3 Lorenzo Ghiberti, *Sacrifice of Isaac,* **competition relief commissioned for the doors of the Baptistery. 1401–02.** Parcel-gilt bronze, 21″ × 17½″. Museo Nazionale del Bargello, Florence. As opposed to Brunelleschi's, Ghiberti's background seems to be real, deep space.

the wilderness to perform the deed, but at the last moment, an angel stopped him, implying that God was convinced of Abraham's faith and would be satisfied with the sacrifice of a ram instead. Brunelleschi and Ghiberti both depicted the same aspect of the story, the moment when the angel intervenes. Brunelleschi placed Isaac in the center of the panel and the other figures, whose number and type were probably prescribed by the judges, all around (Fig. **7.2**). The opposition between Abraham and the angel, as the angel grabs Abraham's arm to stop him from plunging his knife into his son's breast, is highly dramatic and realistic, an effect achieved by the figures' jagged movements. Ghiberti, in contrast, set the sacrifice to one side of the panel (Fig. **7.3**). He replaced a sense of physical strain with graceful rhythms, so that Isaac and Abraham are unified by the bowed curves of their bodies, Isaac's nude body turning on its axis to face Abraham. The angel in the upper right corner is represented in a more dynamic manner than in Brunelleschi's panel. This heavenly visitor seems to have rushed in from deep space. The effect is achieved by **foreshortening**, a technique used to suggest that forms are sharply receding. In addition, the strong diagonal of the landscape, which extends from beneath the sacrificial altar and rises up into a large rocky outcrop behind the other figures, creates a more vivid sense of real space than Brunelleschi's scene.

Despite the artistic differences in the two works, the contest might have been decided by economics. Brunelleschi cast each of his figures separately and then assembled them on the background. Ghiberti cast separately just the body of Isaac, a method that required only two-thirds of the bronze used by his rival. The process also resulted in a more unified panel, and this may have given Ghiberti the edge. Disappointed, Brunelleschi left Florence for Rome and gave up sculpture forever. Their competition highlights the growing emphasis on individual achievement in the young Italian Renaissance: The work of the individual craftsperson was replacing the collective efforts of the guild or workshop in decorating public space. The judges valued the originality of Brunelleschi's and Ghiberti's conceptions. Rather than placing their figures on a shallow platform, as one might expect in the shallow space available in a relief sculpture, both sought to create a sense of a deep, receding space, enhancing the appearance of reality.

As humanists, Ghiberti and Brunelleschi valued the artistic models of antiquity and looked to Classical sculpture for inspiration—notice, for instance, the twisting torso of Ghiberti's nude Isaac. But, above all, the artworks they created captured human beings in the midst of a crisis of faith with which every viewer might identify. In all this, their competition looks forward to the art that defines the Italian Renaissance itself.

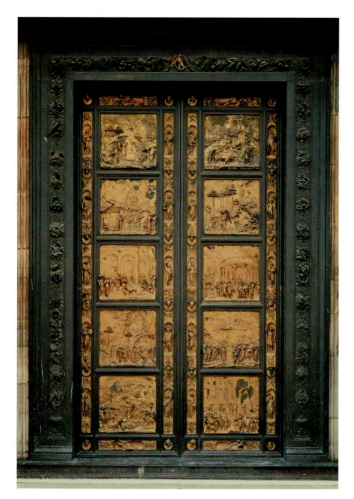

Fig. 7.4 Lorenzo Ghiberti, *Gates of Paradise*, east doors of the Baptistery, Florence. ca. 1425–52. Gilt bronze, height 15'. Ghiberti wrote of the doors in his *Commentaries* (ca. 1450–55): "I strove to imitate nature as clearly as I could, and with all the perspective I could produce, to have excellent compositions with many figures."

The *Gates of Paradise*

Ghiberti worked on the north-side doors for the next 22 years, designing 28 panels in four vertical rows illustrating the New Testament (originally the subject had been the Hebrew Bible, but the guild changed the program). Immediately upon their completion in 1424, the Wool Guild commissioned a second set of doors from Ghiberti for the east side of the Baptistery. These would take him another 27 years. Known as the *Gates of Paradise* because they open onto the *paradiso*, Italian for the area between a baptistery and the entrance to its cathedral, these doors depict scenes from the Hebrew Bible in ten square panels (Fig. **7.4**). The borders surrounding them contain other biblical figures, as well as a self-portrait (Fig. **7.5**). The artist's head is slightly bowed, perhaps in humility, but perhaps, situated as it is just above the average viewer's head, so that he might look out upon his audience. The proud image functions as both a signature and a bold assertion of Ghiberti's own worth as an artist and individual.

Each of the panels in the east doors depicts one or more events from the same story. For instance, the first panel, at the upper left of the doors (Fig. **7.6**), contains four episodes from the book of Genesis: the Creation of Adam, at the bottom left; the Creation of Eve, in the center; the Temptation, in the distance behind the Creation of Adam; and the Expulsion, at the bottom right. This portrayal of sequential events in the same frame harks back to medieval art. But if the content of the space is episodic, the landscape is coherent and realistic, stretching in a single continuum from the foreground into the far distance. The figures themselves hark back to Classical Greek and Roman sculpture. Adam, in the lower left-hand corner, resembles the recumbent god from the east pediment of the Parthenon (see Fig. 2.31 in Chapter 2), and Eve, in the right-hand corner, is a Venus of recognizably Hellenistic origin; compare Praxiteles' fourth-century BCE *Aphrodite of Knidos* (see Fig. 2.39 in Chapter 2).

CONTINUITY & CHANGE

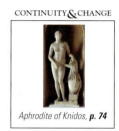

*Aphrodite of Knidos, **p. 74***

Ghiberti meant to follow the lead of the ancients in creating realistic figures in realistic space. As he wrote in his memoirs, "I strove to observe with all the scale and proportion, and to endeavor to imitate Nature . . . on the planes one sees the figures which are near appear larger, and those that are far off smaller, as reality shows." Not only do the figures

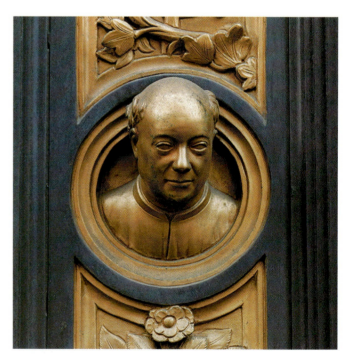

Fig. 7.5 Lorenzo Ghiberti, self-portrait from the *Gates of Paradise*, east doors of the Baptistery, Florence. ca. 1425–52. Gilt bronze. Ghiberti included his self-portrait among the prophets and other biblical figures framing the panels, as he had earlier on the north doors. The extreme naturalism of this self-portrait underscores the spirit of individualism that characterizes the Renaissance.

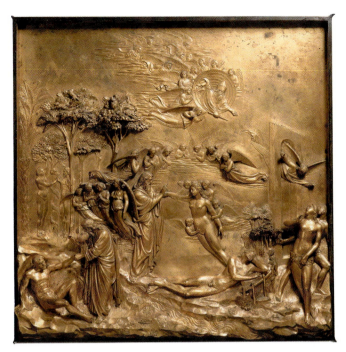

Fig. 7.6 Lorenzo Ghiberti, *The Story of Adam and Eve,* from the *Gates of Paradise,* east doors of the Baptistery, Florence. ca. 1425–52. Gilt bronze, 31¼" × 31¼". The influence of Classical antiquity is clear in the portrayal of Eve, whose pose, at the center, derives from Birth of Venus sculptures, and, on the right, from images of the Venus Pudica, or "modest" Venus.

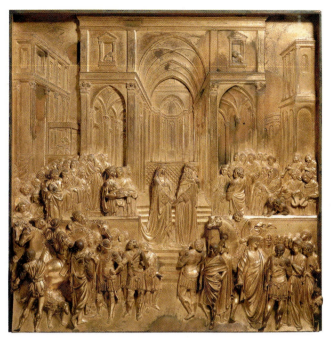

Fig. 7.7 Lorenzo Ghiberti, *Meeting of Solomon and Sheba,* from the *Gates of Paradise,* east doors of the Baptistery, Florence. ca. 1425–52. Gilt bronze, 31¼" × 31¼". The reunification of the Eastern and Western Churches, symbolically represented here, was announced on the steps of Florence Cathedral on July 9, 1439, with the emperor of Byzantium present. The agreement was short-lived, and by 1472, the Eastern church had formally rejected the Florence accords.

farther off appear smaller, but also they decrease in their projection from the panel, so that the most remote are in very shallow relief, hardly raised above the gilded bronze surface.

Whereas medieval artists regarded the natural world as an imperfect reflection of the divine, and hardly worth attention (see Chapter 5), Renaissance artists understood the physical universe as an expression of the divine and thus worth copying in the greatest detail. To understand nature was, in some sense, to understand God. Ghiberti's panel embodies this growing desire in the Renaissance to reflect nature as accurately as possible. It is a major motivation for the development of perspective in painting and drawing.

The work had political significance as well. The only panel to represent a single event in its space is the *Meeting of Solomon and Sheba* (Fig. **7.7**). Here, the carefully realized symmetry of the architecture, with Solomon and Sheba framed in the middle of its space, was probably designed to represent the much-hoped-for reunification of the Eastern Orthodox and Western Catholic branches of the Church. Solomon was traditionally associated with the Western Church, while the figure of Sheba, queen of the Arabian state of Sheba, was meant to symbolize the Eastern. Cosimo de' Medici would finance a Council of Churches that convened in Florence in 1438, and as Ghiberti finished the doors a year earlier it seemed possible, even likely, that reunification might become a reality. This would have restored

symmetry and balance to a divided Church, just as Ghiberti had achieved balance and symmetry in his art. But above all, especially in the context of the other nine panels—all of which depict multiple events with multiple focal points—this composition's focus on a single event reflects the very image of the unity sought by the Church.

Florence Cathedral

Construction of the Duomo (see Fig. 7.1), as Florence Cathedral is known, began in 1296 under the auspices of the Opera del Duomo, which was controlled by the Wool Guild. The cathedral was planned as the most beautiful and grandest in all of Tuscany. It was not consecrated until 140 years later, and even then, was hardly finished. Over the years, its design and construction became a group activity as an ever-changing panel of architects prepared model after model of the church and its details were submitted to the Opera and either accepted or rejected.

Brunelleschi's Dome During visits to Rome, Brunelleschi had carefully measured the proportions of ancient buildings, including the Colosseum, the Pantheon, the remains of the Baths of Caracalla, and the Domus Aurea (Golden Palace) of Nero. Using these studies, Brunelleschi produced the winning design for the dome of Florence Cathedral. The design guaranteed his reputation as one of the geniuses of Renaissance Florence, even in his own day.

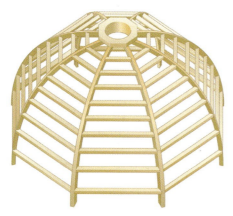

Fig. 7.8 Diagram of ribs and horizontal bands within Brunelleschi's dome. The ribs meet at the oculus, over which Brunelleschi constructed his lantern. The horizontal ribs absorbed the pressure caused by the thrust of the ribs against the wall of the dome.

 Watch an architectural simulation of Brunelleschi's doming of Florence Cathedral on **MyArtsLab**

Brunelleschi's design for the dome solved a number of technical problems. For one thing it eliminated the need for the temporary wooden scaffolding normally used to support the dome vaulting as it was raised. Although critics disagreed, Brunelleschi argued that a skeleton of eight large ribs, visible on the outside of the dome, alternating with eight pairs of thinner ribs beneath the roof, all tied together by only nine sets of horizontal ties, would be able to support themselves as the dome took form (Fig. **7.8**).

Brunelleschi completed the dome in 1436. In yet another competition, he then designed a **lantern** (a windowed turret at the top of a dome, visible in Fig. 7.1) to cover the oculus and thus put the finishing touch on the dome. It was made of over 20 tons of stone. Brunelleschi designed a special hoist to raise the stone to the top of the dome, but construction had barely begun when he died in 1446.

"Songs of Angels": Music for Church and State For the consecration of Florence Cathedral, rededicated as Santa Maria del Fiore (Saint Mary of the Flower) on March 25, 1436, Brunelleschi constructed a 1,000-foot walkway, 6 feet high and decorated with flowers and herbs, on which to guide celebrated guests into the cathedral proper. These included Pope Eugenius IV and his entourage of 7 cardinals, 37 bishops, and 9 Florentine officials (including Cosimo de' Medici), all of whom were observed by the gathered throng. Once inside, the guests heard a new musical work, picking up the floral theme of the day, called *Nuper rosarum flores* ("The Rose Blossoms") (track **7.1**). It was composed especially for the consecration by French composer Guillaume Dufay (ca. 1400–74), who worked in both France and Italy. The piece is a **motet**, the form of polyphonic vocal work that had gained increasing popularity since the mid-thirteenth century (see Chapter 5). Dufay's motet introduced a richer and fuller sonority to the form, combining both voices and instruments. (The use of instruments, other than the organ, in church performance

 Listen at **MyArtsLab**

would remain a matter of controversy for many centuries in the Catholic Church.) The **cantus firmus**—or "fixed melody"—on which the composition is based is stated in not one but two voices, both moving at different speeds.

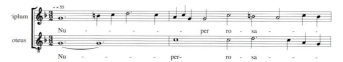

Cantus firmus melody from Dufay's *Nuper rosarum flores*

The melody derives from a chant traditionally used for the dedication of new churches, *Terribilis est locus iste* ("Awesome Is This Place").

Dufay's motet also reflects the ideal proportions of the Temple of Solomon in Jerusalem (see Chapter 1), which, according to I Kings, was laid out in the proportions 6:4:2:3, with 6 being the length of the building, 4 the length of the nave, 2 the width, and 3 the height. Florence Cathedral followed these same proportions, and Dufay mirrors them in his composition by repeating the cantus firmus four times, successively based on 6, 4, 2, and 3 units per *breve* (equivalent to two whole notes in modern notation). Hearing the entire work, one witness wrote: "It seemed as though the symphonies and songs of the angels and divine paradise had been sent forth from Heaven to whisper in our ears an unbelievable celestial sweetness." It is not surprising, given this reaction, that Dufay was regarded as the greatest composer of the fifteenth century. It is even less surprising that the Florentines selected him to celebrate the consecration of their new cathedral and its dome by creating an original work. In performing this service he announced the preeminence of both the cathedral and the city that had built it.

Scientific Perspective and Naturalistic Representation

No aspect of the Renaissance better embodies the spirit of invention evidenced by both Brunelleschi's dome and Dufay's music than **scientific** or **linear perspective**, which allowed artists to translate three-dimensional space onto a two-dimensional surface, thereby satisfying the age's increasing taste for naturalistic representations of the physical world. It was the basis of what would later come to be called *buon disegno*, literally "good design" or "drawing," but the term refers more to the intellectual conception of the work than to literal drawing. Giorgio Vasari, whose *Lives of the Most Excellent Painters, Architects, and Sculptors* is one of our most important sources of information about Italian Renaissance art in the fourteenth, fifteenth, and sixteenth centuries, defined it as follows: "Design (*disegno*) is the imitation of the most beautiful things of nature in all figures whether painted or chiseled, and this requires a hand and genius to transfer everything which the eye sees, exactly and correctly, whether it be in drawings, on paper panel, or other surface, both in relief and sculpture." It distinguished, in his mind, the art of Florence above all others.

Brunelleschi, Alberti, and the Invention of Scientific Perspective It was Brunelleschi who first mastered the art of scientific perspective sometime in the first decade of the fifteenth century. The ancient Greeks and Romans had at least partially understood its principles, but their methods had been lost. Brunelleschi almost certainly turned to them for the authority, at least, to "reinvent" it. His investigation of optics in Arab science also contributed to his understanding, particularly Alhazen's *Perspectiva* (ca. 1000 CE), which integrated the Classical works of Euclid, Ptolemy, and Galen. Their understanding of the principles of geometry, and the sense of balance and proportion that geometry inspired, affected every aspect of Brunelleschi's architectural work.

But it was geometry's revelation of the rules of perspective that most fascinated Brunelleschi. As he surveyed the Roman ruins, plotting three-dimensional architectural forms on flat paper, he mastered its finer points. Back in Florence, he would demonstrate the principles of perspective in his own architectural work. Brunelleschi's findings were codified in 1435 by the architect Leon Battista Alberti (1404–74) in his treatise *On Painting*. Painting, Alberti said, is an intellectual pursuit, dedicated to replicating nature as accurately as possible. A painting's composition should be based on the orderly arrangement of parts, which relies on rendering space in **one-point perspective**. He outlined step-by-step instructions for the creation of such space, and provided diagrams as well (Fig. **7.9**). The basic principles of the system are these: (1) All parallel lines in a visual field appear to converge at a single **vanishing point** on the horizon (think of train tracks merging in the distance); (2) These parallel lines are realized

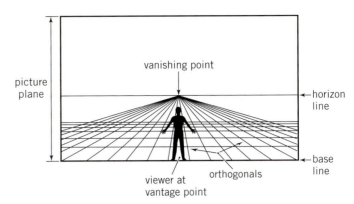

Fig. 7.9 Alberti's perspective diagram.

on the **picture plane**—the two-dimensional surface of the panel or canvas, conceived as a window through which the viewer perceives the three-dimensional world—as diagonal lines called **orthogonals**; (3) Forms diminish in scale as they approach the vanishing point along these orthogonals; and (4) The vanishing point is directly opposite the eye of the beholder, who stands at the **vantage point**, thus, metaphorically at least, placing the individual (both painter and viewer) at the center of the visual field.

Perspective and Naturalism in Painting: Masaccio Although Alberti dedicated *On Painting* first and foremost to Brunelleschi, he also singled out several other Florentine artists. One of these was Masaccio (1401–28), whose masterpiece of naturalistic representation is *The Tribute Money* (Fig. **7.10**). Commissioned by a member of the Brancacci family in the

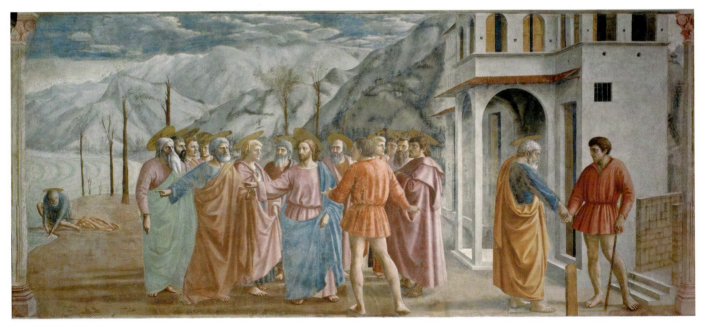

Fig. 7.10 Masaccio, *The Tribute Money*, Brancacci Chapel, Santa Maria del Carmine, Florence. 1420s. Fresco, 8'1¼" × 19'7". When this fresco was restored between 1981 and 1991, cleaning revealed that every character in this scene originally had a gold-leaf halo, except the tax collector, probably not a Christian. Masaccio drew these halos according to the laws of scientific perspective.

 View the Closer Look for *The Tribute Money* on **MyArtsLab**

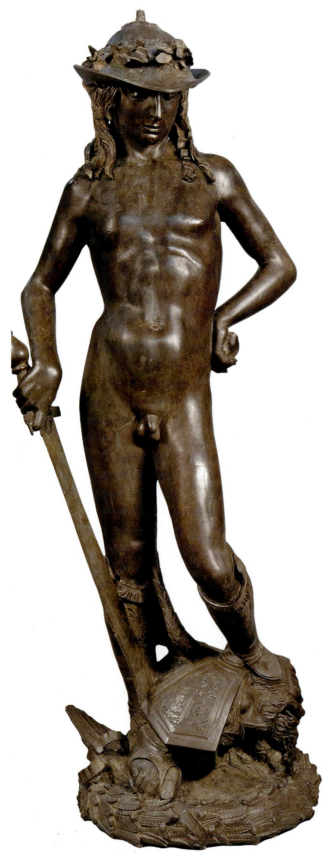

Fig. 7.11 Donatello, *David*. 1440s. Bronze, height 62¼". Museo Nazionale del Bargello, Florence. By 1469, this sculpture stood in the courtyard of the Medici palace as a symbol of the Florentine state.

1420s as part of a program to decorate the family's chapel in the church of Santa Maria del Carmine in Florence, it illustrates an event in the Gospel of Matthew (17:24–27). Christ responds to the demand of a Roman tax collector for money by telling Saint Peter to catch a fish in the Sea of Galilee, where he will find, in its mouth, the required amount. This moment occurs in the center of the painting. Behind the central group, to the left, Saint Peter finds the money, and to the right, he pays the tax. The vanishing point of the painting is behind the head of Christ, where the orthogonals of the architecture on the right converge. In fact, the function of the architecture appears to be to lead the viewer's eyes to Christ, identifying him as the most important figure in the work.

Another device, known as **atmospheric perspective**, also gives the painting the feeling of naturalism. This system depends on the observation that the haze in the atmosphere makes distant elements appear less distinct and bluish in color, even as the sky becomes paler as it approaches the horizon. As a result, the house and trees on the distant hills in this fresco are loosely sketched, as if we see them through a hazy filter of air. The diminishing size of the barren trees at the left also underscores the fact that, in a perspectival rendering of space, far-off figures seem smaller (as does the diminished size of Saint Peter at the edge of the sea).

Perhaps the greatest source of naturalism in the scene comes from the figures themselves, who provide a good imitation of life through their dynamic gestures and poses, their individuality, and their emotional engagement in the events. Here the human figure is fully alive and active. This is especially evident in the *contrapposto* pose of the Roman tax collector, whom we see both with his back to us in the central group of figures and at the far right, where Saint Peter is paying him. Christ, too, throws all of his weight to his right foot. This is a naturalistic device that Masaccio borrowed from antiquity. Indeed, the blond head of Saint John is almost surely a copy of a Roman bust.

The Classical Tradition in Freestanding Sculpture: Donatello Masaccio probably learned about the Classical disposition of the body's weight from Donatello (ca. 1386–1466), who had accompanied Brunelleschi to Rome years before. Many of Donatello's own works seem to have been inspired by antique Roman sculpture.

Although it dates from nearly 15 years after Masaccio's *The Tribute Money*, Donatello's *David* (Fig. **7.11**), which celebrates this Hebrew Bible hero's victory over the giant Goliath, indicates how completely the sculptor had absorbed Classical tradition. The first life-size freestanding nude sculpted since antiquity, it stands in a fully Classical *contrapposto* pose reminiscent of Greek sculpture such as Polyclitus' *Doryphorus* (see Fig. 2.28 in Chapter 2). It is revolutionary in other ways as well. The *contrapposto* pose is almost exaggerated, especially the positioning of the back of the hand against the hip. The young adolescent's youthful

CONTINUITY & CHANGE

*Doryphoros, **p. 63***

gaze stands in marked contrast to the bearded head of Goliath at his feet. Donatello seems to celebrate not just the human body, but also its youthful vitality, a vitality his figure shared with the Florentine state itself.

It is difficult, in other words, to imagine that such a slight, adolescent figure could have slain a giant. It is as if Donatello portrayed David as an unconvincing hero in order to underscore the ability of virtue, in whatever form, to overcome tyranny. And so this young man might represent the vigor and virtue of the Florentine republic as a whole and the city's persistent resistance to domination. In fact, when in 1469 the statue stood in the courtyard of the Medici palace, it bore the following inscription: "The victor is whoever defends the fatherland. All-powerful God crushes the angry enemy. Behold a boy overcame the great tyrant. Conquer, O citizens." The Medici thus secularized the religious image even as they implicitly affirmed their right to rule as granted by an all-powerful God whose might they shared.

The Medici Family and Humanism

The Medici family had been prominent in Florentine civic politics since the early fourteenth century. The family had amassed a fortune by skill in trade—especially the banker's trade in money—and became strong supporters of many of the city's smaller guilds. But their power was only fully cemented by Cosimo de' Medici (1389–1464).

Cosimo inherited great wealth from his father and secured the family's hold on the political fortunes of the city. Without upsetting the appearance of republican government, he mastered the art of behind-the-scenes power by controlling appointments to chief offices. But he also exerted considerable influence through his patronage of the arts. His father had headed the drive to rebuild the church of San Lorenzo, which stood over the site of an early Christian basilica dedicated in 393. San Lorenzo thus represented the entire Christian history of Florence, and after his father's death, Cosimo himself paid to complete its construction and decorate it. In return, it was agreed that no family crest other than the Medici's would appear in the church. Cosimo also rebuilt the old monastery of San Marco for the Dominican Order, adding a library, cloister, chapter room, bell tower, and altarpiece. In effect, Cosimo had made the entire religious history of Florence the family's own.

Marsilio Ficino and Neoplatonism Humanist that he was, Cosimo was particularly impressed by one scholar, the young priest Marsilio Ficino (1433–99). Beginning in about 1453, Cosimo supported Ficino in his translation and interpretation of the works of Plato and later philosophers of Platonic thought. As described in Chapter 2, Platonic thought distinguished between a sphere of being that is eternal and unchanging and the world in which we actually live, in which nothing is fixed forever. Following Plato's lead, Ficino argued that human reason belonged to the eternal dimension, as human achievement in mathematics and moral philosophy demonstrated, and that through human reason we can commune with the eternal sphere of being.

Ficino coined the term **Platonic love** to describe the ideal spiritual (never physical) relationship between two people, based on Plato's insistence on striving for and seeking out the good, the true, and the beautiful. The source of Ficino's thought is his study of the writings of Plotinus (ca. 205–70 CE), a Greek scholar of Platonic thought who had studied Indian philosophy (both Hinduism and Buddhism) and who believed in the existence of an ineffable and transcendent One, from which emanated the rest of the universe as a series of lesser beings. For Plotinus, human perfection (and, therefore, absolute happiness) was attainable in this world through philosophical meditation. This **Neoplatonist** philosophy (a modern usage) recast Platonic thought in contemporary terms. It appealed immensely to Cosimo. He could see everywhere in the great art and literature of antiquity the good, the true, and the beautiful he sought, and so he surrounded himself with art and literature, both contemporary and Classical, and lavished them upon his city.

Domestic Architecture for Merchant Princes In 1444, Cosimo commissioned for the family a new **palazzo** ("palace") that would redefine domestic architecture in the Renaissance. He first rejected a plan by Brunelleschi, considering it too grand, and built instead a palace designed by Michelozzo di Bartolommeo (1396–1472), now known as the Palazzo Medici-Riccardi (Fig. **7.12**). He filled it with the art

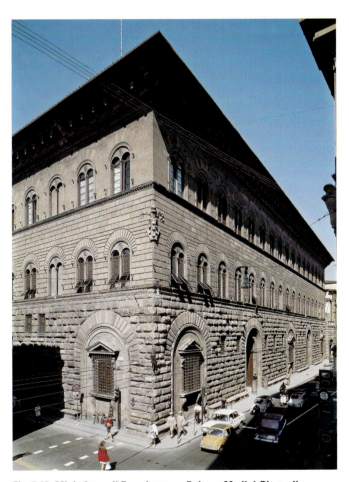

Fig. 7.12 Michelozzo di Bartolommeo, Palazzo Medici-Riccardi, Florence. Begun 1444. If it seems odd to think of such a structure as a palace, it is worth remembering that the Italian word *palazzo* refers to any reasonably large urban house.

For Alberti, architecture is the highest art and all buildings must properly reflect their social "place." Thus the Duomo, which Alberti believed to be the most important building in Florence, is at the heart of the city and rises high above it, the very center of Florentine culture. It follows that leading families should live in houses that reflect those families' stability and strength.

The Palazzo Rucellai does that and more. In direct imitation of the Roman Colosseum (see Fig. 3.11 in Chapter 3), Alberti uses three Classical orders, one for each of the three stories: the Tuscan (substituting for the Doric) at the bottom, the Ionic at the second story, and the Corinthian at the top. As at the Colosseum, the columns are engaged (that is, decorative rather than functional), and an arch is set between them. Many people thought Alberti's plan too grand because, in its reference to the Colosseum, it embodies not Republican but imperial Rome. However, Alberti's design reflects the real state of affairs in Florence at that time. For the city was ruled by what was in fact a hereditary monarchy—the Medici—supported by a wealthy, albeit mercantile, "nobility," consisting of families such as the Rucellai.

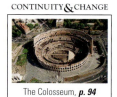

CONTINUITY & CHANGE

The Colosseum, *p. 94*

Lorenzo the Magnificent: ". . . I find a relaxation in learning."

After Cosimo's death in 1464, his son Piero (1416–69) followed in his footsteps, championing the arts, supporting the Platonic Academy, and otherwise working to make Florence the cultural center of Europe. But when Piero died only five years after his father, his 20-year-old son Lorenzo (1449–92) assumed responsibility for leading the family and the city. So great and varied were his accomplishments that in his own time he was known as *il Magnifico*—"the Magnificent."

As a young man, Lorenzo had been tutored by Ficino, and among his favorite pastimes was spending the evening talking with Ficino and other friends. "When my mind is disturbed with the tumults of public business," he wrote Ficino in 1480, "and my ears are stunned with the clamors of turbulent citizens, how would it be possible for me to support such contentions unless I found a relaxation in learning?" In support of learning, he rebuilt the University of Pisa and continued to support the study of Greek philosophy and literature in Florence at the Platonic Academy.

Lorenzo's own circle of acquaintances included many of the greatest minds of the day. Delighted by a copy of an ancient Greek or Roman faun's head made by an unknown adolescent named Michelangelo Buonarroti, Lorenzo invited the sculptor to live in the Medici palace, and the young man was soon a regular in the philosophical discussions that occupied Lorenzo for so many evenings. Besides Ficino, other frequent guests included the composer Heinrich Isaac, the poet Poliziano, the painter Sandro Botticelli, and the philosopher Pico della Mirandola.

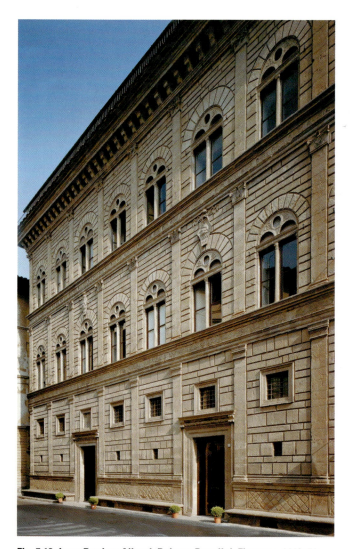

Fig. 7.13 Leon Battista Alberti, Palazzo Rucellai, Florence. 1446–51.
In Alberti's time, the house extended to the right by four more bays and one more doorway, or portal.

of the day (including Donatello's *David*, Fig. 7.11). The bottom story is 20 feet high and made of rough-cut stone meant to imitate the walls of ancient Roman ruins and designed to suggest the Medici's adherence to tradition. The outside of the second story, which housed the living quarters, is cut into smooth stones, with visible joints between them. The outside of the third story, reserved for servants, is entirely smooth, thus giving the facade the appearance of decreasing mass and even airiness.

The Palazzo Medici became the standard for townhouses of wealthy Florentine merchants. Two years later, Leon Battista Alberti, author of *On Painting* and a close friend and advisor to Cosimo, designed a home for the Florentine patrician Giovanni Rucellai that brought the more or less subtle Classical references of Michelozzo's design for Cosimo to full light. The Palazzo Rucellai (Fig. **7.13**) reflects on a domestic level many of the ideas that Alberti would publish in about 1450 in his *On the Art of Building*.

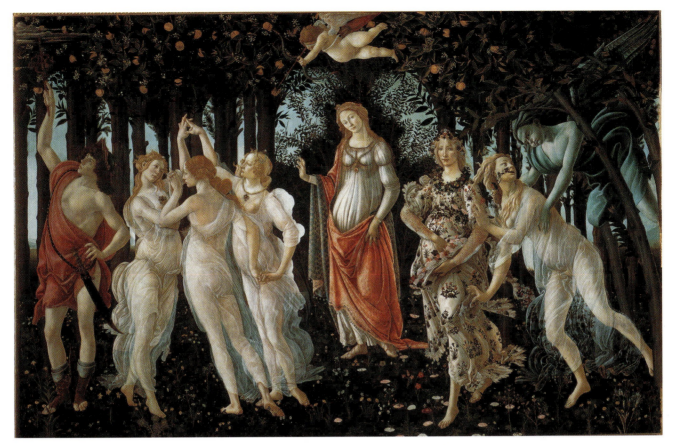

Fig. 7.14 Sandro Botticelli, *Primavera*. Early 1480s. Tempera on panel, 6'8" × 10'4". Galleria degli Uffizi, Florence. *Primavera* means both "spring" and "first truth" in Italian. Although the title is strongly allegorical, its exact meaning is still debated.

View the Closer Look for *Primavera* on **MyArtsLab**

Sandro Botticelli: Humanist Painter It seems very likely that these discussions inspired Sandro Botticelli (1445–1510) to paint his *Primavera* (*Spring*), perhaps on commission from Lorenzo di Pierfrancesco de' Medici, Lorenzo the Magnificent's cousin and a student of Ficino (Fig. **7.14**). In the painting, the nymph stands in the center, depicted as Venus, goddess of Love, surrounded by other mythological characters, who appear to move through the garden setting from right to left. To the humanists in Lorenzo's court, Venus was an allegorical figure who represented the highest moral qualities. According to Ficino, she was the very embodiment of "Humanitas . . . her Soul and mind are Love and Charity, her eyes Dignity and Magnanimity, the hands Liberality and Magnificence, the feet Comeliness and Modesty. The whole, then, is Temperance and Honesty, Charm and Splendor." On the far right of the embodiment of the humanities, Zephyrus, god of the west wind, attempts to capture Chloris, the nymph of spring, in his cold, blue grasp. But Flora, goddess of flowers, who stands beside the nymph, ignores the west wind's threat, and distributes blossoms across the path. To the left of Venus, the three Graces, daughters of Zeus and personifications of beauty, engage in a dance that recalls a specific one created for three people by Lorenzo the Magnificent in the 1460s. Lorenzo called the dance

"Venus" and described it as based on the movement of two figures around a third one:

> First they do a slow side-step, and then together they move with two pairs of forward steps, beginning with the left foot; then the middle dancer turns round and across with two reprises, one on the foot sideways and the other on the right foot, also across; and during the time that the middle dancer is carrying out these reprises the other two go forward with two triplet steps and then give half a turn on the right foot in such a way as to face each other.

Finally, to the left, Mercury, messenger of the gods, holds up his staff as if to brush away the remnants of a stray cloud. Over the whole scene and positioned just above the head of Venus, Cupid reigns.

Primavera captures the spirit of the Medici. It celebrates love, not only in a Neoplatonic sense, as a spiritual, humanist endeavor, but also in a more direct, physical way. For Lorenzo hardly shied away from physical pleasure. He was himself a prolific poet, and his most famous poem, the 1490 "A Song for Bacchus," deliberately invites the kind of carefree behavior we associate with carnivals, lavish festivities that Lorenzo regularly sponsored, complete with floats, processions through mythological settings, dance, and song (**Reading 7.1**):

READING 7.1

"A Song For Bacchus," 1490

How beautiful our Youth is
That's always flying by us!
Who'd be happy, let him be so:
Nothing's sure about tomorrow.

Here are Bacchus, Ariadne,
Lovely, burning for each other:
Since deceiving time must flee,
They seek their delight together.
These nymphs, and other races,
Are full of happiness forever.
Who'd be happy, let him be so:
Nothing's sure about tomorrow.

These delighted little satyrs
With their nymphs intoxicated,
Set a hundred snares now for them,
In the caves and in the bushes:
Warmed by Bacchus, all together
Dancing, leaping there forever,
Who'd be happy, let him be so:
Nothing's sure about tomorrow.

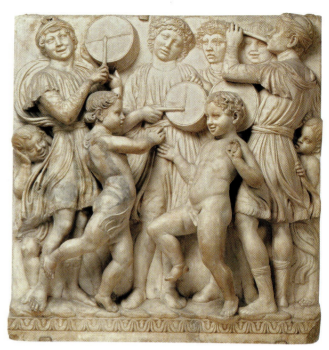

Fig. 7.15 Luca della Robbia, *Drummers* (detail of the *Cantoria*). 1433–40. Marble, 42⅛" × 41". Museo dell'Opera del Duomo, Florence. The 17-foot length of the space containing the *Cantoria* would have accommodated small choirs and portable organs.

In fact, it seems likely that Botticelli's painting decorated Lorenzo di Pierfrancesco's wedding chamber. Clearly, a lighthearted spirit of play tempered all Lorenzo the Magnificent's followers. As Machiavelli would later say of him: "If one examines the light and serious side of his life, one sees in him two different persons joined in an almost impossible conjunction."

Heinrich Isaac: Humanist Composer Lorenzo's love of music was equaled only by his love of painting and poetry, and music was an important part of Florentine life, so much so that in 1433, the Opera del Duomo commissioned a series of eight reliefs from Luca della Robbia celebrating music. The reliefs were to be displayed in a gallery above the north door of the sacristy (Fig. **7.15**). They were conceived to illustrate Psalm 150, which calls for worshipers to praise God "with sound of the trumpet . . . with psaltery and harp . . . with timbrels and dance . . . with stringed instruments and organs . . . upon the high-sounding cymbals." Luca's youthful figures are the very embodiment of the joy and harmony that made music such an ideal manifestation of the humanist spirit.

Lorenzo's household employed its own private music master, and in 1475, Lorenzo appointed the Flemish composer Heinrich Isaac (1450–1517) to the position. Isaac oversaw the Medici's five household organs, taught music to Lorenzo's sons, served as organist and choirmaster at Florence Cathedral, and, before he knew it, found himself collaborating with Lorenzo on songs for popular festivals.

The scores for many of the songs produced by this collaboration survive. They are examples of a musical genre known as the *frottola*, from the Italian for "nonsense" or "fib," and are extremely lighthearted. These *frottole* offer evidence of a strongly Italian movement away from the complex polyphony and counterpoint of church music (see the discussions of music in Chapters 5 and 6) in favor of simple harmonies and dancelike rhythms. Most *frottole* consist of three musical parts, with the melody in the highest register. The melodic line is generally taken by a soprano voice, accompanied in the two lower parts by either a lute and viol, two viols, other instruments, or two other voices. A typical *frottola* rhythm, such as from "Un di Lieto" ("One of Good Cheer"), might go something like this:

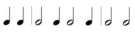

Typical *frottola* rhythm

From Lorenzo's point of view, such songs, sung in his native Italian, not Greek or Latin, demonstrated once and for all that Italian was the most harmonious and beautiful of languages when set to music. This sentiment would have lasting impact, especially on the development of the musical genre known as *opera* in the sixteenth and seventeenth centuries.

Pico della Mirandola: Humanity "at the . . . center of the world . . . ." Cultural life in Lorenzo's court was grounded on moral philosophy. The young humanist philosopher Pico della Mirandola (1463–94) shared Lorenzo's deep interest in the search for divine truth. By age 23, in 1486, Pico had compiled a volume of some 900 theological and philosophical theses, 13 of which Pope Innocent VIII (papacy 1484–92) considered heretical. When Pico refused to recant those few theses, Innocent condemned all 900.

Pico's thinking was based on wide reading in Hebrew, Arabic, Latin, and Greek, and he believed that all intellectual endeavors shared the same purpose—to reveal divine truth. Pico proposed defending his work, in public debate in Rome, against any scholar who might dare to confront him, but the pope banned the debate and even imprisoned him for a brief time in France, where he had fled. Lorenzo offered Pico protection in Florence, defying the pontiff in a daring assertion of secular versus papal authority. As a result, Pico became an important contributor to Lorenzo's humanist court.

In his *Oration on the Dignity of Man* of 1486—the introduction to his proposed debate and one of the great manifestos of humanism—Pico argued that humanity was part of the "great chain of being" that stretches from God to angels, humans, animals, plants, minerals, and the most primal matter. This idea can be traced to the Idea of the Good developed by Plato in Book 7 of the *Republic*, an idea of perfection to which all creation tends. Plotinus' brand of Neoplatonic thought took it a step further in proposing that the material world, including humanity, is but the shadowy reflection of the celestial, a condition that the pursuit of knowledge allows humanity, if it chooses, at least to begin to overcome. According to Pico, humanity finds itself in a middle position in the great chain of being—not by natural law but by the exercise of its own free will. Humans, then, are not fixed in the middle position. They are, in fact, pure potential, able to make of themselves what they wish. Humanity, it follows, is God's greatest miracle: "There is nothing to be seen more wonderful than man," Pico wrote. In his *Oration*, he has God explain to Adam that he has placed him "at the very center of the world" and given him the gift of pure potential to shape himself (**Reading 7.2**):

READING 7.2

from Pico della Mirandola, *Oration on the Dignity of Man* (1486)

We have given you, Oh Adam, no visage proper to yourself, nor any endowment properly your own, in order that whatever place, whatever form, whatever gifts you may, with premeditation, select, these same you may have and possess through your own judgment and decision. The nature of all other creatures is defined and restricted within laws which We have laid down; you, by contrast, impeded by no such restrictions, may, by your own free will, to whose custody We have assigned you, trace for yourself the lineaments of your own nature. I have placed you at the very center of the world, so that from that vantage point you may with greater ease glance round about you on all that the world contains. . . . You may, as the free and proud shaper of your own being, fashion yourself in the

form you prefer. It will be in your power to descend to the lower, brutish forms of life; [or] you will be able, through your own decision, to rise again to the superior orders whose life is divine.

For Pico, the role of the philosopher in this anthropocentric (human-centered) world is as "a creature of heaven and not of earth." This is because "unmindful of the body, withdrawn into the inner chambers of the mind," the philosopher is part of "some higher divinity, clothed with human flesh." It is imperative, therefore, in Pico's view, for individuals to seek out virtue and knowledge, even while knowing their capability of choosing a path of vice and ignorance. Taking the idea of "freedom of judgment" to a new level, Pico argues that humanity is completely free to exercise its free will. And this gift of free will makes humans "the most fortunate of living things."

Such thinking reflects what may be the most important transformation wrought by Renaissance thinkers on medieval ideas. Art, literature, and philosophy, as the free expression of the individual's creative power, can, if they aim high enough, express not only the whole of earthly creation but also the whole of the divine. The human being is a *parvus mundus*, a "small universe."

BEYOND FLORENCE: THE DUCAL COURTS AND THE ARTS

How did the art and literature created in the ducal courts of Italy reflect Florentine humanist values?

Pico's message of individual free will and of humanity's ability to choose a path of virtue and knowledge inspired Lorenzo's circle and the courts of other Italian city-states as well. These leaders were almost all nobles, not merchants like the Medici (who, it must be said, had transformed themselves into nobility in all but name), and each court reflected the values of its respective duke—and, very often, his wife. But if they were not about to adopt the republican form of government of Florence, they all shared the humanistic values that were so thoroughly developed there.

The Montefeltro Court in Urbino

One of the most prominent of these city-states was Urbino, some 70 miles east of Florence across the Apennines (see Map 7.1), where the learned military strategist duke Federigo da Montefeltro (1422–82) ruled. Federigo surrounded himself with humanists, scholars, poets, and artists, from whom he learned and from whom he commissioned works to embellish Urbino. He financed this expenditure through his talents as a *condottiero*, a mercenary soldier who was a valuable and highly paid ally to whomever could afford both him and his army. His court was also a magnet for young men who wanted to learn the principles of noble behavior.

Baldassare Castiglione and "*L'uomo Universale*" One of the most important books of the age, written between 1513 and 1518, recalled conversations, probably imaginary, that took place in 1507 among a group of aristocrats at the Urbino court of Guidobaldo da Montefeltro (1472–1508), the son of Federigo. *The Book of the Courtier* by Baldassare Castiglione (1478–1529) takes the form of a dialogue in which the eloquent courtiers at Urbino compete with one another to describe the perfect courtier—the man (or woman) whose education and deportment are best fashioned to serve the prince. It was not published until 1528, but by 1600, it had been translated into five languages and reprinted in 57 editions.

The Book of the Courtier is, in essence, a nostalgic re-creation of Castiglione's nine years (1504–12) in the Urbino court, which he labeled "the very abode of joyfulness." It takes place on four successive evenings in the spring of 1507. The dialogue is in the form of a dialectic, as the viewpoints of some speakers are challenged and ridiculed by others. The first two books debate the qualities of an ideal gentleman. The goal is to be a completely well-rounded person, *l'uomo universale.* Above all, a courtier must be an accomplished soldier (like Federigo), not only mastering the martial arts but also demonstrating absolute bravery and total loyalty in war. His liberal education must include Latin and Greek, other modern languages such as French and Spanish (necessary for diplomacy), and study of the great Italian poets and writers, such as Petrarch and Boccaccio, so that he might imitate their skill in his own verse and prose, both in Latin and in the vernacular. The courtier must also be able to draw, appreciate the arts, and excel in dance and music (although one must avoid the wind instruments since they deform the face). Above all, the courtier must demonstrate a certain *grazia* ("gracefulness") (**Reading 7.3**):

READING 7.3

from Baldassare Castiglione, *The Courtier*, Book 1 (1513–18; published 1528)

I wish then, that this Courtier of ours should be nobly born and of gentle race; . . . for noble birth is like a bright lamp that manifests and makes visible good and evil deeds, and kindles and stimulates to virtue both by fear of shame and by hope of praise. . . .

Besides this noble birth, then, I would have the Courtier favored in this regard also, and endowed by nature not only with talent and beauty of person and feature, but with a certain grace and (as we say) air that shall make him at first sight pleasing and agreeable to all who see him; and I would have this an ornament that should dispose and unite all his actions, and in his outward aspect give promise of whatever is worthy the society and favor of every great lord.

Grazia must be tempered by *gravitas* ("dignity") in all things. This balanced character trait is obtained, Castiglione explains in *The Book of the Courtier*, by means of "one universal rule":

Flee as much as possible . . . affectation; and, perhaps to coin a word . . . make use in all things of a certain *sprezzatura*, which conceals art and presents everything said and done as something brought about without laboriousness and almost without giving it any thought.

Sprezzatura means, literally, "undervaluing" or "setting a small price" on something. For the courtier, it means simply doing difficult things as if effortlessly and with an attitude of nonchalance. The ideal gentleman, in other words, is a construction of absolute artifice, a work of art in his own right who cuts *una bella figura*, "a fine figure," that all will seek to emulate. Ultimately, Castiglione suggests, a state led by such perfect gentlemen would itself reflect their perfection, and thus the state does not create great individuals so much as great individuals create the perfect state, in the kind of exercise of free will that Pico discussed.

The Sforza Court in Milan and Leonardo da Vinci The Sforza family's control over the court of Milan was somewhat less legitimate than most other ducal city-states in Italy. Francesco Sforza (1401–66) became ruler of Milan by marrying the illegitimate daughter, but sole heir, of the duke of Milan. His own illegitimate son, Ludovico (1451–1508), called *il Moro*, "the Moor," because of his dark complexion, wrested control of the city from the family of Francesco's legitimate brother and proclaimed himself duke of Milan in 1494. Both Francesco and Ludovico understood the tenuousness of their claims to rule, and they actively sought to win the support of the people through the arts. They welcomed artists from throughout central Italy to their city, and embraced humanism.

The most important of these artists was Leonardo da Vinci (1452–1519), who first arrived in Milan in 1482 as the emissary of Lorenzo de' Medici to present a silver lyre, perhaps made by Leonardo himself, to Ludovico Sforza. Ludovico was embroiled in military matters, and Leonardo pronounced himself a military engineer, capable of constructing great "machines of war," including designs for a catapult and covered vehicles that resemble present-day armored cars.

Leonardo's restless imagination, in fact, led him to the study of almost everything: such natural phenomena as wind, storms, and the movement of water; anatomy and physiology; physics and mechanics; music; mathematics; plants and animals; geology; and astronomy, to say nothing of painting and drawing. Leonardo was a humanist, and as such was deeply swayed by Neoplatonic thought. He saw connections among all spheres of existence and wrote of them:

If man has in himself bones, the supports and armature
for the flesh, the world has the rocks, the supports of the
earth; if man has in himself the lake of blood, in which
the lungs increase and decrease in breathing, the body of
the earth has its oceanic sea, which likewise increases and
decreases every six hours with the breathing of the world;
if from the said lake veins arise, which proceed to ramify

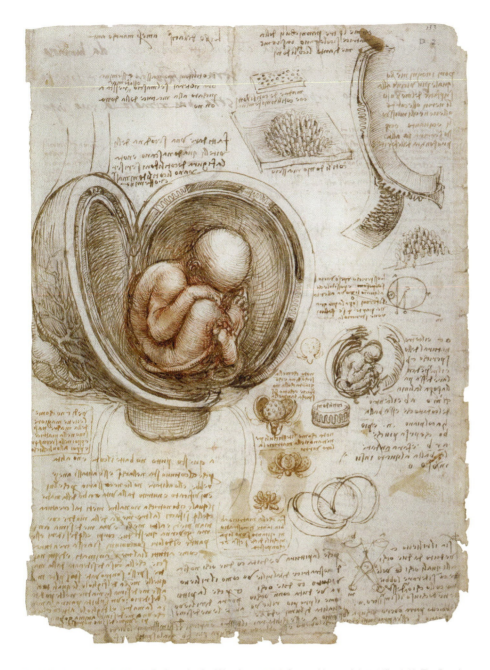

Fig. 7.16 Leonardo da Vinci, _Embryo in the Womb_. ca. 1510. Pen and brown ink, 11¾" × 8½". The Royal Collection © 2011 Her Majesty Queen Elizabeth II. Leonardo's notes on this page from one of his notebooks relate not only to standard questions of anatomy and physiology, including the nourishment of the fetus, but also to the relationship of the fetus's soul to that of its mother.

throughout the human body, the oceanic sea fills the body of the earth with infinite veins of water.

Thus, the miracle of the fetus in the womb, which Leonardo depicts in a famous anatomical study from his notebooks (Fig. **7.16**), is analogous in his mind to the mysteries that lie deep within the body of the earth. "I came to the entrance of a great cavern," he writes in one note. "There immediately arose in me two feelings— fear and desire—fear of the menacing, dark cavity, and desire to see if there was anything miraculous within." Leonardo's fascination with the human body—an image, for him, of both attraction and repulsion—led him to produce this and his other precisely drawn dissections of it in 1510–12, probably working under the direction of a young professor of anatomy.

In his _Lives of the Most Excellent Painters, Architects, and Sculptors,_ which first appeared in 1550 and was subsequently revised and greatly expanded in 1568, Giorgio Vasari underscores the inquisitiveness that Leonardo's dissections reveal.

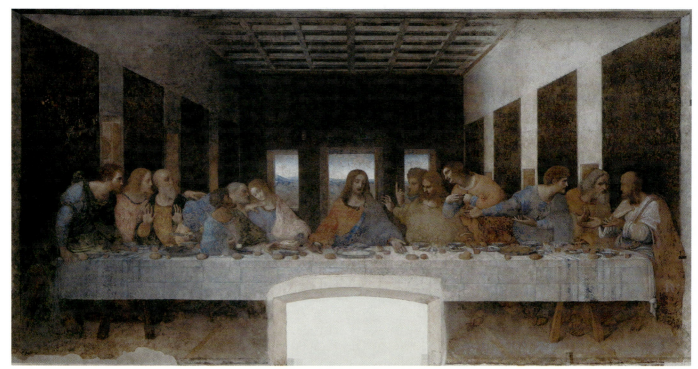

Fig. 7.17 Leonardo da Vinci, _Last Supper_, wall painting in refectory, Convent of Santa Maria delle Grazie, Milan. ca. 1495–98. Fresco, oil, and tempera on plaster, 15'1⅛" × 28'10½". Today, even after "restoration," Leonardo's original painting remains in very bad shape. The fault is almost entirely Leonardo's—or maybe Ludovico Sforza's, who rushed him to complete it. Instead of using the established fresco technique of painting tempera on wet plaster, Leonardo applied oil and tempera to dry plaster. As early as 1517, the paint began to flake off, unable to adhere to the wall.

The CONTINUING PRESENCE
of the PAST

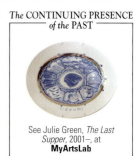

See Julie Green, _The Last Supper_, 2001–, at
MyArtsLab

Born in 1511, Vasari could never have known Leonardo personally, but as a painter and architect, as well as an historian, he did know many other Renaissance artists, including Michelangelo, and his _Lives_ remains one of our primary sources on Renaissance art. He focuses on demonstrating the individual creative genius of each artist he discusses. Vasari's treatment of Leonardo is typical of the other biographies in _Lives_. From the very opening lines, Vasari presents him as a prototypical Renaissance man (**Reading 7.4**):

READING 7.4

from Giorgio Vasari, "Life of Leonardo," in _Lives of the Most Excellent Painters_ . . . (1550, 1568)

The greatest gifts are often seen, in the course of nature, rained by celestial influences on human creatures; and sometimes, in supernatural fashion, beauty, grace, and talent are united beyond measure in one single person, in a manner that to whatever such a one turns his attention, his every action is so divine, that, surpassing all other men, it makes itself clearly known as a thing bestowed by God (as it is), and not acquired by human art. This was seen by all mankind in Leonardo da Vinci, in whom, besides a beauty of body never sufficiently extolled, there was an infinite grace in all his actions; and so great was his genius, and such its growth, that to whatever

difficulties he turned his mind, he solved them with ease. In him was great bodily strength, joined to dexterity, with a spirit and courage ever royal and magnanimous; and the fame of his name so increased, that not only in his lifetime was he held in esteem, but his reputation became even greater among posterity after his death.

In 1495, Ludovico commissioned Leonardo to paint a monumental fresco of the Last Supper for the north wall of the refectory of the Dominican convent of Santa Maria delle Grazie. The intent was that at every meal the monks would contemplate Christ's last meal in a wall-sized painting. The _Last Supper_ illusionistically extends the refectory walls in a modified one-point perspective (the tabletop is tipped toward the viewer), carrying the present of architectural space into the past of the painting's space (Fig. **7.17**).

The moment Leonardo chose to depict is just after Christ has announced to the apostles that one of them will betray him. Each apostle reacts in his characteristic way. Saint Peter grabs a knife in anger, while Judas turns away and Saint John appears to faint. The vanishing point of the painting is directly behind Christ's head, focusing the viewer's attention

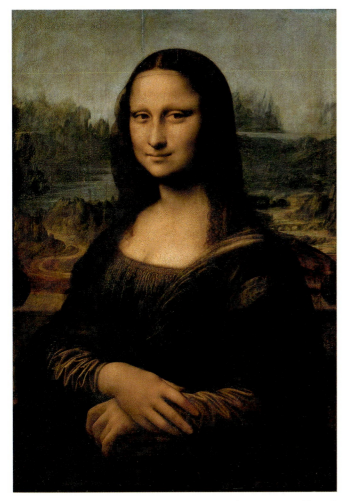

Fig. 7.18 Leonardo da Vinci, *Mona Lisa*. 1503–15. Oil on wood, 30¼″ × 21″. Musée du Louvre, Paris. Recent research tends to suggest that the woman in this picture is the wife of the Florentine patrician Francesco del Giocondo. She is seated on a balcony, originally between two columns that have been cut off (the base of the left column is just visible).

View the Closer Look for the *Mona Lisa* on **MyArtsLab**

and establishing Christ as the most important figure in the work. He extends his arms, forming a perfect equilateral triangle at the center of the painting, an image of balance and a symbolic reference to the Trinity. What is unique about this painting of an otherwise completely traditional subject for a refectory is the psychological realism that Leonardo lends to it. We see this in the sense of agitated doubt and confusion among the apostles, their intertwined bodies twisting and turning as if drawn toward the self-contained and peaceful image of Christ. The apostles, even Judas, are revealed in all their humanity, while Christ is composed in his compassion for them.

Leonardo's fascination with revealing the human personality in portraiture is nowhere more evident than in his *Mona Lisa* (Fig. **7.18**), where he fuses his subject with the landscape behind her by means of light. This technique is called ***sfumato*** ("smokiness"). Its hazy effects, which create

a half-waking, dreamlike quality reminiscent of dusk, could only be achieved by building up color with many layers of transparent oil paint—a process called **glazing**. But it is the mysterious personality of Leonardo's sitter that most occupies the viewer's imagination. For generations, viewers have asked, Who is this woman? What is she thinking about? What is her relation to the artist? Leonardo presents us with a particular personality, whose half-smile suggests that he has captured her in a particular, if enigmatic, mood. And the painting's hazy light reinforces the mystery of her personality. Apparently, whatever he captured in her look he could not give up. The *Mona Lisa* occupied Leonardo for years, and it followed him to Rome and then to France in 1513, where King Louis XII offered him the Château of Cloux near Amboise as a residence. Leonardo died there on May 2, 1519.

In 1499, the French, under Charles VIII, deposed Ludovico and imprisoned him in France, where he died in 1508. Leonardo abandoned Milan, eventually returning to Florence in about 1503. Both of Ludovico's sons would briefly rule as duke of Milan in the early sixteenth century, but both were soon deposed, and the male line of the Sforza family died out.

PAPAL PATRONAGE AND THE HIGH RENAISSANCE IN ROME

How did papal patronage impact the arts in Rome?

When Brunelleschi arrived in Rome in 1402, shortly after the competition for the Baptistery doors in Florence, the city must have seemed a pitiful place. Its population had shrunk from around 1 million in 100 CE to around 20,000. It was located in a relatively tiny enclave across the Tiber from the Vatican and Saint Peter's Basilica, and was surrounded by the ruins of a once-great city. Even 150 years later, in the sixteenth century, the city occupied only a small fraction of the territory enclosed by its third-century CE walls. The ancient Colosseum was now in the countryside, the Forum a pasture for goats and cattle. The ancient aqueducts that had once brought fresh water to the city had collapsed. The popes had even abandoned the city when, in 1309, under pressure from the king of France, who sought to assert secular authority over the clergy, they left Italy and established Avignon as the seat of the Church. When Rome finally reestablished itself as the titular seat of the Church in 1378, succeeding popes rarely chose to visit the city, let alone live in it. The city held little appeal, except perhaps for the ruins themselves, and, as we have already seen, it was to the ruins of Rome that Brunelleschi was most attracted.

After 1420, when Pope Martin V (papacy 1417–31) brought the papacy back to Rome for good, it became something of a papal duty to restore the city to its former greatness. Because as many as 100,000 visitors might swarm into Rome during religious holidays, it was important that they

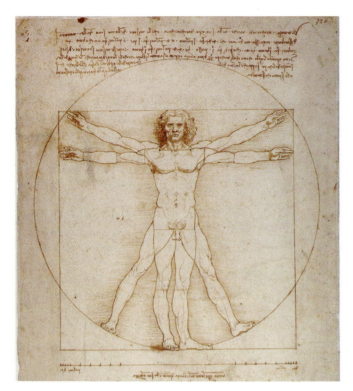

Fig. 7.19 Leonardo da Vinci, *Vitruvian Man.* ca. 1485–90. Pen and ink, 13½" × 9⅝". Gallerie dell'Accademia, Venice. Vitruvius specifically related the harmonious physical proportions of man, which reflect their divine creator, to the proportions of architecture.

Bramante and the New Saint Peter's Basilica

Shortly after he was elected pope in 1503, Julius II made what may have been the most important commission of the day. He asked the architect Donato Bramante (1444–1514) to renovate the Vatican Palace and serve as chief architect of a plan to replace Saint Peter's Basilica with a new church. The pope's chosen architect, Bramante, had worked with Leonardo da Vinci in Milan, and Julius was deeply impressed by Leonardo's understanding of the writings of the ancient Roman architectural historian Vitruvius. For Vitruvius, whose acquaintance with Polyclitus' *Canon* of proportion is our only firsthand account of the now-lost original (see Chapter 2), the circle and square were the ideal shapes. Polyclitus' proportion was the geometrical equivalent of Pythagoras' **music of the spheres**, the theory that each planet produced a musical sound, fixed mathematically by its velocity and distance from Earth, which harmonized with those produced by other planets and was audible but not recognized on Earth. Thus, according to Vitruvius, if the human head is one-eighth the total height of an idealized figure, then the human body itself fits into the ideal musical interval of the **octave**, the interval that gives the impression of duplicating the original note at a higher or lower pitch. Leonardo had captured this notion in his *Vitruvian Man*, a drawing in which he placed the human figure at the center of a perfect circle inscribed over a square (Fig. **7.19**).

In Rome, Bramante quickly applied this emphasis on geometrical figures to one of his earliest commissions, a small freestanding circular chapel in the courtyard of a Spanish church in Rome, San Pietro in Montorio, directly over what was revered as the site of Saint Peter's martyrdom. Because of its small size and the fact that it was modeled on a Classical temple that was excavated in Rome during the reign of Sixtus IV, this structure is known as the Tempietto (Little Temple) (Fig. **7.20**). The 16 exterior columns are Doric—in fact, their shafts are original ancient Roman granite columns— and the frieze above them is decorated with objects of the Christian liturgy in sculptural relief. The diameter of the shafts defines the entire plan. Each shaft is spaced four diameters from the next, and the colonnade they form is two diameters from the circular walls. In its Classical reference, its incorporation of original Classical Roman columns into its architectural scheme, and, above all, the mathematical orderliness of its parts, the Tempietto is the very embodiment of Italian humanist architecture in the High Renaissance.

The task of replacing Old Saint Peter's was a much larger project and Bramante's most important one. Old Saint Peter's was a *basilica*, a type of ancient Roman building with a long central nave, double side aisles set off by colonnades (see Fig. 4.6 in Chapter 4), an apse in the wall opposite the main door, and a transept near the apse so that large numbers of visitors could approach the shrine to Saint Peter. In his plan for a new Saint Peter's (Fig. **7.21a**), Bramante adopted the Vitruvian square, as illustrated in Leonardo's drawing, placing inside it a **Greek cross** (a cross in which

be "moved by its extraordinary sights," as one pope put it, and thus find their "belief continually confirmed and daily corroborated by great buildings . . . seemingly made by the hand of God." In other words, the popes were charged with the sacred duty of becoming great patrons of the arts and architecture of Rome.

By and large, Rome imported its artists from Florence. In 1481, Botticelli and a group of his fellow Florentine painters arrived to decorate the walls of the Vatican's Sistine Chapel. When Pope Julius II (papacy 1503–13) began a massive campaign to rebuild Saint Peter's Basilica and the Vatican, he commanded Michelangelo to leave Florence for Rome in 1505 and commissioned major paintings and monuments from the then 30-year-old artist. In 1508, Michelangelo was followed by Raphael (Raffaello Santi or Sanzio, 1483–1520), a young painter from Urbino who had arrived in Florence in about 1505. Julius set him the task of decorating the papal apartments. Rome must have seemed something of a Florentine place. In November 1494, the domination of Florence by the Medici family had come to an end. But when the Medici returned to power in Florence in 1512, they did so under the sway of two great Medici popes: Leo X (papacy 1513–21), who was Lorenzo the Magnificent's son, Giovanni de' Medici; and Clement VII (papacy 1523–34), who was Lorenzo's nephew, Giulio de' Medici. Whether in the church or the republic, Rome or Florence, the males of this patrician family were the dominant force in the Renaissance political world.

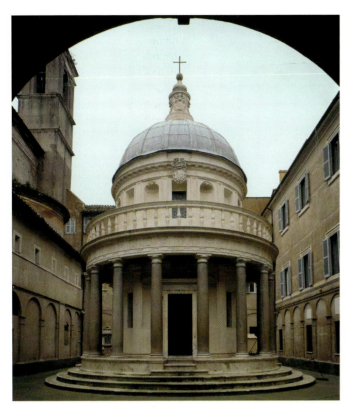

Fig. 7.20 **Donato Bramante, Tempietto. 1502.** San Pietro in Montorio, Rome. This chapel was certainly modeled on a Classical temple. It was commissioned by King Ferdinand and Queen Isabella of Spain, financiers of Christopher Columbus's voyages to America. It was undertaken in support of Pope Alexander VI, who was himself Spanish.

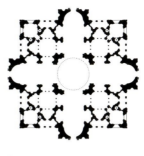

a   b

Fig. 7.21 **Plans for Saint Peter's, Rome, by (a) Donato Bramante and (b) Michelangelo.** Bramante's original plan (a), in the form of a Greek cross, was sporadically worked on after Julius II's death in 1513. The project came to a complete halt for a decade after the Sack of Rome by the troops of the Habsburg Emperor Charles V in 1527. In 1547, Pope Paul III appointed Michelangelo as architect, and he revived Bramante's original plan but added more support for the dome and thickened the walls. He also added a portico consisting of 10 columns in the second row and 4 in the front, which created the feeling of a Latin cross, especially when extended by his other addition to Bramante's scheme, the massive flight of steps rising to the main portal (b).

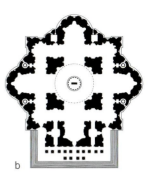 **Watch** an architectural simulation of Saint Peter's on **MyArtsLab**

Michelangelo and the Sistine Chapel

After the fall of the Medici in 1494, a young Michelangelo, not yet 20 years old, had left Florence for Rome. There must have seemed little prospect for him in Florence, where a Dominican friar, Girolamo Savonarola (1452–98), abbot of the monastery of San Marco, wielded tremendous political influence. Savonarola appealed, first and foremost, to a moralistic faction of the populace that saw, in the behavior of the city's upper classes, and in their humanistic attraction to Classical Greek and Roman culture, clear evidence of moral decadence. Savonarola railed against the Florentine nobility—the Medici in particular—going so far as to organize troops of children to collect the city's "vanities"—everything from cosmetics to books and paintings—and burn them on giant bonfires. Finally, in June 1497, an angry Pope Alexander VI excommunicated him for his antipapal preachings and for disobeying his directives for the administration of the monastery of San Marco. Savonarola was commanded not to preach, an order he chose to ignore. On May 28, 1498, he was forcibly removed from San Marco, tortured as a heretic along with two fellow friars, hanged until nearly dead, and then burned at the stake. His ashes were subsequently thrown into the Arno River. Florence felt itself freed from tyranny.

With the fall of Savonarola, the Signoria, Florence's governing body, quickly moved to assert the republic's survival in visual terms. It moved Donatello's *David* (see Fig. 7.11) from the Medici palace to the Palazzo della Signoria, where the governing body met to conduct business. It also asked Michelangelo to return to Florence in 1501 to work on a huge cracked block of marble that all other sculptors had abandoned in dismay. It was to be another freestanding

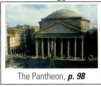

CONTINUITY & CHANGE

The Pantheon, *p. 98*

the upright and transverse shafts are of equal length and intersect at their middles) topped by a central dome purposely reminiscent of the giant dome of the Pantheon (see Fig. 3.18 in Chapter 3). The resultant central plan is essentially a circle inscribed within a square. In Renaissance thinking, the central plan and dome symbolized the perfection of God. Construction began in 1506. Julius II financed the project through the sale of **indulgences**, remissions of penalties to be suffered in the afterlife, especially release from purgatory. This was the place where, in Catholic belief, individuals temporarily reside after death as punishment for their sins. Those wanting to enter heaven more rapidly than they otherwise might could shorten their stay in purgatory by purchasing an indulgence. The Church had been selling these documents since the twelfth century, and Julius's building campaign intensified the practice. (In protest against the sale of indulgences, Martin Luther would launch the Protestant Reformation in Germany in 1517; see Chapter 8.) New Saint Peter's would be a very expensive project, but there were also very many sinners willing to help to pay for it. With the deaths of both pope and architect, in 1513 and 1514 respectively, the project came to a temporary halt. Its final plan would be developed in 1546 by Michelangelo (Fig. **7.21b**).

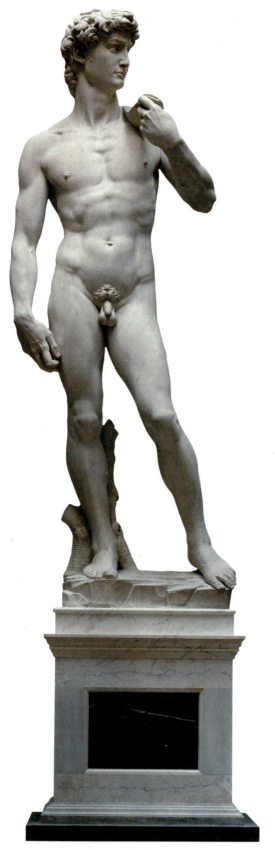

Fig. 7.22 Michelangelo, *David*. 1501–04. Marble, height 17'3". Accademia, Florence. The *David* was originally conceived to be placed high on the facade of Florence Cathedral. It was probably situated in the Piazza della Signoria because it could not be lifted into place.

statue of the biblical hero David, but colossal in scale. Michelangelo rose to the challenge.

The completed figure (Fig. 7.22), over 17 feet high—even higher on its pedestal—intentionally references Donatello's boyish predecessor but then challenges it. Michelangelo represents David before, not after, his triumph, sublimely confident, ready to take on whatever challenge faces him, just as the republic itself felt ready to take on all-comers. The nudity of the figure and the *contrapposto* stance are directly indebted to the Medici celebration of all things ancient Greek. Its sense of self-contained, even heroic individualism captures perfectly the humanist spirit. Michelangelo's triumph over the complexity of the stone transformed it into an artwork that his contemporaries lauded for its almost unparalleled beauty. It was an achievement that Michelangelo would soon equal, in another medium, in his work on the Sistine Chapel ceiling at the Vatican, in Rome.

The fate of the *David* underscores the political and moral turbulence of the times. Each night, as workers installed the statue in the Piazza della Signoria, supporters of the exiled Medici hurled stones at it, understanding, correctly, that the statue was a symbol of the city's will to stand up to any and all tyrannical rule, including that of the Medici themselves. Another group of citizens soon objected to the statue's nudity, and before it was even installed in place, a skirt of copper leaves was prepared to spare the general public any possible offense. The skirt is long gone, but it symbolizes the conflicts of the era, even as the sculpture itself can be thought of as truly inaugurating the High Renaissance.

But it is Michelangelo's work on the Sistine Chapel in Rome that remains one of the era's crowning achievements. Just as the construction of New Saint Peter's was about to get under way, Julius II commissioned Michelangelo to design his tomb. It would be a three-story monument, over 23 feet wide and 35 feet high, and it represents Michelangelo's first foray into architecture. For the next 40 years, Michelangelo would work sporadically on the tomb, but from the beginning he was continually interrupted, most notably in 1506 when Julius himself commanded the artist to paint the 45-by-128-foot ceiling of the Sistine Chapel, named after Sixtus IV, Julius's uncle, who had commissioned its construction in 1473. Ever since its completion, the chapel has served as the meeting place of the conclave of cardinals during the election of new popes. Michelangelo at first refused Julius's commission, but in 1508, he reconsidered, signed the contract, and began the task.

Julius first proposed filling the spandrels between the windows with paintings of the 12 apostles and then decorating the ceiling proper with ornamental designs. But when Michelangelo objected to the limitations of this plan, the pope freed him to paint whatever he liked, and Michelangelo undertook for himself a far more ambitious task—nine scenes from Genesis, the first book of the Hebrew Bible, on the ceiling proper, surrounded by prophets, Sibyls, the ancestors of Christ, and other scenes (Figs. 7.23 and 7.24). Thus, the ceiling would narrate events before the coming of the law of Moses, and would complement the narrative cycles on the walls below.

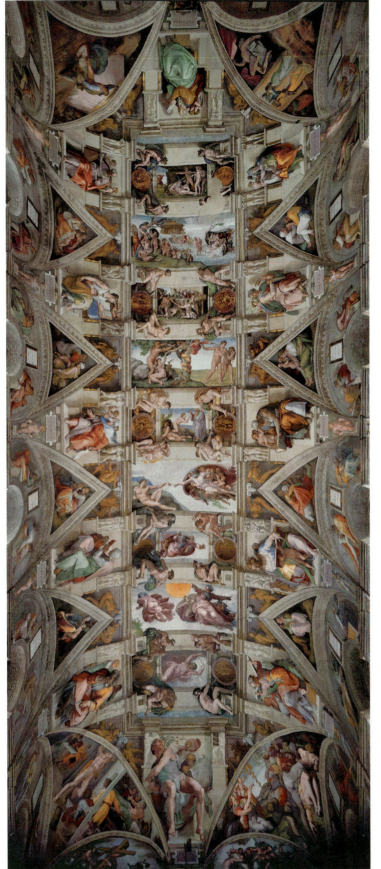

Figs. 7.23 and 7.24 Michelangelo, Sistine Chapel ceiling and plan of its narrative program, Vatican, Rome. 1508–12. Fresco, 45' × 128'. The intense and vibrant colors of the ceiling were revealed after a thorough cleaning, completed in 1990. Centuries of smoke and grime were removed by a process that involved the application of a solvent, containing both a fungicide and an antibacterial agent, mixed with a cellulose gel that would not drip from the ceiling. This mixture was applied in small sections with a bristle brush, allowed to dry for three minutes, and then removed with sponge and water. Until the cleaning, no one for centuries had fully appreciated Michelangelo's daring, even sensual, use of color.

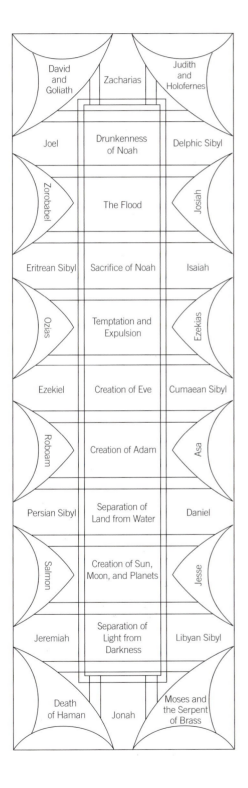

❋ **Explore** an architectural panorama of the Sistine Chapel on **MyArtsLab**

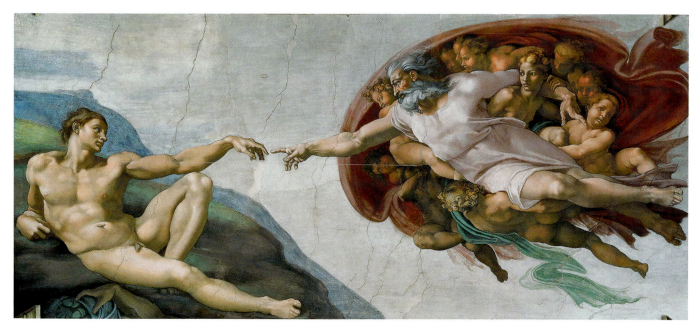

Fig. 7.25 Michelangelo, *Creation of Adam*, Sistine Chapel, Vatican, Rome. 1510. Fresco. Note the analogy Michelangelo creates between Adam and God, between the father of humankind and God the Father. Although they face each other, Adam and God are posed along parallel diagonals, and their right legs are in nearly identical positions. The connection is further highlighted by the fluttering green ribbon in God's space that echoes the colors of the ground upon which Adam lies.

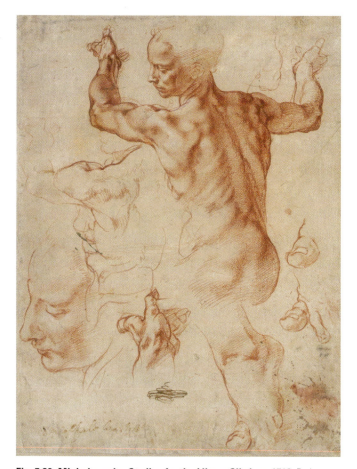

Fig. 7.26 Michelangelo, *Studies for the Libyan Sibyl*. ca. 1510. Red chalk, 11⅜″ × 8⁷⁄₁₆″. The Metropolitan Museum of Art, New York, Joseph Pulitzer Bequest, 1924 (24.197.2). Very few of Michelangelo's drawings for the Sistine Chapel survive, even though he prepared hundreds as he planned the ceiling.

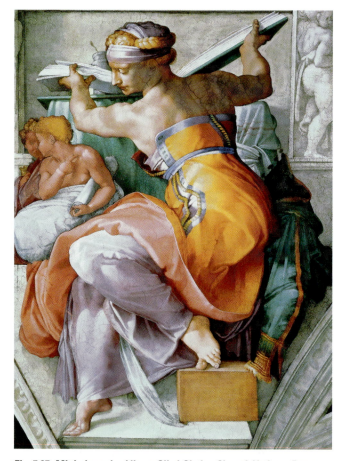

Fig. 7.27 Michelangelo, *Libyan Sibyl*, Sistine Chapel, Vatican, Rome. 1512. Fresco. In Michelangelo's program for the ceiling, the Sibyls alternate with Hebrew Bible prophets around the room. One of the most striking characteristics of these figures is the way they seem to project in front of the decoration and enter into the real space of the chapel, creating a stunning illusionistic effect.

Throughout the ceiling Michelangelo includes the della Rovere heraldic symbols of oak (*rovere*) and acorn to symbolize the pope's patronage, usually in the hands of **ignudi**, nude youths who sit at the four corners of alternate central panels. These same panels are framed by bronze shields that underscore the patron's military prowess. The whole is contained in an entirely illusionistic architecture that appears to open at each end to the sky outside. Only the spandrels over the windows and the **pendentives** (concave triangular sections that form a transition between a rectilinear and a dome shape) at each corner are real.

The nine central panels tell the story, in three panels each, of the Creation, Adam and Eve, and Noah. The series begins over the chapel altar with the Separation of Light from Darkness, a moment associated with the eternal struggle between good and evil, truth and falsehood. In fact, this pairing of opposites characterizes the entire program. At the center of the ceiling is the *Creation of Eve*. Life and death, good and evil, the heavenly and the earthly, the spiritual and the material, pivot around this central scene. Everything between here and the altar represents Creation before the knowledge of good and evil was introduced to the world by the temptation of Eve in the Garden of Eden, a scene represented, together with the Expulsion, in the panel just to the right. From here to the panel over the door to the chapel, we witness the early history of fallen humankind, for viewers entering the chapel look up to see directly above them the Drunkenness of Noah, an image symbolic of their own frailty. They see the goodness and truth of God's creation only at the greatest remove from them, far away at the chapel's other end.

The tension between the spiritual and the material worlds is nowhere better represented on the ceiling than in the *Creation of Adam* (Fig. **7.25**). Adam is earthbound. He seems lethargic, passive, barely interested, while a much more animated God flies through the skies carrying behind him a bulging red drapery that suggests both the womb and the brain, creativity and reason. Under his arm is a young woman, who may be Eve, who prefigures the Virgin, while God's left hand touches the shoulder of an infant, who may symbolize the future Christ. The implication of the scene is that in just one moment, God's finger will touch Adam's and infuse him with not just energy but soul, not just life but the future of humankind.

Michelangelo worked on the ceiling from May 1508 until 1512. His accomplishment becomes even clearer when we compare the final painting to the preparatory studies. In a drawing of one of the later figures painted, the *Libyan Sibyl* (Fig. **7.26**), the figure's hands are balanced evenly, at the same level, but by the time he painted her (Fig. **7.27**), the left hand had dropped below the right to emphasize her downward turn, underlining the fact that she is bringing knowledge down to the viewer. The artist has paid special attention to the left foot, seeing the need to splay the four smaller toes backward. And finally, his model in the drawing was apparently male. In his reworking of the face at the lower left of the drawing, he softens the figure's cheekbones and fills out her lips. In the final painting, he reduces the model's prominent brow, hides the musculature of the model's back, and exaggerates the

buttocks and hips, feminizing the original masculine sketch. As graceful as it is powerful and majestic, the *Libyan Sibyl* is a virtuoso display of technical mastery.

Raphael and the Stanza della Segnatura

Meanwhile, in about 1505, a young painter named Raphael (Raffaello Santi or Sanzio) arrived in Florence from Urbino and began to receive a great deal of attention as a painter of portraits of wealthy Florentine citizens. He also produced a series of small, beautifully executed paintings of the Virgin and Child. The latter, of course, embraced a theme that stretched back to the Byzantine icon, down through the work of the Sienese painters Duccio and Martini and the Florentines Cimabue and Giotto (see Chapter 6). However, the naturalism that these earlier painters had striven to achieve reached new heights in Raphael's work. His paintings were immediately approachable—linearly precise, coloristically rich, and compositionally simple.

The *Small Cowper Madonna* (Fig. **7.28**) is an example. Both Virgin and Child are imbued with an almost celestial serenity—owing in no small part to the fact that their heads are framed by the radiant light of Raphael's sky. But what

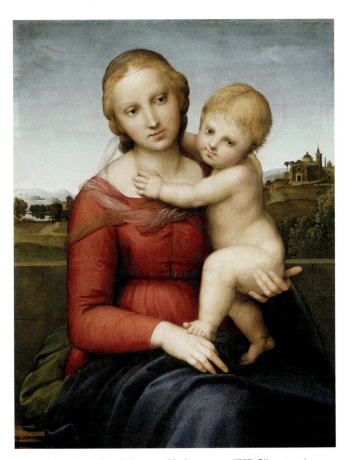

Fig. 7.28 Raphael, Small Cowper Madonna. ca. 1505. Oil on panel, 23⁷⁄₁₆″ × 17⁵⁄₁₆″. National Gallery of Art, Washington, D.C., Widener Collection (1942.9.57). Photograph © Board of Trustees, National Gallery of Art. The painting takes its name from its owner, George Nassau Clavering, the third Earl Cowper (1738–89), who visited Italy in 1760 and remained there for the rest of his life, amassing an extraordinary collection of Italian Renaissance paintings.

strikes us most is their very humanity—the fact that they seem absolutely alive with a sense of touch, the Child's toes resting on her right hand, her left supporting his naked buttocks. Lending the scene a sense of reality is the landscape itself, which is a real one, featuring the church of San Bernardino, 2 miles outside Raphael's native Urbino. But perhaps more than anything else, the self-reflective gaze of the Virgin captures the viewer's imagination, as if we have caught her literally in the moment, thinking who knows what, but deep in thought nonetheless. Divinity and humanity are here perfectly balanced.

In 1508, the young Raphael left Florence to arrive in Rome as Michelangelo was beginning work on the Sistine Chapel ceiling, and he quickly secured a commission from Julius II to paint the pope's private rooms in the Vatican Palace. The first of these rooms was the so-called Stanza della Segnatura (Room of the Signature), where subsequent popes signed official documents, but which Julius used as a library. Julius had determined the subjects. On each of the four walls, Raphael was to paint one of the four major areas of humanist learning: Law and Justice, to be represented by the *Cardinal Virtues*; the Arts, to be represented by *Mount Parnassus*; Theology, to be represented by the *Disputà*, or *Dispute over the Sacrament*; and Philosophy, to be represented by the *School*

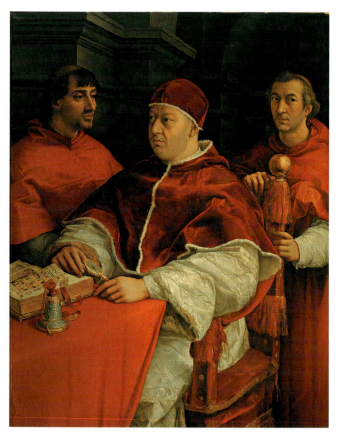

Fig. 7.29 Raphael, *Pope Leo X with Cardinals Giulio de' Medici and Luigi de' Rossi*. 1517. Panel, 60½″ × 47″. Galleria degli Uffizi, Florence. The illuminated manuscript on the table in front of the pope is from his private collection. It contributes significantly to the highly naturalistic feeling of the scene, even as it symbolizes his humanism.

of Athens (see *Closer Look*, pages 234–35). In an apparent attempt to balance Classical paganism and Christian faith, a gesture completely in keeping with Julius's humanist philosophy, two of these scenes—*Mount Parnassus* and the *School of Athens*—had Classical themes, the other two Christian.

The Medici Popes

Pope Julius II died in 1513, not long after Michelangelo had completed the Sistine Chapel ceiling and Raphael the Stanza della Segnatura. He was succeeded by Leo X, born Giovanni de' Medici, son of Lorenzo the Magnificent. Leo's papacy began a nearly 21-year period of dominance from Rome by the Medici popes, which ended with the death of Clement VII in 1534. The patronage of these Medici popes had a significant effect on art.

After Raphael's work in the Stanza, Leo was quick to hire him for other commissions. When Bramante died in 1514, Leo appointed the young painter as papal architect, though Raphael had never worked on any substantial building project. It was not long before Leo asked Raphael to paint his portrait.

Pope Leo X with Cardinals Giulio de' Medici and Luigi de' Rossi (Fig. **7.29**), painted in 1517, suggests a new direction in Raphael's art. The lighting is more somber than in the vibrantly lit paintings of the Stanza della Segnatura. Architectural detail is barely visible as the figures are silhouetted, seated against an intensely black ground. Although posed as a group, the three figures look in different directions, each preoccupied with his own concerns. It is as if they have just heard something familiar but ominous in the distance, something that has given them all pause. There is, furthermore, a much greater emphasis on the material reality of the scene. One can almost feel the slight stubble of Leo's beard, and the beards of the two cardinals are similarly palpable. The velvet of Leo's ermine-trimmed robe contrasts dramatically with the silk of the cardinals' cloaks. And the brass knob on the pope's chair reflects the rest of the room like a mirror, including a brightly lit window that stands in total opposition to the darkness of the rest of the scene. All in all, the painting creates a sense of drama, as if we are witness to an important historical moment.

In fact, in 1517, the papacy faced some very real problems. To the north, in Germany, Martin Luther had published his *Ninety-Five Theses*, attacking the practice of papal indulgences and calling into question the authority of the pope (see Chapter 8). Back in Florence, where the Medici had resumed power in 1512, the family maintained control largely through its connections to Rome, and that control was constantly threatened. Despite these difficulties, as Leo tried to rule the Church in Rome and Florence from the *stanze* of the Vatican, he continued his patronage of the arts unabated. He commissioned Raphael to decorate more rooms in the papal apartments and to develop a series of **cartoons** (full-scale drawings used to transfer a design onto another surface) for tapestries to cover the lower walls of the Sistine Chapel. Leo also celebrated his papacy with a series of commissions at

San Lorenzo, the neighborhood church in Florence that had served as the Medici family mausoleum for nearly 100 years. He hired Michelangelo to design a new funerary chapel there, the so-called New Sacristy, for recently deceased members of the family.

When Leo X died in 1521, he was briefly succeeded by a Dutch cardinal who deplored the artistic patronage of the Medici popes as both extravagant and inappropriate. He died only a year into his reign, and when Giulio de' Medici succeeded him as Clement VII, artists and humanists reacted enthusiastically. As cardinal, he had commissioned major works from Raphael and others, and he had worked closely with Leo on Michelangelo's New Sacristy at San Lorenzo in Florence. But Clement was never able to sustain the scale of patronage in Rome that his uncle had managed. This failure resulted in part from the Sack of Rome by the German mercenary troops of Holy Roman Emperor Charles V in 1527. During this crisis, many of the artists' workshops in the city were destroyed, and many artists abandoned the city altogether.

Josquin des Prez and the Sistine Chapel Choir

The inventiveness that marks the patronage of the Medici popes and cardinals as well as the work of Raphael, Leonardo, and Michelangelo was a quality shared by Renaissance musicians, especially in the virtuosity of their performances. Such originality was the hallmark of the Sistine Chapel Choir, founded in 1473 by Sixtus IV. It performed only on occasions when the pope was present, and typically consisted of between 16 and 24 male singers. The choir's repertory was limited to the polyphonic forms common to the liturgy: motets, masses, and psalm settings. These were arranged in four parts (voices), for boy sopranos, male altos, tenors, and basses. The choir usually sang without instrumental accompaniment,

a cappella, "in the manner of the chapel," an unusual practice at the time, since most chapel choirs relied on at least organ accompaniment.

Composers from all over Europe were attracted to the Sistine Chapel Choir. Between 1489 and 1495, one of the principal members of the choir was the Franco-Flemish composer Josquin des Prez (ca. 1450–1521). Afterward, beginning in about 1503, he served as musical director of the chapel at the court of Ferrara. During his lifetime, he wrote some 18 masses, almost 100 motets (see Chapter 6 and the discussion of Guillaume Dufay earlier in this chapter), and some 70 songs, including three Italian *frottole*.

Josquin's last mass, the *Pange lingua* ("Sing, My Tongue"), written sometime after 1513, is structured by means of **paraphrase**. In paraphrase structure, all voices elaborate on an existing melody. One voice introduces a musical idea that is subsequently repeated with some variation in sequence by each of the other voices throughout the entire work or section of a work, so that all the parts are rhythmically and melodically balanced. This creates the richly polyphonic texture of the whole. This contrasts with **cantus firmus**, which is the plainchant (monophonic) "fixed melody" on which the composition is based (see Chapter 5). The source of Josquin's melody in *Pange lingua* is a very well-known plainchant hymn written in the sixth century by Venantius Fortunatus (ca. 530–609), one of the earliest medieval poets and composers. Josquin transforms the original into a completely new composition, even as he leaves the melody entirely recognizable.

The opening *Kyrie* (Fig. **7.30**) (track **7.2**) is based on the opening of the Fortunatus plainchant. In a technique known as **point of imitation**, this musical theme is taken up by all the voices of Josquin's polyphonic composition in succession so that all four voices weave round one another in imitation. This kind of innovative play upon a more or less

Listen at MyArtsLab

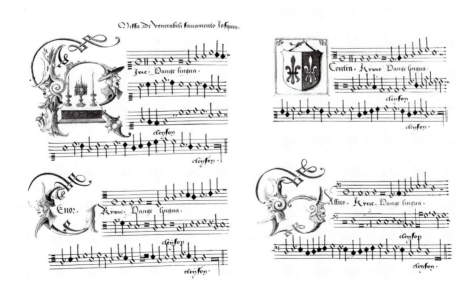

Fig. 7.30 Score of the opening bars of Josquin des Prez's *Pange lingua* mass. 16th century.
The four voices of the mass are represented here, each one indicated by the decorative capital at the beginning of the line.

The *School of Athens*, also known as *Philosophy*, is generally acknowledged as the most important of Raphael's four paintings for the Stanza della Segnatura of the Vatican Palace in Rome. Its Classicism is clearly indicated in several ways: by its illusionistic architectural setting, based on ancient Roman baths; by its emphatic one-point perspective, which directs the viewer's attention to the two central figures, Plato and Aristotle, fathers of philosophy; and by its subject matter, the philosophical foundation of the Renaissance humanistic enterprise. All the figures here—the Platonists on the left, the Aristotelians on the right, although not all have been identified—were regarded by Renaissance humanists as embodying the ideal of continual pursuit of learning and truth. The clarity, balance, and symmetry that distinguish this Raphael composition became a touchstone for painters in centuries to come.

Plato (ca. 428–347 BCE) resembles a self-portrait of Leonardo da Vinci. He points upward to the realm of ideas. (Note the resemblance of this gesture to that of Doubting Thomas in Leonardo's *Last Supper*, Fig. 7.17). He carries the Timaeus, the dialogue on the origin of the universe, in which he argued that the circle is the image of cosmic perfection.

Apollo, holding a lyre, is god of reason, patron of music, and symbol of philosophical enlightenment.

Epicurus (341–270 BCE) reads a text and wears a crown of grape leaves, symbolic of his philosophy that happiness could be attained through the pursuit of pleasures of the mind and body.

Pythagoras (ca. 570–490 BCE), the Greek mathematician, illustrates the theory of proportions to interested students—among them, wearing a turban, the Arabic scholar **Averroës** (1126–98).

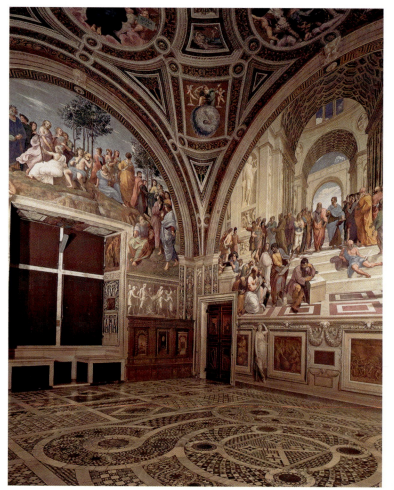

Something to Think About . . .

Why do you suppose that Raphael chose to use so many of his contemporaries as models for the figures from Classical antiquity depicted in the painting?

Stanza della Segnatura, Vatican, Rome.
Fresco on the left lunette, *Parnassus*; on the right lunette, *School of Athens*.

Raphael's *School of Athens*

Aristotle (384–322 BCE) carries his *Nicomachean Ethics* and gestures outward toward the earthly world of the viewer, emphasizing his belief in empiricism—that we can understand the universe only through the careful study and examination of the natural world.

Minerva, the goddess of wisdom, is the traditional patron of those devoted to the pursuit of truth and artistic beauty.

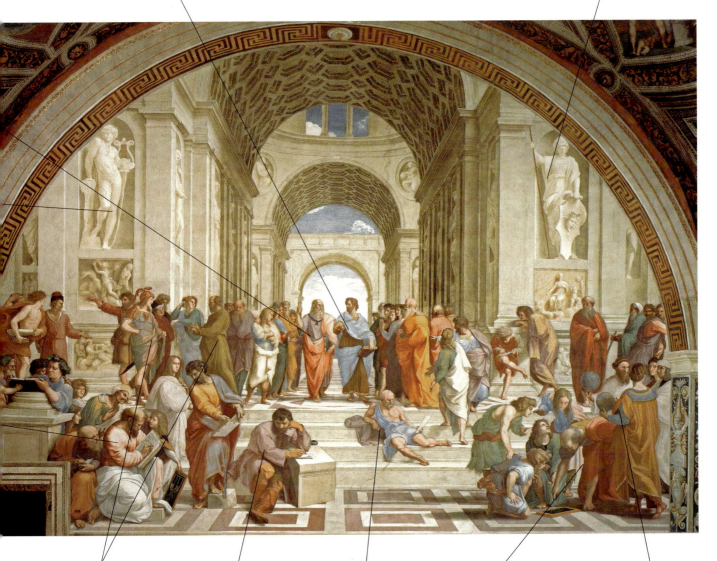

Alexander the Great (356–323 BCE) debates with **Socrates** (469–399 BCE), who makes his points by enumerating them on his fingers.

Heraclitus (ca. 540–480 BCE), the brooding Greek philosopher who despaired at human folly, wears stonecutter's boots and is actually a portrait of **Michelangelo.**

Diogenes the Cynic (ca. 412–323 BCE), who roamed the streets of Athens looking for an honest man, hated worldly possessions, and lived in a barrel.

Euclid (third century BCE), whose *Elements* remained the standard geometry text down to **modern** times, is actually a portrait of **Bramante.**

Ptolemy, the second-century astronomer and philosopher, holds a terrestrial globe, while **Zoroaster** (ca. 628–551 BCE) faces him holding a celestial globe. Both turn toward a young man who looks directly out at us. This is a self-portrait of **Raphael.**

Raphael, *School of Athens.* **1510–11.** Fresco, 19' × 27'. Stanza della Segnatura, Vatican, Rome.

standard theme is testimony to Josquin's ingenuity and humanist individualism. And it brings a level of expressiveness to the liturgy that far exceeds the more or less unemotional character of the plainchant. Largely because of this expressiveness, his compositions were among the first polyphonic works to be widely performed long after the death of their composer.

Niccolò Machiavelli and the Perfect Prince

If Josquin des Prez represents the inventiveness of the Renaissance individual in remaking musical tradition, the political philosopher Niccolò Machiavelli (1469–1527) represents the individual's capacity to ignore tradition altogether and follow the dictates of pragmatic self-interest. Machiavelli's treatise *The Prince* (1513) is part of a long tradition of literature giving advice to rulers that stretches back to the Middle Ages. But Machiavelli's revolutionary political pragmatism sets the work apart. Humanist education had been founded on the principle that it alone prepared people for a life of virtuous action. Machiavelli's *Prince* challenged that assumption.

Machiavelli had served the Florentine city-state for years, assuming the post of second chancellor of the Republic in 1498. He had studied the behavior of ancient Roman rulers and citizens at great length, and he admired particularly their willingness to act in defense of their country. On the other hand, he disdained the squabbling and feuding that marked Italian internal relations in his own day. Assessing the situation in the Italian politics of his day, he concluded that only the strongest, most ruthless leader could impose order on the Italian people.

From Machiavelli's point of view, the chief virtue any leader should display is that of ethical pragmatism. For the statesman's first duty, he believed, was to preserve his country and its institutions, regardless of the means he used. Thus, a prince's chief preoccupation, and his primary duty, says Machiavelli, is to wage war (**Reading 7.5a**):

READING 7.5a

from Niccolò Machiavelli, *The Prince*, Chapter 14 (1513)

A Prince . . . should have no care or thought but for war, and for the regulations and training it requires, and should apply himself exclusively to this as his peculiar province; for war is the sole art looked for in one who rules, and is of such efficacy that it not merely maintains those who are born Princes, but often enables men to rise to that eminence from a private station; while, on the other hand, we often see that when Princes devote themselves rather to pleasure than to arms, they lose their dominions.

His attention turned to war, the prince must be willing to sacrifice moral right for practical gain, for "the manner in which we live, and that in which we ought to live, are things so wide asunder, that he who quits the one to betake himself to the other is more likely to destroy than to save himself." Therefore, "it is essential . . . for a Prince who desires to maintain his position, to have learned how to be other than good." Goodness, from Machiavelli's point of view, is a relative quality anyway. A prince, he says, "need never hesitate . . . to incur the reproach of those vices without which his authority can hardly be preserved; for if he well consider the whole matter, he will find that there may be a line of conduct having the appearance of virtue, to follow which would be his ruin, and that there may be another course having the appearance of vice, by following which his safety and well-being are secured." The well-being of the prince, in other words, is of the utmost importance because upon it rests the well-being of the state.

Machiavelli further argues that the prince, once engaged in war, has three alternatives for controlling a state once he has conquered it: He can devastate it, live in it, or allow it to keep its own laws. Machiavelli recommends the first of these choices, especially if the prince defeats a republic (**Reading 7.5b**):

READING 7.5b

from Niccolò Machiavelli, *The Prince*, Chapter 5 (1513)

In republics there is a stronger vitality, a fiercer hatred, a keener thirst for revenge. The memory of their former freedom will not let them rest; so that the safest course is either to destroy them, or to go and live in them.

This is probably a warning directed at the absentee Medici popes, far away in Rome and not tending to business in Florence, for Machiavelli originally planned to dedicate the book to Giovanni de' Medici, by then Pope Leo X. (He eventually dedicated it to Lorenzo de' Medici, then duke of Florence, hoping to secure political favor.) Its lessons, drawn from Roman history, were intended as a guide to aid Italy in rebuffing the French invasions.

Finally, according to Machiavelli, the prince should be feared, not loved, for "Men are less careful how they offend him who makes himself loved than him who makes himself feared." This is because "love is held by the tie of obligation, which, because men are a sorry breed, is broken on every whisper of private interest; but fear is bound by the apprehension of punishment which never relaxes."

From Machiavelli's point of view, humans are "fickle," "dishonest," "simple," and, as he says here, all in all a "sorry breed." The state must be governed, therefore, by a morality different from that governing the individual. Such moral and ethical pragmatism was wholly at odds with the teachings of the Church. In 1512, Pope Julius II's troops overran the Florentine republic, restored the Medici to power in Florence, and dismissed Machiavelli from his post as second chancellor. Machiavelli was then (wrongfully) accused of involvement in a plot to overthrow the new heads of state, imprisoned, tortured, and finally exiled permanently to a country home

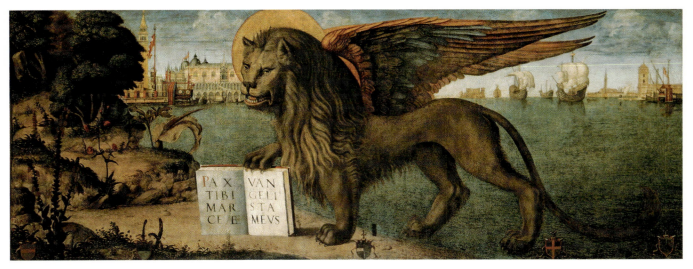

Fig. 7.31 Vittore Carpaccio, *Lion of Saint Mark*. 1516. Oil on canvas, 4'6¾" × 12'1". Doge's Apartments, Doge's Palace, Venice. Venetians believed that an angel visited Saint Mark and prophesied that he would be buried in Venice, on the very spot where Saint Mark's Cathedral stands. So they felt justified in removing his relics from Egypt and bringing them to Venice.

in the hills above Florence. It is there, beginning in 1513, that he wrote *The Prince*.

Although widely circulated, *The Prince* was too much at odds with the norms of Christian morality to be well received in the sixteenth century. Throughout the seventeenth and eighteenth centuries, it was more often condemned than praised, particularly because it appeared to be a defense of absolute monarchy. Today, we value *The Prince* as a pioneering text in political science. As an essay on political power, it provides a rationalization for the political expediency and duplicity that society has all too often witnessed in modern political history.

THE HIGH RENAISSANCE IN VENICE

What distinguishes Venetian culture from that of Florence and Rome?

In a mid-fifteenth-century painting by Vittore Carpaccio (1450–1525) of Saint Mark's lion (Fig. 7.31), symbol of the Republic, the lion stands with its front paws on land and its rear paws on the sea, symbolizing the importance of both elements to the city. In the sixth or seventh century, invading Lombards from the north had forced the local populations of the Po River delta to flee to the swampy lagoon islands that would later become the city of Venice. Ever since, trade had been the lifeblood of Venice.

Not only did the city possess the natural fortification of being surrounded by water (Map 7.2), but also, as a larger

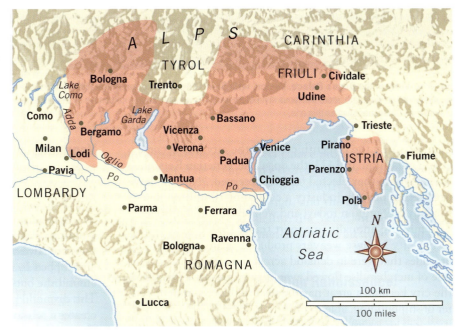

Map 7.2 Venice and the Venetian *Terraferma*, the Venetian-controlled mainland, at the end of the 15th century. Venice controlled all the land inside the red area. Its territories extended almost to Milan in the west, northward into the Alps, and almost as far as Ferrara and Mantua to the south. A causeway connecting Venice to the mainland was constructed in the middle of the nineteenth century. Until then, the city was approachable only by water.

city-state, it controlled the entire floodplain north of the Po River, including the cities of Padua and Verona and extending eastward nearly to Milan. This larger territory was called *Terraferma* (from the Latin *terra firma*, "firm ground"), to distinguish it from the watery canals and islands of the city proper. From *Terraferma*, the Venetians established trade routes across the Alps to the north, and eastward across Asia Minor, Persia, and the Caucasus. As one Venetian historian put it in a thirteenth-century history of the city, "Merchandise passes through this noble city as water flows through

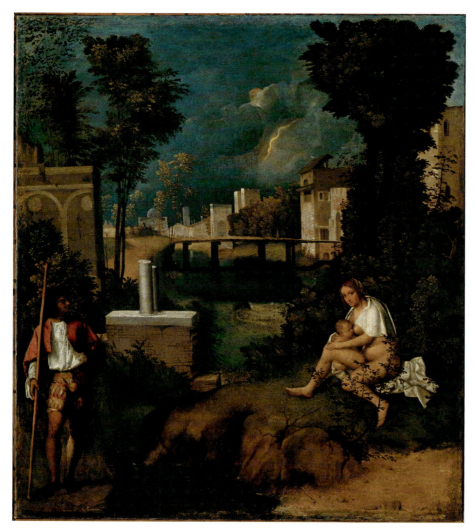

Fig. 7.34 Giorgione, *Tempest.* **ca. 1509.** Oil on canvas, 31¼″ × 28¾″. Gallerie dell'Accademia, Venice. There is nothing about this painting that could be called controlled. The landscape is overgrown and weedy—just as the man and woman are disheveled and disrobed. It is as if, for a moment, the lightning has revealed to the viewer a scene not meant to be witnessed.

View the Closer Look for *Tempest* on **MyArtsLab**

7.18) are fully realized in Giorgione's *Tempest* (Fig. **7.34**). The first known mention of the painting dates from 1530, when it surfaced in the collection of a Venetian patrician. We know almost nothing else about it, which contributes to its mystery. At the right, an almost nude young woman nurses her child. At the left, a somewhat disheveled young man, wearing the costume of a German mercenary soldier, gazes at the woman and child with evident pride. Between them, in the foreground, stands a pediment topped by two broken columns. A creaky wooden bridge crosses the estuary in the middle ground, and lightning flashes in the distance, illuminating a densely built cityscape. What, we must ask, is the relationship between the two figures? Are they husband and wife? Or are they lovers, whose own tempestuous affair has resulted in the birth of a child? These are questions that remain unanswered.

Giorgione evidently began work on his paintings without preliminary drawings, and X-ray examination of this one reveals that in the young man's place there originally stood a second young woman stepping into the pool between the two figures. At the time that the work surfaced in a wealthy Venetian's collection in 1530, it was described simply as a small landscape with a soldier and a gypsy. It seems to have satisfied the Venetian taste for depictions of the affairs of everyday life, and even though its subject remains obscure, the painting continues to fascinate us.

The fact that Giorgione did not make preliminary drawings for his paintings led Vasari, in his *Lives of the Most Excellent Painters, Architects, and Sculptors*, to charge that he was simply hiding his inability to draw well beneath a virtuoso display of surface color and light. The shortcoming of all Venetian artists, Vasari claimed, was their sensuous painterly technique, as opposed to the intellectual pursuits of the Florentines, epitomized by their careful use of scientific perspective and linear clarity.

Titian In a certain sense, Vasari was right. Sensuality, even outright sexuality, would become a primary subject of Venetian art, as many of Titian's paintings make clear. When Giorgione died of the plague in 1510, at only 32 years of age, it seems likely that his friend Titian, 10 years younger, finished several of his paintings. While lacking the sense of intrigue that his elder mentor captured in the *Tempest*, Titian's *Sacred and Profane Love* (Fig. **7.35**) similarly addresses the relations between the sexes, only a little more indirectly. The nude figure at the right holds a lamp, perhaps symbolizing divine light and connecting her to the Neoplatonic ideal of the celestial Venus and thus sacred love. The luxuriously clothed, fully dressed figure on the left, whom we might think of as the "*earthly* lady," or profane love, holds a bouquet of flowers, a symbol of her fecundity. Between the two, Cupid reaches into the fountain.

The painting was a commission from Niccolò Aurelio on the occasion of his marriage to Laura Bagarotto in 1514. Behind the clothed figure on the left, two rabbits cavort in the grass, underscoring the conjugal theme of the image. It seems probable that the two female figures represent two aspects of the same woman, and thus embody the roles that the Renaissance woman filled for her humanist husband, combining Classical learning and intelligence with a candid celebration of sexual love in marriage.

Titian's *Venus of Urbino* (Fig. **7.36**), painted for Duke Guidobaldo della Rovere of Urbino in 1538, more fully

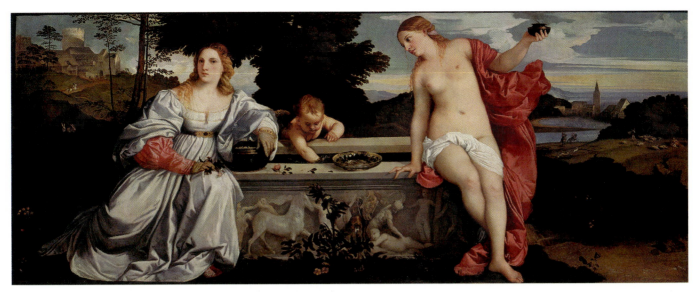

Fig. 7.35 Titian, _Sacred and Profane Love._ ca. 1514. Oil on canvas, 46½" × 1097⁄8". Galleria Borghese, Rome. The painting was commissioned by Niccolò Aurelio, a Venetian, to celebrate his marriage to Laura Bagarotto, and was probably intended for the couple's sleeping chamber. The husband's coat of arms is carved on the fountain; the wife's is inside the silver bowl on the fountain's ledge.

acknowledges the sexual obligations of most Renaissance women. This "Venus"—more a real woman than an ethereal goddess, and referred to by Guidobaldo as merely a "nude woman"—is frankly available. She stares out at the viewer, Guidobaldo himself, with a matter-of-factness suggesting that she is totally comfortable with her nudity.

(Apparently the lady-in-waiting and maid at the rear of the palatial rooms are searching for suitably fine clothing in which to dress her.) Her hand both covers and draws attention to her genitals. Her dog, a traditional symbol of both fidelity and lust, sleeps lazily on the white sheets at her feet. She may be, ambiguously, either a courtesan or a bride. (The chest from which the servant is removing clothes is a traditional reference to marriage.) In either case she is, primarily, an object of desire.

As Titian's work continued to develop through the 1550s, 1560s, and 1570s, his brushwork became increasingly loose and gestural (see Chapter 10). The frank sensuality conveyed by crisp contours in _Sacred and Profane Love_ and the _Venus of Urbino_ found expression, instead, in the artist's handling of paint itself. Indeed, the viewer can feel Titian's very hand in these later works, for he would actually paint with his fingers and the stick end of his brush too. But Titian's mastery of color—the rich varieties of warm reds, the luminosity of his glazes—so evident in these paintings, never altered. In fact, his color came to define the art of Venice itself. When people speak of "Venetian" color, they have Titian in mind.

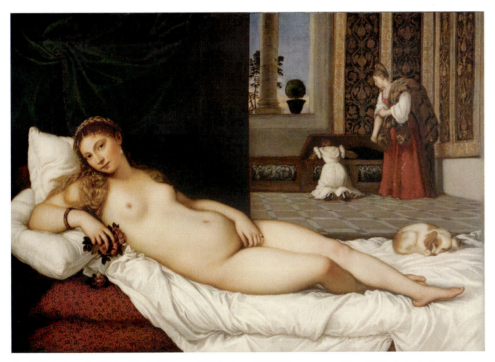

Fig. 7.36 Titian, _Reclining Nude (Venus of Urbino)._ ca. 1538. Oil on canvas, 47" × 65". Galleria degli Uffizi, Florence. Titian's technique contributes significantly to the power of the painting. Although not visible in reproduction, the nude's skin is built up of layers of semitransparent yellow-whites and pinks that contrast with the cooler bluish-whites of the bedsheets. Behind her, the almost black panel and curtain further contrast with the luminous light on her body.

WOMEN IN ITALIAN HUMANIST SOCIETY

How did women fare in the Italian Renaissance?

The paintings of both Giorgione and Titian raise the issue of the place of women in Italian humanist society. It remained commonplace, especially in Venice, to paint portraits of women whose identity was unknown but who represented ideal beauty. Titian's *La Bella* (Fig. **7.37**) seems to be the same person depicted in the *Venus of Urbino* (and she appears in at least two other Titian portraits), but her identity is a mystery, if in fact she was ever a "real" woman and not simply the embodiment of Titian's idea of "true" beauty. Something of a canon of female beauty had been codified by Petrarch, in his sonnets, and Poliziano in his poems (see Reading 6.5 in Chapter 6). In her book *Women in Italian Renaissance Art: Gender, Representation, Identity*, Paola Tinagli sums up the canon: "Writers praised [painters for] the attractions of wavy hair gleaming like gold; of white skin similar to snow, to marble, to alabaster or to milk; they admired cheeks which looked like lilies and roses, and eyes that shone like the sun or the stars. Lips are compared to rubies, teeth to pearls, breasts to snow or apples." Portraits of Venetian women who embodied such traits are emblems of the beautiful more than representations of real beings.

But as humanist values helped to redefine the relation of the individual to the state throughout the Italian city-states and gave male citizens a greater degree of freedom, women began to benefit as well. While at all levels of culture their role might still be relegated to the domestic side of life, they were increasingly better educated and therefore better able to assert themselves. This is particularly true of middle- and upper-class women. And occasionally these women, through their accomplishments, achieved a remarkable level of stature.

The Education of Women

In the Italian humanist courts, the wives of rulers and their daughters—who were, after all, prospective wives of other rulers—received a humanist education. Like the medieval author of the *Book of the City of Ladies*, Christine de Pizan (see Chapter 6), they possessed knowledge of French and Latin, the ability to write in their native language with grace and ease, a close acquaintance with both Classical and vernacular Italian literature, and at least a passing knowledge of mathematics and rhetoric. They were expected to be good musicians and dancers. In addition, the rise of the merchant class to a position of wealth and social responsibility necessitated at least some degree of education for the women whose husbands were members of the guilds and confraternities of the city.

The Florentine mercantile system required of every man a working knowledge of mathematics and accounting and the ability to read. As we have seen, the guilds, where these skills were practiced daily, were also the chief sponsors of public works, from cathedrals and churches to the sculptures and paintings that adorned them. In general, the wives of these merchant guildsmen were not only conversant with their

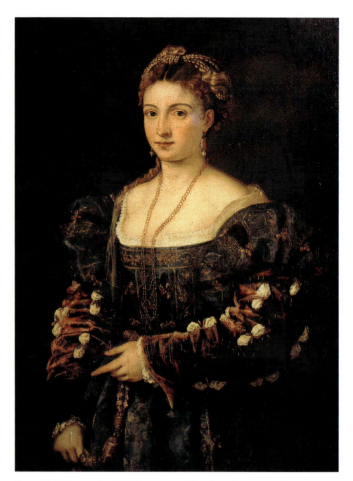

Fig. 7.37 Titian, *La Bella* (*Woman in a Blue Dress*). ca. 1538. Oil on canvas, 39⅜" × 30". Palazzo Pitti, Florence. The sumptuousness of the dress adds considerably to the sense of beauty Titian seeks to convey. It was painted with extremely expensive lapis lazuli pigments.

husbands' affairs, but also with the greater affairs of the city. Many took a more active role in both. Indeed, since women customarily married between the ages of 13 and 17 and to men generally much older than themselves, they often inherited the family businesses. In order to maintain their financial and personal independence, many chose not to remarry.

The most influential women in Rome, for instance, were connected to the Church hierarchy either by blood or by marriage. Their brothers and brothers-in-law, uncles and nephews were the cardinals and popes who lavished the city with their wealth and largesse. As executors of their husbands' estates and as widows, many of these women became important patrons of convents, where they were able to escape the social strictures of widowhood.

Women and Family Life

Still, for most women the husband's role was one of active, public life, and the wife's was to manage domestic affairs. In *On the Family*, a book published in 1443 by the same Leon Battista Alberti whose *On Painting* had outlined the principles of perspective, the author approvingly quotes a young groom introducing his bride to his household:

After my wife had been settled in my house a few days, and after her first pangs of longing for her mother and family had begun to fade, I took her by the hand and showed her around the whole house. . . . At the end there were no household goods of which my wife had not learned both the place and purpose. Then we returned to my room and having locked the door, I showed her my treasures, silver, tapestry, garments, jewels, and where each thing had its place.

For Alberti, clearly, the family is an orderly system. Each thing in the household has its proper place, just as, not coincidentally, each object in a perspectival drawing has its right and proper place. And the woman's proper place was in the service of her husband.

Much of what we know about what was accepted as the proper behavior of ladies of the court derives from Castiglione's *Book of the Courtier*, since, as part of its concern with the conduct of the aristocratic gentleman, it details the gentleman's expectations of his lady. It was generally agreed, for instance, by the conversationalists at the Urbino court that a courtier's lady should profit from most of the rules that serve the courtier. Thus, her accomplishments should demonstrate the casual effortlessness of *sprezzatura*. In one of the book's conversations, for instance, Giuliano de' Medici addresses a gathering of ladies and gentlemen, intent on pointing out what the lady needs *beyond* the accomplishments of her husband (**Reading 7.6**):

READING 7.6

from Baldassare Castiglione, *The Courtier*, Book 3 (1513–18; published 1528)

[The court lady] must have not only the good sense to discern the quality of him with whom she is speaking, but knowledge of many things, in order to entertain him graciously; and in her talk she should know how to choose those things that are adapted to the quality of him with whom she is speaking, and should be cautious lest occasionally, without intending it, she utter words that may offend him. . . . Let her not stupidly pretend to know that which she does not know, but modestly seek to do herself credit in that which she does know. . . . I wish this Lady to have knowledge of letters, music, painting, and to know how to dance and make merry; accompanying the other precepts that have been taught the Courtier with discreet modesty and with the giving of a good impression of herself. And thus, in her talk, her laughter, her play, her jesting, in short, in everything, she will be very graceful, and will entertain appropriately, and with witticisms and pleasantries befitting her, everyone who shall come before her. . . .

Whereas, for Castiglione, the courtier must strive to exemplify the perfectly well-rounded *l'uomo universale*, the court lady must use her breeding and education to further the perfection of the home.

Laura Cereta and Lucretia Marinella: Renaissance Feminists

Many fifteenth-century women strove for a level of education beyond the mere "knowledge of letters, music, painting" called for by Castiglione. One of the most interesting is Laura Cereta (1469–99). She was the eldest child of a prominent family from the city of Brescia in the Venetian *Terraferma*. Until she was 11, she was educated by nuns at a convent school. There, she studied reading, writing, embroidery, and Latin until her father called her home to help to raise her siblings. But he encouraged her to continue her studies, and in his library, she read deeply in Latin, Greek, and mathematics. At 15, however, Cereta chose motherhood over the pursuit of her studies and married a local merchant. When he died, two years later, she returned to her studies. In 1488, at just 19 years of age, she published *Family Letters*, a Latin manuscript containing 82 letters addressed to friends and family, an unusually large number of them women, as well as a mock funeral oration in the Classical style.

Cereta's letter, known as the *Defense of Liberal Instruction for Women*, is one of the most remarkable fifteenth-century Italian documents. It is a response to a critic who had praised her as a prodigy, implying that true women humanist scholars were rare and that, perhaps, her father had authored her letters. In the *Defense*, Cereta explains why so few women were scholars and then defends her own learning (**Reading 7.7**):

READING 7.7

from Laura Cereta, *Defense of Liberal Instruction for Women* (1488)

Only the question of the rarity of outstanding women remains to be addressed. The explanation is clear: women have been able by nature to be exceptional, but have chosen lesser goals. For some women are concerned with parting their hair correctly, adorning themselves with lovely dresses, or decorating their fingers with pearls and other gems. Others delight in mouthing carefully composed phrases, indulging in dancing, or managing spoiled puppies. Still others wish to gaze at lavish banquet tables, to rest in sleep, or, standing at mirrors, to smear their lovely faces. But those in whom a deeper integrity yearns for virtue, restrain from the start their youthful souls, reflect on higher things, harden the body with sobriety and trials, and curb their tongues, open their ears, compose their thoughts in wakeful hours, their minds in contemplation, to letters bonded to righteousness. For knowledge is not given as a gift, but [is gained] with diligence. The free mind, not shirking effort, always soars zealously toward the good, and the desire to know grows ever more wide and deep. It is because of no special holiness, therefore, that we [women] are rewarded by God the Giver with the gift of exceptional talent. Nature has generously lavished its gifts upon all people, opening to all the doors of choice through which reason sends envoys to the will, from which they learn and convey its desires. The will must choose to exercise the gift of reason.

7.1 Discuss the influence of the Medici family on Florentine art and the development of humanist thought.

Florence was the center of the cultural revival that we have come to call the Renaissance, a "rebirth" that amounted to a revolution in human consciousness founded on humanist inquiry. How does the Baptistery Doors competition of 1401 exemplify this new consciousness? How does Lorenzo Ghiberti's new set of doors, the *Gates of Paradise*, articulate Renaissance values even more?

By 1418 Florence Cathedral still lacked a dome above its octagonal crossing. Brunelleschi won the competition for the dome's design, a feat of architectural engineering unsurpassed in his day. For the cathedral's consecration on March 25, 1436, the French composer Guillaume Dufay created a new musical work, a motet called *Nuper rosarum flores* ("The Rose Blossoms"). How does Dufay's composition reflect Brunelleschi's feat?

Brunelleschi was also the first Renaissance artist to master the art of scientific perspective. What values does the interest in scientific perspective reflect? How does the work of the sculptor Donatello also reflect these values?

Medici control of Florentine politics was secured by Cosimo de' Medici, who surrounded himself with humanists. How would you describe Marsilio Ficino's Neoplatonist philosophy? How does it recast Platonic thought? Cosimo's grandson, Lorenzo, "the Magnificent," continued the Medici tradition. His own circle of acquaintances included many of the greatest minds of the day, including the composer Heinrich Isaac, the painter Sandro Botticelli, and the philosopher Pico della Mirandola. Can you describe how the work of each reflects humanistic principles?

7.2 Describe how other Italian courts followed the lead of the humanist court in Florence.

Lorenzo's court inspired the courts of the leaders of other Italian city-states, who were almost all nobles. At the Urbino court of Duke Federigo da Montefeltro, Baldassare Castiglione wrote *The Book of the Courtier*. How does this treatise define *l'uomo universale*? In Milan, Ludovico Sforza commissioned Leonardo da Vinci to paint the *Last Supper* for the Dominican convent of Santa Maria delle Grazie. What would you say is Leonardo's greatest strength as a painter? How does his portraiture reflect humanistic values?

7.3 Examine the impact of papal patronage on the art of the High Renaissance in Rome.

In the fifteenth century, the grandeur that had once distinguished the city of Rome had almost entirely vanished. But beginning with the ascension of Sixtus IV to the papacy in 1471, the patronage of the popes and their cardinals transformed Rome. This period is known as the High Renaissance. Many of the greatest works of the period, including Donato Bramante's Tempietto and his new basilica for Saint Peter's, Michelangelo's ceiling for the Sistine Chapel, and Raphael's frescoes for the Stanza della Segnatura, were commissioned by Pope Julius II. How would you describe Julius II's personality?

Julius II was followed in 1513 by Leo X, born Giovanni de' Medici. Niccolò Machiavelli's treatise *The Prince* reflects the turmoil surrounding papal politics in this era. What does he suggest is the prince's primary duty? Do you think Machiavelli's outlook is applicable today?

Renaissance musicians shared with other artists of the age its spirit of inventiveness. The Sistine Chapel Choir, founded in 1473 by Sixtus IV, usually sang *a cappella* (without instrumental accompaniment). Between 1489 and 1495, one of the principal members of the Sistine Chapel Choir was the Franco-Flemish composer Josquin des Prez. His compositions include 18 masses.

7.4 Compare the social fabric and artistic style of Renaissance Venice to that of both Florence and Rome.

Fifteenth-century Venice defined itself as both the most cosmopolitan and the most democratic city in the world. Its religious and political centers—Saint Mark's Cathedral and the Doge's Palace—stood side by side, symbolizing peace, prosperity, and, above all, unity of purpose. The wealth and general well-being of Venice was displayed along the Grand Canal, where its most important families built their homes. These magnificent homes were Gothic in character. How can we account for the city's taste for this medieval style? Two of the most important Venetian painters of the early fifteenth century were Giorgione and Titian. In what ways does their painting style differ from other High Renaissance painters such as Michelangelo and Raphael?

7.5 Outline the place of women in Renaissance Italy.

In many ways the paintings of both Giorgione and Titian reflect Venetian attitudes toward women. What does Titian's *La Bella* reveal about these attitudes? Several notable women strove for a level of education beyond the mere "knowledge of letters, music, painting" called for by Castiglione. Among these were Laura Cereta and Lucretia Marinella, who frankly rebelled against male attitudes. What is the relation between Cereta's *Defense of Liberal Instruction for Women* and Pico della Mirandola's *Oration on the Dignity of Man*? How would you describe Marinella's sense of women's place?

The Venetian literary scene was dominated by a group of so-called honest courtesans whose reputations were built upon the ability to combine sexual and intellectual pursuits. The poetry of one of these courtesans, Veronica Franco, exemplifies their literary production. Maddalena Casulana, the first professional woman composer to see her own compositions in print, composed madrigals, a form mastered by the choirmaster at Saint Mark's, Adrian Willaerts.

✔️ **Study** and **review** on **MyArtsLab**

Palladio and His Influence

The setting of Titian's *Sacred and Profane Love* represents an escapist tendency that we first saw in Boccaccio's *Decameron* (Chapter 6). In Boccaccio's stories, a group of young men and women flee the onset of the plague in Florence, escape to the country, and for 10 days entertain one another with a series of tales, many of which are alternately ribald and erotic, moral and exemplary. Renaissance humanists considered retreats to the country to be an honored ancient Roman tradition, the pleasures of which were richly documented by such Roman poets as Horace in his *Odes* (Chapter 3):

> How in the country do I pass the time?
> The answer to the question's brief:
> I lunch and drink, I sing
>   and play,
> I wash and dine, I rest.

By the High Renaissance, wealthy Venetian families, following strong Classical precedent, routinely escaped from the heat and humidity of the city to private villas in the countryside. The Villa La Rotonda by Adrea Palladio (1508–80) (Fig. **7.38**), located just outside the city of Vicenza, set the standard for the country villa. As in so much Venetian architecture, the house looks outward, toward the light of the countryside, rather than inward to the shadow of a courtyard. It is situated on the crest of a hill. On each of its four sides Palladio has placed a pedimented loggia, approached by a broad staircase, designed to take advantage of the view.

Built in the 1560s for a humanist churchman, Villa Rotonda has a centralized plan that recalls Leonardo's *Vitruvian Man* (see Fig. 7.19). Palladio was, in fact, a careful student of Vitruvius, as was Leonardo. It is not surprising, then, that the central dome of La Rotonda is modeled on the Pantheon (see Fig. 3.18 in Chapter 3), which was itself known in the sixteenth century as La Rotonda, as was any large, domed, circular room. Although lacking the Pantheon's coffered ceiling and size, Palladio's villa was originally distinguished by a 7-foot-diameter oculus, like that at the Pantheon open to the sky, but today covered by a small cupola. Directly below the oculus, a stone drain in the shape of a faun's face allowed rainwater to fall into the basement. Although Venice depended on the agricultural economy of the *Terraferma*, the Villa Rotonda was not designed to be a working farm. Rather, the house was intended for family life and entertaining.

Palladio built many villas in the vicinity of Venice. Each of them is interesting in a different way, and they constitute an important body of High Renaissance architecture that influenced architects in many countries and later centuries down to our own day. More than 300 years after Palladio's death, Thomas Jefferson would model his own country estate at Monticello (Fig. 7.39) on Palladio's example. Set atop a hill outside Charlottesville, Virginia, it commanded vistas that were in every way comparable to those of the Villa Rotonda. As opposed to La Rotonda, Monticello was the centerpiece of a working farm, where Jefferson continually experimented with agricultural techniques and methods. But Jefferson recognized in Palladio's use of elemental geometric forms—circle, cube, and sphere—a sense of order and harmony that seemed, from his point of view, ideal for the architecture of his new American republic. ■

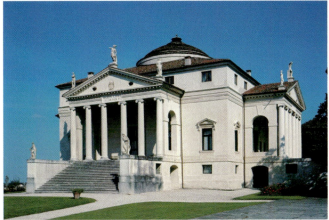

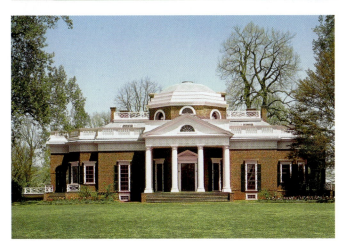

Figs. 7.38 and 7.39 (top) Andrea Palladio, Villa La Rotonda. Begun 1560s. (bottom) Thomas Jefferson, Monticello, Charlottesville, VA. 1770–84, 1796–1806.

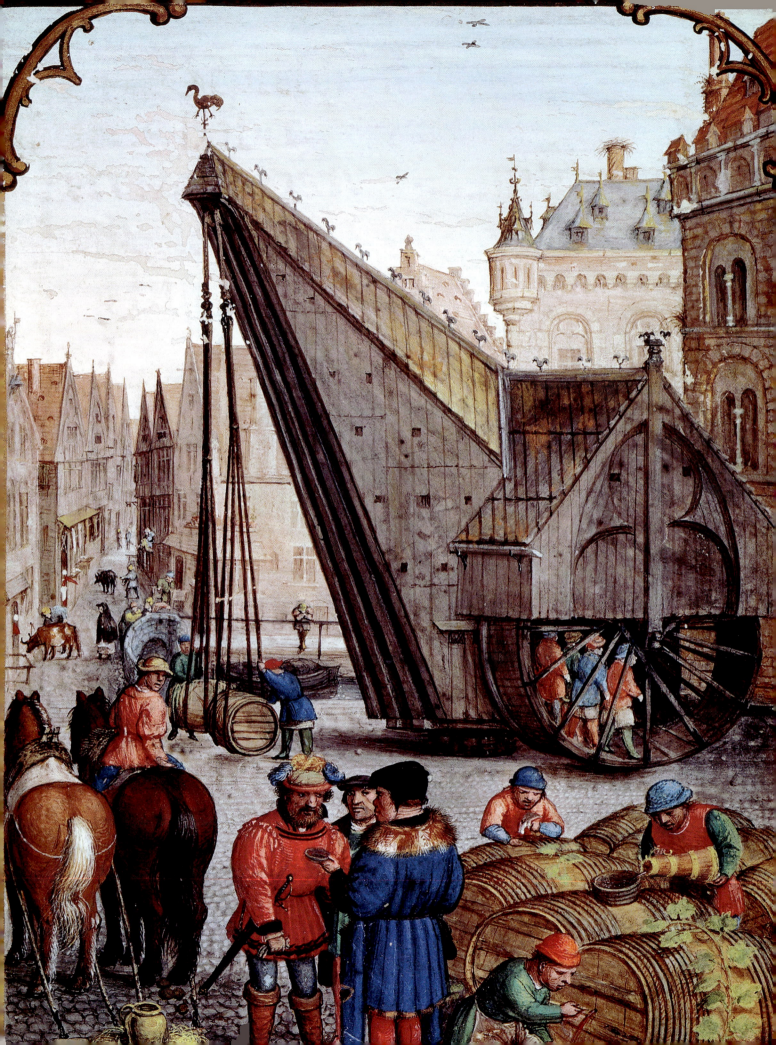

Renaissance and Reformation in the North

8

Between Wealth and Want

LEARNING OBJECTIVES

8.1 Describe the effect of commerce and mercantile wealth on the development of both religious and secular painting in Northern Europe.

8.2 Explain the causes of the Reformation and assess its impact on the art and literature of the era.

Fifteenth- and sixteenth-century Italy did not hold a monopoly on the arts in Europe. To the north, the Flemish city of Bruges was a major center of culture, rivaling the Italian city-states in both art and commerce. The financial capital of the North, the city was home to the Medici banking interests in the region and had a strong merchant class of its own. Although inland, its link to the North Sea gave Bruges access to other mercantile centers by a waterway, closed off at the mouth of the sea by a lock, where, in the words of one sixteenth-century report, "It is a pleasure and a marvel to behold the wild sea let in and out, as it were, through a wooden door, with artfulness and human ingenuity." Waterborne commerce terminated at the Waterhalle in the heart of the city. But heavy cargoes, such as barrels of beer and wine, were unloaded further north on the Kraanrei, "Crane canal," where by 1290, the city had constructed a large wooden crane propelled by "crane children" who powered it by walking on a circular treadmill (Fig. **8.1**).

The city's prosperous merchant class, like the nobility, actively supported the arts. This chapter outlines the development of a commercial art market in several Northern European centers of culture like Bruges—Antwerp, Paris, and London especially—that would permanently change the nature of artistic culture in the West. A spirit of innovation dominated the arts, spurred on largely by competition in the marketplace. Civic and mercantile patronage would begin to rival that of the nobility and Church, and artistic workshops increasingly functioned as businesses. In London, audiences of all classes flocked to the south bank of the Thames River to see plays performed by theatrical companies competing for profits sufficient to support them.

But there was a darker side to the North's growing prosperity. In his classic text on the rise of the Renaissance in the North, *The Autumn of the Middle Ages*, Johan Huizinga describes the tensions that informed life in the North:

> There was less relief available for misfortune and for sickness; they came in a more fearful and more painful way. Sickness contrasted more strongly with health. The cutting cold and the dreaded darkness of winter were more concrete evils. Honor and wealth were enjoyed more fervently and greedily because they contrasted still more than now with lamentable poverty. A fur-lined robe of office, a bright fire in the oven, drink and jest, and a soft bed still possessed . . . high value for enjoyment. . . .
>
> So intense and colorful was life that it could stand the mingling of the smell of blood and roses. Between hellish fears and the more childish jokes, between cruel harshness and sentimental sympathy the people stagger—like the giant with the head of a child, hither and thither. Between the absolute denial of all worldly joys and a frantic yearning for wealth and pleasure, between dark hatred and merry conviviality, they live in extremes.

◀ **Fig. 8.1 Crane in Bruges. 16th century.** Miniature. Bayerishe Staatsbibliothek, Munich, Germany.
The Bruges crane was at once a symbol of mechanical ingenuity and mercantile prosperity. It signaled the preeminence of the city as a center of commercial activity and trade.

The English Portrait Tradition

Hamlet represents the logical outcome of the English taste for portraiture, the dramatic embodiment of the nation's humanist emphasis on individualism. One of the most important portraitists of wealthy society in Europe was Hans Holbein the Younger (ca. 1497–1543). One of the most interesting and ambitious of all Holbein's portraits is *The Ambassadors* (Fig. **8.19**), which depicts two French ambassadors to the court of Henry VIII. Jean de Dinteville, on the left, commissioned the painting, and Georges de Selve, on the right, was the bishop elect of Lauvau. Both represent the interests of Francis I, and, therefore, of the Catholic Church (see Chapter 10). It seems clear that both were present at court to negotiate with Henry about his insistence on annulling his marriage to Katherine of Aragon and marrying Anne Boleyn, and the subsequent separation of the Church

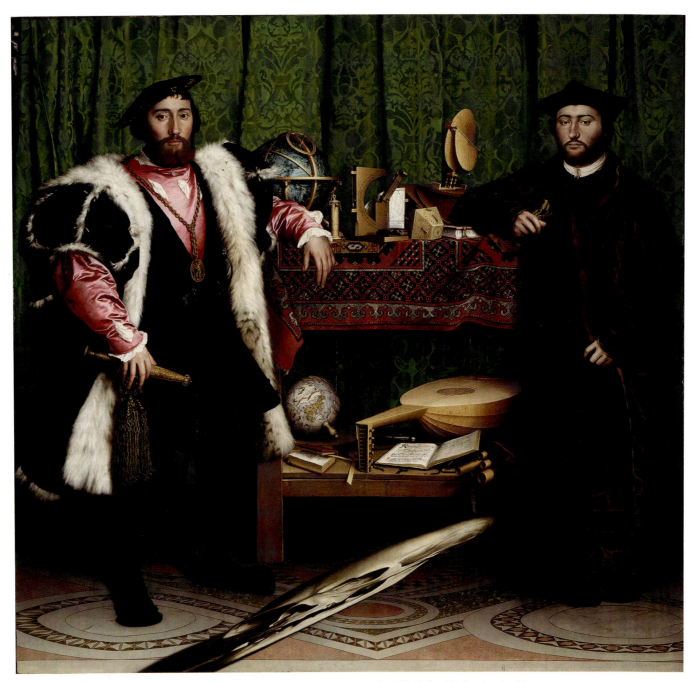

Fig. 8.19 Hans Holbein the Younger, *The Ambassadors*. 1533. Oil on oak panel, 81½" × 82". National Gallery, London. The Lutheran hymnal that lies open beneath the lute is Johannes Walther's *The Little Hymn-Book* (1525). The hymn on the left is "Come, Holy Ghost, our souls inspire," one of Martin Luther's best-known compositions. The hymn on the right is also by Luther: "Man, if thou wouldst live a good life and remain with God eternally."

View the Closer Look for *The Ambassadors* on **MyArtsLab**

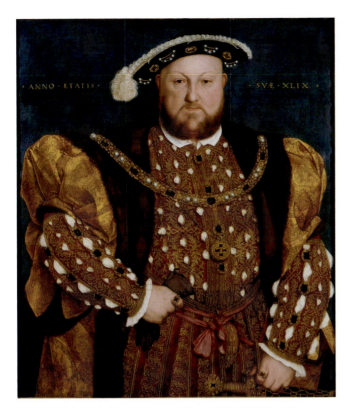

Fig. 8.20 Hans Holbein the Younger, *Henry VIII in Wedding Dress.* 1540. Oil on panel, 32½" × 29". Galleria Barberini, Rome. Henry is in the clothes that he wore when he married the 25-year-old Anne of Cleves in 1540. He was 49.

just as many of London's German merchant community. Each portrait conveyed the sitter's status and captured something of the sitter's identity, in the case of Henry nothing less than his imposing self-confidence—he was, for his time, physically imposing as well, his 6-foot-2-inch frame supporting a 54-inch waistline.

Like her father, Elizabeth was also the subject of many portraits. But few later English painters could match Holbein's skill in depicting volume, texture, and light. Most portraits of Elizabeth, such as the so-called *Darnley Portrait of Elizabeth I* (Fig. **8.21**), tend to concentrate on elaborate decorative effects. Set behind the flat patterning of her lace collar, pearl necklaces, and jewel-encrusted dress, Elizabeth appears almost bodiless—the exact opposite of Holbein's emphatically embodied portrait of Henry VIII. And yet, no other portrait of Elizabeth better conveys her steadfast determination, even toughness, while still capturing something of her beauty. By all accounts, she could alternately swear like a common prostitute and charm like the most refined diplomat, the very embodiment of the tensions that dominated her age.

of England from the Catholic Church. In fact, Henry had married Anne just three months before this work was painted, in January 1533. A cylindrical dial on the table between the two ambassadors tells us that it is April 11, 1533. The tiled floor is a direct copy of the floor of the sacred area in front of the high altar of Westminster Abbey. The tiles are colored glass and stone, from Rome, Egypt, and the Middle East. By using this design, Holbein suggests that his ambassadors stand on holy ground and are engaged in some holy purpose. The skull, placed between the viewer and the ambassadors, in what is known as an anamorphic projection, suggests that the two men understand the fate that awaits us all. The lute is in perfect linear perspective, in contrast to the distorted perspective of the skull, suggesting that one's point of view determines what one is capable of seeing—perhaps the principal lesson of diplomacy. One of the eleven strings is broken, probably symbolizing the lack of harmony between Catholic and Protestant interests. But the other objects on the two-tiered table between the ambassadors—the Lutheran hymnal, the terrestrial globe, the celestial globe, and the astronomical instruments—all indicate the men's willingness to strike a balance between Catholic and Protestant interests.

Holbein painted hundreds of works during his two extended visits to England (1526–28, 1532–43), including many of Henry VIII (Fig. **8.20**), four of Henry's six wives, scores of portraits of English courtiers and humanists, and

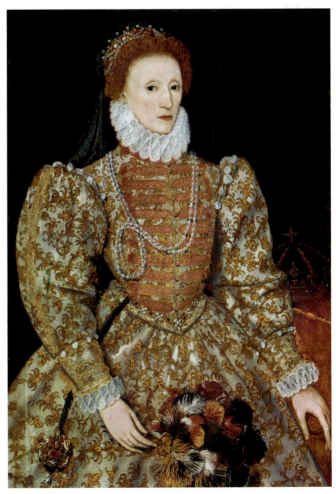

Fig. 8.21 Attributed to Federigo Zuccaro, *The Darnley Portrait of Elizabeth I.* ca. 1575. Oil on panel, 44½" × 31". National Portrait Gallery, London. Behind Elizabeth, on the table at the right, lies her crown.

8.1 Describe the effect of commerce and mercantile wealth on the development of both religious and secular painting in Northern Europe.

The center of commercial activity in Flanders by the beginning of the fifteenth century was Bruges. There, luxury art goods, especially paintings, were sold to a rising merchant class, for both local consumption and export. Flemish painters took oil painting to new heights. Often, the objects depicted in these paintings seem so real that the viewer might actually touch them. What contributes specifically to oil painting's luminosity? What attributes of oil painting make its heightened sense of realism possible? How did Hieronymus Bosch take advantage of these effects?

In Germany, Matthias Grünewald's *Isenheim Altarpiece* is grimly realistic in its portrayal of death, and yet transcendently emotional. How does his work compare to that of the Flemish painters? How does mysticism inform German art and literature? Perhaps the most interesting development in Germany was Nuremburg artist Albrecht Dürer's attempt to synthesize the Northern interest in detailed representation with the traditions of Italian humanism he had assimilated on his visit there in 1505–06. How does this synthesis manifest itself in his art?

8.2 Explain the causes of the Reformation and assess its impact on the art and literature of the era.

On October 31, 1517, the German priest and professor Martin Luther posted his *Ninety-Five Theses* on the door of Wittenberg's Castle Church. His feelings about the Church were in many ways inspired by the writings of the Dutch humanist scholar Desiderius Erasmus, who is most noted for his satirical attack on the corruption of the Roman Catholic Church, entitled *In Praise of Folly*.

In what terms does Erasmus "praise" human folly? What are the characteristics of satire and how does irony contribute to it?

Luther's call for the reform of the Roman Catholic Church unleashed three centuries of social and political conflict. Luther deplored the concept of indulgences and detested the secular spirit apparent in both Church patronage of lavish decorative programs and the moral laxity of the cardinals in Rome. What are indulgences? The Church charged Luther with heresy, but he continued to publish tracts challenging the authority of the pope.

In Germany, Luther's defense of individual conscience against the authority of the pope seemed to peasants a justification for their own independence from their feudal lords. What resulted from this newfound sense of freedom? Ulrich Zwingli, in Zurich, and John Calvin, in Geneva, followed Luther's lead, both convinced that their respective cities could become models of moral rectitude and Christian piety. What was the rationale for the iconoclasm both championed? How did their approach to Church doctrine differ from Luther's? How was Henry VIII's challenge to papal authority in England more different still?

One of the most important contributors to the Reformation was Johannes Gutenberg's printing press. It made the Bible a best seller. How did the widespread distribution of his texts fuel reformist movements? How did Thomas More take advantage of the medium? But, in England, perhaps the greatest artistic achievement of the era was its drama, particularly the plays of William Shakespeare. In what ways is Shakespeare's character Hamlet unique in the theater of the early seventeenth century? How does he reflect England's taste for portraiture?

✓ **Study** and **review** on **MyArtsLab**

The Catholic Church Strikes Back

No movement as radical as the Reformation could take place without a strong reaction from the Roman Catholic Church. The challenge of Protestantism to the moral authority of the pope threatened the Church with downfall, and Rome soon recognized this. Yet the Roman Catholic Church had come to some of the same conclusions about its shortcomings as its Northern critics. In self-defense, therefore, it launched a Counter-Reformation, both to strike back against the fundamental ideas defended by reformists like Luther and to implement reforms of its own.

The Counter-Reformation (see Chapter 10) had the support of clergy and laypeople through newly organized groups such as the Modern Devotion and the Oratory of Divine Love. These groups encouraged a return to the principles of simplicity, ethical living, and piety that Erasmus had championed. The Society of Jesus, known more familiarly as the Jesuits, took a tougher approach. Founded by Ignatius of Loyola in the 1530s, it advocated a return to strict and uncompromising obedience to the authority of the Church and its ecclesiastical hierarchy. The society's Rule 13 sums up its notion of obedience: "I will believe that the white that I see is black if the hierarchical Church so defines it." Then, in 1545, Pope Paul III convened the Council of Trent in order to define Church doctrine and recommend far-reaching reforms in the abuses practiced by the Church, particularly the selling of indulgences.

The Council of Trent, which convened in two more sessions between 1545 and 1563, also decided to counter the Protestant threat "by means of the stories of the mysteries of our Redemption portrayed by paintings or other representations, [so that] the people be instructed and confirmed in the habit of remembering and continually revolving in mind the articles of faith." The arts should be directed, the Council said, toward clarity and realism, in order to increase understanding, and toward emotion, in order to arouse piety and religious fervor. While the Council of Trent generally preached restraint in design, its desire to appeal to the emotions of its audience resulted in increasingly elaborate church architecture, so that the severe simplicity of the Calvinist church (Fig. 8.22), devoid of any art, would seem emotionally empty beside the grand expanse of the Catholic interior (Fig. 8.23). Yet the basic configuration would remain the same. For the next two centuries both churches would vie for the souls of Christians in Europe and the Americas. ∎

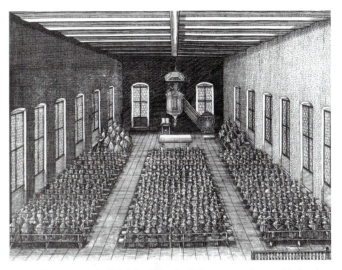

Fig. 8.22 Interior of a Calvinist Church. 17th century. German National Museum, Nuremberg.

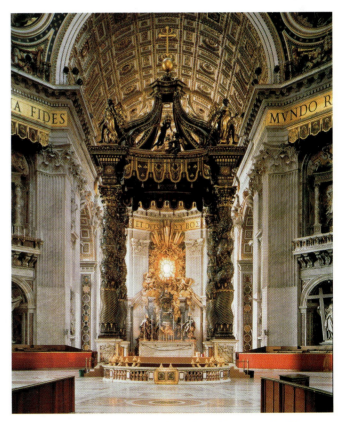

Fig. 8.23 Gianlorenzo Bernini, Baldacchino. Saint Peter's Basilica, Vatican, Rome. 1624–33. Gilt bronze, marble, stucco, and glass, height approx. 100′.

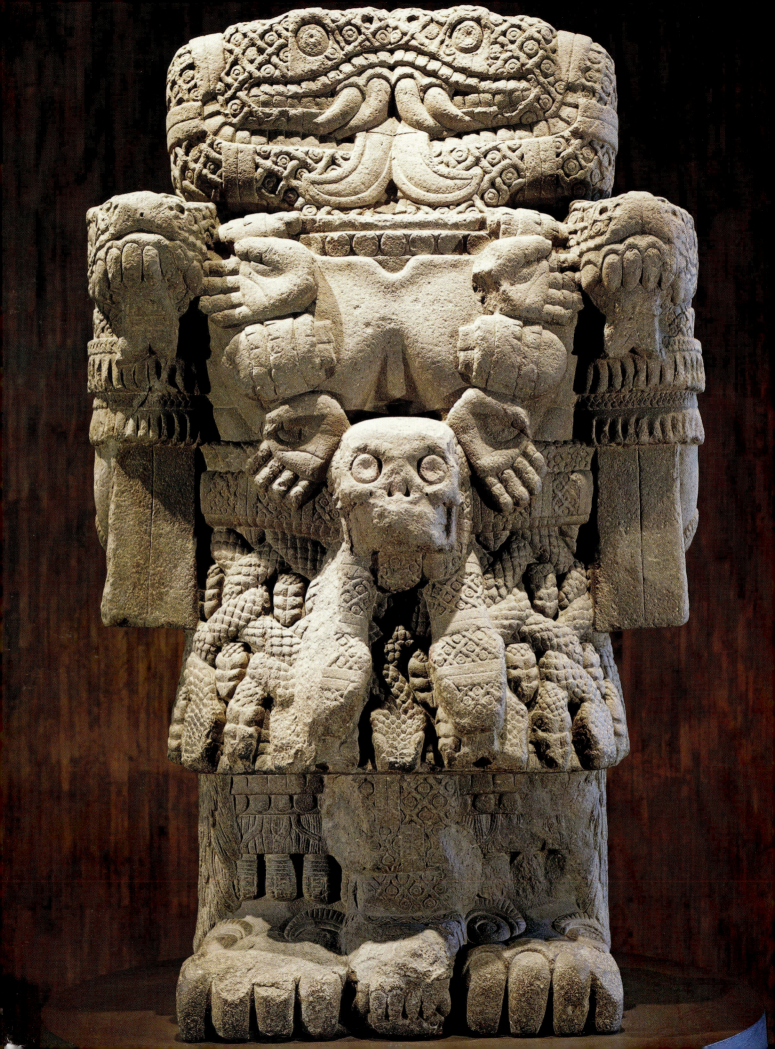

Encounter and Confrontation 9
The Impact of Increasing Global Interaction

LEARNING OBJECTIVES

9.1 Discuss the cultures that preceded that of the Aztecs in the Americas, and the Spanish reaction to Aztec culture.

9.2 Describe the impact of the Portuguese on African life and the kinds of ritual traditions that have contributed to the cultural survival of African communities after contact.

9.3 Outline the ways in which contact with Europe affected Mogul India.

9.4 Assess the impact of contact with the wider world on China and the ways in which the arts reflect the values of the Chinese state.

9.5 Explain the tension between spiritual and military life in Japanese culture and the importance of patronage in Japanese cultural life.

In 1519–21, the Aztec empire of Mexico was conquered by the Spanish conquistador ("conqueror") Hernán Cortés (1485–1547) and his army of 600 men through a combination of military technology (gunpowder, cannon, and muskets), disease inadvertently introduced by his troops, and a series of lies and violations of trust. The Aztecs possessed neither guns nor horses, nor much in the way of clothing or armor, all of which made them appear if not uncivilized, then completely vulnerable. They were also vulnerable because other native populations in Mexico deeply resented the fact that the Aztecs regularly raided their villages to obtain victims for blood sacrifice. According to Aztec legend, at the time of their exile from Tula, the supreme spiritual leadership of the culture was assumed by the bloodthirsty Huitzilopochtli, the god of war, who had emerged fully grown from the womb of his mother Coatlicue, the earth goddess, wielding his weapon, the Fire Serpent, Xiuhcoatl. A sculpture depicting Coatlicue may have originally stood in the temple to Huitzilopochtli at the Aztec capital of Tenochtitlán atop the giant temple at the heart of the city, the Templo Mayor (Fig. **9.1**).

Her head is composed of two fanged serpents, symbolizing two rivers of blood flowing from her decapitated torso. She wears a necklace of human ears, severed hands, and, at the bottom, a human skull. Her skirt is made of interwoven serpents which, to the Aztecs, represent both childbirth and blood—that is, fertility and decapitation.

Huitzilopochtli was born full-grown out of Coatlicue of necessity. Coatlicue was also mother of Coyolxauhqui, the Moon, and one day, while she was sweeping her temple on top of Coatepec hill, symbolically represented in Tenochtitlán by the Templo Mayor, she had been miraculously impregnated with Huitzilopochtli by a ball of feathers that floated down from the sky. Coyolxauhqui viewed the pregnancy of her mother as an affront, and she conspired to kill Coatlicue. At that moment, Huitzilopochtli was born. He decapitated his treacherous sister, and cast her down from the top of Coatepec hill. At each tumble of her fall, she was further dismembered. This is the Aztec explanation for the phases of the moon. As, the moon wanes each month, more and more of it disappears.

◄ **Fig. 9.1 Coatlicue, Aztec. 15th century.** Basalt, height 8'3". National Museum of Anthropology, Mexico City. Coatlicue is represented as headless because, as legend has it, she was decapitated at the beginning of the present creation.

 View the Closer Look for the goddess Coatlicue on **MyArtsLab**

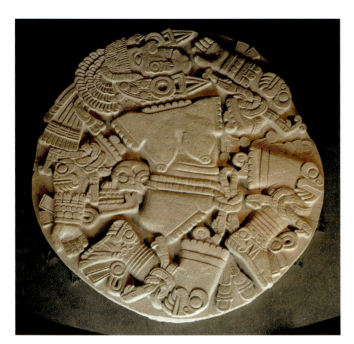

Fig. 9.2 Aztec, *The Moon Goddess Coyolxauhqui*, from the Sacred Precinct, Templo Mayor, Tenochtitlán. ca. 1469. Stone, diameter 10′11″. Museo Templo Mayor, Mexico City. The sculpture was found lying at the base of the Templo Mayor, as if cast down by Huitzilopochtli.

A giant disk, over 10 feet across, found at the base of the Templo Mayor depicts the goddess (Fig. **9.2**) decapitated, arms and legs dismembered. She is adorned with a two-headed serpent belt bearing a skull, like the necklace of her mother, Coatlicue, in Fig. 9.1. Her torso, with flaccid breasts, is shown frontally. Issuing from her mouth is what appears to be her last breath. Thus victorious over the moon, Huitzilopochtli ordered the Aztec priests to search for a cactus with a great eagle perched upon it and there establish a city in his name. They soon found the place on the shores of Lake Texcoco. The cactus bore red fruit in the shape of the hearts that Huitzilopochtli devoured, and the eagle was the symbol of the god himself. The Aztecs proceeded to build their great city, Tenochtitlán, "the place of the prickly pear cactus."

Anthropological evidence suggests that just before Cortés's birth, in about 1450, the Aztecs, in their thirst for blood sacrifice, had wiped out the entire population of Casas Grandes, near present-day Chihuahua in northern Mexico, a trading center containing over 2,000 pueblo apartments. Given such Aztec behavior, other tribes were willing to cooperate with Cortés. Cortés also had the advantage of superior weaponry, and he quickly realized that he could exploit the Aztecs' many vulnerabilities. One of the most important documents of the Spanish conquest, the 1581 *History of the Indies of New Spain*, by Diego de Durán, depicts Cortés's technological superiority (Fig. **9.3**). Durán was a Dominican priest fluent in Nahuatl, the Aztec language. His *History* is the product of extensive interviews and conversations with the Aztecs themselves. It represents a concerted effort to preserve Aztec culture, recounting Aztec history from its creation story through the Spanish conquest. In this illustration, a well-armed force led by

Pedro de Alvarado, one of Cortés's generals, confronts the Aztec military orders of the Eagle and the Jaguar. The Spanish wear armor and fight with crossbows and firearms, while the Aztecs have only spears.

Despite their technological superiority, Alvarado's men were in some jeopardy. Alvarado was besieged by Aztecs angry at the slaughter of hundreds of their kin during the Fiesta of Toxcatl, staged to impress their Spanish visitors. The massacre by the Spaniards is illustrated in Durán's *History* (Fig. **9.4**). Throughout these events, the Aztec king Motecuhzoma (formerly spelled Montezuma) had remained a prisoner of the Spanish forces. Cortés had pledged his friendship, but once he had been admitted into Tenochtitlán itself, he imprisoned Motecuhzoma. The Spanish conquistador had learned of an Aztec myth concerning Quetzalcóatl, the Feathered Serpent, who was widely worshiped throughout Mexico. In this myth, Quetzalcóatl was dethroned by his evil brother, Tezcatlipoca, god of war, and fled to the Gulf of Mexico, where he burst into flames and ascended to the heavens, becoming the Morning Star, Venus. In yet another version, he sailed away across the sea on a raft of serpents, promising to return one day. It was reputed that Quetzalcóatl was fair-skinned and bearded. Evidently, Motecuhzoma believed that Cortés was the returning Quetzalcóatl and welcomed him without resistance. Within two years, Cortés's army had crushed Motecuhzoma's people in

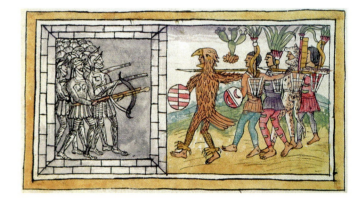

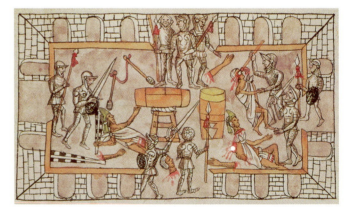

Figs. 9.3 and 9.4 (top) Aztecs confront the Spaniards; and (bottom) the Spanish massacre Aztec nobles in the temple courtyard. Both from Diego de Durán's *History of the Indies of New Spain*. 1581. Biblioteca Nacional, Madrid. Durán's work was roundly criticized during his lifetime for helping the "heathen" Aztecs to maintain their culture.

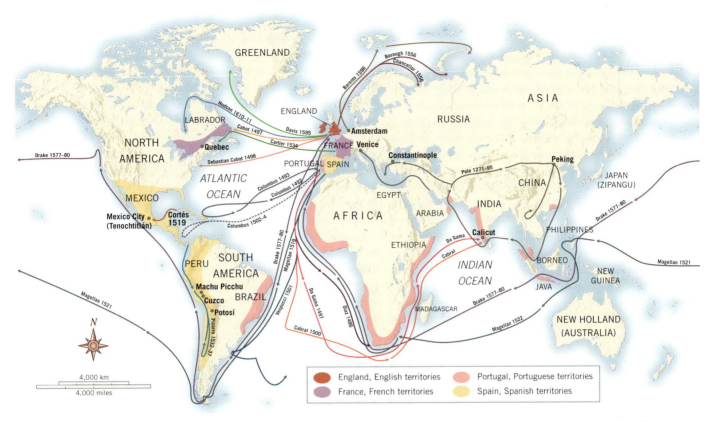

Map 9.1 **World exploration. 1486–1611.** Note Marco Polo's overland route to China in 1271 to 1295, which anticipated the great sea explorations by 200 years.

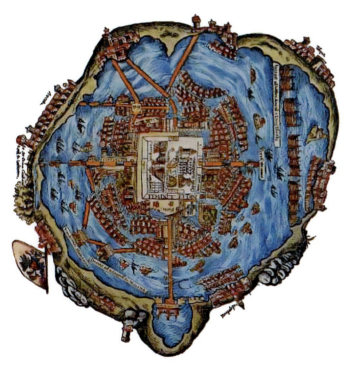

Fig. 9.5 **Plan of Tenochtitlán, from Cortés's first letter to the king of Spain. 1521.** Bernal Díaz, one of Cortés's conquistadors, compared the plan of Tenochtitlán to Venice. Set in the middle of Lake Texcoco, it was crisscrossed by canals. In the center of the island is the Templo Mayor.

the name of Spain. Of the 20 to 25 million inhabitants of Mexico at that time, only about 2 million survived—the remainder were wiped out by war and disease. Their beautiful capital, Tenochtitlán, surrounded by the waters of Lake Texcoco (Fig. 9.5), would be quickly transformed into the capital of New Spain, its Templo Mayor reduced to rubble.

The imperial adventuring of Cortés in the Americas was mirrored around the globe, as Europeans sought to establish their power not only in the Americas, but also in Africa, India, China, and Japan. This chapter considers the cultures of the Americas, Africa, India, China, and Japan in this period, and considers how Europe transformed these cultures as it explored the world (Map **9.1**) and was itself transformed by contact with them. But European contact was not the only interaction these cultures experienced in the era. They also had an impact on one another. From a Western perspective, these cultures represented a wider world with Europe at its center. But from the point of view of these cultures, Europe represented the periphery, a cultural force invading their own centers of culture from the outside.

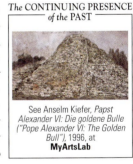

The CONTINUING PRESENCE *of the* PAST

See Anselm Kiefer, *Papst Alexander VI: Die goldene Bulle* ("Pope Alexander VI: The Golden Bull"), 1996, at **MyArtsLab**

THE SPANISH IN THE AMERICAS

What are some of the cultures that preceded the arrival of the Spanish in the Americas and how did the Spanish impact the indigenous cultures they found there?

When Cortés entered the Aztec island capital of Tenochtitlán (see Fig. 9.5), more than 200,000 people lived there. Gold-laden temples towered above the city. Gardens rich in flowers and fruit, and markets with every available commodity dominated the city itself; Bernal Díaz (1492–1584), one of Cortés's conquistadors, would later recall the sight (**Reading 9.1**):

READING 9.1

from Bernal Díaz, *True History of the Conquest of New Spain* (ca. 1568; published 1632)

We were astounded. . . . These buildings rising from the water, all made of stone, seemed like an enchanted vision. . . . Indeed some of our soldiers asked whether it was not all a dream. . . . It was all so wonderful that I do not know how to describe this first glimpse of things never heard of, seen, or dreamed of before. . . .

Let us begin with the dealers in gold, silver, and precious stones, feathers, cloaks, and embroidered goods, and male and female slaves who are also sold there. . . . Next there were those who sold coarser cloth, and cotton goods and fabrics made of twisted threads, and there were chocolate merchants with their chocolate. In this way you could see every kind of merchandise to be found anywhere in New Spain. . . . We were astounded at the great number of people and the quantities of merchandise, and at the orderliness and good arrangements that prevailed.

What most astonished Cortés himself, as it had Díaz, was that Aztec civilization was as sophisticated as his own. "So as not to tire Your Highness with the description of things of this city," Cortés wrote Queen Isabella of Spain, "I will say only that these people live almost like those in Spain, and in as much harmony and order as there, and considering that they are barbarous and so far from the knowledge of God and cut off from all civilized nations, it is truly remarkable to see what they have achieved in all things." This inclination to see a thriving civilization as uncivilized because it is unlike one's own is typical of the attitude of Westerners toward the peoples with whom they came into contact in the Age of Encounter. Other peoples were exactly that—the "Other"—a separate category of being that freed Western colonizers from any obligation to identify these peoples as equal, or even similar, to themselves.

The Americas before Contact

Great cultures had, in fact, developed in the Americas before the arrival of the Spanish. In the arid north of present-day Mexico, a somewhat mysterious but enormously influential civilization centered at Teotihuacán flourished. By the fourth century CE, it was a center of culture comparable in size and influence to Constantinople. In Mesoamerica, comprising present-day Honduras, Guatemala, Belize, and southern Mexico, between 250 and 900 CE the Maya established vast palace complexes that were both the administrative and religious centers of their culture.

These cultures were themselves preceded by others. As early as 1300 BCE, a pre-literary group known as the Olmec came to inhabit the area between Veracruz and Tabasco on the southern coast of the Gulf of Mexico, where they built huge ceremonial precincts in the middle of their communities. In these precincts, they erected giant pyramidal mounds, where an elite group of ruler-priests lived. These pyramids may have been an architectural reference to the volcanoes that dominate Mexico, or they may have been tombs. Excavations may eventually tell us. At La Venta, very near the present-day city of Villahermosa, three colossal stone heads stood guard over the ceremonial center on the south end of the platform (Fig. 9.6), and a fourth guarded the north end by itself. Each head weighs between 11 and 24 tons, and each bears a unique

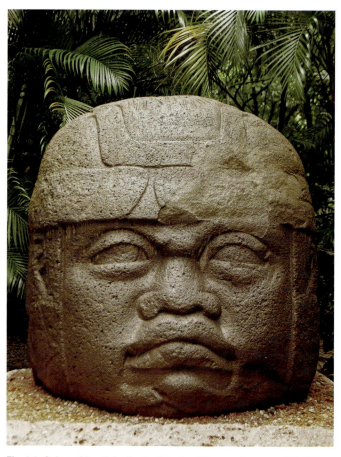

Fig. 9.6 Colossal head, La Venta, Mexico, Olmec culture. ca. 900–500 BCE. Basalt, height 7'5". La Venta Park, Villahermosa, Tabasco, Mexico. The stone heads are generally believed to be portraits of Olmec rulers, and they all share the same facial features, including wide, flat noses and thick lips. They suggest that the ruler was the culture's principal mediator with the gods, literally larger than life.

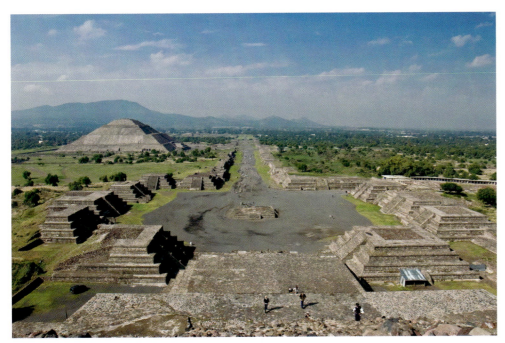

Fig. 9.7 Teotihuacán, Mexico, as seen from the Pyramid of the Moon, looking south down the Avenue of the Dead, the Pyramid of the Sun at the left. ca. 350–650 CE. One of the largest cities in the world by the middle of the first millennium, Teotihuacán covered an area of nearly 9 square miles.

The Pyramid of the Sun is oriented to mark the passage of the sun from east to west and the rising of the stellar constellation the Pleiades on the days of the equinox. Each of its two staircases contains 182 steps, which, when the platform at its apex is added, together total 365. The pyramid is thus an image of time. This representation of the solar calendar is echoed in another pyramid at Teotihuacán, the Temple of Quetzalcóatl, which is decorated with 364 serpent fangs.

At its height, in about 500 CE, about 200,000 people lived in Teotihuacán, making it one of the largest cities in the world. Scholars believe that a female deity, associated with the moon, as well as cave and mountain rituals played an important role in Teotihuacán culture. The placement of the Pyramid of the Moon, in front of the dead volcano Cerro Gordo (see Fig. 9.7), supports this theory. It is as if the mountain, seen from a vantage point looking north up the Avenue of the Dead, embraces the pyramid in its flanks. And the pyramid, in turn, seems to channel the forces of nature—the water abundant on the mountain, in particular—into the heart of the city.

emblem on its headgear, which is similar to old-style American leather football helmets. The heads are carved of basalt, although the nearest basalt quarry is 50 miles to the south in the Tuxtla Mountains. They were evidently at least partially carved at the quarry, then loaded onto rafts and floated downriver to the Gulf of Mexico before going back upriver to their final resting places. Many of the characteristic features of later Mesoamerican culture, such as pyramids, ball courts, mirror-making, and the calendar system, probably originated with the Olmec.

Teotihuacán Certainly the sense of colossal scale is found again and again throughout Pre-Columbian culture in Mesoamerica. The city of Teotihuacán, for instance, is laid out in a grid system, the basic unit of which is 614 square feet, and every detail is subjected to this scheme, conveying a sense of power and mastery. A great broad avenue, known as the Avenue of the Dead, runs through the city (Figs. 9.7 and 9.8). It links two great pyramids, the Pyramids of the Moon and the Sun, each surrounded by about 600 smaller pyramids, 500 workshops, numerous plazas, 2,000 apartment complexes, and a giant market area.

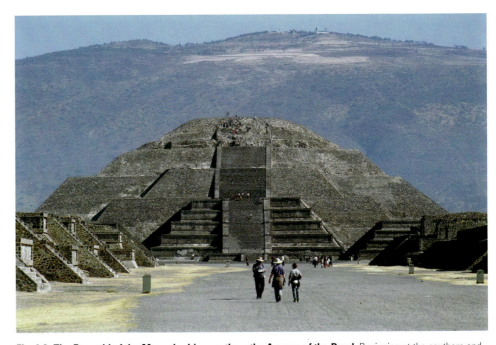

Fig. 9.8 The Pyramid of the Moon, looking north up the Avenue of the Dead. Beginning at the southern end of the city, and culminating at the Pyramid of the Moon, the Avenue of the Dead is 2½ miles long.

👁 Watch an architectural simulation of Teotihuacán on **MyArtsLab**

Mayan Culture To the south, another culture, that of the Maya, both predated and postdated that of Teotihuacán. The Maya occupied several regions: the highlands of Chiapas and Guatemala; the southern lowlands of Guatemala, Honduras, El Salvador, Belize, and the Mexican states of Chiapas; and the northern lowlands in the states of Yucatan, Campeche, and Quintano Roo. These were never unified into a single political entity, but rather consisted of many small kingdoms that engaged in warfare with one another over land and resources.

An elaborate calendar system enabled them to keep track of their history—and, evidence suggests, predict the future. It consisted of two interlocking ways of recording time, a 260-day calendar and a 365-day calendar. The 260-day calendar probably derives from the length of human gestation, from a pregnant woman's first missed menstrual period to birth. When both calendars were synchronized, it took exactly 52 years of 365 days for a given day to repeat itself—the so-called *calendar round*—and the end of each cycle was widely celebrated.

The Mayan calendar was put to many uses. An example is the Madrid Codex (Fig. **9.9**), one of the four surviving Mayan codices. It consists of 56 stucco-coated bark-paper leaves, painted, with the exception of one page, on both sides. Over 250 separate "almanacs" that place events of both a sacred and secular nature within the 260-day Mesoamerican ritual calendar fill its pages. It records events concerning particularly the activities of daily life (planting, tending crops, the harvest, weaving, and hunting), rituals, astronomic events, offerings, and deities associated with them. The four horizontal rows in the lower half of each panel are composed of the glyphs of the 20 named days recycling thirteen times. Sky serpents who send the rain and speak in thunder are shown weaving around the rows of glyphs. In the shorter top two leaves, standard numerology can be seen. The Mayans wrote numbers in two ways: as a system of dots and bars, seen here,

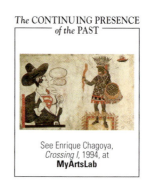

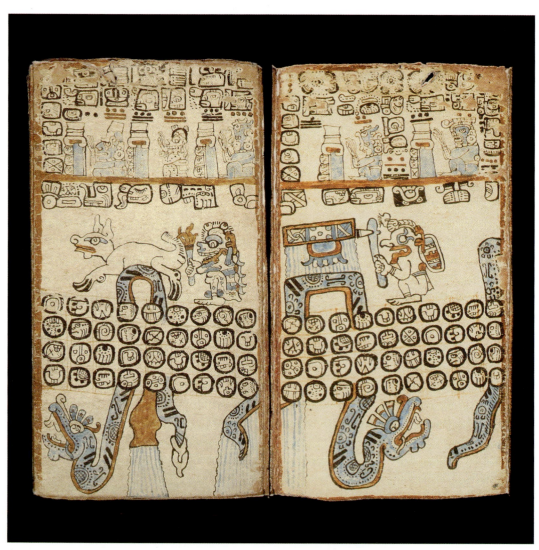

Fig. 9.9 Madrid Codex, leaves 13–16. ca. 1400. Amatl paper, 56 leaves, painted on both sides and screenprinted. Museo de América, Madrid. Diviners would have used this text to predict events such as flood, drought, or an abundant harvest.

and in a set of pictorial variants. Twenty was expressed with a glyph of the moon, and zero with a shell glyph. Zero, incidentally, was used widely in Mesoamerica many centuries before Hindu mathematicians "discovered" it in India.

Among the most important Mayan cities is Palenque, one of the best-preserved of all Mayan sites. Lost in the jungle for centuries following its decline, which occurred around the year 850, Palenque was rediscovered in 1746 by a Spanish priest who had heard rumors of its existence. The Temple of Inscriptions, facing into the main courtyard of the so-called Palace, which may have been an administrative center rather than a royal residence, rises in nine steps, representing the nine levels of the Mayan Underworld (Fig. **9.10**). It is inscribed with the history of the Palenque kings, who were associated with the jaguar. The first recorded king is K'uk B'alam, "Quetzal Jaguar," who, so the inscriptions say, founded the city on March 11, 431. Palenque's most powerful king was K'inich Janaab' Pakal I (Great Sun Shield), known as Pakal (603–83), who ruled for 67 years, and the Temple of Inscriptions was erected over his grave.

In 1952, Alberto Ruz, a Mexican archeologist, discovered the entrance to the tomb of Lord Pakal under the pyramid. It was hidden under large stone slabs in the floor of the temple at the top of the pyramid. Ruz had to clear the passage down to Pakal's tomb, at the very base of the structure, which had been back-filled with stone debris. When he reached the tomb, he found that Pakal's face was covered with a jade death mask. A small tube connected the tomb with the upper level, thus providing the dead king with an eternal source of fresh air. It also functioned as a form of communication between the living and the ancestor. Pakal was buried in a large uterus-shaped stone sarcophagus weighing over five tons and covered with jade and cinnabar.

By 900 CE, the Mayan culture from which the Aztec eventually emerged had collapsed as a result of a wide variety of events, including overpopulation and accompanying ecological degradation, political competition, and war. Its peoples, who survive in large numbers to this day, returned to simple farming around the ruins of their once-great cities. But, after contact, it seemed paramount to the Spanish crown to begin to raise the native population from its "barbarous" condition by bringing Christianity to it. The Spanish essentially obliterated the traditions of the Native American cultures they encountered, burning all their books, destroying

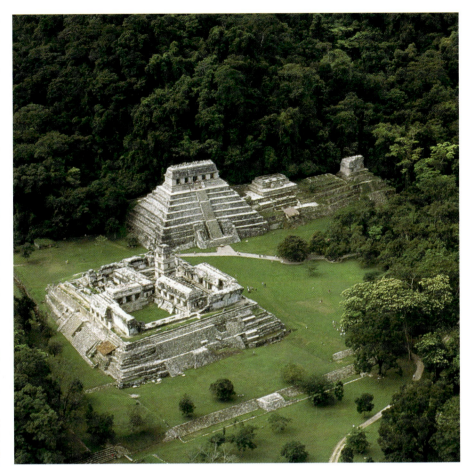

Fig. 9.10 "Palace" (foreground) and Temple of Inscriptions (tomb pyramid of Lord Pakal), Palenque, Mexico. Maya culture. 600–900 CE. These two buildings, along with two other temples not seen in this view, formed the central complex of Palenque. Another complex to the north is composed of five temples and a ball court, and a third group of temples lies to the south. Palenque was the center of a territory that may have been populated by as many as 100,000 people.

View the Closer Look for Palenque, Palace and Temple on **MyArtsLab**

almost every record of their history that they could lay their hands on, and crippling for all time our ability ever to piece together an adequate picture of their culture. Churches were quickly built in Mexico City. And as the Church sought to convert native populations to the Catholic faith, the musical liturgy became a powerful tool. As early as 1523, Spanish monks created a school for Native Americans in Texcoco, Mexico (just east of Mexico City), and began teaching music, including Gregorian chant, the principles of polyphony, and composition, on an imported organ. Throughout the sixteenth century, missionaries used music, dance, and religious dramas to attract and convert the indigenous population to Christianity. A syncretic culture quickly developed, in which European styles were nativized, and native culture was Christianized.

The Spanish in Peru

An interesting example of the Spanish Christianization of native culture is one of the most elaborately decorated of all Inca sites, the Coricancha (literally, "the corral of gold"), the

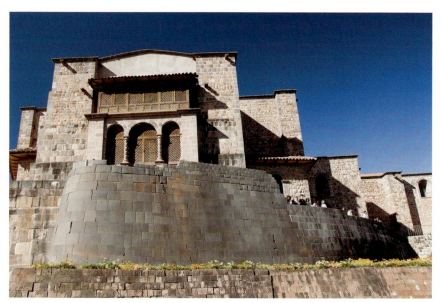

Fig. 9.11 Original Inca stone wall of the Coricancha with a Dominican monastery rising above it, Cuzco, Peru. Inca culture. The extraordinary skill of Inca masons is evident in this surviving granite wall, which was made with stone tools and without mortar, and that has, for centuries, withstood earthquakes that have destroyed many later structures.

treasure were sent home from the New World. When the first Royal Fifth (that is, one-fifth of the treasures collected by Cortés and earmarked by contract for the king) arrived in Brussels, the German artist Albrecht Dürer was present:

I saw the things which were brought to the King from the New Golden Land: a sun entirely of gold, a whole fathom [6 feet] broad; likewise, a moon, entirely of silver, just as big; likewise, sundry curiosities from their weapons, armor, and missiles; very odd clothing, bedding, and all sorts of strange articles for human use, all of which is fairer to see than marvels. These things were all so precious that they were valued at a hundred thousand guilders. But I have never seen in all my days that which so rejoiced my heart, as these things. For I saw among them amazing artistic objects, and I marveled over the subtle ingenuity of the men in these distant lands. Indeed I cannot say enough about the things which were there before me.

Inca Temple of the Sun facing the main plaza of Cuzco, the traditional capital of the Inca empire (Fig. **9.11**). Dedicated to Inti, the sun god, the original temple was decorated with 700 sheets of gold studded with emeralds and turquoise and designed to reflect the sunlight admitted through its windows. Its courtyard was filled with golden statuary—"stalks of corn that were of gold—stalks, leaves, and ears," the Spanish chronicler Pedro de Cieza de León reported in the mid-sixteenth century. "Aside from this," he continued, there were "more than twenty sheep [llamas] of gold with their lambs and the shepherds who guarded them, all of this metal."

Spain conquered Peru in 1533 through the exploits of Francisco Pizarro (1474–1541) with an army of only 180 men. Pizarro's military strategy was aided by simple deceit. He captured the Inca emperor, Atahuallpa, who offered Pizarro a ransom of 13,420 pounds of gold and 26,000 pounds of silver. Pizarro accepted the ransom and then executed the unsuspecting emperor. He next proceeded to plunder Peru of the gold and silver artifacts that were part of its religious worship of the sun (gold) and moon (silver), including the massive decorations at the Temple of the Sun in Cuzco. In addition, Spanish priests quickly adopted the foundations of the temple to their own purposes, constructing a Dominican church and monastery on the original Inca foundations. The Inca traditionally gathered to worship at the circular wall of the Coricancha, and thus the apse of Santo Domingo was purposefully constructed above it to emphasize Christian control of the native site.

Still, whatever the missionary zeal of the Spanish, the acquisition of gold, silver, and other treasure was a major motivation for their colonial enterprise. Great masses of

Accounts like this helped to give rise to the belief in an entire city of gold, El Dorado, which continued to elude the grasp of the conquistadors under royal order who followed in Pizarro's footsteps in Peru, often with unhappy results. The treasures of gold and silver that were brought back would be melted down for currency, far more important than their artistic value to the warring Spanish monarchy. In fact, almost no gold or silver objects survive from the conquest.

WEST AFRICAN CULTURE AND THE PORTUGUESE

What impact did the Portuguese have on West African life, and how did ritual serve to preserve traditional culture?

Portugal was as active as Spain in seeking trading opportunities through navigation, but focused on Africa and the East instead of the Americas. In 1488, Bartholomeu Dias (ca. 1450–1500), investigating the coast of West Africa (Map **9.2**), was blown far south by a sudden storm, and turning northeast, found that he had rounded what would later be called the Cape of Good Hope and entered the Indian Ocean. Following Dias, Vasco da Gama (ca. 1460–1524) sailed around the cape with four ships in 1497 and reached Calicut, India, 10 months and 14 days after leaving Lisbon. Then, in 1500, Pedro Cabral (ca. 1467–ca. 1520), seeking to repeat da Gama's voyage to India, set out from the bulge of Africa. Sailing too far westward, he landed in what is now Brazil, where he claimed the territory for Portugal.

👁 **Watch** an architectural simulation of Inca masonry on **MyArtsLab**

The Indigenous Cultures of West Africa

When the Portuguese arrived, somewhat to their surprise they discovered that thriving cultures had long since established themselves. Several large kingdoms dominated the western African region known as the Sahel, the grasslands that serve as a transition between the Sahara desert and the more temperate zones to the west and south. Among the most important is the kingdom of Mali, discussed in Chapter 4, which shows the great influence Islam had come to have on much of North Africa long before the end of the first millennium CE. Farther south, along the western coast of central Africa, were the powerful Yoruba state of Ife and the kingdom of Benin.

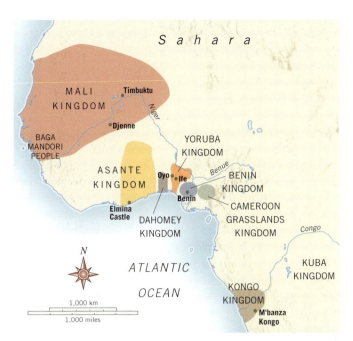

Map 9.2 Sub-Saharan West Africa, 1200–1700. While Muslim traders had extensive knowledge of North Africa, little was known of sub-Saharan Africa before the Portuguese explorations of the fifteenth and sixteenth centuries.

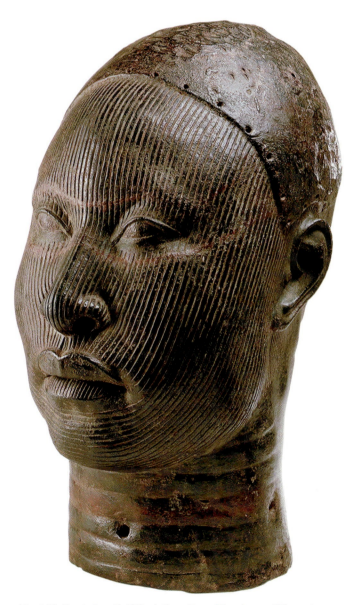

Fig. 9.12 Head of an *Oni* (King). Ife culture, Nigeria. ca. 13th century. Brass, height 11⁷⁄₁₆". Museum of Ife Antiquities, Ife, Nigeria. The metal used to cast this head is an alloy of copper and zinc, and therefore not technically bronze, but brass.

Ife Culture The Ife culture is one of the oldest in West Africa. It developed beginning around the eighth century along the Niger River, in what is now Nigeria. It was centered in the city of Ife. By 1100, it was producing highly naturalistic, sculptural commemorative portraits in clay and stone, probably depicting its rulers, and not long after, elegant brass sculptures as well.

An example of Ife brasswork is the *Head of an Oni* (or *King*) (Fig. **9.12**). The parallel lines that run down the face represent decorative effects made by scarring—**scarification**. A hole in the lower neck suggests that the head may have been attached to a wooden mannequin, and in memorial services, the mannequin may have worn the royal robes of the Ife court. Small holes along the scalp line suggest that hair, or perhaps a veil of some sort, also adorned the head. But the head itself was, for the Ife, of supreme importance. It was the home of the spirit, the symbol of the king's capacity to organize the world and to prosper. Ife culture depended on its kings' heads for its own welfare. Since the Ife did not leave a written record of their cultural beliefs, we can best understand their ancient culture by looking at their contemporary descendants.

The Yoruba people, whose population today is about 11 million, trace their ancestry directly to Ife culture. The Yoruba cosmos consists of the world of the living (*aye*) and the realm of the gods (*orun*). The gods are themselves called *orisha* and among them are the primordial deities, who created the world, as well as forces of nature, such as thunder and lightning, and ancestral heroes who have risen to immortality. Linking these two worlds is the king, who serves as

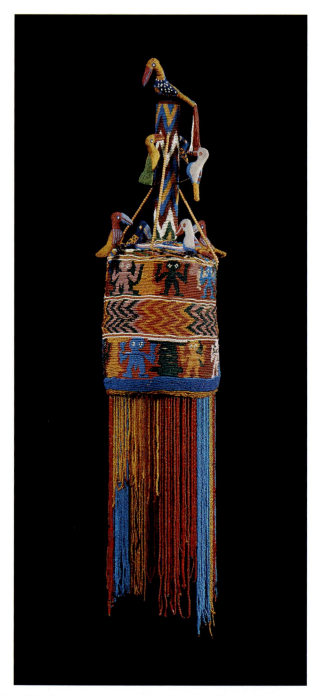

Fig. 9.13 *Ade*, or beaded crown, Yoruba culture, Nigeria. Late 20th century. Beadwork, height 6'1¼". © The Trustees of the British Museum. Today, approximately 50 Yoruba rulers wear beaded crowns and claim descent from King Oduduwa.

the representative in this world of those existing in *orun*. The king's head is thus sacred, and his crown, or *ade* (Fig. **9.13**), rising high above his head, symbolizes his majesty and authority. Rows of beads fall over his face to shield viewers from the power of his gaze. Imagery on the crown varies, but often refers to Ife myths of origin, similar to myths of origin found throughout the world (see Chapter 1). The first Yoruba king, Oduduwa, from whom all subsequent kings descend, is frequently represented. According to legend, Oduduwa was ordered to create a land mass out of the watery reaches of

earth so that it might be populated by people. Oduduwa lowered himself down onto the waters, the legend continues, and emptied earth from a small snail shell onto the water. He then placed a chicken on the sand to spread it and make land. Finally he planted some palm kernels. It was at Ife that he did this, and Ife remains the most sacred of Yoruba sites.

Benin Culture Sometime around 1170, the city-state of Benin, some 150 miles southeast of Ife, also in the Niger basin, asked the *oni* of Ife to provide a new ruler for their territory, which was, legend has it, plagued by misrule and disorder. The *oni* sent Prince Oranmiyan, who founded a new dynasty. Oranmiyan was apparently so vexed by the conditions he found that he named his new state *ibini*, "land of vexation," from which the name Benin derives. After some years, Oranmiyan returned home, but not until after he had impregnated the Benin princess. Their son Eweka would become the first king, or *oba*, as the Benin culture called their ruler, ruling from 1180 to 1246.

Already in place at the capital, Benin City, were the beginnings of a massive system of walls and moats that would become, by the fifteenth century, the world's largest man-made earthwork. According to archeologist Patrick Darling, who has studied the wall and moat system for several decades, they total some 10,000 miles in length, or some four to five times the length of the main Great Wall of China. These earthworks consist of moats, the dirt from which was piled alongside them to make walls up to 60 feet high. They were probably first dug more than a thousand years ago to protect settlements and their farmlands from the nocturnal raids of the forest elephant. But as Benin grew, linear earth boundaries demarcated clan or family territories and symbolically signified the boundary between the real, physical world and the spirit world. When the British arrived in the late nineteenth century, the walls were still largely intact (Fig. **9.14**), but they were soon destroyed by British forces, and what remains of them has been increasingly consumed by modern urbanization.

Like the Ife to the north, the Benin rulers also created lifelike images of their ancestor rulers. In the first half of the twentieth century, recognizing that many of the oral traditions of Benin culture were in danger of being lost, the Benin court historian, Chief Jacob Eghaverba (1893–1981), recorded as many traditional tales and historical narratives as he could find and published them in his *Short History of Benin*. This is his account of the origins of the casting of brass *oba* heads in Benin culture (**Reading 9.2**):

READING 9.2

from Jacob Eghaverba, *A Short History of Benin*

Oba Oguola [r. 1274–87] wished to introduce brass casting into Benin so as to produce works of art similar to those sent him from Ife. He therefore sent to the Oni of Ife for a brass-smith and Iguegha was sent to him. Iguegha was very clever and left many designs to his successors, and

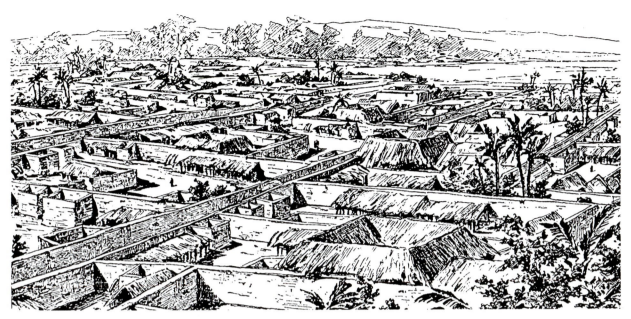

Fig. 9.14 Drawing of Benin City as it appeared to an unknown British officer in 1891. This drawing represents a small portion of the more than 2,500 square miles of walls and moats that made up Benin City in the nineteenth century.

was in consequence deified, and is worshiped to this day by brass-smiths. The practice of making brass-castings for the preservation of the records of events was originated during the reign of Oguola.

The artists, members of the royal casters' guild, lived in their own quarters just outside the palace in Benin, where they are located to this day. Only the *oba* could order brass-work from them. These commissions were usually memorial heads, commemorating the king's royal ancestors in royal costume (Fig. **9.15**). (The head shown in Fig. **9.15** was made in the mid-sixteenth century, but heads like it were made in the earliest years of bronze production in the culture.) As in Ife culture, the *oba*'s head was the home of the spirit and the symbol of the *oba*'s capacity to organize the world and to prosper.

This power could be described and commemorated in an oral form known as a **praise poem**. Praise poems are a major part of West African culture. By praising something—a king, a god, a river—the poet was believed to gain influence over it. Almost everyone in West African culture has praise poems associated with them. These poems often use a poetic device known as **anaphora**, a repetition of words and phrases at the beginning of successive sentences that, owing to the particularities of the West African languages, is almost impossible to duplicate in translation. But the poems are intended to create a powerful and insistent rhythm that forms a crescendo.

West African Music The rhythm-driven crescendo of the Benin praise poem shares much with African music as a whole. In fact, the poem may have been accompanied by music. African music is part of the fabric of everyday life,

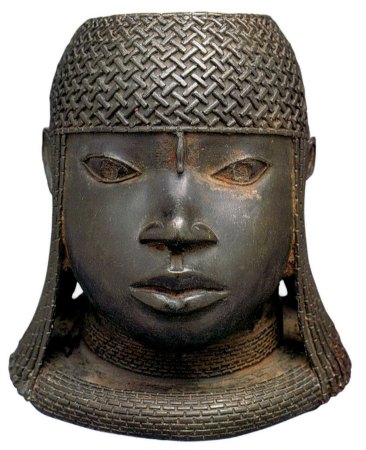

Fig. 9.15 Head of an *Oba*. Nigeria; Edo, Court of Benin. ca. 1550. Brass, 9¼" × 9⅝" × 9". The Metropolitan Museum of Art, New York. Such heads were usually commissioned upon the death of an *oba* by his successor, so that the deceased leader might continue to influence his community.

accompanying work, poetry, ceremony, and dance, and often evoked by visual art. The Western idea that music can be isolated from everyday experience is almost incomprehensible to the African sensibility. Typically consisting of a single line of melody without harmony, African music is generally communal in nature, encouraging a sense of social cohesion by promoting group activity. As a result, one of the most universal musical forms throughout Africa is **call-and-response** music, in which a caller, or soloist, raises the song, and the community chorus responds to it.

Call-and-response music is by no means simple. The Yoruba language, for instance, is tone-based; any Yoruba syllable has three possible tones, and this tone determines its meaning. The Yoruba reproduce their speech in the method of musical signaling known as **talking drums** (track **9.1**), performed with three types of batá drum, which imitate the three tones of the language. In ritual drumming, the drums are played for the Yoruba gods and are essentially praise poems to those gods. Characteristic of this music is its polyrhythmic structure. As many as five to ten different "voices" of interpenetrating rhythms and tones, often repeated over and over again in a call-and-response form, play off against one another. This method of playing against or "off" the main beat is typical of West African music and exists to this day in the "off-beat" practices of Western jazz.

Listen at MyArtsLab

Portugal and the Slave Trade

After Bartholomeu Dias's exploration of the west coast of Africa, it did not take long for European and African traders to extend existing practices of human exploitation that were common on both continents. This trade in human labor would eventually take on a scope and dimension not previously seen. The Portuguese exploitation of African labor was financed principally by a Florentine banker together with a group of other financiers from Genoa. Over the course of four centuries, the Portuguese transported millions of Africans across the Atlantic on the **Middle Passage**, so named because it formed the base of a triangular trade system: Europe to Africa, Africa to the Americas (the Middle Passage), and the Americas to Europe. No one can say with certainty just how many slaves made the crossing, although estimates range between 15 and 20 million (Map **9.3**). Part of the problem is the unknown numbers who died of disease and harsh conditions during the voyage. For instance, in 1717, a ship reached Buenos Aires with only 98 survivors of an original 594 slaves. Such figures were probably not unusual.

For a while, at least, the Portuguese enjoyed a certain status in Benin as divine visitors from the watery world, the realm of Olokun, god of the sea. They were considered to be the equivalent of the mudfish, because they could both "swim" (in their boats) and walk on land. The mudfish was sacred to the people of Benin, who saw it as a symbol of both transformation and power. (It lies dormant all summer on dry mudflats until fall when the rains come and it is "reborn.") (The fish is a symbol of power because it can deliver strong electric shocks and possesses fatal spines.) Likewise, the Portuguese seemed to be born of the sea and possessed fatal "spines" of their own—rifles and musketry.

An example of this association of the mudfish with the Portuguese is a decorative design that forms the tiara of an ivory mask worn as a hip pendant by the *oba* Esigie (r. 1504–50) (Figs. **9.16** and **9.17**). (An *oba* is the supreme traditional head of a Yoruba town.) The pendant probably depicts the queen mother (that is, the *oba*'s mother), or *iyoba*. Esigie's mother was named Idia, and she was the first

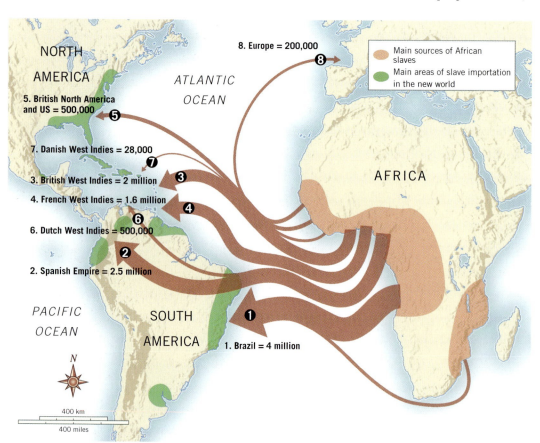

8. Europe = 200,000

Main sources of African slaves

Main areas of slave importation in the new world

NORTH AMERICA

ATLANTIC OCEAN

5. British North America and US = 500,000

7. Danish West Indies = 28,000

3. British West Indies = 2 million

4. French West Indies = 1.6 million

6. Dutch West Indies = 500,000

2. Spanish Empire = 2.5 million

PACIFIC OCEAN

SOUTH AMERICA

1. Brazil = 4 million

AFRICA

N

400 km
400 miles

Map 9.3 Transatlantic Slave Trade, 1450–1870. These numbers are approximate, and subject to much scholarly debate.

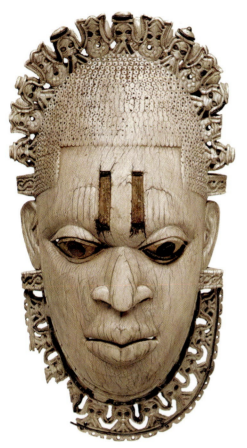

Fig. 9.16 Mask of an *iyoba* (queen mother), probably Idia, Court of Benin, Nigeria. ca. 1550. Ivory, iron, and copper, height 9⅜". The Metropolitan Museum of Art, New York. The Michael C. Rockefeller Memorial Collection, Gift of Nelson A. Rockefeller, 1972. (1978.412.323). The scarification lines on the forehead were originally inlaid with iron, and so were its pupils, both forehead and pupils being symbols of strength.

View the Closer Look for the Hip Pendant representing an Iyoba on MyArtsLab

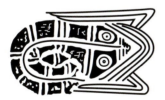

Fig. 9.17 Symbol of a coiled mudfish. Found throughout the art of Benin and in the tiara worn by the *iyoba* in Fig. 9.16.

woman to hold officially the position of *iyoba*. Apparently, when the neighboring Igala people of lower Niger threatened to conquer the Benin, Idia raised an army and by using magical powers helped Esigie to defeat the Igala army. Part of her magic may have been the enlistment of Portuguese help. In acknowledgment of the Portuguese aid, the *iyoba*'s collar bears decorative images of bearded Portuguese sailors and alternating sailors and mudfish at the top of her tiara.

The impact of the Portuguese merchants, and of the Catholic missionaries who followed them, was not transforming,

although it was undeniable and at times devastating. The Benin culture has remained more or less intact since the time of encounter. Today, for instance, during rituals and ceremonies, the *oba* wears at his waist five or six replicas of masks such as the *iyoba*'s, as well as the traditional coral-bead headdress. Oral traditions, like the praise poem, remain in place, despite attempts by Western priests to suppress them. If anything, it has been the last 50 years that have most dramatically transformed the cultures of Africa. But it was the institution of slavery, long practiced in Africa and the Middle East and by the Yoruba of Ife (their founding city) and the Benin peoples, that had the most dramatic impact on Portuguese and Western culture.

At first Benin had traded gold, ivory, rubber, and other forest products for beads and, particularly, brass. The standard medium of exchange was a horseshoe-shaped copper or brass object called a *manilla*, five of which appear in an early sixteenth-century Benin plaque portraying a Portuguese warrior (Fig. 9.18). Such metal plaques decorated the palace and royal altar area particularly, and here the soldier brings with him the very material out of which the plaque is made. If his weapons—trident and sword—suggest his power, it is a power in the service of the Benin king, at least from the Benin point of view.

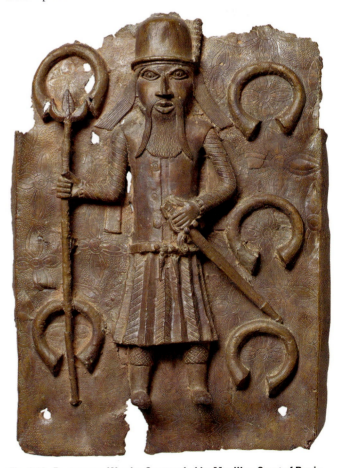

Fig. 9.18 *Portuguese Warrior Surrounded by Manillas,* Court of Benin, Nigeria. 16th century. Bronze, 18" × 13" × 3". Weltmuseum, Vienna. Notice the background of the bronze, which is incised with images of jungle flowers.

The Portuguese also picked up thousands of small objects—amulets, trinkets, and so on—that they termed *fetisso*, a sixteenth-century Afro-Portuguese pidgin word from which derives our word **fetish**, signifying an object believed to have magical powers similar to those of Western objects such as rosaries or reliquaries. But eventually the trade turned to slaves. Africans had long been selling slaves, the victims of war with neighboring territories, to Muslim traders. But the Portuguese dramatically expanded the practice. At the start of the era, around 1492, there were an estimated 140,00 to 170,000 African slaves in Europe, but in about 1551, the Portuguese began shipping thousands more slaves to Brazil to work in the sugar plantations. War captives proved an insufficient source of bodies, and the Portuguese took whomever they could get their hands on. Furthermore, they treated these slaves much more harshly than the Muslims had. They chained them, branded them, and often literally worked them to death. In short, the Portuguese inaugurated a practice of *cultural hegemony* (cultural domination) that set the stage for the racist exploitation that has haunted the Western world ever since.

Strategies of Survival Almost all African cultures emphasized the well-being of the group over the individual, a conviction invoked, guaranteed, and celebrated by the masked dance. In the face of European challenges to the integrity of African cultures, dance became an especially important vehicle in maintaining cultural continuity. The masked dance is, in fact, a ritual activity so universally practiced from one culture to the next across West Africa that it could be called the focal point of the region's cultures. It unites the creative efforts of sculptors, dancers, musicians, and others. Originally performed as part of larger rituals connected with stages in human development, the passing of the seasons, or stages of the agricultural year, the masked dance in recent years has become increasingly commercial—a form of entertainment disconnected from its original social context. A modern photograph of the *banda* mask performed by the Baga Mandori people who live on the Atlantic coastline of Guinea is unique, however, in capturing an actual *banda* dance (Fig. **9.19**). The *banda* mask is always danced at night, with only torches for illumination, but in 1987 villagers agreed, for the sake of photography, to begin the performance at dusk. The photographs taken that evening by Fred Lamp, Curator of African Art at the Yale University Art Gallery, are the only extant photographs of an actual *banda* performance.

The *banda* mask is a sort of amalgam of different creatures, combining the jaws of a crocodile, the face of a human, the elaborate hairstyle of a woman, the body of a serpent, the horns of an antelope, the alert ears of a deer,

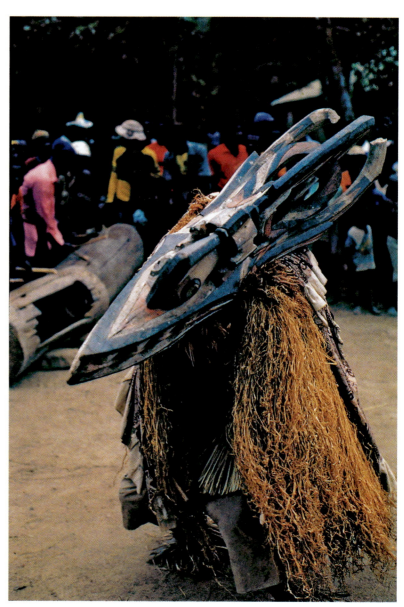

Fig. 9.19 Dance of Banda, Baga Mandori, Guinea, 1987. The choreography of the dance involves the dancer spinning madly while holding the headdress aloft, then twirling the mask in a series of figure eights, finally dashing it down to the ground before returning it to his head, all in one seamless burst of movement.

and, rising between the horns, the tail of a chameleon. The *banda* mask is generally danced at initiations, harvest ceremonies, and funerals, and is renowned for its spectacular acrobatics, with the wearer spinning high in the air and low to the ground as if in defiance of the enormous weight of the mask itself. Like the cave paintings discussed in Chapter 1, the *banda* mask is believed to possess *agency*. That is, it helps to effect change—the transformation (as symbolized by the chameleon's tail) from adolescence to adulthood, from fall to winter, from life to death. And it embodies the collective consciousness of the group by incorporating into its single visage the diversity of the natural world.

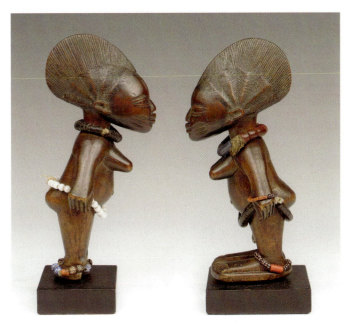

Fig. 9.20 Twin Figures (*ere ibeji*), Yoruba culture, Nigeria. 20th century. Wood, height 7⅞". The University of Iowa Museum of Art, Stanley Collection. This pair of *ere ibeji* appear to have been carved at the same time, by the same artist in the Yoruba city of Abeokuta. A strong case has been made that they are the work of Akiode, who died in 1936.

Interestingly, African cultures do not have a word for "mask." Rather, each mask has a particular name that is generally the word for the ancestor or supernatural being that the mask helps to make manifest. The ritual use of objects connected to the spirit world is a practice that, from the moment of European contact on, has continued to exhibit a strong presence despite the ongoing influence of Western and Islamic cultures. It is almost certain that many, if not most, of these ritual beliefs, practices, and customs date back centuries and help to establish a very real sense of cultural continuity.

The ritualistic use of objects connected with birth, death, and ancestral connections to the spirit world figure prominently in maintaining this sense of continuity. A fascinating example in Yoruba culture is the carving of *ere ibeji*, or "twin figures" (Fig. **9.20**), when a twin dies. Since the Yoruba have one of the highest rates of twin births in the world (45 for every 1,000 births), and since twins are generally smaller and weaker than single-born infants, twin deaths are comparatively common. While the *ere ibeji* are being carved, the mother of the deceased child lavishes gifts of food on the carver, and when the sculpture is finished, she carries it home on her back, wrapped as if it were living, while the women of the village sing songs to accompany her. The mother then performs various tasks to honor the figure, washing it as if it were alive, rubbing its body with powder and oil, offering it what are believed to be the favorite foods of twins—beans and palm oil—and dressing it in rich

garments and beads. Honored in this way, the spirit of the deceased twin will, it is believed, bring to its parents wealth and good fortune.

INDIA AND EUROPE: CROSS-CULTURAL CONNECTIONS

How did European contact affect Mogul India?

The synthesis of cultures so evident in the pluralistic society that developed in New Spain is also apparent in the art of India during roughly the same period. But in India, the synthesis was far less fraught with tension. The reason has much to do with the tolerance shown by India's leaders in the seventeenth and eighteenth centuries toward forces from the outside, which, in fact, they welcomed.

Islamic India: The Taste for Western Art

India's leaders in the seventeenth and eighteenth centuries were Muslim. Islamic groups had moved into India through the northern passes of the Hindu Kush by 1000 and had established a foothold for themselves in Delhi by 1200. In the early sixteenth century, a group of Turko-Mongol Sunni Muslims known as *Moguls* (a variation on the word *Mongol*) established a strong empire in northern India, with capitals at Agra and Delhi, although the Hindus temporarily expelled them from India between 1540 and 1555.

Their exile, in Tabriz, Persia, proved critical. Shah Tamasp Safavi (r. 1524–76), a great patron of the arts who especially supported miniature painting, received them into his court. The Moguls reconquered India with the aid of the shah in 1556. The new Mogul ruler, Akbar (r. 1556–1605), was just 14 years of age when he took the throne, but he had been raised in Tabriz and he valued its arts. He soon established a school of painting in India, open to both Hindu and Islamic artists, taught by Persian masters brought from Tabriz. He also urged his artists to study the Western paintings and prints that Portuguese traders began to bring into the country in the 1570s. By the end of Akbar's reign, a state studio of more than 1,000 artists had created a library of over 24,000 illuminated manuscripts.

Akbar ruled over a court of thousands of bureaucrats, courtiers, servants, wives, and concubines. Fully aware that the population was largely Hindu, Akbar practiced an official policy of religious tolerance. He believed that a synthesis of the world's faiths would surpass the teachings of any one of them. Thus he invited Christians, Jews, Hindus, Buddhists, and others to his court to debate with Muslim scholars. Despite taxing the peasantry heavily to support the luxurious lifestyle that he enjoyed, he also instituted a number of reforms, particularly banning the practice of immolating surviving wives on the funeral pyres of their husbands.

Under the rule of Akbar's son Jahangir (r. 1605–27), the English taste for portraiture (see Chapter 8) found favor in India. The painting *Jahangir in Darbar* is a good example (Fig. **9.21**). It shows Jahangir, whose name means "World Seizer," seated between the two pillars at the top of the painting, holding an audience, or *darbar*, at court. His son, the future emperor Shah Jahan, stands just behind him. The figures in the street are a medley of portraits, composed in all likelihood from albums of portraits kept by court artists. Among them is a Jesuit priest from Europe dressed in his black robes (although nothing in the painting shows a familiarity with Western scientific perspective). The stiff formality of the figures, depicted in profile facing left and right toward a central axis, makes a

sharp contrast to the variety of faces with different racial and ethnic features that fills the scene.

The force behind this growing interest in portraiture was the British East India Company, founded by a group of enterprising and influential London businessmen in 1599. King James I awarded the Company exclusive trading rights in the East Indies. A few years later, James sent a representative to Jahangir to arrange a commercial treaty that would give the East India Company exclusive rights to reside and build factories in India. In return, the company offered to provide the emperor with goods and rarities for his palace from the European market.

Jahangir's interest in all things English is visible in a miniature, *Jahangir Seated on an Allegorical Throne*, by an artist named Bichitr (Fig. **9.22**). The miniaturist depicts Jahangir on an hourglass throne, a reference to the brevity of life. The shah hands a book to a Sufi teacher, evidently preferring the mystic's company to that of the two kings who stand below, an Ottoman Turkish ruler who had been conquered by Jahangir's ancient ancestor Tamerlane and, interestingly,

Fig. 9.21 Attributed to Manohar, *Jahangir in Darbar*. Northern India. Mogul period. ca. 1620. Opaque watercolor and gold on paper, 13¾" × 7⅛". Museum of Fine Arts, Boston. Francis Bartlett Donation of 1912 and Picture Fund 14.654. Photograph © 2013 Museum of Fine Arts, Boston. Nothing underscores the Mogul lack of interest in Western perspective more than the way in which the figure in the middle of the street seems to stand on the head of the figure below him.

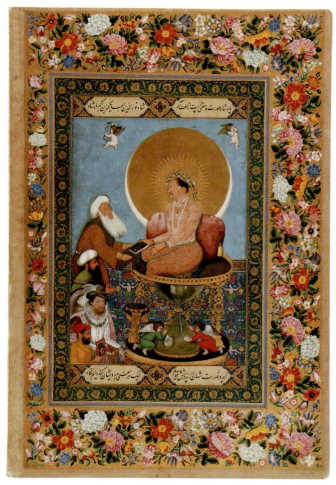

Fig. 9.22 Bichitr. *Jahangir Seated on an Allegorical Throne*, from the *Leningrad Album of Bichitr*. ca. 1625. Opaque watercolor, gold, and ink on paper, 10" × 7⅛". Freer Gallery of Art, Smithsonian Institution, Washington, D.C. (42.15V). Behind the shah is a giant halo or nimbus consisting of the sun and a crescent moon. It recalls those behind earlier images of Buddha.

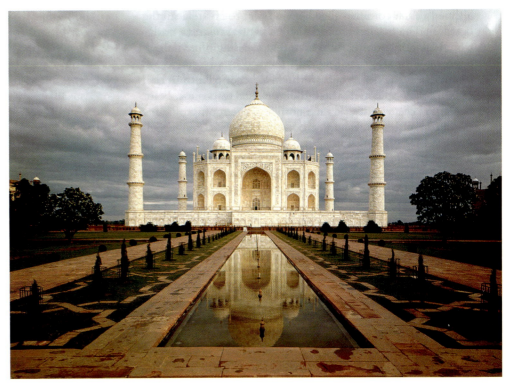

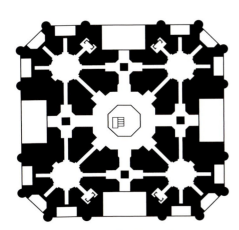

Fig. 9.23 Plan of the Taj Mahal, Agra. ca. 1632–48.

Fig. 9.24 Taj Mahal, Agra. Mogul period. ca. 1632–48. Originally, Shah Jahan planned to build his own tomb across the river, a matching structure in black marble, connected to the Taj Mahal by a bridge. The shah's tomb was never built, however, and he is buried, with his beloved wife, in a crypt in the mausoleum's central chamber.

 View the Closer Look for the Taj Mahal on **MyArtsLab**

King James I of England. The English monarch's pose is a three-quarter view, typical of Western portraiture but in clear contrast to the preferred profile pose of the Mogul court, which Jahangir assumes. The figure holding a picture at the bottom left-hand corner of the composition may be the artist, Bichitr, himself. Two Western-style *putti* (cherubs) fly across the top of the composition: The one at the left is a Cupid figure, about to shoot an arrow, suggesting the importance of worldly love; the one at the right apparently laments the impermanence of worldly power (as the inscription above reads). At the bottom of the hourglass, two Western-style angels inscribe the base of the throne with the prayer, "Oh Shah, may the span of your life be a thousand years." The throne itself is depicted in terms of scientific perspective, but the carpet it rests upon is not. Framing the entire image is a border of Western-style flowers, which stand in marked contrast to the Turkish design of the interior frame. All told, the image is a remarkable blend of stylistic and cultural traditions, bridging the gap between East and West in a single page.

Mogul Architecture: The Taj Mahal

Addicted to wine laced with opium, Shah Jahangir died in 1627, not long after the completion of the miniature wishing him a life of a thousand years. While his son Shah Jahan (r. 1628–58) did not encourage painting to the degree

his father and grandfather had, he was a great patron of architecture. His most important contribution to Indian architecture—and arguably one of the most beautiful buildings in the world—is the Taj Mahal ("Crown of the Palace"), constructed as a mausoleum for Jahan's favorite wife, Mumtaz-i-Mahal (the name means "Light of the Palace"), who died giving birth to the couple's fourteenth child (Figs. **9.23** and **9.24**).

Sited on the banks of the Jumna River at Agra in northern India, the Taj Mahal is surrounded by gardens meant to evoke a vision of paradise as imagined in the Qur'an. Measuring 1,000 by 1,900 feet, the garden is divided up by broad pathways, reflecting pools, and fountains that were originally lined by fruit trees and cypresses, symbols, respectively, of life and death. To the west of the building, in the corner of the property, is a red sandstone mosque, used for worship. Rising above the garden, and reflected in its pools, is the delicate yet monumental mausoleum of Taj Mahal itself.

The white marble tomb is set on a broad marble platform with minarets at each corner, their three main sections corresponding to the three levels of the mausoleum proper, thus uniting them with the main structure. At the top of these minarets are ***chattri***, or small pavilions that are traditional embellishments of Indian palaces, from which muezzins can call the faithful to worship at the property's mosque. The main structure, the Taj Mahal proper, is basically square,

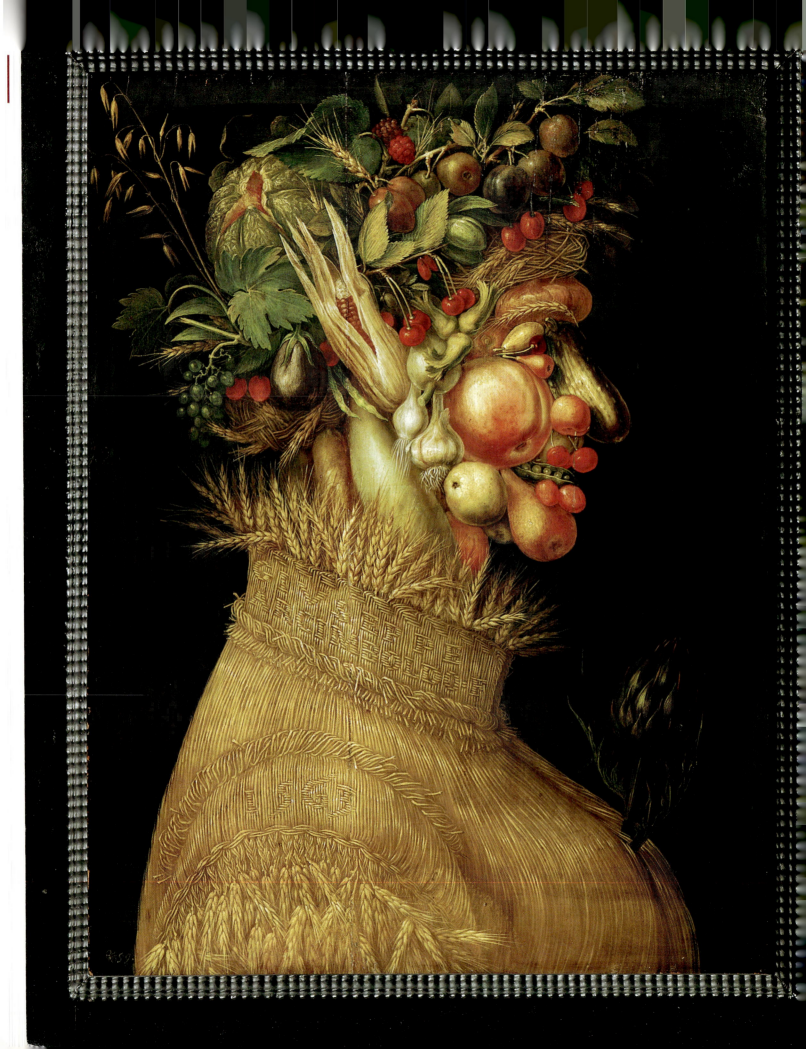

The Counter-Reformation and the Baroque

10

Emotion, Inquiry, and Absolute Power

LEARNING OBJECTIVES

10.1 Explain Mannerism and how it arose out of the Counter-Reformation.

10.2 Describe how the Baroque style manifested itself in the art, music, and literature of the era.

10.3 Discuss the vernacular Baroque style that developed in the North.

10.4 Define absolutism and discuss how it impacted the arts.

In 1562, a 36-year-old artist from Milan, Giuseppe Arcimboldo, left Italy for the Habsburg court in Vienna. The head of the Habsburg court was also the ruler of the Holy Roman Empire, first constituted by the pope in Charlemagne's time (see Chapter 5). He was also king of Spain, and thus in control of most of the Americas, with all the gold and silver the Western Hemisphere had to offer. For Arcimboldo, the prospects must have been enticing. Between 1549 and 1558, he had worked in Milan Cathedral designing stained-glass windows. In 1556 he began work on a fresco for the Cathedral of Monza, and in 1560 he delivered a cartoon for a tapestry for Como Cathedral. He had also made something of a reputation for himself in Milan as an illustrator of animals, birds, flowers, and plants. A drawing depicting a beetle, a caterpillar, a grasshopper, a chameleon, a lizard, and a salamander dates from 1553. But nothing of Arcimboldo's career before leaving for Vienna prepares us for the work he did there—a series of profile busts of the Four Seasons and the Four Elements composed out of vegetative matter arranged to create composite heads.

Summer (Fig. 10.1) is a virtual inventory of the produce readily available to the Habsburg court in the summer months—a currant for the figure's eye, a peach for its cheek, and a pear for its chin—but there are also less common varieties of crops, such as corn, which had been introduced to Europe from the New World in 1525, and eggplant, common

enough in Andalusian Spain but rarely seen in northern climes. Arcimboldo has woven his signature into the grains forming the collar of the coat and dated the composition on the shoulder.

We can only guess at Arcimboldo's motivation for composing such paintings. They were understood in the court of the Holy Roman Emperor Maximilian II (r. 1564–76) in Vienna as political allegories. The Italian humanist scholar Giovanni Battista Fonteo composed a poem of 308 stanzas in praise of them that was presented to Maximilian on New Year's Day 1569. Between them, the Four Seasons and the Four Elements represented the entire universe, the variety of things composing it existing in harmony, as a product of the peace and prosperity that the emperor's reign had bestowed on the world. We know as well that the emperor was devoted to his botanical gardens, filled with exotic trees whose fruits he served at palace dinners, and he maintained a menagerie full of rare animals, including an elephant, which court scientists studied. And it is this taste for the exotic that perhaps tells us most. The Habsburg court relished all things never-before-seen, inventions of wit never-before-heard, entertainments never-before-so-enjoyed. Arcimboldo's paintings satisfied all these tastes. They were, quite literally, fantastic—totally and completely original.

Arcimboldo's work represents a new direction in European art, an art of invention that developed as a kind of

◄ **Fig. 10.1 Giuseppe Arcimboldo, *Summer*. 1563.** Oil on limewood, 26⅜" × 20". Kunsthistorisches Museum, Vienna. The Emperor Maximilian was so enamored of these paintings that he and his court dressed up as the elements and seasons in a 1571 festival orchestrated by Arcimboldo, in which the emperor played Winter.

counter-statement to the decorum and restraint urged upon artists by the Catholic Church as it tried to respond to the Protestant Reformation. The Church recognized that its own excesses had fueled the Reformation, but the Holy Roman Emperor Charles V (r. 1519–58)—Maximilian II became emperor by virtue of marrying Charles's daughter Maria—continued to feud with Francis I of France, thus stymying the Church's efforts to respond politically. Still, despite their ongoing conflict—financed, on the Holy Roman Emperor's side, by gold and silver from the newly discovered Americas—both monarchs understood the necessity of addressing the threat posed by the Protestant Reformation. They convinced the pope to convene the so-called Council of Trent in 1545. Its charge was to outline a path of reform for the Church itself. The Council called for a return to "simplicity, zeal toward God, and a contempt of vanities" in the lifestyles of its bishops. It believed the Church's art and music should reflect these values as well. In Italy, the Church initiated an Inquisition as a method of enforcing the strictures of the Counter-Reformation. In Spain, an Inquisition had been in place since 1478 as a tool to expel or convert all non-Christian Spaniards, especially Spanish Muslims and Jews, but also Catholic nuns and priests who practiced a brand of mysticism closely related to Jewish mystical tracts.

Even as the early Counter-Reformation would seek to impose a sense of restraint in all aspects of life, a more secular approach to art represented by the likes of Arcimboldo arose, originating in the High Renaissance's love for artistic genius and originality. Increasingly, the courts supported the production of works of art devoid of religious themes and without the restraint and decorum called for by Church reform. A clear division arose between the public face of the courts, which were almost uniformly aligned with the Church, and the tastes for the exotic and the inventive that those courts felt free to indulge in private. And in other lesser cultural centers, namely the princely courts of northern Italy, artists were free to pursue the spirit of originality and invention that had defined the High Renaissance, especially in nonreligious imagery. Inspired by the late work of Michelangelo, the style of painting and sculpture that developed in the courts of the Gonzaga in Mantua and the d'Este in Ferrara was notable for its freedom to experiment, its virtuosity and eccentricity, and its often frank sensuality.

We have come to call this style Mannerist, from the Italian word maniera, "style." Mannerism, in general, can be thought of as a style of refined elegance, reflecting the virtuosity and sophistication of its practitioners, often by means of an exaggeration and distortion of proportion that tests the boundaries of the beautiful and ideal. It resulted in an art almost the opposite of that called for by the Council of Trent, and it spawned an equally free and inventive literature. Eventually some artists managed to reconcile the aims of the Counter-Reformation and the inventiveness of Mannerism, creating a style that would pave the way for the Baroque era to come.

The transition from Mannerism to a full-blown Baroque style is the subject of this chapter. Attention to the way viewers would emotionally experience a work of art is a defining characteristic of the Baroque, a term many believe takes its name from the Portuguese barroco, literally a large, irregularly shaped pearl. It was originally used in a derogatory way to imply a style so heavily ornate and strange that it verges on bad taste. We look at the Baroque first as it developed in Rome, and at the Vatican in particular, as a conscious style of art and architecture dedicated to furthering the aims of the Counter-Reformation; then in Venice, which in the seventeenth century was the center of musical activity in Europe. The Baroque also became the defining style of the royal courts of Europe, and by the start of the eighteenth century, almost every royal court in Europe modeled itself on King Louis XIV's court at Versailles. Louis so successfully asserted his authority over the French people, the aristocracy, and the Church that the era in which he ruled has become known as the Age of Absolutism.

Absolutism is a term applied to strong, centralized monarchies that exert royal power over their dominions, usually on the grounds of divine right. The principle had its roots in the Middle Ages, when the pope crowned Europe's kings, and went back even farther to the man/god kings of ancient Mesopotamia and Egypt. But by the seventeenth century, the divine right of kings was assumed to exist even without papal acknowledgment. The most famous description of the nature of absolutism is by Bishop Jacques-Bénigne Bossuet (1627–1704), Louis's court preacher and tutor to his son. While training the young dauphin for a future role as king, Bossuet wrote Politics Drawn from the Very Words of Holy Scripture, a book dedicated to describing the source and proper exercise of political power. In it, he says the following:

> God is infinite, God is all. The prince, as prince, is not regarded as a private person: he is a public personage, all the state is in him; the will of all the people is included in his. As all perfection and all strength are united in God, so all the power of individuals is united in the person of the prince. What grandeur that a single man should embody so much! . . . you see the image of God in the king, and you have the idea of royal majesty.

Absolutism also informs, of course, the politics leading up to the Council of Trent, for although the monarchs of Europe were often at war with one another, they were united in their belief in the power of the throne, their insistence on their actual, if not official authority over the pope, and the role of the arts in sustaining that authority. In France, Louis XIV never missed an opportunity to impress upon the French people (and the other courts of Europe) his grandeur and power. In England, the monarchy struggled to assert its divine right to rule as it fought for power against Puritan factions that denied absolutism. In Spain, the absolute rule of the monarchy was deeply troubled by the financial insolvency of the state, but Philip IV advertised his absolutist position by inviting some of the greatest artists in Europe to his court.

THE EARLY COUNTER-REFORMATION AND MANNERISM

What is Mannerism and how did it arise out of the Counter-Reformation?

In 1493, the year after Columbus arrived in America, Pope Alexander VI decreed that the New World was the property of the Church, and he chose to rent it in its entirety to Spain (he was himself Spanish). Alexander's papal bull made clear that no other country could occupy any of these territories without the pope's permission and, by extension, his direct financial benefit. Thus, the subsequent colonization of North America by France and England was, from the Church's point of view, an act of piracy.

As king of Spain, Charles V was the direct beneficiary of the pope's pronouncements. From his point of view, the Americas served but one purpose—to provide funds for his continuing war against Francis I of France. The two monarchs had been at war since 1521 but never with any clear outcome for any significant period of time. The papacy needed both of them as allies in its campaign against the Protestant Reformation. But it was Charles V whose troops, to his embarrassment, had sacked Rome in 1527 and imprisoned Pope Clement VII (Giulio de' Medici), as a direct response to Clement's alliance with Francis I and Henry VIII of England.

The enmity between Charles V and Francis I went back to the election of Charles as emperor of the Holy Roman Empire in 1521. When, after the death of Emperor Maximilian, Charles out of courtesy informed Francis that he intended to seek election as emperor, Francis had replied, "Sire, we are both courting the same lady." The pope backed Francis, but Charles secured a loan of 500,000 florins from a bank in Augsburg and literally bought the votes of the seven electors.

Charles's empire was immense. By heredity and marriage, it included the Netherlands, where he had been born (in Ghent), the Iberian peninsula, southern Italy, Milan, Austria and parts of present-day Germany, and the Franche-Comté (see brown areas in Map 10.1). To this was added the lands of the Holy Roman Empire (outlined in red in Map 10.1), including all of Germany, Switzerland, and more of Italy. Because of its vast size, Charles's territory was susceptible to attack from virtually all directions, as Suleiman the Magnificent, emperor of the Ottoman Empire, demonstrated when, at Francis's request, he defeated and killed Charles's brother-in-law Louis II of Hungary in 1526. Thus embattled, Charles claimed to want peace so that the Church and its Catholic kings could turn their united attention to the threat of Protestantism. Finally, in 1544, Charles entered France from the Netherlands. Francis was sufficiently frightened, or sufficiently tired of the endless conflict, that he sued for peace. Together the two kings then turned to Pope Paul III and

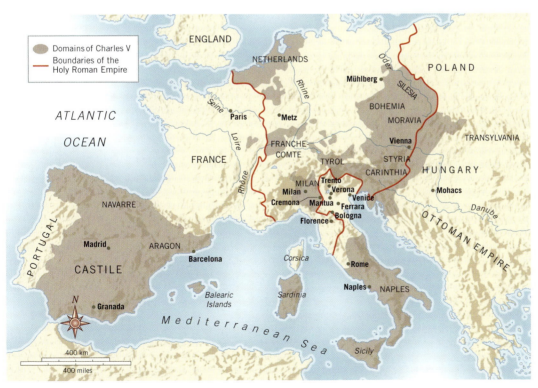

Map 10.1 The empire of Charles V. ca. 1521. The whole of the Holy Roman Empire in Charles V's time lies between the red lines, but Charles was in absolute control of the areas shaded in brown. In addition to the lands shown here, Charles also controlled almost all of the Americas.

pressured him to call a general council to be held at Trento, in northern Italy, beginning on December 3, 1545, to confront their common enemy, the Protestant challenge.

The Council of Trent and Catholic Reform of the Arts

The resolution of the conflict between Charles and Francis marks a moment when historical urgency profoundly affected the direction of humanistic enterprise. The resulting Council of Trent was charged with reforming the Church. It met in three sessions, and owing to war, plague, and the political strategies of the papacy itself, it spanned the careers of four different popes over 18 years: 1545–47, 1551–52, and 1562–63. The Council concentrated on restoring internal Church discipline. It called a halt to the selling of Church offices and religious goods, a common practice used by clergy to pad their coffers. It required bishops, many of whom lived in Rome, to return to their dioceses, where, they were told, they needed to preach regularly, exert discipline over local religious practice, and be active among their parishioners. They were warned not to live ostentatiously:

> It is to be desired that those who undertake the office of bishop shall understand... that they are called, not to their own convenience, not to riches or luxury, but to labors and cares, for the glory of God.... Wherefore ... this Council not only orders that bishops be content with modest furniture and a frugal table and diet, but that they also give heed that in the rest of their manner of living and in their whole house there be nothing seen which is alien to this holy institution, and which does not manifest simplicity, zeal toward God, and a contempt of vanities.

The bishops were to maintain strict celibacy, which they had not been required to do before. And they were to construct a seminary in every diocese.

The Council of Trent's injunction against luxury and its assertion of the principle of simple piety were directly translated to the arts. Contrary to many Protestant sects, the Council of Trent insisted on the use of religious imagery:

> The images of Christ, of the Virgin Mother of God, and of other saints are to be placed and retained especially in churches... [and] set before the eyes of the faithful so that they... may fashion their own life and conduct in imitation of the saints and be moved to adore and love God and cultivate piety.

Subsequent treatises on art, written by clergy, called explicitly for direct treatment of subjects, unencumbered by anything "sensuous," from brushwork to light effects.

The Council of Trent's order for a visual art that would directly affect the souls of the people influenced the direction in which church music developed as well. The function of music in the liturgy, the Council insisted, was to serve the text, and so the text should be clear and intelligible to the congregation:

> The whole plan of singing should be constituted not to give empty pleasure to the ear, but in such a way that the words be clearly understood by all, and thus the hearts of the listeners be drawn to the desire of heavenly harmonies.... They shall also banish from church all music that contains, whether in the singing or in the organ playing, things that are lascivious or impure.

For some, polyphony (two or more voices of equal importance) constituted "lascivious or impure" music, and they argued that only the single line of monophonic plainchant should be performed in the church. The Council rejected this idea.

Legend has it that the Council rejected the replacement of polyphonic music with plainchant because of a particular polyphonic mass, composed in 1567 by Giovanni Pierluigi da Palestrina (ca. 1525–94): *Missa Papae Marcelli*, or *Mass for Pope Marcellus*. The story is not true, but that it was widely believed for centuries testifies to the power of Palestrina's choral work. In his career, which included serving as choirmaster at the Capella Giulia in the Vatican for many years, Palestrina wrote 104 settings of the Mass, 375 motets, 80 hymns, and about 140 songs, both sacred and secular. He was the first composer of the sixteenth century to have his complete works published and was one of the most influential composers of his day.

The *Missa Papae Marcelli* is notable for the way it carries out the requirements of the Council of Trent. Its music is restrained so that the words, when sung by the choir, stand out in utter clarity, especially at the beginning of phrases. Although the voices in the Credo section enunciate each syllable of the text in chordal unison (usually thirds and sixths, or what we have come to recognize as consonant intervals), a constant interplay between **counterpoint**, in which voices imitate the main melody in succession, and **homophony**, in which the subordinate voices simply accompany the melody in unison, enlivens the music (track **10.1**). Likewise, Palestrina often plays one voice sustaining a single note per syllable against a voice engaged in **melisma**, or many notes per syllable. Above all, however, the intelligibility of the text is of paramount concern.

Listen at **MyArtsLab**

This quality is also audible in Palestrina's *Super Flumina Babylonis*, or *By the Rivers of Babylon*, one of his most famous motets (track **10.2**). The **motet**, you will remember, was the most important form of polyphonic vocal music in the Middle Ages and Renaissance. From the Renaissance onward, it normally had a Latin sacred text, and, like a mass, was sung during Catholic service. The text of *Super Flumina Babylonis* is from Psalm 137 of the Bible and expresses the lamentation of the Jewish people:

Listen at **MyArtsLab**

> By the rivers of Babylon, there we sat down and wept,
> When we remembered you, O Zion.
> On the willows, in the midst of everything, we hung up
>   our harps.

The rhythm of each word matches up directly to the musical cadence. The accented syllable of each word is also usually set to a higher note, thus blending text and music with absolute clarity. In Palestrina's own words, the intention is to draw out "the vital impulse given to its words, according to their meaning." In keeping with the thinking of the Council of Trent, Palestrina's music serves to enliven—even glorify—the words, words that the Council believed every member of the congregation must be moved to understand and believe.

The Rise of Mannerism

The demand for clarity and directness that marks the art and music of the Counter-Reformation did not constrain so original an artist as Michelangelo, who introduced a different, more inventive direction in sixteenth-century art. Raphael had already arrived at a new style in the last paintings he executed for the Vatican before his death in 1520. He replaced the clarity, restraint, and order of his *School of Athens* (see *Closer Look*, pages 234–235) with a more active, dynamic, even physically distorted realization of the human figure, probably in response to Michelangelo's own innovations in the same direction in the later frescoes for the Sistine Chapel ceiling—in the *Libyan Sibyl*, for instance (see Fig. 7.27 in Chapter 7). This new Mannerist style resulted in distorted, artificial poses, mysterious or obscure settings, and, very often, elongated proportions. It is marked by the rejection of the Classicizing tendencies of the High Renaissance and by the artist's display of virtuosity through manipulation and distortion of the conventional figure.

Michelangelo's *Pietà*, one of the artist's last works, is a fully realized example of the new Mannerist artistic vocabulary (Fig. 10.2). The traditional *contrapposto* pose that evolved from Classical Greek sculpture in order to give a static figure the illusion of potential movement is here exaggerated by the dynamic, spiral turn of Christ's body as he falls to the ground. The result is what would become known as a **serpentine figure**, with no single predominant view. The right arm twists away from the body even as Christ's right leg seems to fold forward to the right at a 90-degree angle.

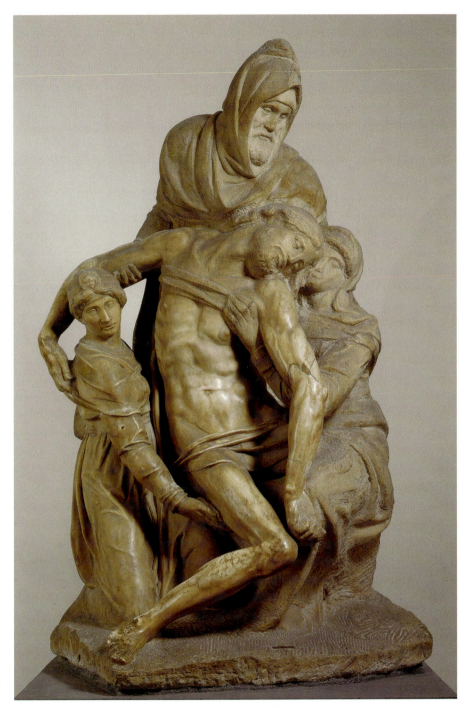

Fig. 10.2 Michelangelo, *Pietà*. 1547–53. Marble, height 89". Museo dell'Opera del Duomo, Florence. The female figure on the left was finished by Tiberio Calcagni, and the whole reconstructed by him, after Michelangelo smashed the sculpture upon discovering, after seven years of work, an imperfection in the marble that he had not previously detected.

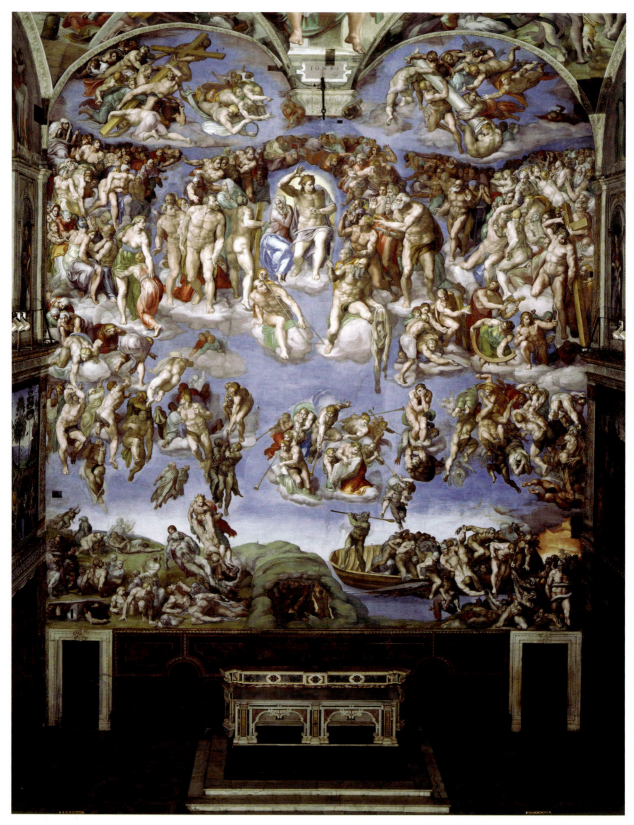

Fig. 10.3 Michelangelo, *Last Judgment*. 1534–41. Fresco, 48' × 44'. Sistine Chapel, Vatican, Rome. Foto Musei Vaticani. Well to Christ's right, past the nude figure of John the Baptist, is a personification of the Church embracing a woman kneeling before her. The personification is bare-breasted to symbolize her ability to nourish the faithful. Balancing her, at the far right of the painting, a man places a large cross on the Sistine Chapel cornice, a symbolic representation of Christ's sacrifice. The pair, male and female, mirror Christ and Mary in the center of the painting.

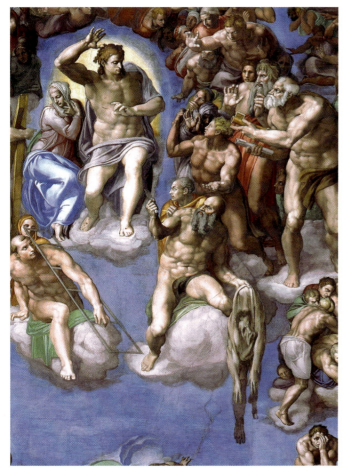

Fig. 10.4 Michelangelo, *Last Judgment*. 1534–41. Detail. Fresco, 48' × 44'. Sistine Chapel, Vatican, Rome. Foto Musei Vaticani. Nudity such as Michelangelo paints here was virtually unheard of in church decorative programs.

them across the River Styx. In the bottom center of the painting, directly behind the altar of the Sistine Chapel, is Hell's Mouth, and above it, angels trumpeting the arrival of the Last Judgment.

Michelangelo's *Last Judgment* almost immediately provoked controversy because of its presentation of religious figures nude. The poet Pietro Aretino sent him a letter in 1545 objecting to the fresco, a letter especially interesting when considered in the context of the Council of Trent, which was then in session (**Reading 10.1**):

READING 10.1

from Pietro Aretino, Letter to Michelangelo (1545)

The pagans when they made statues I do not say of Diana who is clothed, but of naked Venus, made them cover with their hand the parts which should not be seen. And here there comes a Christian who, because he rates art higher than faith, deems a royal spectacle martyrs and virgins in improper attitudes, men dragged down by their genitals, things in front of which brothels would shut their eyes in order not to see them. Your art would be at home in some voluptuous *bagnio* [bathhouse], certainly not in the highest chapel in the world.... Restore it to good repute by turning the indecent parts of the damned to flames, and those of the blessed to sunbeams, or imitate the modesty of Florence, who hides your David's shame beneath some gilded leaves. And yet that statue is exposed upon a public square, not in a consecrated chapel.

When Michelangelo did not respond to this letter, Aretino published it. The letter underscores the growing tension between the developing Mannerist style and the aims of the Counter-Reformation, especially in the context of the Council of Trent, which was then in session. In fact, as long as Paul III remained pope, the *Last Judgment* stayed as Michelangelo had painted it. But with the election of Paul IV in 1555, the first new pope after Paul III had convened the Council of Trent in 1545, the painting fell into ever-increasing disfavor. Shortly after Michelangelo's death in 1564, Daniele da Volterra and others painted draperies over the genital areas of the fresco's nude figures, a feat for which they ignominiously earned the name *braghettoni*, "breeches-painters." Even when the painting was cleaned and restored in 1994, the Vatican chose to leave the draperies in place.

As long as painting confined itself to depicting nonreligious subjects for nonreligious venues, it was more or less free to do as it pleased. Even the nudity of Michelangelo's Sistine Chapel figures would have been tolerable if painted in some less holy place. The Roman cardinal Cirillo Franco summed up the general attitude in a letter: "I hold the painting and sculpture of Michelangelo to be a miracle of nature; but I would praise it so much more if, when he wants to show the supremacy of his art in all that posturing of naked limbs, and all those nudes... he did not paint it on the vault of the

Michelangelo incorporated this serpentine pose somewhat less dramatically into his first commission in Rome after returning in 1534, a *Last Judgment* fresco for the altar wall of the Sistine Chapel (Fig. **10.3**). At the top center of the painting, Mary crouches beside Christ, turning her head away toward the left-hand side of the composition, apparently absorbed in her own thoughts (Fig. **10.4**). Christ himself turns his attention to the saints and martyrs on the right-hand side of the composition, such as white-bearded Saint Peter holding gold and silver keys to Heaven. Saint Bartholomew, who was martyred by being skinned alive, sits just below Christ's feet, holding in his right hand a knife, the instrument of his torture, and in his left hand his own flayed skin.

Many scholars believe that the face on the flayed skin is a self-portrait of Michelangelo, suggesting his sense of his own martyrdom under the unrelenting papal commissions of Pope Paul III. These figures, whose bodies were mutilated and maimed in their martyrdom, have been healed and restored as they rise to heaven. At the bottom of the painting, on the left, angels welcome souls ascending from the grave. At the right, demons drag the damned down into Hell as Charon, the mythological boatman of the Classical world, ferries

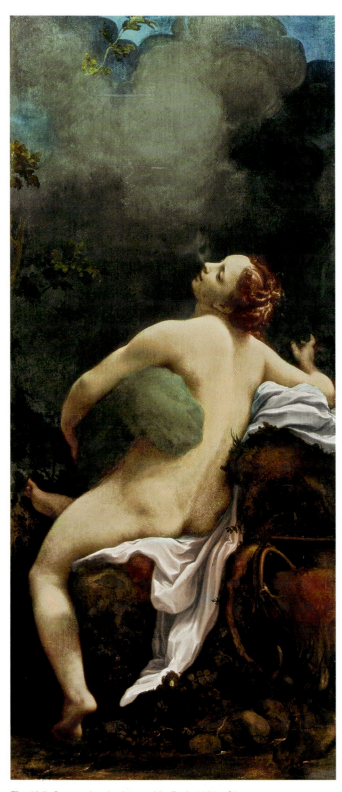

Fig. 10.5 Correggio, *Jupiter and Io*. Early 1530s. Oil on canvas, 69" × 29½". Kunsthistorisches Museum, Vienna. In the myth, Jupiter (Zeus) appears in a dream to Io, daughter of the king of Argos, and takes her to Lerna, a marsh and stream in the eastern Peloponnese, where he seduces her disguised as a cloud. The painting was created for the pleasure chamber of Federico Gonzaga in the Palazzo Ducale, Mantua.

Pope's Chapel, but in a gallery, or some garden loggia." It was a matter of decorum, or propriety. What might be decorous and appropriate in a gallery or garden loggia was absolutely not so in a church.

In the private galleries of the princely courts throughout Europe, this more indecorous but highly inventive imagery thrived. In the early 1530s, for instance, Federico Gonzaga of Mantua commissioned a set of erotic paintings that seem almost intentionally the indecorous embodiment of what the Council of Trent would label "the lascivious or impure." They were the work of the northern Italian artist Correggio (given name Antonio Allegri, ca. 1494–1534) and depicted the loves of Jupiter, or Zeus.

Jupiter and Io, painted in the early 1530s, is one of these (Fig. **10.5**). The painting illustrates Jupiter consummating his love for Io, a priestess of Hera (Jupiter's wife). Jupiter appears to Io in the guise of a cloud, his face barely visible behind her, kissing her lightly on the cheek. His bearlike arm embraces her as she abandons herself, quite visibly, to sensual pleasure. In addition to the unabashed sensuality of the presentation, the somewhat bizarre juxtaposition of Io's fully lit and well-defined body with Jupiter's dark and amorphous form is fully Mannerist in spirit.

This same theme occupied Titian in a series of paintings commissioned by Philip II of Spain in the late 1550s. Philip built a special room to house them in the Escorial, his palace complex near Madrid. In *The Rape of Europa*, Jupiter has assumed the form of a bull to abduct the nymph Europa as she adorns his horns with flowers (Fig. **10.6**). What most distinguishes the work is this Venetian artist's loose, sensual way of handling paint—a far cry from the crisp, even cold linearity of Correggio's Mannerist technique in the drapery beneath Io and in the porcelain-like quality of her skin. Titian's lush brushwork mirrors the sensuality of the image. And yet, in the way Europa falls across the bull's back in a serpentine posture emphasized by the spiraling form of the red robe that flies from her hand, the painting demonstrates just how strongly Mannerist expression had entered the vocabulary of sixteenth-century painting as a whole. Like the Mannerists, the later Titian draws attention to his own virtuosity and skill, to the presence of his so-called **hand**, or stylistic signature through brushwork, in the composition. (The root of *maniera*, not coincidentally, is *mano*, "hand.")

Even when Mannerists did find themselves working in a religious context, they tended to paint works designed to unsettle the viewer. When, for instance, Girolamo Francesco Maria Mazzola (1503–40), known as Parmigianino, was commissioned in 1535 to decorate a family chapel in the church of Santa Maria dei Servi in his native Parma (where, not coincidentally, Correggio spent most of his career), the resulting Madonna and Child must have startled more than one viewer. Known as *The Madonna with the Long Neck* (Fig. **10.7**), the painting seems, from the very first glance, oddly organized. How much space, for instance, is there between the Madonna and her attendants, compressed into the left three-quarters of the painting, and the figure of Saint Jerome

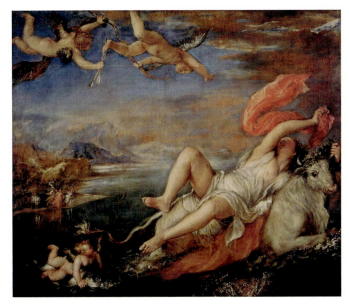

Fig. 10.6 Titian, *The Rape of Europa*. 1559–62. Oil on canvas, 5'9¼" × 7'8¼". Isabella Stewart Gardner Museum, Boston. On the distant shore, Europa's maidservants gesture in vain at her abduction.

reading a scroll in the distant, open space at the right? He appears to be standing just a short step below the Madonna's chair, but because Parmigianino has not accounted for the wide gap between the saint and the foreground group, the space in which he stands is visually almost totally incoherent. In fact, he must be standing far below her. We know that Saint Jerome's presence in the painting was a requirement of the commission—he was famous for his adoration of the Virgin, and Parmigianino had even painted a *Vision of Saint Jerome* in 1527, in which, oddly, the saint is sound asleep—but it is almost as if Parmigianino is scoffing at his patron's wishes, or at least acceding to them in an almost flippant way. The painting, it is worth noting, is over 7 feet high, and thus the miniature Saint Jerome contrasts even more dramatically with the greater-than-life-size Virgin who rises above him almost as if she is analogous in size to the column beside which he stands. Indeed, the Virgin's swanlike neck is a traditional conceit, found in medieval hymns, comparing her neck to an ivory tower or column, a sort of vernacular expression of the Virgin as the allegorical representation of the Church.

But it is not only the spatial ambiguity of the painting that lends it such a sense of the unorthodox. The uncannily long-legged figure at the left inexplicably holds a long, oval amphora, as if he is offering it to the Virgin. It serves no real allegorical purpose. Rather, it defines the compositional principle upon which Parmigianino has organized his painting. Like the amphora, the Virgin's head is oval, and her entire body sweeps across the canvas forming the same oval shape. This oval is transected by the disproportionately long body of the Christ Child, who lies across the Virgin's lap. The Virgin seems to withdraw from the child as if recognizing what will befall him. In one of the painting's oddest effects,

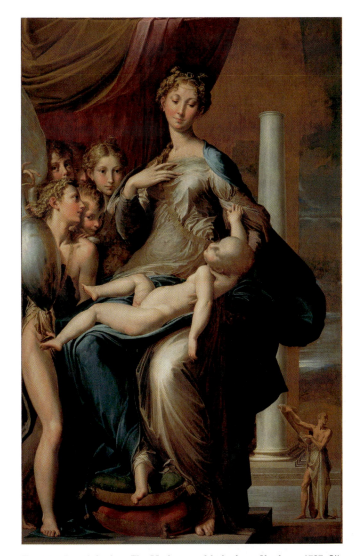

Fig. 10.7 Parmigianino, *The Madonna with the Long Neck*. ca. 1535. Oil on panel, 7'1" × 4'4". Galleria degli Uffizi, Florence. This work was begun in 1535, but the background space above Saint Jerome remained unfinished at Parmigianino's death in 1540.

Parmigianino has posed the Madonna so that, between her glance and the Christ Child's face, the folds of her blouse hang stiffly from a decidedly pointed nipple. Equally unsettling is the way that the Virgin's right foot seems to extend beyond the plane of the support into our own space, so that the gap between ourselves and the world of the painting mirrors the unaccounted-for space that lies between the Virgin and Saint Jerome.

Veronese and the Italian Inquisition A clear example of the need to use invention decorously in art is provided by the fate of a *Last Supper*, now known as the *Feast in the House of Levi*, by the Venetian artist Veronese (1528–88). Veronese was born Paolo Cagliari and nicknamed after the city of his birth, Verona. As early as 1542, Pope Paul III had initiated a Roman **Inquisition**—an official inquiry into possible heresy—and in 1573, Paolo Veronese was called before the Inquisition to answer charges that his

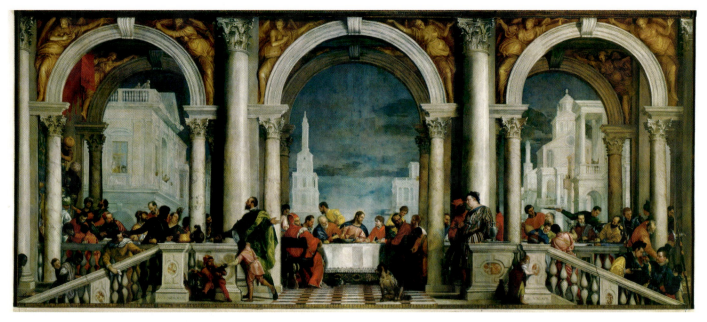

Fig. 10.8 Veronese, *Feast in the House of Levi*. 1573. Oil on canvas, 18′ × 42′. Galleria dell'Accademia, Venice. After his testimony before the Inquisition, Veronese made it clear that his "new" source for the painting was the feast in the house of Levi by citing the biblical reference on the balustrade.

 View the Closer Look for *Feast in the House of Levi* on **MyArtsLab**

Last Supper (Fig. **10.8**), painted with life-size figures for a Dominican monastery in Venice, was heretical in its inappropriate treatment of the subject matter. His testimony before the tribunal illuminates the aesthetic and religious concerns of the era (**Reading 10.2**):

READING 10.2

from *The Trial of Veronese* (1573)

VERONESE: This is a picture of the Last Supper that Jesus Christ took with His Apostles in the house of Simon.
INQUISITOR: At this Supper of Our Lord have you painted other figures?
VERONESE: Yes, milords.
INQUISITOR: Tell us how many people and describe the gestures of each.
VERONESE: There is the owner of the inn, Simon; beside this figure I have made a steward, who, I imagined, had come there for his own pleasure to see how the things were going at the table. There are many figures there which I cannot recall, as I painted the picture some time ago . . .
INQUISITOR: In this Supper which you made for SS. Giovanni e Paolo, what is the significance of the man whose nose is bleeding?
VERONESE: I intended to represent a servant whose nose was bleeding because of some accident.
INQUISITOR: What is the significance of those armed men dressed as Germans, each with a halberd in his hand?
VERONESE: We painters take the same license the poets and the jesters take and I have represented these two

halberdiers, one drinking and the other eating nearby on the stairs. They are placed there so that they might be of service because it seemed to me fitting, according to what I have been told, that the master of the house, who was great and rich, should have such servants.
INQUISITOR: And that man dressed as a buffoon with a parrot on his wrist, for what purpose did you paint him on that canvas?
VERONESE: For ornament, as is customary . . .
INQUISITOR: Are not the decorations which you painters are accustomed to add to paintings or pictures supposed to be suitable and proper to the subject and the principal figures or are they for pleasure—simply what comes to your imagination without any discretion or judiciousness?
VERONESE: I paint pictures as I see fit and as well as my talent permits.
INQUISITOR: Does it seem fitting at the Last Supper of the Lord to paint buffoons, drunkards, Germans, dwarfs and similar vulgarities?
VERONESE: No, milords.

The tribunal concluded that Paolo Veronese should "improve and correct" the painting in three months' time or face penalties. But rather than change the painting, Veronese simply changed the painting's title to *Feast in the House of Levi*. This title refers to a biblical passage: "Levi gave a great banquet for him [Jesus] in his house, and a large crowd of tax collectors and others were at table with them" (Luke 5:29). Through this strategy Veronese could justify the artistic invention in his crowded scene.

The Spanish Inquisition In sixteenth-century Spain, a brand of religious mysticism threatened the Church from within. The *alumbrados*, or "illuminated ones," nuns, monks, and priests lit by the Holy Spirit, practiced an extremely individualistic and private brand of faith, which led to accusations that they also claimed to have no need of the sacraments of the Church. The *alumbrados* were therefore susceptible to charges of heresy. Chief among them were the Carmelite nun Teresa of Ávila (1515–82) and the Carmelite friar Juan de la Cruz (1542–91), known as John of the Cross. Teresa was from a *converso* family—converted Jews—that lived in Ávila, the medieval center of Jewish mystical thought. Dissatisfied with the worldliness that had crept into her Carmelite order, Teresa campaigned to reform it, founding the Discalced (or shoeless) Carmelites, dedicated to absolute poverty and the renunciation of all property. Between 1567 and 1576, she traveled across Spain, founding Discalced convents and a reform monastery for Carmelite men. Juan de la Cruz was one of the first two members, and the two would become close friends. Juan's powers as a teacher, preacher, and poet served to strengthen the movement. Teresa's writings, including an autobiography and *The Way to Perfection*, both written before 1567, and *The Interior Castle*, written in 1577, all describe the ascent of the soul to union with the Holy Spirit in four basic stages. In the final of these stages, "devotion of ecstasy or rapture," consciousness of being in the body disappears and the spirit finds itself alternating between the ecstatic throes of a sweet, happy pain and a fearful, glowing fire.

In 1574, Teresa was denounced to the Inquisition as a restless wanderer who under the pretext of religion lived a life of dissipation. As a result, in 1576, she was confined in a convent. Juan de la Cruz suffered an even worse fate. Calced Carmelites arrested him in Toledo on the night of December 3, 1577. They held him in solitary confinement and lashed him before the community weekly until he escaped eight months later. Among the great works written following his escape is *The Dark Night of the Soul*, a book-length account of the author's mystical union with God.

The moral strictures of the Inquisition and the mysticism of the *alumbrados* are recognizable in the art of one of the most original sixteenth-century painters, El Greco, "The Greek" (born Domenico Theotokopoulos; 1541–1614). He trained as an icon painter in his native Crete, in those days a Venetian possession. In 1567 he went to Venice, then three years later to Rome, and in 1576, to Spain, where he soon developed a style that wedded Mannerism with the elongated, iconic figures of his Byzantine training. He used painting to convey an intensely expressive spirituality.

Painted at the turn of the sixteenth century, El Greco's *Resurrection* is decorous to the extent that draperies carefully conceal all inappropriate nudity (Fig. **10.9**). The poses of the writhing Roman soldiers who surround the vision of the triumphant Christ are as artificial and contrived as any in Mannerist art. The verticality of the composition, popular since the time of Correggio, mirrors the elongated anatomy of El Greco's figures. And yet, El Greco's style is unique, singular in the angularity of its draperies, in the drama of the representation, and in its overall composition. The Roman soldiers rise and fall in

elongated, serpentine poses, twisting around Christ like petals on a blossom, with Christ himself as the flower's stamen. If Christ's sexuality has been repressed, the effect of his presence on the soldiers, who swoon in near-hysterical ecstasy, is unmistakable. Above all, this painting celebrates raw physicality, even as it presents the greatest spiritual mystery of the Christian faith. Here the aspirations of the Counter-Reformation and the inventiveness of the Mannerist style are fully united, as they would come to be in the Baroque art of the seventeenth century.

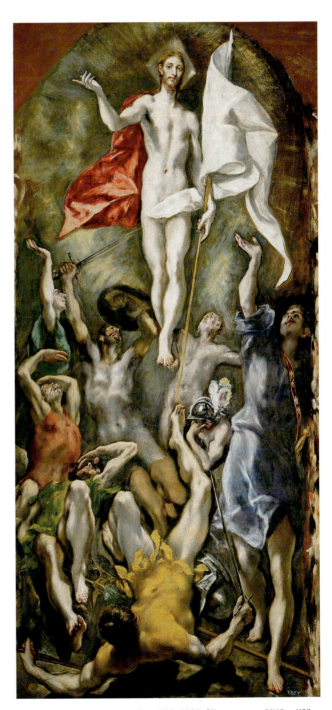

Fig. 10.9 El Greco, *Resurrection*. 1597–1604. Oil on canvas, 9′¼″ × 4′2″. Museo del Prado, Madrid. The image was probably painted for the Colegio de Doña Maria, Madrid, and paired with a depiction of the Pentecost, the descent of the Holy Spirit upon the apostles on the seventh Sunday after Easter.

Cervantes and the Picaresque Tradition

In the last half of the sixteenth century, a literary genre originated in Spain that celebrated inventiveness, particularly suited to Spanish taste, and had a strong effect on literary events in the seventeenth century. This was the **picaresque** novel, a genre of prose that narrates, in a realistic way, the adventures of a *picaro*, a roguish hero of low social rank living by his wits in a corrupt society. The first book to introduce the picaresque tradition in Spain was *Lazarillo de Tormes*, published anonymously in 1554. Raised by beggars and thieves, Lazarillo is a frankly common man, particularly bent on ridiculing and satirizing the Catholic Church and its officials. For that reason and probably because its hero was not highborn, the Spanish crown banned the book and listed it in the Index of Forbidden Books of the Inquisition. A much more complex *picaro* and undoubtedly the greatest hero of the picaresque tradition in Spanish literature is Don Quixote, the creation of the novelist, poet, and playwright Miguel de Cervantes (1547–1616).

Cervantes was himself a hero in the army of Philip II at the Battle of Lepanto in 1569 (where Spain defeated the Turks, gaining control of the Mediterranean), a captive of Barbary pirates for five years (1575–80), a supplier of provisions for the ill-fated Spanish Armada, and several times imprisoned for debt. In 1605, when he was 58 years of age, he published *The Ingenious Hidalgo Don Quixote de la Mancha*. (A *hidalgo* is a member of the lower Spanish nobility, generally exempt from paying taxes but not necessarily owning any real property.) A second part followed a decade later, a year before his death. The novel is more familiarly known today simply as *Don Quixote*.

Don Quixote is often considered the first great modern novel. It is set in La Mancha, a great arid plain southeast of Madrid. Into this landscape Cervantes places his two principal characters, Don Quixote and his servant Sancho Panza. Don Quixote is obsessed with the old stories of romance literature about questing knights and decides to become one himself. Cervantes presents him as a highly satiric re-creation of the conquistadors, whose exploits in the Americas were, Cervantes understood, similarly inspired by a thirst for romantic adventuring. Don Quixote's enthusiasm and self-deception unintentionally produce comic results. Sancho Panza, on the other hand, is a down-to-earth realist who believes the Don to be a bit crazy but plays along and accompanies him as squire on his adventures, hoping to get rich. The two search for the Don's ideal—and imaginary—lady, Dulcinea. Sancho convinces the Don that she is a plain, poorly dressed peasant riding a donkey and that he cannot recognize her for the beauty he knows Dulcinea to be because his vision has been bewitched by an enchantress. In other scenes, the Don mistakes a common country inn for a castle, a herd of sheep for a pagan army at battle with Christian forces, and two windmills for battling giants sent by an evil enchanter. This last is his most famous adventure, and in it Don Quixote, ever the noble conquistador, proceeds to tilt at the two windmills with his lance.

All these episodes are parables of the relation between illusion and reality, art and life. They anticipate the psychological complexities that will come to define the novel as a form. Don Quixote cannot reconcile his dreams with the realities of life itself, and his comic adventuring becomes his tragic fate. Above all, Don Quixote's adventures underscore both the marvelous possibilities that come from unleashing the imagination and the dangers of leaving the world behind.

THE BAROQUE IN ITALY

What is the Baroque style and how does it manifest itself in art and music?

By the middle of the seventeenth century, then, artists like Bernini were increasingly comfortable working in the inventive and exuberant style that had been inaugurated by Mannerism, while, at the same time, they still fully accepted the edicts of the Council of Trent. The Church's point of view was emphatically supported by the teachings of the Society of Jesus, founded by the Spanish nobleman Ignatius of Loyola (1491–1556). From their headquarters at the Church of Il Gesù in Rome, the Jesuits, as they were known, led the Counter-Reformation in the seventeenth century and the revival of the Catholic Church worldwide. All agreed that the purpose of religious art was to teach and inspire the faithful, that it should always be intelligible and realistic, and that it should be an emotional stimulus to piety.

In his *Spiritual Exercises*, published in 1548, Loyola had called on Jesuits to develop all their senses—an idea that surely influenced the many and richly diverse elements of the Baroque style. For instance, in the Fifth Exercise, a meditation on the meaning of Hell, Loyola invokes all five senses (**Reading 10.3**):

READING 10.3

from Ignatius Loyola, *Spiritual Exercises*, Fifth Exercise (1548)

FIRST POINT: This will be to see *in imagination the vast fires, and the souls enclosed, as it were, in bodies of fire.*

SECOND POINT: To hear *the wailing, the howling, cries, and blasphemies against Christ our Lord and against His saints.*

THIRD POINT: With the sense of smell *to perceive the smoke, the sulphur, the filth, and corruption.*

FOURTH POINT: To taste *the bitterness of tears, sadness, and remorse of conscience.*

FIFTH POINT: With the sense of touch *to feel the flames which envelop and burn the souls.*

Such a call to the senses would manifest itself in increasingly elaborate church decoration, epitomized by a ceiling fresco painted by Andrea Pozzo (1642–1709) for the church of Sant'Ignazio in Rome depicting the *Apotheosis of Saint Ignatius of Loyola* (Fig. **10.10**). The fresco employs a technique used on the ceilings of many Roman churches and palaces in the

Baroque era to create dynamic and dramatic spatial effects—foreshortening. Foreshortening allowed artists to make the ceiling appear larger than it actually was. To create the illusion of greater space, the artist would paint representations of architectural elements—such as vaults, arches or niches—and then fill the remaining space with foreshortened figures that seem to fly out of the top of the building into the heavens above. Because of Pozzo's masterful use of foreshortening, it is difficult for a visitor to Sant'Ignazio to tell that the space above the nave is a barrel vault. Pozzo painted it over with a rising architecture that seems to extend the interior walls an extra story. A white marble square in the pavement below indicates to the viewer just where to stand to appreciate the perspective properly. On each side of the space overhead are allegorical figures representing the four continents. America is at the upper left, crowned by a feathered headdress of red, white, and blue. Just below the center of the painting, Saint Ignatius, in gray robes, is transported on a cloud toward the waiting Christ, just above him. Other Jesuit saints rise to meet them. In Pozzo's ceiling, the faithful are invited to see not Hell, as Loyola outlines in his *Spiritual Exercises*, but Heaven. They are invited to hear "in imagination" not wailing but hosannas, smell not smoke but perfume, taste not bitter tears but sweet tears of joy, and touch not flames but the glorious light of God.

Baroque Sculpture: Bernini

Probably nothing sums up the Baroque movement better than Bernini's sculptural program for the Cornaro Chapel. Located in Carlo Maderno's Church of Santa Maria della Vittoria in Rome, the work was a commission from the Cornaro family and executed by Bernini in the middle of the century, at about the same time he was working on the colonnade for Saint Peter's Square. Bernini's theme is a pivotal moment in the life of Teresa of Ávila. Teresa was steeped in the mystical tradition of the Jewish Kabbalah, the brand of mystical Jewish thought that seeks to attain the perfection of Heaven while still living in this world by transcending the boundaries of time and space. Bernini illustrates the vision she describes in the following passage (**Reading 10.4**):

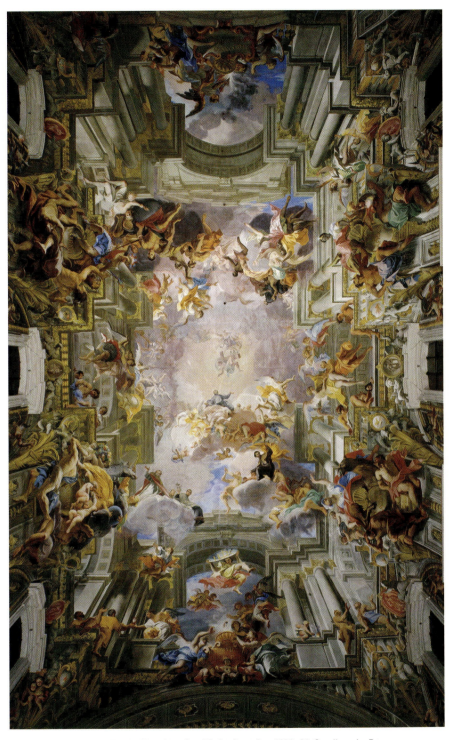

Fig. 10.10 Fra Andrea Pozzo, ***Apotheosis of Saint Ignatius.*** **1691–94.** Sant'Ignazio, Rome. Ceiling fresco, ca. 56' x 115'. Allegorical works in each corner represent the four continents—Europe, Asia, Africa, and America—where the Society of Jesus carried out its missionary work.

 View the Closer Look for Andrea Pozzo, *Apotheosis of Saint Ignatius* on **MyArtsLab**

READING 10.4

from Teresa of Ávila, "Visions," Chapter 29 of *The Life of Teresa of Ávila* (before 1567)

It pleased the Lord that I should sometimes see the following vision. I would see beside me, on my left hand, an angel in bodily form.... He was not tall, but short, and very beautiful, his face so aflame that he appeared to be one of the highest types of angel who seem to be all afire. They must be those who are called cherubim; they do not tell me their names but I am well aware that there is a great difference between certain angels and others, and between these and others still, of a kind that I could not possibly explain. In his hands I saw a long golden spear and at the end of the iron tip I seemed to see a point of fire. With this he seemed to pierce my heart several times so that it penetrated to my entrails. When he drew it out, I thought he was drawing them out with it and he left me completely afire with a great love for God. The pain was so sharp that it made me utter several moans; and so excessive was the sweetness caused me by this intense pain that one can never wish to lose it, nor will one's soul be content with anything less than God. It is not bodily pain, but spiritual, though the body has a share in it—indeed, a great share. So sweet are the colloquies of love which pass between the soul and God that if anyone thinks I am lying I beseech God, in His goodness, to give him the same experience.

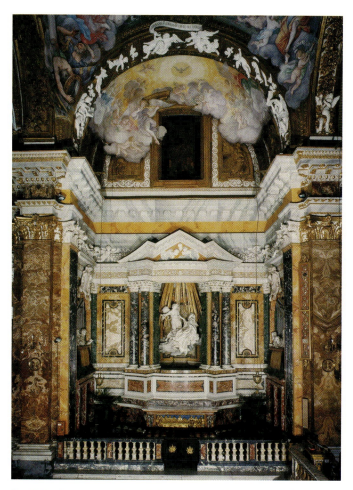

Fig. 10.12 Gianlorenzo Bernini, Cornaro Chapel, Santa Maria della Vittoria, Rome. 1647–52. The Cornaro family portraits are just visible on the left and right walls of the chapel.

Watch an architectural simulation of the Cornaro Chapel on **MyArtsLab**

Bernini might not have recognized in Teresa's words a thinly veiled description of sexual orgasm. But he probably did understand that the sexuality that Protestantism and the Catholic Counter-Reformation had deemed inappropriate to religious art, but which had survived in Mannerism, had found, in Saint Teresa's vision, a properly religious context, uniting the physical and the spiritual. Thus, the sculptural centerpiece of his chapel decoration is Teresa's ecstatic swoon, the angel standing over her, having just withdrawn his penetrating arrow from her "entrails," as Teresa throws her head back in the throes of spiritual passion (Fig. 10.11).

Bernini's program is far more elaborate than just its sculptural centerpiece (Fig. 10.12). The angel and Teresa are positioned beneath a marble canopy from which gilded rays of light radiate, following the path of the real light entering the chapel from the yellow panes of a window hidden from view behind the canopy pediment. Painted angels, sculpted in stucco relief, descend across the ceiling, bathed in a similarly yellow light that appears to emanate from the dove of Christ at the top center of the composition. On each side of

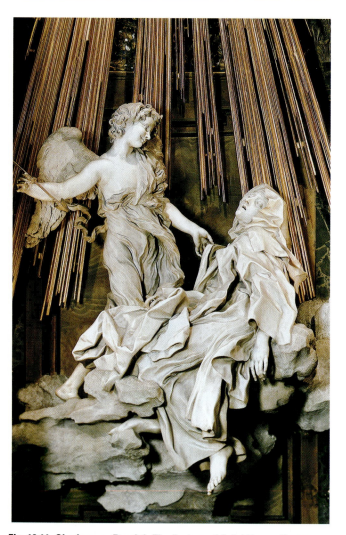

Fig. 10.11 Gianlorenzo Bernini, *The Ecstasy of Saint Teresa*, Cornaro Chapel, Santa Maria della Vittoria, Rome. 1647–52. Marble, height of group 11'6".

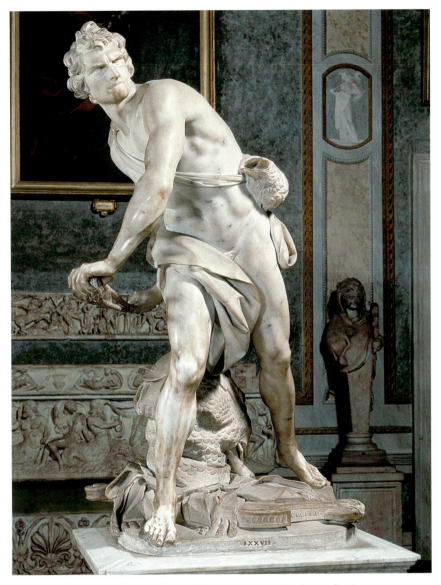

Fig. 10.13 Gianlorenzo Bernini, *David*. 1623. Marble, height 5'7". Galleria Borghese, Rome. Bernini carved this work when he was 25 years old, but he was already carving sculptures of remarkable quality by age 8.

the chapel, life-size marble re-creations of the Cornaro family lean out of what appear to be theater boxes into the chapel proper, as if witnessing the vision of Saint Teresa for themselves. Indeed, Bernini's chapel is nothing less than high drama, the stage space of not merely religious vision, but visionary spectacle. Here is an art designed to appeal to the feelings and emotions of its audience and draw them emotionally into the theatrical space of the work.

The Cornaro Chapel program suggests that the Baroque style is fundamentally theatrical in character, and the space it creates is theatrical space. It also demonstrates how central action was to Baroque representation. Bernini's *David* (Fig. 10.13), commissioned by a nephew of Pope Paul V, appears to be an intentional contrast to Michelangelo's sculpture of the same subject (see Fig. 7.22 in Chapter 7). Michelangelo's hero is at rest, in a moment of calm anticipation before confronting Goliath. In contrast, Bernini's sculpture captures

the young hero in the midst of action. David's body twists in an elaborate spiral, creating dramatic contrasts of light and shadow. His teeth are clenched, and his muscles strain as he prepares to launch the fatal rock. So real is his intensity that viewers tend to avoid standing directly in front of the sculpture, moving to one side or the other in order, apparently, to avoid being caught in the path of his shot.

In part, David's action defines Bernini's Baroque style. Whereas Michelangelo's David seems to contemplate his own prowess, his mind turned inward, Bernini's David turns outward, into the viewer's space, as if Goliath were a presence, although unseen, in the sculpture. In other words, the sculpture is not self-contained, and its active relationship with the space surrounding it—often referred to as its **invisible complement**—is an important feature of Baroque art. (The light source in his Cornaro Chapel Saint Teresa is another invisible complement.)

The Drama of Painting: Caravaggio and the Caravaggisti

Ever since the Middle Ages, when Abbot Suger of Saint-Denis, Paris, had insisted on the power of light to heighten spiritual feeling in the congregation, particularly through the use of stained glass, light had played an important role in church architecture (see Chapter 6). Bernini used it to great effect in his *Ecstasy of Saint Theresa* (see Fig. 10.11), and Baroque painters, seeking to intensify the viewer's experience of their paintings, sought to manipulate light and dark to great advantage as well. The acknowledged master of light and dark, and perhaps the most influential painter of his day, was Michelangelo Merisi, known as Caravaggio (1571–1610) after the town in northern Italy where he was born. His work inspired many followers, who were called the Caravaggisti.

Master of Light and Dark: Caravaggio Caravaggio arrived in Rome in about 1593 and began a career of revolutionary painting and public scandal. His first major commission in Rome was *The Calling of Saint Matthew* (Fig. **10.14**), arranged for by his influential patron Cardinal del Monte and painted about 1599–1600 for the Contarelli Chapel in the Church of San Luigi dei Francesi, the church of the French community (dei Francesi) in Rome. The most dramatic element in this work is light. The light that streams in from an unseen window at the upper right of the painting is almost palpable. It falls onto the table where the tax collector Levi (Saint Matthew's name before he became one of Jesus' apostles) and his four assistants count the day's take, highlighting their faces and gestures. They are dressed in a style not of Jesus' time, but of Caravaggio's, making it more possible for his audience to identify with them. With Saint Peter at his side, Christ enters from the right, a halo barely visible above his head.

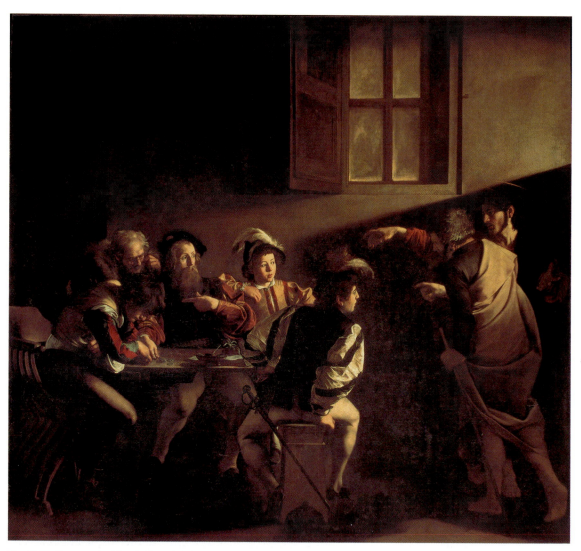

Fig. 10.14 Caravaggio, *The Calling of Saint Matthew*. ca. 1599–1600. Oil on canvas, 11'1" × 11'5". Contarelli Chapel, San Luigi dei Francesi, Rome. The window at the top of the painting is covered by parchment, often used by painters to diffuse light in their studios. This makes the intensity of light entering the room from the right especially remarkable.

View the Closer Look for The Calling of Saint Matthew on **MyArtsLab**

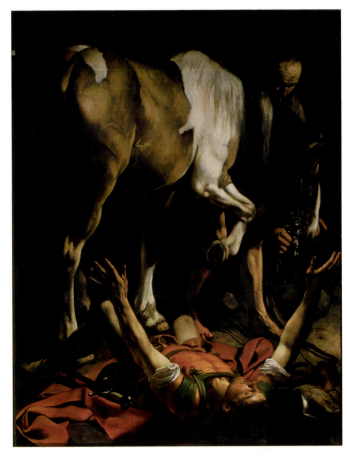

Fig. 10.15 Caravaggio, *Conversion of Saint Paul.* ca. 1601. Oil on canvas, 90½″ × 68⅞″. Santa Maria del Popolo, Rome. This painting was designed to fill the right wall of the narrow Carasi family chapel in Santa Maria del Popolo. Caravaggio had to paint it to be seen at an angle of about 45 degrees, a viewpoint that can be replicated by tipping this page inward about half open to an angle of 45 degrees to the reader's face. The resulting space is even more dramatic and dynamic.

He reaches out with his index finger extended in a gesture derived from Adam's gesture toward God in the Sistine Chapel ceiling *Creation*—an homage, doubtless, by the painter to his namesake (see Fig. 7.25). One of the figures at the table—it is surely Levi, given his central place in the composition—points with his left hand, perhaps at himself, as if to say, "Who, me?" or perhaps at the young man bent over at the corner of the table intently counting money, as if to say, "You mean him?" All in all, he seems to find the arrival of Jesus uninteresting. In fact, the assembled group is so ordinary—reminiscent of gamblers seated around a table— that the transformation of Levi into Saint Matthew, which is imminent, takes on the aspect of a miracle, just as the light flooding the scene is reminiscent of the original miracle of creation: "And God said, 'Let there be light: and there was light'" (Gen. 1:3). The scene also echoes the New Testament, specifically John 8:12, where Christ says: "I am the light of the world; he that followeth me shall not walk in darkness, but shall have the light of life."

Caravaggio's insistence on the reality of his scene is thus twofold: He not only depicts real people of his own day engaged in real tasks (by implication, Christ himself assumes

a human reality as well), but also insists on the reality of its psychological drama. The revelatory power of light—its ability to reveal the world in all its detail—is analogous, in Caravaggio's painting, to the transformative power of faith. Faith, for Caravaggio, fundamentally changes the way we *see* the world, and the way we *act* in it. Time and again, his paintings dramatize this moment of conversion through use of the technique known as **tenebrism**. As opposed to chiaroscuro, which many artists employ to create spatial depth and volumetric forms through slight gradations of light and dark, a tenebrist style is not necessarily connected to modeling at all. Tenebrism makes use of large areas of dark, contrasting sharply with smaller, brightly illuminated areas. In *The Calling of Saint Matthew*, Christ's hand and face rise up out of the darkness, as if his very gesture creates light itself—and by extension Matthew's salvation.

One of the clearest instances of Caravaggio's use of light to dramatize moments of conversion is the *Conversion of Saint Paul*, painted around 1601 (Fig. **10.15**). Although painted nearly 50 years before Bernini's *Ecstasy of Saint Teresa* (see Fig. 10.11), its theme is essentially the same, as is its implied sexuality. Here, Caravaggio portrays the moment when the Roman legionnaire Saul (who will become Saint Paul) has fallen off his horse and hears the words, "Saul, Saul, why persecutest thou me?" (Acts 9:4). Neither Saul's servant nor his horse hears a thing. Light, the visible manifestation of Christ's words, falls on the foreshortened soldier. Saul reaches into the air in both a shock of recognition and a gesture of embrace. A sonnet, "Batter My Heart," by the English metaphysical poet John Donne (1572–1631), published in 1618 in his *Holy Sonnets*, captures Saul's experience in words (**Reading 10.5**):

READING 10.5

John Donne, "Batter My Heart" (1618)

Batter my heart, three-person'd God, for you
As yet but knock, breathe, shine, and seek to mend;
That I may rise and stand, o'erthrow me, and bend
Your force to break, blow, burn, and make me new.
I, like an usurp'd town to' another due,
Labor to' admit you, but oh, to no end;
Reason, your viceroy in me, me should defend,
But is captiv'd, and proves weak or untrue.
Yet dearly' I love you, and would be lov'd fain,
But am betroth'd unto your enemy;
Divorce me,' untie or break that knot again,
Take me to you, imprison me, for I,
Except you' enthrall me, never shall be free,
Nor ever chaste, except you ravish me.

There is no reason to believe the English poet—who was raised a Catholic but converted to the Anglican Church for his own safety and prosperity—knew the Italian's painting, but the fact that the two men share so completely in the ecstasy of the moment of conversion, imaged as physical ravishment, suggests how widespread such conceits were in the seventeenth century. Both share with Teresa of Ávila a profound mysticism, the pursuit of achieving communion or identity with the divine through direct experience, intuition, or insight. All three believe that such experience is the ultimate source of knowledge or understanding, and they seek to convey that in their art. Such mystical experience, in its extreme physicality and naturalistic representation, also suggests how deeply the Baroque as a style was committed to sensual experience.

Artemisia Gentileschi and Caravaggisti Painting One of Caravaggio's most important followers, and one of the first women artists to achieve an international reputation, was Artemisia Gentileschi (1593–1652/53). Born in Rome,

she was raised by her father, Orazio, himself a painter and Caravaggisto. Orazio was among Caravaggio's closest friends. As a young girl, Artemisia could not have helped but hear of Caravaggio's frequent run-ins with the law—for throwing a plate of artichokes at a waiter, for street brawling, for carrying weapons illegally, and, ultimately, in 1606, for murdering a referee in a tennis match. Artemisia's own scandal would follow. It and much of her painting must be understood within the context of this social milieu—the loosely renegade world of Roman artists at the start of the seventeenth century. In 1612, when she was 19, she was raped by Agostino Tassi, a Florentine artist who worked in her father's studio and served as her teacher. Orazio filed suit against Tassi for injury and damage to his daughter. The transcript of the seven-month trial survives. Artemisia accused Tassi of repeatedly trying to meet with her alone in her bedroom and, when he finally succeeded, of raping her. When he subsequently promised to marry her, she freely accepted his continued advances, naïvely assuming marriage would follow. When he refused to marry her, the lawsuit followed.

At trial, Tassi accused her of having slept with many others before him. Gentileschi was tortured with thumbscrews to "prove" the validity of her testimony, and was examined by midwives to ascertain how recently she had lost her virginity. Tassi further humiliated her by claiming that Artemisia was an unskilled artist who did not even understand the laws of perspective. Finally, a former friend of Tassi's testified that Tassi had boasted about his exploits with Artemisia. Ultimately, he was convicted of rape but served only a year in prison. Soon after the long trial ended, Artemesia married an artist and moved with him to Florence. In 1616, she was admitted to the Florentine Academy of Design.

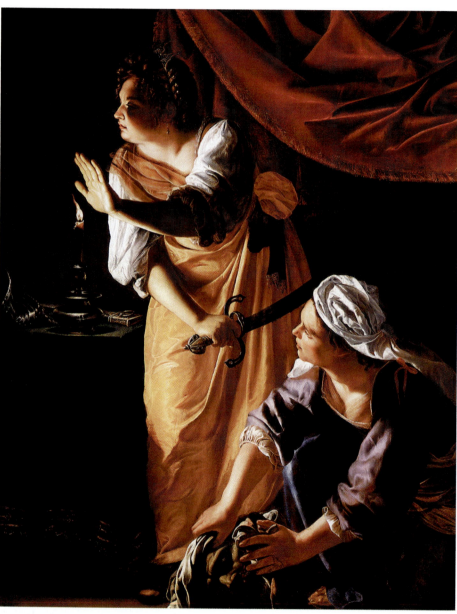

Fig. 10.16 Artemisia Gentileschi, *Judith and Maidservant with Head of Holofernes*.
ca. 1625. Oil on canvas, 72½" × 55¾". The Detroit Institute of Arts. Gift of Leslie H. Green. 52.253. Judith is a traditional symbol of fortitude, a virtue with which Artemisia surely identified.

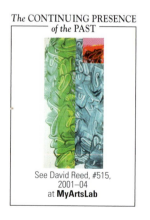

The CONTINUING PRESENCE of the PAST

See David Reed, #515, 2001–04 at **MyArtsLab**

Beginning in 1612, Artemisia painted five separate versions of the biblical story of Judith and Holofernes. The subject was especially popular in Florence, which identified with both the Jewish hero David and the Jewish heroine Judith (both of whom had been celebrated in sculptures by Donatello and Michelangelo). When Artemisia moved there, her personal investment in the subject found ready patronage in the city. Nevertheless, it is nearly impossible to see the paintings outside the context of her biography. She painted her first version of the theme during and just after the trial itself, and the last, *Judith and Maidservant with Head of Holofernes*, in about 1625 (Fig. **10.16**), suggesting that in this series she transforms her personal tragedy in her painting. In all of them, Judith is a self-portrait of the artist. In the Hebrew Bible's Book of Judith, the Jewish heroine enters the enemy Assyrian camp intending to seduce their lustful leader, Holofernes, who has laid siege to her people. When Holofernes falls asleep, she beheads him with his own sword and carries her trophy back to her people in a bag. The Jews then go on to defeat the leaderless Assyrians.

Gentileschi lights the scene by a single candle, dramatically accentuating the Caravaggesque tenebrism of the presentation. Judith shades her eyes from its light, presumably in order to look out into the darkness that surrounds her. Her hand also invokes our silence, as if danger lurks nearby. The maid stops wrapping Holofernes's head in a towel, looking on alertly herself. Together, mistress and maid, larger than life-size and heroic, have taken their revenge on not only the Assyrians, but also lust-driven men in general. As is so often the case in Baroque painting, the space of the drama is larger than the space of the frame. The same invisible complement outside Bernini's *David* (see Fig. 10.13) hovers in the darkness beyond reach of our vision here.

Gentileschi was not attracted to traditional subjects like the Annunciation. She preferred biblical and mythological heroines and women who played major roles. In addition to Judith, she dramatized the stories of Susannah, Bathsheba, Lucretia, Cleopatra, Esther, Diana, and Potiphar's wife. A good businesswoman, Gentileschi also knew how to exploit the taste for paintings of female nudes.

Venice and Baroque Music

In the sixteenth century, the Council of Trent had recognized the power of music to convey moral and spiritual ideals, at the same time rejecting the use of secular music, which by definition it deemed lascivious and impure, as a model for sacred compositions. Renaissance composers such as Guillaume Dufay and Josquin des Prez (see Chapter 7) had routinely used secular music in composing their masses, and Protestants had adapted the chorales of their liturgy from existing melodies, both religious and secular.

The division between secular and religious music was far less pronounced in Venice, a city that had traditionally chafed at papal authority. As a result, Venetian composers felt freer to experiment and work in a variety of forms, so much so that in the seventeenth century, the city became the center of musical innovation and practice in Europe.

Giovanni Gabrieli and the Drama of Harmony Venice earned its place at the center of the musical world largely through the efforts of Giovanni Gabrieli (1556–1612), the principal organist at Saint Mark's Cathedral. Gabrieli composed many secular madrigals, but he also responded to the Counter-Reformation's edict to make church music more emotionally engaging. To do this, he expanded on the polychoral style that Adrian Willaert had developed at Saint Mark's in the mid-1500s (see Chapter 7). Gabrieli located contrasting bodies of sound in different areas of the cathedral's interior, which already had two organs, one on each side of the chancel (the space containing the altar and seats for the clergy and choir). Playing them against one another, he was able to produce effects of stunning sonority. Four choirs—perhaps a boys' choir, a women's ensemble, basses and baritones, and tenors in another group—sang from separate balconies above the nave. Positioned in the alcoves were brass instruments.

Gabrieli was among the first to write religious music intended specifically for wind ensemble—music that was independent of song and that could not, in fact, be easily sung. One such piece is his *Canzona Duodecimi Toni* (*Canzona in the Twelfth Mode [or Tone]*) of 1597, in which two brass ensembles create a musical dialogue (track **10.3**). A **canzona** is a type of contrapuntal instrumental work, derived from Renaissance secular song, like the madrigal, which was increasingly performed in the seventeenth century in church settings. It is particularly notable for its dominant rhythm, LONG-short-short, known as the "canzona rhythm." In Saint Mark's, the two ensembles would have been placed across from each other in separate lofts. The alternating sounds of cornet and trombone or, in other compositions, brass ensemble, choir, and organ, coming from various parts of the cathedral at different degrees of loudness and softness, create a total effect similar to stereo "surround sound."

Listen at MyArtsLab

For each part of his composition, Gabrieli chose to designate a specific voice or instrument, a practice we have come to call **orchestration**. Furthermore, he controlled the **dynamics** (variations and contrast in force or intensity) of the composition by indicating, at least occasionally, the words *piano* ("soft") or *forte* ("loud"). In fact, he is the first known composer to specify dynamics. The dynamic contrasts of loud and soft in the *Canzona Duodecimi Toni*, mirroring the taste for tenebristic contrasts of light and dark in Baroque painting, make it a perfect example of Gabrieli's use of dynamic variety. As composers from across Europe came to Venice to study, they took these terms back with them, and Italian became the international language of music.

Finally, and perhaps most important, Gabrieli organized his compositions around a central note, called the **tonic note** (usually referred to as the **tonality** or **key** of the composition). This tonic note provides a focus for the composition. The ultimate resolution of the composition into the tonic, as in the *Canzona Duodecimi Toni*, where the tonic note is C, the twelfth mode (or "tone") in Gabrieli's harmonic system, provides the heightened sense of harmonic drama that typifies the Baroque.

Claudio Monteverdi and the Birth of Opera

A year after Gabrieli's death, Claudio Monteverdi (1567–1643) was appointed musical director at Saint Mark's in Venice. A violinist, Monteverdi had been the music director at the court of Mantua. In Venice, he proposed a new relation of text (words) and music. Where traditionalists favored the subservience of text to music—"Harmony is the ruler of the text," proclaimed Giovanni Artusi, the most ardent defender of the conservative position—Monteverdi proclaimed just the opposite: "Harmony is the mistress of the text!" Monteverdi's position led him to master a new, text-based musical form, the **opera**, a term that is the plural of *opus*, or "work." Operas are works consisting of many smaller works. (The term *opus* is used, incidentally, to catalogue the musical compositions of a given composer, usually abbreviated *op.*, so that "*op.* 8" would mean the eighth work or works published in the composer's repertoire.)

The form itself was first developed by a group known as the Camerata of Florence (*camerata* means "club" or "society"), a group dedicated to discovering the style of singing used by the ancient Greeks in their drama, which had united poetry and music but was known only through written accounts. Over the course of the 1580s and 1590s, Giulio Caccini and others began to write works that placed a solo vocal line above an instrumental line, known as the ***basso continuo***, or "continuous bass," usually consisting of a keyboard instrument (organ, harpsichord, etc.) and bass instrument (usually a cello), that was conceived as a supporting accompaniment, not as the harmonic equivalent, to the vocal line. This combination of solo voice and *basso continuo* came to be known as **monody**.

The inspiration for Monteverdi's first opera, *Orfeo* (1607), was the musical drama of ancient Greek theater. The **libretto** (or "little book") for Monteverdi's opera was based on the Greek myth of Orpheus and Eurydice. In the opera, shepherds and nymphs celebrate the love of Orfeo (Orpheus) and Eurydice in a dance that is interrupted by the news that Eurydice has died of a snake bite. The grieving Orpheus, a great musician and poet, travels to the underworld to bring Eurydice back. His plea for her return so moves Pluto, the god of the underworld, that he grants it, but only if Orpheus does not look back at Eurydice as they leave. But, anxious for her safety, he does glance back and loses her forever. Monteverdi did, however, offer his audience some consolation (if not really a happy ending): Orpheus's father, Apollo, comes down to take his son back to the heavens where he can behold the image of Eurydice forever in the stars.

Although *Orfeo* is by no means the first opera, it is generally accepted as the first successfully to integrate music and drama. Monteverdi tells the story through a variety of musical genres—choruses, dances, and instrumental interludes. Two particular forms stand out—the **recitativo** and the **aria**. *Recitativo* (or recitative) is a style of singing that imitates very closely the rhythms of speech. Used for dialogue, it allows a more rapid telling of the story than might be possible otherwise. The aria would eventually develop into an elaborate solo or duet song that expresses the singer's emotions and feelings, expanding on the dialogue of the recitative (in Monteverdi's hands, the aria could still be sung in recitative style).

Orfeo required an orchestra of three dozen instruments—including 10 viols, 3 trombones, and 4 trumpets—to perform the overture, interludes, and dance sequences, but generally only a harpsichord or lute accompanied the arias and recitatives so that the voice would remain predominant. For the age, this was an astonishingly large orchestra, financed together with elaborate staging by the Mantuan court where it was composed and first performed, and it provided Monteverdi with a distinct advantage over previous opera composers. He could achieve what his operatic predecessors could only imagine—a work that was both musically and dramatically satisfying, one that could explore the full range of sound and, with it, the full range of psychological complexity.

Antonio Vivaldi and the Concerto

Perhaps Venice's most important composer of the early eighteenth century was Antonio Vivaldi (1678–1741). In 1703, Vivaldi, son of the leading violinist at Saint Mark's, assumed the post of musical director at the Ospedale della Pietà, one of four orphanages in Venice that specialized in music instruction for girls. (Boys at the orphanages were not trained in music since it was assumed they would enter the labor force.) As a result, many of the most talented harpsichordists, lutenists, and other musicians in Venice were female, and many of Vivaldi's works were written specifically for performance by orphanage girls' choirs and instrumental ensembles. By and large, the orphanage musicians were young girls who would subsequently go on to either a religious life or marriage, but several were middle-aged women who remained in the orphanage, often as teachers, for their entire lives. The directors of the orphanages hoped that wealthy members of the audience would be so dazzled by the performances that they would donate money to the orphanages. Audiences from across Europe attended these concerts, which were among the first in the history of Western music that took place outside a church or theater and were open to the public. People were, in fact, dazzled by the talent of these female musicians; by all accounts, they were as skilled and professional as any of their male counterparts in Europe.

Vivaldi specialized in composing **concertos**, a three-movement secular form of instrumental music, popular at court. But he systematized the form. The first movement of a concerto is usually *allegro* (quick and cheerful), the second slower and more expressive, like the pace of an opera aria, and the third a little livelier and faster than the first. Concertos usually feature one or more solo instruments that, in the first and third movements particularly, perform passages of material, called episodes, that contrast back and forth with the orchestral score—a form known as ***ritornello***, "something that returns" (i.e., returning thematic material). At the outset, the entire orchestra performs the *ritornello* in the tonic—the specific home pitch around which the composition is organized. Solo episodes interrupt alternating with the *ritornello*, performed in partial form and in different keys, back and forth, until the *ritornello* returns again in its entirety in the tonic in the concluding section.

In the course of his career, Vivaldi composed nearly 600 concertos—for violin, cello, flute, piccolo, oboe, bassoon, trumpet, guitar, and even recorder. Most of these were performed by the Ospedale ensemble. The most famous is a group of four violin concertos, one for each season of the year, called *The Four Seasons*. It is an example of what would later come to be known as **program music**, or purely instrumental music in some way connected to a story or idea. The program of the first of these concertos, *Spring* (track **10.4**), is supplied by a sonnet, written by Vivaldi himself, at the top of the score. The first eight lines suggest the text for the first movement, and the last six lines, divided into two groups of three, the text for the second and third movements:

Listen at MyArtsLab

> Spring has arrived, and full of joy
> The birds greet it with their happy song.
> The streams, swept by gentle breezes,
> Flow along with a sweet murmur.
> Covering the sky with a black cloak,
> Thunder and lightning come to announce the season.
> When all is quiet again, the little birds
> Return to their lovely song.

The *ritornello* in this concerto is an exuberant melody played by the whole ensemble. It opens the movement, and corresponds to the poem's first line. Three solo violins respond in their first episode—"the birds greet it with their happy song"—imitating the song of birds. In the second episode, they imitate "streams swept by gentle breezes," then, in the third, "thunder and lightning," and finally the birds again, which "Return to their lovely song." The whole culminates with the *ritornello*, once again resolved in the tonic.

In its great rhythmic freedom (the virtuoso passages given to the solo violin), and the polarity between orchestra and solo instruments (the contrasts of high and low timbres, or sounds, such as happy bird song and clashing thunder), Vivaldi's concerto captures much of what differentiates Baroque music from its Renaissance predecessors. Gone are the balanced and flowing rhythms of Palestrina and the polyphonic

composition in which all voices are of equal importance. Perhaps most of all, the drama of beginning a composition in a tonic key, moving to different keys and then returning to the tonic—a process known as **modulation**—could be said to distinguish Baroque composition from what had come earlier. The dramatic effect of this modulation, together with the rich texture of the composition's chord clusters, parallels the dramatic lighting of Baroque painting, just as the embellishment of the solo voice finds its equivalent in the ornamentation of Baroque architecture.

THE SECULAR BAROQUE IN THE NORTH

A more austere Baroque style dominated northern Europe in the seventeenth century. Amsterdam was at its center. The city's economy thrived, sometimes too hotly, as in 1636 when mad speculation sent the market in tulip bulbs skyrocketing (a single bulb in Amsterdam sold for 4,600 florins, 15 or 20 times the annual income of a skilled craftsman). But this tendency to excess was balanced by the conservatism of the Dutch Reformed Church. The Calvinist fathers of the Dutch Reformed Church found no place for art in the Calvinist liturgy, by and large banning art from its churches.

But the prosperous Dutch populace avidly collected pictures. A visiting Englishman, John Evelyn, explained their passion for art this way, in 1641: "The reason of this store of pictures and their cheapness proceeds from want of land to employ their stock [wealth], so that it is an ordinary thing to find a common farmer lay out two or three thousand pounds in this commodity. Their houses are full of them and they vend them at their fairs to very great gains." If Evelyn exaggerates the sums invested in art—a typical landscape painting sold for only three or four guilders, still the equivalent of two or three days' wages for a Delft clothworker—he was accurate in his sense that almost everyone owned at least a few prints and a painting or two.

New Imagery: Still Life, Landscape, and Genre Painting

Despite Dutch Reformed distaste for religious history painting—commissions from the Church had dried up almost completely by 1620—about a third of privately owned paintings in the city of Leiden (one of the most iconoclastic in Holland) during the first 30 years of the seventeenth century represented religious themes. But other, more secular forms of painting thrived. Most Calvinists did not object to sitting for their portraits, as long as the resulting image reflected their Protestant faith. And most institutions wanted visual documentation of their activities, resulting in a thriving industry in group portraiture. Painting also came to reflect the matter-of-fact materialism of the Dutch character—its interest in all manner of things, from carpets, to furnishings, to clothing, collectibles, foodstuffs, and everyday activities. And the Dutch artists themselves were particularly interested in technical developments in the arts, especially

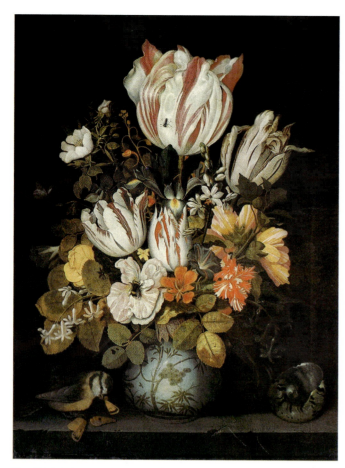

Fig. 10.17 Johannes Goedaert, *Flowers in a Wan-li Vase with Blue-Tit.* ca. 1660. Oil on panel, 21⅜″ × 14½″. Photo: Charles Roelofsz/RKD Images. Bob P. Haboldt & Co., Inc. Art Gallery, New York. The shell in the lower right corner is a symbol of worldly wealth, but as it is broken and empty, it is also a reminder of our vanity and mortality.

The CONTINUING PRESENCE of the PAST

See Pat Steir, *The Brueghel Series: A Vanitas of Style,* 1983–84 at **MyArtsLab**

Caravaggio's dramatic lighting. To accommodate the taste of the buying public, Dutch artists developed a new visual vocabulary that was largely vernacular, reflecting the actual time and place in which they lived.

Still Life Among the most popular subjects were **still lifes**, paintings dedicated to the representation of common household objects and food. At first glance, they seem nothing more than a celebration of abundance and pleasure. But their subject is also the foolishness of believing in such apparent ease of life. *Flowers in a Wan-li Vase with Blue-Tit* (Fig. **10.17**) by Johannes Goedaert (1617–68) is, on the one hand, an image of pure floral exuberance. The arrangement contains four varieties of tulip—somewhat ominously, given the memories of tulipomania—and a wide variety of other flowers, including a Spanish iris, nasturtiums from Peru, *fritillaria* from Persia, a striped York and Lancaster rose— a whole empire's worth of blossoms. The worldliness of the

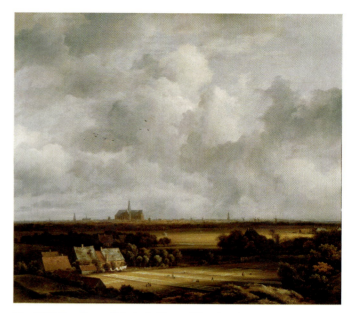

Fig. 10.18 Jacob van Ruisdael, *View of Haarlem from the Dunes at Overveen.* ca. 1670. Oil on canvas, 22″ × 24⅜″. Mauritshuis, The Hague. The play of light and dark across the landscape can be understood in terms of the rhythms of life itself.

blooms is underscored by the Wan-li vase in which they are placed, a type of Ming dynasty porcelain (see Fig. 9.30) that became popular with Dutch traders around the turn of the century. The short life of the blooms is suggested by the yellowing leaves, and the impermanence of the scene by the fly perched on one of the tulips. But perhaps the most telling detail is the bird at the bottom left of the painting, a blue-tit depicted in the act of consuming a moth. Dutch artists of this period used such details to remind the viewer of the frivolous quality of human existence, our vanity in thinking only of the pleasures of the everyday. Such **vanitas paintings**, as they are called, remind us that pleasurable things in life inevitably fade, that the material world is not as long-lived as the spiritual, and that the spiritual should command our attention. They are, in short, examples of the *memento mori*—reminders that we will die. Paintings such as Goedaert's were extremely popular. Displayed in the owner's home, they were both decorative and imbued with a moral sensibility that announced to a visitor the owner's upright Protestant ethic.

Landscapes Another popular subject was landscapes. Landscape paintings such as *View of Haarlem from the Dunes at Overveen* by Jacob van Ruisdael (ca. 1628–82) reflect national pride in the country's reclamation of its land from the sea (Fig. **10.18**). The English referred to the United Provinces as the "united bogs," and the French constantly poked fun at the baseness of what they called the *Pays-Bas* (the "Low Countries"). But the Dutch themselves considered their transformation of the landscape from hostile sea to tame farmland, in the century from 1550 to 1650, as analogous to God's recreation of the world after the Great Flood.

In Ruisdael's landscape painting, this religious undertone is symbolized by the great Gothic church of Saint Bavo at Haarlem, which rises over a flat, reclaimed landscape where figures toil in a field lit by an almost celestial light. It is no accident that two-thirds of Ruisdael's landscape is devoted to sky, the infinite heavens. In flatlands, the sky and horizon are simply more evident, but more symbolically, the Dutch thought of themselves as *Nederkindern*, the "children below," looked after by an almighty God with whom they had made an eternal covenant.

Genre Scenes Paintings that depict events from everyday life—or **genre scenes**—were another favorite of the Dutch public. *The Dancing Couple* (Fig. **10.19**) by Jan Steen (1626–79) is typical. Like many of Steen's paintings, it depicts festivities surrounding some sort of holiday or celebration. Steen was both a painter and a tavernkeeper, and the scene here is most likely a tavern patio in midsummer. An erotic flavor permeates the scene, an atmosphere of flirtation and licentiousness. To the right, musicians play as a seated couple drunkenly watch the dancers. To the left, two men enjoy food at the table, a woman lifts a glass of wine to her lips, and

a gentleman—a self-portrait of the artist—gently touches her chin. Steen thus portrays his own—and, by extension, the Dutch—penchant for merry making, but in typical Dutch fashion he also admonishes himself for taking such license. On the tavern floor lie an overturned pitcher of cut flowers and a pile of broken eggshells, both *vanitas* symbols. Together with the church spire in the distance, they remind us of the fleeting nature of human life as well as the hellfire that awaits those who have fallen into the vices so openly displayed in the rest of the painting.

One of the masters of this type of painting was Johannes Vermeer (1632–75). His paintings illuminate—and celebrate—the material reality of Dutch life. We know very little of Vermeer's life, and his painting was largely forgotten until the middle of the nineteenth century. But today he is recognized as one of the great masters of the Dutch seventeenth century. Vermeer painted only 34 works that modern scholars accept as authentic, and most depict intimate genre scenes that reveal a moment in the domestic world of women.

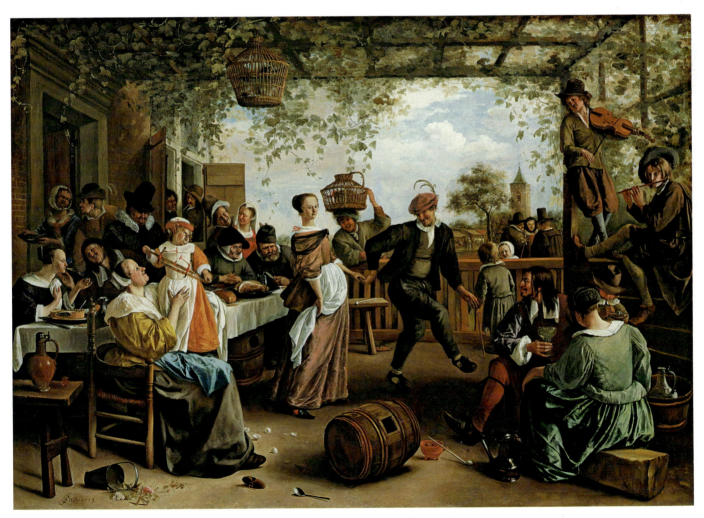

Fig. 10.19 Jan Steen, *The Dancing Couple*. 1663. Oil on canvas, 40⅜" × 56⅛". National Gallery of Art, Washington, D.C., Widener Collection. 1942.9.81. Photography © Board of Trustees, National Gallery of Art. Steen's paintings, whatever their moralizing undercurrents, remind us that the Dutch were a people of great humor and happiness. They enjoyed life.

The example here is *Woman with a Pearl Necklace* (Fig. 10.20). Light floods the room from a window at the left, where a yellow curtain has been drawn back, allowing the young woman to see herself better in a small mirror beside the window. She is richly dressed, wearing an ermine-trimmed yellow satin jacket. On the table before her are a basin and a powder brush; she has evidently completed the process of putting on makeup and arranging her hair as she draws the ribbons of her pearl necklace together and admires herself in the mirror. From her ear hangs a pearl earring, glistening in the light. The woman brims with self-confidence, and nothing in the painting suggests that Vermeer intends a moralistic message of any sort. While the woman's pearls might suggest her vanity—to say nothing of pride because of the way she gazes at them—they also traditionally symbolize truth, purity, even virginity. This latter reading is supported by the great, empty, and white stretch of wall that extends between her and the mirror. It is as if this young woman is a *tabula rasa*, a blank slate, whose moral history remains to be written.

Rembrandt van Rijn and the Drama of Light

Yet another popular genre of the era was the **group portrait**, a large canvas commissioned by a civic institution to document or commemorate its membership at a particular time. In the hands of Rembrandt van Rijn (1606–69), the group portrait took on a heightened sense of drama. The leading painter in Amsterdam, Rembrandt was a master at building up the figure with short dashes of paint or, alternately, long, fluid lines of loose, gestural brushwork. The

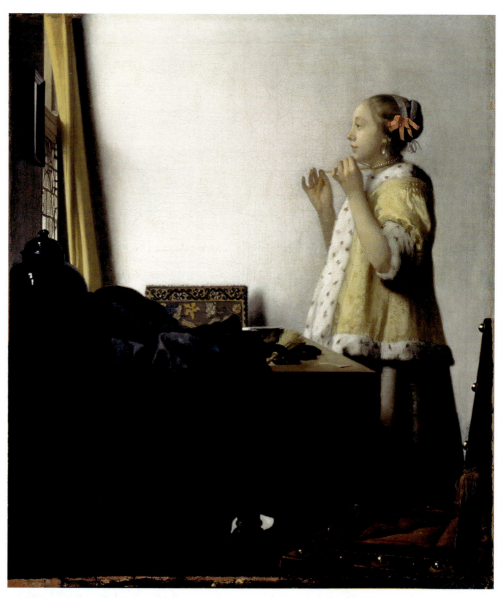

Fig. 10.20 Johannes Vermeer, *Woman with a Pearl Necklace*. ca. 1664. Oil on canvas, 22⁵⁄₃₂″ × 17¾″. Post-restoration. Inv.: 912 B. Photo: Joerg P. Anders. Gemäldegalerie, Staatliche Museen, Berlin. The mirror can symbolize both vanity—self-love—and truth, the accurate reflection of the world.

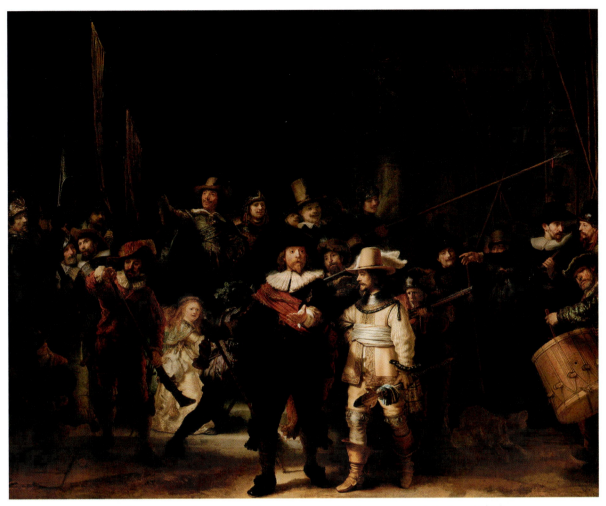

Fig. 10.21 Rembrandt van Rijn, *Captain Frans Banning Cocq Mustering His Company (The Night Watch)*. 1642. Oil on canvas, 11'11" × 14'4". Rijksmuseum, Amsterdam. Recently, the Dutch scholar Dudok van Heel has made a convincing case that the main character in the painting is not Frans Banning Cocq but Frans Bannink Cocq, a member of a much richer and more influential family than Banning Cocq.

result, paradoxically, is an image of extreme clarity, a clarity that has not always been apparent in his group portrait of *Captain Frans Banning Cocq Mustering His Company* (Fig. 10.21). The enormous canvas (which was originally even larger) was so covered by a layer of grime and darkened varnish that for years it was thought to represent the Captain's company on a night patrol of Amsterdam's streets, and it was known, consequently, as *The Night Watch*. But after a thorough cleaning and restoration in 1975–76, its true subject revealed itself—the company forming for a parade in a side street of the city. Perhaps more important, the cleaning also revealed one of Rembrandt's important contributions to the art of portraiture—his use of light to animate his figures. Captain Cocq's hand extends toward us in the very center of the painting, casting a shadow across the lemon-yellow jacket of his lieutenant. Competing for our attention is a young woman, also dressed in yellow satin studded with pearls, to the captain's right. A chicken hangs from her waist, and below it a money-bag, as if she has encountered the company on her way home from the market. She is such

an odd addition to the scene that scholars have for years tried to account for her presence as, for instance, a symbolic representation of the company itself or, alternatively, an ironic commentary on the company's relation to mercantile interests. That said, she certainly adds a dimension of liveliness to the scene, asserting herself as a dramatic presence who underscores the motion and action of the painting as a whole. Everyone seems to be looking in different directions; different conversations abound; the figure in red, at the left, seems to have just discharged his rifle; a dog barks at a drummer entering from the right. Compared to the standard group portrait of the time, in which everybody seems literally to sit still for the portraitist, Rembrandt's group is animated, even noisy. As his figures move in and out of light and shadow, it seems as if the artist has barely managed to capture them.

In one of his most famous group portraits, *The Anatomy Lesson of Dr. Tulp* (see *Closer Look*, pages 338–339), Rembrandt would use this symbolic light for ironic effect. But in his religious works, especially, it would come to stand for the redemption offered to humankind by the example of Christ.

CLOSER LOOK

The Anatomy Lesson of Dr. Tulp was commissioned by Dr. Tulp to celebrate his second public anatomy demonstration, performed in Amsterdam on January 31, 1632. Public dissections were always performed in the winter months in order to preserve the cadaver better from deterioration. The body generally was that of a recently executed prisoner. The object of these demonstrations was purely educational—how better to understand the human body than to inspect its innermost workings? By understanding the human body, the Dutch believed, one could come to understand God. As the Dutch poet Barlaeus put it in 1639, in a poem dedicated to Rembrandt's painting:

> Listener, learn yourself! And while you proceed through
>   the parts,
> believe that, even in the smallest, God lies hid.

Public anatomies, or dissections, were extremely popular events. Town dignitaries would generally attend, and a ticket-buying public filled the amphitheater. As sobering as the lessons of an anatomy might be, the event was also an entertaining spectacle. An example of the Dutch group portrait, this one was designed to celebrate Tulp's medical knowledge as well as his following. He is surrounded by colleagues, all of whom are identified on the sheet of paper held by the figure standing behind the doctor. Their curiosity underscores Tulp's prestige and the scientific inquisitiveness of the age.

The figures are arranged in a triangle. Dr. Tulp, in the bottom right corner, holds forceps that are the focus of almost everyone's attention. As is characteristic of Rembrandt's work, light plays a highly symbolic role. It shines across the room, from left to right, directly lighting the faces of the three most inquisitive students, suggesting the light of revelation and learning. And it terminates at Tulp's face, almost as if he himself is the source of their light. Ironically, the best-lit figure in the scene is the corpse. Whereas light in Rembrandt's work almost always suggests the kind of lively animation we see on the students' brightly lit faces, here it illuminates death.

Dr. Frans van Loenen points at the corpse with his index finger as he engages the viewer's eyes. The gesture is meant to remind us that we are all mortal.

The pale, almost bluish skin tone of the cadaver contrasts dramatically with the rosy complexions of the surgeons. Typically, the cadaver's face was covered during the anatomy, but Rembrandt unmasked the cadaver's face for his painting. In fact, we know the identity of the cadaver. He is Adriaen Adriaenszoon, also known as "Aris Kindt"—"the Kid"—a criminal with a long history of thievery and assault who was hanged for beating an Amsterdam merchant while trying to steal his cape. Dr. Tulp and his colleagues retrieved the body from the gallows. In another context, a partly draped nude body so well lit would immediately evoke the entombment of Christ with its promise of resurrection. It is the very impossibility of that fate for Adriaen Adriaenszoon that the lighting seems to underscore here.

Dr. Tulp is displaying the flexor muscles of the arm and hand and demonstrating their action by activating various muscles and tendons. It is the manual dexterity enabled by these muscles that physically distinguishes man from beast.

Something to Think About...

While it is the hand that distinguishes man from beast, why would an artist like Rembrandt be especially drawn to representing its dissection?

Rembrandt's *The Anatomy Lesson of Dr. Tulp*

Dr. Hartman Hartmanszoon holds in his hand a drawing of a flayed body upon which someone later added the names of all the figures in the scene.

Dr. Tulp was born Claes Pieterszoon but took the name *Tulp*—Dutch for "tulip"—sometime between 1611 and 1614 when still a medical student in Leiden, where he encountered the flower in the botanical gardens of the university. Throughout his career, a signboard painted with a single golden yellow tulip on an azure ground hung outside his house.

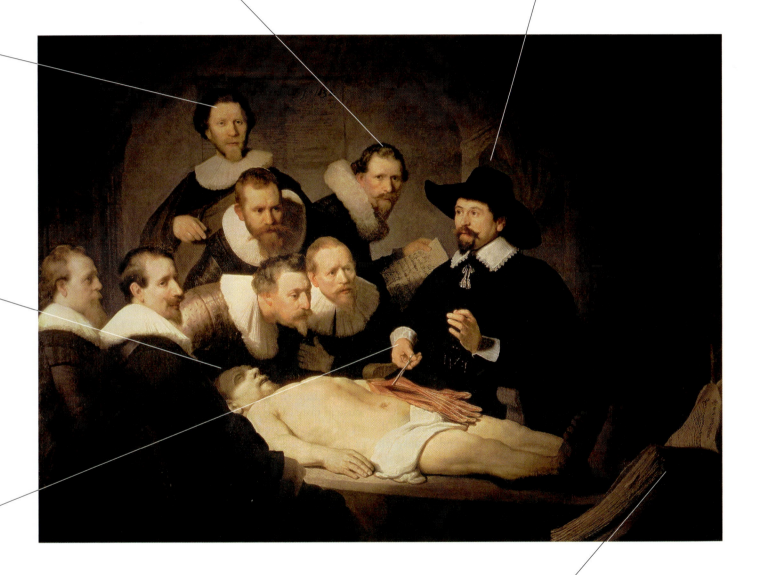

This large book may be the *De humani corporis fabrica*, the first thorough anatomy, published in 1543 by the Dutch scientist Andreis van Wesel (1514–64), known as Vesalius, who had taught anatomy at the University of Padua. Tulp thought of himself as *Vesalius redivivus*, "Vesalius revived."

Rembrandt van Rijn, ***The Anatomy Lesson of Dr. Tulp***. **1632.** Oil on canvas, 5'3¾" × 7'1¼".
Royal Cabinet of Paintings, Mauritshuis, The Hague.

 View the Closer Look for *The Anatomy Lesson of Dr. Tulp* on **MyArtsLab**

ABSOLUTISM AND THE BAROQUE COURT

What is absolutism and how did it impact the arts?

By the start of the eighteenth century, almost every royal court in Europe modeled itself on the court of King Louis XIV of France (r. 1643–1715). Louis detested the Louvre, the royal palace in Paris that had been the seat of French government and home to French kings since the Middle Ages. In 1661 he began construction of a new residence in the small town of Versailles, 12 miles southeast of Paris. For 20 years, some 36,000 workers labored to make Versailles the most magnificent royal residence in the world. Landscape architect André Le Nôtre (1613–1700) was in charge of the grounds at Versailles. He believed in the formal garden, and his methodical, geometrical design has come to be known as the **French garden**. The grounds were laid out around a main axis, emphasized by the giant cross-shaped Grand Canal, which stretched to the west of the palace (Fig. **10.24**). Pathways radiated from this central axis, circular pools and basins surrounded it, and both trees and shrubbery were groomed into abstract shapes to match the geometry of the overall site. The king himself took great interest in Le Nôtre's work, even writing a guide to the grounds for visitors. Neat boxwood hedges lined the flower beds near the chateau, and a greenhouse provided fresh flowers to be planted in the gardens as the seasons changed. Over 4 million tulip bulbs, imported from Holland, bloomed each spring, and Louis's gardener had over 2 million flowerpots at his disposal. When Louis permanently moved his court and governmental offices there in 1682, Versailles became the unofficial capital of France and symbol of Louis's absolute power and authority.

The elaborate design of the palace was intended to leave the attending nobility in awe. Charles Le Brun (1619–1690) served as chief painter to the king, and directed the team of artists who decorated the palace's interior. The Hall of Mirrors (Fig. **10.25**) was begun in

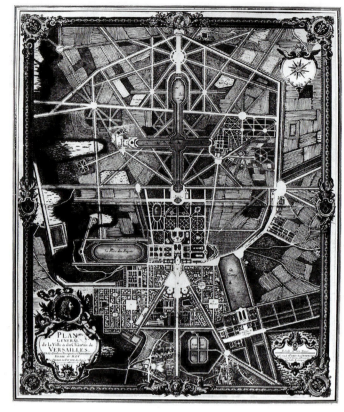

Fig. 10.24 André Le Nôtre, plan of the gardens and park, Versailles. Designed 1661–68, executed 1662–90. Drawing by Leland Roth after Delagive's engraving of 1746. To the right are the main streets of the town of Versailles. Three grand boulevards cut through it to converge on the palace itself.

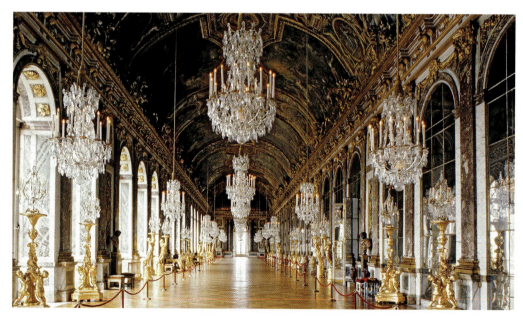

Fig. 10.25 Jules Hardouin-Mansart and Charles Le Brun, Galerie des Glaces (Hall of Mirrors), Palace of Versailles. Begun 1678. The Galerie des Glaces is 233 feet long and served as a reception space for state occasions. It gets its name from the Venetian-style mirrors—extraordinarily expensive at the time—that line the wall opposite windows of the same shape and size, creating by their reflection a sense of space even vaster than it actually is.

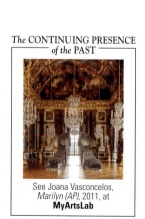

The CONTINUING PRESENCE *of the* PAST

See Joana Vasconcelos, *Marilyn (AP)*, 2011, at **MyArtsLab**

1678 to celebrate the high point of Louis XIV's political career, the end of six years of war with Holland. Louis asked Le Brun to depict his government's accomplishments on the ceiling of the hall in 30 paintings, framed by stucco, showing the monarch as a Roman emperor, astute administrator, and military genius. Le Brun balanced the 17 windows that stretch the length of the hall and overlook the garden with 17 arcaded mirrors along the interior wall, all made in a Paris workshop founded to compete with Venice's famous glass factories. Originally, solid silver tables, lamp holders, and orange-tree pots adorned the gallery. Louis later had them all melted down to finance his ongoing war efforts.

The Court at Versailles

At court, Louis fully regulated the lives of the nobility. He thought of himself as *Le Roi Soleil*, "the Sun King," because like the sun (associated with Apollo, god of peace and the arts) he saw himself dispensing bounty across the land. His ritual risings and retirings (the *levée du roi* and the *couchée du roi*) symbolized the actual rising and setting of the sun. They were essentially state occasions, attended by either the entire court or a select group of fawning aristocrats who eagerly entered their names on waiting lists. Louis encouraged the noble-women at court to consider it something of an honor to sleep with him; he had many mis-tresses and many illegitimate children. Life in his court was entirely formal, governed by custom and rule, so etiquette became a way of social advancement. He required the use of a fork at mealtimes instead of using one's fingers. Where one sat at dinner was determined by rank. In fact, rank determined whether foot-men opened one or two of Versailles's glass-paneled "French doors" for each guest passing through the palace. Louis's control over the lives of his courtiers had the political benefit of making them financially dependent on him. According to the memoirs of the duc de Saint-Simon, Louis de Rouvroy (1675–1755):

> He loved splendor, magnificence, and profusion in all things, and encouraged similar tastes in his Court; to spend money freely on equipages and buildings, on feast-ing and at cards, was a sure way to gain his favour, perhaps to obtain the honor of a word from him. Motives of pol-icy had something to do with this; by making expensive habits the fashion, and, for people in a certain position, a necessity, he compelled his courtiers to live beyond their income, and gradually reduced them to depend on his bounty for the means of subsistence.

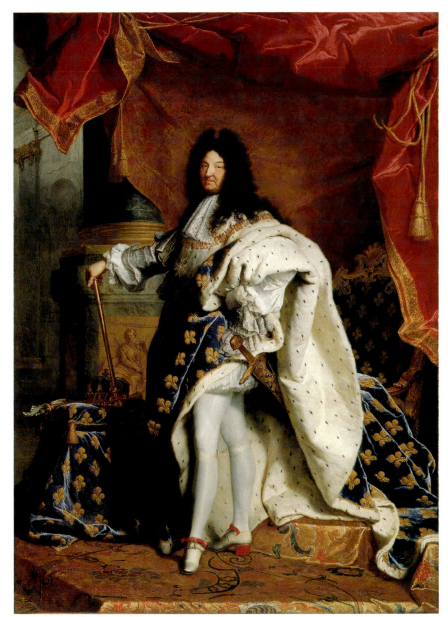

Fig. 10.26 Hyacinthe Rigaud, *Louis XIV, King of France.* **1701.** Oil on canvas, 9'1" × 6'4⅜". Musée du Louvre, Paris. In his ermine coronation robes, Louis both literally and figuratively looks down his nose at the viewer, his sense of superiority fully captured by Rigaud.

View the Closer Look for *Louis XIV, King of France* on **MyArtsLab**

Louis's sense of his own authority—to say nothing of his notorious vanity—is wonderfully captured in Hyacinthe Rigaud's official state portrait of 1701 (Fig. **10.26**). The king has flung his robes over his shoulder in order to reveal his white stockings and shoes with high, red heels. He designed the shoes himself to compensate for his 5-foot-4-inch height. He is 63 years old in this portrait, but he means to make it clear that he is still a dashing courtier.

The Painting of Peter Paul Rubens: Color and Sensuality One of Louis's favorite artists was the Flemish painter Peter Paul Rubens (1577–1640). Louis's grandmother Marie de' Medici had commissioned Rubens in 1621 to celebrate her life in a

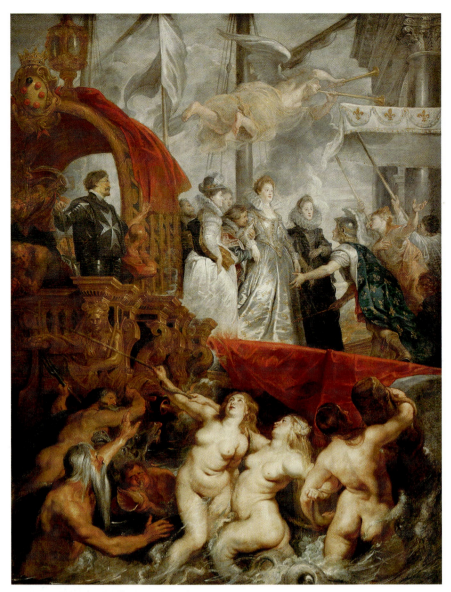

Fig. 10.27 Peter Paul Rubens and his workshop, *The Arrival and Reception of Marie de' Medici at Marseilles.* **1621–25.** Oil on canvas, 13′ × 10′. Musée du Louvre, Paris. The point of view here is daringly low, perhaps in the water, or oddly floating above it. This creates a completely novel relationship between viewer and painting.

series of 21 monumental paintings. The cycle took four years (1621–25) to complete with the help of studio assistants.

Rubens's pictorial approach to such self-promoting biographical commissions was through lifelike allegory. *The Arrival and Reception of Marie de' Medici at Marseilles* depicts the day Marie arrived in France from her native Italy en route to her marriage to King Henry IV (Fig. **10.27**). The figure of Fame flies above her, blowing a trumpet, while Neptune, god of the sea, and his son Triton, accompanied by three water nymphs, rise from the waves to welcome her. A helmeted allegorical figure of France, wearing a *fleur-de-lis* robe like that worn by Louis XIV in his portrait

of 1701, bows before her. Marie herself, not known for her beauty, is so enveloped by rich textures, extraordinary colors, and sensuous brushwork that she seems transformed into a vision as extraordinary as the scene itself.

The fleshy bodies of the nymphs in this painting are a signature stylistic component of Rubens's work. In fact, Rubens's style is almost literally a "fleshing out" of the late Italian Renaissance tradition. It is so distinctive that it came to be known as "Rubenesque." His nudes, which often startle contemporary viewers because we have developed almost entirely different standards of beauty, are notable for the way in which their flesh folds and drapes across their bodies. Their beauty rests in the sensuality of this flesh, which in some measure symbolizes the sensual life of self-indulgence and excess. Rubens pushed to new extremes the Mannerist sensibilities of Michelangelo's *Last Judgment* (see Fig. 10.3), the color and textures of the Venetian school as embodied in Titian's *Rape of Europa* (see Fig. 10.6), and the play of light and dark of the Caravaggisti (see Fig. 10.14). He brought to the Italian tradition a northern appreciation for observed nature—in particular, the realities of human flesh—and an altogether inventive and innovative sense of space and scale. Only rarely are Rubens's paintings what might be called frontal, where the viewer's position parallels the depicted action. Rather, the action moves diagonally back into space from either the front left or front right corner of the composition.

In a painting like *The Kermis*, or *Peasant Wedding*, Rubens transforms a simple tavern gathering—a genre common to northern painting (see Fig. 10.19)—into a monumental celebration (Fig. **10.28**). *The Kermis* is over 8 feet wide. Its wedding celebration spills in a diagonal out of the confines of the tavern into the panoramic space of the Flemish countryside. At the pinnacle of this sideways pyramid of entwined flesh, a young man and a disheveled woman, her blouse fallen fully from her shoulders, run off across the bridge, presumably to indulge their appetites behind some hedge. Like the Hall of Mirrors at Versailles, with its mathematical regularity overlaid with sumptuously rich ornamentation, Rubens's painting seems at once moralistic and libertine. Arms and legs interlace in a swirling, twirling riot that can be interpreted as either a descent into debauchery or a celebration of sensual pleasure, readings that Rubens seems to have believed were not mutually exclusive.

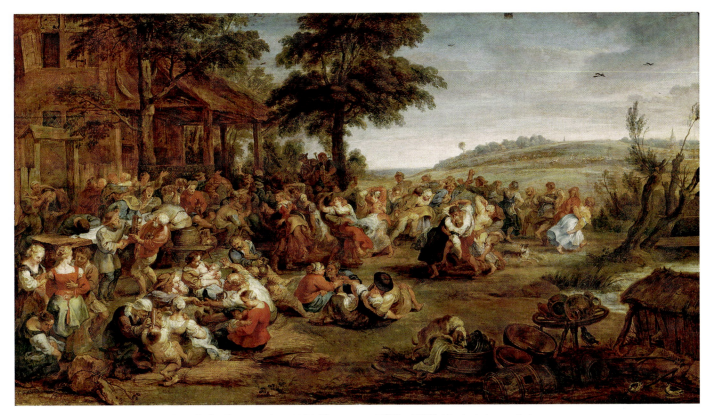

Fig. 10.28 Peter Paul Rubens, *The Kermis (La Kermesse)*. ca. 1635. Oil on canvas, 56⅝" × 102¾". Musée du Louvre, Paris. In this painting, Rubens reveals his Flemish heritage, taking up the traditional subject matter of Jan Steen and others, a genre scene of everyday life.

Such frank sensuality is a celebration of the simple joy of living in a world where prosperity and peace extend even to the lowest rungs of society. Yet in keeping with his Northern roots, Rubens gave the painting moralistic overtones. The posture of the dog with its nose in the cloth-draped tub at the bottom center of the canvas echoes the form of the kissing couple directly behind it and the dancing couples above it and, once more, represents the base, animal instincts that dominate the scene. The nursing babes at breast throughout the painting do not so much imply abundance as animal hunger, the desire to be fulfilled. Rubens knew full well that the bacchanal was not merely an image of prosperity but also one of excess. In his later years, excess enthralled him, and *The Kermis* is a product of this sensibility.

Some 50 years later, in April 1685, Louis XIV purchased *The Kermis* for Versailles. What did the monarch see in this painting? For one thing, it was probably important to the man who considered himself Europe's greatest king to possess the work of the artist widely considered to be Europe's greatest painter. For another, Louis must have appreciated the painting's frank sexuality, which the artist emphasized by his sensual brushwork and color. It recalled the king's own sexual exploits.

The Painting of Nicolas Poussin: Classical Decorum By the beginning of the eighteenth century, 14 other Rubens

paintings had found their way to the court of Louis XIV. Armand-Jean du Plessi, duc de Richelieu (1629–1715), the great-nephew of Cardinal Richelieu (1585–1642), who had served as artistic advisor to Marie de' Medici and Louis XIII, purchased the 14 paintings that had remained in Rubens's personal collection after his death in 1640. Before he acquired his own collection of Rubens's work, Richelieu had wagered and lost his entire collection of paintings by Nicolas Poussin (1594–1665) against Louis's own collection of works by Rubens in a tennis match between the two. A debate had long raged at court as to who was the better painter—Poussin or Rubens. Charles Le Brun had gone so far as to declare Poussin the greatest painter of the seventeenth century. Although a Frenchman, Poussin had spent most of his life in Rome. He particularly admired the work of Raphael and, following Raphael's example, advocated a Classical approach to painting. A painting's subject matter, he believed, should be drawn from Classical mythology or Christian tradition, not everyday life. There was no place in his theory of painting for a genre scene like Rubens's *The Kermis*, even if portrayed on a monumental scale. Painting technique itself should be controlled and refined. There could be no loose brushwork, no "rough style." Restraint and decorum had to govern all aspects of pictorial composition.

The Court Arts of England and Spain

Although the monarchs of Europe were often at war with one another, they were united in their belief in the power of the throne and the role of the arts in sustaining their authority. In England, the arts were dramatically affected by tension between the absolutist monarchy of the English Stuarts and the much more conservative Protestant population. As in France, throughout the seventeenth century, the English monarchy sought to assert its absolute authority, although it did not ultimately manage to do so. The first Stuart monarch, James I (r. 1603–1625), succeeded Queen Elizabeth I in 1603. "There are no privileges and immunities which can stand against a divinely appointed King," he quickly insisted.

James's son Charles I (r. 1625–1649) shared these absolutist convictions, but Charles's reign was beset by religious controversy. Although technically head of the Church of England, he married a Catholic, Henrietta Maria, sister of the French king Louis XIII. Charles proposed changes in the Church's liturgy that brought it, in the opinion of many, dangerously close to Roman Catholicism. Puritans (English Calvinists) increasingly dominated the English Parliament and strongly opposed any government that even remotely appeared to accept Catholic doctrine.

Parliament raised an army to oppose Charles, and civil war resulted, lasting from 1642 to 1648. The key political question was who should rule the country—the king or the Parliament? Led by Oliver Cromwell (1599–1658), the Puritans defeated the king in 1645, and executed him for treason on January 30, 1649, a severe blow to the divine right of kings. Meanwhile, Cromwell tried to lead a commonwealth—a republic dedicated to the common well-being of the people—but he soon dissolved the Parliament and assumed the role of Lord Protector. His protectorate occasionally called the Parliament into session, but only to ratify his own decisions. Cromwell's greatest difficulty was requiring the people to obey "godly" laws—in other words, Puritan doctrine. He forbade swearing, drunkenness, and cockfighting. No shops or inns could do business on Sunday. The country, used to the idea of a freely elected parliamentary government, could not tolerate such restriction, and when, in September 1658, Cromwell died, his system of government died with him.

The monarchy was restored, but the threat of the monarchy adopting Catholicism continued to cause dissension among Puritans. Finally, in September 1688, William of Orange, married to the Protestant daughter of James II, who had become king in 1685, invaded Britain from Holland at the invitation of the Puritan population. James II fled, and what has come to be called the Glorious Revolution ensued. Parliament enacted a Bill of Rights endorsing religious tolerance and prohibiting the king from annulling parliamentary law. Constitutional monarchy was reestablished once and for all in Britain, and the divine right of kings permanently suspended.

Anthony van Dyck in England The tension between the Catholic-leaning English monarchy and the Puritan-oriented

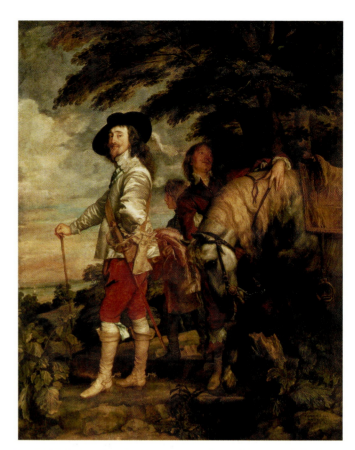

Fig. 10.31 Anthony Van Dyck, _Portrait of Charles I Hunting._ 1635. Oil on canvas, 8′11″ × 6′11″. Musée du Louvre, Paris. Inv.1236. Charles's posture, his left hand on his hip, and his right extended outward where it is supported by a cane, adopts the positions of the arms in court dance.

Parliament was exacerbated by the flamboyant style of the court, which offended more austere Puritan tastes. The court style is embodied in _Portrait of Charles I Hunting_ (Fig. **10.31**), by the Flemish artist Anthony Van Dyck (1599–1641), court painter to Charles I. Sometime in his teens, Van Dyck went to work in Rubens's workshop in Antwerp, and he led the studio by the time he was 17. Van Dyck's great talent was portraiture. After working in Italy in the 1620s, in 1632 he accepted the invitation of Charles I of England to come to London as court painter. He was knighted there in 1633. He often flattered his subjects by elongating their features and portraying them from below to increase their stature. In the case of the painting shown here, Van Dyck positioned Charles so that he stands a full head higher than the grooms behind him, lit in a brilliant light that glimmers off his silvery doublet. The angle of his jauntily cocked cavalier's hat is echoed in the trees above his head and the neck of his horse, which seems to bow to him in respect. He is, in fact, the very embodiment of the **Cavalier** (from the French _chevalier_, meaning "knight"), as his royalist supporters were known. Like the king here, Cavaliers were famous for their style of dress—long, flowing hair, elaborate clothing, and large, sometimes feathered hats.

Diego Velázquez in Spain Even as England endured its divisive religious wars, Spain remained dogmatically Catholic. But despite the wealth flowing into the country from its American empire, by 1600 Spain had entered a period of decline during which deteriorating economic and social conditions threatened the absolutist authority of its king. Severe inflation, a shift of population away from the countryside and into the cities, and a loss of population and therefore tax revenue brought the absolutist Spanish court to bankruptcy. To make matters worse, Philip IV (r. 1621–65), great-grandson of the Holy Roman Emperor Charles IV, embarked on a number of disastrous, highly costly military campaigns, culminating in 1659 with Spain accepting a humiliating peace with France. Nevertheless, even as the Spanish throne seemed to crumble, the arts flourished under the patronage of a court that recklessly indulged itself. So remarkable was the outpouring of Spanish arts and letters in the seventeenth century that the era is commonly referred to as the Spanish Golden Age.

The Spanish court understood that in order to assert its absolutist authority, it needed to impress the people through its patronage of the arts. So when Philip IV assumed the Spanish throne at the age of 16, his principal advisor suggested that his court should strive to rival all the others of Europe by employing the greatest painters of the day. The king agreed, hiring Rubens in the 1630s to paint a cycle of 112 mythologies for his hunting lodge. But when the 24-year-old Diego Rodríguez de Silva y Velázquez (1599–1660) was summoned to paint a portrait of the king in the spring of 1623, both the king and his advisor recognized that one of the great painters of seventeenth-century Europe was homegrown. An appointment as court painter quickly followed, and Velázquez became the only artist permitted to paint the king.

In 1628, when Rubens visited the Spanish court, Velázquez alone among artists in Madrid was permitted to visit with the master at work. And Velázquez guided Rubens through the royal collection, which included Bosch's *Garden of Earthly Delights* (see *Closer Look*, Chapter 8) and, most especially, Titian's *The Rape of Europa* (see Fig. 10.6), which had been painted expressly for Philip II. Rubens copied both. He also persuaded Velázquez to go to Italy from 1629 to 1630, where he studied the work of Titian in Venice. In Florence and Rome, Velázquez disliked the paintings of Raphael, whose linear style he found cold and inexpressive.

Velázquez's chief occupation as painter to Philip IV was painting court portraits and supervising the decoration of rooms in the various royal palaces and retreats. Most were portraits of individuals, but *Las Meninas* (*The Maids of Honor*) is a life-size group portrait and his last great royal commission (Fig. 10.32). It elevates the portrait to a level of complexity almost unmatched in the history of art. The source of this complexity is the competing focal points of the composition. At the very center of the painting, bathed in light, is the Infanta Margarita, beloved daughter of King Philip IV and Queen Mariana. In one sense, the painting is the Infanta's portrait, as she seems the primary focus. Yet the title *Las Meninas*, "The Maids of Honor," implies that her attendants are the painting's real subject. However, Velázquez has painted himself into the composition at work on a canvas, so the painting is, at least partly, also a self-portrait. The artist's gaze, as well as the gaze of the Infanta and her dwarf lady-in-waiting, and perhaps also of the courtier who has turned around in the doorway at the back of the painting, is focused on a spot outside the painting, in front of it, where we as viewers stand. The mirror at the back of the room, in which Philip and Mariana are reflected, suggests that the king and queen also occupy this position, acknowledging their role as Velázquez's patrons. This work continues to inspire artists to this day.

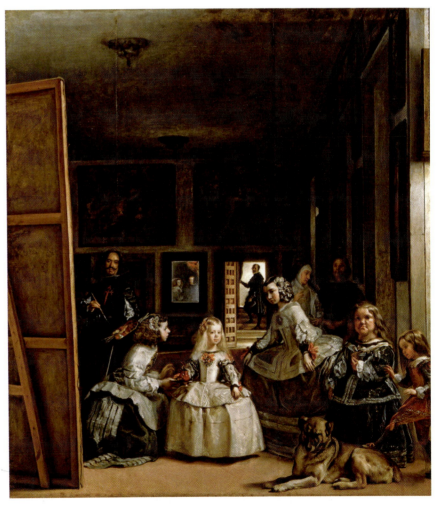

Fig. 10.32 Diego Velázquez, *Las Meninas (The Maids of Honor)*. 1656. Oil on canvas, 10'3¾" × 9'¾". Museo del Prado, Madrid. No other Velázquez painting is as tall as *Las Meninas*, which suggests that the back of the canvas in the foreground is, in fact, *Las Meninas* itself. Velázquez thus paints himself painting this painting.

View the Closer Look for *Las Meninas* on **MyArtsLab**

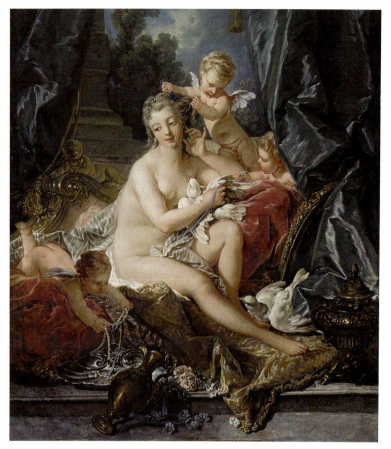

Fig. 11.14 François Boucher, _The Toilet of Venus_. 1751. Oil on canvas, 42⅝" × 33⅛". Signed and dated (lower right): f-Boucher-1751. The Metropolitan Museum of Art, New York. Bequest of William K. Vanderbilt, 1920 (20.155.9). Boucher's contemporaries likened his palette, which favored pinks, blues, and soft whites, to "rose petals floating in milk."

king's mistress. (Boucher was notoriously famous for such nudes.) _The Toilet of Venus_, for instance, was commissioned by Madame de Pompadour for the bathing suites of the chateau of Bellevue, one of six residences just outside Paris that Louis built for her (Fig. **11.14**). She had played the title role in a production called _La Toilette de Vénus_ staged at Versailles a year earlier, and evidently this is a scene—or more likely an idealized version of one—from that production. The importance of the work is that it openly acknowledges both Madame de Pompadour's sexual role in the court and the erotic underpinnings of the Rococo as a whole.

Jean-Honoré Fragonard Boucher's student Jean-Honoré Fragonard (1732–1806) carried his master's tradition into the next generation. Fragonard's most important commission was a series of four paintings for Marie-Jeanne Bécu, comtesse du Barry, the last mistress of Louis XV. Entitled _The Progress of Love_, it was to portray the relationship between Madame du Barry and the king, but in the guise of young people whose romance occurs in the garden park of the countess's chateau at Louveciennes, itself a gift from Louis.

The series was inspired by an earlier painting, _The Swing_ (Fig. **11.15**), a work that suggests an erotic intrigue between

two lovers. It implies as well the aesthetic intrigue between the artist and the patron, a conspiracy emphasized by the sculpture of Cupid to the left, holding his finger to his mouth as if to affirm the secrecy of the affair. The painting's subject matter was in fact suggested by another artist, Gabriel-François Doyen, who was approached by the baron de Saint-Julien to paint his mistress "on a swing which a bishop is setting in motion. You will place me in a position in which I can see the legs of the lovely child and even more if you wish to enliven the picture." Doyen declined the commission but suggested it to Fragonard.

Much of the power of the composition lies in the fact that the viewer shares, to a degree, the voyeuristic pleasures of the reclining lover. The entire image is charged with an erotic symbolism that would have been commonly understood at the time. For instance, the lady on the swing lets fly her shoe—the lost shoe and naked foot being a well-known symbol of lost virginity. The young man reaches toward her, hat in hand—the hat that in eighteenth-century erotic imagery was often used to cover the genitals of a discovered lover. Even more subtly, and ironically, the composition echoes the central panel of Michelangelo's Sistine Chapel ceiling, the _Creation of Adam_ (see Fig. 7.25 in Chapter 7). The male lover assumes Adam's posture, and the female lover God's, although she reaches toward Adam—to bring him to life, as it were—with her foot, not her hand.

Art Criticism and Theory

Art was in fact one of the most carefully cultivated pursuits of French intellectuals (and those with intellectual pretensions). By the last half of the eighteenth century, it was becoming increasingly fashionable for educated upper-class people to experience what the English called the "Grand Tour" and the French and Germans referred to as the "Italian Journey." Art and architecture were the focal points of these travels, along with picturesque landscapes and gardens. A new word was coined to describe the travelers themselves—"tourist."

Tourists then, as they do today, wanted to understand what they were seeing. Among the objects of their travel were art exhibitions, particularly the Paris Salon—the official exhibition of the French Royal Academy of Painting and Sculpture. It took place in the Salon Carré of the Louvre, which lent the exhibition its name. It ran from August 25 until the end of September almost every year from 1737 until 1751, and every other year from 1751 to 1791. But few visitors were well-equipped to appreciate or understand what they were seeing, so a new brand of writing soon developed in response: art criticism.

The _philosophe_ Denis Diderot (1717–83) began reviewing the official exhibitions of the Paris Salon in 1759 for a private newsletter circulated to a number of royal houses outside France. Many consider these essays (there are nine of them) the first art criticism. Boucher and his fellow Rococo

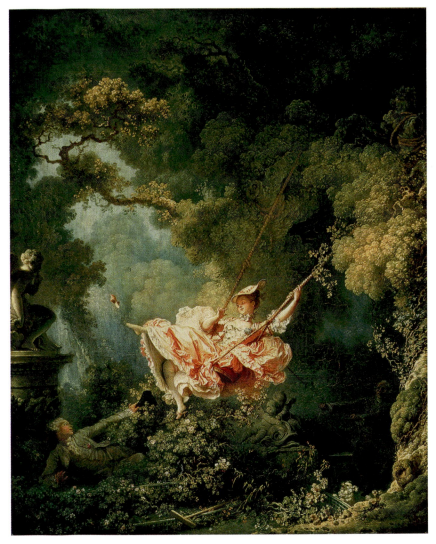

Fig. 11.15 Jean-Honoré Fragonard, *The Swing*. 1767. Oil on canvas, 32⅝″ × 26″. Wallace Collection, London. Contributing to the erotic overtones of the composition is the lush foliage of the overgrown garden into which the male lover has inserted himself.

View the Closer Look about Jean-Honoré Fragonard on **MyArtsLab**

(1699–1779). Considering the small Chardin still life *The Brioche* (Fig. **11.16**), a painting of the famous French bread or cake eaten at the breakfast table, Diderot in the *Salon of 1767* wrote: "One stops in front of a Chardin as if by instinct, as a traveler tired of his journey sits down almost without being aware of it in a spot that offers him a bit of greenery, silence, water, shade, and coolness." What impressed Diderot most was Chardin's use of paint: "Such magic leaves one amazed. There are thick layers of superimposed color and their effect rises from below to the surface.... Come closer, and everything becomes flat, confused, and indistinct; stand back again, and everything springs back into life and shape." What Diderot valued especially in Chardin's work was its detail, what amounts to an almost encyclopedic attention to the everyday facts of the world. As opposed to the Rococo artists of the court, whose *fêtes galantes*, he complained, conveyed only the affected and therefore false manners and conventions of polite society, Chardin was able to convey the truth of things. "I prefer rusticity to prettiness," Diderot proclaimed.

Despite Diderot's preference for subject matter of a "truthful" kind, he was fascinated with the individual work of art. He expressed this fascination in his description of its painterly surface beyond whatever "subject matter" it might possess. This fascination was part of a broader change in the way that the eighteenth century approached the arts in general.

artists were the object of his wrath. In 1763, Diderot asked: "Haven't painters used their brushes in the service of vice and debauchery long enough, too long indeed?" Painting, he argued, ought to be "moral." It should seek "to move, to educate, to improve us, and to induce us to virtue." And in his *Salon of 1765*, Diderot would complain about Boucher:

> I don't know what to say about this man. Degradation of taste, color, composition, character, expression, and drawing have kept pace with moral depravity.... And then there's such a confusion of objects piled one on top of the other, so poorly disposed, so motley, that we're dealing not so much with the pictures of a rational being as with the dreams of a madman.

An artist who did capture Diderot's imagination was the still-life and genre painter Jean-Baptiste Chardin

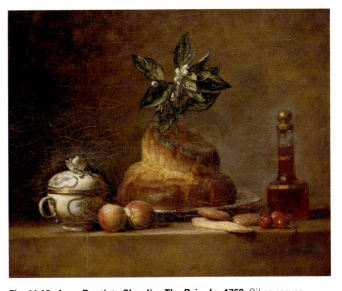

Fig. 11.16 Jean-Baptiste Chardin, *The Brioche*. 1763. Oil on canvas, 18½″ × 22″. Musée du Louvre, Paris. Chardin painted from dark to light, the brightest parts of the canvas coming last.

The Declaration of the Rights of Man and Citizen

In France, the situation leading to the signing of the Declaration of the Rights of Man and Citizen was somewhat more complicated. It was, in fact, the national debt that abruptly brought about the events leading to revolution, the overthrow of the royal government, and the country becoming a republic. In the 15 years after Louis XVI ascended to the throne in 1774, the debt tripled. In 1788, fully one-half of state revenues were dedicated to paying interest on debt already in place, despite the fact that two years earlier bankers had refused to make new loans to the government. The cost of maintaining Louis XVI's court was enormous, so the desperate king attempted to levy a uniform tax on all landed property. Riots, led by aristocrat and bourgeois alike, forced the king to bring the issue before an Estates General, an institution little used and indeed half-forgotten (it had not met since 1614).

The Estates General convened on May 5, 1789, at Versailles. It was composed of the three traditional French **estates**. The First Estate was the clergy, which comprised a mere 0.5 percent of the population (130,000 people) but controlled nearly 15 percent of French lands. The Second Estate was the nobility, consisting of only 2 percent of the population (about 500,000 people) but controlling about 30 percent of the land. The Third Estate was the rest of the population, composed of the bourgeoisie (around 2.3 million people), who controlled about 20 percent of the land, and the peasants (nearly 21 million people), who controlled the rest of the land, although many owned no land at all.

Traditionally, each estate deliberated separately and each was entitled to a single vote. Any issue before the Estates General thus required a vote of at least 2:1—and the consent of the crown—for passage. The clergy and nobility usually voted together, thus silencing the opinion of the Third Estate. But from the outset, the Third Estate demanded more clout, and the king was in no position to deny it. The winter of 1788 to 1789 had been the most severe in memory. In December, the temperature had dropped to −19° Celsius (or −2° Fahrenheit), freezing the Seine over to a considerable depth. The ice blockaded barges that normally delivered grain and flour to a city already filled by unemployed peasants seeking work. With flour already in short supply after a violent hailstorm had virtually destroyed the crop the previous summer, the price of bread almost doubled. As the Estates General opened, Louis was forced to appease the Third Estate in any way he could. First he "doubled the third," giving the Third Estate as many deputies as the other two estates combined. Then he was pressured to bring the three estates together to debate and "vote by head," each deputy having a single vote. Louis vacillated on this demand, but on June 17, 1789, the Third Estate withdrew from the Estates General, declared itself a National Assembly, and invited the other two estates to join it.

A number of the First Estate, particularly parish priests who worked closely with the common people, accepted the Third Estate's offer, but the nobility refused. When the king banned the commoners from their usual meeting place, they gathered nearby at the Jeu de Paume, an indoor tennis court at Versailles that still stands, and there, on June 20, 1789, swore an oath never to disband until they had given France a constitution. Jacques-Louis David recreated the scene a year later in a detailed sketch for a painting that he would never finish, as events overtook its subjects (Fig. **12.3**). David's plan, like Trumbull's celebration of the signing of the Declaration of Independence, was to combine exact observation (he drew the major protagonists from life) with monumentality on a canvas where everyone would be life-size (many of his subjects would soon fall out of favor with the revolution itself and be executed). The "winds of freedom" blow in through the windows as commoners look on. At the top left, these same winds turn an umbrella inside out, signaling the change to come. In the middle of the room, the man

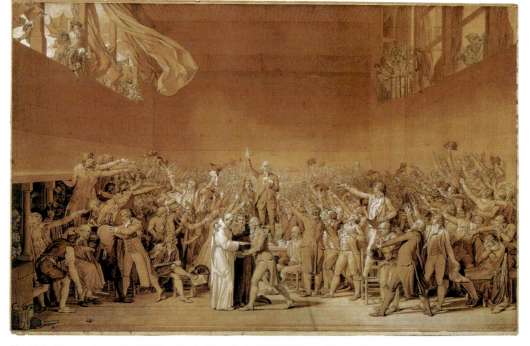

Fig. 12.3 Jacques-Louis David, *The Tennis Court Oath*. 1789–91. Pen and brown ink and brown wash on paper, 26″ × 42″. Musée National du Château, Versailles. MV 8409: INV Dessins. Note how the figures in this painting, all taking an oath, stretch out their hands in the manner of David's earlier Neoclassical masterpiece, *The Oath of the Horatii* (see Fig. 12.5).

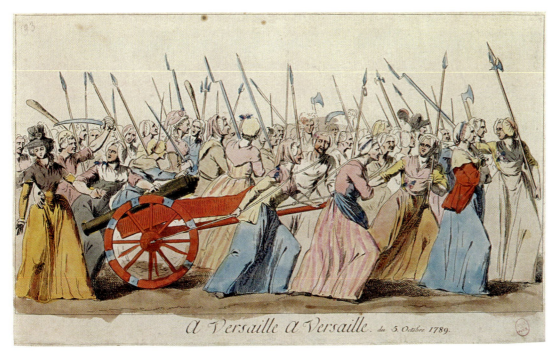

Fig. 12.4 *To Versailles, To Versailles, October 5, 1789.* Engraving. Musée de la Ville de Paris, Musée Carnavalet, Paris. The despair on the face of the aristocratic woman at the left contrasts sharply with the determined working-class women heading for Versailles.

who would soon become mayor of Paris reads the proclamation aloud. Below him a trio of figures, representing each of the three estates, clasp hands as equals in a gesture of unity. At the actual event, all the members of the National Assembly marched in alphabetical order and signed the Tennis Court Oath, except for one. He signed, but wrote after his name the word "opposed." David depicts him, an object of ridicule, seated at the far right, his arms folded despairingly across his chest. Faced with such unanimity, Louis gave in, and on June 27 he ordered the noble and clerical deputies to join the National Assembly.

But the troubles were hardly over. While the harvest was good, drought had severely curtailed the ability of watermills to grind flour from wheat. Just as citizens were lining up for what bread was available, a false rumor spread through the Paris press that the queen, Marie Antoinette, had flippantly remarked, on hearing that the people lacked bread, "Let them eat cake!" The antiroyalists so despised the queen that they were always willing to believe anything negative said about her. Peasant and working-class women, responsible for putting bread on the table, had traditionally engaged in political activism during times of famine or inflation, when bread became too expensive, and would march on the civic center to demand help from the local magistrates. But now, on October 5, 1789, about 7,000 Parisian women, many of them armed with pikes, guns, swords, and even cannon, marched on the palace at Versailles demanding bread (Fig. **12.4**). The next day, they marched back to the city with the king and queen in tow. The now essentially powerless royal couple lived as virtual prisoners of the people in their Paris palace at the Tuileries.

The National Assembly, which also relocated to Paris after the women's march on Versailles, had passed, on August 26, 1789, the Declaration of the Rights of Man and Citizen. It was a document deeply influenced by Jefferson's Declaration of Independence, as well as the writings of John Locke. It listed 17 "rights of man and citizen," among them these first three, which echo the opening of the American document (**Reading 12.2**):

Due process of law was guaranteed, freedom of religion was affirmed, and taxation based on the capacity to pay was announced.

READING 12.2

from the Declaration of the Rights of Man and Citizen (1789)

1. Men are born and remain free and equal in rights....
2. The aim of every political association is the preservation of the natural and imprescriptible [inherent or inalienable] rights of man. These rights are liberty, property, security, and resistance to oppression.
3. The principle of all sovereignty resides essentially in the nation. No body nor individual may exercise authority which does not proceed from the nation.

For a time, the king managed to appear as if he were cooperating with the National Assembly, which was busy drafting a constitution declaring a constitutional monarchy on the model of England. Then, in June 1791, just a couple of months before the new constitution was completed, Louis tried to flee France with his family, an act that seemed treasonous to most Frenchmen. The royals were evidently planning to join a large number of French nobility who had removed themselves to Germany, where they were actively seeking the support of Austria and Russia in a counter-revolution. A radical minority of the National Assembly, the **Jacobins**, had been lobbying for the elimination of the monarchy and the institution of egalitarian democracy for months. Louis's actions strengthened their position. When the Constitutional Convention met, it immediately declared France a republic, the only question being just what kind. Moderates favored executive and legislative branches independent of each other and laws that would be submitted to the people for approval. But Jacobin extremists, led by Maximilien Robespierre (1758–94), argued for what he called a "Republic of Virtue," a dictatorship led by a 12-person Committee for Public Safety, of which he was a member. A second Committee for General Security sought out enemies of the republic and turned them over to the new Revolutionary Tribunal, which over the course of the next three years executed as many as 25,000 citizens of France. These included not only royalists and aristocrats, but also good republicans whose moderate positions were in opposition to Robespierre. Louis XVI himself was tried and convicted as "Citizen Louis Capet" (the last of the Capetian dynasty) on January 21, 1793, and his queen, Marie Antoinette, referred to as "the widow Capet," was executed 10 months later. As Robespierre explained, defending his Reign of Terror:

> If virtue be the spring of popular government in times of peace, the spring of that government during a revolution is virtue combined with terror.... Terror is only justice prompt, severe, and inflexible; it is then an emanation of virtue....
>
> It has been said that terror is the spring of despotic government.... The government in revolution is the despotism of liberty against tyranny.

The Constitutional Convention instituted many other reforms as well. Some bordered on the silly—expunging the king and queen from the deck of cards and eliminating use of the formal *vous* ("thou") in discourse, substituting the informal *tu* ("you") in its place. Others were of greater import. The delegates banned slavery in all the French colonies. They de-Christianized the country, requiring that all churches become "Temples of Reason." The calendar was no longer to be based on the year of the birth of Christ, but on the first day of the Republic. Year one began, then, on September 21, 1792. New names, associated with the seasons and the climate, were given to the months. "Thermidor," for instance, was the month of Heat, roughly late July through early August. Finally, the idea of the Sunday sabbath was eliminated, and every tenth day was a holiday.

📖 **Read** the document by Jacques-Louis David on **MyArtsLab**

The Reign of Terror ended suddenly in the summer of 1794. Robespierre pushed through a law speeding up the work of the Tribunal, with the result that in six weeks some 1,300 people were sent to their deaths. Finally, he was hounded out of the Convention to shouts of "Down with the tyrant!" and chased to city hall. There he tried to shoot himself, but he succeeded only in shattering his lower jaw. He was executed the next day with 21 others.

The last act of the convention was to pass a constitution on August 17, 1795. It established France's first bicameral (two-body) legislature, led by a five-person executive Directory. Over the next four years, the Directory improved the lot of French citizens, but its relative instability worried moderates. So, in 1799, the successful young commander of the army, Napoleon Bonaparte (1769–1821), conspired with two of the five directors in the *coup d'état* that ended the Directory's experiment with republican government. This coup would put Napoleon in a position to assume control of the country. He dreamed that he might lead a new classical empire—a Neoclassical empire—modeled on that of Rome.

THE NEOCLASSICAL SPIRIT

What is Neoclassicism in art and architecture?

The rise of the Neoclassical in France, with its regularity, balance, and proportion, can be attributed to the same ideals that would lead to the overthrow of the aristocracy in the French Revolution. The civilizations of Greece and Rome were considered as close to a Golden Age as the Western world had ever come, and the aim of any revolution was to restore the intellectual and artistic values that those Classical civilizations embodied. But France had more recent examples of order and balance as well in, for instance, the formal symmetry of the gardens at Versailles (see Fig. 10.24 in Chapter 10). The Neoclassical could also claim descent from Poussin (see Fig. 10.29) and Palladio, not coincidentally Jefferson's favorite architect (see Fig. 7.38 in Chapter 7). But it was in the painting of Jacques-Louis David (1748–1825) that the Neoclassical found its first full expression.

Jacques-Louis David and the Neoclassical Style

David's career stretches from pre-Revolutionary Paris, through the turmoil of the Revolution and its aftermath, and across the reign of Napoleon Bonaparte. He was, without doubt, the most influential artist of his day. "I do not feel an interest in any pencil but that of David," Thomas Jefferson wrote in a flush of enthusiasm from Paris during his service as minister to the court of Louis XVI from 1885 to 1889. And artists flocked to David's studio for the privilege of studying with him. In fact, many of the major artists of the following century were his students.

David abandoned the traditional complexity of composition that had defined French academic history painting for decades and substituted a formal balance and simplicity that are fully Neoclassical. His works had a frozen

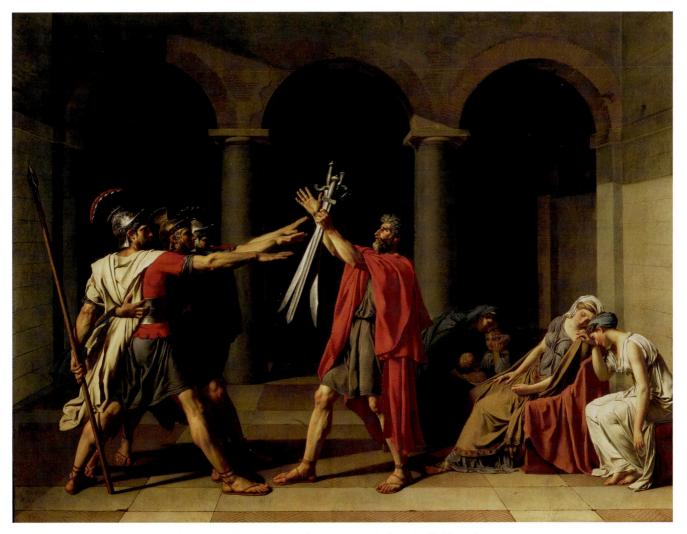

Fig. 12.5 Jacques-Louis David, *The Oath of the Horatii*. 1784–85. Oil on canvas, 10'10" × 13'11½". Musée du Louvre, Paris. The clarity of David's composition is also attributable to the fact that he has reintroduced a frontal, one-point perspective largely abandoned in European painting since Raphael. Compare, for instance, Raphael's *School of Athens* (see *Closer Look*, Chapter 7).

 View the *Closer Look* for *The Oath of the Horatii* on **MyArtsLab**

quality to emphasize rationality, and the brushstrokes were invisible to create a clear focus and to highlight details. At the same time, his works had considerable emotional complexity. A case in point is his painting *The Oath of the Horatii* (Fig. **12.5**), commissioned by the royal government in 1784 to 1785. The story is a sort of parable or example of loyal devotion to the state. It concerns the conflict between early Rome, led by Horatius, and neighboring Alba, led by Curatius. In order to spare a war that would be more generally destructive, the two civic leaders agreed to send their three sons—the Horatii and the Curatii—to battle each other. David was contemplating painting the battle's aftermath, when Horatius's youngest son, the sole survivor of the conflict, murders his sister Camilla, whom he discovered mourning the loss of her husband, one of the Curatii.

But David chose instead to present the moment *before* the battle when the three sons of Horatius swear an oath to their father, promising to fight to the death. The sons on the left, the father in the middle, and the sisters to the right are each clearly and simply contained within the frame of one of three arches behind them. Except for Horatius's robe, the colors are muted and spare, the textures plain, and the paint itself almost flat. The male figures stand rigidly in profile, their legs extending forward tensely, as straight as the spear held by the foremost brother, which they parallel. Their orderly Neoclassical arrangement contrasts with that of the women, who are disposed in a more conventional, Baroque grouping. Seated, even collapsing, while the men stand erect, the women's soft curves and emotional despair contrast with the male realm of the painting. David's message here is that civic responsibility must eclipse the joys of domestic life, just as reason supplants emotion and Classical order supplants Baroque complexity. Sacrifice is the price of citizenship (a message that Louis XVI would have been wise to heed).

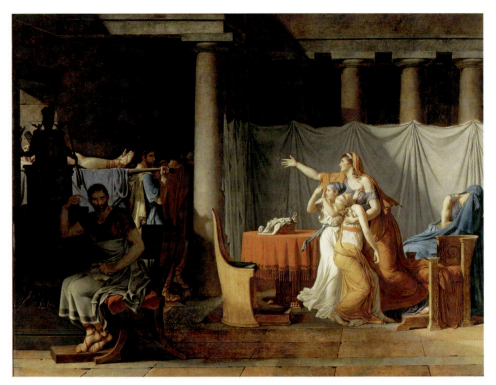

Fig. 12.6 Jacques-Louis David, *The Lictors Returning to Brutus the Bodies of His* Sons. 1789. Oil on canvas, 10′7¼″ × 13′10¼″. Musée du Louvre, Paris. Brutus' emotional exile from his proper place at the table as patriarch is signaled by the empty chair and the subtle analogy between Brutus' own toes and the scrolling decoration at the base of the table where he once sat.

 View the *Closer Look* for *The Lictors Returning to Brutus the Bodies of His Sons* on **MyArtsLab**

David's next major canvas, *The Lictors Returning to Brutus the Bodies of His Sons* (Fig. **12.6***)*, was painted in 1789, the year of the Revolution but before it had begun. It is a more complex response to the idea of sacrifice for the state. The painting shares with the *Oath of the Horatii* the theme of a stoic father's sacrifice of his sons for the good of the state, as Brutus' lictors (the officers in his service as ruler) return the sons' bodies to him after their execution.

The hero of the historical tale that is the subject of this painting is the founder of the Roman republic, Lucius Junius Brutus (sixth century BCE; not to be confused with the Brutus who would later assassinate Julius Caesar). He had become head of Rome and inaugurated the republic by eliminating the former monarch, Tarquinius, who himself had assumed the throne by conspiring with the wife of the former king. She murdered her husband, and he his own wife, and the two married. Brutus' sons had conspired to restore the monarchy—their mother was related to Tarquinius—and under Roman law Brutus was required not only to sentence them to death but also to witness the execution.

In David's painting, Brutus sits in shadow at the left, his freshly beheaded sons passing behind him on stretchers carried by the lictors. Brutus points ignominiously at his own head, as if affirming his responsibility for the deed, the sacrifice of family to the patriotic demands of the state. In contrast to the dark shadows in which Brutus sits, the boys' mother, nurse, and sisters await the bodies in a fully lighted stage space framed by a draperied colonnade. The mother reaches out in a gesture reminiscent of Horatius's in the *Oath of the Horatii*. The nurse turns and buries her head in the mother's robe. One of the sisters appears to faint in her mother's arms, while the other shields her eyes from the terrible sight. Their spotlit anguish emphasizes the high human cost of patriotic sacrifice, whereas the *Oath of the Horatii* more clearly celebrates the patriotic sacrifice itself.

Although David would serve the new French Republic with verve and loyalty as its chief painter after the Revolution, his paintings are rarely as straightforward as they at first appear. In his work, it would seem, the austerity of the Neoclassical style is something of a mask for an emotional turbulence within, a turbulence that the style holds in check.

Napoleon's Neoclassical Tastes

If it was the threat of economic and international chaos—including a new coalition formed against France by England, Austria, Russia, and the Ottomans—that guaranteed Napoleon's successful *coup d'état*, it was, perhaps, his understanding of the power of the Neoclassical style to reflect not chaos but order that led him to adopt it—quite intentionally for propagandistic purposes—as the image of the state. Order was the call of the day, and Napoleon was bent on restoring it.

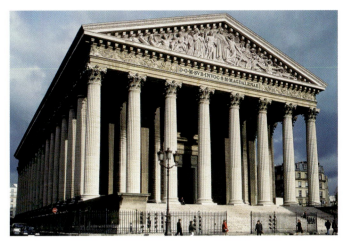

Fig. 12.7 Pierre-Alexandre Vignon, La Madeleine, Paris. 1806–42. Length 350′, width 147′, height of podium 23′, height of columns 63′. The church of La Madeleine was built to culminate a north–south axis that began on the Left Bank of the Seine at the Chamber of Deputies (newly refurbished with a facade of Corinthian columns), crossing a new bridge northward into the Place de la Concorde.

Seeking to lend Paris a sense of order and reason, he soon commissioned the construction of Roman arches of triumph and other classically inspired monuments to commemorate his victories and convey the political message of the glory of his rule. One of the most impressive works was the redesign of a church that had been started under Louis XVI but that Napoleon wanted to see reinterpreted as a new Temple of the Glory of the Grand Army. This work, commissioned in 1806 from Pierre-Alexandre Vignon (1763–1828), was to have been identified by the following dedicatory inscription: "From the Emperor to the soldiers of the Great Army." It was another of the many Parisian churches that were converted to secular temples during the revolution. Ironically, Napoleon reversed his decision to honor the army in 1813 after the unfortunate Battle of Leipzig and the loss of Spain. Although work continued on the building, its original name, the church of La Madeleine, was restored.

Not completed until after Napoleon's downfall, but nevertheless to Vignon's original design, La Madeleine is imperially Roman in scale and an extraordinary example of Neoclassical architecture (Fig. **12.7**). Eight 63-foot-high Corinthian columns dominate its portico, and 18 more rise to the same height on each side. Beneath the Classical roof line of its exterior, Vignon created three shallow interior domes that admit light through *oculi* at their tops that are hidden by the roofline. They light a long nave without aisles that culminates in an apse roofed by a semidome. This interior evokes traditional Christian architecture, even as the exterior announces its Classicism through the Roman temple features.

Napoleon also modeled his government on ancient Roman precedents. By 1802, he had convinced the legislators to declare him First Consul of the French Republic for life, with the power to amend the constitution as he saw fit. In 1804, he persuaded the Senate to go a step further and declare that "the government of the republic is entrusted to an emperor." This created the somewhat paradoxical situation of a "free" people ruled by the will of an individual. But Napoleon was careful to seek the consent of the electorate in all these moves. When he submitted his constitution and other changes to the voters in a plebiscite (a "yes" or "no" vote), they ratified them by an overwhelming majority.

Napoleon justified voter confidence by moving to establish stability across Europe by force. To this end, in 1800 he crossed into Italy and took firm control of the regions of Piedmont and Lombardy. Although Napoleon never defeated the British, his principal enemy, from 1805 to 1807 he launched a succession of campaigns against Britain's allies, Austria and Prussia. He defeated both, and by 1807 the only European countries outside Napoleon's sphere of influence were Britain, Portugal, and Sweden. Everywhere he was victorious, he brought the reforms that he had established in France and overturned much of the old political and social order.

David, who had survived the revolutionary era and painted many of its events, went on to portray many of the major moments of Napoleon's career. He celebrated the Italian campaign in *Napoleon Crossing the Saint-Bernard* (Fig. **12.8**). Here he depicts Napoleon on horseback leading his troops across the pass at Saint-Bernard in the Alps. In its

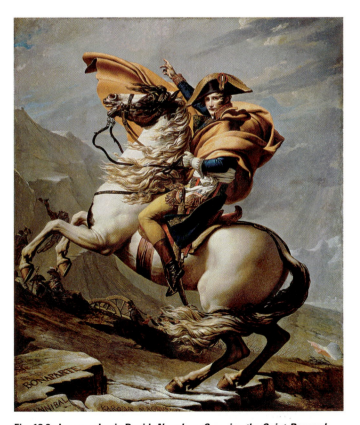

Fig. 12.8 Jacques-Louis David, *Napoleon Crossing the Saint-Bernard.* 1800–01. Oil on canvas, 8′11″ × 7′7″. Musée National du Château de la Malmaison, Rueil-Malmaison, France. David would claim to everyone, "Bonaparte is my hero!" This is one of five versions of the painting, which differ significantly in color, painted by David and his workshop. There are also many copies in French museums and elsewhere done by others.

clearly drawn central image and its emphasis on right angles (consider Napoleon's leg, the angle of his pointing arm to his body, the relation of the horse's head and neck, and the angle of its rear legs), the painting is fully Neoclassical. In the background, as is typical of David, is a more turbulent scene as Napoleon's troops drag a cannon up the pass. In the foreground, inscribed on the rocks, are the names of the only generals who crossed the Alps into Italy: Hannibal, whose brilliance in defeating the Romans in the third century BCE Napoleon sought to emulate; Karolus Magnus (Charlemagne); and Napoleon.

Actually, Napoleon did not lead the crossing of the pass but crossed it with his rear guard, mounted on a mule led by a peasant. So the work is pure propaganda, designed to create a proper myth for the aspiring leader. Although still four years from crowning himself emperor, the First Consul in his identification with the great Frankish emperor of the Holy Roman Empire, Charlemagne, makes clear his aspirations to unite Europe and rule it. Napoleon was boldly creating a myth that is probably nowhere better expressed than by the great German philosopher Georg Wilhelm Friedrich Hegel (1770–1831) in a letter of October 13, 1806: "I have seen the emperor, that world soul, pass through the streets of the town on horseback. It is a prodigious sensation to see an individual like him who, concentrated at one point, seated on a horse, spreads over the world and dominates it."

Neoclassicism in America

The founders of the newly created United States of America modeled their new republic on Classical precedents. Their democracy would be modeled on what they believed were the first democracies, those of Athens and Rome. On October 27, 1787, a Federal Convention presented the states with a new constitution. James Madison (1751–1836) had been responsible for drafting the constitution itself, and his inspiration came from ancient Greece and Rome. (Among his papers was a list of books he thought were essential for understanding the American political system, among them Edward Gibbon's *On the Decline of the Roman Empire*, Basil Kennett's *Antiquities of Rome*, Plutarch's *Lives*, Plato's *Republic*, and Aristotle's *A Treatise on Government*.)

The Neoclassical style of architecture dominated the architecture of the new American republic, where it became known as the **Federal style**. Its foremost champion was, of course, Jefferson. Like almost all leaders of the American colonies, Jefferson was well-educated in the classics and knew such works as James Stuart and Nicholas Revett's *Antiquities of Athens* (1758) and Robert and James Adam's *Works in Architecture* well. His taste for the classical would affect the design, the furniture, and even the gardens at his home, Monticello, outside Charlottesville, Virginia (see Fig. 7.37 in Chapter 7).

Jefferson's Neoclassical tastes were not limited to his private life. He designed the Virginia State Capitol in Richmond, which was, first of all, a "capitol," the very name derived from Rome's Capitoline Hill (Fig. 12.9). The building was a literal copy of the Maison Carrée in Nîmes, France, a Roman temple built in the first century BCE. To ensure that the country grew in an orderly manner, Jefferson proposed in 1785 that Congress pass a land ordinance requiring all new communities to be organized according to a grid. The measure resulted in a regular system of land survey across the North American continent. It effectively imposed a Neoclassical pattern on the American landscape.

The nation's new capitol in Washington, D.C., would, however, modify Jefferson's rectilinear scheme. President George Washington believed that the swampy, humid site along the Potomac River required something magnificent, so he hired Major Pierre Charles L'Enfant (1754–1825) to create a more ambitious design. The son of a court painter at Versailles, L'Enfant had emigrated to America from Paris in 1776 to serve in the Continental army. His plan (Fig. 12.10) is a conscious echo of the diagonal approaches and garden pathways at Versailles (see Fig. 10.24 in Chapter 10), superimposed on Jefferson's grid. The result is an odd mixture of angles and straightaways that mirrored, though unintentionally, the complex workings of the new American state. Visiting in 1842, a half century later, the English novelist Charles Dickens would be struck by the city's absurdity: "Spacious avenues... begin in nothing, and lead nowhere; streets, mile-long, that only want houses, roads, and inhabitants; public buildings that need but a public to be complete." It was, he wrote, a city of "Magnificent Intentions," as yet unrealized.

Fig. 12.9 Benjamin Henry Latrobe, *View of Richmond Showing Jefferson's Capitol from Washington Island.* 1796. Watercolor on paper, ink and wash, 7" × 10⅜". Maryland Historical Society, Baltimore. No view of an American capitol in the eighteenth century better captures the almost audacious aspirations of the new nation.

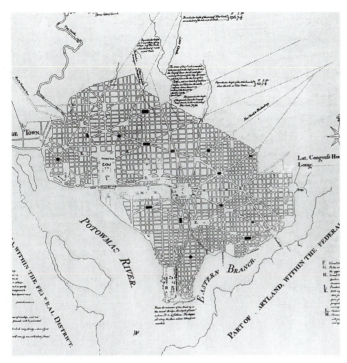

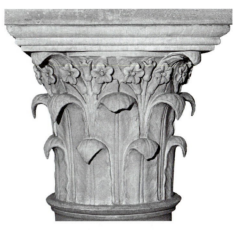

Fig. 12.11 Benjamin Henry Latrobe, tobacco-leaf capital for the U.S. Capitol, Washington, D.C. ca. 1815. Despite this unique design, Latrobe used more traditional capitals elsewhere in the Capitol. For the Supreme Court area of the building, he designed Doric capitals in proportions similar to those at Paestum (see Fig. 2.13 in Chapter 2).

Fig. 12.10 Pierre Charles L'Enfant, plan for Washington, D.C. (detail). 1791. Published in the *Gazette of the United States*, Philadelphia, January 4, 1792. Engraving after the original drawing, Library of Congress, Washington, d.c. The architect, L'enfant, had served as a volunteer in the Revolutionary War. He also designed Federal Hall in New York City, which hosted the first Continental Congress in 1789.

CONTINUITY & CHANGE

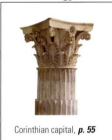

Corinthian capital, *p. 55*

The city somewhat oddly combined Neoclassical cultivation with what might be called rural charm. When Jefferson's disciple the architect Benjamin Henry Latrobe (1764–1820) was hired to rebuild the Capitol after the British burned it during the war of 1812, he invented a new design for the capitals of the Corinthian columns in the vestibule and rotunda of the Senate wing, substituting corncobs and tobacco for the Corinthian acanthus leaves (Fig. **12.11**).

The Issue of Slavery

The high-minded idealism reflected in the American adoption of Neoclassicism in its art and architecture was clouded, from the outset, by the issue of slavery. In the debates leading up to the Revolution, slavery had been lumped into the debate over free trade. Americans had protested not only the tax on everyday goods shipped to the colonies from Britain, including glass, paint, lead, paper, and tea, but also the English monarchy's refusal to allow the colonies to trade freely with other parts of the world, and that included the trade in enslaved Africans.

The Atlantic slave trade followed an essentially triangular pattern (see Map 9.3, p. 288). Europe exported goods to Africa, where they were traded for African slaves, who were then taken to the West Indies and traded for sugar, cotton, and tobacco; these goods were then shipped either

back to Europe or north to New England for sale. Since the slaves provided essentially free labor for the plantation owners, these goods, when sold, resulted in enormous profits. Although a port like Boston might seem relatively free of the slave trade, Boston's prosperity and the prosperity of virtually every other port on the Atlantic depended on slavery as an institution. And the American taste for Neoclassical art, epitomized by Josiah Wedgwood's assertion that for "North America we cannot make anything too rich and costly," was in very large part satisfied by the slave trade.

The conditions on board slave ships were described by Olaudah Equiano, a native of Benin, in West Africa, who was kidnapped and enslaved in 1756 at age 11. Freed in 1766, he traveled widely, educated himself, and mastered the English language. In his autobiography, published in England in 1789, he describes the transatlantic journey (**Reading 12.3**):

READING 12.3

from Olaudah Equiano, *The Interesting Narrative of the Life of Olaudah Equiano, or Gustavus Vassa the African* (1789)

The stench of the hold while we were on the coast [of Africa] was so intolerably loathsome that it was dangerous to remain there for any time, and some of us had been permitted to stay on the deck for the fresh air, but now that the whole ship's cargo were confined together it became absolutely pestilential. The closeness of the place and the heat of the climate, added to the number in the ship, which was so crowded that each had scarcely room to turn himself, almost suffocated us. This produced copious perspirations, so that the air soon became unfit for respiration from a variety of loathsome smells, and brought on a sickness among the slaves, of which many died, thus falling victims to the improvident avarice, as I may call it, of their purchasers. This wretched situation was again aggravated by the galling of the chains, now become insupportable; and the filth of the necessary tubs, into which the children often fell and were almost suffocated. The shrieks of the women and the groans of the dying soon rendered the whole a scene of horror almost inconceivable.

Recent biographical discoveries cast doubt on Equiano's claim that he was born and raised in Africa and that he endured the Middle Passage (the name given to the slave ships' journey across the Atlantic Ocean) as he describes. Baptismal and naval records suggest, instead, that he was born around 1747 in South Carolina. Still, if Equiano did fabricate his early life, it appears that he did so based on the verbal accounts of his fellow slaves, for the story he tells, when compared to other sources, is highly accurate. Whatever the case, Equiano's book became a best seller among the over 100 volumes on the subject of slavery published the same year, and it became essential reading for the ever-growing abolitionist movement in both England and the Americas.

The lot of the slaves, once they were delivered to their final destination, hardly improved. One of the most interesting accounts is *Narrative of a Five Years' Expedition against the Revolted Negroes of Surinam, in Guiana, on the Wild Coast of South America, from the Year 1772 to 1777*, written by John Gabriel Stedman (1747–97) and illustrated by William Blake (1757–1827) (Fig. **12.12**). Blake was already an established engraver and one of England's leading poets. Stedman had been hired by the Dutch to suppress rebel slaves in Guiana, but once there, he was shocked to see the conditions the slaves were forced to endure. Their housing was deplorable, but worse, they were routinely whipped, beaten, and otherwise tortured for the nonperformance of impossible tasks, as a means of instilling a more general discipline. Female slaves endured sexual abuses that were coarse beyond belief. The planters maintained what amounted to harems on their estates and freely indulged their sexual appetites.

Slavery pitted abolitionist sentiments against free-thinking economic theory. Free-trade economists, such as Adam Smith (1723–90), would argue that people should be free to do whatever they might to enrich themselves. Thus Smith would claim that a **laissez-faire**, "let it happen as it will," economic policy was the best. "It is the maxim of every prudent master of a family," Smith wrote in *The Wealth of Nations*, published in 1776, "never to make at home what it will cost him more to make than to buy.... What is prudence in the conduct of every private family, can scarce be folly in that of a great kingdom. If a foreign country can supply us with a commodity cheaper than we ourselves can make it, better buy it of them." Labor, it could be argued, was just such a commodity and slavery its natural extension.

In 1776, arguments for and against slavery seemed, to many people, to balance each other out. Economics and practicality favored the practice of slavery, while human sentiment and, above all, the idea of freedom denied it. Although at the time he wrote the Declaration

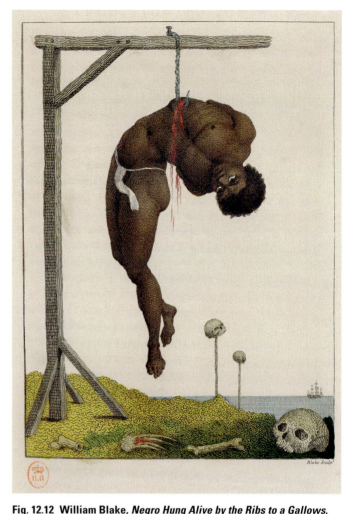

Fig. 12.12 William Blake, *Negro Hung Alive by the Ribs to a Gallows*, engraved illustration to John Gabriel Stedman's *Narrative of a Five Years' Expedition against the Revolted Negroes of Surinam*. 1796. Private collection. Blake executed the etchings for Stedman's volume after original drawings by Stedman himself. Stedman was impressed that the young man being tortured here stoically endured the punishment in total silence.

of Independence, Jefferson himself owned about 200 slaves and knew that other Southern delegates supported slavery as necessary for the continued growth of their agricultural economy, in his first draft he had forcefully repudiated the practice. Abigail Adams (1744–1818), who, like her husband, John, knew and respected Jefferson, but unlike him owned no slaves, was equally adamant on the subject: "I wish most sincerely," she wrote her husband in 1774, as he was attending the First Continental Congress in Philadelphia, "that there was not a slave in the province. It always seemed a most iniquitous scheme to me—to fight ourselves for what we are daily robbing and plundering from those who have as good a right to freedom as we have."

The CONTINUING PRESENCE
of the Past

See Kara Walker, *Insurrection! (Our Tools Were Rudimentary, Yet We Pressed On)*, 2000, at **MyArtsLab**

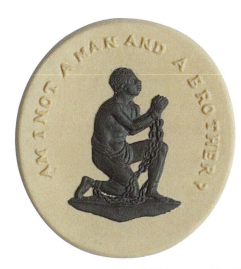

Fig. 12.13 William Hackwood, for Josiah Wedgwood, "Am I Not a Man and a Brother?" 1787. Black-and-white jasperware, 1⅜" × 1⅜". The Wedgwood Museum, Barlaston, Staffordshire, England. The image illustrated Erasmus Darwin's poem "The Botanic Garden," which celebrates not only the natural world, but also the rise of British manufacturing at the dawn of the Industrial Revolution. The poem nevertheless severely criticized British involvement in the slave trade, which it deemed highly "unnatural."

Many Britons, looking from across the Atlantic at the American Revolution, shared Abigail Adams's sentiments. As long as the colonies tolerated slavery, their demand for their own liberty seemed hypocritical. The English poet Thomas Day (1748–89) described the typical American as "signing resolutions of independence with one hand, and with the other brandishing a whip over his affrighted slaves."

Abolitionist opposition to slavery in both England and the American colonies began to gain strength in 1771 when Granville Sharp pled the case of an escaped American slave, James Somerset, before the Lord Chief Justice, Lord Mansfield. Somerset's American owner had recaptured him in England, but the Lord Chief Justice set Somerset free, ruling that the laws governing another country carried no weight in England. Leading the fight against slavery were the Quakers as well as the members of the Lunar Society (see Chapter 11). In 1787, Josiah Wedgwood made hundreds of ceramic cameos of a slave in chains, on bent knee, pleading, "Am I Not a Man and a Brother?" (Fig. **12.13**). He distributed them widely, and the image quickly became the emblem for the abolitionist movement as a whole. In Philadelphia, Benjamin Franklin, president of the Philadelphia Abolitionist Society, received a set.

THE ROMANTIC IMAGINATION

What is Romanticism and how does it manifest itself in both literature and painting?

Originally coined in 1798 by the German writer and poet Friedrich von Schlegel (1772–1829), the term "Romanticism" described an overt reaction against the Enlightenment and Classical culture of the eighteenth century. For Schlegel, Romanticism refers mainly to his sense that the common cultural ground of Europe—the Classical past from which it had descended, and the values of which it shared—was disintegrating, as Europeans formed new nation-states based on individual cultural identities.

Schlegel's own thinking was deeply influenced by the philosopher Immanuel Kant. In his *Critique of Judgment* (1790), Kant defined the pleasure we derive from art as "disinterested satisfaction." By this he meant that contemplating beauty, whether in nature or in a work of art, put the mind into a state of free play in which things that seemed to oppose each other—subject and object, reason and imagination—are united. Schlegel was equally influenced by the perspective on Greek art offered by Johann Winckelmann (1717–68) in his *History of Ancient Art* (1764)—the first book to include the words "history" and "art" in its title. What the Greeks offered were not works of art to be slavishly imitated, in the manner of Neoclassical artists. For Winckelmann, and for Schlegel, the Greeks provided a new way for the Romantic artist to approach nature: The Greeks studied nature in order to discover its essence. Nature only occasionally rises to moments of pure beauty. The lesson taught by the Greeks, Winckelmann argued, was that art might capture and hold those rare moments.

As a way of approaching the world, the Romantic movement amounts to a revolution in human consciousness. Dedicated to the discovery of beauty in nature, the Romantics rejected the truth of empirical observation, which John Locke and other Enlightenment thinkers had championed. The objective world mattered far less to them than their subjective experience of it. The poet Samuel Taylor Coleridge (1772–1834), one of the founders of the Romantic movement, offered a pithy summary in a letter to a friend: "My opinion is this—that deep Thinking is attainable only by a man of deep Feeling, and that all Truth is a species of Revelation." Knowing the exact distance between the earth and the moon mattered far less than how it *felt* to look at the moon in the dark sky. And it must be remembered that for Romantics, the night was incomparably more appealing, because it was more mysterious and unknowable, than the daylight world.

Nor did they believe that the human mind was necessarily a thinking thing, as René Descartes had argued, when he wrote, "I think, therefore I am." For the Romantics, the mind was a feeling thing, not distinct from the body as Descartes had it, but intimately connected to it. Feelings, they believed, led to truth, and most of the major writers and artists of the early nineteenth century used their emotions as a primary way of expressing their imagination and creativity. Indeed, since nature stimulated the emotions as it did the imagination, the natural world became the primary subject of Romantic poetry, and landscape the primary genre of Romantic painting. In nature the Romantics discovered not just the wellspring of their own creativity, but the very presence of God, the manifestation of the divine on earth.

The Romantic Poem

The Romantic imagination found its first—and certainly its most articulate—expression in poetry. Poetry by its nature is almost inherently intuitive and personal. It is a medium capable of expressing the most deeply felt emotions. And in the beauty of its expression—the eloquence of its sounds and cadences—it might capture, even mirror, the beauty of nature itself.

William Wordsworth's "Tintern Abbey" Perhaps the most eloquent expression of the Romantic imagination is a poem by William Wordsworth (1770–1850) generally known by the shortened title "Tintern Abbey." Its complete title is "Lines Composed a Few Miles above Tintern Abbey, on Revisiting the Banks of the Wye during a Tour, July 13, 1798." Tintern Abbey is a ruined medieval monastery on the banks of the Wye River in South Wales, Britain. Its roofless buildings were open to the air and its skeletal Gothic arches overgrown with weeds and saplings (Fig. **12.14**). In the late eighteenth century, it was common for British travelers to tour the beautiful Wye River, and the final destination of the journey was the abbey itself.

Wordsworth had visited the valley of the Wye five years before he wrote the poem, and he begins his poem by thinking back to that earlier trip (**Reading 12.4**):

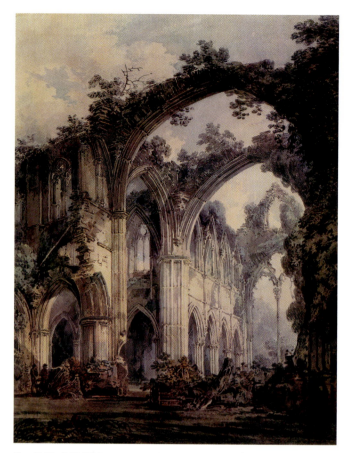

Fig. 12.14 J. M. W. Turner, *Interior of Tintern Abbey*. 1794. Watercolor, 12⅝" × 9⅞". Victoria and Albert Museum, London. Turner toured South Wales and the Wye Valley in 1792, when he was 19 years old. This watercolor is based on a sketch made on that trip.

READING 12.4

from William Wordsworth, "Tintern Abbey" (1798)

Five years have passed; five summers, with the length
Of five long winters! and again I hear
These waters, rolling from their mountain-springs
With a soft inland murmur. —Once again
Do I behold these steep and lofty cliffs,
That on a wild secluded scene impress
Thoughts of more deep seclusion; and connect
The landscape with the quiet of the sky.

The implication is that the scene evokes thoughts "more deep" than mere appearance, thoughts in which landscape and sky—and perhaps the poet himself—are all connected, united as one.

After describing the scene before him at greater length, the poet then recalls the solace that his memories of the place had brought him in the five intervening years as he had lived "in lonely rooms, and 'mid the din/ Of towns and cities." His memories of the place, he says, brought him "tranquil restoration," but even more important, "another gift," in which "the weary weight/Of all this unintelligible world,/ Is lightened" by allowing the poet to "see into the life of things." Wordsworth does not completely comprehend the power of the human mind here. What the mind achieves at such moments remains to him something of a "mystery." But it seems to him as if his breath and blood, his very body—that

"corporeal frame"—is suspended in a "power /Of harmony" that informs all things.

Wordsworth next describes how he reacted to the scene as a boy. The scene, he says, was merely "an appetite." But now, as an adult, he looks on the natural world differently. He finds in nature a connection between landscape, sky, and thought that is intimated in the opening lines of the poem. Humankind and Nature are united in total harmony:

A motion and a spirit, that impels
All thinking things, all objects of all thought,
And rolls through all things.

In this perception of the unity of all things, Wordsworth is able to define nature as his "anchor" and "nurse," "The guide, the guardian of my heart, and soul /Of all my mortal being." Wordsworth's vision is informed not just by the scene itself, but by his memory of it, and by his imagination's understanding of its power. As the poem moves toward conclusion, Wordsworth turns to his sister beside him, praying that she too will know, as he does, that "Nature never did betray / The heart that loved her." Indeed, Wordsworth's prayer for his sister Dorothy is really intended as a prayer for us all. We should each of us become, as he is himself, "a worshipper of Nature."

"Tintern Abbey" can be taken as one of the fullest statements of the Romantic imagination. In the course of its 159 lines, it argues that in experiencing the beauty of nature, the imagination dissolves all opposition. Wordsworth suggests that the mind is an active participant in the process of human perception, rather than a passive vessel. There is an ethical dimension to aesthetic experience, a way to stand above, or beyond, the "dreary intercourse of daily life," both literally and figuratively on higher ground. Perhaps most of all, the poem provides Wordsworth with the opportunity for communion, not merely with the natural world, but with his sister beside him, and by extension his readers as well. In individual experience, Wordsworth makes contact with the whole.

The Romantic Landscape

The most notable landscape painting in Europe had developed in Italy and the Netherlands 200 years earlier. Even the term "landscape" derives from the Dutch word *landschap*, meaning a patch of cultivated ground. Although influenced by Italian artists' use of light and color, the great seventeenth-century Dutch landscape painters, including Jacob van Ruisdael (see Fig. 10.18 in Chapter 10), were also inspired by a dramatically changing physical geography sparked by the reclamation of hundreds of thousands of acres of land along the coast. The Dutch landscape painters in turn influenced later English landscape painters.

John Constable: Painter of the English Countryside Tension between the timeless and the more fleeting aspects of nature deeply informs the paintings of John Constable (1776–1837). Constable focused most of his efforts on the area around the valley of the Stour River in his native East Bergholt, Suffolk. Like Wordsworth, Constable believed that his art could be traced back to his childhood, back to the Stour, a place that he had known his whole life. "I should paint my own places best," he wrote to a friend in 1821, "I associate my 'careless boyhood' to all that lies on the banks of the Stour. They made me a painter (& I am grateful)." Also like Wordsworth, Constable wished to depict incidents and situations from common life, including villages, churches, farmhouses, and cottages. But most of all, Constable was, like Wordsworth, "a worshipper of Nature." As Constable wrote in a letter of May 1819, "Every tree seems full of blossom of some kind & the surface of the ground seems quite living—every step I take & on whatever object I turn my Eye that sublime expression of the Scripture 'I am the resurrection and the life' &c, seems verified about me." In fact, the cathedral at the center of so many Constable landscapes symbolizes the permanence of God in nature.

From 1819 to 1825, Constable worked on a series of what he referred to as his "six-footers," all large canvases depicting scenes on the Stour painted in his London studio from sketches and drawings done earlier. *The Hay Wain* (Fig. **12.15**) is one. The painting contains more than one state of mind—the passing storm, indicated by the darkened clouds on the left, contrasts with the brightly lit field below the billowing clouds at the right; the longevity of the tree behind the house with its massive trunk contrasts with the freshly cut hay at the right; the gentleman fisherman contrasts with

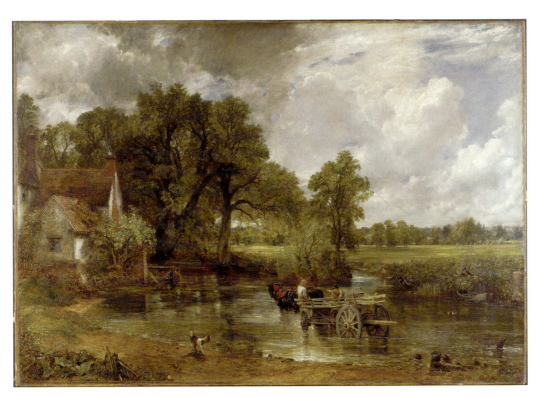

Fig. 12.15 John Constable, *The Hay Wain*. 1821. Oil on canvas, 51⅜" × 73". National Gallery, London. Constable failed to sell *The Hay Wain* when it was exhibited at the Royal Academy in 1821, although he turned down an offer of £70 for it.

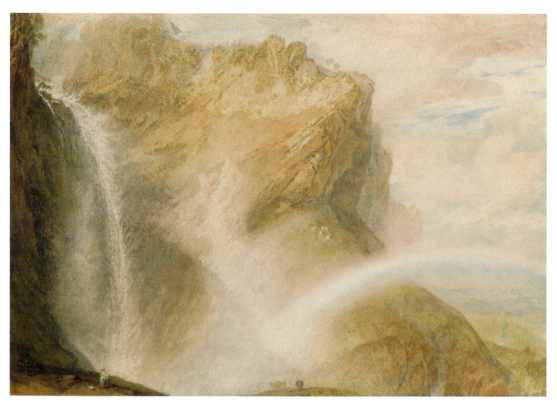

Fig. 12.16 J. M. W. Turner, *The Upper Falls of the Reichenbach*. ca. 1810–15. Watercolor, 10⅞″ × 15⁷⁄₁₆″. Yale Center for British Art, Paul Mellon Collection. B1977.14.4702. Turner achieved the transparent effect of the rainbow and the spray rising from the falls by scraping away the watercolor down to the white paper beneath.

the hard-working cart drivers. The house is Willy Lott's. Lott lived in the house his entire 80 years, spending only four nights of his life away from it. For Constable, the house symbolized a stability and permanence that contrasts dramatically with the impermanence of the weather, the constant flux of light and shadow, sun and cloud.

When the painting was first exhibited at the Royal Academy in 1821, Londoners could not accept that this was a "finished" painting because it had been painted in economical, almost abstract terms. Constable used short, broken strokes of color in a variety of shades and tints to produce a given hue (the green of foliage, for example). Nor did they understand how such a common theme deserved so monumental a canvas. Constable subsequently complained to a friend: "Londoners with all their ingenuity as artists know nothing of the feeling of a country life (the essence of Landscape)—any more than a hackney coach horse knows of pasture."

Joseph Mallord William Turner: Colorist of the Imagination The other great English landscape painter of the day, Joseph Mallord William Turner (1775–1851) freely explored what he called "the colors of the imagination." Even his contemporaries recognized, in the words of the critic William Hazlitt (1778–1830), that Turner was interested less in "the objects of nature than . . . the medium through which they are seen." In Turner's paintings, earth and vegetation seem to dissolve into light and water, into the very medium—gleaming oil or translucent watercolor—with

which he paints them. In *The Upper Falls of the Reichenbach*, for instance, Turner's depiction of the falls, among the highest in the Swiss Alps, seems to animate the rocky precipice (Fig. **12.16**). Turner draws our attention not to the rock, cliff, and mountain, but to the mist and light through which we see them.

Perhaps the best way to understand the difference between Constable and Turner is to consider the *scale* of their respective visions. Constable's work is "close," nearby and familiar, with an abundance of human associations. Turner's is exotic, remote, and even alienating. The human figure in Constable's paintings is an essential and elemental presence, uniting man and nature. The human figure in Turner's paintings is minuscule, almost irrelevant to the painting except insofar as its minuteness underscores nature's very indifference. Not only is *The Upper Falls of the Reichenbach* removed from the close-at-hand world of Constable's paintings, but also the cowherd and his dog, barely visible at the lower left of the painting, are dwarfed by the immensity of the scene. Cattle graze on the rise at the bottom middle, and another herd is on the ridge across the gorge. The effect is similar to that described by Wordsworth in "Tintern Abbey":

And I have felt
A presence that disturbs me with the joy
Of elevated thought; a sense sublime
Of something far more deeply interfused,

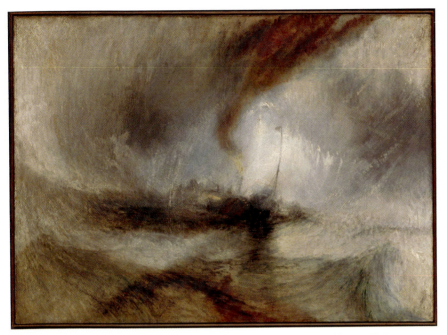

Fig. 12.17 **J. M. W. Turner,** *Snow Storm—Steam-Boat off a Harbour's Mouth.* **1842.** Oil on canvas, 36″ × 48″. © Tate, London 2014. Turner bequeathed 19,049 drawings and watercolors to the British nation. Many of these works anticipate the gestural freedom of this painting, with its sweeping linear rhythms.

Whose dwelling is the light of setting suns,
And the round ocean and the living air
And the blue sky, and in the mind of man:
A motion and a spirit, that impels
All thinking things, all objects of all thought,
And rolls through all things.

We must keep in mind, though, that the sublime is never altogether benign or kind. The viewer has nowhere to stand, except in the path of this mammoth demonstration of nature's force. A painting like *Snow Storm—Steam-Boat off a Harbour's Mouth* (Fig. **12.17**) suggests the "extinction" of the very "hope of man"—a sentiment far removed from Constable's pastoral landscapes or Wordsworth's "natural piety." Originally subtitled *The author was in this storm on the night the Ariel left Harwich,* the painting is the record of the immersion of the self (and the viewer) into the primal forces of nature. "I wished to show," Turner said, "what such a scene was like. I got the sailors to lash me to the mast to observe it... and I did not expect to escape: but I felt bound to record it if I did."

We have no evidence confirming a ship named *Ariel.* Most likely, Turner imagined this scene of a maelstrom of steam and storm that deposits us at its very heart. We descend into Turner's chaos of light and dark, the very opposite of the Enlightenment ideal of the natural world characterized by clarity, order, and harmony.

The Romantic in Germany: Friedrich and Kant Although Constable and Turner's approaches are very different, both believed that nature provoked their imaginations. In the German Romantic tradition, the imagination is also the fundamental starting point. The painter Caspar David Friedrich (1774–1840) represents the imaginative capacities of the Romantic mind by placing figures, often solitary ones, before sublime landscapes (see *Closer Look,* pages 400–401). In *Monk by the Sea* (Fig. **12.18**), a figure stands alone, engulfed in the vast expanse of sand and storm, as if facing the void. His is a crisis of faith. How do I know God? he seems to ask. And how, in the face of this empty vastness, do I come to belief? Can I even believe?

These sentiments echo the philosopher Immanuel Kant's *Critique of Pure Reason* (1781), in which he had argued that the mind is not a passive recipient of information—not, that is, the "blank slate" that Locke had claimed. For Kant, the mind was an active agent in the creation of knowledge.

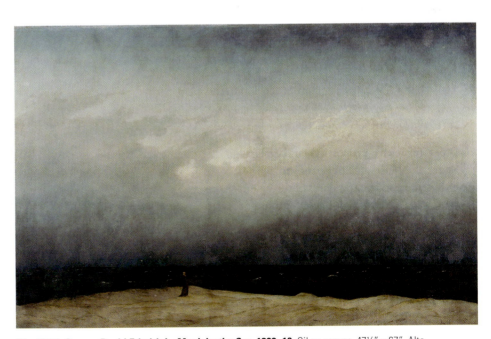

Fig. 12.18 **Caspar David Friedrich,** *Monk by the Sea.* **1809–10.** Oil on canvas, 47½″ × 67″. Alte Nationalgalerie, Staatliche Museen, Berlin. Some art historians believe that the monk is Friedrich himself, which would make this a self-portrait.

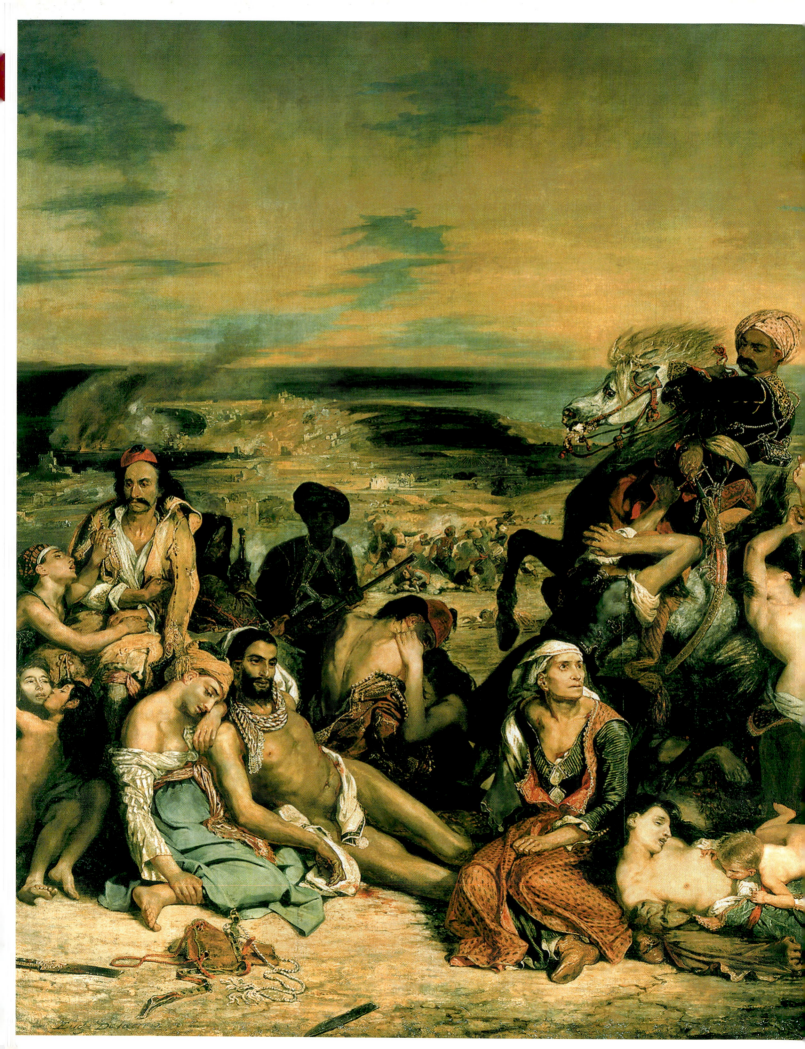

The Working Class and the Bourgeoisie

The Conditions of Modern Life

LEARNING OBJECTIVES

13.1 Describe how realism manifested itself in nineteenth-century art and literature.

13.2 Describe the various ways in which French artists and writers attacked bourgeois values in the 1850s and 1860s.

13.3 Define Impressionism and examine how it transformed conventional assumptions about style and content in painting.

13.4 Outline the characteristics of the American sense of self as it developed in the nineteenth century.

13.5 Examine the impact of Western imperial adventuring on the non-Western world.

After the defeat of Napoleon in 1815, Louis XVIII (r. 1814–24), whose rule had been restored the year before when Napoleon had been exiled to Elba, could not ignore the reforms implemented by both the revolution and Napoleon himself. His younger brother, the count of Artois, disagreed, and almost immediately a so-called Ultra-royalist movement, composed of families who had suffered at the hands of the revolution, established itself. Advocating the return of their confiscated estates and the abolition of revolutionary and Napoleonic reforms, the Ultraroyalists imprisoned and executed hundreds of revolutionaries, Bonaparte sympathizers, and Protestants in southern France. (The artist Jacques-Louis David, who had supported Napoleon, was in exile during this period.) In order to solidify his control, Louis dissolved the largely Ultraroyalist Chamber of Deputies and called for new elections, which resulted in a more moderate majority.

Relative calm prevailed in France for the next four years, but in February 1820, the son of the count of Artois, who was the last of the Bourbons and heir to the throne, was assassinated, initiating ten years of repression. The education system was placed under the control of Roman Catholic bishops,

press censorship was inaugurated, and "dangerous" political activity banned. At the death of Louis XVIII, the count of Artois assumed the throne as Charles X (r. 1824–30).

In the midst of this turmoil, at the Salon of 1824, a young painter by the name of Eugène Delacroix (1798–1863) exhibited a large painting entitled *Scenes from the Massacres at Chios* (Fig. **13.1**). Delacroix had studied with Théodore Géricault, and had actually served as the model for the face-down nude in the bottom center of *The Raft of the "Medusa"* (see Fig. 12.23 in Chapter 12). He shared his master's disillusionment with Royalist politics. The full title of Delacroix's painting—*Scenes from the Massacres at Chios; Greek Families Awaiting Death or Slavery, etc.—See Various Accounts and Contemporary Newspapers*—reveals its close association with journalistic themes. It depicts events of April 1822, after the Greeks had initiated a War of Independence from Turkey, a cause championed by all of liberal Europe. In retaliation, the sultan sent an army of 10,000 to the Greek island of Chios, several miles off the west coast of Turkey. The troops killed 20,000 and took thousands of women and children into captivity, selling them into slavery across North Africa. In the left foreground, defeated Greek families await their fate. To

◀ **Fig. 13.1 Eugène Delacroix, *Scenes from the Massacres at Chios*. 1824.** Oil on canvas, 165″ × 139¼″. Musée du Louvre, Paris. Delacroix relied on the testimony of a French volunteer in the Greek cause for the authenticity of his depiction.

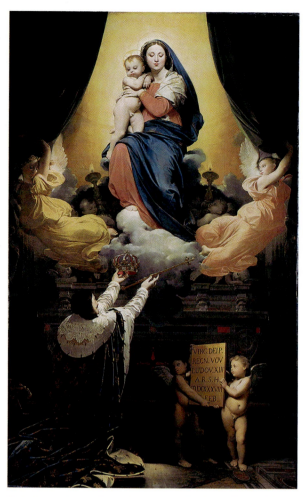

Fig. 13.2 Jean-Auguste-Dominique Ingres, *The Vow of Louis XIII*. 1824. Oil on canvas, 165¾" × 103⅛". Montauban Cathedral, France. The plaque in the hands of the *putti* reads "Louis XIII puts France under the protection of the Virgin, February 1638."

the right a grandmother sits dejectedly by what is perhaps her dead daughter, even as her grandchild tries to suckle at its dead mother's breast. A prisoner vainly tries to defend a Greek woman tied to a triumphant Turk's horse. The vast space between the near foreground and the far distance is startling, almost as if the scene transpires before a painted tableau.

The stark contrast between Delacroix's *Scenes from the Massacres at Chios* and an equally large painting by Jean-Auguste-Dominique Ingres (1780–1867) exhibited at the same Salon, *The Vow of Louis XIII* (Fig. **13.2**), emphatically underscores the competing styles of the two artists. Especially in the context of the times, Ingres's painting is a deeply royalist work. It depicts Louis XIII placing France under the protection of the Virgin in February 1638 in order to end a Protestant rebellion. The painting is divided into two distinct zones, the religious and the secular, or the worlds of Church and State. The king kneels in the secular space of the foreground, painted in almost excruciating detail. Above him, the Virgin, bathed in a spiritual light, is a monument to Renaissance Classicism, directly referencing the Madonnas of Raphael. In every way, the painting is a monument to tradition—to the traditions of the Bourbon throne, the Catholic Church, and Classical art.

In his paintings, Ingres never hesitated to adjust the proportions of the body to the overall composition. A good example is his *La Grande Odalisque* of 1814 (Fig. **13.3**). An **odalisque** is a female slave or concubine in a Middle Eastern, particularly Turkish, harem. When the painting was exhibited at the Salon of 1819, viewers immediately recognized that his figure's back is endowed with too many vertebrae, that her right arm extends to too great a length, as if disjointed at the elbow, and that her right foot appears amputated from a rather too distant right knee. Ingres could

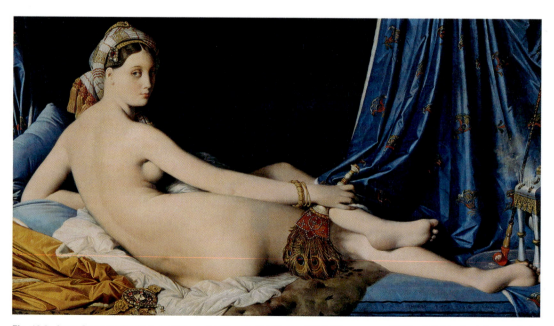

Fig. 13.3 Jean-Auguste-Dominique Ingres, *La Grande Odalisque*. 1814. Oil on canvas, 35⅞" × 63". Musée du Louvre, Paris. Inv. Rf1158. The painting was commissioned by Napoleon's sister Caroline Murat, queen of Naples.

hardly have cared less. For him, the composition demanded the sweeping curve of both back and arm, the curve of which continues into the folds of the hanging drapery, even as it crosses and works against the emphatic diagonal created by his figure's legs. Equally appealing to him was the dramatic contrast between the dark background and the brilliantly lit flesh of the body, his stunningly realistic realization of satin and silk, and the almost palpable sense of touch elicited by the peacock-feather fan—all rendered without so much as the trace of a brushstroke.

The odalisque continued to occupy Ingres for the rest of his career, as in fact it did nineteenth-century French artists as a group. But when Delacroix took up the theme in the *Odalisque* painted in 1845–50 (Fig. 13.4), the effect was dramatically different. Both works employ the standard iconography of the harem—the unkempt bed, the hashish pipe or hookah, the curtained room. Both figures address the viewer with their eyes. But where the cool blues of Ingres's painting underscore the equally cool, even icy sexual aloofness of his model, the reds of Delacroix's are charged with an intense eroticism, underscored by the fact that his model is turned toward the viewer rather than away. In fact, where Ingres's odalisque seems untainted, almost pure, Delacroix's appears lasciviously postcoital. And Delacroix's brushwork, the wild, energetic gesture of his touch, is the very opposite of Ingres's traceless

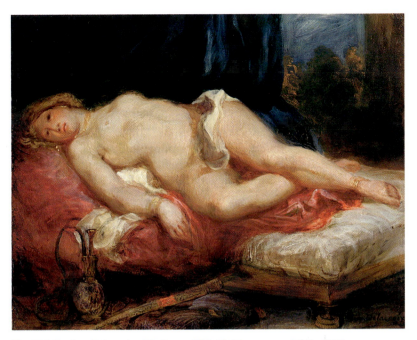

Fig. 13.4 Eugène Delacroix, *Odalisque*. 1845–50. Oil on canvas, 14⅞" × 18¼". © Fitzwilliam Museum, University of Cambridge, England. The comparatively small size of Delacroix's painting lends it a sense of sketchlike immediacy.

mark. In 1854, Delacroix wrote in his journal, "I pity those who work tranquilly and coldly [by whom he means Ingres]. I am convinced that everything they do can only be cold and tranquil." Delacroix preferred what he called "the fury of the brush," a fury especially evident in paintings such as this one. Described by a contemporary as "plunged deep like sword thrusts," his brushwork in this painting is indeed almost violently sexual.

Thus, Delacroix and Ingres reenact the aesthetic debate that had marked French painting since the time of Louis XIII, the debate between the intellect and emotion, between the school of Poussin and the school of Rubens (see Chapter 10). But Ingres's Neoclassicism and Delacroix's Romanticism entered into this debate not merely as expressions of aesthetic taste but as a political struggle, which already in 1830 had erupted again in a revolution that Delacroix would celebrate in his monumental painting *Liberty Leading the People* (Fig. 13.5).

Three years earlier, after liberals won a majority in the Chamber of Deputies, King Charles X responded by relaxing censorship of the press and government control of education. But these concessions irked him, and in the spring of 1830 he called for new elections. The liberals won a large majority, but Charles was not to be thwarted.

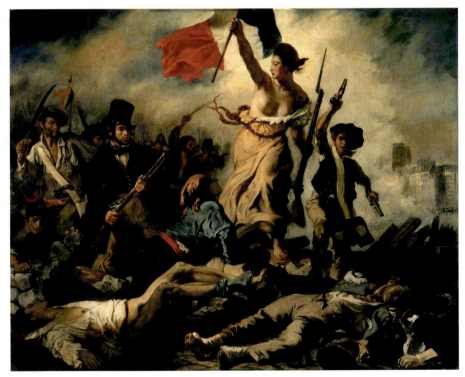

Fig. 13.5 Eugène Delacroix, *Liberty Leading the People*. 1830. Oil on canvas, 8'6" × 10'7". Musée du Louvre, Paris. Note one of the towers of Notre-Dame Cathedral in the right background of the painting, which contributes to the realism of the image.

 View the *Closer Look* for *Liberty Leading the People* on **MyArtsLab**

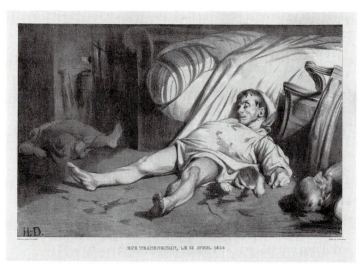

Fig. 13.7 Honoré Daumier, *Rue Transnonain, April 15, 1834*. 1834. Lithograph, 11½″ × 17⅝″. Private collection. A few days after the police killed the residents of 12 rue Transnonain, Daumier exhibited this image in the window of a Paris store, drawing huge crowds.

newspapers possible. He could literally create a drawing and publish it the same day. In his focus on ordinary life, Daumier openly lampooned the idealism of both Neoclassical and Romantic art. No longer was the object of art to reveal some "higher" truth; what mattered instead was the truth of everyday experience, and in Louis-Philippe's France, everyday experience was not always an attractive proposition.

👁 **Watch** a studio technique video on lithography on **MyArtsLab**

Daumier's *Rue Transnonain* is not a cartoon; it was, rather, widely understood as direct reportage of the killings committed by government troops during an insurrection by Parisian workers in April 1834 (Fig. **13.7**). After a sniper's bullet killed one of their officers, the police claimed it had come from 12 rue Transnonain and they killed everyone inside. Daumier's illustration shows the father of the family, who had been sleeping, lying dead by his bed, his child crushed beneath him, his dead wife to his left and an elder parent to his right. The strong diagonal of the scene draws us into its space, a working-class recasting of Géricault's *Raft of the "Medusa"* (see Fig. 12.23 in Chapter 12). The impact of such images on the French public was substantial, as the king clearly understood. Louis-Philippe eventually declared that freedom of the press extended to verbal but not pictorial representation.

By focusing on laborers and common country folk rather than on the Parisian aristocracy and bourgeoisie, French realist painting is implicitly political, reflecting the social upheaval that in 1848 rocked almost all of Europe. But Daumier's painting is relatively modest in size. When Gustave Courbet (1819–77) exhibited his painting *The Stonebreakers* (Fig. **13.8**) at the Salon of 1850–51, the public was genuinely astonished by the monumental scale of the painting. Such a grand size was usually reserved for paintings of historical events, but Courbet's subjects were the mundane and the everyday.

A farmer's son and largely self-taught artist, Courbet's goal was to paint the world just as he saw it, without any taint of Romanticism or idealism. "To know in order to be able to

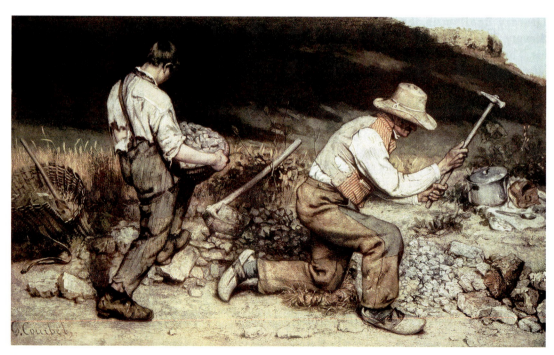

Fig. 13.8 Gustave Courbet, *The Stonebreakers*. 1849 (Salon of 1850–51). Oil on canvas, 5′3″ × 8′6″. (destroyed in 1945). Galerie Neue Meister, Dresden. © Staatliche Kunstsammlungen Dresden. The painting is believed to have been destroyed during the American fire-bombing of Dresden in World War II.

create," Courbet wrote in his Realist Manifesto of 1855, "that was my idea. To be in a position to translate the customs, the ideas, the appearance of my epoch, according to my own estimation; to be not only a painter, but a man as well; in short, to create living art—this is my goal." In fact, he rejected the traditional political and moral dimensions of realism in favor of a more subjective and apolitical approach to art. This new brand of realism would dominate the art of the following generations.

In *The Stonebreakers*, Courbet depicts two workers outside his native Ornans, a town at the foot of the Jura Mountains near the Swiss border. They are pounding stones to make gravel for a road. Everything in the painting seems to be pulled down by the weight of physical labor—the strap pulling down across the boy's back, the basket of stones resting on his knee, the hammer in the older man's hand descending, the stiff, thick cloth of his trousers pressing against his thigh, even the shadows of the hillside behind them descending toward them. Only a small patch of sky peeks from behind the rocky ridge in the upper right-hand corner, the ridge itself following the same downward path as the hammer. Together, the older man and his younger assistant seem to suggest the unending nature of their work, as if their backbreaking work has afflicted generation after generation of Courbet's rural contemporaries—"a complete expression of human misery," as Courbet explained it.

Representing Slavery and the Civil War

Many in Europe and across the globe were surprised that war erupted in the United States, believing that some sort of compromise was likely. In no small part, this delusion resulted from a romanticized view of slavery embedded even in abolitionist literature such as *Uncle Tom's Cabin*. For every Simon Legree there is an Augustine St. Clare and his daughter, Little Eva; for every runaway slave, a grateful Christian convert.

A prime example of blindness to the full implications of slavery in antebellum America is evident in the painting *Negro Life in the South* by Eastman Johnson (1824–1906) (Fig. **13.9**). The painting achieved instant success when it was exhibited in New York in 1859. Much of its realism was contributed by the models Johnson employed—the household slaves owned by his father in Washington, D.C.

Negro Life in the South was a curious painting in that it was highly ambiguous—it could be read as either for or against slavery. For some, Johnson's painting seemed to depict slaves as contented with their lot. A banjo-picker plays a song for a mother and child who are dancing together. A young man and woman flirt at the left, while another woman and child look out on the scene from the window above. The white mistress of the house steps through the gate at the right as if to join in the party. However, to an abolitionist, the contrast

The CONTINUING PRESENCE
of the PAST

See Fred Wilson,
Mining the Museum, 1992,
at **MyArtsLab**

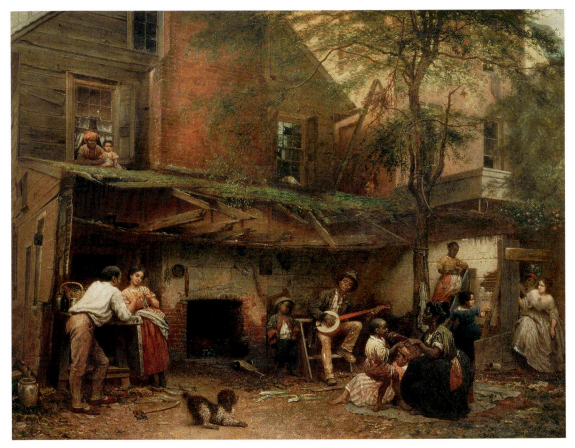

Fig. 13.9 Eastman Johnson, *Negro Life in the South (Kentucky Home)*. 1859. Oil on canvas, 36" × 45". Collection of the New-York Historical Society. Johnson studied in Europe from 1849 to 1855, culminating in a period in the studio of Thomas Couture in Paris, where Édouard Manet was also a student (see Figs. 13.12 and 13.14).

Renoir's *Luncheon of the Boating Party* required the painter to take a slightly different tack than was usual for him. We can identify many of the figures from his circle of friends and acquaintances at Chatou, including members of the Fournaise family at whose restaurant the painting is set. To represent such recognizable figures, Renoir had to abandon the gestural brushwork of Monet and Pissarro except in the background landscape. He composed his figures with firm outlines and modeled them in subtle gradations of light and dark, which clearly define their anatomical and facial features. And he carefully structured the group in a series of interlocking triangles, the largest of which is made up of

Aline Charigot, his future wife, sitting at the table holding her dog. Scholars believe that the painting, begun in the summer of 1880, may represent Renoir's response to Émile Zola's critique in his review of the 1880 Salon charging the Impressionists with selling "sketches that are hardly dry" and challenging them to make more complex paintings that would be the result of "long and thoughtful preparation." For this reason, the theory goes, Renoir assimilates into this single work landscape, still life, and genre painting in a manner probably intentionally recalling seventeenth-century Dutch and Flemish paintings like Rubens's *The Kermis* (see Fig. 10.28 in Chapter 10), which Renoir would have seen at the Louvre.

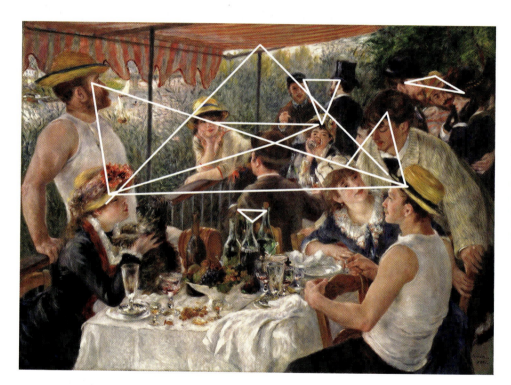

Grounding the interplay of triangles upon which Renoir's painting is based is the still-life composition of three bottles in the center of the table. Outlined here are the various sets of triangular relationships determined by groupings of figures and their visual or verbal interchanges. While the entire composition moves off into space at an angle from left to right, another compositional pyramid is formed by the angles of Caillebotte's and Charigot's hats, meeting roughly at the top of the post supporting the awning at the top middle of the painting.

Something to Think About...

Given the wide variety of people in this composition, how might you describe its social politics? In other words, what sort of broader society does it suggest?

Pierre-Auguste Renoir, *Luncheon of the Boating Party*. 1880–81. Oil on canvas, 51¼" × 69⅛". Acquired 1923. Phillips Collection, Washington, D.C.

The Italian journalist Adrien Maggiolo, the only male not wearing a hat, leans over an actress by the name of Angèle Legault and the painter Gustave Caillebotte. Maggiolo was a writer for *Le Triboulet* (*The King's Dunce*), a journal dedicated to theater and cabaret in Paris.

Alphonsine Fournaise, the proprietor's daughter, rests her elbow on the railing. She is talking with Baron Raoul Barbier, Renoir's friend and a notorious womanizer.

Charles Euphussi, in the top hat, editor of the *Gazette des Beaux-Arts*, and an avid art collector, chats with a young man in a mariner's cap, perhaps the poet Jules Laforgue, who served as Euphussi's personal secretary.

The actress Jeanne Samary, a star of the Comédie Française, covers her ears as two of Renoir's best friends, the writer Paul Lhote, in the red-striped hat, and Eugène Pierre Lestringuez, who had known Renoir since childhood, flirt with her.

Leaning against the rail and overseeing the entire luncheon is Alphonse Fournaise, son of the restaurant's proprietor.

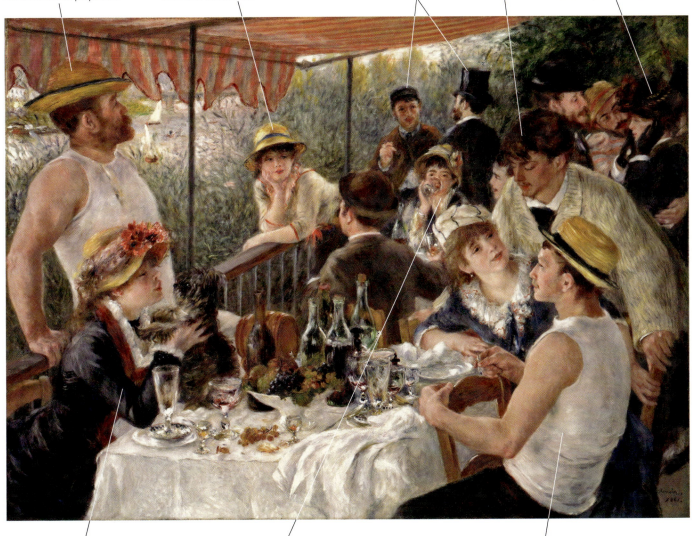

Renoir would marry Aline Charigot in 1890. Serving as their witnesses were Lhote and Lestringuez, depicted in the opposite corner of the painting flirting with the actress Jeanne Samary.

The actress Ellen Andrée was a close friend of Aline Charigot. She performed in the most avant-garde plays of the day at the Théâtre-Libre.

At age 32, when Renoir painted this scene, Caillebotte was the youngest of the Impressionists. He was also by far the wealthiest, having inherited his father's considerable fortune, and he thought it his God-given duty to support his Impressionist colleagues. As a result, he amassed a very substantial collection of works by Degas, Paul Cézanne, Manet, Monet, Pissarro, Renoir, and Alfred Sisley, which he bequeathed to the state upon his death in 1894. His bequest—Renoir was his estate's executor—became the basis for the great collection of Impressionist painting today housed in the Musée d'Orsay in Paris.

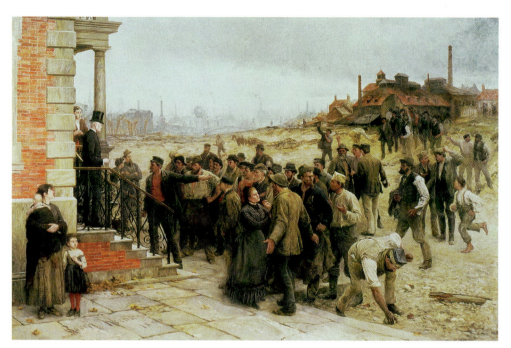

Fig. 13.22 Robert Koehler, *The Strike.* **1886.** Oil on canvas, 5'11½" × 9⅝". Deutsches Historisches Museum, Berlin. Koehler's father was a machinist, and he identified with the plight of the working class. The painting was exhibited at the National Academy of Design in 1886, to general approval.

Impromptu strikes, walkouts, and the beginnings of organized labor unions signaled the changing economic and social climate. When the Baltimore & Ohio Railroad cut wages in 1877, its workers staged spontaneous strikes, which spread rapidly to other railroads. In Baltimore, the state militia shot and killed 11 strikers and wounded 40 others.

Owners of railroads and other corporations, together with the political leaders they supported, made sure wage reductions remained in place. The federal government aided them when the U.S. War Department created the National Guard as a quick-reaction force to put down future disturbances. It was an era of unparalleled political unrest, and *The Strike* by Robert Koehler (1850–1917) suggests something of the mood of the workers and their bosses, as well as the grim environment of industrial-age America (Fig. **13.22**). The painting depicts an angry crowd confronting an employer, demanding a living wage from the stern top-hatted man and a worried younger man standing behind him. An impoverished woman with her children looks on at the left; another woman, more obviously middle class, tries to talk with one of the workers, but behind him a striker bends down to pick up a stone to throw. Koehler's realism is evident in the diversity of his figures, each possessing an individual identity. But the background of the work, with its smoky, factory-filled landscape on the horizon, owes much to the Impressionist style.

The May 1, 1886, issue of *Harper's Weekly* included the painting as its central feature. On the same day, a national strike called for changing the standard workday from 12 hours to 8. More than 340,000 workers stopped work at 12,000 companies across the country. In Chicago, a bomb exploded as police broke up a labor meeting in Haymarket Square. A police officer was killed by the blast and police retaliated, firing into the crowd of workers, killing one and wounding many more. Four labor organizers were charged with the policeman's death and subsequently hanged, demoralizing the national labor movement and energizing management to resist labor's demands.

The Romantic Song of the American Self: Landscape and Experience

The alienation of the urban worker contrasted sharply with the national belief in the healing power of the natural world, so remote, it seemed, from the reality of the factory and tenement. In the first half of the nineteenth century, the American wilderness had inspired a sense of wonder at the natural world, with which American writers shared with artists like Thomas Cole (1801–48) and Asher B. Durand (1796–1886) an almost ecstatic communion. In many ways, they were shaped by the nation's emphasis on individualism and individual liberty. Free to think for themselves, their imaginations were equally free to discover the self in nature.

The Hudson River Painters Born in England in 1801, Thomas Cole, who would come to be known as the founding father of American landscape painting, emigrated with his family to America in 1818. By 1824, he was painting regularly in the Hudson River valley north of New York City. He loved, especially, Kaaterskill Clove, a deep gorge carved by a stream emptying two lakes at the top of the Catskill escarpment, southwest of Albany, and in 1836 he moved to Catskill, New York, nestled on the left side of the river, just below the escarpment itself. His chief subject, he said, was the tension between "the improvements of cultivation and the sublimity of the wilderness," and no painting better captures that tension than *The Oxbow* (Fig. **13.23**). It shows a famous bend in the Connecticut River in Massachusetts, which describes the boundary between the cultivated fields below and the wilderness of Mt. Holyoke, upon which Cole has positioned himself, going so far as to paint himself into the scene—he is at his easel below the rocks to the left of his pack and umbrella. Thus he acts as mediator between the neatly fenced sunny fields of the valley below and the rugged wilderness behind him, symbolized by the blasted tree stump and the dark clouds of the thunderstorm in the distance.

When Cole died unexpectedly from pneumonia in 1848, he was eulogized by his long-time friend the poet William Cullen Bryant (1794–1878). "To us who remain," Bryant lamented, "the region of the Catskills, where he wandered

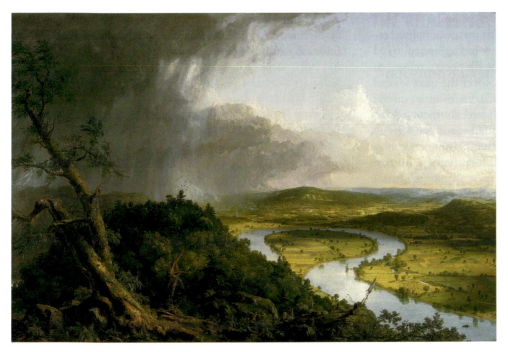

Fig. 13.23 Thomas Cole, *The Oxbow (View from Mount Holyoke, Northampton, Massachusetts, After a Thunderstorm)*. 1836. Oil on canvas, 4'3½" × 6'4". The Metropolitan Museum of Art, New York. Gift of Mrs. Russell Sage, 1908 (08.228). The painting suggests, as the storm departs to the left, that civilization will eventually overwhelm the wilderness, a prospect Cole anticipated with distress.

View the Closer Look for Thomas Cole, *The Oxbow* on **MyArtsLab**

and studied and sketched, and wrought his sketches into such glorious creations, is saddened by a certain desolate feeling, when we behold it or think of it. The mind that we knew was abroad in those scenes of grandeur and beauty, and which gave them a higher interest in our eyes, has passed from the earth, and we see that something of power and greatness is withdrawn from the sublime mountain tops and the broad forests and the rushing waterfalls." Upon hearing Bryant's eulogy, the New York City art collector Jonathan Sturges (1802–74) immediately commissioned Cole's friend and fellow-painter Durand to paint the poet and the painter standing together in Kaaterskill Clove (Fig. **13.24**). The two are depicted as "kindred spirits," a reference to the English romantic poet John Keats's "Sonnet to Solitude," in which Keats imagines how the wild beauties of the natural world—there "where the deer's swift leap / Startles the wild bee from the foxglove bell"—are even sweeter when shared with a friend: "it sure must be/ Almost the highest bliss of human-kind,/ When to thy haunts two kindred spirits flee." They stand on a rock outcropping that, like the brush in Cole's hand, points up the gorge; the course of the meandering creek is mirrored in the crooked branches of the tree that frames the top of the painting; an American bald eagle floats over the scene; tree trunks presumably shattered by lightning, wind, or both testify to the force of raw nature, as do the boulders that have tumbled into the stream. The two figures represent the highest order of civilization, but they are shown taking their inspiration from the wilderness itself.

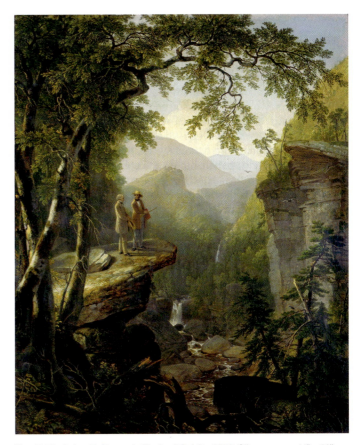

Fig. 13.24 Asher B. Durand, *Kindred Spirits*. 1848. Oil on canvas, 44" × 36". Crystal Bridges Museum of American Art, Bentonville, AK. As if to comment ironically on the desecration of the wilderness wrought by the burgeoning tourist industry in the Hudson River valley, Durand has painted, as if carved into the birch tree at the left, the names "Bryant" and "Cole."

Sergei Eisenstein would cram 155 separate shots into a four-minute sequence of his film *The Battleship Potemkin*—a shot every 1.6 seconds. In 1900, France had produced 3,000 automobiles; by 1907, it was producing 30,000 a year. The technological advances represented by the automobile were closely connected to the development of the internal combustion engine, pneumatic tires, and, above all, the rise of the assembly line. After all, building 30,000 automobiles a year required an efficiency and speed of production unlike any ever before conceived. Henry Ford (1863–1947), the American automobile maker, attacked the problem. Ford asked Frederick Taylor (1856–1915), the inventor of "scientific management," to determine the exact speed at which the assembly line should move and the exact motions workers should use to perform their duties; in 1908, assembly-line production as we know it was born.

Amid all this speed and motion, the world also suddenly seemed a less stable and secure place. Discoveries in science and physics confirmed this. In 1900, the German physicist Max Planck (1858–1947) proposed the theory of matter and energy known as quantum mechanics. In quantum mechanics, the fundamental particles are unknowable, and are only hypothetical things represented by mathematics. Furthermore, the very technique of measuring these phenomena necessarily alters their behavior. Faced with the fact that light appeared to travel in absolutely contradictory ways, as both particles and waves, depending upon how one measured it, in 1913, the Danish physicist Niels Bohr (1885–1962) built on quantum physics to propose a new theory of complementarity: two statements, apparently contradictory, might at any moment be equally true. At the very end of the nineteenth century, in Cambridge, England, J. J. Thompson detected the existence of separate components in the previously indivisible atom. He called them "electrons," and by 1911, Ernest Rutherford had introduced a new model of the atom—a small, positively charged nucleus containing most of the atom's mass around which electrons continuously orbit. Suddenly matter itself was understood to be continuously in motion. Meanwhile, in 1905, Albert Einstein had published his theory of relativity and by 1915 had produced the *General Principles of Relativity*, with its model of the non-Euclidean, four-dimensional space-time continuum. Between 1895 and 1915, the traditional understanding of the physical universe had literally been transformed—and it was not a universe of entities available to the human eye.

THE RISE OF MODERNISM IN THE ARTS

What are some characteristic features of modernism in art and literature?

The arts responded to this radical shift in understanding. In painting, those who followed upon the Impressionist generation—the Post-Impressionists, as they were soon known—saw themselves as inventing a new future for painting, one that reflected the spirit of innovation that defined modernity. In Paris, the studio of Spanish-born Pablo Picasso (1881–1973) was quickly recognized by artists and intellectuals as the center of artistic innovation in the new century. From around Europe and America, artists flocked to see his work, and they carried his spirit—and the spirit of French painting generally—back with them to Italy, Germany, and America. New art movements—new "isms," including Delaunay's Simultanism—succeeded one another in rapid fire. Picasso's work also encouraged radical approaches to poetry and to music, where the discordant, sometimes violent distortions of his paintings found expression in sound.

Post-Impressionist Painting

Among the Post-Impressionists were Paul Cézanne, Paul Gauguin, and Georges Seurat, all of whom exhibited at various Impressionist shows, and Vincent van Gogh, who arrived in Paris only in time to see the eighth and last Impressionist exhibition. But rather than creating Impressionist works that captured the optical effects of light and atmosphere and

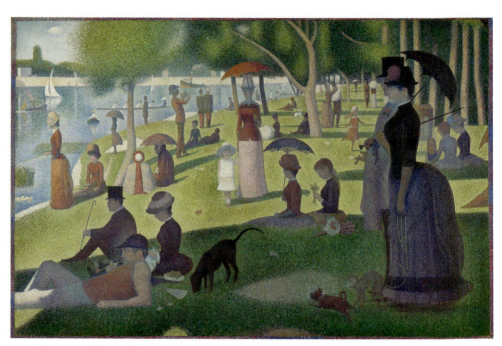

Fig. 14.2 Georges Seurat, *A Sunday on La Grande Jatte*. 1884–86. Oil on canvas, 81¾" × 121¼". Helen Birch Bartlett Memorial Collection, 1926.224. Photograph © 2006, The Art Institute of Chicago. All rights reserved. Capuchin monkeys like the one held on a leash by the woman on the right, were a popular pet in 1880s Paris.

View the Closer Look for *A Sunday on La Grande Jatte* on **MyArtsLab** the fleeting qualities of sensory experience, they sought to capture something transcendent in their act of vision, something that captured the essence of their subject.

Pointillism: Seurat and the Harmonies of Color One of the most talented of the Post-Impressionist painters was Georges Seurat (1859–91), who exhibited his masterpiece, *A Sunday on La Grand Jatte*, in 1886, when he was 27 years old (Fig. **14.2**). It depicts a Sunday crowd of Parisians enjoying the weather on the island of La Grand Jatte in the Seine River, just northeast of the city. The subject matter is typically Impressionist, but it lacks that style's sense of spontaneity and the immediacy of its brushwork. Instead, *La Grand Jatte* is a carefully controlled, scientific application of tiny dots of color—*pointilles*, as Seurat called them—and his method of painting became known as pointillism to some, and Neo-Impressionism to others.

In setting his "points" of color side by side across the canvas, Seurat determined that color could be mixed, as he put it, in "gay, calm, or sad" combinations. Lines extending upward could also reflect these same feelings, he explained, imparting a cheerful tone, as do warm and luminous colors of red, orange, and yellow. Horizontal lines that balance dark and light, warmth and coolness, create a sense of calm. Lines reaching in a downward direction and the dark, cool hues of green, blue, and violet evoke sadness.

With this symbolic theory of color in mind, we can see much more in Seurat's *La Grand Jatte* than simply a Sunday crowd enjoying a day at the park. There are 48 people of various ages depicted, including soldiers, families, couples, and singles, some in fashionable attire, others in casual dress. A range of social classes is present as well, illustrating the mixture of people on the city's day of leisure. Although overall the painting balances its lights and darks and the horizontal dominates, thus creating a sense of calm, all three groups in the foreground shadows are bathed in the melancholy tones of blue, violet, and green. With few exceptions—a running child, and behind her a couple—almost everyone in the painting is looking either straight ahead or downward. Even the tails of the pets turn downward. This solemn feature is further heightened by the toy-soldier rigidity of the figures. Seurat's painting *suggests* more than it portrays. As one critic of the time wrote of *La Grande Jatte*, "one understands then the rigidity of Parisian leisure, tired and stiff, where even recreation is a matter of striking poses."

Symbolic Color: Van Gogh Seurat's influence on French painting was profound. The Dutch painter Vincent van Gogh (1853–90) studied Seurat's paintings while living in Paris in 1886–87, and experimented extensively with Seurat's color combinations and pointillist

technique, which extended even to his drawings, as a means to create a rich textural surface.

Van Gogh was often overcome with intense and uncontrollable emotions, an attribute that played a key role in the development of his unique artistic style. Profoundly committed to discovering a universal harmony in which all aspects of life were united through art, he found Seurat's emphasis on contrasting colors appealing. It became another ingredient in his synthesis of techniques. He began to apply complementary colors in richly painted zones using dashes and strokes that were much larger than Seurat's *pointilles*. In a letter to his brother Theo in 1888, Van Gogh described the way the complementary colors in *Night Café* (Fig. **14.3**) work to create visual tension and emotional imbalance:

> In my picture of the *Night Café* I have tried to express the idea that the café is a place where one can ruin oneself, run mad, or commit a crime. I have tried to express the terrible passions of humanity by means of red and green. . . . Everywhere there is a clash and contrast of the most alien reds and greens. . . . So I have tried to express, as it were, the powers of darkness in a low wine shop, and all this in an atmosphere like a devil's furnace of pale sulphur. . . . It is a color not locally true from the point of view of the stereoscopic realist, but color to suggest the emotion of an ardent temperament.

Color, in Van Gogh's paintings, becomes symbolic, charged with feelings. Added to the garish conflict of colors

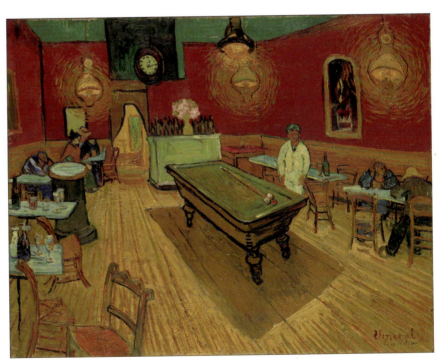

Fig. 14.3 Vincent Van Gogh, ***Night Café.*** **1888.** Oil on canvas, 28½″ × 36¼″. Yale University Art Gallery. Bequest of Stephen Carlton Clark, B.A. 1903. 1961.18.34. Van Gogh frequented this café on the Place Lamartine in Arles. Gas lighting, only recently introduced, allowed it to stay open all night. Drifters and others with no place to stay would frequent it at night. Notice how many patrons seem to be asleep at the tables.

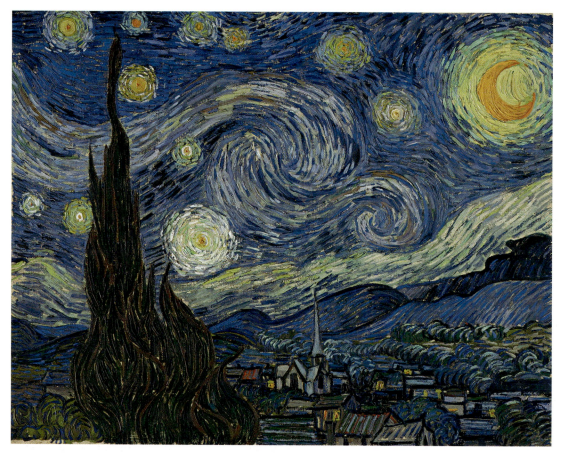

The CONTINUING PRESENCE
of the PAST

See Robert Colescott,
*Auvers-sur-Oise (Crow in the
Wheat Field)*, 1981,
at **MyArtsLab**

Fig. 14.4 Vincent Van Gogh, ***The Starry Night.*** **1889.** Oil on canvas, 28¾″ × 36¼″. Museum of Modern Art, New York. Acquired through the Lillie P. Bliss Bequest. (472.1941). Saint-Rémy, where Van Gogh painted this work, lies at the foot of a small range of mountains between Arles and Aix-en-Provence. This part of France is plagued in the winter months by the mistral, strong winds that blow day after day out of the Alps down the Rhône River valley. The furious swirls of Van Gogh's sky and the blowing cypress trees suggest that he might be representing this wind, known to drive people mad, in contrast to the harmony of the painting's color scheme.

View the Closer Look for *The Starry Night* on **MyArtsLab**

is Van Gogh's peculiar point of view, elevated above the room, which sweeps away from the viewer in exaggerated and unsettling perspective. *Night Café* in this regard reflects not just a mundane view of the interior of a café lit by lamps, but also Van Gogh's "ardent" reaction to it.

For many viewers and critics, Van Gogh's paintings are the most personally expressive in the history of art, offering unvarnished insights into the painter's unstable psychological state. As he was painting *Night Café*, Van Gogh was living in the southern French town of Arles, where, over the course of 15 months, he produced an astounding quantity of work: 200 paintings, over 100 drawings and watercolors, and roughly 200 letters. Many of these letters, especially those addressed to his brother Theo, help us to interpret his paintings, which have become treasured masterpieces, each selling for tens of millions of dollars. Yet at the time he painted them, almost no one liked them, and he sold almost none of his art.

To viewers at the time, the dashes of thickly painted color, an effect known as *impasto*, seemed thrown onto the canvas as a haphazard and unrefined mess. And yet, the staccato rhythms of this brushwork seemed to Van Gogh himself deeply autobiographical, capturing almost stroke by stroke

the pulse of his own volatile personality. Although his work grew ever bolder and more creative as the years passed, Van Gogh continued to suffer from the emotional instability and depression that had tormented him most of his adult life. In December 1888, his personal emotional turmoil reached fever pitch when he sliced off a section of his earlobe and presented it to an Arles prostitute as a present. After a brief stay at an Arles hospital, he was released, but by the end of January, the city received a petition signed by 30 townspeople demanding his committal. In early May, he entered a mental hospital in Saint-Rémy, not far from Arles, and there he painted *Starry Night*, perhaps his most famous composition (Fig. **14.4**). Here the swirling cypresses (in which red and green lie harmoniously side by side) and the rising church steeple unite earth and sky. Similarly, the orange and yellow stars and moon unite with the brightly lit windows of the town. Describing his thoughts about the painting in a letter to his brother, Van Gogh wrote, "Is it not emotion, the sincerity of one's feeling for nature, that draws us?" But finally, in July 1890, after a number of stays in hospitals and asylums, he committed suicide in the fields outside Auvers-sur-Oise, where he was being treated by Dr. Paul Gachet, who was the subject of several of the great artist's last portraits.

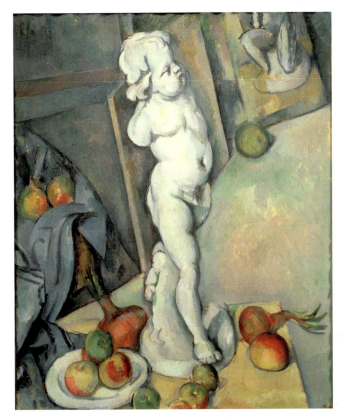

Fig. 14.5 Paul Cézanne, *Still Life with Plaster Cast*. ca. 1894. Oil on paper on board, 26½″ × 32½″. The Samuel Courtauld Trust, Courtauld Institute of Art Gallery, London. Cézanne's challenge to tradition is highlighted by the tension between his radical approach to the representation of space and his inclusion, at the heart of the painting, of a plaster cast of a seventeenth-century Cupid sculpted by Pierre Puget (1620–94).

View the Closer Look for Paul Cézanne, *Still Life with Plaster Cast* on **MyArtsLab**

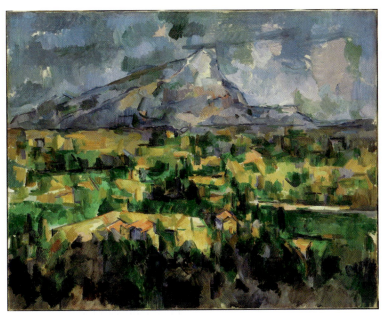

Fig. 14.6 Paul Cézanne, *Mont Sainte-Victoire*. 1902–04. Oil on canvas, 28¾″ × 36³⁄₁₆″. Photo: Graydon Wood. Philadelphia Museum of Art: The George W. Elkins Collection, 1936. E1936-1-1. Cézanne painted this from the top of the steep hill known as Les Lauves, just north of Aix-en-Provence but within walking distance of the city center. He built his own studio on a plot of land halfway up the hill, overlooking the city.

The Structure of Color: Cézanne Of all the Post-Impressionists, Paul Cézanne (1839–1906) was the only one who, after 1890, continued to paint *en plein air*. In this regard, he remained an Impressionist, and he continued to paint what he called "optics." The duty of the painter, he said, was "to give the image of what we see," but innocently, "forgetting everything that has appeared before." Since the Renaissance, Western art had been dedicated to representing the world as the eye sees it—that is, in terms of perspectival space. But Cézanne realized that we see the world in far more complex terms than just the retinal image before us. We see it through the multiple lenses of our lived experience. This multiplicity of viewpoints, or perspectives, is the dominant feature of *Still Life with Plaster Cast* (Fig. **14.5**). Nothing in the composition is spatially stable. Instead we wander through the small space in the corner of Cézanne's studio just as the painter's eye would do. His viewpoint constantly moves, contemplating its object from this angle, then that one. The result of this vision is a representation of nature as a series of patches of color that tend to flatten the surface of his paintings. Note, for instance, how the fruit and onions on the table are modeled by radical shifts in color rather than gradations from light to dark (traditional chiaroscuro).

Cézanne returned to the same theme continually—particularly still lifes and Mont Sainte-Victoire, the mountain overlooking his native Aix-en-Provence in the south of France (Fig. **14.6**). In the last decade of his life, the mountain became something of an obsession, as he climbed the hill behind his studio to paint it day after day. He especially liked to paint after storms, when the air was clear and the colors of the landscape were at their most saturated and uniform intensity. Cézanne acknowledges the illusion of space in the mountain scene by means of three bands of color. Patches of gray and black define the foreground, green and yellow-orange the middle ground, and violets and blues the distant mountain and sky. Yet in each of these areas, the predominant colors of the other two are repeated—the green brushstrokes of the middle ground in the sky, for instance—all with a consistent intensity. The distant colors possess the same strength as those closest. Together with the uniform size of Cézanne's brushstrokes—his patches do not get smaller as they retreat into the distance—this use of color makes the viewer very aware of the surface qualities and structure of Cézanne's composition. It is this tension between spatial perspective and surface flatness that would become one of the chief preoccupations of modern painting in the forthcoming century.

Escape to Far Tahiti: Gauguin In 1891, the painter Paul Gauguin (1848–1903) left France for the island of Tahiti, part of French Polynesia, in the South Pacific. A frustrated businessman and father of five children, he had taken up art with a rare dedication a decade earlier, studying with Camille Pissarro and Paul Cézanne. Gauguin was also a friend of Van Gogh, with whom he spent several months painting in

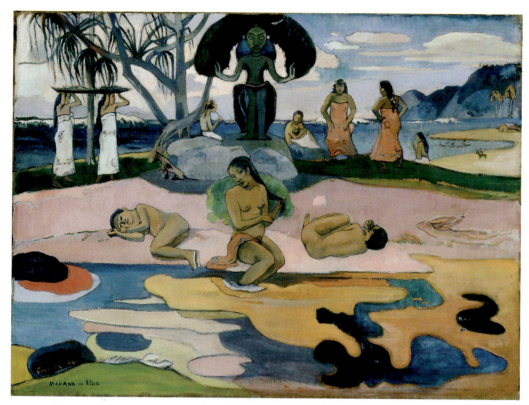

Fig. 14.7 Paul Gauguin, _Mahana no atua (Day of the God)_. 1894. Oil on canvas, 27⅜" × 35⅝". The Art Institute of Chicago. Helen Birch Bartlett Memorial Collection (1926.198). Photograph © 2007 The Art Institute of Chicago. All rights reserved. There is no record of Gauguin ever exhibiting this work. It was first exhibited at the Boston Art Club in 1925.

Arles during the Dutch artist's most productive period. He had also been inspired by the 1889 _Exposition Universelle_, where indigenous peoples and housing from around the world were displayed. "I can buy a native house," he wrote his friend Émile Bernard, "like those you saw at the World's Fair. Made of wood and dirt with a thatched roof." To other friends he wrote, "I will go to Tahiti and I hope to finish out my life there… far from the European struggle for money… able to listen in the silence of beautiful tropical nights to the soft murmuring music of my heartbeats in loving harmony with the mysterious beings in my entourage."

Gauguin's first trip to Tahiti was not everything he dreamed it would be, since by March 1892 he was penniless. When he arrived back in France, he had painted 66 pictures but had only four francs (about $12 today) to his name. He spent the next two years energetically promoting his work and writing an account of his journey to Tahiti, entitled _Noa Noa_ (_noa_ means "fragrant" or "perfumed"). It is a fictionalized version of his travels and bears little resemblance to the details of his journey that he recorded more honestly in his letters. But _Noa Noa_ was not meant to be true so much as sensational, with its titillating story of the artist's liaison with a 13-year-old Tahitian girl, Tehamana, offered to him by her family. He presents himself as a _primitif_. In French, the word _primitif_ suggests the primal, original, or irreducible. Gauguin believed that "primitive" ways

of thinking offered an entry into the primal powers of the mind, and he considered his paintings visionary glimpses into the primal forces of nature.

Gauguin arranged for two exhibitions at a Paris gallery in November 1893 and another in December 1894. He opened a studio of his own, painted olive green and a brilliant chrome yellow, and decorated it with paintings, tropical plants, and exotic furnishings. He initiated a regular Thursday salon where he lectured on his paintings and regaled guests with stories of his travels, as well as playing music on a range of instruments.

In this studio, he painted _Mahana no atua_ (_Day of the God_) of 1894 (Fig. **14.7**). Based on idealized recollections of his escape to Tahiti, the canvas consists of three zones. In the top zone or background, figures carry food to a carved idol, representing a native god, a musician plays as two women dance, and two lovers embrace beside the statue of the deity. Below, in the second zone, are three nude figures. The one to the right assumes a fetal position suggestive of birth and fertility. The one to the left appears to be daydreaming or napping, possibly an image of reverie. The middle figure appears to have just emerged from bathing in the water below, which constitutes the third zone. She directs her gaze at the viewer and so suggests an uninhibited sexuality. The bottom, watery zone is an irregular patchwork of color, an abstract composition of sensuous line and fluid shapes. As in Van Gogh's

View the Closer Look for _Mahana no atua_ on **MyArtsLab**

work, color is freed of its representational function to become an almost pure expression of the artist's feelings.

Gauguin returned to Tahiti in June 1895 and never came back to France, completing nearly 100 paintings and over 400 woodcuts in the eight remaining years of his life. He moved in 1901 to the remote island of Hivaoa, in the Marquesas, where in the small village of Atuona he built and decorated what he called his House of Pleasure. Taking up with another young girl, who like Tehamana gave birth to his child, Gauguin alienated the small number of priests and colonial French officials on the islands but attracted the interest and friendship of many native Marquesans, who were fascinated by his nonstop work habits and his colorful paintings. Having suffered for years from heart disease and syphilis, he died quietly in Hivaoa in May 1903.

Pablo Picasso's Paris: At the Heart of the Modern

Picasso's Paris was centered at 13 rue Ravignon, at the Bateau-Lavoir ("Laundry Barge"), so nicknamed by the poet Max Jacob. This was Picasso's studio from the spring of 1904 until October 1909, and he continued to store his paintings there until September 1912. Anyone wanting to see his work would have to climb the hill topped by the great white cathedral of Sacre Coeur in the Montmartre quarter, beginning from the Place Pigalle, and finally climb the stairs to the great ramshackle space, where the walls were piled deep with canvases. Or they might see his work at the Saturday evening salons of expatriate American writer and art collector Gertrude Stein (1874–1946) at 27 rue de Fleurus behind the Jardin du Luxembourg on the Left Bank of the Seine. If you knew someone who knew someone, you would be welcome enough. Many Picassos hung on her walls, including his portrait of her, painted in 1906 (Fig. **14.8**).

In her book *The Autobiography of Alice B. Toklas* (1932)—actually her own memoir disguised as that of her friend and lifelong companion—Stein described the making of this picture in the winter of 1906 (**Reading 14.1**):

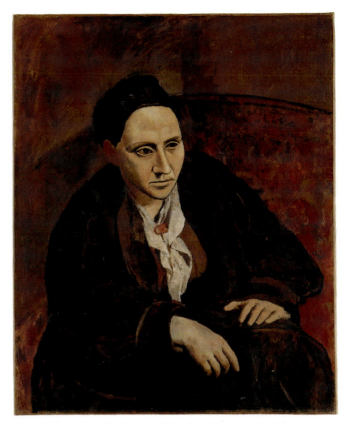

Fig. 14.8 Pablo Picasso, *Gertrude Stein*. Autumn–Winter 1906. Oil on canvas, 39⅜" × 32". Bequest of Gertrude Stein, 1946 (47.106). The Metropolitan Museum of Art, New York. © 2014 Estate of Pablo Picasso/Artists Rights Society (ARS), New York. According to Stein, in painting her portrait, "Picasso passed [on]... to the intensive struggle which was to end in Cubism."

READING 14.1

from Gertrude Stein, *The Autobiography of Alice B. Toklas* (1932)

Picasso had never had anybody pose for him since he was sixteen years old. He was then twenty-four and Gertrude had never thought of having her portrait painted, and they do not know either of them how it came about. Anyway, it did, and she posed for this portrait ninety times. There was a large broken armchair where Gertrude Stein posed. There was a couch where everybody sat and slept. There was a little kitchen chair where Picasso sat to paint. There was a large easel and there were many canvases. She took her pose, Picasso sat very tight in his chair and very close to his canvas and on a very small palette, which was of a brown gray color, mixed some more brown gray and

the painting began. All of a sudden one day Picasso painted out the whole head. I can't see you anymore when I look, he said irritably, and so the picture was left like that.

Picasso actually finished the picture early the following fall, painting Stein's face in large, masklike masses in a style very different from the rest of the picture. No longer relying on the visual presence of the sitter before his eyes, Picasso painted not his view of her, but his idea of her. When Alice B. Toklas later commented that some people thought the painting did not look like Stein, Picasso replied, "It will."

The Aggressive New Modern Art: *Les Demoiselles d'Avignon* In a way, the story of Gertrude Stein's portrait is a parable for the birth of modern art. It narrates the shift in painting from an optical art—painting what one sees—to an imaginative construct—painting what one thinks about what one sees. The object of painting shifts, in other words, from the literal to the conceptual. The painting that most thoroughly embodied this shift was *Les Demoiselles d'Avignon*, which Picasso began soon after finishing his portrait of Stein (Fig. **14.9**).

Completed in the summer of 1907, *Les Demoiselles d'Avignon* was not exhibited in public until 1916. So if you wanted to see it, you had to climb the hill to the Bateau-Lavoir. And many did, because the painting was notorious, seen—correctly—as an assault on the idea of painting as it had always been understood. At the Bateau-Lavoir, a common insult hurled by Picasso and his friends at one another was "Still much too symbolist!" No one said this about *Les Demoiselles*. It seemed entirely new in every way.

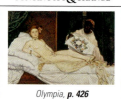

CONTINUITY & CHANGE

Olympia, **p. 426**

The painting represents five prostitutes in a brothel on the carrer d'Avinyo (Avignon Street) in Picasso's native Barcelona. As the figure on the left draws back a curtain as if to reveal them, the prostitutes address the viewer with the frankness of Manet's *Olympia* (see Fig. 13.14

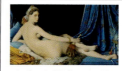

CONTINUITY & CHANGE

La Grande Odalisque, **p. 414**

in Chapter 13), a painting Picasso greatly admired. In fact, in January 1907, as Picasso was planning *Les Demoiselles*, *Olympia* was hung, for the first time, in the Louvre, to much public comment and controversy. It was placed, not coincidentally, alongside Ingres's *La Grande Odalisque* (see Fig. 13.3 in Chapter 13). Both figures turn to face the viewer, and the distortions both painters work upon their figures—Manet's flat paint, Ingres's elongated spine and disconnected extremities—probably inspired Picasso to push the limits of representation even further.

Also extremely important to Picasso was the example of Cézanne, who, a year after his death in October 1906, was honored with a huge retrospective at the 1907 Salon d'Automne. Cézanne, Picasso would say, "is the father of us all." In the way Picasso shows one object or figure from two different points of view, the compressed and concentrated space of *Les Demoiselles* is much like Cézanne's (see Fig. 14.5). Consider the still-life grouping of melon, pear, apple, and grapes in the center foreground. The viewer is clearly looking down at the corner of a table, at an angle completely inconsistent with the frontal view of the nude who is parting the curtain. And note the feet of the nude second from the left. Could she possibly be standing? Or is she, in fact, reclining, so that we see her from the same vantage point as the still life?

Picasso's subject matter and ambiguous space were disturbing to viewers. Even more disturbing were the strange faces of the left-hand figure and the two to the right. X-ray analysis confirms that originally all five of the figures shared the same facial features as the two in the middle left, with their almond eyes and noses drawn in an almost childlike profile. But sometime in May or June 1907, after he visited the ethnographic museum at the Palais du Trocadéro, across the river from the Eiffel Tower, Picasso painted over the faces of the figure at the left and the two on the right, giving them instead what most scholars agree are the characteristics of African masks. But equally important to Picasso's creative process was a retrospective of Gauguin's painting and sculpture, at the 1906 Salon d'Automne, with their Polynesian imagery (see Fig. 14.7). At any rate, Picasso's intentions were clear. He wanted to connect his prostitutes to the seemingly authentic—and emotionally energizing—forces that Gauguin had discovered in the "primitive." Many years later, he described the meaning of African and Oceanic masks to *Les Demoiselles*:

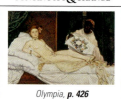

Fig. 14.9 Pablo Picasso, *Les Demoiselles d'Avignon*. May–July 1907. Oil on canvas, 95⅛" × 91⅛". Acquired through the Lillie P. Bliss Bequest. The Museum of Modern Art/Licensed by SCALA/ Art Resource, New York. © 2008 Artists Rights Society (ARS), New York. Central to Picasso's composition is the almond shape, first used for Gertrude Stein's eyes and repeated in the eyes of the figures here and in other forms—thighs and arms particularly. The shape is simultaneously rounded and angular, reinforcing the sense of tension in the painting.

View the Closer Look for *Les Demoiselles d'Avignon* on **MyArtsLab**

The masks weren't just like any other pieces of sculpture. Not at all. They were magic things.... They were against everything—against unknown, threatening spirits. I always looked at fetishes. I understood; I too am against everything. I too believe that everything is unknown, that everything is an enemy!... All the fetishes were used for the same thing. They were weapons. To help people avoid coming under the influence of spirits again, to help them become independent. They're tools. If we give spirits a form, we become independent.... I understood why I was a painter. All alone in that awful museum [the Trocadéro] with masks, with dolls made by the redskins, dusty manikins. *Les Demoiselles d'Avignon* must have come to me that very day, but not because of the forms; because it was my first exorcism painting—yes absolutely!

Les Demoiselles, then, was an act of liberation, an exorcism of past traditions, perhaps even of painting itself. It would allow Picasso to move forward into a kind of painting that was totally new.

Picasso scholar Patricia Leighten has argued convincingly that the African masks in *Les Demoiselles* are designed not only to challenge and mock Western artistic traditions but also to evoke and criticize the deplorable exploitation by Europeans of black Africans, particularly in the Congo—a theme taken up by Joseph Conrad in his 1899 novella *Heart of Darkness* (see Chapter 13). A scandal had erupted in 1905 when the French government's administrators in the Congo, Fernand Gaud and Georges Toqué, were accused of a wide variety of atrocities. In addition to their salaries, these administrators received bonuses for rubber collected under them, and they coerced natives to furnish them with rubber by pillaging their villages, executing "lazy" or uncooperative villagers, kidnapping their wives and children, and perpetrating even more scandalous assaults. Gaud and Toqué were accused specifically of dynamiting an African guide in celebration of Bastille Day and of forcing one of their servants to drink soup they had made from a native's head. Thus Picasso's painting confronts a variety of idealizations: the idealization of the world as reflected in traditional European art, the idealization of sexuality—and love—and the idealization of the colonizing mission of the European state. It acknowledges, in other words, the artist's obligation to confront the horrific truths that lie behind and support bourgeois complacency.

The Invention of Cubism: Braque's Partnership with Picasso

When the French painter Georges Braque (1882–1963) first saw *Les Demoiselles*, in December 1907, he said that he felt burned, "as if someone were drinking gasoline and spitting fire." He was, like Picasso, obsessed with Cézanne, so much so that he went to paint the following summer in Cézanne country in the south of France. When he returned to Paris in September, he brought with him a series of landscapes, among them *Houses at l'Estaque* (Fig. 14.10). Picasso was fascinated with their spatial ambiguity and cubelike shapes.

Note in particular the central house, where (illogically) the two walls that join at a right angle are shaded on both sides of the corner yet are similarly illuminated. And the angle of the roof line does not meet at the corner, thus flattening the roof. Details of windows, doors, and moldings have been eliminated, as have the lines between planes, so that one plane seems to merge with the next in a manner reminiscent of Cézanne. The tree that rises on the left seems to merge at its topmost branch into the distant houses. The curve of the bush on the left echoes that of the tree, and its palmlike leaves are identical to the trees rising between the houses behind it. The structure of the foreground mirrors that of the houses. All this serves to flatten the composition even as the lack of a horizon causes the whole composition to appear to roll toward the viewer rather than recede in space.

Seeing Braque's landscapes at a gallery in November 1908, the critic Louis Vauxcelles wrote: "He [Braque] is contemptuous of form, reduces everything, sites and figures and houses to geometric schemas, to cubes." But the movement known as **Cubism** was born out of collaboration. "Almost every evening," Picasso later recalled, "either I went to Braque's studio or Braque came to mine. Each of us had to see what the other had done during the day." The two men were inventors, brothers—Picasso even took to calling Braque "Wilbur," after the aeronautical brothers Orville

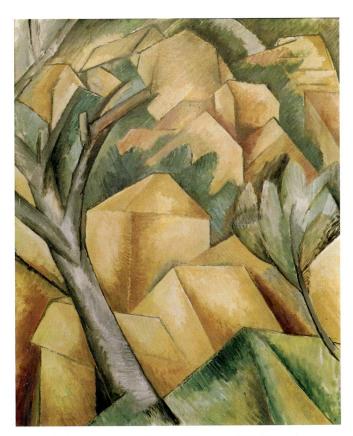

Fig. 14.10 Georges Braque, *Houses at l'Estaque*. 1908. Oil on canvas, 28¾″ × 23¾″. Estate of Georges Braque. © 2014 Artists Rights Society (ARS), New York/ADAGP, Paris. Hermann and Margit Rupf Foundation. Braque's trip to l'Estaque in the summer of 1908 was a form of homage to Cézanne, whose style he consciously radicalized in such works as this.

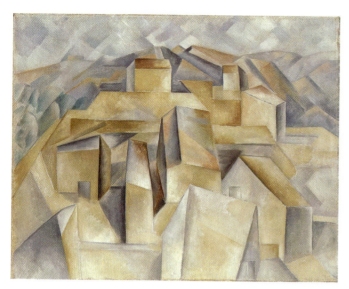

Fig. 14.11 Pablo Picasso, *Houses on a Hill, Horta de Ebro*. 1909. Oil on canvas, 25⅝″ × 31⅞″. Jens Ziehe/Nationalgalerie, Museum Berggruen, Staatliche Museen, Berlin. © 2014 Estate of Pablo Picasso/Artists Rights Society (ARS), New York. This is one of a series of some 15 paintings Picasso executed at Horta de Ebro (known today as Horta de Sant Joan) in the hills above Valencia during the summer of 1909.

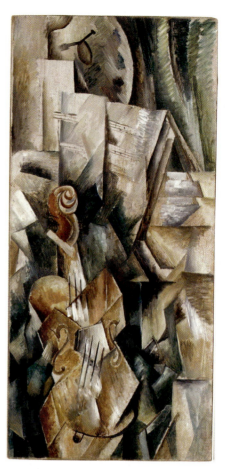

Fig. 14.12 Georges Braque, *Violin and Palette*. Autumn 1909. Oil on canvas, 36⅛″ × 16⅞″. The Solomon R. Guggenheim Museum, New York. 54.1412. © 2014 Artists Rights Society (ARS), New York/ADAGP, Paris. As in Picasso's *Les Demoiselles*, the primary tension in the painting is created by the juxtaposition of the rounded and angular forms.

and Wilbur Wright. When Picasso returned to Paris from Spain in the fall of 1909, he brought with him landscapes that showed just how much he had learned from Braque (Fig. 14.11).

Picasso and Braque pushed on, working so closely together that their work became indistinguishable to most viewers. They began to decompose their subjects into faceted planes, so that they seem to emerge down the middle of the canvas from some angular maze, as in Braque's *Violin and Palette* (Fig. 14.12). Gradually they began to understand that they were questioning the very nature of reality, the nature of "truth" itself. This is the function of the *trompe-l'oeil* nail casting its shadow onto the canvas at the top of Braque's painting. It announces its own artifice, the practice of illusionistically representing things in three-dimensional space. But the nail is no more real than the violin, which is about to dissolve into a cluster of geometric forms. Both are painted illusions, equally real as art.

From 1910 to 1912, Picasso and Braque took an increasingly abstract approach to depicting reality through painting. They were so experimental, in fact, that the subject nearly disappeared. Only a few cues remained to help viewers understand what they were seeing—a moustache, the scroll of a violin, a treble clef.

Increasingly, Picasso and Braque added a few words here and there. Picasso used words from a popular song, "*Ma Jolie*" ("My pretty one"), to identify portraits of his current lover, or "*Jou*," to identify the newspaper *Le Journal*. "*Jou*" was also a pun on the word *jeu* ("play"), and it symbolized the play

The CONTINUING PRESENCE of the PAST

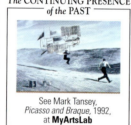

See Mark Tansey, *Picasso and Braque*, 1992, at **MyArtsLab**

between the reality of the painting as an object and the reality of the world outside the frame. This kind of ambiguity led Braque and Picasso to introduce actual two- and three-dimensional elements into the space of the canvas, in what they came to call **collage**, from the French *coller*, "to paste or glue." These elements—paper, fabric, rope, and other material—at least challenged, if they did not completely obliterate, the space between life and art.

Thus in Picasso's 1912 *Guitar, Sheet Music, and Wine Glass* (Fig. 14.13), at the bottom of the page, the headline of *Le Journal* reads, "*La bataille s'est engagé*," "The battle is joined." Literally, it refers to a battle in the Balkans, where Bulgaria attacked the Turks, November 17 through 19. But the "battle" is also metaphorical, the battle between art and reality (and perhaps between Braque and Picasso as they explored the possibilities of collage). Similarly, the background's trellis-and-rose wallpaper is no more or less real than the fragment of the actual musical score, the *faux-bois* ("false wood") guitar, and the Cubist drawing of a glass, cut out of some preexisting source like the other collage elements in the work. Collage is the great equalizer, in which all the elements are united on the same plane, both the literal plane of the canvas and the figurative plane of reality.

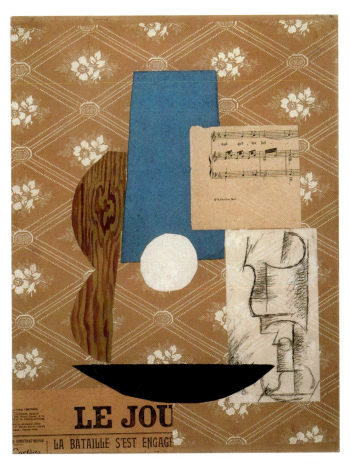

Fig. 14.13 **Pablo Picasso,** *Guitar, Sheet Music, and Wine Glass.* 1912. Charcoal, gouache, and *papiers-collé*, 18⅞″ × 14⅜″. The McNay Art Museum, San Antonio, TX. Bequest of Marion Koogler McNay. Art © 2014 Estate of Pablo Picasso/Artists Rights Society (ARS), New York. The newspaper fragment at the bottom of the painting derives from the front page of *Le Journal*, November 18, 1912.

Futurism: The Cult of Speed

News of the experimental fervor of Picasso and Braque spread quickly through avant-garde circles across Europe, and other artists sought to match their endeavors in independent but related ways. On February 20, 1909, for instance, the Paris newspaper *Le Figaro* published on its front page the *Founding and Manifesto of Futurism*, written by the Italian Filippo Marinetti (1876–1944). It rejected the political and artistic traditions of the past and called for a new art. Marinetti quickly attracted a group of painters and sculptors to invent it. These included the Italian artists Giacomo Balla (1871–1958), Umberto Boccioni (1882–1916), Carlo Carrà (1881–1966), Luigi Russolo (1885–1947), who was also a musician, and Gino Severini (1883–1966). The new style was called Futurism. The Futurists repudiated static art and sought to render what they thought of as the defining characteristic of modern urban life—speed. But it was not until Marinetti took Boccioni, Carra, and Russolo to Paris for two weeks in the fall of 1911, arranging visits to the studios of Picasso and Braque, that the fledgling Futurists discovered *how* they might represent it—in the fractured idiom of Cubism.

📖 **Read** the document from Filippo Marinetti on **MyArtsLab**

However, the work the Futurists created was philosophically remote from Cubism. It reflected Marinetti's *Manifesto*, which affirmed not only speed, but also technology and violence. In the manifesto, Futurism is born out of a high-speed automobile crash in the "maternal ditch" of modernity's industrial sludge, an intentionally ironic image of rebirth and regeneration. Where the Cubist rejection of tradition had largely been the invention of two men working in relative isolation, the Futurist rejection was public, bombastic, and political. As the Futurists traveled around Europe between 1910 and 1913 promoting their philosophy in public forums and entertainments, their typical evening featured insult-slinging and scuffles with the audience, usually an arrest or two, and considerable attention in the press. In fact, it could be said that Marinetti was among the first artists to understand the power of publicity in stimulating public interest, in creating what we have come to call "buzz."

One of the great masterpieces of Futurist art is Boccioni's *Unique Forms of Continuity in Space* (Fig. **14.14**), a work oddly evocative of the very *Nike of Samothrace* (see Fig. 2.45 in Chapter 2) that Marinetti in his manifesto found less compelling than a speeding car. Boccioni probably intended to represent a nude, her musculature stretched and

CONTINUITY&CHANGE

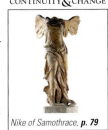

Nike of Samothrace, **p. 79**

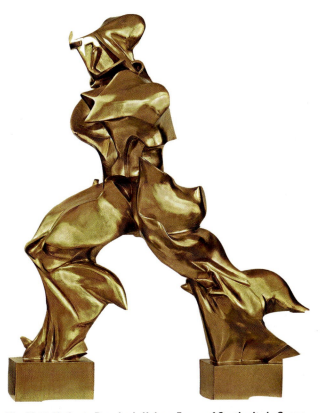

Fig. 14.14 **Umberto Boccioni,** *Unique Forms of Continuity in Space.* **1913.** Bronze, 43⅞″ × 34⅞″ × 15¾″. The Museum of Modern Art, New York. Acquired through the Lillie P. Bliss Bequest. (231.1948). Between 1912 and 1914, Boccioni made 12 important sculptures. Five have survived, of which this is one.

drawn out as she moves through space. "What we want to do," he explained, "is show the living object in its dynamic growth."

A New Color: Matisse and the Expressionists

When the painter Henri Matisse (1869–1954) saw *Les Demoiselles*, he is said to have considered it an "audacious hoax," an "outrage [ridiculing] the modern movement." It is little wonder, as the two painters' aesthetic visions were diametrically opposed. Gertrude Stein had introduced the two men in April 1906. Twelve years older than Picasso, Matisse was the favorite of Gertrude Stein's brother Leo. He had established himself, at the Salon des Indépendants in 1904, as the leader of a radical new group of experimental painters known as the Fauves—or "Wild Beasts." **Fauvism** was known for its radical application of arbitrary, or unnatural, color, anticipated in a few of Van Gogh's paintings and in the pool of color in the foreground of Gauguin's *Mahana no atua* (see Fig. 14.7). Picasso and Matisse saw each other regularly at the Steins' apartment, but their relationship was competitive. In fact, it is useful to think of Matisse's monumental *Dance* (Fig. **14.15**) as something of a rebuttal of the upstart Picasso's *Demoiselles*. Matisse had painted a similar circular dance before, with six figures, but when he repeated the motif in *Dance*, the number is five, like Picasso's five prostitutes. Matisse also replaces Picasso's squared and angular composition with a circular and rounded one. Where Picasso's painting seems static, as if asking us to hold our breath at the scene before us,

Matisse's is active, moving as if to an unheard music. Most astonishing is Matisse's color—vermilion (red-orange), green, and blue-violet, the primary colors of light. In effect, Matisse's modernism takes place in the light of day, Picasso's in the dark of night; Matisse's with joy, Picasso's with fear and trepidation.

Like that of the Fauves, the German Expressionists' interest in color can be traced to the art of Van Gogh and Gauguin. But unlike the Fauves, they often drew their subject matter from their own psychological makeup. They laid bare in paint the torment of their lives. There were Expressionist groups throughout Europe that encompassed the visual arts and other media, but the most important in Germany was *Der Blaue Reiter* ("The Blue Rider"), based in Munich.

Der Blaue Reiter did not come into being until 1911. It was headed by the Russian émigré Wassily Kandinsky (1866–1944) and by Franz Marc (1880–1916), an artist especially fond of painting animals, because he believed they possessed elemental energies. They were joined by a number of other artists, and although they shared no common style, all were obsessed with color. "Color," Kandinsky wrote in *Concerning the Spiritual in Art*, first published in 1912 in the *Blaue Reiter Almanac*, "directly influences the soul. Color is the keyboard, the eyes are the hammers, the soul is the piano with many strings. The artist is the hand that plays... to cause vibrations of the soul." The color blue, Kandinsky wrote, is "the typical heavenly color." Marc saw in blue what he thought of as the masculine principle of spirituality. So his *Large Blue*

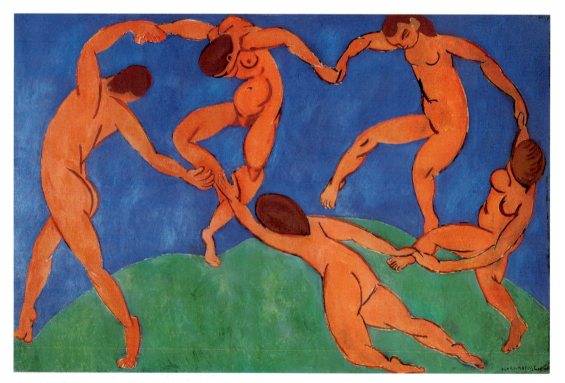

Fig. 14.15 Henri Matisse, *Dance II*. 1910. Oil on canvas. 8'5⅝" × 12'9½". Inv. no. 9673. The State Hermitage Museum, Saint Petersburg. © 2014 Succession H. Matisse/Artists Rights Society (ARS), New York. This work and another similarly colored painting of musicians called *Music* were commissioned by the Russian collector Sergei Shchukin to decorate the staircase of his home in Moscow.

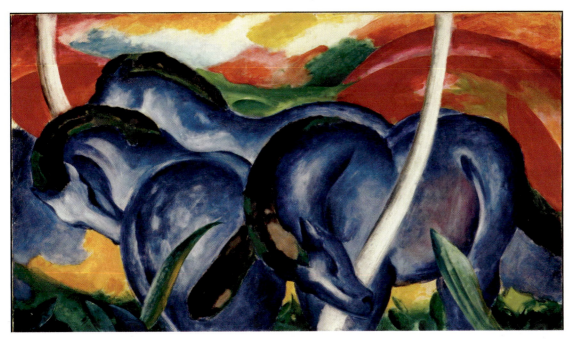

Fig. 14.16 Franz Marc, *The Large Blue Horses*. 1911. Oil on canvas, 3'5⅜" × 5'11¼". Walker Art Center, Minneapolis. Gift of T. B. Walker Collection, Gilbert M. Walter Fund, 1942. The painting is meant to contrast the beauty of the untainted natural world with the sordidness of modern existence, very much in the spirit of Gauguin.

Horses, with its seemingly arbitrary color and interlocking rhythm of fluid curves and contours, very much influenced by Matisse, is the very image of the spiritual harmony in the natural world (Fig. **14.16**).

Kandinsky's chief theme was the biblical Apocalypse, the moment when, according to a long tradition in the Byzantine church, Moscow would become the New Jerusalem. "Der Reiter," in fact, was the popular name for Saint George, patron saint of Moscow, and the explosions of contrasting colors across *Composition VII* (Fig. **14.17**) suggest that the fateful moment has arrived. Earthly yellow competes with heavenly blue, and red with green. Red, Kandinsky wrote, "rings inwardly with a determined and powerful intensity," while green "represents the social middle class, self-satisfied, immovable, narrow." Linear elements, he felt, were equivalent to dance, and the painting can be interpreted as a rendering of dance set to music. But *Composition VII* is the last of a series of "compositions"—the title in fact refers to music—on the biblical themes of war and resurrection, deluge and apocalypse, with each painting becoming more and more abstract. Certain passages, however, remain legible, especially when seen in light of the earlier works, such as a boat with three oars at the bottom left, which is, for Kandinsky, an emblem of the deluge. But above all, the painting remains a virtually nonobjective orchestration of line and color.

Modernist Music and Dance

The dynamism and invention evident in modern painting also appeared in music and dance. On May 29, 1913, the Ballets Russes, a company under the direction of the impresario Sergei Diaghilev (1872–1929), premiered the ballet *Le Sacre du printemps* (*The Rite of Spring*) at the Théâtre des Champs-Élysées in Paris. The music was by the cosmopolitan Russian composer Igor Stravinsky (1882–1971) and the

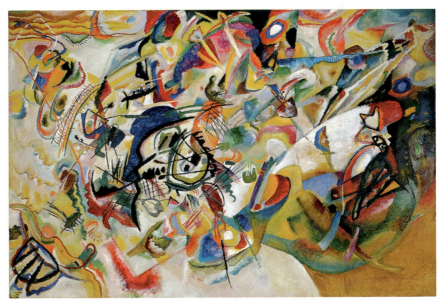

Fig. 14.17 Wassily Kandinsky, *Composition VII. 1913*. Oil on canvas, 6'6¾" × 9'11⅛". Tretyakov Gallery, Moscow. © 2014 Artists Rights Society (ARS), New York/ADAGP, Paris. Among practitioners of nonfigurative abstract art, Kandinsky was perhaps unique in not forcing his point of view on his colleagues. If his was what he called "the Greater Abstraction," theirs was "the Greater Realism," equally leading to "the spiritual in art."

choreography by his countryman Vaslav Nijinsky (1890–1950). The performance was a scandal. Together with the Futurists' confrontational performances and, earlier, the public outrage at Manet's *Luncheon on the Grass* and *Olympia* in the 1860s, it helped to define modern art as antagonistic to public opinion and an affront to the public's values.

The events of that evening surprised everyone. The night before, a dress rehearsal performed before an audience, in Stravinsky's words, "of actors, painters, musicians, writers, and the most cultured representatives of society" had proved uneventful. But on the night of the public premiere, the first notes of Stravinsky's score evoked derisive laughter. Hissing, booing, and catcalls followed, and at such a level that the dancers could not hear the music. Diaghilev ordered the lights to be turned on and off, hoping to quiet the crowd, but that just incensed the audience further. Finally the police had to be called, as Stravinsky himself crawled to safety out of a backstage window.

What seemed most radically new to Stravinsky's audience was the music's angular, jarring, sometimes violent rhythmic inventiveness. The ballet's story—it is subtitled *Pictures from Pagan Russia*—centers on a pre-Christian ritual welcoming the beginning of spring that culminates in a human sacrifice. The music reflects the brutalism of the pagan rite with savage dissonance. Part 1 of the work, "The Adoration of the Earth," culminates in a spirited dance of youths and maidens in praise of the earth's fertility. In Part 2, "The Sacrifice," one of the maidens is chosen to be sacrificed in order to guarantee the fertility celebrated in Part 1. All dance in honor of the Chosen One, invoking the blessings of the village's ancestors, culminating in the frenzied Sacrificial Dance of the Chosen One herself (see track **14.1**). Just before the dancer collapses and dies, Stravinsky shifts the meter eight times in 12 measures; the men then carry the Chosen One's body to the foot of a sacred mound and offer her up to the gods.

Sometimes different elements of the orchestra play in different meters simultaneously. Such **polyrhythms** contrast dramatically with other passages where the same rhythmic pulse repeats itself persistently—such as when at the end of the ballet's first part the orchestra plays the same eighth-note chords 32 times in succession. (This technique is known as *ostinato*—Italian for "obstinate.") In addition to its rhythmic variety, Stravinsky's ballet was also **polytonal**: Two or more keys are sounded by different instruments at the same time, and the traditional instruments of the orchestra are used in startlingly unconventional ways, so that they sound raw and strange. Low-pitched instruments, such as bassoons, play at the top of their range, for instance, and clarinets at the gravelly bottom of their capabilities. Integrated with these jarring juxtapositions are passages of recognizable Russian folk songs. Stravinsky's music was enormously influential on subsequent composers, who began to think about rhythmic structure in a totally different way.

If the first Paris audience found Stravinsky's music offensive, Nijinsky's choreography seemed a downright provocation to riot: "They repeat the same gesture a hundred times over," wrote one critic, "they paw the ground, they stamp, they stamp, they stamp, they stamp and they stamp.... Evidently all of this is defensible; it is prehistoric dance." It certainly was not recognizable as ballet. It moved away from the traditional graceful movements of ballerinas dancing *en pointe* (on their toes in boxed shoes) toward a new athleticism. Nijinsky's choreography called for the dancers to assume angular, contorted positions that at once imitated ancient bas-relief sculpture and Cubist painting, to hold these positions in frozen stillness, and then burst into wild leaps and whirling circle dances.

Meanwhile, in Germany, audiences were equally challenged by the work of Arnold Schoenberg (1874–1951). Schoenberg was from Vienna, where he led a group of composers, including Alban Berg and Anton Webern, who believed that the long reign of tonality, the harmonic basis of Western music, was over. On January 2, 1911, the *Blaue Reiter* painters Kandinsky and Marc attended a Schoenberg concert in Munich. Marc later wrote to a friend, "Can you imagine a music in which tonality is completely suspended? I was constantly reminded of Kandinsky.... Schoenberg seems, like [us], to be convinced of the irresistible dissolution of the European laws of art and harmony."

Schoenberg did in fact abandon **tonality**, the organization of the composition around a home key (the tonal center). In its place, he created a music of complete **atonality**, a term he hated (since it implied the absence of musical tone altogether), preferring instead "pantonal." His 1912 setting of a cycle of 21 poems by Albert Giraud, *Pierrot lunaire*, is probably the first atonal composition to be widely appreciated, although to many it represented, as one critic put it, "the last word in cacophony and musical anarchy" (see track **14.2**). Pierrot is a character from the Italian commedia dell'arte, the improvisational traveling street theater that first developed in the fifteenth century. He is a moonstruck clown whose mask conceals his deep melancholy, brought on by living in a state of perpetually unrequited desire. (Picasso often portrayed himself as Pierrot, especially early in his career.) In *Pierrot lunaire*, five performers play eight instruments in various combinations in accompaniment to a voice that does not sing but instead employs a technique that Schoenberg calls *Sprechstimme* or "speech-song." "A singing voice," Schoenberg explained, "maintains the pitch without modification; speech-song does, certainly, announce it [the pitch], only to quit it again immediately, in either a downward or an upward direction." In the "Madonna" section of *Pierrot lunaire*, which addresses Mary at the moment of the *pietà*, when she mourns over the dead body of her son, the lyrics focus on the blood of Christ's wounds, which "seem like eyes, red and open." The atonality of Schoenberg's music reflects this anguish with explosive force.

Creating long works without the resources of tonality was a very real challenge to Schoenberg—hence the usefulness of 21 short works in the *Pierrot lunaire* series. By 1924, Schoenberg had created a system in which none of the 12 tones of the chromatic scale could be repeated in a composition until each of the other 11 had been played. This **12-tone system** reflected his belief that every tone was equal to every other. The 12 notes in their given order are called a **tone row**, and audiences soon grew accustomed to not hearing a tonal center in the progression and variation of the tone row as it developed in Schoenberg's increasingly **serial composition**. The principal tone row can be played upside down, backward, or upside down and backward. While the possibilities for writing an extended composition with a single tone row and its variations might at first seem limited, by adding rhythmic and dynamic variations, as well as contrapuntal arrangements, the development of large-scale works became feasible.

Early Twentieth-Century Literature

If one word could express the literature of the early twentieth century, it would be innovation. Like visual artists and composers, writers too were drawn to uncharted ground and experimented with creating new forms in an effort to embrace the multiplicity of human experience. Like Picasso in his *Demoiselles d'Avignon*, they sought a way to capture the simultaneous and often contradictory onslaught of information and feelings that characterized the fabric of modern life. And writers understood that these multiple impulses from the real world struck the brain randomly, inharmoniously, in rhythms and sounds as discordant as the music of Stravinsky and Schoenberg.

Guillaume Apollinaire and Cubist Poetics Picasso's good friend and a champion of his art, Guillaume Apollinaire (1880–1918), was one of the leaders in the "revolution of the word," as this new approach to poetry and prose has been called. Modeling his work on the example of Picasso, Apollinaire quickly latched on to the principle of collage. In his poem "Lundi, rue Christine" ("Monday in the rue Christine"), snatches of conversation overheard on a street in Paris, not far from the École des Beaux Arts, follow one another without transition or thematic connection (**Reading 14.2**):

READING 14.2

from Guillaume Apollinaire, "Lundi, rue Christine" (1913)

Those pancakes were delicious
The tap is running
A dress as black as her nails
It's absolutely impossible
Look sir
The malachite ring
The ground is covered with sawdust
So it's true

The redhaired waitress was abducted by a bookseller
A journalist whom by the way I know only very vaguely
Listen Jacques I'm going to tell you something very
    serious
Goods and passenger steam navigation company

In this short, representative fragment from the poem, Apollinaire has transformed this collage of voices into poetry by the act of arranging each phrase into poetic lines.

Ezra Pound and William Carlos Williams Apollinaire's strategy of juxtaposing fragments of speech heard simultaneously, thereby combining two (or more) unlike words, objects, or images, was, in fact, a fundamental strategy of modern art. It informs, as well, the poetry of the Imagists, a group of English and American poets who sought to create precise images in clear, sharp language. Imagism was the brainchild of American poet Ezra Pound (1885–1972), who in October 1912 submitted a group of poems under the title *Imagiste* to the new American journal *Poetry*. The poet and critic F. S. Flint would succinctly define the Imagist poem in the March 1913 issue of the magazine. Its simple rules were:

1. Direct treatment of the "thing," whether subjective or objective.

2. To use absolutely no word that does not contribute to the presentation.

3. As regarding rhythm: to compose in sequence of the musical phrase, not in sequence of the metronome.

Pound's "In a Station of the Metro," which first appeared in *Poetry* in 1913, is in many ways the classic Imagist poem (**Reading 14.3**):

READING 14.3

Ezra Pound, "In a Station of the Metro" (1913)

The apparition of these faces in the crowd;
Petals on a wet, black bough.

Pound was an avid scholar of Chinese and Japanese poetry, and the poem is influenced both by the Japanese *waka* tradition, with its emphasis on the changing seasons, and formally, in its brevity at least, by the haiku tradition (see Chapter 9). (Haiku normally consist of 3 lines in 17 syllables, while Pound's poem is made up of 19 syllables in 2 lines.) The poem's first line seems relatively straightforward—except for the single word "apparition." It introduces Pound's predisposition, his sense that Paris is inhabited by the "living dead." It contrasts dramatically with the poem's second and final line, which is an attractive picture of nature. The first line's six-beat iambic meter—da-duh, da-duh, and so on—is transformed into a five-beat line that ends in three long strophes—that is, single beats—"wet, black bough." The semicolon at the end of the first line acts as a kind of hinge, transforming the bleak vision of the moment into a vision of possibility and hope, the implicitly "white" apparition of the faces of the ghostlike crowd transformed into an image of spring itself, the petals on the wet, black bough. The poem moves from the literal subway underground, from burial, to life, reborn in the act of the poetic vision itself. It captures that moment, as Pound said, when a thing "outward and objective" is transformed into a thing "inward and subjective."

In 1934, Pound would publish a collection of essays titled *Make It New*, and his "make it new" mantra soon became something of a rallying cry for the new American poetry. The sentiment was shared especially by his friend, the poet William Carlos Williams (1883–1963). Williams met Pound when they were both students at the University of Pennsylvania in 1902. Williams was a physician in Rutherford, New Jersey, across the Hudson River from New York City. He was immediately attracted to Imagism when Pound defined it in the pages of *Poetry* magazine, particularly to the Imagist principle of verbal simplicity: "Use absolutely no word that does not contribute to the presentation." He praised Imagism for "ridding the field of verbiage." His own work has been labeled "Radical Imagism," for concentrating on the stark presentation of commonplace objects to the exclusion of inner realities. His famous poem "The Red Wheelbarrow" is an example (**Reading 14.4**):

READING 14.4

William Carlos Williams, "The Red Wheelbarrow," from *Spring and All* (1923)

so much depends
upon

a red wheel
barrow

glazed with rain
water

beside the white
chickens

The first line of each stanza of Williams's poem raises expectations which the second line debunks in two syllables. Thus a mere preposition, "upon," follows the urgency of "so much depends." A "red wheel" conjures images of Futurist speed, only to fall flat with the static "barrow." "Rain/water" approaches redundancy. Our expectations still whetted by the poem's first line, the word "white" suggests purity, only to modify the wholly uninspiring image, "chickens." Williams's aesthetic depends upon elevating the commonplace and the everyday into the realm of poetry, thus transforming them, making them new.

THE GREAT WAR AND ITS AFTERMATH

What was the impact of the Great War on the art and literature of the era?

On June 28, 1914, a young Bosnian nationalist assassinated Archduke Francis Ferdinand, heir to the Austrian throne, in the Bosnian capital of Sarajevo. Europe was outraged, except for Serbia, which had been at war with Bosnia for years. Austria suspected that Serbian officials were involved (as in fact they were). With Germany's support, Austria declared war on Serbia, Russia mobilized in Serbia's defense, and France mobilized to support its ally, Russia. Germany invaded Luxembourg and Belgium, and then pushed into France. Finally, on August 4, Britain declared war on Germany, and Europe was consumed in battle.

Although the Germans advanced perilously close to Paris in the first month of the war, the combined forces of the British and French stopped them. From then on, along the Western Front on the French/Belgian border, both sides dug in behind zigzagging rows of trenches protected by barbed wire that stretched from the English Channel to Switzerland, some 25,000 miles of them. In the three years after its establishment, the Western Front moved only a few miles either east or west.

Stagnation accompanied carnage. Assaults in which thousands of lives were lost would advance the lines only a couple of hundred yards. Poison mustard gas was introduced in the hope that it might resolve the stalemate, but it changed nothing, except to permanently maim or kill thousands upon thousands of soldiers. Mustard gas blinded those who encountered it, but it also slowly rotted the body from within and without, causing severe blistering and damaging the bronchial tubes, so that its victims slowly choked to death. Most affected by the gas died within four to five weeks. British troops rotated trench duty. After a week behind the lines, a unit would move up, at night, to the front-line trench, then after a week there, back to a support trench, then after another week back to the reserve trench, and then, finally, back to a week of rest again. Attacks generally came at dawn, so it was at night, under the cover of darkness, that most of the work in the trenches was done—wiring, digging, moving ammunition. It rained often, so the trenches were often filled with water. The troops were plagued by lice, and huge rats, which fed on cadavers and dead horses, roamed through the encampments. The stench was almost as unbearable as the weather, and lingering pockets of gas might blow through at any time. As Germany tried to push both east and west, the human cost was staggering. By the war's end, casualties totaled around 10 million dead—it became impossible to count accurately—and somewhere around twice that many wounded.

Trench Warfare and the Literary Imagination

At the outset of the war, writers responded to the conflict with buoyant enthusiasm, along with thousands of others, their patriotic duty calling them to arms. Life in the trenches soon brought the meaninglessness of such rhetoric crashing down around this new generation of soldiers. Words like "glory" and "honor" suddenly rang hollow. The tradition of viewing warfare as an arena in which heroes exhibit what the Greeks called *areté*, or virtue (see Chapter 2)—that is, realize their full human potential—no longer seemed applicable to experience, and a new kind of writing about war, an antiwar literature far removed from the heroic battle scenes of poems like Homer's *Iliad*, soon appeared.

Wilfred Owen: "The Pity of War"   A notable example is the poetry of 25-year-old Wilfred Owen (1893–1918), killed in combat just a week before the armistice was signed in 1918. His work caused a sensation when it first appeared in 1920. "My subject is War, and the pity of War," he wrote in a manuscript intended to preface his poems, "and the Poetry is in the pity." The poems drew immediate attention for Owen's horrifying descriptions of the war's victims, as in "Dulce et Decorum Est," its title drawn from Ode 13 of the Roman poet Horace (see Chapter 3), "It is sweet and fitting to die for one's country." But Owen's reference to Horace is bitterly ironic (**Reading 14.5**):

READING 14.5
Wilfred Owen, "Dulce et Decorum Est" (1918)

Bent double, like old beggars under sacks,
Knock-kneed, coughing like hags, we cursed through
    sludge,
Till on the haunting flares we turned our backs
And towards our distant rest began to trudge.
Men marched asleep. Many had lost their boots
But limped on, blood-shod. All went lame; all blind;
Drunk with fatigue; deaf even to the hoots
Of disappointed shells that dropped behind.

GAS! Gas! Quick, boys!—An ecstasy of fumbling,
Fitting the clumsy helmets just in time;
But someone still was yelling out and stumbling
And floundering like a man in fire or lime.—
Dim, through the misty panes and thick green light
As under a green sea, I saw him drowning.

In all my dreams, before my helpless sight,
He plunges at me, guttering, choking, drowning.

If in some smothering dreams you too could pace
Behind the wagon that we flung him in,
And watch the white eyes writhing in his face,
His hanging face, like a devil's sick of sin;
If you could hear, at every jolt, the blood
Come gargling from the froth-corrupted lungs,
Obscene as cancer, bitter as the cud
Of vile, incurable sores on innocent tongues,—
My friend, you would not tell with such high zest
To children ardent for some desperate glory,
The old Lie: Dulce et decorum est
Pro patria mori.

The quotation from Horace in the last lines is, notably, labeled by Owen a "Lie." And the fact is, Owen's intent is that

the reader should share his horrific dreams. His rhetorical strategy is to describe the drowning of this nameless man in a sea of green gas in such vivid terms that we cannot forget it either.

T. S. Eliot: The Landscape of Desolation   The American poet T. S. (Thomas Stearns) Eliot (1888–1965) was studying at Oxford University in England when World War I broke out. Eliot had graduated from Harvard with a degree in philosophy and the classics, and his poetry reflects both the erudition of a scholar and the depression of a classicist who feels that the tradition he so values is in jeopardy of being lost. In Eliot's poem *The Waste Land*, the opening section, called "The Burial of the Dead," is a direct reference to the Anglican burial service, performed so often during and after the war. "April is the cruelest month," the poem famously begins (**Reading 14.6**):

READING 14.6a
from T. S. Eliot, *The Waste Land* (1921)

April is the cruelest month, breeding
Lilacs out of the dead land, mixing
Memory and desire, stirring
Dull roots with spring rain.
Winter kept us warm, covering
Earth in forgetful snow, feeding
A little life with dried tubers.

The world, in short, has been turned upside down. Spring is cruel, winter consoling. Eliot sees London as an "Unreal City" populated by the living dead (**Reading 14.6b**):

READING 14.6b
from T. S. Eliot, *The Waste Land* (1921)

Unreal City,
Under the brown fog of a winter dawn,
A crowd flowed over London Bridge, so many,
I had not thought death had undone so many.
Sighs, short and infrequent, were exhaled,
And each man fixed his eyes before his feet.
Flowed up the hill and down King William Street,
To where Saint Mary Woolnoth kept the hours
With a dead sound on the final stroke of nine.

In the crucial middle section of the poem, "The Fire Sermon," Eliot depicts modern love as reduced to mechanomorphic tedium. He describes the sexual encounter between a typist and her "young man carbuncular"—that is, covered with boils—as overseen by the figure of Tiresias. In a note, Eliot insists that Tiresias is "the most important personage in the poem," despite the fact that he is a "mere spectator." In his *Metamorphoses* (see Chapter 3), Ovid describes how Tiresias spent seven years as a woman. Later, he was asked to settle a quarrel between Zeus and Hera over who enjoyed sex more, men or women. When Tiresias

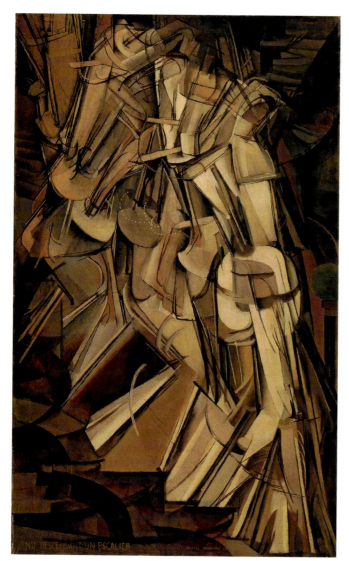

Fig. 14.19 Marcel Duchamp, *Nude Descending a Staircase, No. 2*. 1912. Oil on canvas, 58" × 35". Philadelphia Museum of Art, Louise and Walter Arenberg Collection. Photo: Graydon Wood, 1994. © 2014 Artists Rights Society (ARS), New York/ADAGP, Paris/Succession Marcel Duchamp. Interestingly, when Duchamp submitted this painting to the 1912 Salon des Indépendants in Paris, the selection committee objected to its literal title and traditional subject matter.

 View the Closer Look for Marcel Duchamp, *Nude Descending a Staircase, No.2* on **MyArtsLab**

already notorious for his *Nude Descending a Staircase, No. 2* (Fig. **14.19**), which had been the focus of critical debate in February 1913 at the International Exhibition of Modern Art at the 69th Infantry Regiment Armory in New York. Known simply as the Armory Show, the exhibit displayed nearly 1,300 pieces, including 17 Matisses, 7 Picassos, 15 Cézannes (plus a selection of lithographs), 13 Gauguins (plus, again, a number of lithographs and prints), 18 Van Goghs, 4 Manets, 5 Monets, 5 Renoirs, 2 Seurats, a Delacroix, and a Courbet. It was the first time that most Americans were able to view French modernist painting. One newspaper writer called Duchamp's *Nude* "an explosion in a shingle factory." *American Art News* called it "a collection of saddlebags" and offered a $10 reward to anyone

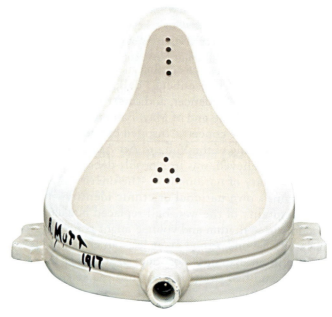

Fig. 14.20 Marcel Duchamp, *Fountain*. 1917; replica 1963. Porcelain, height 14". Purchased with assistance from the Friends of the Tate Gallery 1999. © Tate, London 2014. © 2014 Artists Rights Society (ARS), New York/ADAGP, Paris/Succession Marcel Duchamp. It is important to recognize that Duchamp has turned the urinal on its side, thus undermining its utility.

who could locate the nude lady it professed to portray. President Theodore Roosevelt compared it to the Navajo rug in his bathroom. Considering the European artists shown at the exhibition as a whole, he concluded that they represented the "lunatic fringe." But if Duchamp's nude seemed inexplicable to Americans in 1913, today we can easily identify several influences that shaped the work. Duchamp was familiar with Picasso and Braque's Cubist reduction of the object into flat planes (see Figs. 14.10 and 14.11). He also knew of the Futurists' ideas about depicting motion, and, perhaps more important, he was familiar with the burgeoning motion-picture industry.

Thus, when Duchamp introduced what he dubbed his "ready-mades," the New York art world was prepared to be shocked. And *Fountain* (Fig. **14.20**) shocked them indeed. An upside-down urinal purchased by Duchamp in a New York plumbing shop, signed with the pseudonym "R. Mutt," it was submitted by Duchamp to the New York Society of Independent Artists exhibition in April 1917. The exhibition committee, on which Duchamp served, had agreed that all work submitted would be shown, and was therefore unable to reject the piece. To Duchamp's considerable amusement, they decided instead to hide it behind a curtain. Over the course of the exhibition, Duchamp gradually let it be known that he was "R. Mutt," and in a publication called *The Blind Man* defended the piece:

The CONTINUING PRESENCE *of the* PAST

See Sherrie Levine, *Fountain (After Marcel Duchamp: A.P.)*, 1991, at **MyArtsLab** Cast bronze, 14" × 25" × 15".

Whether Mr Mutt with his own hands made the fountain or not has no importance. He CHOSE it. He took an ordinary article of life, placed it so that its useful significance disappeared under the new title and point of view—created a new thought for the object.

But Duchamp's ready-made was equally an attack on art and culture as a whole. If *Fountain* is, indeed, a work of art, it is also, insistently, a bathroom fixture, a commodity. By extension, Duchamp seemed to be arguing, works of art had increasingly become commodities in their own right, objects to be bought and sold at will, and were, subsequently, degraded by the marketplace.

The Harlem Renaissance

Soon after Reconstruction, the period immediately following the Civil War, Southern states passed a group of laws that effectively established a racial caste system that relegated black Americans to second-class status and institutionalized segregation. In the South, the system was known as Jim Crow. In the years before the outbreak of World War I, nearly 90 percent of all African Americans lived in the South, three-quarters of them in the rural South. Lured by a huge demand for labor in the North once the war began, impoverished after a boll weevil infestation ruined the cotton crop, and threatened especially by the rise of white terrorists like the Ku Klux Klan, whose membership reached some 4 million by the early 1920s, blacks flooded into the North. In the course of a mere 90 days early in the 1920s, 12,000 African Americans left Mississippi alone. An average of 200 left Memphis every night. Many met with great hardship, but there was wealth to be had as well, and anything seemed better than life under Jim Crow in the South. From 1915 through 1918, as war raged in Europe, between 200,000 and 350,000 Southern blacks moved north in what came to be called the Great Migration.

As the Great Migration proceeded, racial tension erupted. The jobs that black workers were promised by recruiters in the South often turned out to be jobs as strikebreakers, and striking workers retaliated. In addition, as veterans returned home after the war to jobs now occupied by blacks, animosity flared. In East St. Louis, Illinois, in 1917, as blacks were arriving at a rate of about 2,000 a week, finding work at the Aluminum Ore Company and American Steel Company where white workers were on strike, riots broke out that resulted in somewhere between 40 and 200 dead, and as many as 6,000 blacks left homeless. In Tulsa, Oklahoma, in 1921, whites burned down 40 city blocks of what was the most prosperous black business district in the Southwest, destroying 23 African-American churches and over 1,000 homes and businesses. The number of African-American dead is today estimated at over 100. Nevertheless, in New York, the Great Migration inspired a cultural community so robust, and so new, that the era has come to be known as the Harlem Renaissance.

"The New Negro" Perhaps the first self-conscious expression of the Harlem Renaissance took place at a dinner party on March 21, 1924, hosted by Charles S. Johnson (1893–1956) of the National Urban League. The League was dedicated to promoting civil rights and helping black Americans address the economic and social problems they encountered as they settled in the urban North. At Johnson's dinner, young writers from Harlem were introduced to New York's white literary establishment. A year later, the *Survey Graphic*, a national magazine dedicated to sociology, social work, and social analysis, produced an issue dedicated exclusively to Harlem. The issue, subtitled *Harlem: Mecca of the New Negro*, was edited by Alain Leroy Locke (1886–1954), an African-American professor of philosophy at Howard University in Washington, D.C. He was convinced that a new era was dawning for black Americans, and wrote a powerful introduction to a new anthology. In his essay, sometimes referred to as the manifesto of the New Negro Movement, Locke argued that Harlem was the center of this new arena of creative expression (**Reading 14.9**):

> ## READING 14.9
> ### Alain Locke, *The New Negro* (1925)
>
> [There arises a] consciousness of acting as the advance-guard of the African peoples in their contact with Twentieth Century civilization... [and] the sense of a mission of rehabilitating the race in world esteem from that loss of prestige for which the fate and conditions of slavery have so largely been responsible. Harlem, as we shall see, is the center of both these movements.... The pulse of the Negro world has begun to beat in Harlem.... The New Negro... now becomes a conscious contributor and lays aside the status of beneficiary and ward for that of a collaborator and participant in American civilization. The great social gain in this is the releasing of our talented group from the arid fields of controversy and debate to the productive fields of creative expression.... And certainly, if in our lifetime the Negro should not be able to celebrate his full initiation into American democracy, he can at least, on the warrant of these things, celebrate the attainment of a significant and satisfying new phase of group development, and with it a spiritual Coming of Age.

In Locke's view, each ethnic group in America had its own identity, which it was entitled to protect and promote, and this claim to cultural identity need not conflict with the claim to American citizenship. Locke further emphasized that the spirit of the young writers who were a part of this anthology would drive this new Harlem-based movement by focusing on the African roots of black art and music, but they would, in turn, contribute mightily to a new, more inclusive American culture.

Langston Hughes and the Poetry of Jazz As the young poet Langston Hughes (1902–67) later put it, "Negro was in vogue." Hughes was among the new young poets whom Locke published in *The New Negro*, and the establishment publishing house Knopf would publish his book of poems, *Weary Blues*, in 1926. Twenty-two years of age in 1924, Hughes had gone to Paris seeking a freedom he could not find at home. He was soon writing poems inspired by the jazz rhythms he was hearing played by the African-American bands in the clubs where he worked as a busboy and dishwasher. The music's syncopated rhythms can be heard in poems such as "Jazz Band in a Parisian Cabaret" (**Reading 14.10**):

READING 14.10

from Langston Hughes, "Jazz Band in a Parisian Cabaret" (1925)

Play that thing,
Jazz band!
Play it for the lords and ladies,
For the dukes and counts,
For the whores and gigolos,
For the American millionaires,
And the school teachers
Out for a spree.
......
You know that tune
That laughs and cries at the same time
......
May I?
Mais oui,
Mein Gott!
Parece una rumba.
Play it, jazz band!

In these last lines, Hughes's poem captures all the voices of the Parisian cabaret, just as Apollinaire had captured the cacophony of conversation at his Parisian café on rue Christine (see Reading 14.2).

African Americans like Hughes had been drawn to Paris by reports of black soldiers who had served in World War I, in the so-called Negro divisions, the 92nd and 93rd infantries. Jazz itself was introduced to the French by Lieutenant Jimmy Europe, whose 815th Pioneer Infantry band played in city after city across the country. They had experienced something they never had in the United States—total acceptance by people with white skin. Paris presented itself after the war as the new land of freedom—and opportunity. But Harlem, largely because of the efforts of Johnson and Locke, soon replaced Paris in the African-American imagination.

In Harlem, Hughes quickly became one of the most powerful voices. His poems narrate the lives of his people, capturing the inflections and cadences of their speech. In fact, the poems celebrate, most of all, the inventiveness of African-American culture, especially the openness and ingenuity of its music and language. Hughes had come to understand that his cultural identity rested not in the grammar and philosophy of white culture, but in the vernacular expression of the American black, which he could hear in its music (the blues and jazz especially) and its speech.

The Blues and Jazz

By the time of the Great Migration, jazz had established itself as the music of African Americans. So much did it seem to define all things American that the novelist F. Scott Fitzgerald (1896–1940) entitled a collection of short stories published in 1922 *Tales of the Jazz Age*, and the name stuck. By the end of the 1920s, jazz was *the* American music, and it was almost as popular in Paris and Berlin as it was in New York, Chicago, and New Orleans. It originated in the 1890s in New Orleans, probably the most racially diverse city in America, particularly in the ragtime piano music of Scott Joplin and others. But it had deep roots as well in the blues.

The Blues If syncopated rhythm is one of the primary characteristics of jazz, another is the **blue note**. Blue notes are slightly lower or flatter than conventional pitches. In jazz, blues instrumentalists or singers commonly "bend" or "scoop" a blue note—usually the third, fifth, or seventh note of a given scale—to achieve heightened emotional effects. Such effects were first established in the blues proper, a form of song that originated among enslaved black Americans and their descendants.

The **blues** are by definition laments bemoaning loss of love, poverty, or social injustice, and they contributed importantly to the development of jazz. The standard blues form consists of three sections of four bars each. Each of these sections corresponds to the single line of a three-line stanza, the first two lines of which are the same.

Dixieland and Louis Armstrong in Chicago The bands that played around 1910–20 in the red-light district of New Orleans, the legendary Storyville, quickly established a standard practice. A "front line," consisting of trumpet (or cornet), clarinet, and trombone, was accompanied by banjo (later guitar), piano, bass, and drums. In **Dixieland jazz**, as it came to be known, the trumpet carried the main melody and the clarinet played off against it with a higher countermelody, while the trombone played a simpler, lower tune. The most popular forms of Dixieland were the standard 12-bar blues and a 32-bar AABA form. The latter consists of four 8-measure sections. Generally speaking, the trumpet plays the basic tune for the first 32 measures of the piece, then the band plays variations on the tune in a series of solo or collective improvisations, keeping to the 32-bar format. Each 32-bar section is called a "chorus."

When Storyville was shut down in 1917 (on orders from the U.S. Navy, whose sailors' discipline they believed was threatened by its presence), many of the bands that had played in the district joined the Great Migration and headed north. Among them was the trumpeter Louis Armstrong (1901–71), who arrived in Chicago in 1922 to play for Joe Oliver's Creole Jazz Band. The pianist and composer Lil Hardin (1898–1971) was the pianist and arranger for Oliver's band, and Hardin and Armstrong were married in 1924. Soon, Armstrong left Oliver's band to play on his own. He formed two studio bands composed of former New Orleans colleagues, the Hot Five and the Hot Seven, with whom he made a series of groundbreaking recordings. One, *Hotter Than That* (see track **14.3**), written by Hardin and recorded in 1927, is based on a 32-bar form over which the performers improvise. In the

Listen at **MyArtsLab**

third chorus, Armstrong sings in nonsense syllables, a method known as **scat**. This is followed by another standard form of jazz band performance, a **call-and-response** chorus between Armstrong and guitarist Lonnie Johnson, the two imitating one another as closely as possible on their two different instruments.

Swing: Duke Ellington at the Cotton Club The same year that Armstrong recorded *Hotter Than That*, Duke Ellington, born Edward Kennedy Ellington in Washington, D.C. (1899–1974), began a five-year engagement at Harlem's Cotton Club. The Cotton Club itself was owned by a gangster who used it as an outlet for his "Madden's #1 Beer," which, like all alcoholic beverages, was banned after National Prohibition was introduced in 1920. The Club's name was meant to evoke leisurely plantation life for its "white-only" audience, who came to listen to its predominantly black entertainers.

Ellington had formed his first band in New York in 1923. His 1932 *It Don't Mean a Thing (If It Ain't Got That Swing)* (see track **14.4**) introduced the term **swing** to jazz culture. (A particularly clear example of a "blue note" can be heard, incidentally, on the first "ain't" of the first chorus of *It Don't Mean a Thing*.) Swing is characterized by big bands—as many as 15 to 20 musicians, including up to five saxophones (two altos, two tenors, and a baritone)—resulting in a much bigger sound. Its rhythm depends on the subtle avoidance of downbeats, with the solo instrument attacking the beat either just before or just after it.

By the time Ellington began his engagement at the Cotton Club, commercial radio was seven years old, and many thousands of American homes had a radio. Live radio broadcasts from the Cotton Club brought Ellington national fame, and he was widely imitated throughout the 1930s by bands who toured the country. These included bands led by clarinetist Benny Goodman, soon known as "the King of Swing"; trumpeter Harry James; trombonist Glenn Miller; trombonist Tommy Dorsey; pianist Count Basie; and clarinetist Artie Shaw. These bands also featured vocalists, and they introduced the country to Frank Sinatra, Bing Crosby, Perry Como, Sarah Vaughan, Billie Holiday, Peggy Lee, Doris Day, Rosemary Clooney, and Ella Fitzgerald.

The Visual Arts in Harlem The leading visual artist in Harlem in the 1920s was Aaron Douglas (1898–1979), a native of Topeka, Kansas, who arrived in Harlem in 1925 with a Bachelor of Fine Arts degree from the University of Nebraska, where he had been the only black student in his class. "My first impression of Harlem," he would later write, "was that of an enormous stage swarming with humanity....

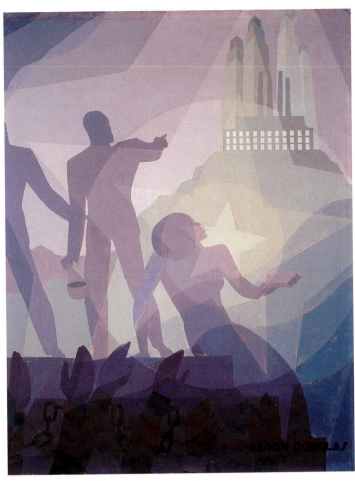

Fig. 14.21 Aaron Douglas, *Aspiration.* **1936.** Courtesy Fine Arts Museum of San Francisco. Art © Heirs of Aaron Douglas/Licensed by VAGA, New York, NY. Douglas's painting is composed as a series of stars within stars, all pointing toward the future and the promise he believed it held for African Americans.

Here one found a kaleidoscope of rapidly changing colors, sounds, movements—rising, falling, swelling, contracting, now hurrying, now dragging along without end and often without apparent purpose. And yet beneath the surface of this chaotic incoherent activity one sensed an inner harmony, one felt the presence of a mysterious hand fitting all these disparate elements into a whole." Douglas's work is a celebration of the African-American contribution to American culture (Fig. **14.21**), and his two-dimensional silhouetted figures would become the signature style of Harlem Renaissance art, in which a sense of rhythmic movement and sound is created by abrupt shifts in the direction of line and mass. *Aspiration* depicts the progression out of slavery, represented by the shackled arms that rise out of the bottom of the painting, out of the South, and toward the promise of the industrial North.

But as Douglas well knew, the realization of such aspiration was hard won. The jazz clubs that were at the center of African-American culture in Harlem were, in fact, restricted to white customers—blacks could enter only as performers or waiters. Access to satisfactory housing was extremely limited as whites created de facto white-only neighborhoods. Except in Harlem, landlords in New York City were unwilling to rent to black tenants, and as early as 1920, a one-room apartment in Harlem rented to whites for $40 and to blacks for between $100 and $125. These high rental expenses led to extreme population density—in 1920s Harlem, there were over 215,000 people per square mile (by way of comparison, today there are fewer than 70,000 people per square mile in Manhattan as a whole).

These were realities that Jacob Lawrence (1917–2000) did not shy from representing. Lawrence moved to Harlem in 1924 at the age of seven and trained as a painter at the Harlem Art Workshop, where he studied Aaron Douglas's work. When he was just 23 years old, he created a series of 60 paintings narrating the history of the Great Migration. Among the paintings are images of race riots, including the East St. Louis riots of 1917, the bombing of black homes, overcrowded housing, and tuberculosis outbreaks, but he also saw the same kind of hope and aspiration as Douglas, as is evident in his illustration of three girls writing on a chalkboard at school (Fig. 14.22). Using the same angularity and rhythmic repetition of forms that Douglas introduced, the intellectual growth of the girls, as each reaches higher on the board, is presented as a musical crescendo in a syncopated, four-beat, rhythmic form where the first beat, as it were, is silent and unplayed. The *Migration* series won Lawrence immediate fame. In 1942, the Museum of Modern Art in New York and the Phillips Collection in Washington, D.C., each bought 30 panels. That same year Lawrence became the first black artist represented by a prestigious New York gallery—the Downtown Gallery.

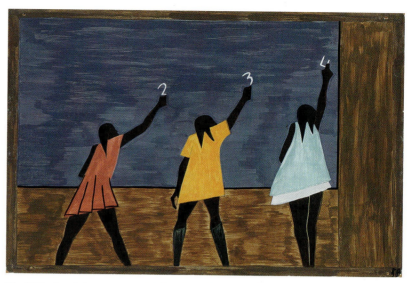

Fig. 14.22 Jacob Lawrence, *In the North the Negro had Better Educational Facilities*, panel 58 from *The Migration of the Negro.* 1940–41. Casein tempera on hardboard, 12″ × 18″. Gift of Mrs. David M. Levy. Museum of Modern Art, New York. © 2014 The Jacob and Gwendolyn Lawrence Foundation, Seattle/Artists Rights Society (ARS), New York. Note that Lawrence dresses the girls in the primary colors of red, yellow, and blue, thus emphasizing the fundamental nature of primary education.

Russia: Art and Revolution

In 1914, Russia entered the war ill-prepared for the task before it; within the year, Tsar Nicholas II (1868–1918) oversaw the devastation of his army. One million men had been killed, and another million soldiers had deserted. Famine and fuel shortages gripped the nation. Strikes broke out in the cities, and in the countryside, peasants seized the land of the Russian aristocrats. The tsar was forced to abdicate in February 1917.

Vladimir Lenin and the Soviet State Through a series of astute, and sometimes violent, political maneuvers, the Marxist revolutionary Vladimir Ilyich Lenin (1870–1924) assumed power the following November. Lenin headed the most radical of Russian postrevolutionary groups, the Bolsheviks. Like Marx, he dreamed of a "dictatorship of the proletariat," a dictatorship of the working class. Marx and Lenin believed that the oppression of the masses of working people resulted from capitalism's efforts to monopolize the raw materials and markets of the world for the benefit of the privileged few. He believed that all property should be held in common, that every member of society would work for the benefit of the whole and would receive, from the state, goods and products commensurate with their work. "He who does not work," he famously declared, "does not eat."

Lenin was a utopian idealist. He foresaw, as his socialist state developed, the gradual disappearance of the state: "The state," he wrote in *The State and Revolution* (1917), "will be able to wither away completely when society has realized the rule: 'From each according to his ability: to each according to his needs,' *i.e.,* when people have become accustomed to observe the fundamental rules of social life, and their labor is so productive that they voluntarily work *according to their ability.*" But he realized that certain pragmatic changes had to occur as well. He emphasized the need to electrify the nation: "We must show the peasants," he wrote, "that the organization of industry on the basis of modern, advanced technology, on electrification... will make it possible to raise the level of culture in the countryside and to overcome, even in the most remote corners of land, backwardness, ignorance, poverty, disease, and barbarism." And he was, furthermore, a political pragmatist. When, in 1918, his Bolshevik party received less than a quarter of 1 percent of the vote in free elections, he dissolved the government, eliminated all other parties, and put the Communist party into the hands of five men, a committee called the Politburo, with himself at its head. He also systematically eliminated his opposition: Between 1918 and 1922, his secret police arrested and executed as many as 280,000 people in what has come to be known as the Red Terror.

The Arts of the Revolution Before the Revolution in March 1917, avant-garde Russian artists, in direct communication with the art capitals of Europe, particularly Paris, Amsterdam, and Berlin, established their own brand of modern art. Most visited Paris, and saw Picasso and Braque's Cubism in person, but Kazimir Malevich (1878–1935), perhaps

📖 **Read** the document from Kazimir Malevich on **MyArtsLab**

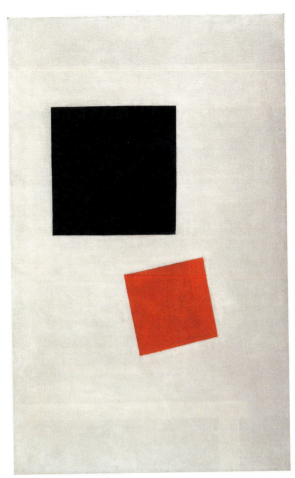

Fig. 14.23 Kazimir Malevich, *Painterly Realism: Boy with Knapsack—Color Masses in the Fourth Dimension*. 1915. Oil on canvas, 28" × 17½". Museum of Modern Art, New York. 1935 Acquisition confirmed in 1999 by agreement with the Estate of Kazimir Malevich and made possible with funds from the Mrs. John Hay Whitney Bequest (by exchange). 816.1935. Malevich always insisted that he painted not in three, but in four dimensions—that time, in other words, played a role in creating a work. Later, he claimed to work in five dimensions, the fifth being "economy," or minimal means.

the most inventive of them all, never did. By 1912, he had created "Cubo-Futurism," a style that applied modernist geometric forms to Russian folk themes. But Malevich was soon engaged, as he wrote, in a "desperate attempt to free art from the ballast of objectivity." To this end, he says, "I took refuge in the square," creating in 1913 a completely nonobjective painting, consisting of nothing more than a black square on a white ground. He called his new art Suprematism, defining it as "the supremacy of . . . feeling in . . . art."

The "feeling" of which Malevich speaks is not the kind of personal or private emotion that we associate with, say, German Expressionism. Rather, it lies in what he believed was the revelation of an absolute truth—a utopian ideal not far removed from Lenin's political idealism—discovered through the most minimal means. Thus, his *Painterly Realism: Boy with Knapsack—Color Masses in the Fourth Dimension* (Fig. **14.23**) is not really a representation of a boy with a knapsack, nor is it an example of realism. The title is deeply ironic, probably intended to jolt any viewer expecting to see

representational work. The painting is, rather, about the two forms—a black square and a smaller red one—that appear to float above a white ground, even, it seems, at different heights. The painting was first exhibited in December 1915 at an exhibition in Petrograd entitled *0.10: The Last Futurist Exhibition of Paintings*. The exhibition's name refers to the idea that each of the 10 artists participating in the show were seeking to articulate the "zero degree"—that is, the irreducible core—of painting. What, in other words, most minimally makes a painting? In this particular piece, Malevich reveals that in relation, these apparently static forms—two squares set on a rectangle—are energized in a dynamic tension.

One of the greatest of Russia's revolutionary innovators was the filmmaker Sergei Eisenstein (1898–1948). After the Revolution, he had worked on the Russian agit-trains, special propaganda trains that traveled the Russian countryside bringing "agitational" materials to the peasants. ("Agitational," in this sense, means presenting a political point of view.) The agit-trains distributed magazines and pamphlets, presented political speakers and plays, and, given the fact that the Russian peasantry was largely illiterate, perhaps most important of all presented films, known as *agitkas*. These films were characterized by their fast-paced editing style, designed to keep the attention of an audience that, at least at first, had never before seen a motion picture.

Out of his experience making *agitkas*, Lev Kuleshov (1899–1970), one of the founders of the Film School in Moscow in the early 1920s, developed a theory of **montage**. He used a close-up of a famous Russian actor and combined it with three different images—a bowl of soup, a dead woman lying in a coffin, and a girl playing with a teddy bear. Although the image of the actor was the same in each instance, audiences believed that he was hungry with the soup, sorrowful with the woman, joyful toward the girl—a phenomenon that came to be known as the *Kuleshov effect*. Shots, Kuleshov reasoned, acquire meaning through their relation to other shots. Montage was the art of building a cinematic composition out of such shots.

Eisenstein learned much from Kuleshov, although he disagreed about the nature of montage. Rather than being used to build a unified composition, Eisenstein believed that montage should be used to create tension, even a sense of shock, in the audience, which he believed would lead to a heightened perception and a greater understanding of the film's action. His aim, in a planned series of seven films depicting events leading up to the Bolshevik Revolution, was to provoke his audience into psychological identification with the aims of the Revolution.

None of his films accomplishes this better than *The Battleship Potemkin*, the story of a 1905 mutiny aboard a Russian naval vessel and the subsequent massacre of innocent men, women, and children on the steps above Odessa harbor by tsarist troops. The film, especially the famous "Odessa Steps Sequence," which is a virtual manifesto of montage, tore at the hearts of audiences and won respect for the Soviet regime around the world (see *Closer Look*, pages 472–473).

Freud and the Workings of the Mind

Eisenstein's emphasis on the viewer's psychological identification with his film was inspired in no small part by the theories of the Viennese neurologist Sigmund Freud (1856–1939). By the start of World War I, Freud's theories about the nature of the human psyche and its subconscious functions were gaining wide acceptance. As doctors and others began to deal with the sometimes severely traumatized survivors of the war, the efficacy of Freud's psychoanalytic techniques—especially dream analysis and "free association"—were increasingly accepted by the medical community.

But Freud understood that free association required interpretation, and increasingly, he began to focus on the obscure language of the unconscious. By 1897, he had formulated a theory of infantile sexuality based on the proposition that sexual drives and energy already exist in infants. One of the keys to understanding the imprint of early sexual feeling upon adult neurotic behavior was the interpretation of dreams. Freud concluded that dreams allow unconscious wishes, desires, and drives censored by the conscious mind to exercise themselves. "The dream," he wrote in his 1900 *The Interpretation of Dreams*, "is the (disguised) fulfillment of a (suppressed, repressed) wish." And the wish, by extension, is generally based in the sexual.

World War I provided Freud with evidence of another, perhaps even more troubling source of human psychological dysfunction—society itself. In 1920, in *Beyond the Pleasure Principle*, he speculated that human beings had death drives (*Thanatos*) that were in conflict with sex drives (*Eros*). Their opposition, he believed, helped to explain the fundamental forces that shape both individuals and societies; their conflict might also explain self-destructive and outwardly aggressive behavior. To this picture he added, in his 1923 work *The Ego and the Id*, a model for the human mind that would have a lasting impact on all subsequent psychological writings, at least in their terminology. According to Freud, human personality is organized by the competing drives of the id, the ego, and the superego. The **id** is the seat of all instinctive, physical desire—from the need for nourishment to sexual gratification. Its goal is immediate gratification, and it acts in accord with the pleasure principle. The **ego** manages the id. It mediates between the id's potentially destructive impulses and the requirements of social life, seeking to satisfy the needs of the id in socially acceptable ways. For Freud, civilization itself is the product of the ego's endless effort to control and modify the id. But Freud's recognition of yet a third element in the psyche—the **superego**—is crucial. The superego is the seat of what we commonly call "conscience," the psyche's moral base. The conscience comes from the psyche's consideration of criticism or disapproval leveled at it by the family, where "family" can be understood broadly as parents, clan, and culture. But since the superego does not distinguish between thinking a deed and doing it, it can also instill in the id enormous subconscious guilt.

The Dreamwork of Surrealist Painting

In his 1924 *Surrealist Manifesto*, the French writer, poet, and theorist André Breton (1896–1966) credited Freud with encouraging his own creative endeavors: "It would appear that it is by sheer chance that an aspect of intellectual life—and by far the most important in my opinion—about which no one was supposed to be concerned any longer has, recently, been brought back to light. Credit for this must go to Freud. On the evidence of his discoveries a current of opinion is at last developing which will enable the explorer of the human mind to extend his investigations, since he will be empowered to deal with more than merely summary realities." Breton had trained as a doctor and had used Freud's technique of free association when treating shell-shock victims in World War I. As his definition indicates, he had initially conceived of Surrealism as a literary movement, with Breton himself at its center. Many of the Surrealists had been active Dadaists, but as opposed to Dada's "anti-art" spirit, their new "surrealist" movement believed in the possibility of a "new art." Nevertheless, Surrealism retained much of Dada's spirit of revolt. They were committed to verbal automatism, a kind of writing in which the author relinquishes conscious control of the production of the text. In addition, the authors wrote dream accounts, and

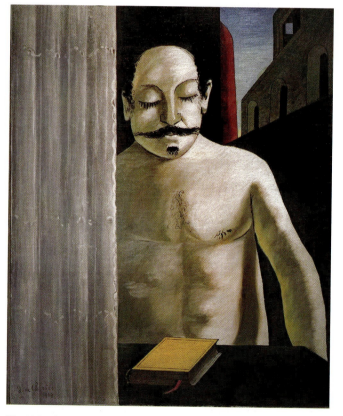

Fig. 14.24 Giorgio de Chirico, *The Child's Brain*. 1914. Oil on canvas, 31⅛" × 25⅝". Moderna Museet, Stockholm. © 2014 Artists Rights Society (ARS), New York/SIAE, Rome. De Chirico actually knew almost nothing about Freud, a fact that made his art seem even more authentic to the Surrealists, as if he had arrived at Freudian psychology intuitively rather than intellectually.

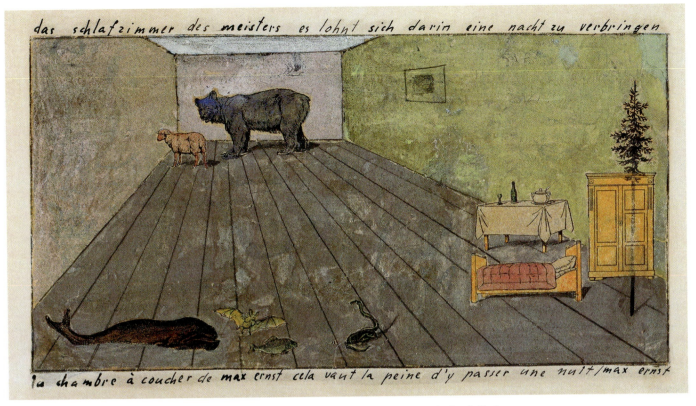

das schlafzimmer des meisters es lohnt sich darin eine nacht zu verbringen

la chambre à coucher de max ernst cela vaut la peine d'y passer une nuit/max ernst

Fig. 14.25 Max Ernst, *The Master's Bedroom, It's Worth Spending a Night There* (Letter from Katherine S. Dreier to Max Ernst, May 25, 1920). Collage, gouache, and pencil on paper, 6⅜″ × 8⅝″. Yale Collection of American Literature, Beinecke Rare Book and Manuscript Library. Translation from German by John W. Gabriel. From *Max Ernst, Life and Work* by Werner Spies, published by Thames & Hudson, page 67. © 2014 Artists Rights Society (ARS), New York/ADAGP, Paris. Prior to World War I, Ernst studied philosophy and abnormal psychology at the University of Bonn. He was well acquainted with the writings of Freud.

Breton's colleague Louis Aragon (1897–1982), especially, emphasized the importance of chance operations: "There are relations other than reality that the mind may grasp and that come first, such as chance, illusion, the fantastic, the dream," Aragon wrote. "These various species are reunited and reconciled in a genus, which is surreality."

The Surrealists also found precedent for their point of view not only in Freud, but in the painting of Giorgio de Chirico (1888–1978) and the Dadaist Max Ernst (1891–1976). When Breton saw de Chirico's painting *The Child's Brain* (Fig. **14.24**) in the window of Paul Guillaume's gallery in March 1922, he jumped off a bus in order to look at it. He bought the canvas and immediately published a reproduction in his magazine *Littérature*. The painting seemed to embody, precisely, Freud's theory of the dream. Here, the child's dreaming brain (the id) confronts the repressive threat of both the father figure (the ego)—who, half-naked, is also sexually threatening— and the broader, more societal moral authority represented by the book before him (the superego).

Breton would later look back at Ernst's 1921 exhibition of small collage-paintings like the aptly titled *The Master's Bedroom* (Fig. **14.25**) as the first Surrealist work in the visual arts. This painting consists of two pages from a small pamphlet of clip art, on the left depicting assorted animals and on the right various pieces of furniture. Ernst painted over most of the spread to create his perspective view, leaving unpainted the whale, fish, and snake at the bottom left, the bear and sheep at the top, and the bed, table, and bureau at the right. This juxtaposition of diverse elements, which would normally never occupy the same space—except perhaps in the dreamwork—is one of the fundamental stylistic devices of Surrealist art.

Picasso's Surrealism Breton argued that Picasso led the way to Surrealist art in his *Les Demoiselles d'Avignon* (see Fig. **14.9**), which jettisoned art's dependence on external reality. The great founder of Cubism, Breton said, possessed "the facility to give materiality to what had hitherto remained in the domain of pure fantasy." Picasso was attracted to the Surrealist point of view because it offered him new directions and possibilities. His Surrealism would assert itself most fully in the late 1920s and early 1930s, especially in a series of monstrous bonelike figures that alternated with sensuous portraits of his mistress Marie-Thérèse Walter (1909–77), whom he had met when she was only 17 in January 1927. For eight years, until 1935, he led a double life, married to Olga Khokhlova (1891–1955) while conducting a secret affair with Marie-Thérèse.

Picasso was indeed obsessed in these years with the duality of experience, the same opposition between Thanatos (the death drive) and Eros (the sex drive) that Freud had outlined in *Beyond the Pleasure Principle*. His 1932 double portrait of Marie-Thérèse, *Girl before a Mirror* (Fig. 14.26), expresses this—she is the moon, or night, at the right, and the sun, or light, on the left, where her own face appears in both profile and three-quarter view. Her protruding belly on the left suggests her fertility (indeed, she gave birth to their child, Maya, in 1935, soon after Picasso finally separated from Olga), although in the mirror, in typical Picasso fashion, we see not her stomach but her buttocks, her raw sexuality. She is the conscious self on the left, with her subconscious self revealing itself in the mirror. Picasso's work addresses Surrealism's most basic theme—the self in all its complexity. And he adds one important theme—the self in relation to the Other, for Picasso is present himself in the picture, not just as its painter, but in his symbol, the harlequin design of the wallpaper. But the painting also suggests that the self, in the dynamic interplay between the conscious and unconscious selves, might actually be the Other to itself.

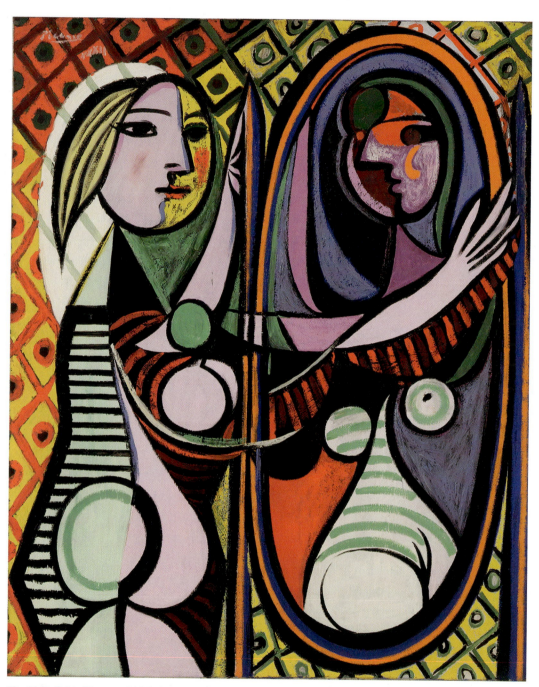

Fig. 14.26 Pablo Picasso, *Girl Before a Mirror.* **1932.** Oil on canvas, 64 × 51¼". Gift of Mrs. Simon Guggenheim (2.1938). Museum of Modern Art, New York. © 2014 Estate of Pablo Picasso/Artists Rights Society (ARS), New York. The long oval mirror into which Marie-Thérèse gazes, supported on both sides by posts, is known as a *psyche*. Hence Picasso paints her psyche both literally and figuratively.

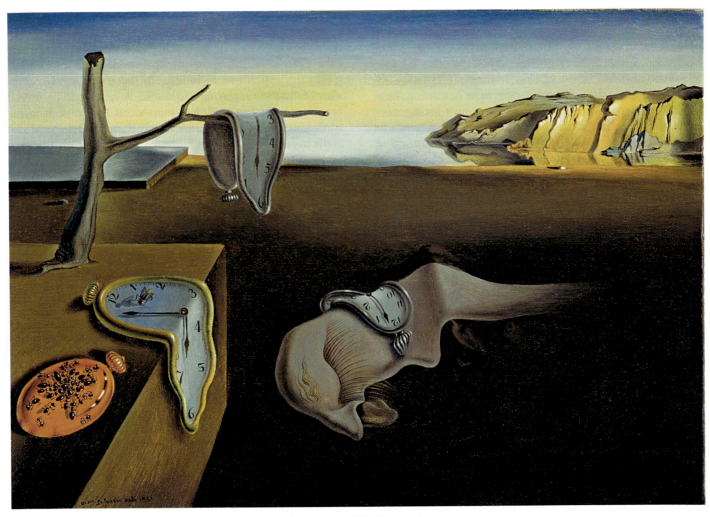

Fig. 14.27 Salvador Dalí, *The Persistence of Memory*. 1931. Oil on canvas, 9½″ × 13″. The Museum of Modern Art, New York. Given anonymously. © Salvador Dalí, Fundació Gala-Salvador Dalí, Artists Rights Society (ARS), New York 2014. Dalí called such paintings "hand-painted dream photographs."

View the Closer Look for Salvador Dalí, *The Persistence of Memory* on **MyArtsLab**

Salvador Dalí's Menacing Vision This sense of self-alien-ation is central to the work of the Spanish artist Salvador Dalí (1904–89), who in 1928, at age 24, was introduced to the Surrealists. Already eccentric and flamboyant, Dalí had been expelled from the San Fernando Academy of Fine Arts two years earlier for refusing to take his final examination, claiming that he knew more than the professor who was to examine him. He brought this same daring self-confidence to the Surrealist movement.

Dalí followed, he said, a "paranoiac critical method," a brand of self-hypnosis that he claimed allowed him to hal-lucinate freely. "I believe the moment is at hand," he wrote in a description of his method, "when, by a paranoiac and active advance of the mind, it will be possible (simultaneously with automatism…) to systematize confusion and thus to help to discredit the world of reality." He called his images "new and menacing," and works such as the famous *Persistence of Memory* (1931; Fig. **14.27**) are precisely that. This is a self-portrait of the sleeping Dalí, who lies sluglike in the middle of the painting, draped beneath the coverlet of time. Ants, which

are a symbol of death, crawl over a watchcase on the left. A fly alights on the watch dripping over the ledge, and another limp watch hangs from a dead tree that gestures toward the sleeping Dalí.

By the mid-1930s, Breton and the Surrealists parted ways with Dalí over his early admiration for Adolf Hitler and his reluctance to support the Republic in the Spanish Civil War. To this could be added Dalí's love of money, for which he earned the name Avida Dollars (Greedy Dollars), an ana-gram of his name created by Breton. In 1938, he was formally expelled from the Surrealist movement.

The Stream-of-Consciousness Novel

Perhaps the most important literary innovation of the era was the **stream-of-consciousness** novel. The idea had arisen in the late nineteenth century, in the writings of both Wil-liam James (1842–1910), the novelist Henry James's older brother, and the French philosopher Henri Bergson (1859–1941). For Bergson, human consciousness is composed of two somewhat contradictory powers: intellect, which sorts and

Cassady advocated a brand of writing that amounted to, as he put it in a letter to Kerouac, "a continuous chain of undisciplined thought." In fact, Kerouac wrote the novel in about three weeks on a single long scroll of paper, improvising, he felt, like a jazz musician, only with words and narrative. But, like a jazz musician, Kerouac was a skilled craftsman, and if the novel seems a spontaneous outburst, it nevertheless reflects the same careful attention to craft as that reflected in Robert Frank's *The Americans*. Frank, after all, had taken over 2,800 photographs, but he had published only 83 of them. One senses, in reading Kerouac's rambling adventure, something of the same editorial control.

Ginsberg and "Howl" The work that best characterizes the Beat generation is "Howl," a poem by Allen Ginsberg (1926–97). This lengthy poem in three parts and a footnote has a memorable opening (**Reading 15.3**):

READING 15.3

from Allen Ginsberg, "Howl" (1956)

I saw the best minds of my generation destroyed by madness, starving hysterical naked,
dragging themselves through the negro streets at dawn looking for an angry fix,
angelheaded hipsters burning for the ancient heavenly connection to the starry dynamo in the machinery of night,
who poverty and tatters and hollow-eyed and high sat up smoking in the supernatural darkness of cold-water flats floating across the tops of cities contemplating jazz
who bared their brains to Heaven under the El and saw Mohammedan angels staggering on tenement roofs illuminated,
who passed through universities with radiant cool eyes hallucinating Arkansas and Blake-light tragedy among the scholars of war,
who were expelled from the academies for crazy & publishing obscene odes on the windows of the skull,
who cowered in unshaven rooms in underwear, burning their money in wastebaskets and listening to the Terror through the wall . . .

Ginsberg's spirit of inclusiveness admitted into art not only drugs and alcohol but also graphic sexual language, to say nothing of his frank homosexuality. Soon after "Howl" was published in 1956 by Lawrence Ferlinghetti's City Lights bookstore in San Francisco, federal authorities charged Ferlinghetti with obscenity. He was eventually acquitted. Whatever the public thought of it, the poem's power was hardly lost on the other Beats. The poet Michael McClure (1932–) was present the night Ginsberg first read it at San Francisco's Six Gallery in 1955:

Allen began in a small and intensely lucid voice. At some point Jack Kerouac began shouting "GO" in cadence as Allen read it. In all of our memories no one had been so outspoken in poetry before—we had gone beyond a point of no return—and we were ready for it, for a point of no return. None of us wanted to go back to the gray, chill, militaristic silence, to the intellective void—to the land without poetry—to the spiritual drabness. We wanted to make it new and we wanted to invent it and the process of it as we went into it. We wanted voice and we wanted vision. . . .

Ginsberg read on to the end of the poem, which left us standing in wonder, or cheering and wondering, but knowing at the deepest level that a barrier had been broken, that a human voice and body had been hurled against the harsh wall of America and its supporting armies and navies and academies and institutions and ownership systems and power-support bases.

Here, in fact, in the mid-1950s were the first expressions of the forces of rebellion that would sweep the United States and the world in the following decade.

Cage and the Aesthetics of Chance

Ginsberg showed that anything and everything could be admitted into the domain of art. This notion also informs the music of the composer John Cage (1912–92), who by the mid-1950s was proposing that it was time to "give up the desire to control sound . . . and set about discovering means to let sounds be themselves." Cage's notorious *4'33"* (*4 minutes 33 seconds*) is a case in point. First performed in Woodstock, New York, by the pianist David Tudor on August 29, 1952, it consists of three silent movements, each of a different length, but when added together totaling 4 minutes and 33 seconds. The composition was anything but silent, however, admitting into the space framed by its duration all manner of ambient sound—whispers, coughs, passing cars, the wind. Whatever sounds happened during its performance were purely a matter of chance, never predictable. Like Frank's, Cage's is an art of inclusiveness.

That summer, Cage organized a multimedia event at Black Mountain College near Asheville, North Carolina, where he occasionally taught. One of the participants was the 27-year-old artist Robert Rauschenberg (1925–2008). By the mid-1950s, Rauschenberg had begun to make what he called **combine paintings**, works in which all manner of material—postcards, advertisements, tin cans, pinups—are combined. If Rauschenberg's work does not literally depend upon matters of chance in its construction, it does incorporate such a diverse range of material that it creates the aura of representing Rauschenberg's chance encounters with the world around him. And it does, above all, reflect Cage's sense of all-inclusiveness. *Bed* literally consists of a sheet, pillow, and quilt raised to the vertical and then dripped not only with paint but also with toothpaste and fingernail polish in what amounts to a parody of Abstract Expressionist introspection (Fig. **15.7**). Even as it juxtaposes highbrow art-making with the vernacular quilt, abstraction with realism, *Bed* is a wryly perceptive transformation of the dream space evoked by Surrealism.

The Art of Collaboration *Theater Piece #1*, as the multimedia event at which Rauschenberg first met Cage in 1952 came to be known, is remembered by almost everyone who took part somewhat differently. It seems certain that the poets M. C. Richards (1916–99) and Charles Olson (1910–70) read poetry from ladders, Rauschenberg played Edith Piaf records on an old windup phonograph with his almost totally "White Paintings" hanging around the room, and Merce Cunningham (1919–2009) danced through the audience, a dog at his heels, while Cage himself sat on a stepladder, sometimes reading a lecture on Zen Buddhism, sometimes just listening. "Music," Cage declared at some point in the event, "is not listening to Mozart but sounds such as a street car or a screaming baby."

The event inaugurated a collaboration between Cunningham (dance), Cage (music), and Rauschenberg (decor and costume) that would span many years. Their collaboration is unique in the arts because of its insistence on the *independence*, not interdependence, of each part of the dance's presentation. Cunningham explains:

> In most conventional dances there is a central idea to which everything adheres. The dance has been made to the piece of music, the music supports the dance, and the decor frames it. The central idea is emphasized by each of the several arts. What we have done in our work is to bring together three separate elements in time and space, the music, the dance and the decor, allowing each one to remain independent.

So Cunningham created his choreography independently of Cage's scores, and Rauschenberg based his decor on only minimal information offered him by Cunningham and Cage. The resulting dance was, by definition, a matter of music, choreography, and decor coming together (or not) as a chance operation.

The music Cage composed for Cunningham was also often dependent on chance operations. For instance, in 1959, Cage recorded an 89-minute piece entitled *Indeterminacy* (track **15.1**). It consisted of Cage narrating short, humorous stories while, in another room, out of earshot, David Tudor performed selections from Cage's 1958 *Concert for Piano and Orchestra* and also played pre-recorded tape from another 1958 composition, *Fontina Mix*. For a later collaboration, *Variations V*, Cage's score consisted of sounds randomly triggered by sensors reacting to the movements of Cunningham's dancers. This resulted in what Gordon Mumma, a member of Cunningham's troupe, called "a superbly poly: -chromatic, -genic, -phonic, -morphic, -pagic, -technic, -valent, multi-ringed circus."

Johns and the Obvious Image Whereas the main point for Cunningham, Cage, and Rauschenberg was the idea of composition without a central focus, Rauschenberg's close friend and fellow painter Jasper Johns (1930–) took the opposite

 Listen at **MyArtsLab**

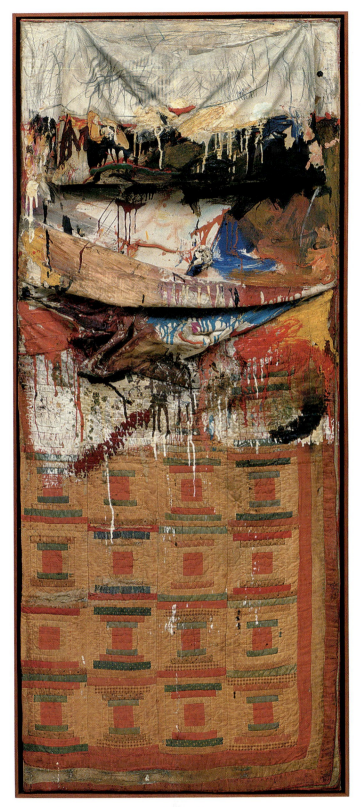

Fig. 15.7 **Robert Rauschenberg, *Bed*. 1955.** Combine painting: oil and pencil on pillow, quilt, and sheet on wood supports, 6′3¼″ × 31½″ × 8″. Gift of Leo Castelli in honor of Alfred H. Barr, Jr. (79.1989). Art © Robert Rauschenberg Foundation/Licensed by VAGA, New York, NY. The mattress, pillow, quilt, and sheets are believed to be Rauschenberg's own and so may be thought of as embodying his famous dictum: "Painting relates to both art and life. . . . (I try to act in that gap between the two)."

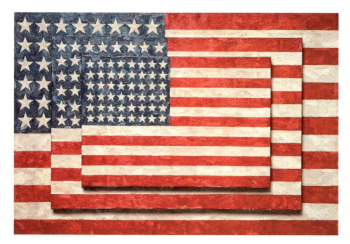

Fig. 15.8 Jasper Johns, *Three Flags*. 1958. Encaustic on canvas, 30⅞" × 45½" × 5". 50th Anniversary Gift of the Gilman Foundation, Inc., The Lauder Foundation, A. Alfred Taubman, an anonymous donor, and purchase. 80.32. Collection of Whitney Museum of American Art, New York. Photo by Geoffrey Clements. Art © Jasper Johns/Licensed by VAGA, NY. Each of the three flags diminishes in scale by about 25 percent from the one behind. Because the flags project outward, getting smaller each time, they reject pictorial perspective's illusion of depth and draw attention to the surface of the painting itself.

tack. Throughout the 1950s, he focused on the most common, seemingly obvious subject matter—numbers, targets, maps, and flags—in a manner that in no way suggests the multiplicity of meaning in his colleagues' work. Johns's painting *Three Flags* is nevertheless capable of evoking in its viewers emotions ranging from patriotic respect to equally patriotic outrage, from anger to laughter (Fig. 15.8). But Johns means the imagery to be so obvious that viewers turn their attention

to the wax-based paint itself, to its almost sinuous application to the canvas surface. In this sense, the work—despite being totally recognizable—is as abstract as any Abstract Expressionist painting, but without Abstract Expressionism's assertion of the primacy of subjective experience.

Architecture in the 1950s

If the Beat generation was antiestablishment in its sensibilities, the architecture of the 1950s embodied the very opposite. What is known as the *International Style*—characterized by pure forms, severe, flat surfaces, and a lack of ornamentation—dominated architectural taste. One of its principal practitioners was Ludwig Mies van der Rohe (1886–1969). His aesthetic use of refined austerity, summed up by the phrase "less is more," is clearly evident in his 1950 Farnsworth House (Fig. 15.9), with its insistence on the vertical and the horizontal elements. It is virtually transparent, opening out to the surrounding countryside, with views of the Fox River, and also inviting the countryside in.

The design of the American architect Frank Lloyd Wright (1867–1959) for the Solomon R. Guggenheim Museum in New York is a conscious counter-statement to Mies's severe rationalist geometry, which, in fact, Wright despised (Fig. 15.10). Situated on Fifth Avenue directly across from Central Park, the museum's organic forms echo the natural world. The plan is an inverted spiral ziggurat, or stepped tower, that dispenses with the right-angle geometry of standard urban architecture and the conventional approach to museum design, which led visitors through a series of interconnected rooms. Instead, Wright whisked museumgoers to the top of the building via elevator, allowing them to proceed downward on a continuous spiral ramp from

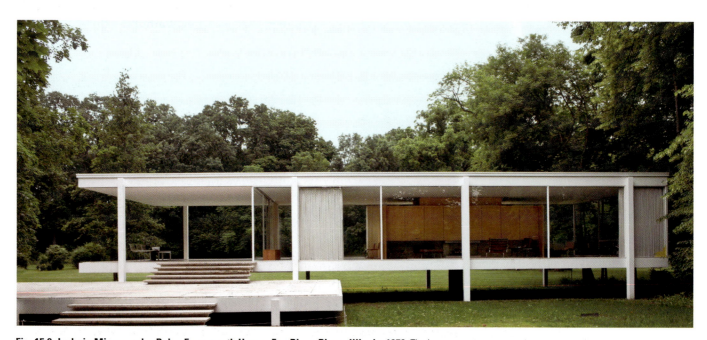

Fig. 15.9 Ludwig Mies van der Rohe, Farnsworth House, Fox River, Plano, Illinois. 1950. The house was commissioned as a weekend retreat. Its bathroom and storage areas are behind non-load-bearing partitions that divide the interior space.

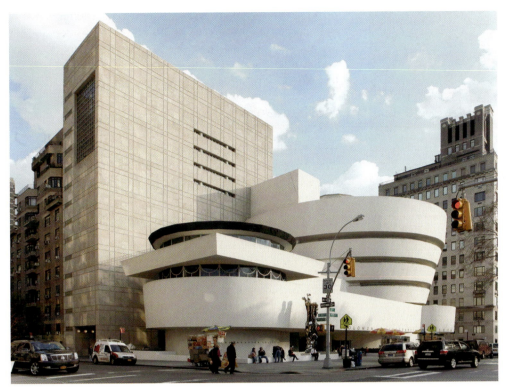

Fig. 15.10 Frank Lloyd Wright, The Solomon R. Guggenheim Museum, New York, 1956–1959. The tower behind Wright's original building was designed much later, in 1992, by Gwathmey Siegel and Associates. It contains 51,000 square feet of new and renovated gallery space, 15,000 square feet of new office space, a restored theater, a new restaurant, and retrofitted support and storage spaces. Wright had originally proposed such an annex to house artists' studios and offices, but the plan was dropped for financial reasons.

which, across the open rotunda in the middle, they could review what they had already seen and anticipate what was to come. The ramp is cantilevered to such an extent that several contractors were frightened off by Wright's plans. The plans were complete in 1943, but construction did not begin until 1956 because of a prohibition of new building during World War II and permit delays stemming from the radical nature of the design. It was still not complete at the time of Wright's death in 1959. In many ways Wright's Guggenheim Museum represents the spirit of architectural innovation that still pervades the practice of architecture to this day.

Pop Art

In the early 1960s, especially in New York, a number of artists created a "realist" art that represented reality in terms of the media—advertising, television, comic strips—the imagery of mass culture. The famous paintings of Campbell's Soup cans created by Andy Warhol (1928–87) were among the first of these to find their way into the gallery scene

(Fig. **15.11**). In the fall of 1962, Warhol exhibited 32 uniform 20″ × 16″ canvases at the Ferus Gallery in Los Angeles. Each depicted one of the 32 different Campbell's Soup "flavors." Even as the paintings debunked the idea of originality—are they Campbell's or Warhol's?—their literalness

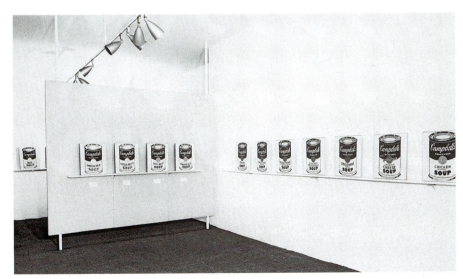

Fig. 15.11 Andy Warhol, installation view of *Campbell's Soup Cans*, Ferus Gallery, Los Angeles. 1962. Founding Collection, The Andy Warhol Museum, Pittsburgh. © 2014 The Andy Warhol Foundation for the Visual Arts, Inc./Artists Rights Society (ARS), New York. In order to evoke the way we encounter Campbell's soup on the grocery shelf, Warhol placed the cans on narrow shelves on the gallery walls.

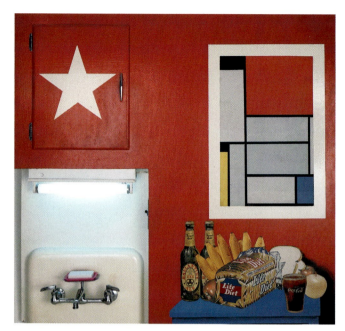

Fig. 15.12 Tom Wesselmann, *Still Life #20*. 1962. Mixed media, 48" × 48" × 5½". Albright-Knox Art Gallery, Buffalo, New York. Gift of Seymour H. Knox, Jr. Art © Estate of Tom Wesselmann/Licensed by VAGA, New York, NY. An actual sink faucet and soap dish are incorporated into the composition. Its fluorescent light can be turned on or off.

redefined the American landscape as the visual equivalent of the supermarket aisle. The works were deliberately opposed to the self-conscious subjectivity of the Abstract Expressionists. It was, in fact, as if the painter had no personality at all. As Warhol himself put it, "If you want to know all about Andy Warhol, just look at the surface of my paintings and films and me, and there I am. There's nothing behind it."

The term Pop Art quickly became attached to work like Warhol's. Coined in England in the 1950s, it soon came to refer to any art whose theme was essentially the commodification of culture—that is, the marketplace as the dominant force in the creation of "culture." Thus, *Still Life #20* (Fig. 15.12) by Tom Wesselmann (1931–2004) is contemporaneous with Warhol's *Soup Cans*, although neither artist was aware of the other until late in 1962, and both are equally "pop." Inside the cabinet with the star stenciled on it—which can be shown either opened or closed—are actual household items, including a package of SOS scouring pads and a can of Ajax cleanser. Above the blue table on the right, covered with two-dimensional representations (cut out of magazines) of various popular varieties of food and drink, is a reproduction of a highly formalist painting by the Dutch artist Piet Mondrian. The implication, of course, is that art—once so

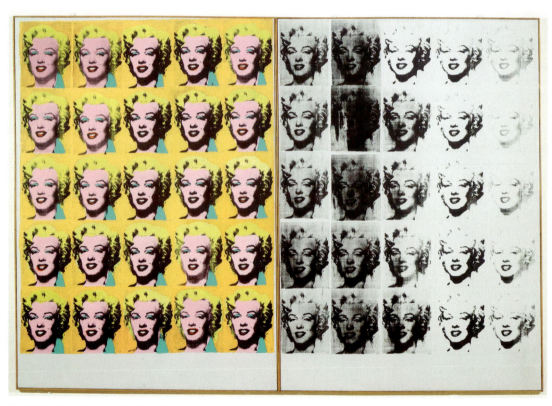

Fig. 15.13 Andy Warhol, *Marilyn Diptych*. 1962. Oil, acrylic, and silkscreen on enamel on canvas, 6'8⅞" × 4'9". Tate, London. © 2014 Tate, London. © 2014 The Andy Warhol Foundation for the Visual Arts/Artists Rights Society (ARS), New York. Warhol was obsessed with Hollywood, especially with the false fabric of fame that it created. The image of Marilyn is a direct transfer of a 1953 publicity shot for the film *Niagara*.

The CONTINUING PRESENCE of the PAST

See Mike Bidlo, *Not Warhol (Brillo Boxes)*, 2005, at **MyArtsLab**

 View the Closer Look for *Marilyn Diptych* on **MyArtsLab**

 Watch a studio technique video on silkscreen on **MyArtsLab**

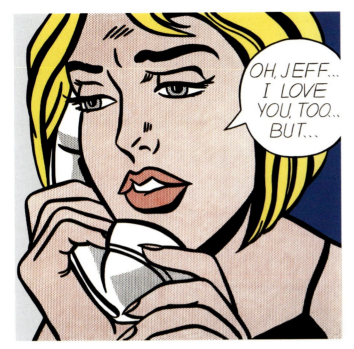

Fig. 15.14 Roy Lichtenstein, *Oh, Jeff . . . I Love You, Too . . . But. . . . 1964.* Oil on magma on canvas, 4' × 4'. © Estate of Roy Lichtenstein. The large size of these paintings mirrors the scale of the Hollywood screen and the texture of the common billboard.

Fig. 15.15 Roy Lichtenstein, *Little Big Painting.* 1965. Oil on synthetic polymer on canvas, 70" × 82" × 2¼". Purchase, with funds from the Friends of the Whitney Museum of American Art. 66.2. Collection of the Whitney Museum of American Art, New York. © Estate of Roy Lichtenstein. This "detail" of an imaginary larger painting is nonetheless a giant in its own right.

far removed from everyday life, not even, in this case, refer-ring to the world—has itself become a commodity, not so very different from Coke or a loaf of Lite Diet bread. In fact, the structure and color of Wesselmann's collage subtly reflect the structure and color of Mondrian's painting, as if the two are simply two different instances of "the same."

By late 1962, Warhol had stopped making his paintings by hand, instead using a photo-silkscreen process to create the images mechanically and employing others to do the work for him in his studio, The Factory. One of the first of these is the *Marilyn Diptych* (Fig. **15.13**). Marilyn Mon-roe had died, by suicide, in August of that year, and the painting is at once a memorial to her and a commentary on the circumstances that had brought her to despair. She is not so much a person as she is a personality, the creation of a Hollywood studio system whose publicity shot War-hol would repeat over and over again here to the point of erasure.

The enlarged comic-strip paintings of Roy Lichtenstein (1923–97) are replete with heavy outlines and Ben Day dots, the process created by Benjamin Day at the turn of the century to produce shading effects in mechanical printing. Widely used in comic strips, the dots are, for Lichtenstein, a conscious parody of Seurat's pointillism (see Chapter 14). But they also reveal the extent to which "feeling" in popu-lar culture is as "canned" as Campbell's Soup. In *Oh, Jeff . . .* (Fig. **15.14**), "love" is emptied of real meaning, as the real weight of the message is carried by the final "But. . ." Even the feelings inherent in Abstract Expressionists' brushwork came under Lichtenstein's attack (Fig. **15.15**). In fact, Lichtenstein had taught painting to college students, and

he discovered that the "authentic" gesture of Abstract Expressionism could easily be taught and replicated with-out any emotion whatsoever—as a completely academic enterprise.

One of the most inventive of the Pop artists was Claes Oldenburg (1929–), born in Sweden but raised in New York and Chicago. In 1961, he converted the storefront studio in New York's Lower East Side into *The Store*, which he filled with life-size and over-life-size enameled plaster sculptures of everything from pie à la mode to hamburgers, hats, caps, 7-Up bottles, shirt-and-tie combinations, and slices of cake. "I am for an art," he wrote in a statement accompanying the exhibition,

> that is political-erotica-mystical, that does something other than sit on its ass in a museum.
>
> I am for an art that grows up not knowing it is art at all, an art given the chance of having a starting point of zero.
>
> I am for an art that embroils itself with the everyday crap & still comes out on top. I am for an art that imitates the human, that is comic, if necessary, or violent, or what-ever is necessary.
>
> I am for an art that takes its form from the lines of life itself, that twists and extends and accumulates and spits and drips, and is heavy and coarse and blunt and sweet and stupid as life itself.

Admiring the way that cars filled the space of auto show-rooms, Oldenburg soon enlarged his objects to the size of cars and started making them out of vinyl stuffed (or not) with foam rubber. These objects toy not only with our sense of scale—a 5-foot-high toilet, for instance, or a giant

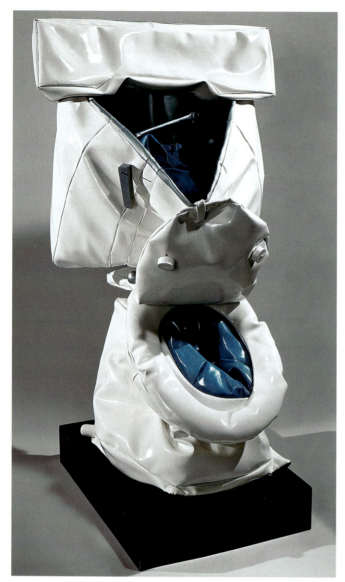

Fig. 15.16 Claes Oldenburg, *Soft Toilet*. 1966. Vinyl, kapok, Liquitex, wood, 55½" × 28¼" × 30". Collection of the Whitney Museum of American Art, New York. © 1966 Claes Oldenburg. Oldenburg's art is epitomized by his slightly but intentionally vulgar sense of humor.

lightplug—but with the tension inherent in making soft something meant to be hard (Fig. **15.16**). They play, further, in almost Surrealist fashion, with notions of sexuality as well—the analogy between inserting a lightplug into its socket and sexual intercourse was hardly lost on Oldenburg, who delighted even more in the image of cultural impotence that his "soft" lightplug implied.

THE WINDS OF CHANGE

What role did politics play in the art and literature of the 1960s and 1970s?

In 1954, the U.S. Supreme Court ruled that racially segregated schools violated the Constitution. In *Brown v. Board of Education*, the Court found that it was not good enough to provide "separate but equal" schools. "Separate educational facilities are inherently unequal," the Court declared, and were in violation of the Fourteenth Amendment to the Constitution's guarantee of equal protection. The Justices called on states with segregated schools to desegregate "with all deliberate speed."

Within a week, the state of Arkansas announced that it would seek to comply with the court's ruling. The state had already desegregated its state university and its law school. Now it was time to desegregate elementary and secondary schools. The plan was for Little Rock Central High School to open its doors to African-American students in the fall of 1957. But on September 2, the night before school was to start, Governor Orval Faubus ordered the state's National Guard to surround the high school and prevent any black students from entering. Faubus claimed he was trying to prevent violence. Eight of the nine black students who were planning to attend classes that day decided to arrive together on September 4. Unaware of the plan, Elizabeth Eckford arrived alone (Fig. **15.17**). The others followed, but were all turned away by the Guard. Nearly three weeks later, after a federal injunction ordered Faubus to remove the Guard, the nine finally entered Central High School. Little Rock citizens then launched a campaign of verbal abuse and intimidation to prevent the black students from remaining in school. Finally, President Dwight D. Eisenhower ordered 1,000 paratroopers and 10,000 National Guardsmen to Little Rock, and on September 25, Central High School was officially desegregated. Nevertheless, chaperoned throughout the year by the National Guard, the nine black students were spat at and reviled every day, and none of them returned to school the following year.

By April 1963, the focal point of racial tension and strife in the United States had shifted to Birmingham, Alabama. In protest over desegregation orders, the city had closed its parks and public golf courses. In retaliation, the black community called for a boycott of Birmingham stores. The city responded by halting the distribution of food normally given to the city's needy families. In this progressively more heated atmosphere, the Southern Christian Leadership Conference (SCLC), led by the Reverend Martin Luther King, Jr. (1929–68), decided that Birmingham would be their battlefield. In the spring of 1963, groups of protesters, gathering first at local churches, descended on the city's downtown both to picket businesses that continued to maintain "separate but equal" practices, such as different fitting rooms for blacks and whites in clothing stores, and to take seats at "whites-only" lunch counters. The city's police chief, Eugene "Bull" Connor, responded by threatening to arrest anyone marching on the downtown area. On April 6, 50 marchers were arrested. The next day, 600 marchers gathered, and police confronted them with clubs, attack dogs, and the fire department's new water hoses, which, they bragged, could rip the bark off a tree. But day after day, the marchers kept coming, their ranks

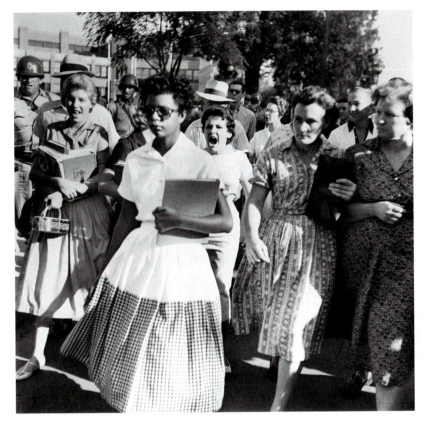

Fig. 15.17 One of the "Little Rock Nine," Elizabeth Eckford, braves a jeering crowd, September 4, 1957. Alone, as school opened in 1957, Elizabeth Eckford faced the taunts of the crowd defying the Supreme Court order to integrate Central High School in Little Rock, Arkansas. The image captures perfectly the hatred—and the determination—that the civil rights movement inspired.

The youth returned, with reinforcements, over the next few days. By May 6, over 2,000 demonstrators were in jail, and police patrol cars were pummeled with rocks and bottles whenever they entered black neighborhoods. As the crisis mounted, secret negotiations between the city and the protesters resulted in change: Within 90 days, all lunch counters, restrooms, department-store fitting rooms, and drinking fountains would be open to all, black and white alike. The 2,000 people under arrest would be released immediately.

It was a victory, but Birmingham remained uneasy. On Sunday, September 15, a dynamite bomb exploded in the basement of the 16th Street Baptist Church, a center for many civil rights rallies and meetings, killing four girls— one 11-year-old and three 14-year-olds. As news of the tragedy spread, riots and fires broke out throughout the city and two more teenagers were killed.

The tragedy drew many moderate whites into the civil rights movement. Popular culture had put them at the ready. In June 1963, the folk-rock trio Peter, Paul, and Mary released "Blowin' in the Wind," their version of the song that Bob Dylan (1941–) had written in April 1962. The Peter, Paul, and Mary record sold 300,000 copies in two weeks. The song famously ends:

How many years can some people exist,
Before they're allowed to be free?
How many times can a man turn his head,
Pretending he just doesn't see?
The answer, my friend, is blowin' in the wind,
The answer is blowin' in the wind.

At the March on Washington later that summer—an event organized by A. Philip Randolph, who had conceived of a similar event over 20 years earlier, that time to promote passage of the Civil Rights Act—Peter, Paul, and Mary performed the song live before 250,000 people, the largest gathering of its kind to that point in the history of the United States. Not many minutes later, Martin Luther King delivered his famous "I Have a Dream" speech to the same crowd. The trio's album *In the Wind*, released in October, quickly rose to number one on the charts. The winds of change were blowing across the country.

Black Identity

It is probably fair to say that an important factor contributing to the civil rights movement was the growing sense of ethnic identity among the African-American population. Its origins can be traced back to the Harlem Renaissance (see Chapter 14), but throughout the 1940s and 1950s, a growing

swelling. A local judge issued an injunction banning the marches, but on April 12, King led a march of 50 people in defiance of the injunction. Crowds gathered in anticipation of King's arrest, and, in fact, he was quickly taken into custody and placed in solitary confinement in the Birmingham jail.

Soon after King's incarceration, the situation in Birmingham worsened. A local disc jockey urged the city's African-American youth to attend a "big party" at Kelly Ingram Park, across from the 16th Street Baptist Church. It was no secret that the "party" was to be a mass demonstration. At least 1,000 youths gathered to face the police, most of them teenagers but some as young as seven or eight years old. As the chant of "Freedom, freedom *now!*" rose from the crowd, the Birmingham police closed in with their dogs, ordering them to attack those who did not flee.

Police wagons and squad cars were quickly filled with arrested juveniles, and as the arrests continued, the police used school buses to transport over 600 children and teenagers to jail. By the next day, the entire nation—in fact, the entire world—had come to know Connor, as televised images documented his dogs attacking children and his fire hoses literally washing them down the streets.

sense of cultural self-awareness and self-definition was taking hold, even though African Americans did not share in the growing wealth and sense of well-being that marked postwar American culture.

Sartre's "Black Orpheus" One of the most important contributions to this development was existentialism, with its emphasis on the inevitability of human suffering and the necessity for the individual to act responsibly in the face of that predicament. Jean-Paul Sartre's 1948 essay "Orphée Noir" or "Black Orpheus" was especially influential. The essay defined "blackness" as a mark of authenticity:

> A Jew, a white among whites, can deny that he is a Jew, declaring himself a man among men. The black cannot deny that he is black nor claim for himself an abstract, colorless humanity: he is black. Thus he is driven to authenticity: insulted, enslaved, he raises himself up. He picks up the word "black" ["Négre"] that they had thrown at him like a stone, he asserts his blackness, facing the white man, with pride.

If, like the Jews, blacks had undergone a shattering diaspora, or dispersion, across the globe, traces of the original African roots were evident in everything from American blues and jazz to the African-derived religious and ritual practices of the Caribbean that survived as Vodun, Santeria, and Condomblé. For Sartre, these were all manifestations of an original "Orphic" voice, which, like the master musician and poet Orpheus of Greek legend, who descended into Hades to rescue his beloved Eurydice, had descended into the "black substratum" of their African heritage to discover an authentic—and revolutionary—voice.

Ralph Ellison's Invisible Man Probably the book most instrumental in introducing existentialist attitudes to an American audience was the novel *Invisible Man* by Ralph Waldo Ellison (1913–94), published in 1952 and written over a period of about seven years in the late 1940s and early 1950s. In part, the novel is an ironic reversal of the famous trope of Ellison's namesake, Ralph Waldo Emerson, in his essay *Nature* (see Chapter 13): "I become a transparent eye-ball. I am nothing. I see all." "I am an invisible man," Ellison's prologue to the novel begins (**Reading 15.4a**):

> ### READING 15.4a
>
> **from Ralph Ellison, *Invisible Man* (1952)**
>
> No, I am not a spook like those who haunted Edgar Allan Poe; nor am I one of your Hollywood-movie ectoplasms. I am a man of substance, of flesh and bone, fiber and liquid—and I might even be said to possess a mind. I am invisible, understand, simply because people refuse to see me. . . . That invisibility to which I refer occurs because of a peculiar disposition of the eyes of those with whom I come in contact. A matter of the construction of their inner eyes, those eyes with which they look through their physical eyes upon reality.

Ellison's story is told by a narrator who lives in a subterranean "hole" in a cellar at the edge of Harlem into which he has accidentally fallen in the riot that ends the novel. As "underground man," his self-appointed task is to realize, in the narrative he is writing (the novel itself), the realities of black American life and experience. At the crucial turning point of the novel, after seeing three boys in the subway, dressed in "well-pressed, too-hot-for-summer suits. . . . walking slowly, their shoulders swaying, their legs swinging from their hips in trousers that ballooned from cuffs fitting snug about their ankles; their coats long and hip-tight with shoulders far too broad to be those of natural western men," he muses (**Reading 15.4b**):

> ### READING 15.4b
>
> **from Ralph Ellison, *Invisible Man* (1952)**
>
> Moving through the crowds along 125th Street, I was painfully aware of other men dressed like the boys, and of girls in dark exotic-colored stockings, their costumes surreal variations of downtown styles. They'd been there all along, but somehow I'd missed them. . . . They were outside the groove of history, and it was my job to get them in, all of them. I looked into the design of their faces, hardly a one that was unlike someone I'd known down South. Forgotten names sang through my head like forgotten scenes in dreams. I moved through the crowd, the sweat pouring off me, listening to the grinding roar of traffic, the growing sound of a record shop loudspeaker blaring a languid blues. I stopped. Was this all that would be recorded? Was this the only true history of the times, a mood blared by trumpets, trombones, saxophones and drums, a song with turgid, inadequate words?

The blues is not enough. The narrator's new self-appointed task is to take the responsibility to find words adequate to the history of the times. Up to this point, his own people have been as invisible to him as he to them. He has opened his own eyes as he must now open others'. At the novel's end, he is determined to come out of his "hole." "I'm shaking off the old skin," he says, "and I'll leave it here in the hole. I'm coming out, no less invisible without it, but coming out nevertheless. And I suppose it's damn well time. . . . Perhaps that's my greatest social crime, I've overstayed my hibernation, since there's a possibility that even an invisible man has a socially responsible role to play."

Asserting Blackness in Art and Literature One of Ellison's narrator's most vital realizations is that he must, above all else, assert his blackness instead of hiding from it. He must not allow himself to be absorbed into white society. "Must I strive toward colorlessness?" he asks.

> But seriously, and without snobbery, think of what the world would lose if that should happen. America is woven of many strands; I would recognize them and let it so remain. . . . Our fate is to become one, and yet many—This is not prophecy, but description.

There could be no better description of the collages of Romare Bearden (1911–88), who had worked for two decades in an almost entirely abstract vein, but who in the early 1960s began to tear images out of *Ebony*, *Look*, and *Life* magazines and assemble them into depictions of black experience. *The Dove* (Fig. **15.18**)—named for the white dove that is perched over the central door, a symbol of peace and harmony—combines forms of shifting scale and different orders of fragmentation. For example, a giant cigarette extends from the hand of the dandy sporting a cap at the right, and the giant fingers of a woman's hand reach over the windowsill at the top left. The resulting effect is almost kaleidoscopic, an urban panorama of a conservatively dressed older generation and hipper, younger people gathered into a scene bursting with energy—the "one, and yet many." As Ellison wrote of Bearden's art in 1968:

> Bearden's meaning is identical with his method. His combination of technique is in itself eloquent of the sharp breaks, leaps of consciousness, distortions, paradoxes, reversals, telescoping of time and surreal blending of styles, values, hopes, and dreams which characterize much of [African] American history.

The sense of a single black American identity, one containing the diversity of black culture within it that Bearden's work embodies, is also found in the work of the poet and playwright Amiri Baraka (1934–2014). Baraka changed his name from LeRoi Jones in 1968 after the assassination of the radical black Muslim minister Malcolm X in 1965. Malcolm X believed that blacks should separate themselves from whites in every conceivable way, that they should give up integration as a goal and create their own black nation. As opposed to Martin Luther King, who advocated nonviolent protest, Malcolm advocated violent action if necessary: "How are you going to be nonviolent in Mississippi," he asked a Detroit audience in 1963, "as violent as you were in Korea? How can you justify being nonviolent in Mississippi and Alabama, when your churches are being bombed, and your little girls are being murdered? . . . If violence is wrong in America, violence is wrong abroad."

Baraka's chosen Muslim name, Imamu Amiri Baraka, refers to the divine blessing associated with Muslim holy men that can be transferred from a material object to a person, so that a pilgrim returning from Mecca is a carrier of *baraka*. Baraka's 1969 poem "Ka'Ba" seeks to bestow *baraka*

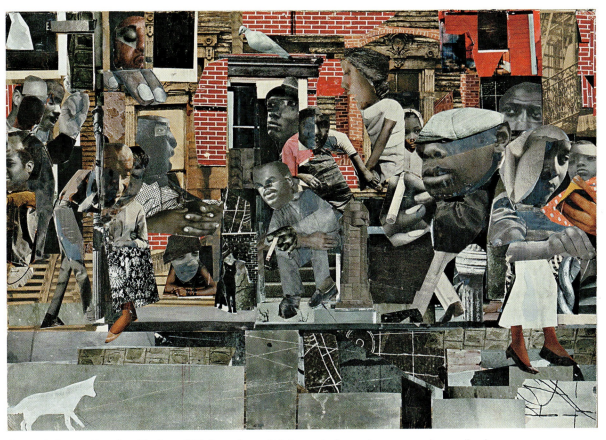

Fig. 15.18 Romare Bearden, *The Dove*. 1964. Cut-and-pasted photoreproductions and papers, gouache, pencil and colored pencil on board, 13⅜″ × 18¾″. Blanchette Rockefeller Fund (377.1971). Museum of Modern Art, New York. Art © Romare Bearden Foundation/Licensed by VAGA, New York, NY. The white dog at the lower left appears to be stalking the black cat at the foot of the steps in the middle, in counterpoint to the dove above the door.

Read the document from Romare Bearden on **MyArtsLab**

upon the people of Newark, New Jersey, where Baraka lived (**Reading 15.5**):

READING 15.5

Amiri Baraka, "Ka'Ba" (1969)

A closed window looks down
on a dirty courtyard, and Black people
call across or scream across or walk across
defying physics in the stream of their will.

Our world is full of sound
Our world is more lovely than anyone's
tho we suffer, and kill each other
and sometimes fail to walk the air.

We are beautiful people
With African imaginations
full of masks and dances and swelling chants
with African eyes, and noses, and arms
tho we sprawl in gray chains in a place
full of winters, when what we want is sun.

We have been captured,
and we labor to make our getaway, into
the ancient image; into a new
Correspondence with ourselves
and our Black family. We need magic
now we need the spells, to raise up
return, destroy, and create. What will be
the sacred word?

The sacred word, the poem's title suggests, is indeed "Ka'Ba." But, despite the spiritual tone of this poem, Baraka became increasingly militant during the 1960s. In 1967, he produced two of his own plays protesting police brutality. A year later, in his play *Home on the Range*, his protagonist Criminal breaks into a white family's home only to find them so immersed in television that he cannot communicate with them. The play was performed as a benefit for the leaders of the Black Panther party, a black revolutionary political party founded in 1966 by Huey P. Newton (1942–89) and Bobby Seale (1936–) and dedicated to organizing support for a socialist revolution.

Other events, too, reflected the growing militancy of the African-American community. In August 1965, violent riots in the Watts district of South Central Los Angeles lasted for six days, leaving 34 dead, over 1,000 people injured, nearly 4,000 arrested, and hundreds of buildings destroyed. In July 1967, rioting broke out in both Newark and Detroit. In Newark, six days of rioting left 23 dead, over 700 injured, and close to 1,500 people arrested. In Detroit, five days of rioting resulted in 43 people dead, 1,189 injured, over 7,000 people arrested, and 2,509 stores looted or burned. Finally, it seemed to many that Martin Luther King's pacifism had come back to haunt him when he was assassinated on April 4, 1968.

It was directly out of this climate that the popular poetry/music/performance/dance phenomenon known as rap, or hip-hop, came into being. Shortly after the death of King, on

Malcolm X's birthday, May 19, 1968, David Nelson, Gylan Kain, and Abiodun Oyewole founded the group the Last Poets, named after a poem by the South African poet Willie Kgositsile (1938–) in which he had claimed that it would soon be necessary to put poetry aside and take up guns in the looming revolution. "Therefore we are the last poets of the world," Kgositsile concluded. In performance, the Last Poets were deeply influenced by the musical phrasings of Amiri Baraka's poetry. They improvised individually, trading words and phrases back and forth like jazz musicians improvising on one another's melodies, until their voices would come together in a rhythmic chant and the number would end. Most of all, they were political, attacking white racism, black bourgeois complacency, the government, and the police—whoever or whatever seemed to stand in the way of significant progress for African Americans. As Oyewole put it, "We were angry, and we had something to say."

Equally influential was the performer Gil Scott-Heron (1949–2011), whose recorded poem "The Revolution Will Not Be Televised" appeared on his 1970 album *Small Talk at 125th and Lenox* (**Reading 15.6**):

READING 15.6

from Gil Scott-Heron, "The Revolution Will Not Be Televised" (1970)

You will not be able to stay home, brother.
You will not be able to plug in, turn on and cop out.[1]
You will not be able to lose yourself on skag[2] and
skip out for beer during commercials because
The revolution will not be televised.

The revolution will not be televised.
The revolution will not be brought to you by Xerox in
    4 parts without commercial interruptions. . . .
There will be no highlights on the Eleven O'Clock News
and no pictures of hairy armed women liberationists
and Jackie Onassis blowing her nose.
The theme song will not be written by Jim Webb or
    Francis Scott Key,
nor sung by Glen Campbell, Tom Jones, Johnny Cash,
Englebert Humperdinck, or Rare Earth.
The revolution will not be televised.

[1] **turn on and cop out:** A play on the motto of Timothy Leary (1920–96), advocate and popularizer of the psychedelic drug LSD, who in the 1960s urged people to "turn on, tune in, drop out."
[2] **skag:** Slang for heroin.

Scott-Heron's poems, spoken to music, would influence the development of hip-hop even more than the Last Poets, and his work was often "sampled" by later hip-hop disc jockeys who created rhythmic musical works by looping small portions of recorded songs on two turntables. Equally important to hip-hop were break dancing and graffiti writing. Although widely condemned as destruction of public and private property, by the early 1980s graffiti had entered the mainstream art market, particularly in the work of Jean-Michel Basquiat (see *Closer Look*, pages 502–503).

The Vietnam War: Rebellion and the Arts

Even as the civil rights movement took hold, the Cold War tensions with the Soviet Union were increasingly exacerbated by the United States' involvement in the war in Vietnam. By the mid-1960s, fighting between the North Vietnamese Communists led by Ho Chi Minh and the pro-Western and former French colony of South Vietnam had led to a massive troop buildup of American forces in the region, fueled by a military draft that alienated many American youth, the population of 15- to 24-year-olds that over the course of the 1960s increased from 24.5 million to 36 million.

Across the country, the spirit of rebellion that fueled the civil rights movement took hold on college campuses and in the burgeoning antiwar community. Events at the University of California at Berkeley served to link, in the minds of many, the antiwar movement and the fight for civil rights. In 1964, the university administration tried to stop students from recruiting and raising funds on campus for two groups dedicated to ending racial discrimination. Protesting the administration's restrictions, a group of students organized the Free Speech Movement, which initiated a series of rallies, sit-ins, and student strikes at Berkeley. The administration backed down, and the Berkeley students' tactics were quickly adapted by groups in the antiwar movement, which focused on removing the Reserve Officers' Training Corps from college campuses and helped to organize antiwar marches, teach-ins, and rallies across the country. By 1969, feelings reached fever pitch, as over a half million protesters, adopting the tactics of the civil rights movement in 1963, marched on Washington.

Kurt Vonnegut's *Slaughterhouse-Five*

Antiwar sentiment was reflected in the arts in works primarily about earlier wars, World War II and the Korean War, as if it were impossible to deal directly with events in Southeast Asia, which could be seen each night on the evening news. Joseph Heller's novel *Catch-22* was widely read, and the Robert Altman (1925–2006) film *M*A*S*H*, a smash-hit satiric comedy about the 4077th Mobile Army Surgical Hospital in Korea, opened in 1970 and spawned an 11-year-long television series that premiered in 1972. But perhaps the most acclaimed antiwar work was the 1969 novel *Slaughterhouse-Five* by Kurt Vonnegut (1922–2007). It is the oddly narrated story of ex-World War II GI Billy Pilgrim, a survivor, like Vonnegut himself, of the Allied fire-bombing of Dresden (where 135,000 German civilians were killed, more than at Hiroshima and Nagasaki combined). Pilgrim claims to have been abducted by extraterrestrial aliens from the planet of Trafalmadore. At the beginning of the book, the narrator (more or less, Vonnegut himself) is talking with a friend about the war novel he is about to write (*Slaughterhouse-Five*), when the friend's wife interrupts (**Reading 15.7**):

READING 15.7

from Kurt Vonnegut, *Slaughterhouse-Five* (1969)

"You'll pretend that you were men instead of babies, and you'll be played in the movies by . . . John Wayne. . . . And war will look just wonderful, so we'll have a lot more of them. And they'll be fought by babies. . . ." She didn't want her babies or anyone else's babies killed in wars. And she thought wars were partly encouraged by books and movies.

In response, Vonnegut creates, in Pilgrim, the most innocent of heroes, and subtitles his novel *The Children's Crusade: A Duty-Dance with Death*. Pilgrim's reaction to the death he sees everywhere—"So it goes"—became a mantra for the generation that came of age in the late 1960s. The novel's fatalism mirrored the sense of pointlessness and arbitrariness that so many felt in the face of the Vietnam War.

Artists Against the War

By the fall of 1969, a large number of artists had organized in opposition to the war. In a speech at an opening hearing that led to the creation of the antiwar Art Workers' Coalition, art critic and editor Gregory Battcock outlined how the art world was complicit in the war effort:

> The trustees of the museums direct NBC and CBS, the *New York Times*, and the Associated Press, and that greatest cultural travesty of modern times—the Lincoln Center. They own AT&T, Ford, General Motors, the great multi-billion dollar foundations, Columbia University, Alcoa, Minnesota Mining, United Fruit, and AMK, besides sitting on the boards of each other's museum. The implications of these facts are enormous. Do you realize that it is those art-loving, culturally committed trustees of the Metropolitan and the Modern museums who are waging the war in Vietnam?

In other words, the museums embodied, in the minds of many, the establishment politics that had led to the war in the first place. On October 15, 1969, the first Vietnam Moratorium Day, artists managed to close the Museum of Modern Art, the Whitney Museum, and the Jewish Museum, but the Metropolitan and the Guggenheim refused to close.

The Art Workers' Coalition also quickly reacted to reports that American soldiers, the men of Charlie Company, had slaughtered men, women, and children in the Vietnam village of My Lai on March 16, 1968. More than a year later, in November 1969, as the army was investigating Charlie Company's platoon leader, First Lieutenant William L. Calley, Jr., photographs taken at My Lai by the army photographer Ron Haeberle appeared in the *Cleveland Plain Dealer*. Four days later, in an interview by Mike Wallace on CBS-TV, Paul Meadlo, who had been at My Lai, reported that Calley had rounded up 40 or 45 villagers and ordered them shot. "Men, women, and children?" Wallace

Charles the First by Jean-Michel Basquiat (1960–88) is an homage to the great jazz saxophonist Charlie Parker, one of a number of black cultural heroes celebrated by the graffiti-inspired Basquiat. Son of a middle-class Brooklyn family (his father was a Haitian-born accountant, his mother a black Puerto Rican), Basquiat left school in 1977 at age 17 and lived on the streets of New York for several years, during which time he developed the "tag"—or graffiti pen-name—SAMO, a combination of "Sambo" and "same ol' shit." SAMO was most closely associated with a three-pointed crown (as self-anointed "king" of the graffiti artists) and the word "TAR," evoking racism (as in "tar baby"), violence ("tar and feathers," which he would entitle a painting in 1982), and, through its anagram, the "art" world as well. A number of his paintings exhibited in the 1981 *New York/New Wave* exhibit at an alternative art gallery across the 59th Street Bridge from Manhattan attracted the attention of several art dealers, and his career exploded.

Central to his personal iconography is the crown, which is a symbol of not only his personal success but also that of the other African-American heroes that are the subject of many of his works—jazz artists, as is the case here, and "famous Negro athletes," as he calls them, such as the boxer Sugar Ray Leonard and baseball's Hank Aaron.

The price of a halo at 59¢ suggests that martyrdom is "for sale" in Basquiat's world.

Beneath the crown that Basquiat had introduced in his SAMO years is a reference to Thor, the Norse god; below it, the Superman logo; and above it, a reference to the Marvel comic *X-Men* heroes. Thor is, in fact, another X-Man hero. Marvel describes the X-Men as follows: "Born with strange powers, the mutants known as the X-Men use their awesome abilities to protect a world that hates and fears them." Basquiat clearly means to draw an analogy between the X-Men and his African-American heroes.

The "X" in Basquiat's work is never entirely negative. In Henry Dreyfuss's *Symbol Sourcebook: An Authoritative Guide to International Graphic Symbols*, Basquiat discovered a section on "Hobo Signs," marks left, graffiti-like, by hobos to inform their brethren about the lay of the local land. In this graphic language, an "X" means "O.K.; All right."

This phrase is a reference to the other "Charles the First"—King Charles I of England, beheaded by Protestants in the English Civil War in 1649 (see Chapter 10). But it also suggests, especially considering the crossed-out word "young," Basquiat's sense of his own martyrdom. In fact, four months before his 28th birthday, in 1988, he would become the victim, according to the medical examiner's report, of "acute mixed drug intoxication (opiates–cocaine)."

Something to Think About . . .

Many viewers are at least initially put off by the apparent sloppiness of Basquiat's distinctive style. But Basquiat adopted this style for a purpose. What do you imagine his purpose might have been?

The "S," especially crossed out, also suggests dollars, $.

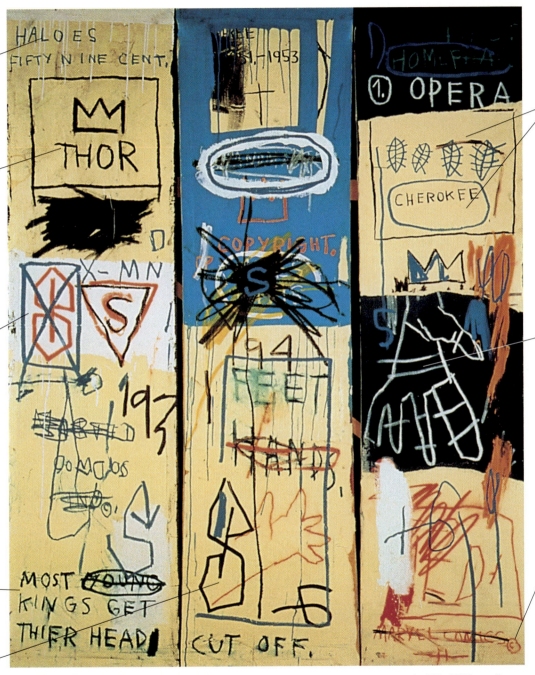

Beneath the word "Opera," and apparently on a par with the most aristocratic of musical genres, is the title of one of Charlie Parker's greatest tunes, "Cherokee," topped by four feathers in honor of Parker's nickname, "Bird." The feathers and song also evoke the Cherokee Indians' forced removal from Georgia to Oklahoma on the so-called Trail of Tears in 1838.

The hand probably represents the powerful hand of the musician, and equally the painter.

The copyright sign, ©, which also appears spelled out at the top of the middle panel, is repeated again and again in Basquiat's work and suggests not just ownership but the exercise of property rights and control in American society, which Basquiat sees as the root cause of the institution of slavery (to say nothing of the removal of the Cherokee nation to Oklahoma).

Jean-Michel Basquiat, *Charles the First*. **1982.** Acrylic and oil paintstick on canvas, three panels, 78" × 62¼" overall. © 2014 The Estate of Jean-Michel Basquiat/ADAGP, Paris/ARS, New York.

 View the Closer Look for *Charles the First* on **MyArtsLab**

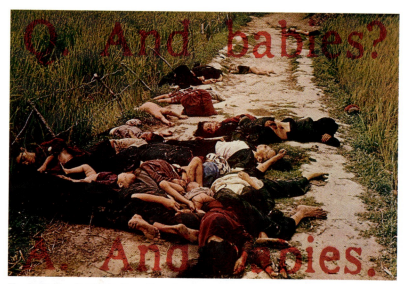

Fig. 15.19 Ron Haeberle, Peter Brandt, and the Art Workers' Coalition, *Q. And Babies? A. And Babies.* 1970. Offset lithograph, 24" × 38". Museum of Modern Art, New York. Gift of the Benefit for the Attica Defense Fund. Brandt was the poster's designer.

asked. "Men, women, and children," Meadlo answered. "And babies?" "And babies." The transcript of the interview was published the next day in the *New York Times*, accompanied by the photograph. Quickly, the Art Workers' Coalition added Wallace's question and Meadlo's response to the image (Fig. **15.19**), printed a poster, and distributed it around the world.

The Feminist Movement

At the same time that the antiwar and civil rights movements galvanized political consciousness among both men and women, "the Pill" was introduced in the early 1960s. As women gained control over their own reproductive functions, they began to express the sexual freedom that men had always taken for granted. The struggle for gender equality in the United States found greater and greater expression throughout the 1960s until, by the early 1970s, a full-blown feminist era emerged.

The Theoretical Framework: Betty Friedan and NOW In 1963, a freelance journalist and mother of three, Betty Friedan (1921–2006), published *The Feminine Mystique*. In many ways, hers was an argument with Freud, or at least with the way Freud had been understood, or misunderstood. While she admits that "Freudian psychology, with its emphasis on freedom from a repressive morality to achieve sexual fulfillment, was part of the ideology of women's emancipation," she is aware that some of Freud's writings had been misused as a tool for the suppression of women. Latent in Friedan's analysis, but central to the feminist movement, is her understanding that in Freud, as in Western discourse as a whole, the term "woman" is tied, in terms of its construction as a word, to man (its medieval root is "*wifman*," or "wife [of] man"). It is thus a contested term that does not refer to the biological female but to the sum total of all the patriarchal society expects of the female,

including behavior, dress, attitude, and demeanor. "Woman," said the feminists, is a cultural construct, not a biological one. In *The Feminine Mystique*, Friedan rejects modern American society's cultural construction of women. But she could not, in the end, reject the word "woman" itself. Friedan would go on to become one of the founders of the National Organization for Women (NOW), the primary purpose of which was to advance women's rights and gender equity in the workplace. In this, she dedicated herself to changing, in American culture, her society's understanding of what "woman" means.

Feminist Poetry The difficulties that women faced in determining an identity outside the patriarchal construction of "woman" became, in the 1960s, one of the chief subjects of poetry by women, particularly in the work of the poets Anne Sexton (1928–74), Sylvia Plath (1932–63), and Adrienne Rich (1929–2012). Sexton's work is exemplary. She was an affluent housewife and mother, living in a house with a sunken living room and a backyard swimming pool in the Boston suburb of Weston, Massachusetts. But she was personally at odds with her life, and as her husband saw his formerly dependent wife become a celebrity, their marriage dissolved into a fabric of ill will, discord, and physical abuse. The poem with which she opened most readings, the ecstatically witty "Her Kind," published in 1960 in her first book of poems, *To Bedlam and Part Way Back*, captures the sense of independence that defined her from the beginning (**Reading 15.8**):

READING 15.8

Anne Sexton, "Her Kind" (1960)

I have gone out, a possessed witch
haunting the black air, braver at night;
dreaming evil, I have done my hitch
over the plain houses, light by light:
lonely thing, twelve-fingered, out of mind.
A woman like that is not a woman, quite.
I have been her kind.

I have found the warm caves in the woods,
filled them with skillets, carvings, shelves,
closets, silks, innumerable goods;
fixed the suppers for the worms and the elves:
whining, rearranging the disaligned.
A woman like that is misunderstood.
I have been her kind.

I have ridden in your cart, driver,
waved my nude arms at villages going by,
learning the last bright routes, survivor
where your flames still bite my thigh
and my ribs crack where your wheels wind.
A woman like that is not ashamed to die.
I have been her kind.

Feminist Art Despite the advances made by women in the arts in the 1960s, real change was slow in coming. Although in 1976 approximately 50 percent of the professional artists in the United States were women, only 15 in 100 one-person shows in New York's prestigious galleries were devoted to work by women. Eight years later, the Museum of Modern Art reopened its enlarged facilities with a show entitled *An International Survey of Painting and Sculpture*. Of the 168 artists represented, only 13 were women.

So used was the public to seeing art in purely formalist terms—in terms, that is, of line, color, and composition—that when an artist like Judy Chicago (1939–) tried to invest her work with feminist content, the public refused to recognize it. Her series of *15 Pasadena Lifesavers* (Fig. **15.20**) exhibited in 1970 at Cal State Fullerton expressed, she felt, "the range of my own sexuality and identity, as symbolized through form and color." Their feminist content was affirmed by a statement on the gallery wall directly across from the entrance, which read:

> Judy Gerowitz hereby divests herself of all names imposed upon her through male social dominance and freely chooses her own name Judy Chicago.

But male reviewers ignored the statement. As Chicago says in her 1975 autobiography, *Through the Flower: My Struggle as a Woman Artist*: "[They] refused to accept that my work was intimately connected to my femaleness." But, in part, their misapprehension was her own doing. As she explains in *Through the Flower*, "I had come out of a formalist

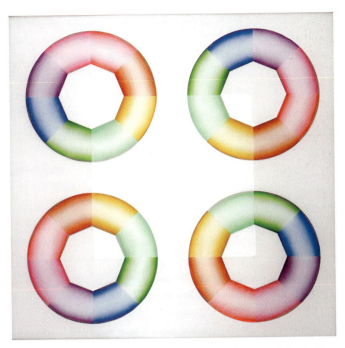

Fig. 15.20 Judy Chicago, *Pasadena Lifesavers Red Series #3*. 1969–70. Sprayed acrylic lacquer on acrylic, 60" × 60". Collection of Locks Gallery, Philadelphia, PA. Photo © Donald Woodman. © 2014 Judy Chicago/Artists Rights Society (ARS), New York. To many viewers, the geometry of Chicago's forms completely masked their sexual meaning.

background and had learned to neutralize my subject matter. In order to be considered a 'serious' artist, I had had to suppress my femaleness. . . . I was still working in a frame of reference that people had learned to perceive in a particular, non-content-oriented way."

Chicago's great collaborative work of the 1970s, *The Dinner Party* (Fig. **15.21**), changed all that. In its bold assertion of woman's place in social history, the piece announced the growing power of the women's movement itself. More than 300 women worked together over a period of five years to create the piece, which consists of a triangular table, set with 39 places, 13 on a side, each celebrating a woman who has made an important contribution to world history. The first plate is dedicated to the Great Goddess, and the third to the Cretan Snake Goddess. Around the table the likes of Eleanor of Aquitaine and Artemisia Gentileschi are celebrated. Where the *Pasadena Lifesavers* had sheltered their sexual content under the cover of their symbolic abstraction, in *The Dinner Party*, the natural forms of the female anatomy were fully expressed in the ceramic work, needlepoint, and drawing. But, as Chicago is quick to point out, "the real point of the vaginal imagery in *The Dinner Party* was to say that these women are not known because they have vaginas. That is all they had in common, actually. They were from different periods, classes, ethnicities, geographies, experiences, but what kept them within the same historical space was the fact that they had vaginas."

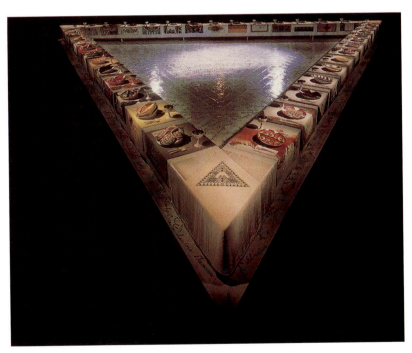

Fig. 15.21 Judy Chicago, *The Dinner Party*. 1979. Mixed media, 48' × 48' × 3' installed. Collection of the Brooklyn Museum of Art, Gift of the Elizabeth A. Sackler Foundation. Photograph © Donald Woodman. © 2014 Judy Chicago/Artists Rights Society (ARS), New York. The names of 999 additional women are inscribed in ceramic tiles along the table's base.

 View the Closer Look for *The Dinner Party* on **MyArtsLab**

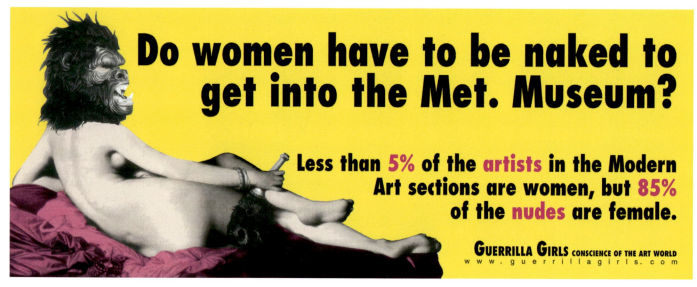

Fig. 15.22 Guerrilla Girls, *Do women have to be naked to get into the Met. Museum?* 1989. Poster. © 1989, 1995 by the Guerrilla Girls, Inc. The figure is a parody of Jean-Auguste-Dominique Ingres' 1814 Neoclassical painting *La Grande Odalisque*, in the collection of the Louvre, Paris (see Fig. 13.3).

Despite Chicago's success with *The Dinner Party*, it remained very difficult for women to enter the art world. In 1985 an anonymous group of women who called themselves the Guerrilla Girls began hanging posters in New York City to draw attention to the problem (Fig. **15.22**). They listed the specific galleries who represented less than 1 woman out of every 10 men. Another poster asked: "How Many Women Had One-person Exhibitions at NYC Museums Last Year?" The answer:

Guggenheim	0
Metropolitan	0
Modern	1
Whitney	0

One of the Guerrilla Girls' most daring posters was distributed in 1989. It asked, "When racism & sexism are no longer fashionable, what will your art collection be worth?" It listed 67 women artists and pointed out that a collection of works by all of them would be worth less than the art auction value of any *one* painting by a famous living male artist. Its suggestion that the value of the male artists' work might be drastically inflated struck a chord with many.

By the late 1990s, the situation had changed somewhat. Many more women were regularly exhibited in New York galleries and more major retrospectives were devoted to their work. But, internationally especially, women continued to get short shrift. Where a retrospective by a major male artist—Robert Rauschenberg, for instance—might originate in New York at the Guggenheim and travel to international venues around the world, most retrospectives of women artists remained much more modest—a single nontraveling show at, say, the New Museum in New York or the Los Angeles County Museum of Art.

THE POSTMODERN ERA

How are pluralism and diversity reflected in postmodern art and literature?

It is difficult to pinpoint exactly when "modernism" ended and "postmodernism" began, but the turning point came in the late 1960s. Architects began to reject the pure, almost hygienic uniformity of the International Style, represented by the work of Mies van der Rohe (see Fig. 15.9), favoring more eclectic architectural styles that were anything but pure. A single building might incorporate a classical colonnade and a roof line inspired by a piece of Chippendale furniture. Or it might look like the Rasin Building in Prague (Fig. **15.23**). Built on the site of a Renaissance structure destroyed in World War II, the building in its teetering sense of collapse evokes the postwar cityscape of twisted I-beams, blown-out facades with rooms standing open to the sky, and sunken foundations, all standing next to a building totally unaffected by the bombing. But that said, the building is also a playful, almost whimsical celebration, among other things, of the marvels of modern engineering—a building made to look as if it is at the brink of catastrophe, even as it is completely structurally sound. So lighthearted is the building that it was called the "Dancing House," or, more specifically, "Ginger and Fred," after the American film stars Ginger Rogers and Fred Astaire. The more solid tower on the corner seems to be leading the transparent tower—Ginger—by the waist, as the two spin around the corner.

The building was the idea of the Czech architect Vlado Milunić (1941–), and he enlisted the American architect Frank Gehry (1929–) to collaborate on the project. To many eyes in Prague, a city renowned for its classical architecture, it seemed an absolutely alien American element dropped into the city. But Milunić conceived of the

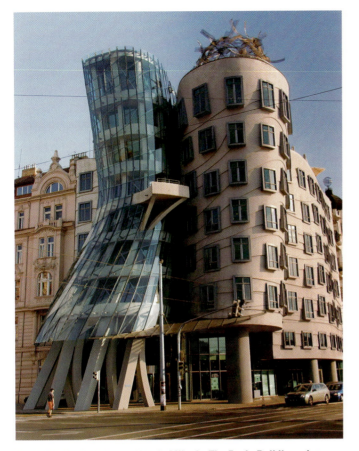

Fig. 15.23 Frank Gehry and Vlado Milunić, The Rasin Building, also known as the "Dancing House" or "Ginger and Fred," Prague, Czech Republic. 1992–96. The building was championed by Vaclav Havel (1936–2011), the Czech playwright who served as president of first Czechoslovakia and then the Czech Republic from the fall of the Soviet Union in 1989 until 2003. Havel had lived next door since childhood.

building as addressing modern Prague even as it engaged the city's past. He wanted the building to consist of two parts: "Like a society that forgot its totalitarian past—a static part—but was moving into a world full of changes. That was the main idea. Two different parts in dialogue, in tension, like plus and minus, like Yang and Yin, like man and woman." It was Gehry who nicknamed it "Ginger and Fred."

The use of many different, even contradictory elements of design is the hallmark of **postmodern** architecture. The English critic Peter Fuller explained the task of the postmodern architect this way:

> The west front of Wells Cathedral, the Parthenon pediment, the plastic and neon signs on Caesar's Palace in Las Vegas, even the hidden intricacies of a Mies curtain wall, are all equally "interesting." Thus the Post-Modern designer must offer a shifting pattern of changing strategies and substitute a shuffling of codes and devices, varying ceaselessly according to audience, and/or building type, and/or environmental circumstance.

But perhaps the clearest and most seminal statement of the postmodern aesthetic is that of the architect Robert Venturi

(1925–), whose 1966 "Gentle Manifesto" described criteria for a new eclectic approach to architecture that abandoned the clean and simple geometries of modern architecture. In its place, Venturi argued for "an architecture of complexity and contradiction. . . . It must embody the difficult unity of inclusion rather than the easy unity of exclusion."

Pluralism and Diversity in Postmodern Painting

By the end of the 1960s, artists felt free to engage in a wide spectrum of experimental approaches to painting, ranging from the stylized imagery introduced by Pop artists to the street style of graffiti writers (see the *Closer Look* on Jean-Michel Basquiat, pp. 502–503), and from full-blown abstraction to startlingly naturalistic realism. Indeed, the exchange of ideas between proponents of realism and those of abstraction during the post-World War II era had far-reaching effects. Rather than an either/or proposition, there is abundant cross-fertilization between the approaches. We can see this in the work of the contemporary German artist Gerhard Richter (1932–), who moves freely between the two—sometimes repainting photographs, black-and-white and color, and sometimes creating large-scale abstract works. Richter uses photographs, including amateur snapshots and media images, because, he says, they are "free of all the conventional criteria I had always associated with art . . . no style, no composition, no judgment." To him, they are "pure" pictures, unadulterated by the intervention of conscious aesthetic criteria. *Meadowland* (Fig. 15.24), an oil painting on canvas, might as well have been taken from the window of a passing car. The questions it raises

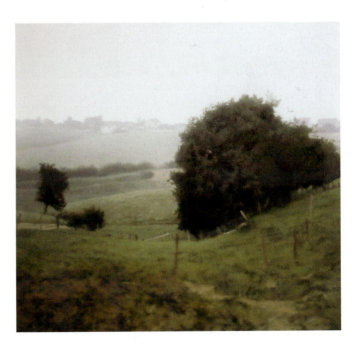

Fig. 15.24 Gerhard Richter, *Meadowland*. 1992. Oil on canvas, 35⅝" × 37½". The Museum of Modern Art, New York. Blanchette Rockefeller, Betsy Babcock, and Mrs. Elizabeth Bliss Parkinson Funds (350.1985). © Gerhard Richter 2014. In 1964, Richter began collecting the source photos for all his paintings and arranging them on panels. When the resulting work, *Atlas,* was exhibited in 1995 at the Dia Center for the Arts in New York, it contained 683 panels and close to 5,000 photographs.

are quite simple: Why did he select this photograph to translate into a painting? How and when does the eye sense the difference between a painting and a photographic surface?

In comparing *Meadowland* to the artist's abstractions, which he concentrated on throughout the 1980s and 1990s, we can begin to answer these questions. Works such as *Ice (2)* (Fig. **15.25**) are obviously paintings. One senses that Richter begins with a realistic image, and before the ground completely dries, he drags another layer of paint through it with a squeegee or palette knife. The result is like viewing an object close up while passing it at high speed. But the resulting work is above all a painterly surface, not a photographic one. Nevertheless, in Richter's words,

> abstract paintings . . . visualize a reality which we can neither see nor describe but which we may nevertheless conclude exists. We attach negative names to this reality; the unknown, the ungraspable, the infinite, and for thousands of years we have depicted it in terms of substitute images like heaven and hell, gods and devils. With abstract painting we create a better means of approaching what can be neither seen nor understood because abstract painting illustrates with the greatest clarity, that is to say with all the means at the disposal of art, "nothing." . . . [Looking at abstract paintings] we allow ourselves to see the un-seeable, that which has never before been seen and indeed is not visible.

Given this artistic strategy, Richter's photograph-based works are paintings of the graspable and visible. Why did he select the photograph upon which *Meadowland* is based? Precisely because it is so mundane, a prospect we have so often seen before. How and when do we recognize *Meadowland* as a painting and not a photograph? When we accept photographic clarity—or photographic blurring, for that matter—as one of the infinite methods of painting. Richter's photographic paintings are thus the very antithesis of his abstractions, except that both styles are equal statements of the artist's vision. Together, in them, Richter explores not only the conditions of seeing but also the possibilities of painting. Richter might be the ultimate postmodernist: "I pursue no objects, no system, no tendency," he writes. "I have no program, no style, no direction. . . . I steer clear of definitions. I don't know what I want. I am

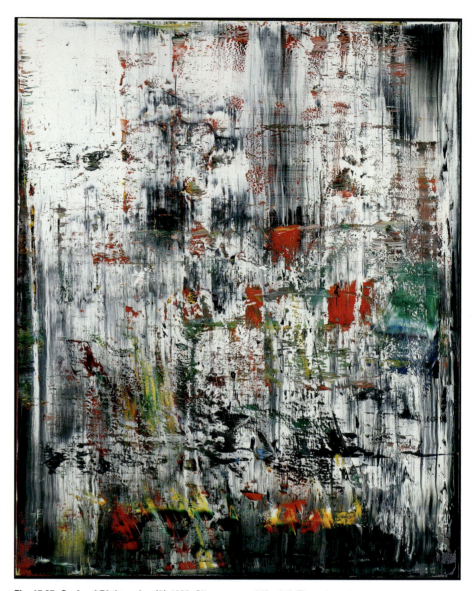

Fig. 15.25 Gerhard Richter, *Ice (2).* **1989.** Oil on canvas, 80″ × 64″. Through prior gift of Joseph Winterbotham; gift of Lannan Foundation, 1997.168. Reproduction, the Art Institute of Chicago. All rights reserved. © Gerhard Richter 2014. In the abstractions, the blurred effect of the photograph-based work has been heightened. We seem to be looking at the world through a sheet of ice.

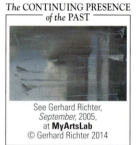

The CONTINUING PRESENCE
of the PAST

See Gerhard Richter,
September, 2005,
at **MyArtsLab**
© Gerhard Richter 2014

inconsistent, non-committal, passive; I like the indefinite, the boundless; I like continued uncertainty."

Another approach to the question of the relation between abstraction and representation is seen in the works of Pat Steir (1940–). In 1989, she adapted Pollock's drip technique to her own ends, allowing paint to flow by force of gravity down the length of her enormous canvases to form recognizable waterfalls. *Yellow and Blue One-Stroke Waterfall* (Fig. **15.26**) is 14 feet high, its format reminiscent of Chinese scroll paintings of waterfalls. Steir explained

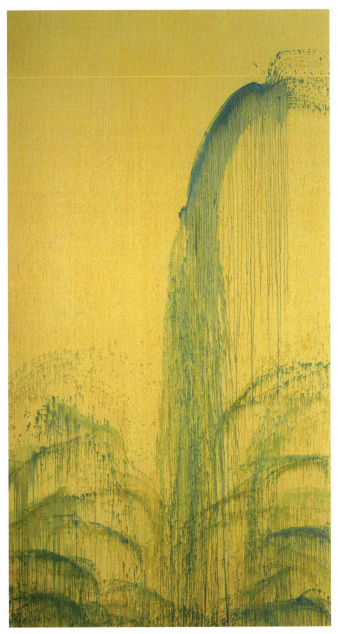

Fig. 15.26 Pat Steir, *Yellow and Blue One-Stroke Waterfall*. 1992. Oil on canvas, 14'6¼" × 7'6¾". The Solomon R. Guggenheim Museum, New York. Gift, John Eric Cheim, 1999. 99.5288. Steir's work is deeply informed by her interest in Tibetan and Chinese religious lore, and she is interested in creating something of their meditative space.

the rationale behind her series of waterfall paintings in an interview in 1992:

> I don't think of these paintings as abstract. . . . These are not only drips of paint. They're paintings of drips which form waterfall images: pictures. . . . [Nor are] they realistic . . . I haven't sat outdoors with a little brush, trying to create the illusion of a waterfall. The paint itself makes the picture. . . . Gravity make the image. . . .
>
> These paintings are, in a sense a comment on the New York School [i.e., the first generation of Abstract Expressionists, including Pollock and de Kooning], a dialogue and a wink.

They [her waterfall paintings] say, "You didn't go far enough. You stopped when you saw abstraction." . . . I've taken the drip and tried to do something with it that the Modernists denied.

The painting is thus at once, and paradoxically, both abstract and representational.

Pluralism and Diversity in Postmodern Literature

In a world of complexity and contradiction, the pursuit of meaning is equally difficult. For the postmodern writer, meaning is always plural and fleeting, and attempting to find any permanent or stable meaning can lead only to frustration. The postmodern hero seeks meaning, but accepts the fact that the search is never-ending. At the beginning of his study of the Western experience of order, entitled *The Order of Things* (in English translation), French historian Michel Foucault (1926–84) quotes a passage from an essay by the Latin American writer Jorge Luis Borges (1899–1986) that embodies, from Foucault's point of view, the profusion of meaning that defines postmodern thought, an impossible taxonomy from "a certain Chinese encyclopedia" entitled *Celestial Emporium of Benevolent Knowledge* (**Reading 15.9**):

READING 15.9

from Jorge Luis Borges, "The Analytical Language of John Wilkins," in *Other Inquisitions 1937–1952*, trans. Ruth L. C. Simms (1964)

On those remote pages it is written that animals are divided into (a) those that belong to the Emperor, (b) embalmed ones, (c) those that are trained, (d) suckling pigs, (e) mermaids, (f) fabulous ones, (g) stray dogs, (h) those that are included in this classification, (i) those that tremble as if they were mad, (j) innumerable ones, (k) those drawn with a very fine camel's hair brush, (l) others, (m) those that have just broken a flower vase, (n) those that resemble flies from a distance.

The impossibility of Jorge Luis Borges's (1899–1986) encyclopedia is based on how impossible it is for contemporary thought to recognize difference with no relation to opposition or relation to a common ground. Each element in Borges's taxonomy requires a complete shift in the reader's point of view. There is, as Foucault points out, "no common locus" beneath this taxonomy, no center around which to organize its elements. But it is precisely this possibility of "thinking that" that is the goal of postmodern literature. To this point in this survey of the Western humanities, we have referred to a historical series of shifting geographic centers, each one providing a common cultural locus for thought. Postmodern thought alters the situation. The postmodern world consists of multiple centers of thought, each existing simultaneously with and independently of the others.

Borges's short story "Borges and I" may be the first postmodern exploration of this state of affairs. Although he published widely in almost every imaginable form, his reputation as one of the leaders of modern Latin-American literature rests almost entirely on a series of some 40 short stories, tales, and sketches—"fictions," as he called them. Many of these sometimes very brief fictions take on a quality of dreamlike mystery (**Reading 15.10**):

READING 15.10

Jorge Luis Borges, "Borges and I" (1967)
Translated by J. E. I.

The other one, the one called Borges, is the one things happen to. I walk through the streets of Buenos Aires and stop for a moment, perhaps mechanically now, to look at the arch of an entrance hall and the grillwork on the gate; I know of Borges from the mail and see his name on a list of professors or in a biographical dictionary. I like hourglasses, maps, eighteenth century typography, the taste of coffee and the prose of Stevenson; he shares these preferences, but in a vain way that turns them into the attributes of an actor. It would be an exaggeration to say that ours is a hostile relationship; I live, let myself go on living, so that Borges may contrive his literature, and this literature justifies me. It is no effort for me to confess that he has achieved some valid pages, but those pages cannot save me, perhaps because what is good belongs to no one, not even to him, but rather to the language and to tradition. Besides, I am destined to perish, definitively, and only some instant of myself can survive in him. Little by little, I am giving over everything to him, though I am quite aware of his perverse custom of falsifying and magnifying things. Spinoza knew that all things long to persist in their being; the stone eternally wants to be a stone and the tiger a tiger. I shall remain in Borges, not in myself (if it is true that I am someone), but I recognize myself less in his books than in many others or in the laborious strumming of a guitar. Years ago I tried to free myself from him and went from the mythologies of the suburbs to the games with time and infinity, but those games belong to Borges now and I shall have to imagine other things. Thus my life is a flight and I lose everything and everything belongs to oblivion, or to him.
I do not know which of us has written this page.

This is the story in its entirety. Borges describes himself as a bodily self divided from his persona as a writer. In the postmodern world, meaning shifts according to place and time and, Borges teaches us, point of view—not only the writer's but also our own. Meaning might well be determined by a myriad of semantic accidents or misunderstandings, or by a reader whose mood, gender, or particular cultural context defines, for the moment, how and what he or she understands. Postmodern writing produces texts that willingly place themselves in such an open field of interpretation, subject to uncertainty.

The literature of Latino and Hispanic culture in the Americas is infused with a sense of cross-fertilization—like Borges, a sense of different, even competing selves. From the beginning of the sixteenth century, the Hispanization of Indian culture and the Indianization of Hispanic culture in Latin and South America created a unique cultural pluralism. By the last half of the twentieth century, Latino culture became increasingly Americanized, and an influx of Hispanic immigrants helped to Latinize American culture. The situation has been summed up by the Puerto Rico-born poet Aurora Levins Morales (1954–) in "Child of the Americas," a poem in which she comes to the same "difficult unity of inclusion" as that described by Robert Venturi in relation to postmodern architecture (**Reading 15.11**):

READING 15.11

Aurora Levins Morales, "Child of the Americas" (1986)

I am a child of the Americas,
a light-skinned mestiza of the Caribbean,
a child of many diaspora, born into this continent at a
    crossroads.
I am a U.S. Puerto Rican Jew,
a product of the ghettos of New York I have never known.
An immigrant and the daughter and granddaughter of
    immigrants.
I speak English with passion: it's the tongue of my
    consciousness,
a flashing knife blade of crystal, my tool, my craft.

I am Caribeña, island grown. Spanish is my flesh,
Ripples from my tongue, lodges in my hips:
the language of garlic and mangoes,
the singing of poetry, the flying gestures of my hands.
I am of Latinoamerica, rooted in the history of my
    continent:
I speak from that body.

I am not African. Africa is in me, but I cannot return.
I am not taína. Taíno[1] is in me, but there is no way back.
I am not European. Europe lives in me, but I have no
    home there.

I am new. History made me. My first language was
    spanglish.
I was born at the crossroads
and I am whole.

[1] **Taíno:** The first Native American population encountered by Christopher Columbus.

Cross-Fertilization in the Visual Arts

"Language is a virus," declared the American author William S. Burroughs (1914–97), referring, at least in part, to the fact that American English has become the international language of business, politics, the media, and culture—a plague upon indigenous languages, threatening their extinction. In this context, the collision of global cultures could hardly be ignored. Increasingly, artists have responded by acknowledging that life in a global world increasingly demands that they accept multiple identities as Aurora Levins Morales has. Many find themselves in a double bind—how, they ask, can they remain true to their native or ethnic identities and still participate in the larger world market? What happens to their work when it enters a context where it is received with little or no understanding of its origins? How, indeed, does the global threaten the local? Is the very idea of the "self" threatened by technology and technological innovation?

The postmodern blurring of the boundaries between classical art and contemporary culture is epitomized in art by the controversial painting *The Holy Virgin Mary* by the British-born Nigerian painter Chris Ofili (1968–) which is a case in point (Fig. **15.27**). Ofili portrays the Virgin as a black woman, and surrounding her are *putti* (winged cherubs) with bare bottoms and genitalia cut out of pornographic magazines. Two balls of elephant dung, acquired from London Zoo, support the painting, inscribed with the words "Virgin" and "Mary," a third clump defining one of her breasts. The son of black African Catholic parents, both of whom were born in Lagos, Nigeria, and whose first language was Yoruba, Ofili has used this West African culture as a source of inspiration for his art.

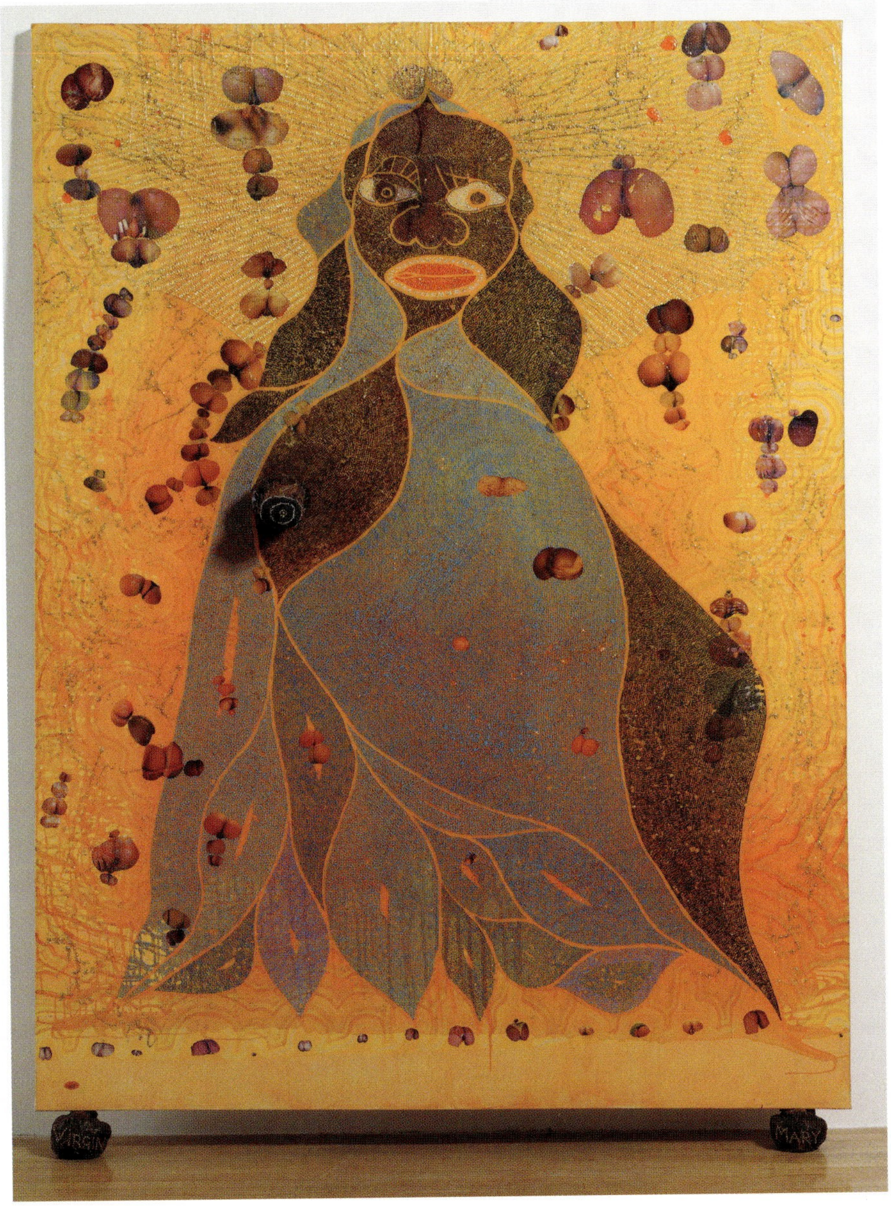

The display of sexual organs, especially in representations of female divinities, is common in Yoruba culture, and Ofili's *putti* are meant to represent modern examples of this indigenous tradition, symbolizing the fertility of the Virgin Mary. As for elephant dung, in 1992, during a trip to Zimbabwe, Ofili was struck by its beauty after it was dried and varnished. He also came to understand that it was worshiped as a symbol of fertility in Zimbabwe, and he began to mount his paintings on clumps of dung as a way, he said, "of raising the paintings up from the ground and giving them a feeling that they've come from the earth rather than simply being hung on a wall."

The Holy Virgin Mary artwork thus reflects Ofili's African heritage. But he understood that the African association of genitalia and dung with fertility and female divinities would be lost on his Western audience. Indeed it was. When the painting was exhibited at the Brooklyn Museum in late 1999, it provoked a stormy reaction. The Catholic cardinal in New York called it a blasphemous attack on religion, and the Catholic League called for demonstrations at the Museum. New York's Mayor Rudolph W. Giuliani threatened to cut off the museum's funding as well as evict it from the city-owned building it leased. (He was forced to back down by the courts.) For Ofili, the conflict his painting generated was itself emblematic of the collision of cultures that define his own identity. At the same time, it can be said that the controversy helped to make Ofili even more prominent and did little to diminish the "marketability" of his art. In 2003, he was chosen to represent Great Britain at the Venice Biennale, perhaps the most prominent contemporary global art exhibition.

Fig. 15.27 Chris Ofili, *The Holy Virgin Mary*. 1996. Acrylic, oil, polyester resin, paper collage, glitter, map pins, and elephant dung on linen, 96″ × 72″. (CO 24.) Collection: Museum of Old and New Art, Hobart, Australia. Courtesy the Artist and Victoria Miro, London. © Chris Ofili. While on display in Brooklyn, the painting was smeared with white paint by an angry 72-year-old spectator.

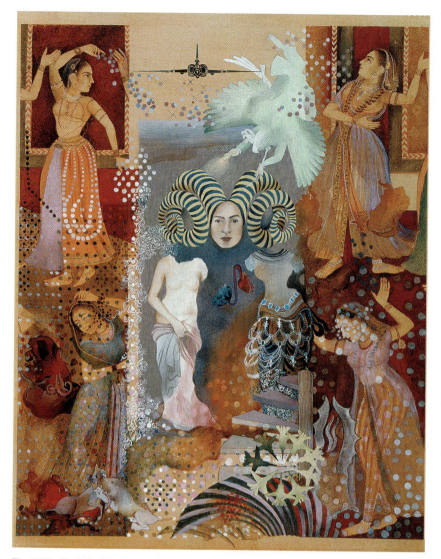

Fig. 15.28 Shahzia Sikander, *Pleasure Pillars*. 2001. Watercolor, dry pigment, vegetable color, tea, and ink on wasli paper, 12" × 10". Courtesy Sikkema Jenkins & Co., New York. As part of her ongoing investigation of identity, Sikander has taken to wearing the veil in public, something she never did before moving to America, in what she labels "performances" of her Pakistani heritage.

👁 **Watch** an Art21 video of Shahzia Sikander discussing her work on **MyArtsLab**

Similarly, the Pakistani painter Shahzia Sikander (1969–) addresses her heterogeneous background in works such as *Pleasure Pillars* (Fig. **15.28**) by reinventing the traditional genre of miniature painting in a hybrid of styles. Combining her training as a miniature artist in her native Pakistan with her focus on contemporary art during her studies at the Rhode Island School of Design, Sikander explores the tension inherent in Islam's encounter with the Western world, Christianity, and the neighboring South Asian tradition of Hinduism. In the center of *Pleasure Pillars*, Sikander portrays herself with the spiraling horns of a powerful ram. Below her head are two bodies, one

CONTINUITY & CHANGE

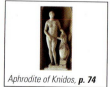

Aphrodite of Knidos, *p. 74*

a Western Venus, the other Devi, the Hindu goddess of fertility, rain, health, and nature, who is said to hold the entire universe in her womb. Between them, two hearts pump blood, a reference to her dual sources of inspiration, East and West. Eastern and Western images of power also inform the image as a lion kills a deer at the bottom left, a direct artistic quotation from an Iranian miniature of the Safavid dynasty (1501–1736), and, at the top, a modern fighter jet roars past. For Sikander and Ofili both, identity is itself contested ground, the very condition of being in a postmodern world.

Of all the world's indigenous peoples, native North Americans have been among the most isolated and marginalized. Diverse but sequestered on arid reservations, enmeshed in poverty and unemployment, their traditions and languages on the brink of extinction, Native Americans seemed the consummate "Other." However, in 1968, in Minneapolis, Minnesota, a gathering of local Native Americans, led by Dennis Banks, George Mitchell, and Clyde Bellecourt, decided to address these problems through collective action, and founded the American Indian Movement (AIM). Almost a quarter-century later, Banks recalled what motivated them:

> Because of the slum housing conditions; the highest unemployment rate in the whole of this country; police brutality against our elders, women, and children, Native Warriors came together from the streets, prisons, jails and the urban ghettos of Minneapolis to form the American Indian Movement. They were tired of begging for welfare, tired of being scapegoats in America and decided to start building on the strengths of our own people; decided to build our own schools; our own job training programs; and our own destiny. That was our motivation to begin. That beginning is now being called "the Era of Indian Power."

AIM was, from the outset, a militant organization. On Thanksgiving Day 1970, AIM members boarded the *Mayflower II* at its dock in Plymouth harbor as a countercelebration of the 350th anniversary of the Pilgrims' landing at Plymouth Rock. A year later, they occupied Mount Rushmore National Monument. In AIM's point of view, the site, which was sacred to their culture, had been desecrated by the carving of the American presidents Washington, Jefferson, Roosevelt, and Lincoln into the mountain. The occupation was designed to draw attention to the 1868 Treaty of Fort Laramie, which had deeded the Black Hills, including Mount Rushmore, to the Lakota Sioux. The U.S. military had ignored the treaty, forcing the Lakota onto the Pine

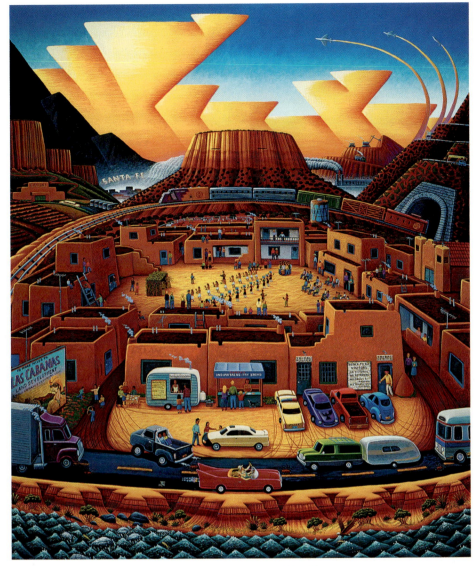

Fig. 15.29 David P. Bradley (Ojibwe), *Indian Country Today*. 1996–97. Acrylic on canvas, 70″ × 60″. Museum purchase through the Mr. and Mrs. James Krebs Fund. Photograph courtesy Peabody Essex Museum. In the foreground is the Rio Grande River, teeming with fish, the lifeblood of the region.

Fe, New Mexico. Behind the pueblo, to the left, the parking lot of an Indian-run casino is filled with tourist buses. Behind it, in the distance, is the city of Santa Fe. The train passing behind the pueblo is the Santa Fe Railroad's "Chief"—the very image of Anglo-American culture's appropriation of Native traditions. To the right of the central mesa is the Four Corners Power Plant in northwestern New Mexico, one of the largest coal-fired generating stations in the United States and one of the greatest polluters. (Note the smoke reemerging on the far side of the mesa.) Behind the plant is an open-pit strip mine. Fighter jets rise over the landscape, reminders of the nearby Los Alamos National Laboratory, where classified work on the design of nuclear weapons is performed.

In the center of the pueblo, Bradley depicts a traditional kachina dance taking place. Performed by male dancers who impersonate kachinas, the spirits who inhabit the clouds, the rain, crops, animals, and even ideas such as growth and fertility (see Chapter 1), the dances are sacred and, although tourists are allowed to view them, photography is strictly prohibited. The actual masks worn in ceremonies are not considered art objects by the Pueblo. Rather, they are thought of as active agents in the transfer of power and knowledge between the gods and the men who wear them in dance. Kachina figurines are made for sale to tourists, but they are considered empty of any ritual power or significance. This commercialization of native tradition is the real subject of Bradley's painting. The native peoples' ability to withstand this onslaught is suggested by the giant mesa, endowed with kachina-like eyes and mouth, that overlooks the entire scene, suggesting that the spirits still oversee and protect their people.

A Multiplicity of Media: New Technology

Just as the electronic media have revolutionized modern culture, ranging from Thomas Edison's first audio recording to the motion picture, radio, television, and digital technology, and from the Internet to the iPod, so too have the arts been revolutionized by these media. This transformation was most fundamentally realized in the visual arts through the medium of video.

Ridge reservation on the plains south of the Black Hills. There, on December 29, 1890, with the Battle of Wounded Knee, conflict erupted (see Chapter 13). In 1973, AIM militants took control of Wounded Knee and were quickly surrounded by federal marshals. For over two months, they exchanged gunfire, until the AIM militants surrendered. Of course, not everyone agreed with AIM's tactics, but the group did help to revitalize Native American cultures throughout the hemisphere and furthered an interest in traditional art forms.

Although Native American communities are arguably better off today than they were in 1970—in no small part because of the emergence of reservation-based casino gambling—many concerns remain. Contemporary life in the Southwestern pueblos is the subject of *Indian Country Today* (Fig. **15.29**) painted by David P. Bradley (1954–), a Native American of Ojibwe descent who has lived for the last 30 years in Santa

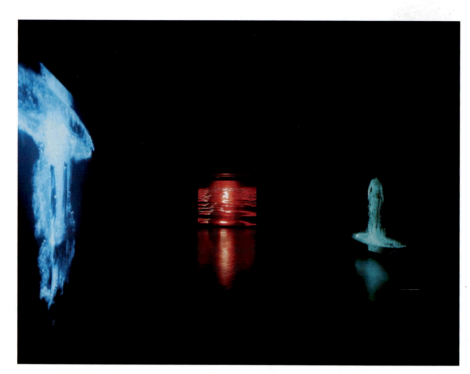

Fig. 15.30 Bill Viola, *Five Angels for the Millennium*. 2001. Video/sound installation, five channels of color video projection on walls in a large, dark room (room dimensions variable); stereo sound for each projection; image size 7'5" × 10'6" each. Edition of three. Photo: Mike Bruce, courtesy Anthony d'Offay, London.

Temporal media like video art are often concerned with the passing of time itself, the life cycle from birth to death. Video artist Bill Viola (1951–) has been fascinated, throughout his career, by the passage of time. His principal metaphor for this passage is water, which flows, like time, but can also be seen, and seems to make both time and space tangible and palpable. His video installation piece *Five Angels for the Millennium* (Fig. **15.30**) is composed of five individual video sequences that show a clothed man plunging into a pool of water. The duration of each video is different, with long sequences of peaceful aqueous landscape suddenly interrupted by the explosive sound of the body's dive into the water. Viola describes the process of making the piece:

Five Angels came out of a three-day shoot in Long Beach that I had undertaken for several other projects. All I knew was that I wanted to film a man plunging into water, sinking down, below, out of frame—drowning. A year or so later, going through this old footage, I came across five shots of this figure and started working with them—intuitively and without a conscious plan. I became completely absorbed by this man sinking in water, and by the sonic and physical environment I had in mind for the piece.

When I showed the finished work to Kira [Perov], my partner, she pointed out something I had not realized until that moment: this was not a film of a drowning man. Somehow, I had unconsciously run time backwards in the five films, so all but one of the figures rush upwards and out of the water. I had

inadvertently created images of ascension, from death to birth.

Because the videos are continuously looped and projected onto the gallery walls, their different durations make it impossible to predict which wall will suddenly become animated by the dive—the one behind you, the one in front of you, the one at your side. The experience is something like being immersed in both water and time simultaneously, in the flow of the moment. For Viola, video differs from film in exactly this sense. The most fundamental aspect of video's origin as a medium is the *live* camera. Video is in the moment. And Viola's installation literally spatializes time, even as time becomes as palpable as the watery surfaces he depicts.

Today, of course, video art per se no longer exists—the medium has become entirely digital, and, in fact, although it is far more expensive, artists working with time-based media have preferred, given the higher quality of the image, to work with film. One of the most remarkable experiments with the medium of film is the nine-screen installation *Ten Thousand Waves* (Fig. **15.31**) by the British artist and filmmaker Isaac Julien (1960–). *Ten Thousand Waves* was inspired by the drowning of 23 Chinese cockle pickers from Fujian province in southeast China in Morecambe Bay, Lancashire, on the evening of February 5, 2004. Their tragedy is juxtaposed with a Chinese fable, "The Tale of Yishan Island," in which the Chinese goddess and protector of sailors, the Fujian goddess Mazu—played by Chinese actress Maggie Chung—saves five boats of fishermen from a storm at sea by directing them to an island that, after they are saved, they can never find again. Layered on these two stories is a third story of a contemporary goddess—a sort of reenactment of Wu Yonggang's 1934 silent film *The Goddess* (about a woman who became a prostitute to support herself and her son), which tracks her as she moves from the historic Shanghai Film Studio sets of the 1930s into the present-day Pudong district of Shanghai.

Julien's multiscreen images at first seem chaotic, but they underscore that the fixed viewpoint of cinematic experience is highly institutionalized—the onslaught of visual stimulus in Julien's installation is actually very much like "the architecture of complexity" that Robert Venturi described. In that sense, Julien's installation thus represents a kind of "visual liberation." Its Dolby surround sound environment—the dialogue of helicopter pilots attempting their rescues of the cockle pickers, the poetry of Wang Ping, the atonal music of Maria de Alvear and fusion mix of Jah Wobble & the Chinese Dub Orchestra—immerses us in a cacophony of sonic

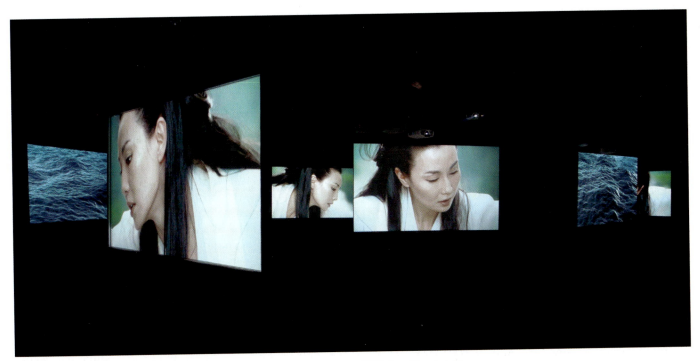

Fig. 15.31 Isaac Julien, *Ten Thousand Waves I*. 2010. Installation view, ShanghART Gallery, Shanghai. Nine-screen installation. 35mm film, transferred to High Definition, 9.2 surround sound. Duration 49 mins, 41 secs. Edition of 6 plus 1AP. Courtesy the Artist and Victoria Miro, London, Metro Pictures, New York, and Galería Helga de Alvear, Madrid. © Isaac Julien. Photography © Adrian Zhou. Here, Maggie Chung, in her role as Mazu, flies over Morecambe Bay searching for the drowning cockle pickers. Julien shot the scene by hoisting Chung on pulleys and filming her flying against a green screen, rendering the ropes invisible.

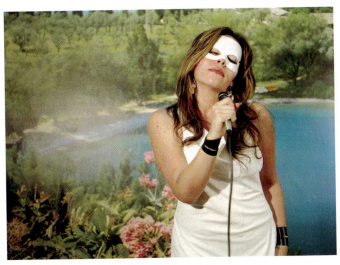

Fig. 15.32 Phil Collins, still from part one of The Smiths karaoke trilogy, *The World Won't Listen*. 2004–07. Synchronized three-channel color video projection with sound, 56 minutes. FILM STILL. Courtesy Shady Lane Productions and Tanya Bonakdar Gallery, New York. The music for the Smiths karaoke was performed by Columbia's biggest rock group, Aterciopelados ("The Velvety").

structures that parallels aurally the visual constructedness of the film. We are caught up in the "ten thousand waves" of Chinese history.

Julien's work is emphatically a condemnation of the exploitation of workers in the new global marketplace, a global marketplace in which culture itself has become a commodity. And perhaps no cultural commodity has traversed global boundaries more effectively than rock and roll. Beginning in 2004, the English artist Phil Collins created posters inviting people to perform karaoke renditions of all the songs from the Smiths' classic 1987 album *The World Won't Listen*, first in Bogotá, Colombia, then in Istanbul, Turkey, and finally in Jakarta and Bandung, Indonesia. "In all the locations," Collins told the Dallas Museum's curator of contemporary art, where the three sessions were first screened simultaneously, "some people had a very rudimentary grasp of English. But they knew the songs so devastatingly well through repetition, every breath and every ad lib, which, considering the importance of lyrics in the songs . . . is pretty amazing." The performers sing in front of travelogue leisure-world backdrops (Fig. **15.32**) ranging from lakeside villas to tropical resorts to American national parks, each entering, as they sing, even if only for a moment, the glamorous world of pop idols. "Other people sometimes find karaoke embarrassing, or laughable, or delusional," Collins explains, "but I find it moving and incredibly courageous. . . . It's like a mild form of heroism." What Collins's trilogy suggests, finally, is a human community of far-flung "fans," but believers, too, in lyrics like those that conclude the song "Rubber Ring": "Don't forget the songs/ That made you cry/ And the songs that saved your life."

There can be little doubt that rock-and-roll culture has had a considerable impact on the arts over the course of

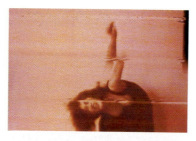

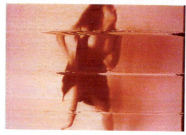

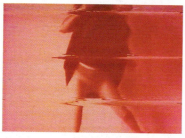

Fig. 15.33 Pipilotti Rist, three stills from *I'm Not The Girl Who Misses Much*. 1986. Single-channel video (color, sound), 5 min. © Pipilotti Rist. Courtesy the artist, Hauser & Wirth, and Luhring Augustine. As much as Rist's video is a parody of music videos in general, it also evokes the horror of John Lennon's assassination in 1980 and the terrible irony that would come to inform the lyrics of "Happiness is a Warm Gun."

the last 50 years. Pipilotti Rist (1962–) began working with video in 1986 with a single-track video, *I'm Not The Girl Who Misses Much* (Fig. 15.33), a parody of the videos that had begun to air on television with the advent of MTV in 1983. The video transforms the lyrics to John Lennon's song *Happiness Is a Warm Gun* (1968) from "She's not a girl," to "I'm not the girl." Rist, who played percussion, bass, and flute in the all-girl rock band Les Reines Prochaines (The Next Queens) from 1988 to 1994, bounces up and down as she dances, manipulating her voice by speeding it up to a frenetic pace and slowing it down to the pace of a funeral march, her image sliding in and out of focus. Her blatant dismissal of high production values is equally a dismissal of the social values of MTV itself, where women had quickly been diminished to mere sexual objects.

In an installation by Rist first screened at the Venice Biennale in 1997, *Ever Is Over All* (Fig. 15.34), a woman is seen walking down a street, dressed in a conservative blue dress and bright red shoes à la Dorothy in *The Wizard of Oz*. She is carrying a large red flower—in fact, a flower known as a red-hot poker, images of which are simultaneously projected around the corner of the room. A soft, even soothing "la, la, la" of a song accompanies her. With a broad smile on her face, she lifts the long-stemmed flower in her hand and smashes it into the passenger window of a parked car. Glass shatters. She moves on, smashing more car windows. Up from behind her comes a uniformed woman police officer, who passes her by with a smiling salute. Her stroll down the boulevard plays in a continuous loop in the gallery. This is the new Oz, the Emerald City that

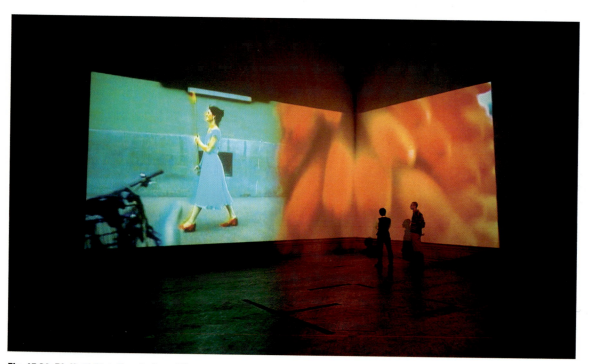

Fig. 15.34 Pipilotti Rist, *Ever Is Over All*. 1997. Audio video installation, National Museum of Foreign Art, Sofia, Bulgaria, 1999; sound with Anders Guggisberg; single-channel video. Museum of Modern Art, New York. Courtesy the artist, Hauser & Wirth, and Luhring Augustine. The person playing the part of the hit woman is the Swiss journalist and documentary filmmaker Silvana Ceschi.

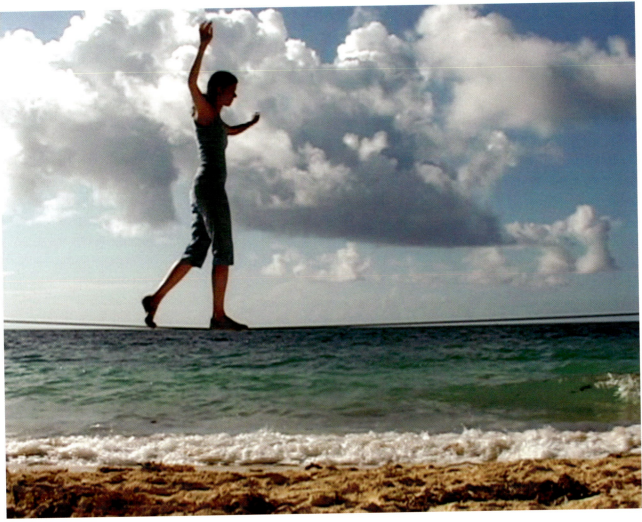

Fig. 15.35 Janine Antoni, *Touch.* **2002.** Color video, sound (projection), 9:36 min. loop. The Art Institute of Chicago. Gift of Donna and Howard Stone, 2007.43. A short segment of *Touch*, narrated by Antoni, is included in the Art21 segment "Janine Antoni in 'Loss and Desire'" at www.pbs.org/art21/artists/antoni/index.html.

we discover "somewhere over the rainbow," where the tensions between nature and civilization, violence and pleasure, the legal and the criminal, impotence and power all seem to have dissolved.

The artist Janine Antoni (1964–) works in a variety of media, including performance and video, often making art out of everyday activities such as eating, bathing, and sleeping. The tension between the mundane qualities of her activities and the technical sophistication of their recording results in a sense of almost magical transformation comparable to that of the Surrealists. In the video *Touch* (Fig. **15.35**), Antoni appears to walk along the horizon, an illusion created by her walking on tightrope stretched between two backhoes on the beach directly in front of her childhood home on Grand Bahama Island. She had learned to tightrope walk, practicing about an hour a day, as an exercise in bodily control and meditation. As she practiced, she realized, she says, that "it wasn't that I was getting more balanced, but that I was getting more comfortable with being out of balance." This she took as a basic lesson in life. In *Touch*, this sense of teetering balance is heightened by the fact that she appears to be walking on an horizon line that we know can never be reached as it continuously moves away from us as we approach it. We know, in other words, that we are in an impossible place, and yet it is a place that we have long contemplated and desired as a culture—the same horizon that Romantic painters such as Caspar David Friedrich looked out upon in paintings like *Monk by the Sea* (see Fig. **12.18** in Chapter 12). When, in the course of the full-length video, both Antoni and the rope disappear, we are left, as viewers, contemplating this illusory line and what it means. And we come to understand that the horizon represents what is always in front of us. "It's a very hopeful image," Antoni says, "it's about the future, about the imagination."

15.1 Outline the principles of existentialism and how they manifest themselves in art and literature.

After World War II, Europe was gripped by a profound pessimism. The existential philosophy of Jean-Paul Sartre was a direct response. What did Sartre mean by the phrase "Existence precedes essence"? He agreed that the human condition is defined by alienation, anxiety, lack of authenticity, and a sense of nothingness, but he said that this did not abrogate the responsibility to act and create meaning. Sartre's play *No Exit* and Samuel Beckett's *Waiting for Godot* are examples of the Theater of the Absurd. What are the characteristics of this brand of theater?

15.2 Compare and contrast the varieties of Abstract Expressionism and describe how the Beats and Pop Art challenged its ascendency.

In America, Jackson Pollock and Willem de Kooning inspired a generation of artists to abandon representation in favor of directly expressing their emotions on the canvas in totally abstract terms. How did Abstract Expressionist painters like Mark Rothko and Helen Frankenthaler differ from Pollock and de Kooning?

At the same time, the Beat generation, a younger, more rebellious generation of writers and artists, began to critique American culture. The Swiss photographer Robert Frank's *The Americans* revealed a side of American life that outraged a public used to seeing the country through the lens of a happy optimism. Allen Ginsberg lashed out in his poem "Howl" with a forthright and uncensored frankness that seemed to many an affront to decency. What was the nature of the collaboration between the composer John Cage, the dancer Merce Cunningham, and the artist Robert Rauschenberg? What characterizes Rauschenberg's combine paintings? What defines Cage's *4'33"* as music? In what ways do the American Beats reflect the existentialism of Jean-Paul Sartre?

Pop Art reflected the commodification of culture and the marketplace as a dominant cultural force. In what terms did Andy Warhol compare Marilyn Monroe to Campbell's Soup? How did Tom Wesselmann suggest that painting itself was a commodity? How did Roy Lichtenstein parody Abstract Expressionist painting? Claes Oldenberg created witty reproductions of American goods. How did he change them?

15.3 Examine the role politics played in the art and literature of the 1960s and 1970s.

By 1963, the Southern Christian Leadership Conference (SCLC), led by the Reverend Martin Luther King, Jr., had decided that Birmingham, Alabama, would be the focal point of the burgeoning civil rights movement. One of the most important factors contributing to the success of the civil rights movement was the growing sense of ethnic identity among the African-American population. How did Jean-Paul Sartre contribute to this newfound sense of self? How did it find expression in the writings of Ralph Ellison and Amiri Baraka?

As American involvement in the war in Vietnam escalated throughout the 1960s, artists and writers responded in a number of ways. What tack did Kurt Vonnegut take in his 1969 novel *Slaughterhouse-Five*? How did the Art Workers' Coalition respond? What steps did they take?

In 1963, in her book *The Feminine Mystique*, Betty Friedan attacked the patriarchal construction of the idea of "woman." What was the primary object of her attack? Poets and painters fought to find a place in an art world that almost totally excluded women from exhibition and even gallery representation. How did Judy Chicago and the Guerrilla Girls address the situation?

15.4 Characterize the ways in which pluralism and diversity are reflected in postmodern art and literature.

Postmodern architecture is characterized by a condition of contradiction that is inclusive and not exclusive. In the arts, this sense of inclusiveness authorizes works in which identity and meaning are plural and multiplicitous, crossing stylistic and cultural boundaries. In Jorge Luis Borges's short parable "Borges and I," the "I" accuses "Borges" of falsification and exaggerating. Whom are we to trust, or are we to trust anyone, and how would you say that defines the postmodern condition? How does "spanglish" reflect cross-cultural negotiation in Aurora Levins Morales's poem "Child of the Americas"?

The globalization of culture has led many to feel they have multiple identities. How do artists like Chris Ofili mediate between their British training and their Nigerian roots? In the late 1960s, the American Indian Movement (AIM) sought to restore power to Native American peoples, the plurality of whose cultures was itself enormous. How does David P. Bradley address the confrontation between native and Anglo cultures? Finally, how does Shahzia Sikander negotiate the boundaries between Islam and the West?

Artists have also used new electronic media to create new artistic spaces. Bill Viola creates video installations that take advantage of the medium's ability to evoke the world of dreams, memories, and reflections, and Viola's work in particular immerses the viewer in the flow of time and the cycle of life and death. How do installations such as Isaac Julien's *Ten Thousand Waves* and Phil Collins's *The World Won't Listen* address the contemporary historical moment? How do Pipilotti Rist's videos address popular culture?

✓ **Study** and **review** on **MyArtsLab**

CONTINUITY & CHANGE

The Environment and the Humanist Tradition

What is the role of art today? What does the museum offer us? What about literature, the book, the poem? Is the museum merely a repository of cultural artifacts? Is the poem a tired and self-indulgent form of intellectual narcissism? Can opera move us even more meaningfully than popular music? How can the arts help us to understand not only our past, but also our present and our future? These are questions that artists, writers, and musicians are continually asking themselves, and questions that students of the humanities, coming to the end of a project such as this one, might well ask themselves as well.

Consider an installation by the Danish artist Olafur Eliasson (1967–), *The Weather Project* (Fig. **15.36**). When he installed it in the mammoth Turbine Hall of Tate Modern, London, in the winter of 2003, it was roundly criticized as "mere" entertainment, in no small part because it attracted over 2 million visitors. At the end of the 500-foot hall hung a giant yellow orb, 90 feet above the floor. The ceiling itself was covered with mirrors, thus apparently doubling the size of the space. The "sun" was actually a semicircle of some 200 yellow sodium streetlights, which, when reflected in the ceiling mirrors, formed a circle. Artificial mist machines filled the hall with a dull, wintry fog. What was the attraction?

In no small part, it seemed to reside in the very artificiality of the environment. Visitors to the top floor of the gallery could easily see the trussing supporting the mirrored ceiling as well as the construction of the sun shape. The extraordinary visual effects of Eliasson's installation were, in the end, created by rather ordinary means. But this ordinariness, in turn, suggested profound and somewhat disturbing truths about our world and our environment. If Eliasson could create this almost postapocalyptic environment—with its dead, heatless sun, perpetual fog, and cold stone ground— with such minimal means, what might we, as a world, create with the advanced technology so readily at our disposal? In other words, as viewers lay on the floor of the museum, and saw themselves reflected on the ceiling above, were they viewing themselves in the present, or seeing themselves in the future? What hath humanity wrought?

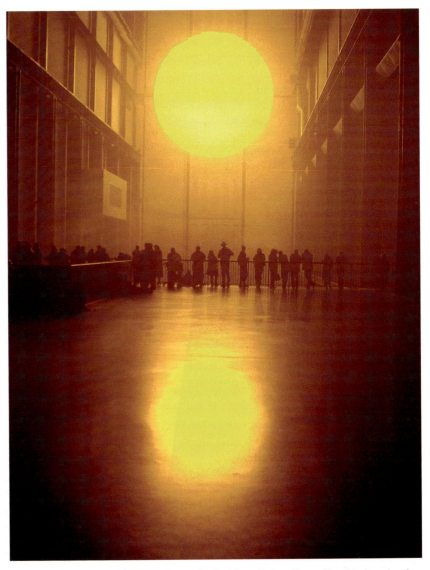

Fig. 15.36 Olafur Eliasson, *The Weather Project*, installation view at Tate Modern, London. 2003. Monofrequency lights, projection foil, haze machine, mirror oil, aluminum, and scaffolding. Courtesy of the artist, Tanya Bonakdar Gallery, New York, and neugerriemschneider, Berlin. © Olafur Eliasson 2003.

The Weather Project was, then, something of a chilling experience, both literally and figuratively. "I regard . . . museums," Eliasson has said, "as spaces where one steps even deeper into society, from where one can scrutinize society." It is perhaps relevant for you to consider this book as such a space. To conclude, what is it about your world that you have come to understand and appreciate more deeply and fully? ■

PHOTO CREDITS

Front Cover Prado, Madrid, Spain/Bridgeman Images
Back Cover © Photo Scala, Florence

Chapter 1

1.1 akg-images; **1.2** © Ministère de la Culture - Médiathèque du Patrimoine, Dist. RMN-Grand Palais/image IGN; **1.3** Erich Lessing/akg-images; **1.4, 1.5** Gianni Dagli Orti/Museum of Anatolian Civilisations Ankara/The Art Archive; **1.6** © RMN-Grand Palais (musée du Louvre)/Droits réservés; **1.7, p32 CL A & B** © Werner Forman Archive; **1.8** Yan Arthus-Bertrand/Altitude/Photo Researchers, Inc.; **1.9** © English Heritage. NMR Aerofilms Collection; **Map 1.3** Courtesy of National Geographic; **1.10** Christopher Gable and Sally Gable © Dorling Kindersley; **1.11** John Deeks/Photo Researchers, Inc.; **1.13** age fotostock/SuperStock; **1.14** © Nik Wheeler/Corbis; **1.16** Courtesy of the Oriental Institute of the University of Chicago; **1.17a & b, 1.23** © The Trustees of The British Museum; **1.18, 1.26, 1.27** © Photo Scala, Florence; **1.19** © RMN-Grand Palais (musée du Louvre)/Franck Raux; **1.20** Soprintendenza Archeologica/IKONA; **p27 (CPP)** © Marjane Satrapi/L'Association, photograph Westimage; **1.21** © Livius.Org; **1.22** © Tibor Bognar/Photononstop/Corbis; **page 29 (CPP)** © Andy Goldsworthy. Courtesy Galerie Lelong, New York. Photo by Julian Calder; **1.24** Photograph © 2015 Museum of Fine Arts, Boston; **1.25** © Photo Scala, Florence/BPK Bildagentur für Kunst, Kultur und Geschichte, Berlin; **1.28** Craig & Marie Mauzy, Athens mauzy@otenet.gr; **1.29** Alfredo Dagli Orti/Musée Archéologique Naples/The Art Archive.

Chapter 2

2.1, 2.2, 2.5, 2.6, 2.9, 2.11, 2.14a, 2.18, 2.19a, 2.20, 2.24a, 2.26, 2.35 Craig & Marie Mauzy, Athens mauzy@otenet.gr; **2.3, 2.34** © 2013. Photo Scala, Florence/BPK, Bildagentur für Kunst, Kultur und Geschichte, Berlin; **2.4, 2.15, p55 CL C, 2.27, 2.39** Nimatallah/akg-images; **2.7** Stephen Conlin © Dorling Kindersley; **2.10, 2.25** Studio Kontos Photostock; **2.12, 2.21** Photograph © 2015 Museum of Fine Arts, Boston; **2.13** © Marco Cristofori/Corbis; **2.16, 2.17** Image copyright © The Metropolitan Museum of Art/Art Resource/Photo Scala, Florence; **p53, 2.38, 2.46** © Photo Scala, Florence; **p54 CL A** Canali Photobank, Milan, Italy; **p55 CL D** © Gianni Dagli Orti/The Art Archive/Alamy; **p55 CL E** Courtesy of the Library of Congress; **2.19b** Museum of Classical Archaeology, University of Cambridge; **2.22** © Photo Scala, Florence /Ministero per i Beni e le Attività culturali; **2.23, 2.37, 2.41, 2.42** Erich Lessing/akg-images; **2.28** Alfredo Dagli Orti/Musée Archéologique Naples/The Art Archive; **2.30, 2.31, 2.32** © The Trustees of The British Museum; **2.33** © Martin von Wagner Museum, University of Wurzburg, Photo P. Neckermann/E Oehrlein; **2.40** © Vanni Archive/Corbis; **p77 (CPP)** © Thomas Struth; **2.43** © DeAgostini Picture Library/Scala, Florence; **2.44** © Photo Scala, Florence - courtesy of Sovraintendenza di Roma Capitale; **2.45** © RMN-Grand Palais (musée du Louvre).

Chapter 3

3.1 Henri Stierlin/akg-images; **3.2** ©1996 Harry N. Abrams, Inc.; **3.3, 3.21** Erich Lessing/akg-images; **3.4, 3.6, 3.12** © Araldo de Luca/Corbis; **3.5, 3.27, 3.33** Image copyright © The Metropolitan Museum of Art/Art Resource/Photo Scala, Florence; **3.7** © Photo Scala, Florence - courtesy of Sovraintendenza di Roma Capitale; **3.8** Gianni Dagli Orti/Musée Archéologique Naples/The Art Archive; **3.09** Walter Bibikow/Getty Images; **3.11** © Patrick Durand/Sygma/Corbis; **3.13** Dr. James E. Packer; **3.14** © Roberto Matassa/age fotostock/Robert Harding World Imagery; **3.15** © Werner Forman Archive; **3.16** © Dennis Cox/Alamy; **3.17, 3.36** © Photo Scala, Florence - courtesy of the Ministero Beni e Att. Culturali; **3.18, 3.23, 3.24** © Vincenzo Pirozzi, Rome fotopirozzi@inwind.it; **3.20** © Hemera Technologies/Alamy; **3.25** D. E. Cox/Stone/Getty Images; **p103 (CPP)** © Cai Guo-Qiang. Photo by Masanobu Moriyama, courtesy Cai Studio; **p108 CL A** O. Louis Mazzatenta/National Geographic Stock; **p109 CL B** Keren Su/Getty Images; **p109 CL C** Laurent Lecat/akg-images; **3.28** The Nelson-Atkins Museum of Art, Kansas City, Missouri. Photo: John Lamberton; **3.29** © Asian Art & Archaeology, Inc./Corbis; **3.30** Gerard Degeorge/akg-images; **3.31** © Photo Scala, Florence; **3.32** National Museum of Karachi, Karachi, Pakistan/Giraudon/Bridgeman Images; **3.34** © Atlantide Phototravel/Corbis.

Chapter 4

4.1 A.F.Kersting/akg-images; **4.2** Erich Lessing/akg-images; **p125** Alfredo Dagli Orti/Musée Archéologique Naples/The Art Archive; **4.4, 4.6, 4.9** © Photo Scala, Florence; **4.8** Bibliotheque des Arts Decoratifs, Paris, France/Archives Charmet/Bridgeman Images; **4.11** © Alfredo Dagli Orti/The Art Archive/Corbis; **4.12, p137 CL D** Image copyright © The Metropolitan Museum of Art/Art Resource/Photo Scala, Florence; **4.13, 4.14** © Altun Images, Istanbul; **4.16** Studio Kontos Photostock; **4.17, 4.18** © Cameraphoto Arte, Venice; **p136 CL A** Seattle Art Museum, Eugene Fuller Memorial Collection. Photo: Paul Macapia; **p136 CL B** Cincinnati Art Museum, Fanny Bryce Lehmer Fund. Acc. #1977.65/Bridgeman Images; **p137 (CPP)** © Wijdan, Courtesy October Gallery, London. © The Trustees of the British Museum; **4.19** © Ahmed Jadallah/Reuters/Corbis; **4.20** © Peter Langer - Associated Media Group - All rights reserved; **4.21** © Achim Bednorz, Cologne; **4.22** © Ian Griffiths/Robert Harding World Imagery; **4.23** © Wolfgang Kaehler/Corbis; **4.24** © Guenter Rossenbach/Corbis.

Chapter 5

5.1 © Werner Forman Archive; **5.2, 5.21** © The Trustees of The British Museum; **5.3** © The British Library Board: Cotton Nero D., f.94v; **5.4** © The Board of Trinity College, Dublin, Ireland/Bridgeman Images; **5.5** © The British Library Board: Cotton Vespasian A. I, f.30v; **5.6, 5.8, 5.11** Erich Lessing/akg-images; **5.9** Stephen Biesty © Dorling Kindersley; **p160 CL A, B, C, D** Musée de la Tapisserie, Bayeux, France/With special authorisation of the city of Bayeux/Bridgeman Images; **p161 CL E, 5.10** Erich Lessing/akg-images; **p163** © Roberto Matassa/age fotostock/Robert Harding World Imagery; **p163 (CPP)** © 2014 Artists Rights Society (ARS), New York/VG Bild-Kunst, Bonn. Image copyright © The Metropolitan Museum of Art/Art Resource/Photo Scala, Florence; **5.12** © Photo Scala, Florence; **5.15** Photononstop/SuperStock; **5.16** © White Images/Scala, Florence; **5.17** Stephen Conlin © Dorling Kindersley; **5.19** © Michael Jenner/Robert Harding World Imagery; **5.20** Joanna Cameron © Dorling Kindersley; **5.22** © Photo Pierpont Morgan Library/Art Resource/Scala, Florence; **5.23** © Achim Bednorz, Cologne; **5.24** © Angelo Hornak.

Chapter 6

6.1 © Adam Woolfitt/Corbis; **6.2, 6.3, 6.10, 6.11, 6.15** © Achim Bednorz, Cologne; **6.4** © Dean Conger/Corbis; **6.5** © Angelo Hornak; **6.7** John Bryson/Photo Researchers, Inc.; **6.9** © Stuart Black/Robert Harding World Imagery/Corbis; **6.12, 6.20** © Photo Scala, Florence; **6.13** Museo Civico, Bologna, Italy/Giraudon/Bridgeman Images; **6.14** Sonia Halliday Photographs; **6.16, 6.17** © RMN-Grand Palais (domaine de Chantilly)/René-Gabriel Ojéda; **6.18a & b, 6.19, 6.21, 6.22, p196-7 CL A, B & C** © Quattrone, Florence; **p191 (CPP)** Courtesy Ronald Feldman Fine Arts, New York/www.feldmangallery.com; **p193** Studio Kontos Photostock; **6.23** Image copyright © The Metropolitan Museum of Art/Art Resource/Photo Scala, Florence; **6.24** Erich Lessing/akg-images; **6.25** Eileen Tweedy/Victoria and Albert Museum London/The Art Archive; **6.26** Bibliothèque nationale de France, Paris; **6.27** Courtesy of the Library of Congress.

Chapter 7

7.1 Folco Quilici © Fratelli Alinari; **7.2** © Arte & Immagini srl/Corbis; **7.3, 7.5** Erich Lessing/akg-images; **7.4, 7.25** Canali Photobank, Milan, Italy; **p212** Nimatallah/akg-images; **7.6** © Museo dell'Opera del Duomo, Florence/Photo Scala, Florence; **7.7, 7.12, p239** © Photo Scala, Florence; **7.10, 7.11, 7.14, 7.17, 7.22, 7.29, 7.36** © Quattrone, Florence; **p216** Alfredo Dagli Orti/Musée Archéologique Naples/The Art Archive; **7.13** © Achim Bednorz, Cologne; **p218** © Patrick Durand/Sygma/Corbis; **7.15** © Museo dell'Opera del Duomo, Florence/Photo Scala, Florence; **7.16** Royal Collection © 2011 Her Majesty Queen Elizabeth II/Bridgeman Images; **p244 (CPP)** © Julie Green; **7.18** © RMN-Grand Palais (musée du Louvre)/Michel Urtado; **7.19, 7.31, 7.32, 7.33a, 7.34, 7.38** © Cameraphoto Arte, Venice; **7.20, p227** © Vincenzo Pirozzi, Rome fotopirozzi@inwind.it; **7.23, p234 CL A** Foto Musei Vaticani/IKONA; **7.26** Image copyright © The Metropolitan Museum of Art/Art Resource/Photo Scala, Florence; **7.27** A. Bracchetti/P. Zigrossi/Foto Musei Vaticani/IKONA; **7.28** Courtesy National Gallery of Art, Washington, DC; **7.30** ONB Vienna: Cod. 4809, fol. 1v-2r; **p234 CL B** IAM/akg-images; **7.35** © Photo Scala, Florence - courtesy of the Ministero Beni e Att. Culturali; **7.37** Alfredo Dagli Orti/Palazzo Pitti, Florence/The Art Archive; **7.39** Courtesy of the Library of Congress.

Chapter 8

8.1 De Agostini Picture Library/Bridgeman Images; **8.2, 8.10, 8.12, 8.15, 8.16, 8.21** © Photo Scala, Florence/BPK Bildagentur für Kunst, Kultur und Geschichte, Berlin; **8.3, 8.4** Image copyright © The Metropolitan Museum of Art/Art Resource/Photo Scala, Florence; **8.6, 8.7, 8.19** © National Gallery, London/Scala, Florence; **p256-7 CL (all)** Prado, Madrid, Spain/Bridgeman Images; **p257 (CPP)** © Raqib Shaw. Courtesy White Cube. Image copyright © The Metropolitan Museum of Art/Art Resource/Photo Scala, Florence; **8.8** Unterlinden Museum Colmar/The Art Archive; **8.9** © Musee D'Unterlinden/Photo Scala, Florence; **8.11** Yale University Art Gallery. Library Transfer, Gift of Paul Mellon, B.A. 1929, L.H.D.H 1967; **8.13** Erich Lessing/akg-images; **8.14** © Bettmann/Corbis; **8.17** British Library, London/Giraudon/Bridgeman Images; **8.18** Trevor Hill © Dorling Kindersley; **8.20** © Vincenzo Pirozzi, Rome fotopirozzi@inwind.it; **8.22** German National Museum, Nuremberg; **8.23** © Photo Scala, Florence.

Chapter 9

9.1 De Agostini Picture Library/G. Dagli Orti/Bridgeman Images; **9.2** © Gianni Dagli Orti/Corbis; **9.3, 9.4** Biblioteca Nacional, Madrid/Bridgeman Images; **9.5** akg-images; **p279 (CPP)** © Anselm Kiefer. Collection of the Modern Art Museum of Fort Worth, Museum purchase, The Friends of Art Endowment Fund; **9.6** Carlos S Pereyra/age Fotostock/Superstock; **9.7** © MJ Photography/Alamy; **9.8** Francesca Yorke © Dorling Kindersley; **9.9** Museo de América, Madrid; **p282 (CPP)** © Enrique Chagoya. Photo: Ruben Guzmán; **9.10** © Danny Lehman/Corbis; **9.11** © Richard Maschmeyer/Robert Harding World Imagery/Corbis; **9.12** © Dirk Bakker/Bridgeman Art Library; **9.13** © The Trustees of The British Museum; **9.15, 9.16** Image copyright © The Metropolitan Museum of Art/Art Resource/Photo Scala, Florence; **9.18** Weltmuseum, Vienna; **9.19** Photograph by Ruben Guzmán courtesy of Frederick John Lamp. The Frances and Benjamin Benenson Foundation Curator of African Art. Yale University Art Gallery; **9.20** The University of Iowa Museum of Art, Iowa City. The Stanley Collection X1986.489 and X1986.488; **9.21, 9.32** Photograph © 2015 Museum of Fine Arts, Boston; **9.22** Freer Gallery of Art, Smithsonian Institution, Washington, DC: Purchase, F1942.15a; **9.24** © Photo Scala, Florence; **9.26** Photo Galileo Picture Services LLC, NY; **9.27** © View Stock/Alamy; **p298 CL B, C, D** © Corbis; **9.28** Photo © The Cleveland Museum of Art. 1974.31; **9.29, 9.30** The Nelson-Atkins Museum of Art, Kansas City, Missouri. Photograph by John Lamberton; **9.31** © Photo Art Resource/Scala, Florence; **9.33** Demetrio Carrasco © Dorling Kindersley; **9.34** © Paul Quayle; **9.35** Steve Vidler/SuperStock, Inc.; **9.36** Photo Galileo Picture Services LLC, NY; **9.37** © Estate of Nam June Paik. Collection Stedelijk Museum Amsterdam.

Chapter 10

10.1, 10.9, 10.27, 10.28 Erich Lessing/akg-images; **10.2** © Museo dell'Opera del Duomo, Florence/Photo Scala, Florence; **10.3, 10.4** Foto Musei Vaticani/IKONA; **10.5** Kunsthistorisches Museum, Vienna; **10.6** © Isabella Stewart Gardner Museum, Boston, MA/Bridgeman Images; **10.7** © Quattrone, Florence; **10.8** © Cameraphoto Arte, Venice; **10.10, 10.12, 10.15** © Vincenzo Pirozzi, Rome fotopirozzi@inwind.it; **10.11, 10.14** Canali Photobank, Milan, Italy; **10.13** © Photo Scala, Florence - courtesy of the Ministero Beni e Att. Culturali; **10.16** The Detroit Institute of Arts. Gift of Leslie H. Green. 52.253. Photo © 1984 Detroit Institute of Arts/Bridgeman Images; **p330 (CPP)** Courtesy the artist. © Albright Knox Art Gallery/Art Resource, NY/Scala, Florence; **10.17** Photo: Charles Roelofsz/RKD Images. Bob P. Haboldt & Co., Inc. Art Gallery, NY; **p334 (CPP)** Courtesy the artist and Cheim & Read; **10.18, 10.32** © Photo Scala, Florence; **10.19** Courtesy National Gallery of Art, Washington, DC; **10.20** © Photo Scala, Florence/BPK, Bildagentur für Kunst, Kultur und Geschichte, Berlin; **10.21** Collection Rijksmuseum, Amsterdam. On loan from the City of Amsterdam; **p338 CL A** Mauritshuis, The Hague, The Netherlands/Bridgeman Images; **10.22** Yale University Art Gallery, New Haven. Fritz Achelis Memorial Collection, Gift of Frederic George Achelis, B.A. 1907; **10.23** The Royal Collection © 2011 Her Majesty Queen Elizabeth II/Bridgeman Images; **10.24** © The Art Gallery Collection/Alamy; **p342 (CPP)** Photo Luís Vasconcelos/Courtesy Unidade Infinita Projectos; **10.25**Artedia/Leemage.com; **10.26** © RMN-Grand Palais (Château de Versailles)/Daniel Arnaudet/Gérard Blot; **10.29** © RMN-Grand Palais (musée du Louvre)/René-Gabriel Ojéda; **10.30** Bibliotheque Nationale, Paris, France/Bridgeman Images; **10.31** © RMN-Grand Palais (musée du Louvre)/Christian Jean; **10.33** Chateau de Versailles/Lauros-Giraudon/Bridgeman Images.

Chapter 11

11.1 By permission of the Trustees of the Goodwood Collection; **11.2** © Angelo Hornak; **11.3a & b** © Photo Scala Florence/Heritage Images; **11.4** © National Gallery, London/Photo Scala, Florence; **11.5** © Graham Jordan/Adams Picture Library/Alamy; **11.6** Private Collection; **11.7** © The Trustees of the British Museum; **11.8** © Krzysztof Melech/Alamy; **11.9** Hermitage, St. Petersburg/Bridgeman Images; **11.10** © RMN-Grand Palais/Agence Bulloz; **11.11** © Peter Willi/Bridgeman Images; **11.12, p370-371 CL A** Erich Lessing/akg-images; **11.13** Alte Pinakothek, Munich/Bridgeman Images; **p370 (CPP)** © Jeff Koons; **p371 CL B** © Photo Scala, Florence; **11.14, 11.22** Image copyright © The Metropolitan Museum of Art/Art Resource/Photo Scala, Florence; **11.15** The Wallace Collection, London/Bridgeman Images; **11.16** © RMN-Grand Palais (musée du Louvre)/Stéphane Maréchalle; **11.17** © RMN-Grand Palais (musée du Louvre)/Hervé Lewandowski; **11.18** British Library/The Art Archive; **11.19** © Victoria and Albert Museum, London; **11.20** The David Collection, inv.B275. Photo: Pernille Klemp; **11.21** Photo © The Cleveland Museum of Art, John L. Severance Fund. 1998.103.14; **11.23** akg-images; **11.24** © RMN-Grand Palais (musée du Louvre)/Thierry Le Mage.

Chapter 12

12.1 © Massachusetts Historical Society, Boston, MA/Bridgeman Images; **12.2** Yale University Art Gallery. Trumbull Collection; **12.3** © RMN-Grand Palais (Château de Versailles)/Gérard Blot; **12.4** Giraudon/Bridgeman Images; **12.5, 12.6** © RMN-Grand Palais (musée du Louvre)/Gérard Blot/Christian Jean; **12.7** © Lebrecht Music and Arts Photo Library/Alamy; **12.8** © RMN-Grand Palais (musée des châteaux de Malmaison et de Bois-Préau)/Gérard Blot; **12.9** Courtesy of the Maryland Historical Society (1960-108-1-1-36); **12.10** Courtesy of the Library of Congress; **p393** © Gianni Dagli Orti/The Art Archive/Alamy; **12.11** Courtesy of the Architect of the Capitol, Washington, DC; **12.12** Private Collection, Archives Charmet/Bridgeman Images; **p394 (CPP)** © 2000 Kara Walker. Photo: Ellen Labenski. Courtesy of Sikkema Jenkins & Co., New York. Solomon R. Guggenheim Museum, New York. Purchased with funds contributed by the International Director's Council and Executive Committee Members: Ann Ames, Edythe Broad, Henry Buhl, Elaine Terner Cooper, Dimitris Daskalopoulos, Harry David, Gail May Engelberg, Ronnie Heyman, Dakis Joannou, Cindy Johnson, Barbara Lane, Linda Macklowe, Peter Norton, Willem Peppler, Tonino Perna, Denise Rich, Simonetta Seragnoli, David Teiger, Ginny Williams, and Elliot K. Wolk 2000.68; **12.13** Image by courtesy of the Wedgwood Museum Trustees, Barlaston, Stafford-shire, (England); **12.14** © Victoria and Albert Museum, London; **12.15** © National Gallery, London/Photo Scala, Florence; **12.16** Yale Center for British Art, Paul Mellon Collection. B1977.14.4702; **12.17** © Tate, London 2014; **12.18, 12.19** © Photo Scala, Florence/BPK, Bildagentur für Kunst, Kultur und Geschichte, Berlin; **p400 CL A** © Roy Rainford/Robert Harding; **p401 CL B** Smith College Museum of Art, Northampton, Massachusetts; **12.20** © RMN-Grand Palais (musée du Louvre)/Thierry Le Mage; **12.21, 12.22** © White Images/Scala, Florence; **p405 (CPP)** Courtesy Devorah Sperber. Limited edition prints commissioned by CALCO-GRAFÍA NACIONAL de Madrid; **12.23** © RMN-Grand Palais (musée du Louvre)/Michel Urtado.

Chapter 13

13.1, 13.3 © RMN-Grand Palais (musée du Louvre)/Thierry Le Mage; **13.2** Lauros-Giraudon/Bridgeman Images; **13.4** © Fitzwilliam Museum, University of Cambridge, UK/Bridgeman Images; **13.5** © RMN-Grand Palais (musée du Louvre)/Hervé Lewandowski; **13.6, 13.13** © RMN-Grand Palais (musée du Louvre)/Droits réservés; **13.7** Private Collection; **13.8** Galerie Neue Meister, Dresden, Germany. © Staatliche Kunstsammlungen Dresden/Bridgeman Images; **13.9** © Collection of the New-York Historical Society/Bridgeman Images; © Fred Wilson. Photography courtesy the artist and Pace Gallery; **13.10** © Brooklyn Museum of Art, New York; **13.11, 13.27** Courtesy of the Library of Congress; **13.12, 13.14** © RMN-Grand Palais (musée du Louvre)/Hervé Lewandowski; **p425 (CPP)** Courtesy of the artist; **13.15, 13.16, 13.18** Erich Lessing/akg-images; **p430 (CPP)** © ART LEE Leenam; **13.17** © National Gallery, London/Photo Scala, Florence; **13.19** Courtesy National Gallery of Art, Washington, DC; **13.20, 13.23** Image copyright © The Metropolitan Museum of Art/Art Resource/Photo Scala, Florence; **13.21** Photograph © 2015 Museum of Fine Arts, Boston; **p434 CL A & B** © The Phillips Collection, Washington, DC/Bridgeman Images; **13.22** Deutsches Historisches Museum, Berlin/Bridgeman Images; **13.24** © White Images/Scala, Florence; **13.25** Museum of the North American Indian, New York/Bridgeman Images; **13.26** © Historical Picture Archive/Corbis; **13.28** akg-images.

Chapter 14

14.1 Collection Van Abbemuseum. Photo: Peter Cox, Eindhoven; **14.2** Photograph © 2006, The Art Institute of Chicago. All Rights Reserved; **14.3** Yale University Art Gallery. Bequest of Stephen Carlton Clark, B.A. 1903; **14.4** Image copyright © The Metropolitan Museum of Art/Art Resource/Photo Scala, Florence; **p450 (CPP)** © Estate of Robert Colescott, courtesy Laura Russo Gallery. Corcoran Gallery of Art, Washington DC/Gift of the Women's Committee of the Corcoran Gallery of Art/Bridgeman Images; **14.5** © Samuel Courtauld Trust, The Courtauld Gallery, London/Bridgeman Images; **14.6** © Photo The Philadelphia Museum of Art/Art Resource/Scala, Florence; **14.7** Photograph © The Art Institute of Chicago; **14.8** © 2014 Estate of Pablo Picasso/Artists Rights Society (ARS), New York. Image copyright © The Metropolitan Museum of Art/Art Resource/Photo Scala, Florence; **p454** © RMN-Grand Palais (musée d'Orsay)/Hervé Lewandowski; **14.9** © 2014 Artists Rights Society (ARS), New York/VG Bild-Kunst, Bonn. Image copyright © The Metropolitan Museum of Art/Art Resource/Photo Scala, Florence; **p454** © RMN-Grand Palais (musée du Louvre)/Thierry Le Mage; **14.10** © 2014 Artists Rights Society (ARS), New York/ADAGP, Paris. Rupf Foundation, Bern/Giraudon/Bridgeman Images; **14.11** © 2014 Artists Rights Society (ARS), New York/VG Bild-Kunst, Bonn. © Photo Scala, Florence/BPK, Bildagentur für

Kunst, Kultur und Geschichte, Berlin; **p456 (CPP)** © Mark Tansey. Courtesy Gagosian Gallery. Digital Image Museum Associates/LACMA/Art Resource NY/Scala, Florence; **14.12** © 2014 Artists Rights Society (ARS), New York/ADAGP, Paris. Photo: Solomon R. Guggenheim Museum, New York; **14.13** © 2014 Artists Rights Society (ARS), New York/VG Bild-Kunst, Bonn. © McNay Art Museum/Art Resource, NY/Scala, Florence; **14.14, 14.23** © Digital image, The Museum of Modern Art, New York/Scala, Florence; **14.15** © 2014 Succession H. Matisse/Artists Rights Society (ARS), New York. Photo © The State Hermitage Museum. Photo by Vladimir Terebenin, Leonard Kheifets, Yuri Molodkovets; **14.16** Walker Art Center, Minneapolis, Gift of T. B. Walker Collection, Gilbert M. Walker Fund, 1942; **14.17** © 2014 Artists Rights Society (ARS), New York/ADAGP, Paris. Erich Lessing/akg-images; **14.18** © 2014 Artists Rights Society (ARS), New York/VG Bild-Kunst, Bonn. Haags Gemeentemuseum, The Hague, Netherlands/Bridgeman Images; **14.19** © Succession Marcel Duchamp/ADAGP, Paris/Artists Rights Society (ARS), New York 2014. © Photo The Philadelphia Museum of Art/Art Resource/Scala, Florence; **14.20** © Succession Marcel Duchamp/ADAGP, Paris/Artists Rights Society (ARS), New York 2014. Photo © Tate, London 2014; **p466 (CPP)** © Sherrie Levine. Courtesy Paula Cooper Gallery, New York and Simon Lee Gallery, London. Walker Art Center, Minneapolis. T.B. Walker Acquisition Fund, 1992; **14.21** Art © Heirs of Aaron Douglas/Licensed by VAGA, New York, NY. Fine Arts Museums of San Francisco. Museum purchase, the estate of Thurlow E. Tibbs Jr., The Museum Auxiliary, American Art Trust Fund, Unrestricted Art Trust Fund, partial gift of Dr. Ernest A Bates, Sharon Bell, Jo-Ann Berverly, Barbara Carleton, Dr. & Mrs. Arthur H. Coleman, Dr. & Mrs. Coyness Ennix, Jr, Nicole Y. Ennix, Mr & Mrs Gary Francois, Dennis L. Franklin, Mr. & Mrs. Maxwell C. Gillette, Zuretti L. Goosby, Mr. & Mrs. Richard Goodyear, Marion E. Greene, Mrs Vivian S. W. Hambrick, Laurie Gibbs Harris, Arlene Hollis, Louis A. & Letha Jeanpierre, Daniel & Jackie Johnson, Jr, Stephen L. Johnson, Mr. & Mrs. Arthur Lathan, Mr. & Mrs. Gary Love, Lewis & Ribbs Mortuary Garden Chapel, Glenn R. Nance, Mr. & Mrs. Harry S. Parker III, Mr. & Mrs. Carr T. Preston, etc.; **14.22** © 2014 The Jacob and Gwendolyn Lawrence Foundation, Seattle/Artists Rights Society (ARS), New York. © Digital image, The Museum of Modern Art, New York/Scala, Florence; **p472 CL A, C, p473 CL E, H, K** Goskino/The Kobal Collection; **p472 CL B, p473 CL D, G** Courtesy Everett Collection/Rex Features; **p473 CL F, I, J** Henry M. Sayre; **14.24** © 2014 Artists Rights Society (ARS), New York/SIAE, Rome. © Cameraphoto Arte, Venice; **14.25** © 2014 Artists Rights Society (ARS), New York/ADAGP, Paris. Letter from Katherine S. Dreier to Max Ernst, May 25, 1920. Yale Collection of American Literature, Beinecke Rare Book and Manuscript Library. Translation from German by John W. Gabriel. From "Max Ernst, Life and Work" by Werner Spies, published by Thames & Hudson, Page 67; **14.26** © 2014 Artists Rights Society (ARS), New York/VG Bild-Kunst, Bonn. © Digital image, The Museum of Modern Art, New York/Scala, Florence; **14.27** © Salvador Dalí, Fundació Gala-Salvador Dalí, Artists Rights Society (ARS), New York 2014. © Digital image, The Museum of Modern Art, New York/Scala, Florence; **14.28** © 2014 Artists Rights Society (ARS), New York/VG Bild-Kunst, Bonn. © Photo Art Resource/Scala, Florence/John Bigelow Taylor.

Chapter 15

15.1 © 1998 Kate Rothko Prizel & Christopher Rothko/Artists Rights Society (ARS), New York. The University of Arizona Museum of Art, Tucson, Gift of E. Gallagher, Jr. Acc. 64.1.1; **15.2**

Neue Galerie - Sammlung Ludwig, Aachen, Germany. Art © Estate of Duane Hanson/Licensed by VAGA, New York, NY; **15.3** © 2014 The Pollock-Krasner Foundation/Artists Rights Society (ARS), New York. Whitney Museum of American Art, NY. Purchase. © 2008 ARS Artists Rights Society, NY; **15.4** © 2014 The Willem de Kooning Foundation/Artists Rights Society (ARS), New York. Reproduction, The Art Institute of Chicago. All Rights Reserved; **15.5** © Estate of Joan Mitchell. Image courtesy National Gallery of Art, Washington, DC; **15.6** © 2014 Estate of Helen Frankenthaler, Inc./Artists Rights Society (ARS), New York. The Detroit Institute of Arts, Founders Society Purchase, Dr. & Mrs. Hilbert H. DeLawter Fund/Bridgeman Images; **15.7** Art © Robert Rauschenberg Foundation/Licensed by VAGA, New York, NY. © Digital image, The Museum of Modern Art, New York/Scala, Florence; **15.8** Art © Jasper Johns/Licensed by VAGA, New York, NY. Whitney Museum of American Art, New York; 50th Anniversary Gift of the Gilman Foundation, Inc., The Lauder Foundation, A. Alfred Taubman, Laura-Lee Whittier Woods and purchase. 80.32; **15.9** © 2014 Artists Rights Society (ARS), New York/VG Bild-Kunst, Bonn. Grant Smith/VIEW Pictures/akg-images; **15.10** © Andrew Garn; **15.11** © 2014 The Andy Warhol Foundation for the Visual Arts Inc./Artists Rights Society (ARS), New York; **15.12** Art © Estate of Tom Wesselmann/Licensed by VAGA, New York, NY. © Albright Knox Art Gallery/Art Resource, NY/Scala, Florence; **15.13** © 2014 The Andy Warhol Foundation for the Visual Arts Inc./Artists Rights Society (ARS), New York. © Tate, London 2014; **p494 (CPP)** © Mike Bidlo, photo © Jesse David Harris; **15.14** © Estate of Roy Lichtenstein; **15.15** © Estate of Roy Lichtenstein. Collection of the Whitney Museum of American Art, New York. Purchase, with funds from the Friends of the Whitney Museum of American Art. 66.2; **15.16** Copyright © 1966 Claes Oldenburg. Whitney Museum of American Art, NY; **15.17** © Bettmann/Corbis All Rights Reserved; **15.18** Art © Romare Bearden Foundation/Licensed by VAGA, New York, NY. © Digital image, The Museum of Modern Art, New York/Scala, Florence; **15-CL** © The Estate of Jean-Michel Basquiat/ADAGP, Paris/ARS, New York 2014; **15.19** © Digital image, The Museum of Modern Art, New York/Scala, Florence; **15.20, 15.21** © 2014 Judy Chicago/Artists Rights Society (ARS), New York. Photo © Donald Woodman; **15.22** Copyright © by Guerrilla Girls, Inc. Courtesy www.guerrillagirls.com; **15.23** © Curva de Luz/Alamy; **15.24, p508 (CPP)** © Gerhard Richter. Digital image, The Museum of Modern Art, New York/Scala, Florence; **15.25** © Gerhard Richter. Reproduction, The Art Institute of Chicago. All Rights Reserved; **15.26** © Pat Steir. Courtesy the artist and Cheim & Read. Photo: Solomon R. Guggenheim Museum, New York; **15.27** The Saatchi Gallery, London. Courtesy the Artist and Victoria Miro, London. © Chris Ofili; **p511** Nimatallah/akg-images; **15.28** © Shahzia Sikander, Courtesy of Sikkema Jenkins & Co., New York; **15.29** © David Bradley. Museum Purchase 1999. Peabody Essex Museum, Salem, Massachusetts. Acq. 06/17/1999; **15.30** Mike Bruce/Courtesy Anthony d'Offay, London; **15.31** Courtesy the artist and Victoria Miro, London, Metro Pictures, New York and Galería Helga de Alvear, Madrid © Isaac Julien. Photography © Adrian Zhou; **15.32** Courtesy Shady Lane Productions and Tanya Bonakdar Gallery, New York; **15.33a, b, c** © Pipilotti Rist. Courtesy the artist, Hauser & Wirth and Luhring Augustine; **15.34** Courtesy the artist, Hauser & Wirth and Luhring Augustine. Photograph: Angel Tzvetanov. **15.35** Courtesy of the artist and Luhring Augustine, New York; **15.36** Courtesy the artist; neuggerriemschneider, Berlin and Tanya Bonkadar Gallery, New York © Olafur Eliasson 2003.

TEXT CREDITS

Chapter 1

Reading 1.2, page 20: From "The Law Code of Hammurabi" from LAW COLLECTIONS FROM MESOPOTAMIA AND ASIA MINOR, 2/e, 1997 by Martha T. Roth. Reprinted by permission of the Society of Biblical Literature; **Reading 1.3a, 1.3b and 1.3c**, pages 21–24: Excerpts from THE EPIC OF GILGAMESH, translated, with an Introduction and Notes, by Maureen Gallery Kovacs. Copyright © 1985, 1989 by the Board of Trustees of the Leland Stanford Jr. University. All rights reserved. With the permission of Stanford University Press, www.sup.org; **Reading 1.4**, page 25: Deuteronomy 6:6–9, from the NEW REVISED STANDARD VERSION BIBLE, copyright 1985, 1989, Division of Christian Education of the National Council of the Churches of Christ in the United States of America. Used by permission. All rights reserved; **Reading 1.5**, page 30: From ANCIENT EGYPTIAN LITERATURE: A BOOK OF READINGS, vol. 1, The Old and Middle Kingdoms by Miriam Lichtheim. Copyright © 1973 by University of California Press. Reproduced with permission of University of California Press.

Chapter 2

Reading 2.1, page 48: "Achilles and Priam" from THE ILIAD by Homer, translated by Robert Fagles, translation copyright © 1990 by Robert Fagles. Used by permission of Viking Penguin a division of Penguin Group (USA) LLC; **Reading 2.2a and b**, page 58: From SAPPHO: A NEW TRANSLATION by Mary Barnard. Copyright © 1958 by The Regents of the University of California. © renewed 1986 by Mary Barnard. Print reproduced with permission of University of California Press via Copyright Clearance Center. Electronic rights by permission of Barnardworks; **Reading 2.5a and b**, pages 69–70: "Antigone" by Sophocles, from THREE THEBAN PLAYS by Sophocles, trans. by Robert Fagles, translation copyright © 1982 by Robert Fagles. Used by permission of the Penguin Group (USA) Inc.

Chapter 3

Reading 3.4, page 105: From THE BOOK OF SONGS translated by Arthur Waley (Allen & Unwin, 1937). © Copyright by permission of The Arthur Waley Estate; **Reading 3.5**, page 105: "There are ways but the Way is uncharted" from THE WAY OF LIFE by Lao Tzu, trans. by Raymond B. Blakney, translation copyright © 1955 by Raymond B. Blakney, renewed © 1983 by Charles Philip Blakney. Used by permission of Dutton Signet, a division of Penguin Group (USA) LLC and the Estate of Raymond Bernard Blakney; **Reading 3.6**, page 107: LAMENT by Liu Xijun, copyright © 2003 by Tony Barnstone and Chou Ping, from LITERATURES OF ASIA, ed. by Tony Barnstone, Pearson Education 2003; **Reading 3.7**, page 107: "To Be a Woman" by Fu Xuan, copyright © 2003 by Tony Barnstone and Willis Barnstone, from LITERATURES OF ASIA, ed. by Tony Barnstone, Pearson Education 2003.

Chapter 4

Reading 4.1, page 123: Romans 5:1–11, from the NEW REVISED STANDARD VERSION BIBLE, copyright 1985, 1989, Division of Christian Education of the National Council of the Churches of Christ in the United States of America. Used by permission. All rights reserved; **Reading 4.4**, page 135: Surah 76. From HOLY QUR'AN trans. by M.H. Shakir (1982). Reprinted by permission of Tahrike Tarsile Qur'an, Inc., New York.

Chapter 5

Reading 5.1, page 150: From BEOWULF, translated by Burton Raffel, copyright © 1962, 1963, renewed © 1990, 1991 by Burton Raffel. Used by permission of Dutton Signet, a division of Penguin Group (USA) LLC, and of Russell & Volkening as agents for the author; **Reading 5.2**, page 154: Terry, Patricia, SONG OF ROLAND, 2nd Ed., © 1992, Reprinted and Electronically reproduced by permission of Pearson Education, Inc., Upper Saddle River, New Jersey; **Reading 5.4**, page 166: Howard, Donald R.; Dietz, Margaret Mary, Translators, ON THE MISERY OF THE HUMAN CONDITION—POPE INNOCENT III, 1st Ed., © 1969. Reprinted and Electronically reproduced by permission of Pearson Education, Inc., Upper Saddle River, New Jersey; **Reading 5.5**, page 170: From Comtessa de Dia's "Cruel are the Pains I've Suffered" trans. by Robert Kehew, from LARK IN THE MORNING: THE VERSES OF THE TROUBADOURS, ed. by Robert Kehew, trans. by Ezra Pound, W.D. Snodgrass, and Robert Kehew. Copyright © 2005 by The University of Chicago. Reprinted by permission of the University of Chicago Press. All rights reserved.

Chapter 6

Reading 6.2, pages 198–199: "Inferno" from THE DIVINE COMEDY by Dante Alighieri, translated by John Ciardi. Copyright 1954, 1957, 1959, 1960, 1961, 1965, 1967, 1970 by the Ciardi Family Publishing Trust. Used by permission of W. W. Norton & Company, Inc. This selection may not be reproduced, stored in a retrieval system, or transmitted in any form or by any means without the prior written permission of the publisher; **Reading 6.3**, pages 200–201: From THE DECAMERON OF GIOVANNI BOCCACCIO, trans. Frances Winwar, Modern Library Edition 1955; copyright © 1930 by The Limited Editions Club, Inc.; renewed 1957. Used with the permission of Easton Press; **Reading 6.4**, page 202: "Sonnet 134" from THE POETRY OF PETRARCH trans. David Young. Translation copyright © 2004 by David Young. Reprinted by permission of Farrar, Straus and Giroux, LLC: Excerpts from Sonnet 134 and Sonnet 338 from THE POETRY OF PETRARCH, trans. by David Young. Translation copyright © 2004 by David Young. CAUTION: Users are warned that this work is protected under copyright laws. The right to reproduce or transfer the work via any medium must be secured with Farrar, Straus and Giroux, LLC; **Reading 6.5**, page 203: "Prologue" from the THE PORTABLE CHAUCER, edited and translated by Theodore Morrison, translation copyright 1949, © 1975, renewed © 1977 by Theodore Morrison. Used by permission of Viking Penguin, a division of Penguin Group (USA) LLC.

Chapter 7

Reading 7.1, page 220: The poem "A Song for Bacchus" by Lorenzo de Medici, translated by A.S. Kline, copyright © 2004 and used by permission. All Rights Reserved; **Reading 7.2**, page 221: From the book ORATION ON THE DIGNITY OF MAN by Giovanni Pico della Mirandola, translated by A. Robert Caponigri. Copyright © 1956. Published by Regnery Publishing. All rights reserved. Reprinted by special permission of Regnery Publishing, Washington, D.C.; **Reading 7.8**, page 244: From THE NOBILITY AND EXCELLENCE OF WOMEN, AND THE DEFECTS AND VICES OF MEN by Lucrezia Marinella, ed. and trans. by Anne Dunhill. Copyright © 1999 by The University of Chicago. Reprinted by permission of the University of Chicago Press. All rights reserved; **Reading 7.9**, page 244–245: "Terze Rime, Capitolo 13" from POEMS AND SELECTED LETTERS by Veronica Franco, ed. and trans. by Ann Rosalind Jones and Margaret F. Rosenthal. Copyright © 1998 by The University of Chicago. Reprinted by permission of the University of Chicago Press. All rights reserved.

Chapter 8

Page 249: THE AUTUMN OF THE MIDDLE AGES by Johan Huizinga, translated by Rodney J. Payton and Ulrich Mammitzsch. Copyright © 1996 University of Chicago Press.

Chapter 9

Reading 9.4, page 295: "Summer Day in the Mountains" by Li Bai, copyright © 2003 by Willis Barnstone, Tony Barnstone and Chou Ping; "Broken Lines" by Du Fu, copyright © 2003 by Tony Barnstone and Chou Ping, from LITERATURES OF ASIA, ed. by Tony Barnstone, Pearson 2003; **Reading 9.7**, page 303: "This Perfectly Still" by Tomonori from ANTHOLOGY OF JAPANESE LITERATURE, compiled and edited by Donald Keene, copyright © 1955 by Grove Press, Inc. Used by permission of Grove/Atlantic, Inc. Any third party use of this material, outside of this publication, is prohibited.

Chapter 10

Reading 10.2, page 322: "The Trial of Veronese" from Holt, Elizabeth Gilmore, LITERARY SOURCES OF ART HISTORY. © 1947 Princeton University Press, 1975 renewed PUP. Reprinted by permission of Princeton University Press; **Reading 10.4**, pages 325–326: From THE COMPLETE WORKS OF SAINT TERESA OF JESUS, Vol. 1, trans. and ed. by E. Allison Peers. New York: Sheed & Ward, 1946. Reprinted by permission of the Rowman & Littlefield Publishing Group; **Reading 10.6**, page 347: Excerpt from TARTUFFE by Moliere, translated into English verse by Richard Wilbur. English translation copyright © 1963, 1962, 1961 and renewed 1991, 1990 and 1989 by Richard Wilbur. Reprinted by permission of Houghton Mifflin Harcourt Publishing Company. All rights reserved.

Chapter 11

Reading 11.10, page 375: Extract from THE SOCIAL CONTRACT AND DISCOURSE by Jean-Jacques Rousseau, trans. by Maurice Cranston, reprinted by permission of Peters Fraser & Dunlop (www.petersfraserdunlop.com) on behalf of the Estate of Maurice Cranston.

Chapter 12

Reading 12.7, page 408: "Heiligenstadt Testament" (1802) from Forbes, Elliott, THAYER'S LIFE OF BEETHOVEN 2 VOLUMES, © 1964 Princeton University Press, 1992 renewed PUP. Reprinted by permission of Princeton University Press.

Chapter 13

Reading 13.4, page 424: From *Les Fleurs du mal* by Charles Baudelaire. Trans. from the French by Richard Howard. Reprinted by permission of David R. Godine, Publisher, Inc. Translation Copyright © 1982 by Richard Howard.

Chapter 14

Reading 14.2, page 461. Extract from "Rue Christine Monday" is taken from GUILLAUME APOLLINAIRE: SELECTED POEMS trans. by Oliver Bernard. New edition published by Anvil Press Poetry in 2004. Reprinted by permission of the publisher; **Reading 14.3**, page 461. "In a Station of the Metro" by Ezra Pound, from PERSONAE, copyright ©1926 by Ezra Pound. Published by Faber and Faber Ltd. Reprinted by permission of Faber and Faber Ltd and New Directions Publishing Corp; **Reading 14.4**, page 462. "The Red Wheelbarrow" by William Carlos Williams from THE COLLECTED POEMS: VOLUME 1, 1909–1939, copyright © 1938 by New Directions Publishing Corp. Reprinted by permission of New Directions Publishing Corp. and Carcanet Press Ltd; **Reading 14.6a, b, c, and d**, pages 463–464: From COLLECTED POEMS 1909–1962 by T.S. Eliot. Published and reprinted by permission of Faber and Faber Ltd. Copyright © the Estate of T.S. Eliot; **Reading 14.9**, page 467: Reprinted with the permission of Scribner Publishing Group from THE NEW NEGRO by Alain Locke. Copyright © 1925 by Albert & Charles Boni, Inc. All rights reserved; **Reading 14.10**, page 468: "Jazz Band in a Parisian Cabaret" from THE COLLECTED POEMS OF LANGSTON HUGHES by Langston Hughes, edited by Arnold Rampersad with David Roessel, Associate Editor, copyright © 1994 by the Estate of Langston Hughes. Used by permission of Alfred A. Knopf, an imprint of the Knopf Doubleday Publishing Group, a division of Random House LLC and David Higham Associates. All rights reserved. Any third party use of this material, outside of this publication, is prohibited. Any third party use of this material, outside of this publication, is prohibited. Interested parties must apply directly to the above for permission.

Chapter 15

Reading 15.1 and text, page 485: Excerpt from NO EXIT AND THE FLIES by Jean-Paul Sartre, copyright © 1946 by Stuart Gilbert. Copyright renewed 1974, 1975 by Maris Agnes Mathilde Gilbert. Published in Great Britain as IN CAMERA AND OTHER PLAYS by Jean-Paul Sartre, trans. by Stuart Gilbert and Kitty Black. Translation copyright © 2000 by Stuart Gilbert, published by Hamish Hamilton 1952. Used and reproduced by permission of Alfred A. Knopf, an imprint of the Knopf Doubleday Publishing Group, a division of Random House LLC, and Penguin Books, Ltd. All rights reserved. French language edition published as HUIS CLOS © 1945 and 1976 by Editions Gallimard. Electronic rights by permission of Editions Gallimard, www.gallimard.fr. Used by permission. Any third party use of this material, outside of this publication, is prohibited. Interested parties must apply directly to Random House LLC, Penguin Books, Ltd, and Editions Gallimard for permission; **Reading 15.3**, page 490: First twenty-one lines from "Howl" from COLLECTED POEMS 1947–1980 by Allen Ginsberg. Copyright © 1955, 1984, 1985 and 2006 by Allen Ginsberg and Allen Ginsberg LLC. Reprinted by permission of HarperCollins Publishers and The Wylie Agency (UK) Ltd; Page 495: Copyright © Claes Oldenburg 1961. Reprinted by permission of Oldenburg van Bruggen Studio, New York; Page 497: Excerpt from "Blowin' in the Wind" by Bob Dylan copyright © 1962 by Warner Bros. Inc.; renewed 1990 by Special Rider Music. All rights reserved. International copyright secured. Reprinted by permission; **Reading 15.4a and b**, page 498: Excerpts from INVISIBLE MAN by Ralph Ellison, copyright © 1947, 1948, 1952 by Ralph Ellison. Copyright renewed 1975, 1976, 1980 by Ralph Ellison. Used by permission of Random House, a division of Random House LLC. All rights reserved; **Reading 15.5**, page 500: Copyright © Nov 22, 1999 Amiri Baraka. Reprinted by permission of Basic Books, a member of the Perseus Books Group.; **Reading 15.6**, page 500: From SO FAR, SO GOOD "The Revolution Will Not Be Televised" copyright © 1990, by Gil Scott-Heron, reprinted by permission of Third World Press, Inc., Chicago, Illinois; **Reading 15.8**, page 504: "Her Kind" from TO BEDLAM AND PART WAY BACK by Anne Sexton. Reprinted by permission of SLL/Sterling Lord Literistic, Inc. Copyright by Anne Sexton; **Reading 15.9**, page 509: "The Analytical Language of John Wilkins" from OTHER INQUISITIONS: 1937–1952, by Jorge Luis Borges, trans. by Ruth L.C. Simms, copyright © 1964, renewed 1993. By permission of the University of Texas Press; **Reading 15.10**, page 510: "Borges and I" by Jorge Luis Borges, trans. by James E. Irby, from LABYRINTHS, copyright © 1962, 1964 by New Directions Publishing Corp. Reprinted by permission of New Directions Publishing Corp. and Pollinger, Ltd (www.pollingerltd.com) on behalf of the Estate of Jorges Louis Borges, collected in SELECTED POEMS, copyright © 1962, 1999 by Maria Kodama. Electronic rights administered by The Wylie Agency LLC, used by permission. All rights reserved; **Reading 15.11**, page 510: Aurora Levins Morales, "Child of the Americas" from Aurora Levins Morales and Rosario Morales, GETTING HOME ALIVE (Firebrand Books, 1986). Copyright © 1986 by Aurora Levins Morales and Rosario Morales. Reprinted with the permission of The Permissions Company, Inc., on behalf of Aurora Levins Morales, www.permissionscompany.com.

INDEX

Note: Boldface names refer to artists. Pages in italics refer to illustrations.